Publications of

₩he Colonial ₩ociety of ₩assachusetts

Volume 62

LAW IN COLONIAL
MASSACHUSETTS
1630-1800

A conference held 6 and 7 November 1981 by

The Colonial Society of Massachusetts

Boston: The Colonial Society of Massachusetts

Distributed by the University Press of Virginia

1984

Printed from the Income of the Sarah Louise Edes Fund

Frontispiece: An engraving of Justice from Murphy v. Pinchbeck, Inferior Court of Common Pleas, Suffolk, 1805 JAN c. 392. Courtesy, Social Law Library.

Title Page: Figure of Justice with Scales. From the Title Page of Ioanne Imberto, *Enchiridion Juris Scripti Galliae* (Utrecht, 1647). Courtesy, Collection of Daniel R. Coquillette.

Volume Editor	DANIEL R. COQUILLETTE
Assistant Editors	ROBERT J. BRINK
	CATHERINE S. MENAND
Editor of Publications	FREDERICK S. ALLIS, JR.

PRINTED AT THE ANTHOENSEN PRESS, PORTLAND, MAINE

Dedicated to the Memory of
JOHN NOBLE, 1829–1909

CLERK OF THE SUPREME JUDICIAL COURT FOR SUFFOLK COUNTY,
1875–1908

A LEADING MEMBER OF THE COLONIAL SOCIETY OF MASSACHUSETTS
DURING ITS EARLY DAYS

A PIONEER IN THE CONSERVATION AND UNDERSTANDING OF
EARLY COURT RECORDS

Photograph Courtesy Social Law Library.

Contents

List of Illustrations   xi

Foreword   xvii
    FREDERICK S. ALLIS, JR.

Introduction: The "Countenance of Authoritie"   xxi
    DANIEL R. COQUILLETTE

Biographical Notes on Contributors   lxv

PART I: CONFERENCE PAPERS
    Thomas Lechford and the Earliest Lawyering in Massachusetts, 1638–1641   3
       THOMAS G. BARNES

    Lay Judges: Magistrates and Justices in Early Massachusetts   39
       GEORGE L. HASKINS

    Nathaniel Byfield, 1653–1733   57
       BARBARA A. BLACK

    John Clark, Esq., Justice of the Peace, 1667–1728   107
       RUSSELL K. OSGOOD

    The Transformation of the Law of Poverty in Eighteenth-Century Massachusetts   153
       DOUGLAS LAMAR JONES

    Criminal Practice in Provincial Massachusetts   191
       DAVID H. FLAHERTY

    Legal Literature in Colonial Massachusetts   243
       MORRIS L. COHEN

    Law and Authority to the Eastward: Maine Courts, Magistrates, and Lawyers, 1690–1730   273
       NEAL W. ALLEN, JR.

Massachusetts Lawyers on the Eve of the American Revolution: The State of the Profession   313
  CHARLES R. McKIRDY

Justinian in Braintree: John Adams, Civilian Learning, and
  Legal Elitism, 1758–1775   359
  DANIEL R. COQUILLETTE

The American Revolution and the Emergence of Modern
  Doctrines of Federalism and Conflict of Laws   419
  WILLIAM E. NELSON

PART II: ARTICLES ON SOURCES
  "Immortality brought to Light": An Overview of Massa-
  chusetts Colonial Court Records   471
  ROBERT J. BRINK

Court Records as Sources for Historical Writing   499
  WILLIAM E. NELSON

A Guide to the Court Records of Early Massachusetts   519
  MICHAEL S. HINDUS

A "magistracy fit and necessary": A Guide to the Massachusetts Court System   541
  CATHERINE S. MENAND

PART III: SOURCES FOR STUDY
  Sources for the Study of Law in Colonial Massachusetts at
  the American Antiquarian Society, Worcester, Massachusetts   551
  KATHLEEN A. MAJOR

Sources for the Study of Law in Colonial Massachusetts at
  the Essex Institute, Salem, Massachusetts   555
  CAROLINE PRESTON

Sources for the Study of Law in Colonial Massachusetts at
  the Harvard Law School, Cambridge, Massachusetts   559
  EDITH G. HENDERSON

Sources for the Study of Law in Colonial Massachusetts at
the Massachusetts Historical Society, Boston, Massachusetts   569
    JOHN D. CUSHING

Index   589

Illustrations

PAGE

1. *Frontispiece.* An Engraving of Justice from Murphy v. Pinchbeck, Inferior Court of Common Pleas, Suffolk, 1805 JAN c. 392. Courtesy, Social Law Library.

2. *Title Page.* Figure of Justice with Scales. From the Title Page of Ioanne Imberto, *Enchiridion Juris Scripti Galliae* (Utrecht, 1647). Courtesy, Collection of Daniel R. Coquillette.

3. John Noble (1829–1900), Clerk of the Supreme Judicial Court for Suffolk County, 1875–1908. A leading member of the Colonial Society of Massachusetts during its early days. A pioneer in the conservation and understanding of early court records. Photograph, courtesy Social Law Library.   v

4. John Winthrop (1587/88–1649), Governor, Chief Magistrate, Member of the Court of Assistants. Member, Gray's Inn and Inner Temple. Admitted, Court of Wards and Liveries. Courtesy, Massachusetts Historical Society, from a copy of a portrait painted in England before 1630.   8

5. Passport for the *Sparrow*, 20 December 1638, from Thomas Lechford's Scrivener's Book, page 29. Courtesy, American Antiquarian Society.   22

6. John Endicott (1589–1665), Governor, Magistrate, Member of the Court of Assistants. From a portrait by an unknown artist. Courtesy, Massachusetts Historical Society.   49

7. Simon Bradstreet (1603–1697), Governor, Member of the Court of Assistants, Member of the Council for the Safety of the People and the Conservation of the Peace. From a portrait by an unknown artist. Courtesy, Commonwealth of Massachusetts.   50

8. Nathaniel Byfield (1653–1733) by John Smibert (*circa* 1729). Judge of the Court of Common Pleas, Bristol; Judge of the Probate Court, Bristol; Judge of the Court of Common Pleas, Suffolk; Judge of the Vice Admiralty Court; Justice of the Peace, Suffolk. Courtesy, Collection of Mr. and Mrs. S. Vagnino. Information and photographs courtesy of Vose Galleries of Boston and R. H. Love Galleries, Inc., Chicago.   56

9. Byfield Coat of Arms. Taken from "A Roll of Arms," Part II, a pamphlet published by the New England Historic-Genealogical Society (1932), Plate 137.   105

10. Title Page, Book of Records belonging to John Clark (1667–1728), Justice of the Peace, Suffolk. Courtesy, Collection of James A. Henderson, Jr.   112

11. Entries, 7 May to 14 May 1711, Book of Records belonging to John Clark, Justice of the Peace, Suffolk. Courtesy, Collection of James A. Henderson, Jr.   131

12. Boston Selectmen to Constable, "Warning Out" dated 1 June 1765, Court of General Sessions of the Peace, Suffolk, 1765 JUL 245. Courtesy, Supreme Judicial Court.   177

13. Return dated 3 June 1765, on "Warning Out" dated 1 June 1765, Court of General Sessions of the Peace, Suffolk, 1765 JUL 245. Courtesy, Supreme Judicial Court.   178

14. Broadside depicting the confinement in the pillory, the whipping, and public confessional of a "rogue," Seth Hudson, in Boston, 1762. Courtesy, Boston Public Library.   185

15. Paul Dudley (1675–1751) by an unknown artist (*circa* 1720). Chief Justice, Superior Court of Judicature; Attorney General. Courtesy, Supreme Judicial Court.   196

16. Ezekiel Goldthwait (1710–1782) by John Singleton Copley (1771). Registrar of Deeds, Suffolk; Clerk, Inferior Court of Common Pleas, Suffolk; Clerk, City of Boston. Courtesy, Museum of Fine Arts, Boston.   203

17. Samuel Sewall (1652–1730) by John Smibert (1729). Chief Justice, Superior Court of Judicature; Judge of the Probate Court, Suffolk. Courtesy, Museum of Fine Arts, Boston.   208

18. Reconstruction of the content and typography of the first printing (1639) of the Glover-Day Press in Cambridge, Massachusetts, *The Oath of a Free-Man*, as appearing in Lawrence C. Wroth, *Oath of a Free-Man* (New York, Woolly Whale Press, 1939). Courtesy of The Press of the Woolly Whale Collection, Beinecke Rare Book and Manuscript Library, Yale University.   249

19. Title Page of Matthew Day's printing of *The Book of the General Lawes and Libertyes* (Cambridge, 1648), now at the Huntington Library, San Marino, California. Courtesy, Huntington Library.   252

20. Title Page of Henry Care, *English Liberties*, from its first American edition, printed in Boston by James Franklin, 1712. Courtesy, Yale Law School.   259

21. Portion of "An Exact Mapp of New England and New York" showing the "Pascatoway River" [Piscataqua] from Cotton Mather, *Magnalia Christi Americana* (1702).   274

22. Gravestone portrait of Colonel John Wheelwright of Wells (1745). 295

23. A deposition of 2 July 1725, York County Court Records. The body of the deposition is in the hand of William Pepperrell, Jr. The signature of the deponent, Samuel Hill, is attested by both William Pepperrell, Jr. and his father, Colonel William Pepperrell, Sr. Courtesy, York County Court Records. 298

24. Entries in the York County Court Records demonstrating the change of clerks. The top entry is in the hand of Joseph Hammond, Jr., Clerk, 1700–1720, and the lower entry is in the hand of William Pepperrell, Jr., Clerk, 1720–1725. Courtesy, York County Court Records. 300

25. James Otis, Jr. (1725–1783) by Joseph Blackburn (1755), from a photographic copy, courtesy of the Harvard Law School Art Collection. 320

26. Stephen Sewall (1702–1760) by Benjamin Feke (*circa* 1755). Chief Justice, Superior Court of Judicature. Courtesy, Harvard Law School Art Collection. 331

27. Theodore Sedgwick (1746–1813) by an unknown artist. Justice, Supreme Judicial Court. Courtesy, Harvard Law School Art Collection. 353

28. John Adams (1735–1826) by Benjamin Blyth (*circa* 1766). The earliest portrait of Adams, painted after he had started his career as a lawyer. Courtesy, Massachusetts Historical Society. 361

29. Purported to be Jeremiah Gridley (1701/1702–1767), Attorney General, Justice of the Peace and of the Quorum. Courtesy, Harvard Law School Art Collection. 364

30. The Gridley-Adams copy of Johannis Van Muyden's *Compendiosa Institutionum Justiniani Tractatio* (Utrecht, 1707). This book was loaned by Jeremiah Gridley to John Adams in 1758 and bought by Adams from Gridley's estate after 1767. Courtesy, Boston Public Library. 365

31. Robert Treat Paine (1731–1814) by Edward Savage and John Coles (*circa* 1796–1801). Justice, Supreme Judicial Court; Attorney General. Courtesy, Massachusetts Historical Society. 375

32. Benjamin Prat (1711–1763) attributed to John Smibert. Chief Justice, Province of New York; Moderator, Boston Town Meeting. Courtesy, Harvard Law School Art Collection. 378

33. First page of the Bar Book, Suffolk County (1770), in the hand of John Adams, its first Secretary. Courtesy, Massachusetts Historical Society. 396

34. Old State House, Boston, by James B. Marston (1801). Built 1713, burned 1748, and rebuilt within the original walls. For many years it served as the seat of the Superior Court of Judicature, and was the heart of the "legal district." John Adams and other lawyers lived near by. Courtesy, Massachusetts Historical Society. 420

35. Fourth Court House, Harvard Square, Cambridge, 1758. Served as Courthouse until 1816. Moved 1841. Demolished 1930. Courtesy, Cambridge Historical Commission. 434

36. Council Chamber, Old State House, Boston. The Superior Court of Judicature met in this room on frequent occasions in the eighteenth century. Courtesy, Bostonian Society. 438

37. Inscription on 1749 October Docket Book. Although the page is entitled "Superior Court," it was used for the Inferior Court of Common Pleas, Suffolk. Courtesy, Social Law Library, Boston. 470

38. Colonial Court records of the Inferior Court of Common Pleas, Suffolk. Illustrated are a minute book, a record book, and file papers. In other counties, colonial file papers are still in their original case rolls. Courtesy, Social Law Library, Boston. 480

39. Docket Book, Inferior Court of Common Pleas, Suffolk, 1758 October, showing the admission of John Adams and Samuel Quincy as attorneys on 6 November 1758. Note the signature of Ezekiel Goldthwait, Clerk, and the names of Jeremiah Gridley, Foster Hutchinson, and Robert Treat Paine. Courtesy, Social Law Library, Boston. 483

40. Watermark, Inferior Court of Common Pleas, Suffolk, 1790 OCT c. 288. Courtesy, Social Law Library, Boston. 486

41. Watermark, Inferior Court of Common Pleas, Suffolk, 1797 OCT 88. Courtesy, Social Law Library, Boston. 486

42. Embossed four-penny filing stamp, Inferior Court of Common Pleas, Suffolk, 1771 OCT c. 49. Courtesy, Social Law Library, Boston. 488

43. Embossed tuppence filing stamp, Inferior Court of Common Pleas, Suffolk, 1761 JAN 128. Courtesy, Social Law Library, Boston. 488

44. Heraldic embossed seal of Richard Jenneys "Notary & Tabellion Publick by Royal Authority . . . in Boston," Inferior Court of Common Pleas, Suffolk, 1760 OCT 134. Courtesy, Social Law Library, Boston. 488

45. Embossed three-penny filing stamp, Inferior Court of Common Pleas, Suffolk, 1755 OCT 173. Courtesy, Social Law Library, Boston. 488

46. Billhead, engraved by Paul Revere, Inferior Court of Common

Pleas, Suffolk, 1772 JUL Misc. *Joy v. Brackett*. Courtesy, Social
Law Library, Boston.   491

47. Engraved billhead illustrating the basic steps in making wallpaper.
It encourages customers to buy American goods. See above, 490. The
Inferior Court of Common Pleas, Suffolk, 1801 APR c. 380. Cour-
tesy, Social Law Library, Boston.   492

48. Wax Seal from His Majesty's Superior Court of Judicature for the
Province of New Brunswick, found on documents delivered to the
Massachusetts Courts in October 1758. Suffolk Files, Cabinet Col-
lection No. 143101. Kathryn M. Carey, Chief Conservator, Su-
preme Judicial Court, restored this seal. Courtesy, Supreme Judicial
Court.   503

49. Case files of the Inferior Court of Common Pleas, Suffolk, showing
the tins in which many colonial court records are still stored. Courtesy, Social Law Library, Boston.   527

50. Section of Writ of Attachment, 25 June 1776, Inferior Court of
Common Pleas, Suffolk. It shows George III's title crossed out and
replaced with "The Government and People of the Massachusetts
Bay in New England." This, and similar writs, were issued before
the signing of the Declaration of Independence on 4 July 1776.
See above, 487. Courtesy, Social Law Library, Boston.   544

51. Samuel Quincy (1734–1789) by John Singleton Copley (*circa*
1767). Solicitor General, Justice of the Peace. Proscribed in 1778,
Quincy became a tory refugee. His brother was Josiah Quincy, Jr.
(1744–1775). Courtesy, Museum of Fine Arts, Boston.   580

52. William Cushing (1732–1810) by Max Rosenthal (1889) from a
portrait by James Sharples. Associate Justice, Supreme Court of the
United States; Chief Justice, Supreme Judicial Court. Cushing was
appointed Chief Justice, Supreme Court of the United States, but
could not serve for health reasons. Courtesy, Harvard Law School
Art Collection.   583

53. Attorney's Bill, 1760. When this volume was in page proof, the editors discovered that there was no illustration to indicate that colonial
lawyers ever got paid. To remedy this oversight we close the volume
with an attorney's bill. The litigious Samuel Phillips, who owed this
substantial sum for legal expenses, was "Esquire" Phillips, the father
of the founder of Phillips Academy, Andover, and one of the wealthiest men in the Province. Inferior Court of Common Pleas, Suffolk,
1760 APR 166. Courtesy, Social Law Library.   585

Foreword

IN the first chapter of his admirable book *The Birth of the Re-public*, Edmund S. Morgan, Sterling Professor of History at Yale University and an Honorary Member of this Society, sets out to describe pre-Revolutionary Americans. In the very first paragraph he has this to say about one of their most striking characteristics:

> The American colonists were reputed to be a quarrelsome, litigious, di-visive lot of people and historical evidence bears out this reputation. The records of the local courts in every colony are cluttered with such a host of small lawsuits that one receives from them the impression of a people who sued each other almost as regularly as they ate or slept.[1]

When some one of Professor Morgan's stature singles out for special emphasis a particular aspect of colonial history, one can have confidence that that aspect is well worth study. The Colonial Society of Massachusetts, therefore, can present this volume — *Law in Colonial Massachusetts* — with the assurance that it will be focusing on one of the most important aspects of colonial life.

Over sixty years ago Roscoe Pound, later Dean of the Harvard Law School, wrote, "For most practical purposes American judicial history begins after the Revolution."[2] To be sure Pound qualified his remark to a certain extent, but as is so often the case with broad statements of this kind, the qualifications have tended to disappear. Certainly for many years after the first appearance of this dictum it was considered virtually gospel by most legal scholars. More recently fresh investigations have challenged the Pound statement until today it no longer has currency. In a sense this volume, representing as it does the latest researches in the field of colonial law, is one continuous refutation of Dean Pound's judgment.

This volume is by no means the first on a legal subject that the Colonial Society has published. Volumes 29 and 30 of the Society's publications contain the records of the Suffolk County Court during

[1] Edmund S. Morgan, *The Birth of the Republic, 1763–1789*, Revised Edition (Chicago, 1977), 4.

[2] Roscoe Pound, *The Spirit of the Common Law* (Boston, 1921), 113. See also Pound, *The Formative Era of American Law* (Boston, 1938), 3–8.

the period 1671–1680, together with a distinguished introduction by Zechariah Chafee, Jr. Volume 4 contains a section of bibliographies of Massachusetts laws. And the indexes to almost every volume bristle with references to colonial legal matters. Thus this volume is continuing a tradition of interest in colonial legal history that is almost as old as the Society itself.

An important editorial decision had to be reached at the very start of this venture—namely, whether to use the legal form of citation or the historical one. Since most of the articles in the volume were historical in treatment, the decision was made to follow the historical rather than the legal form of citation. There is one exception to this general policy. Professor William E. Nelson's article entitled "The American Revolution and the Emergence of Modern Doctrines of Federalism and Conflict of Laws" had so many citations to both British and American court cases that it was thought wiser to follow the legal form of citation in this one instance. One other point: limitations of space have in some instances necessitated the use of shortened captions under the actual illustrations; the full caption, in all cases, appears in the List of Illustrations starting on page xi.

Colonial Society conference volumes are cooperative ventures involving a number of people of good will whose sole aim is the advancement of knowledge. At the head of the list of those who have contributed to this book are, of course, the individual authors, who have produced such a splendid run of papers. In addition the two assistant editors have performed yeoman's service. Robert J. Brink and Catherine S. Menand, both experts in the study and preservation of court records, have not only contributed their expertise and insight in the field of colonial legal history, but have also gone way beyond the call of duty in addressing and solving a host of special problems incident to a book dealing with the law. Their share in this volume is a substantial one. Lois R. Krieger, who produced the magnificent index to the second volume of the Records of Trinity Church, has done an equally outstanding job with this book. Harry Milliken and his staff at The Anthoensen Press, Portland, Maine, have patiently coped with manuscripts and galleys covered with almost illegible editorial scrawls and have reduced the whole to order. All of those connected with this volume can be proud of the quality of book-making that it represents.

The Colonial Society of Massachusetts has been extraordinarily fortunate in the editors for its conference volumes—never more so than with this one on law. Our fellow-member Daniel R. Coquillette brings to his editorial task a rare combination of talents. He is at one and the same time a practicing lawyer, a teacher of law, and a legal scholar. Thus he is not limited to the point of view of any one part of the legal profession, but can approach editorial work from a number of different perspectives. In addition to this, he has a contagious enthusiasm for the job at hand that cannot help spreading to all who work with him. Dan Coquillette was also the man primarily responsible for making the arrangements for the conference itself. In a very real sense, as the conference was his conference, so this volume is his book.

FREDERICK S. ALLIS, JR.
Editor of Publications

87 Mount Vernon Street
Boston, Massachusetts
April 1984

Introduction:
The "Countenance of Authoritie"

[N]o mans goods or estaite shall be taken away from him, nor any way indammaged under colour of law or Countenance of Authoritie, unless it be by vertue or equitie of some expresse law of the country warranting the same, established by a generall Court and sufficiently published, or in case of the defect of a law in any partecular case by the word of God.

> The Liberties of the Massachusetts Collonie in New England, 1641, section 1.[1]

I have wrote you the want we have of two, or three, honest attorneys, (if any such thing in nature).

> Edward Randolph, Secretary to Governor Andros, Letter to England 1689.[2]

The *Reformation of the Law,* and more *Law* for the *Reformation of the World,* is what is mightily called for.

> Cotton Mather, *Bonifacius — An Essay Upon the Good that is to be Devised and Designed of those who Desire to Answer the Great End of Life* ... (Boston, 1710), 165.[3]

"MASSACHUSETTS was a legalistic society from beginning to end...."[4] From the arrival of the visible saints to the edge of the Revolution, the lives of the people of Colonial Massachu-

---

[1] "The Body of Liberties of 1641" from *The Colonial Laws of Massachusetts,* W. H. Whitmore, ed. (Boston, 1889).

[2] See Charles Warren, *A History of the American Bar* (Boston, 1911), 73.

[3] See Dennis R. Nolan, *Readings in the History of the American Legal Profession* (New York, 1980), 2.

[4] Barbara A. Black, "Community and Law in Seventeenth-Century Massachusetts," *Yale Law Journal,* XC (1980), 246, reviewing David T. Konig, *Law and Society in Puritan Massachusetts* (Chapel Hill, 1979). This is not to say law was always the *only,* or dominant, form of social control, but that it was always *a* substantial form of social control. Daniel Boorstin put it particularly well. "The Colonists, though not lawyers, were of a decidedly legalistic turn of mind...." Daniel J. Boorstin, *The Americans: The Colonial Experience* (New York, 1958), 20.

setts were touched in countless ways by law and legal ideology, by the "Countenance of Authoritie." Second only to law's close relatives, theology and ecclesiastical polity, legal issues dominated the intellectual life of the colony and defined the realities of power and social control.[5]

Yet, "the colonial period is, for most lawyers and laymen, the dark ages of American law."[6] Almost as true today as when Samuel Eliot Morison wrote the Preface to the last legal volume of this society fifty years ago, "legal development is probably the least known aspect of American colonial history."[7] Despite pioneering work by great scholars like George Haskins, Joseph Smith, Richard B. Morris, Zechariah Chafee, Jr., and Julius Goebel, the factual map is full of empty quarters illustrated only by decorative conjecturing.[8] Indeed, even the few attempts to draw basic outlines—on issues as fundamental as the primary social functions of the law— have led to controversy and doubt.[9]

The primary curse on these scholarly pioneers was the nature and state of the original sources, "either disappeared or become virtually inaccessible—buried in poorly organized manuscript collections at local archives."[1] What is worse, they had to fight off patriotic and professional romanticism on the one hand, and dogmatic, narrow bickering about the "scope" of legal history and its "proper" relationship to history and law on the other.[2] "Little wonder, then, that

---

[5] See George Haskins' seminal book, *Law and Authority in Early Massachusetts* (New York, 1960), 1–8. "Few others equaled [Massachusetts Bay's] contribution to theology, letters, and education; none paralleled its early achievements in government and law." Ibid., 1.

[6] Lawrence M. Friedman, *A History of American Law* (New York, 1973).

[7] S. E. Morison, "Preface," The Colonial Society of Massachusetts, *Publications*, XXIX (Boston, 1933), ix.

[8] See Stanley N. Katz's bold and stimulating "The Problem of a Colonial Legal History" in *Colonial British America*, Jack P. Greene, J. R. Pole, eds. (Baltimore, 1984), 457–484; and David H. Flaherty's excellent "Introduction" to his *Essays in the History of Early American Law* (Chapel Hill, 1969), 8–17.

[9] As Flaherty puts it, "The field is not barren . . . yet it has not yielded a bountiful harvest." Ibid., 14.

[1] Stephen Botein, *Early American Law and Society* (New York, 1983), 1. See also S. E. Morison, Colonial Society of Massachusetts, *Publications*, XXIX, ix.

[2] See Stanley N. Katz, "The Problem of a Colonial Legal History," 478. Katz believes contemporary ideological disputes could also be "diversions from the main task

a previous generation of scholars tended to dismiss the legal experience of the colonies as mere 'frontier' justice rendered in a kind of 'dark age' antedating the gloriously 'formative' era of American jurisprudence from the revolution to the civil war."[3]

But for the last two decades, dawn has been slowly breaking over this scholarly brave new world. The empirical tools and the objectives of colonial legal scholarship have been changing, bringing fundamental new opportunities. There has even been basic change in perceptions as to what legal history is all about.

Beginning with the brilliant work of Joseph Smith, James Willard Hurst, and George Haskins, it has become increasingly plain that conventional doctrinal and institutional studies do not ask the most important questions about so-called "frontier" law.[4] Rather, only by studying legal developments in the context of social and economic power are significant insights achieved. Further, the great contributions of Perry Miller have taught a generation of scholars that legal ideologies — ideas about law — have a power of their own, a power which cannot be understood in isolation from the political and religious convictions of those who used the law.[5] Sophisticated cross-disciplinary work, ranging from statistical techniques to theological studies, promises great advances in the quality of this "new legal history."[6]

of understanding the past." Ibid. *Cf.* Charles M. Andrews, *The Colonial Period of American History* (New Haven, 1938), IV, 222–223, n.1.

[3] Stephen Botein, *Early American Law and Society*, 1.

[4] See George L. Haskins, *Law and Authority*, x–xiii; James W. Hurst, *Law and the Conditions of Freedom* (Madison, 1967), 4–9; David T. Konig, *Law and Society*, xiii.

[5] *Cf.* Perry Miller, "Errand into the Wilderness" from *Errand Into the Wilderness*, P. Miller ed. (New York, 1956); *The New England Mind* (Boston, 1953), II, 130–131; and *The Life of the Mind in America* (New York, 1956), 99–116. *Cf.* Lawrence M. Friedman, "Heart Against Head: Perry Miller and the Legal Mind," *Yale Law Journal*, LXXVII (1968), 1244–1259, reemphasizing the need to study legal ideology in a social context.

[6] This, of course, does not denigrate the need for "conventional" legal expertise. "The fact that many 'legal scholars' do not explore extensively the social background and context of legal conflict leads some to think that their works say nothing about 'law and society.' The tendency is to put these books in their place: excellent reference books on rules, not roles. But even the narrowest of these works may contribute substantially to one's understanding of the role as well as the rule." Barbara A. Black, "Community and Law in Seventeenth-Century Massachusetts," *Yale Law Journal*, XC (1980), 245–246.

A second radical development has been the so-called "archival revolution." In Massachusetts, the progress has been stunning. Under the leadership of Chief Justice Edward Hennessey, the Massachusetts Judicial Records Committee, and the Colonial Court Records Project of the Social Law Library, all Massachusetts colonial court records are gradually being united in a single, scientific repository. The Plymouth Court Records Project, edited by David T. Konig, is another major achievement.[7] Many of these documents are from the lower courts, and show us much more about the lives of ordinary people, and about the poor and the oppressed, than previously printed sources. As the splendidly practical articles of Robert J. Brink, William E. Nelson, Catherine S. Menand, and Michael S. Hindus in the "sources" section of this book demonstrate, these new archival developments can and should work hand in glove with the newest ideas in legal history.[8] One of the major reasons for this book and conference was to describe the extent and promise of this "revolution" in Massachusetts and to give practical guidance to scholars who wish to use these archives.

The final radical change is perhaps the least important—but it is surely one of the most emotionally charged and controversial. As Perry Miller said, "Americans were the most litigious people in the world, as well as the most contemptuous, or at least distrustful, of the lawyers they employed."[9] Who were these legal "professionals"? How early did they show up, and how important were they? Were they the founders of American civil liberties, or the instruments of political and economic exploitation? Or both?

[7] The Massachusetts Judicial Records Committee has been aided by the National Historical Publications and Records Commission. See Robert J. Brink, "Boston's Great Anthropological Documents"; Hiller B. Zobel, "The Pompeii of Paper"; and Robert S. Bloom, "Judicial Records—The Foundation of a Statewide Records Preservation Program"; all in Boston Bar Journal, XXII (Sept. 1978), 6–33. The Plymouth Court Records Project, funded by a number of grants, was carried out in association with the Pilgrim Society. See William E. Nelson's "Introductory Essay," Plymouth Court Records 1686–1859 (ed. David T. Konig), I, 3–138.

[8] David H. Flaherty, Essays, 29. As Flaherty observes, "[T]he fact remains that few court records have ever been employed in analytical and general studies. Quantifying methods can now be used to great advantage. ...." Ibid., 32. See also David H. Flaherty, "A Select Guide to the Manuscript Court Records of Colonial New England," American Journal of Legal History, XI (1967), 107.

[9] Perry Miller, The Legal Mind in America (New York, 1962), 17.

Only very recently has anyone attempted adequate, scientific study of these "professional" issues. The conventional "bar" histories, such as those of Anton-Hermann Chroust and Charles Warren,[1] did not make extensive use of the range of original sources now available, nor did they ask the hard questions. New work by scholars such as Gerard Gawalt, Stephen Botein, Maxwell Bloomfield, John Reid, Robert Stevens, John Murrin, Daniel Calhoun, Charles McKirdy, Dennis Nolan, and Erwin Surrency—again inspired by James Willard Hurst—is opening doors to more candid and meaningful discussion.[2]

Further, this new professional history has helped to address another charged issue—"law without lawyers." Commencing with John P. Dawson's great *A History of Lay Judges* (Cambridge, Mass., 1960) it has become increasingly obvious that conventional ideas of professionalism have blinded us to the actual use of law in both England and colonial America. We have ignored the widespread role of "amateurs" in the enforcement and development of legal ideas. As George Haskins forcefully demonstrates in this book, an absence of lawyers hardly was an absence of law.[3] The central issues are, rather, what effect "lay" justice has on law and society—and how professionalism changes that.

The essays that follow in this book will illustrate all of these changes in approach and sources. To appreciate their significance,

[1] See Anton-Hermann Chroust, *The Rise of the Legal Profession in America* (Norman, Oklahoma, 1965), 2 vols.; Charles Warren, *A History of the American Bar* (Boston, 1911). Paul Hamlin's *Legal Education in Colonial New York* (New York, 1939) did use extensive original sources. See also David H. Flaherty, *Essays*, 16; Morton J. Horwitz, "The Conservative Tradition in the Writing of American Legal History," *American Journal of Legal History*, XVII (1973), 275.

[2] See Gerard W. Gawalt, *The Promise of Power: The Emergence of the Legal Profession in Massachusetts 1760–1840* (Westport, Conn., 1979); John P. Reid, *In a Defiant Stance* (London, 1977); Maxwell Bloomfield, *American Lawyers in a Changing Society, 1776–1876* (Cambridge, Mass., 1976); Stephen Botein, "Professional History Reconsidered," *American Journal of Legal History*, XXI (1977), 60–79; Dennis R. Nolan, *Readings in the History of the American Legal Profession* (New York, 1980); and Daniel H. Calhoun, *Professional Lives in America: Structure and Aspiration 1750–1850* (Cambridge, Mass., 1965). On the great influence of Hurst, see Robert W. Gordon, "J. Willard Hurst and the Common Law Tradition in American Legal Historiography," *Law and Society Review*, X (1976), 9–56.

[3] George L. Haskins, "Lay Judges: Magistrates and Justices in Early Massachusetts," below, 39–40.

it is useful to outline the primary problems of Massachusetts colonial legal history.

THE MAJOR PROBLEMS OF MASSACHUSETTS COLONIAL LEGAL HISTORY

I. *The Earliest Period: 1620–1648*

The signing of the Mayflower Compact on the waters off Cape Cod on 11 November 1620 and the arrival of the ship *Arbella*, with the Massachusetts Bay Colony Charter on board, at Naumkeag (Salem) on 12 June 1630 are the starting points of Massachusetts legal history—and the perpetual debates about the role of colonial law. The primary issue of the early period has always been the extent and duration of what David Konig has called the "Puritan ideal of communalism." Also hotly debated is the extent of direct importation of English laws and legal expertise, and the degree to which law, as opposed to other community institutions, was used for social control.[4]

There are certain striking facts about early colonial Massachusetts. The first, and perhaps most important, is that England was rapidly approaching civil war. In 1629 Charles I had resolved to govern without Parliament, and by 1640 the royal government was close to complete breakdown. Thus, despite the various crises that beset the colony—such as Dr. Robert Child's remonstrance and the Antinomian crisis—the colonists, with their Charter safely in their hands on this side of the ocean, were largely left alone. There were also bold initiatives by the colonials. The founding of Harvard College (1636) and the first public schools in British America (1642, 1647), the establishment of the first printing press in the American colonies (1639), and the adoption of the great Cambridge Platform (1648) have overshadowed legal developments. But these, too, were remarkable by any standard.

Three of the most notable legal initiatives are analyzed in detail in this book. Thomas Lechford was, without a doubt, the first practicing lawyer in Massachusetts.[5] Lechford's law practice, which

---

[4] See David T. Konig, *Law and Society*, xiii.

[5] The "practicing" limitation excludes colonists with legal backgrounds who acted as magistrates and legislators, but who probably never took clients in the Bay Colony,

spanned the years 1638 until his return to England in 1641, can obviously tell us much about the early legal atmosphere in the colonies — both in terms of Puritan "communalism" and the importation of English law. Thomas G. Barnes' essay, "Thomas Lechford and the Earliest Lawyering in Massachusetts, 1638–1641," is the first detailed analysis of this early practice. It establishes that Lechford was a skilled conveyancer and pleader, familiar with English legal forms and devices; that his services were much in demand; and that he left for England more for religious than professional reasons. Lechford's experience indicated both a society with a concrete need for law of a fairly technical type, even at a very early date, and the ability of a lawyer to prosper there, even though somewhat at odds with the religious order.

George L. Haskins' essay "Lay Judges: Magistrates and Justices in Early Massachusetts" traces the adaptation of that remarkable English institution to American conditions. It is true that some of the original leaders of the colony were trained in law. A notable example was John Winthrop, who was a member of Gray's Inn and Inner Temple, an attorney to the Court of Wards and Liveries, and a steward experienced in running the court leet at his father's Groton manor.[6] Winthrop's son, John Winthrop, Jr., three of the first As-

including John Winthrop, formerly of Gray's Inn and Inner Temple, Richard Bellingham, Recorder of Boston, England, and Reverend Nathaniel Ward, formerly of Lincoln's Inn. In an odd way, it is also hard to overlook that lecherous, alcoholic *bon vivant*, "proud and indolent" Thomas Morton with his "Maypole at Merry-Mount (Wollaston)." He certainly had a legal background, and claimed to be "a gentleman of Cliffords Inn." He was also described as "a kind of pettiefogger of Furnefells Inn" by a rather prejudiced Governor Bradford. See Anton-Hermann Chroust, *The Rise of the Legal Profession,* 72 ; Samuel Eliot Morison, *Builders of the Bay Colony* (Boston, 1930), 16–17. Morton's "practice" seemed to involve selling guns and liquor to the Indians for furs. As Morison observed, some of us have "met more spiritual descendants of Thomas Morton than of John Winthrop." Ibid., 19.

[6] Winthrop was an English justice of the peace at eighteen and held court leet for his father at little more than twenty. Ibid., 53 ; Edmund S. Morgan, *The Puritan Dilemma: The Story of John Winthrop* (Boston, 1958), 15–16. He also was admitted in the Court of Wards and Liveries, as was John Humfry. See G. W. Robinson, *John Winthrop as Attorney* (Cambridge, Mass., 1930). There is some question whether Winthrop was a member of Gray's Inn, Inner Temple, or both. Morgan says he was admitted to Gray's Inn in 1613 and took up bachelor residence in Inner Temple. Edmund S. Morgan, *The Puritan Dilemma,* 15, 23. *The Dictionary of American National Biography* (New York, 1960), X, 408 says that Winthrop was "admitted" at Gray's Inn 25 October 1613 and at Inner Temple in 1628. That explanation is probably correct. Some lawyers were members of one inn, but "mi-

sistants, Isaac Johnson, John Humfry, and Roger Ludlow, together with Richard Bellingham, Simon Bradstreet, Herbert Pelham, Thomas Dudley, and Nathaniel Ward all received some legal education in England.[7] Yet none of them were practicing "professionals." Instead, they served as legislators and/or lay magistrates. Haskins' analysis confirms John P. Dawson's thesis, developed in other contexts, that the institution of lay magistrates provided "further cohesion within the colony beyond that fostered by the churches and by the general 'due forme of Government,'" and that non-professional, local justice would represent, paradoxically, both a major English legal heritage and a model for future colonial independence.[8]

Morris L. Cohen's essay, "Legal Literature in Colonial Massachusetts" focuses on what must be the most astonishing legal development of the fruitful early period — Nathaniel Ward's "The Body of Liberties" (1641) and *The Book of the General Lawes and Libertyes* (1648). These compilations were extraordinary — there was nothing like them in England or anywhere else in the colonies. They anticipated the parallel, but quite separate, law reform efforts during the English Civil War.[9] Their most important feature was their in-

grated" to another. The name of Winthrop's uncle, Emmanuel Downing, appears next to Winthrop's entry in the Inner Temple register in 1628/29. Downing was also an attorney of the Wards, and Winthrop was probably joining his uncle's chambers. Winthrop's eldest son, John, joined Inner Temple in 1624/25. I owe this information to the kind help of J. H. Baker. *Cf.* E. Alfred Jones, *American Members of the Inns of Court* (London, 1924), 219–220, Wilfrid R. Prest, *The Inns of Court Under Elizabeth I and the Early Stuarts, 1590–1640* (London, 1972), 208.

[7] Ward practiced and studied law in London for nearly ten years before entering the ministry. Ibid., 221. See Charles Warren, *A History of the American Bar*, 59; Massachusetts Historical Society, *Proceedings* (Boston, 1878), 3.

[8] See George L. Haskins, "Lay Judges: Magistrates and Justices in Early Massachusetts," below, 53. See J. P. Dawson, *A History of Lay Judges* (Cambridge, Mass., 1960), 3–4.

[9] See George L. Haskins, "Codification of the Law in Colonial Massachusetts: A Study in Comparative Law," *Indiana Law Journal*, XXX (1954), 1; George L. Haskins, Samuel E. Ewing, 3d "The Spread of Massachusetts Law in the Seventeenth Century," *Pennsylvania Law Review*, CVI (1958), 413; George L. Haskins, "Influence of New England Law on the Middle Colonies," *Law and History Review*, I (1983), 238; Thorp L. Wolford, "The Laws and Liberties of 1648," *Boston University Law Review*, XXVIII (1948), 426. As to law reform in England, see Donald Veall, *The Popular Movement for Law Reform 1640–1660* (Oxford, 1970), 97–240; G. B. Nourse, "Law Reform Under the Commonwealth and Protectorate," *Law Quarterly Review*, LXXV (1959), 512–529; Stuart E. Prall, *The Agitation for Law*

herent assumption that both ruling power and societal pluralism should be legally limited. In this sense, they reflected political developments in early seventeenth-century England, before the voyages of 1629–1630, and also anticipated the "modern scientific concept of sovereignty."[1] As John D. Eusden has observed in the English context, "The convictions of the Puritans and the lawyers about the nature and functions of laws and the relation of legal norms to ultimate authorities formed a prototype for modern pluralist thought."[2]

These contributions of Barnes, Haskins, and Cohen reinforce Haskins' original thesis in *Law and Authority in Early Massachusetts*. The early period was remarkably creative. There was both ingenious adaptation of English legal institutions to new conditions and genuinely original ideas, such as "The Body of Liberties" and the *Lawes and Libertyes*.[3] These ideas cannot be seen in isolation from Puritan innovation in religious thought and ecclesiastical polity—and it is

---

Reform During the Puritan Revolution 1640–1660 (Hague, 1960). The law reform movement in England had an interest in the codification of customary law and in establishing a relatively pluralistic and local basis of justice, but its development and character were quite different from anything in the Bay Colony. It was politically more democratic and more radical in its objectives. See Donald W. Hanson, *From Kingdom to Commonwealth: The Development of Civic Consciousness in English Political Thought* (Cambridge, Mass., 1970), 300–301, 332–339; Gerard Winstanley, *The Law of Freedom in a Platform* (London, 1652—reprinted 1941 with Introduction by Robert W. Kenny).

[1] John D. Eusden, *Puritans, Lawyers and Politics in Early Seventeenth-Century England* (New Haven, Conn., 1968), 177.

[2] Ibid., 174. In Massachusetts, this conviction included notions of recording judgments for use as precedents. As early as 1639, the General Court enacted that

Whereas many judgments have bene given in our courts, whereof no records are kept of the evidence and reasons whereupon the verdit and judgment did passe, the records whereof being duely entered and kept would bee of good use for president [precedent] to posterity, and a releife to such as shall have just cause to have their causes reheard and reviewed, it is therefore by this Court ordered and decreed that thenceforward every judgment, with all the evidence, bee recorded in a booke, to bee kept to posterity.

Records of the Governor and Company of Massachusetts Bay in New England (Boston, 1853), I, 275 (1639). See Edwin Powers, *Crime and Punishment*, 437. Nevertheless, while what might be called the first statutory compilation to be printed in Massachusetts, *Lawes and Libertyes*, appeared in 1648, there were no printed reports of Massachusetts cases until 1804. See Laurence M. Friedman, *A History of American Law*, 282–283. The General Court sent to England for two copies of *Cokes Reports* in 1647. See below, xxxi, note 7.

[3] George L. Haskins, *Law and Authority*, 125–136.

hardly a coincidence that the *Lawes and Libertyes* were printed in 1648, the year of the Cambridge Platform.[4] A valuable legal heritage was confronted with rough social challenges, and there was a high degree of actual independence. This was fertile ground for legal innovation. It was none the less a remarkable achievement on the edge of a wilderness.

II. *The Later Bay Colony and the Inter-Charter Period: 1649–1691*

The next forty years remain a "mystery" period. Extending from the publication of the *Lawes and Libertyes* and the death of John Winthrop to the Second Charter, this period represents a great gap in our knowledge about Massachusetts law and lawyers. Despite three outstanding specialized studies: David T. Konig's *Law and Society in Puritan Massachusetts* (Chapel Hill, 1979) limited to Essex County 1629–1692; Joseph H. Smith's *Colonial Justice in Western Massachusetts* (1639–1702) limited to the Pynchon Court Record in frontier Springfield; and the Colonial Society's own *Records of the Suffolk County Court* 1671–1680 (*Publications,*, xxix, xxx, Boston, 1933) with Zechariah Chafee, Jr.'s outstanding Introduction,[5] there remain very substantial questions as to the state of the legal profession, the sources of the law, and the actual operation of the justice system.

It is regrettable, but typical, that none of the papers presented at this conference addressed the period directly. Barbara A. Black touches on its end in "Nathaniel Byfield: 1653–1733," and Morris L. Cohen's "Legal Literature in Colonial Massachusetts" emphasizes the very important legal printing of the period, including supplements to the *General Lawes and Libertyes* in 1650, 1654 and

---

[4] "In their respective religious and civil spheres, the Cambridge Platform and *The Law and Liberties* represented the culmination of an extraordinarily creative period during which the colonists applied conscious design to received tradition. . . ." Ibid., 136. Nevertheless, "little has been done to interpret the Hebraic laws of early New England within a wider context of religious theory and practice." Stephen Botein, *Early American Law and Society*, 2. This includes possible talmudic influences.

[5] Daniel J. Boorstin describes Chafee's Introduction as "brilliant." *The American: The Colonial Experience*, 381. See also Edwin Powers, *Crime and Punishment in Early Massachusetts: 1620–1692* (Boston, 1966), a documentary history limited to the punishment of crime.

1657, *The Book of the General Lawes* in 1660, *The General Laws and Liberties* ... *revised and reprinted* of 1672, the *Book of the General Laws of* ... *New-Plymouth* in 1672 and 1685, and statutory printings for Connecticut in 1673. Most important, the annual printing of the *Several Laws and Orders* began in 1663.

It is not just that there was a very great deal of legal printing. References to legal topics were common in the religious and political literature, as Cohen points out.[6] Further, in 1649, 1650, 1656 and 1673 important statutes were passed regulating hiring of counsel, sources of mercantile law, representation by attorney, length of legal arguments, and barratry.[7] Yet detailed studies are few.

The conventional professional histories either skip this period or give the following picture. The Bay Colony was resting on the laurels of its earlier creative period. The legal printings, admittedly impressive, merely repeated and consolidated earlier gains. The

[6] See Morris Cohen, "Legal Literature in Colonial Massachusetts," below, 245.

[7] In 1649 it became "unlawful for any person to ask a counsellor advice of any magistrate in any case wherein he shall be a plaintiffe," despite the observation by the magistrates that "we must then provide lawyers to direct men in their causes." *Records of the Governor and Company of Massachusetts Bay* (Boston, 1853), III, 168. See also Edwin Powers, *Crime and Punishment*, 434. In the 1660 version of the Massachusetts statutes, this provision was essentially reenforced by adding the words "shall or *may be* plaintiff." *Massachusetts Colonial Laws* (Boston, 1887), 141. To whom would a plaintiff now turn for legal advice? The presence of a practicing bar was acknowledged by a 1663 statute that "No person who is an usuall and common attorney in any inferior court, shall be admitted to sitt as a Deputy in this [General] Court." *Records*, IV, 87. In 1673, it was enacted "that it shall be lawful for any person by his lawfull attorney ... to sue in any of our Courts for any right or interest...." *Records*, IV, 563. The barratry statute of 1656 also took a backhanded notice of legal practice by prohibiting attorneys from fomenting reckless or vexatious litigations. Ibid., 82; *Massachusetts Colonial Laws*, 9.
   Perhaps the most interesting statute was the order in 1650 that "whereas this Commonwealth is much defective for want of laws for maritime affairs ... the said laws printed and published in a book called *Lex Mercatoria* shall be perused and duly considered and such of them as are approved by this court shall be declared and published to be in force in this jurisdiction." *Records*, III, 193. This reference to Gerald Malynes' great commercial law text, *Consuetudo, vel, Lex Mercatoria*, follows closely on the General Court's order to England in 1647 for the importation of two copies each of Coke's *Reports*, Coke's *First Institutes* ("Coke upon Littleton"), [Rastell's] "*Newe Tearmes of the Lawe*," Coke's *Second Institutes* ("Coke upon Magna Carta"), Dalton's *Justice of the Peace*, and [Coke's] "*Book of Entryes*" "to the end we may have the better light for making and proceeding about laws...." *Records*, III, 212. These enactments hardly evidence a lack of interest in law or legal development.

English civil war stopped immigration—the population actually de-
creased—and the economy was depressed. The silver lining was
the forced development of trade, increasingly independent of England. The collapse of peaceful Indian relations and the subsequent
ravages of King Philip's War (1675–1676), together with uneasi-
ness concerning the restored Stuart monarchy, resulted in a "low
profile" for the Bay Colony government and severe rifts among its
leaders. Throughout this period, and right up to the dreaded revocation of the Charter in 1684 and the Andros regime, there was allegedly little or no evidence of legal education, legal practice, or legal
thought.[8] Indeed, several historians have gone so far as to claim that
both the loss of the Charter in 1684 and the Salem witchcraft crisis
in 1692 were due to a lack of lawyers and legal expertise in the Bay
Colony![9]

The limited evidence we have casts severe doubt on this bleak
reconstruction. Not only the printed legal publications, but the court
records and surviving judicial note books give a very different impression. The limited analytical work done with these records, most
notably that of Joseph H. Smith, Zechariah Chafee, Jr., David T.
Konig, and Edwin Powers, indicates a high rate of litigation. This
included relatively sophisticated and complex legal disputes that
were systematically—although not quickly—resolved.[1] Barbara A.
Black's essay in this volume, "Nathaniel Byfield: 1653–1733," although focused on Byfield's personal legal problems, strongly confirms this view. As Black observes, "the inhabitants of Bristol were
embroiled in controversy among themselves from virtually the mo-

[8] See Anton-Hermann Chroust, *The Rise of the Legal Profession*, I, 77–79; Charles
Warren, *A History of the American Bar*, 69–74; Edwin Powers, *Crime and Punishment*, 528; F. W. Grinnell, "The Bench and Bar in Colony and Province (1630–
1776) in *Commonwealth History of Massachusetts* (New York, 1928), II, 161–
164; Henry E. Clay, "The Development of the Legal Profession in the Bay Colony
at the Commonwealth—the First 200 Years," *Massachusetts Law Review* (Summer,
1981), 115, 116; Nathan Mathews, "The Results of Prejudice Against Lawyers in
Massachusetts in the 17th Century," Address Before the Bar Association of the City
of Boston, 9 December 1926, *Boston Bar Journal* (1926), 73–94.

[9] See F. W. Grinell, "Bench and Bar," 161–164; Nathan Mathews, *Results of
Prejudice*, 80–87 (revocation of charter), 88–89 (witchcraft). "Thus ended the
Puritan Commonwealth—a result virtually, and I think literally, due to the absence
of an educated Bar." Ibid., 87.

[1] See above, xxx, note 5 and accompanying text.

ment of settlement. They squabbled, and sued, over rates and roads, mills and ministers, over land and water. . . . No Puritan Eden this."[2] Byfield's personal legal struggles were also technical and highly involved. They required the aid of expert counsel, and seemed to go on forever.[3] Black's study adds credence to the similar descriptions by Chafee, relying on the Suffolk records of 1671–1680, and by Konig, relying on the Essex records of 1629–1692.[4] As Chafee observed, "The most disagreeable characteristic of the colonists which is revealed in these pages is their unwillingness to end a lawsuit."[5] It would be most surprising if this were a society where legal development stood still, and legal expertise was non-existent.

Further, the negotiations with England after the revocation of the Charter, and the arrangements following the overthrow of the Andros regime in 1689, hardly speak of legal naiveté. On the contrary, Increase Mather's mission to England and the activities of the Council for the Safety of the People and the Conservation of the Peace were secular in emphasis and sophisticated in technique. The end result, the signing of the new charter on 7 October 1691, may have been attacked by some of the clergy, but it established a new legal order which preserved some previous gains, at least in terms of localism and limitation of central authority by law.[6]

There is another mystery. Was there a legal profession? The conventional bar histories say there was practically none — and that what "attorneys" existed were untrained, incompetent, and really only "attorneys in fact" in the sense that they appeared on another's behalf, like the simple exercise of a "power of attorney" today.[7] According to this view, the separation of the colony from England by

---

[2] Barbara Black, below, 71, note 5.

[3] As to the retention of Paul Dudley, William Shirley, and Robert Auchmuty in Byfield's later legal affairs, see ibid., 87, 101, 103. There is every reason to suppose similar use of counsel in earlier cases.

[4] See David T. Konig, *Law and Society*, xi–xiii, 89–116; Zechariah Chafee, Jr., Colonial Society of Massachusetts, *Publications*, XXIX, xxxvi–xxxvii.

[5] Ibid., xxxvi.

[6] See Marcus W. Jernegan, "The Province Charter (1689–1715)" in *Commonwealth History of Massachusetts* (New York, 1928), II, 1–28.

[7] See Anton-Hermann Chroust, *The Rise of the Legal Profession*, I, 77–79.

the Civil War had cut it off from English legal training, and nothing had developed indigenously to take its place.

What evidence can be adduced to support this view? An examination of the careers of Harvard graduates, set out in table form in this book as "Appendix II" to Charles R. McKirdy's article, shows only one self-styled "lawyer" between 1648 and 1684. But there is a major "boom" in the Inter-Charter period of 1685–1692 with four law career choices—including the distinguished names of Benjamin Lynde, Addington Davenport, and Paul Dudley—all destined to be among the earliest professionally trained justices of the Superior Court.[8] During the Andros regime, Andros' personal secretary, Edward Randolph, wrote in 1689 to England of the "want we have of two, or three, honest attorneys."[9] "We have but two, one is West's creature,—came with him from New York, and drives all before. He who takes extravagant fees, and for want of more, the country cannot avoid coming to him. . . ." Randolph was not, of course, an unbiased source, and was actually writing to plead for "judges from England," but his letter shows a demand for legal services.

In 1686 a table of attorney's fees was established by the Andros regime, and attorneys were obliged, upon admission to the bar, to take an oath.[1] These seem like strange requirements if there were no professional lawyers. The first five to take the oath, Giles Masters, Nathaniel Thomas, Anthony Checkley, Christopher Webb, and John Watson, have never been carefully studied. Whether or not they had any formal legal training, the oath was an important step toward some professional structure.[2]

More important, it is now established that the court records, at least those that have been examined from Essex and Suffolk, contain many names of those purporting to act as "attornies" during this period. Some names occur very frequently, and it can be shown that they were more than agents or "attorneys-in-fact," at least in the few cases that have been closely examined.[3] Chroust, while appar-

---

[8] See Charles R. McKirdy, "Massachusetts Lawyers on the Eve of the Revolution: The State of the Profession," below, 329–330, 334.

[9] Charles Warren, *A History of the American Bar*, 73.

[1] Ibid., 72. See Anton-Hermann Chroust, *The Rise of the Legal Profession*, 77–83.

[2] See Charles Warren, *A History of the American Bar*, 72–73.

[3] See Zechariah Chafee, Colonial Society of Massachusetts, *Publications*, xxiv–xxvi.

ently acknowledging this fact, claims that "none of these men . . . could be called lawyers in England, and some of them were probably the persons whom Governor Winthrop had in mind when he referred to attorneys as 'mean men.'"[4] But Chroust gives no conclusive evidence for this view, while an examination of the few known lawyer discipline cases — such as that of Daniell Ela for charging excessive fees in 1669, and of Peter Goulding, barred from pleading any cause but his own for "antedating writings" and stirring up vexatious litigation in 1680 — merely confirm that law practice for money was indeed taking place, and that there were abuses, some not unfamiliar to our "modern" profession.[5]

More convincing are the conclusions of Zechariah Chafee, Jr., albeit limited to his study of the Suffolk County Court records from 1671–1680. Chafee found that "There can be no question . . . that many of the attorneys in the cases which follow, do correspond to the lawyers of today" and that "technical arguments in many of the Reasons of Appeal and answers show that they were written by men accustomed to legal problems."[6] Not only do specific names "keep recurring with varying principal [clients]" but, despite the lack of systematic professional training, the records demonstrate skill in litigation.[7] Equally important, the instruments contained in the records — including complex leases, deeds, indentures, bonds, partnership articles, charter-parties, bills of lading, and trusts — were impressive. One set of instruments, trust deeds for the benefit of creditors executed in 1659, were said to be "made by the advice and councell of one whose judgment in the law was accoumpted a bond."[8] Chafee emphasized that "conveyancing, a phase of the modern

---

[4] Anton-Hermann Chroust, *The Rise of the Legal Profession*, 79.

[5] See *Records and Files of the Quarterly Courts of Essex County (1636–1683)* (Salem, 1911–1921), IV, 198 (1669), VII, 416 (1680). See also Edwin Powers, *Crime and Punishment*, 438. Cf. Anton-Hermann Chroust, *The Rise of the Legal Profession*, 80–81. One individual, Hudson Leverett, did have a pretty bad record, but Chroust is much too facile in assuming that lack of a "liberal education" and formal legal education necessarily created technically incompetent and dishonest attorneys. Ibid., 76–77, 80. While we who teach in formal law schools might wish to believe this is true, elitist prejudice is another possibility.

[6] Zechariah Chafee, Jr., Colonial Society of Massachusetts, *Publications*, xxv.

[7] Ibid., xxv. Chafee states that "by the year 1671, when these records begin, paid attorneys were a recognized, but hardly reputable, class." Ibid., xxvi.

[8] Ibid., xxvi.

xxxvi   INTRODUCTION

lawyer's work no less important than appearing in court, was also well developed."[9]

In this book, Thomas G. Barnes completely demolishes the "accepted" picture of Thomas Lechford as an unsuccessful pettifogger.[1] The desire of orthodox bar historians to see an evolutionary "rise" over time in the legal profession appears to have blinded some to the actual state of the profession during this second period as well.[2] At the very least, more genuine research in the original sources is required.

Finally, Chafee's analysis of the Suffolk records challenged "the view that Massachusetts remained until after 1700 in a period of rude, untechnical, popular law." "Before the colony was half a century old, its courts are shown busy with trusts for the benefit of creditors and their annulment for fraud, difficult questions of inheritance, and complex mercantile transactions afloat and ashore."[3] Chafee also raised the possibility that reliance on some forms of English law — particularly in drafting instruments — may have been greater than often assumed, and that slavish attachment to scriptural "laws" was, at least by this period, a myth.[4]

Much, however, remains to be done. Assumptions regarding the state of law and the legal system during this 1648 to 1691 period are fundamental to some of the most important theories about the development of American law,[5] but we really know very little about it. Not only are many court records unexamined, but the significance of colonial statutory drafting and the contribution of Calvinist theology to colonial jurisprudence remain largely unexplored.[6]

[9] Ibid., xxvi.

[1] *Cf.* Anton-Hermann Chroust, *The Rise of the Legal Profession*, 73–75; Charles Warren, *A History of the American Bar*, 68–69.

[2] See Stanley N. Katz, "Looking Backward: The Early History of American Law," *University of Chicago Law Review*, XXXIII (1966), 867, 870–873; Stephen Botein, "The Legal Profession in Colonial North America," *Lawyers in Early Modern Europe and America*, Wilfrid Prest, ed. (New York, 1981), 129–130.

[3] Zechariah Chafee, Colonial Society of Massachusetts, *Publications*, XXIX, xxviii.

[4] Ibid., xxviii–xxxv.

[5] For example, the actual state of the seventeenth-century legal system must be central to John M. Murrin's famous thesis that the eighteenth century saw the "Anglicization" of that system. See page xxxix, below.

[6] See David D. Hall, "Understanding the Puritans" in *Colonial America: Essays in Politics and Social Development*, Stanley N. Katz, ed. (Boston, 1971), 31. "It was

Fortunately, the work of David T. Konig and Barbara A. Black, building on that of Joseph H. Smith and Zechariah Chafee, Jr., points the way. Equally important, the archival advances described in this volume by Robert J. Brink, William E. Nelson, Michael S. Hindus, and Catherine S. Menand should make the task easier and ultimately more accurate.[7] In my opinion, such work will establish that legal process was critically important during the period 1649–1691, particularly in dealing with the high rate of actual social change within the colony. As Barbara Black observes, "Once upon a time the historians of Massachusetts exhibited a tendency to concentrate on the beginning and the end, according short shrift to the middle. Founding and Revolution hypnotized us, and we leaped merrily from John Winthrop to John Adams. . . . Today, of course, the general history of this period is brightly illuminated. But the legal history is not. There the Age remains Dim, if not Dark."[8]

III. The "Second Charter" Period: 1692–1760

Law in Colonial Massachusetts makes its primary contribution in analyzing this important period. The seventy years between the arrival of the Second Charter (1692) and the Writs of Assistance case (1760) saw greater social and economic change. The population exploded from roughly 44,000 (1691) to 280,000 (1765). The economic basis of the colony certainly shifted. Religious, social, and ethnic divisions multiplied, and basic changes occurred throughout the mechanics of governance.[9] Three terrible small pox epidemics in

Calvin, to be sure, who taught the Puritans their legalism, but the political situation in which they found themselves encouraged the development of this legalism beyond the point where he had stopped." Ibid., 43. See generally Perry Miller, *The New England Mind: From Colony to Province* (Cambridge, Mass., 1953), 19–67.

[7] See Robert J. Brink, "'Immortality Brought to Light': An Overview of Massachusetts Colonial Court Records," below, 471; William E. Nelson, "Court Records as Sources for Historical Writing," below, 499; Michael S. Hindus, "A Guide to the Court Records of Early Massachusetts," below, 519 and Catherine S. Menand, "A 'magistracy fit and necessary': A Guide to the Massachusetts Court System," below, 541.

[8] See Barbara Black, "Nathaniel Byfield, 1653–1733," below, 104.

[9] See Douglas L. Jones, below, 153–154, and sources cited. There was also severe inflation. Ibid., 154. See "An Overview of Massachusetts History to 1820" in the companion volume to this book, *Medicine in Colonial Massachusetts*, The Colonial Society of Massachusetts, *Publications*, LVII (1980), 3–19; James A. Henretta,

1720, 1729, and 1759 and a string of savage local wars against the French and Indians—King William's War (1689–1697), Queen Anne's War (1702–1713), the War of Jenkin's Ear (1739–1748) and the French and Indian War (1754–1763)—caused cruel hardship and major dislocations in towns throughout the colony.[1] We must ask what happened to the legal structure—to the lay magistrates, localism, the statutory systems, and the legal profession.

Half of the essays in this book make this period their special concern. Two, the essays of Barbara A. Black and Russell K. Osgood, examine entirely new data on lay magistrates—focusing respectively on the careers and records of Nathaniel Byfield of Bristol (1653–1733) and John Clark of Boston (1667–1728). Two more, by Douglas L. Jones and David H. Flaherty, focus on the law of coercive social control, namely poverty law and criminal law. Flaherty also examines the early history of the criminal bar, while Jones' study of "warning out" records gives us new understanding of who the poor were and how they lived. Morris L. Cohen's article continues to give new perspectives on the printed legal literature of the period, while Neal W. Allen's study of the actual operation of courts in "The Eastern Parts" (Maine) adds flesh and blood to our knowledge of dispute resolution in local courts, of local court procedures, and of the personnel, both lay and professional, who were involved.

There are significant, unresolved historical questions about this period, too. The most obvious is the extent to which Puritan ideals and institutions survived the massive structural and social changes after the revocation of the First Charter.[2] This is linked closely to a

---

"Economic Development and Social Structure in Colonial Boston" in *Colonial America*, Stanley N. Katz ed. (1971), 450–465; Marcus W. Jernegan, "The Province Charter (1689–1715)" in *Commonwealth History of Massachusetts*, II, 1–28; and Bernard Bailyn, *The New England Merchants in the Seventeenth Century* (Cambridge, Mass., 1955), 143–197. The colony was "buffeted by demographic and social changes." See Adam J. Hirsch, "From Pillory to Penitentiary," *Michigan Law Review*, LXXX (1982), 1128.

[1] The Colonial Society of Massachusetts, *Publications*, LVII, 5–11.

[2] Even the bizarre, traumatic Salem witchcraft trials of 1692–1693 have been blamed in part on the dislocation surrounding the revocation of the First Charter. See David T. Konig, *Law and Society*, 169–185. The Second Charter arrived in Boston on 14 May 1692. On 2 June 1692 Governor Phips and his council commissioned the infamous special court of "oyer and terminer," without waiting for

second question, the extent to which the sources of the law and the actual operation of the legal system changed. Was there still indigenous innovation in lawmaking? Were the lay magistrates still central to problems of social control? Was there a continuing contribution of theology to legal theory?

The work of John M. Murrin has stimulated debate on these questions. Murrin's thesis is that the "American colonies experienced a rapid and pervasive Anglicization during the middle of the eighteenth century."[3] Murrin's primary support for this thesis is the growth of the legal profession in Massachusetts during these years. According to Murrin, in the period 1692 to 1702 "the General Court adopted practically the entire court system of the hated Dominion."[4] The practicing bar, emerging from "the undistinguished reality of 1692," grew around a nucleus of royal-sympathizers, like Thomas

the newly authorized legislature to convene, which alone had the necessary powers under the Charter to create courts. Ibid., 170. By 22 September 1692 the last of the terrible executions had occurred. Ironically, witchcraft accusations in Andover were halted by a defamation suit. Ibid., 184.

The causes of the "witchcraft outbreak" remain the focus of a torrent of scholarly work beyond the scope of this conference, but a high rate of social change doubtless contributed to the kind of anxiety that, in the same year, sent sixty armed men from Gloucester into the woods to "intercept a spectral force of French and Indians." Ibid., 167. It is ridiculous to blame the prosecutions on the lack of "trained lawyers of courage and force to challenge the legality of the special court," cf. Anton-Hermann Chroust, I, 77, and equally unavailing to blame the trials on the colonial legal system. The witch proceedings were terminated by Governor Phips in May 1693, never to occur again. The King's Privy Council refused to approve the General Court's effort in the 1692–1693 session to place witchcraft back on the list of capital crimes. The recantation of Judge Samuel Sewall, read for him by the Reverend Samuel Willard during a service at the Old South Church on 14 January 1697, a day of fasting and prayer designated in memory of "the late tragedie," marked the end of an era. Judge Sewall stood silently in the church as the recantation was read. It is sobering to recall that the "Second Charter" period, with its legal and professional growth, began with such a symbol. See Edwin Powers, *Crime and Punishment*, 455–509; John Demos, "Underlying Themes in the Witchcraft of Seventeenth-Century New England," *Colonial America*, Stanley N. Katz ed. (1971), 113–133; Demos, *Entertaining Satan: Witchcraft and the Culture of Early New England* (New York, 1982); Paul Boyer, Steven Nissenbaum, *Salem Possessed: The Social Origins of Witchcraft* (Cambridge, Mass., 1974). As to the considerable extent of colonial witchcraft persecutions at other times and places, see E. W. Taylor "The Witchcraft Episode (1692–1694)," *Commonwealth History*, II, 29–62.

[3] John M. Murrin, "The Legal Transformation: The Bench and Bar of Eighteenth-Century Massachusetts" in *Colonial America*, Stanley N. Katz ed., 415 (Katz's summary).

[4] Ibid., 416.

Newton, or out-right British imports, like John Menzies, a Scot, and John Valentine, an English immigrant. True, Anthony Checkley was a native, but even Checkley was, like Valentine and Newton, an Anglican.[5] Murrin has concluded that the Revolution of 1775 "utterly reversed the trend of the whole previous century" and that — except for revolution — the "trend of the whole eighteenth century was not towards the common lawyer of the nineteenth, but away from the uncommon lawyer of the seventeenth and towards England's hierarchical model instead."[6]

This is a powerful and categorical thesis. It has important implications as to the nature of the American Revolution and the motives of the lawyers involved. Is it true, or is Daniel Boorstin right that the conditions in "pragmatic" America would have led inevitably to the structure of our current system and the values it represents, Revolution or not?[7]

The period 1691 to 1760 did see the establishment of a prosperous and powerful legal elite. Three increasingly prominent generations of true professionals came and went: first the generation of Thomas Newton, Paul Dudley, and John Read, followed by Jeremiah Gridley and Edmund Trowbridge; then the generation of their protégés, Benjamin Prat, Samuel Fitch, and James Otis, Jr.; and finally the generation of "household names" — John Adams, Josiah Quincy, Samuel Quincy, Robert Treat Paine, and William Cushing. These critical generations saw the first professionally trained judges, such as Benjamin Lynde, the first major professional law libraries, the first attempt at law reporting (Quincy), the first bar associations, the first regular appointment of counsel in criminal cases, the first attempts to formalize an indigenous legal training program, and the first attempts to establish hierarchial professional monopolies.[8]

[5] Ibid., 421–425.

[6] Ibid., 448.

[7] See ibid., 448; Daniel J. Boorstin, *The Americans*, 195–205.

[8] See the sources cited in note 2, xxv, above, and the articles of David H. Flaherty and Charles R. McKirdy, below. In the "companion" volume to this book, *Medicine in Colonial Massachusetts 1620–1820*, The Colonial Society of Massachusetts, *Publications*, LVII (Boston, 1980), the editors set out criteria for establishing true "professionalism" among doctors, such as "how doctors in eighteenth-century New

The bar was beginning to demonstrate economic success, political power, and social prestige. The first problem, of course, is why and how this occurred. Was it the inevitable result of the social and economic conditions? Was it "Anglicization"? What did this development owe to the sixty years of colonial legal development that came before? A second, and perhaps more interesting question is whose interests did these developments serve? Who were the clients? Did this professional class serve royal power, indigenous entrepreneurs, the church, the towns and cities, the poor and accused, the "average person"?

Barbara A. Black's article leaves no doubt but that complex civil litigation had come of age by 1730 and that indigenous entrepreneurs, like Nathaniel Byfield, used both the legal process and professional lawyers ruthlessly to pursue their political and financial ends. Russell K. Osgood looks at a different stratum of society. Working from an important new discovery—a hitherto unknown judicial notebook of a magistrate in Boston's North End covering the period 1700 to 1726 with 1,379 entries—Osgood describes the continuing social control function of the lay magistrate in the rapidly developing city. The picture is limited to the bottom levels of society—and to petty crime and small claims—but is all the more interesting for that. From the pages of the notebook emerge sailors, abused women, blacks, the poor, and the small businessmen of an increasingly diverse and fragmented society.[9] Osgood finds that the old lay magistrate ideal proved durable in these new conditions, and he sheds im-

England identified themselves," how they "differentiated themselves from other healers," their development of professional education, what doctor-patient relations were "expected," and "what colonial doctors exploited from their own past." Ibid., 32. It is obvious that comparative study of these two professional developments, legal and medical, would be most fruitful, and it is hoped that the publication of these two "companion" volumes will encourage such study.

[9] There were approximately 1,500 blacks, slave and free, in Boston in 1750. See Sherwin L. Cook, "Boston: The Eighteenth Century Town," *Commonwealth History*, II, 229. There was also racism. In 1723 the Boston Town Meeting voted to recommend to the General Court an act for the restraint of "Indians, Negroes and Mulattoes" that prohibited, among other things, their possession of firearms, visits from slaves, street gatherings, and loitering. They would be required to bind out their children at four years of age to a white master. Ibid., 227–228. Slaves were sold in Boston in 1746. Ibid., 228. There is an obvious contrast here to the Puritan statute of 1647 limiting bond slavery. See Anton-Hermann Chroust, *The Rise of the Legal Profession*, I, 52.

portant light on colonial society, sources of the law, and the use of law to ensure social order.

Douglas L. Jones' article, "The Transformation of the Law of Poverty in Eighteenth Century Massachusetts," continues the focus on lay justice, localism, and the harsh reality of life for the poor. His thesis—that the dramatic increase in poor and dependent people during this period resulted in a redefinition of the "law of poverty" —has important implications. In particular, Jones maintains that the earlier systems of private, local, and religious charity, administered by selectmen, overseers of the poor and the general sessions of the peace, were unable to cope with the new challenges. New balances between the need for welfare and for social control of "strolling poor" were worked out, as formal institutionalization emerged as a major alternative to old concepts of custodial care through place-ment with individual families. Jones describes the development of the almshouse and workhouse, and the restructuring of the system by both court supervision of disputes and new legislation. The grad-ual decriminalization of transiency and the linking up of social con-trol directly with the provision of institutionalized welfare was a major change in the public attitude toward poverty and the position of the poor in the legal system. Most striking, the major reforms before and after the Revolution appear part of an unbroken develop-ment culminating in the revised Poor Law of 1794. The Revolution itself appears to have made little difference, except that the war's economic dislocations heightened concern over defining and con-trolling transients and deciding who would pay their welfare bills. The Poor Law of 1794 was "the resolution of a long history of tension over the allocation of economic resources for poor relief and the control of transients."[1]

David H. Flaherty's article, "Criminal Practice in Provincial Mas-

---

[1] Douglas L. Jones, below, 190. James A. Henretta has observed that, in 1687, "the distribution of political power and influence in Boston conformed to ... a wider, more inclusive hierarchy of status, one which purported to include the entire social order within the bonds of its authority. But the lines of force which had emerged on the eve of the American Revolution ... now failed to encompass a significant portion of the population.... Society had become more stratified and unequal. Influential groups, increasingly different from the small property owners who constituted the center portion of the community, had arisen at either end of the spectrum." *Colonial America*, Stanley N. Katz ed., 462–463.

sachusetts," provides a wealth of detail about criminal law doctrine and the court structure for prosecuting crime. It particularly focuses on the careers of leading criminal lawyers. Flaherty establishes that "[a]fter the creation of the superior court, a small number of lawyers were seemingly present at each session" and were definitely employed in criminal cases.[2] By reviewing these cases, Flaherty paints an intriguing picture of these lawyers, who they were, who their criminal clients were, and what the lawyers could do for them. He demonstrates that this bar consisted of about eleven attorneys, and had elite members—such as Thomas Newton, John Valentine, John Read, Robert Auchmuty, and John Overing—who were highly competent and highly regarded, even before 1720. Flaherty's conclusion challenges views that the early eighteenth century bar was incompetent, unpopular, or only represented the rich. "[M]ost defendants at the assizes, except for the most indigent, probably could afford to retain defense counsel."[3] Further, the "innovation of allowing unrestricted use of defense counsel"—a remarkable Massachusetts development—meant that "[b]y the middle of the eighteenth century persons in Massachusetts accused of a serious crime were in the fortunate position of having talented defense counsel available."[4]

But what about the countryside away from Boston? Neal W. Allen's powerful description of legal authority in the rural country, "Law and Authority to the Eastward: Maine Courts, Magistrates, and Lawyers, 1690–1730," answers this critical question. Complementing Osgood's work on the urban magistrate's role, Allen confirms the tremendous versatility and tenacity of the rural lay magistracy. He also carefully traces the development of professional legal practice in Maine. Maine was a rough place, with refugees from Indian raids "that threatened to weaken dangerously the fragile and extended defenses of the eastern settlements."[5] The earliest lawyers were largely "unprofessional," linked with "the equally unprofessional judges by family and business." But lawyers there were,

---

[2] David H. Flaherty, below, 193.

[3] Ibid., 240.

[4] Ibid., 241.

[5] Neal W. Allen, Jr., below, 275.

and at least eight were admitted and sworn soon after the 1701 "Act Relating to Attorneys." Moreover, lawyers came up from Boston for big cases—"elite" names like Paul Dudley, Thomas Newton, John Valentine, and Addington Davenport, and all this before 1720. Finally, there were many humble people of a "practical bent" who acted as agents or gave legal advice, and, on the other extreme of society, "those more eminent men [sworn or unsworn] who, usually officeholders themselves, also served on the side as advisers, as drafters of legal papers, and as givers of legal opinions."[6]

Allen's detailed reconstruction of a day in the "Court of General Sessions of the Peace for York," namely 6 July 1725, describes both cases which were routinely resolved without any professional input, and those in which counsel were retained and appeals taken to higher authority. The scope of the magistrates' responsibilities—including supervision and granting of tavern licenses, deciding civil and criminal cases of every variety, setting assessments for villages ravaged by the Indian wars, and maintaining the highways—is simply astonishing. Cases involved issues as different as common drunkenness, religious dissent, and serious contempt charges resulting from disruption of town meetings. Yet they were all decided at the same time and place. Further, the standard of legal procedure appeared quite high in the serious cases, and hired counsel were active in important matters, including the drafting of reasons of appeal.[7] The final picture is not one of rampant "Anglicization," nor of primitive Puritan communalism. Rather, it is of a remarkably efficient, practical, and surprisingly legalistic system that had deep American roots, even in 1725. As Allen observes:

Not all the participants of events on that day would have found appealing the idea of a future American democracy. But all shared in a legal tradition whose roots went deep. Unruly and "rude" they often appear in these records, but the institutional framework and the inherited traditions gave force and meaning to the idea that law ruled.[8]

There is one last feature of this period which has never received

---

[6] Ibid., 287.

[7] Ibid., 309.

[8] Ibid., 312.

proper attention, the legislation. Morris L. Cohen's conference essay emphasizes the scale of its printed production. The years 1692 to 1742 saw one hundred and forty-six separate issues of the *Laws and Orders* of the General Court, and the years 1742 to 1775 saw two hundred and eight issues of *Acts and Laws*. "Government printing was an established practice in the colony. Virtually all of it was legal in nature."[9] Seven reprintings of the Charter occurred (1689, 1692, 1699, 1725, 1742, 1759, 1775), five compilations of the *Charter, Acts and Laws* (1699, 1714, 1726, 1742, 1759), three collections of *Temporary Acts and Laws* (1742, 1755, 1763) and, from 1715 to 1774, one hundred and fifty separate issues of the *Journal of the House of Representatives*.[1] Yet the number of reprints of English treatises was very scanty, and no English statutes, law reports or collections of state papers were printed in the colony.[2] Importation of English treatises may have been the answer, but "[a]lthough the publication of technical and doctrinal legal treatises was substantial in England in this period, none was reissued in Massachusetts."[3] This certainly raises doubts about the extent of "Anglicization."

More significantly, the substance of the legislation has been inadequately studied. It was the law of Massachusetts, not of England. The legalism of the Puritan tradition, which turned in its earliest days to codification, continued under the Second Charter in the production of statutes. Massachusetts was, of course, one of His Majesty's provinces but, as its statutory order made explicit, it also stood apart, legally.[4]

IV. *The "Revolutionary Period": 1760–1789*

James Otis' fiery polemics in the Writs of Assistance case, argued in February 1761, left a young, rather awed John Adams convinced that things would never be the same.[5] Indeed, by the time of the

[9] Morris L. Cohen, below, 253.

[1] Ibid., 253–254.

[2] Ibid., 256–261.

[3] Ibid., 256.

[4] This argument certainly was not missed by John Adams. See Daniel R. Coquillette, below, 412–416.

[5] See *Diary and Autobiography of John Adams* ed. L. H. Butterfield (Cambridge, Mass., 1961), I, 210–211, III, 275–276. For an old man's recollection of the

1765 Stamp Act every legal institution in Massachusetts was becoming distracted by the approaching political crisis, and by the time of the Boston Massacre of 1770 most active lawyers were forced to take a political position of some kind.[6]

The impact on the legal system was inevitable. One can call the American Revolution "conservative and non-socially disruptive" and question whether, except for the disruptions of the war itself, there was any fundamental social or economic impact that would not have occurred in all events.[7] But it cannot be seriously doubted that the Revolution hit hard at the unity of the bar, and that it accelerated new political and legal ideas.

The rival political ideologies all invoked concepts of legal order. In the pre-Revolutionary maneuvers and propaganda, the whigs invoked the local gods: the "tradition of local government—the magistrates, the grand and traverse jurors, the representatives to the general court, and the citizens in their town meetings," and the tories invoked the Anglican gods of parliamentary supremacy and "imperial law."[8] As John Reid put it, "law played an all-pervasive . . . role . . . both sides of the political debate were committed to the forms of law."[9] Some, like George Dargo, have gone so far as to call it "a lawyers' revolution."[1]

But the effects of revolution on the law and the bar were surpris-

famous day of his youth, see John Adams' letter to William Tudor, 29 March 1817, in John Adams, *Works*, Charles Francis Adams ed. (Boston, 1817), X, 244–245.

[6] See Charles R. McKirdy, below, 337–358. (Appendices III and IV.)

[7] See David Flaherty's review of William Nelson's *Americanization of the Common Law* in the *University of Toronto Law Journal* (1976), 116. James Henretta has argued that the Revolution was "in reality the completion of a long process of social evolution, simply speeded up and given a positive articulation by the war. . . . Except for the disruptions caused by the war itself and the Loyalist emigration . . . most of the changes . . . represented the culmination of previous trends." James A. Henretta, *The Evolution of American Society, 1700–1815, An Interdisciplinary Analysis* (Lexington, 1973), 169. See also Flaherty, "Review," 116–117; Stanley Katz, "Looking Backward: The Early History of American Law," *Chicago Law Review*, XXXIII (1966), 884.

[8] John P. Reid, "A Lawyer Acquitted: John Adams and the Boston Massacre Trials," *American Journal of Legal History*, XVIII (1974), 189, 191.

[9] Ibid., 191. See also Erwin C. Surrency, "The Lawyer and the Revolution," *American Journal of Legal History*, VIII (1964), 125.

[1] George Dargo, *Law in the New Republic* (New York, 1983), 7.

ingly "uneven."[2] For example, consider one of the terrible ironies of the war, the direct personal effects on the elite bar. Life-long friends, even brothers, were torn apart. Consider lawyers such as John Adams, Josiah Quincy, Samuel Quincy, Samuel Fitch, Daniel Leonard, and Jonathan Sewall, men who belonged to the same select dining clubs and who pursued the same policies for increasing the "professionalism" and meritocracy of the bar.[3] Many of their plans, such as attempts to establish regular "progressions" of legal training (1769), to suppress unauthorized practice (1765–1768), to found a formal Suffolk bar association (3 January 1770), and to adopt uniform regulation with Essex and other counties (1771), were pursued together to the very outbreak of hostilities.[4]

But then they were dramatically and terribly sundered. Most of the loyalists — nearly half the profession — left to permanent exile in Halifax, the West Indies, and England. The Superior Court too was decimated, with only one survivor, William Cushing, of the original five.[5] Yet, during the war itself, every effort was made to shore up the legal institutions and few opportunities were lost "to attempt to induce respect for all lawfully constituted authority."[6] Indeed, within ten years after the hostilities were over, the phenomenal growth of the legal profession had resumed, and the growing importance of lawyers and legal education certainly was anchored, at least in part, on the professional foundations laid just before the war.[7] True, as Murrin would argue, the form of the profes-

[2] "[The changes] affected some legal institutions and not others, and some areas of American Law more than others." Ibid., 7. Dargo has argued that the Revolution had a "deep, abiding, and immediate impact on American *public* law," ibid., 8 (emphasis supplied), but that in terms of private law the changes were much more gradual—although eventually very important. "What is striking, in fact, is the strong continuity of private law in the revolutionary era." Ibid., 8. This view is quite compatible with that of Morton J. Horwitz, set out below, lii.

[3] See Daniel R. Coquillette, below, 376–382, 395–400; Charles R. McKirdy, below, 339–358, [Appendix IV].

[4] Ibid., 318–323. See also Daniel R. Coquillette, below, 395–400.

[5] See John D. Cushing, "The Judiciary and Public Opinion in Revolutionary Massachusetts," in *Law and Authority in Colonial America*, George A. Billias ed. (Barre, Mass., 1965), 173–182, 185, n.19.

[6] Ibid., 182. These efforts included careful charges to the grand juries which explained "the social compact and its violation by Great Britain." Ibid., 174.

[7] See George Dargo, *Law in the New Republic*, 48–59, for an excellent description of the "sudden increase of lawyers" and the new "private" law schools.

sion and the courts might not have been exactly the same, but the consolidation of professional power missed only a beat.[8]

There were other ironies. Whole forests have literally been destroyed to publish histories of this period; yet, as Reid correctly observes, "historians have largely neglected or not understood the role played by law in both setting the stage for rebellion and formulating the conditions under which it would be fought."[9] Reid's *In a Defiant Stance* (London, 1977) and Gerard Gawalt's *The Promise of Power* (London, 1979) have done much to fill this gap, but important, nagging questions remain. Was the prominent role of Massachusetts in the Revolution because of, or despite, its traditions of legalism and its legal profession? To what extent were legal disputes and controversies about the nature of law the cause of ultimate revolution, as opposed to being simply the means and vehicles of political conflict?[1] Some scholars have called the Boston mob a "quasi-legal" institution.[2] Is it true that there was "no evidence of a deterioration of respect for law," even at the height of political dislocation, and "no quarrel with the quality of local justice"?[3] Finally, Gerard Gawalt and George Dargo have presented compelling evidence that the Revolution opened up unprecedented "new vistas" of power and wealth for Massachusetts lawyers, even in an astonish-

---

[8] See John M. Murrin, "The Legal Transformation: The Bench and Bar of Eighteenth-Century Massachusetts," 446–448.

[9] John P. Reid, "A Lawyer Acquitted," 191.

[1] "Both sides were dedicated to following the forms of law but both were prepared to manipulate those forms for their own advantage. It was the forms of law and the idea of legality that mattered, for they kept the situation from escalation into violence; manipulation was a matter of strategy not of abuse." Ibid., 194.

[2] See Reid's analysis of John Adams' personal view of the Tea Party. "Adams was a lawyer, a conservative lawyer, and it is significant that . . . he found, as did so many other whigs, that constitutional legality was at times determined by political necessity." John P. Reid, *In a Defiant Stance*, 99. The political pressure on the entire Massachusetts legal system by the years 1769–1771 was so great that Hiller B. Zobel has concluded "[I]n cases involving political subjects, the Massachusetts judicial system . . . was under such powerful pressure from both sides that a fair trial was, without extra legal assistance, unlikely, if not impossible." Hiller B. Zobel, "Law Under Pressure: Boston 1769–1771" in *Law and Authority in Colonial America*, George A. Bellias ed. (1965), 204. See also Michael S. Hindus, *Prison and Plantation: Crime, Justice, and Authority in Massachusetts and South Carolina, 1767–1878* (Chapel Hill, 1980), 33–36.

[3] Ibid., 65, 67.

ingly short time. By 1785 the losses of the loyalist exiles had been completely replaced by new lawyers, and by shortly after 1790, the total number of lawyers had doubled over 1765.[4] The number of lawyers, according to one estimate, grew from 1783 to 1820 "four times faster than the general population, which itself was expanding at an enormous rate. . . ."[5] It has been said that a central result of the American Revolution was a growth "of the power the legal profession exercised over the American mind."[6] If so, why?

Essential to approaching any of these major questions is a thorough understanding of the education, social composition, and politics of the Massachusetts bar at the outset of revolution. This is the purpose of Charles R. McKirdy's essay "Massachusetts Lawyers on the Eve of the American Revolution: The State of the Profession." To achieve this purpose, McKirdy first attempts a meaningful definition of a "professional," and then applies this definition to analyze the entire known bar as of 1775. In the process, he provides biographical sketches of the eighty-one known lawyers practicing in Massachusetts in 1775 (Appendix IV), including all their known educational backgrounds, bar admissions, judicial positions, and political affiliations. This is an invaluable resource, complementing the biographical sketches in the *Legal Papers of John Adams* (Kinvin Wroth, Hiller Zobel eds., Cambridge, Mass., 1965). It also gives a complete "crosscut" of the profession at a single, crucial point in time. McKirdy also tabulates the occupation and education of Superior Court judges 1692–1774 (Appendix I), the professional choices of Harvard graduates 1642–1760 (Appendix II), and the geographical distribution of lawyers by bar admission "status" and political loyalty (Appendix

---

[4] "What had appeared to be utopian plans for a large prosperous, well-trained legal profession before the war became a reality in the postwar period." Gerard W. Gawalt, *The Promise of Power*, 36.

[5] George Dargo, *Law in the New Republic*, 48.

[6] Ibid., 59. The extremely high growth rates in the legal profession recall the very rapid expansion of the Inns of Court in the period 1500–1600, when the annual rate of admission quadrupled. The growth rate continued to be high until the Civil War. See Wilfrid R. Prest, *The Inns of Court*, 1–70. Morton Horwitz, in a different context, suggests that we should be alert to recapitulation of English experience, but no major comparative studies of the rate of growth of the legal profession and the causes and consequences have ever been undertaken. *Cf.* Morton Horwitz, *Transformation of American Law, 1780–1860* (Cambridge, Mass., 1977), 17.

III). This is exactly the kind of empirical data needed to test conjecture about lawyers at this critical time.

Some of McKirdy's conclusions are really surprising. In particular, the late development of the colonial bar does not really follow Murrin's thesis of "Anglicization," but supports Boorstin's view of an indigenous—and somewhat peculiar—"professional" ideal.[7] "If these [colonial] lawyers were part professionals, they also were part free-wheeling legal entrepreneurs."[8] Further, the extraordinary post-Revolutionary gains of the profession, as emphasized by Gawalt, seem to have been founded on professional advances achieved by the Massachusetts bar right through the pre-Revolutionary period, with patriot and tory lawyers working side by side until the war. The emphasis seems to be on the process of "professionalization" itself—which McKirdy subjects to careful analysis.[9] This analysis assists in explaining why the legal profession recovered so quickly after the war, and why major advances in professional education, such as the famous Litchfield Law School (1784) and Wythe's Law School in Virginia (1779), and Van Schaak's Law School in New York (1786), could have occurred so soon.

My own article, "Justinian in Braintree: John Adams, Civilian Learning, and Legal Elitism, 1758–1775" has a more limited scope: it focuses on the legal education, early practice, and legal ideology of only one lawyer—John Adams. But, thanks to the work of the editors of the Adams papers, his career and writings cast a particularly detailed and vivid—if not utterly unprejudiced—light on this critical time. My conclusions support those of McKirdy and Gawalt, that the development of professional identity went to the edge of conflict—and emphasized notions of meritocracy and elit-

---

[7] See Daniel J. Boorstin, *The Americans: The Colonial Experience*, 195–205.

[8] Charles R. McKirdy, 328.

[9] In particular, McKirdy draws on W. E. Moore's *The Professions: Roles and Rules* (New York, 1970) and B. Bledstein's *The Culture of Professionalism* (New York, 1978) to isolate and describe five characteristics that measure "professionalism:" 1) full-time earning occupation, 2) need for useful, theoretical knowledge and requirement of formal education, 3) group "identity" by members, 4) "service" orientation, and 5) autonomy from outside control. These factors compare closely with those set out by the editors of our companion volume, *Medicine In Colonial Massachusetts, 1620–1820*, The Colonial Society of Massachusetts, *Publications*, LVII, 32.

ism now familiar to the most powerful sectors of the modern bar.[1] I also find support for the conclusions of John Reid that the participation of lawyers in the Revolution followed predetermined paths based on their legal ideology, and support for Daniel Boorstin's conclusion that these paths were particularly American.[2] In Adams' case, the significant influence of classical civil law jurisprudence on his education, his early law practice, and his intellectual life with other lawyers had profound repercussions in his professional and political acts — including the foundation of the Suffolk bar association and Adams' important "Novanglus" exchange with Daniel Leonard, later described as the "climactic duel" of the competing legal models.[3]

There was also a hidden agenda. I have been led by Perry Miller to believe that shared legal education and professional identity among lawyers can create ideologies that are peculiar to them — and which are not necessarily predetermined by the economic motives

[1] John Adams was an elitist, but one who looked to academic performance and formal professional requirements to block the nepotistic careers of the sons of the leading tory families, as well as to eliminate "pettifoggers." See Daniel R. Coquillette, below, 395–400. Among McKirdy's most interesting Appendices is his "Appendix II—Professional Choices of Harvard Graduates: 1642–1760." Before 1684, and the "Intercharter Period," there was but one "law" career choice. During the 1685–1691 "Intercharter Period," there were four. But during the 1692–1760 "Second Charter Period," there were seventy-six Harvard graduates who ultimately would call themselves "lawyers," with twenty-seven alone in the ten-year period 1751–1760. While this was still well behind the clergy (the most popular choice) and medicine (nearly twice as popular as law), it was a most impressive indicator as to the growing prestige of the profession and its expectations for education. See Charles R. McKirdy, below, 333–336 (Appendix II).

[2] See John P. Reid, "A Lawyer Acquitted," 191–194; and Daniel J. Boorstin, *The Americans: The Colonial Experience*, 191–205. As Reid observed: "[I]n the functioning of eighteenth century constitutional legality, local institutions defined the meaning of 'law' as much as did imperial institutions." John P. Reid, *In a Defiant Stance*, 72.

[3] See Janice Potter and Robert M. Calhoon, "The Character and Coherence of the Loyalist Press" in *The Press and the American Revolution*, Bernard Bailyn, John B. Hench eds. (Boston, 1981), 231. On the peculiar influence of classical studies on the American colonial mind, including minds as distinct as John Winthrop and John Adams, see Richard M. Gummere, *The American Colonial Mind and the Classical Tradition* (Cambridge, Mass., 1963). See also Bernard Bailyn, *The Ideological Origins of the American Revolution* (Cambridge, Mass., 1967), 23–24; Stephen Botein "Cicero as Role Model for Early American Lawyers: A Case Study in Classical Influence," *Classical Journal*, LXXIII (1977–1978), 314–318; Charles F. Mullett, "Classical Influences on the American Revolution," *Classical Journal*, XXXV (1939–1940), 93–94.

of their clients or by political forces.[4] Indeed, this legal ideology itself can help to shape political and economic events.[5] My article attempts to demonstrate, in a very limited way, how this occurred in the early professional life of a most important American.[6]

The Revolution presents one final, immensely difficult problem for legal history. What direct effect did the Revolution have on the sources of American law and the development of American legal doctrines and legal institutions? There certainly have been theories enough for all. John Murrin's important thesis focuses solely on the bench and the bar and finds that Massachusetts was experiencing "rapid and pervasive Anglicization," cut off only by the trauma of the war.[7] Morton Horwitz, in his famous and original book, *Transformation of American Law, 1780–1860* (Cambridge, Mass., 1977), sets out a different thesis. Looking solely at doctrine, he perceives a period of stability right up to and through the Revolution.[8] There was, to be sure, an "inevitable and rapid reception of the body of English common law," but only on the terms of the Americans and almost solely by local statute, not judicial activism.[9] Real legal

---

[4] See Perry Miller, *The Legal Mind in America* (New York, 1962), 20–21, 31–32, 41–43; Felix Gilbert "Intellectual History: Its Aims and Methods," *Historical Studies Today*, eds. Felix Gilbert, Stephen R. Graubard (New York, 1972), 141–158; Patrick Gardiner, *The Nature of Historical Explanation* (London, 1952), 115–139. See also William E. Nelson's original essay "The Eighteenth-Century Background of John Marshall's Constitutional Jurisprudence," *Michigan Law Review*, XXVI (1978), 893, 900–901, 917–924.

[5] See Daniel R. Coquillette, "Legal Ideology and Incorporation I: The English Civilian Writers, 1523–1607," *Boston University Law Review*, LXI (1981), 1–2, 3–10; "Legal Ideology and Incorporation II: Sir Thomas Ridley, Charles Molloy, and the Literary Battle for the Law Merchant, 1607–1676," *Boston University Law Review*, LXI (1981), 317–320, 371.

[6] Of course, in focusing on ideology, one must not forget the historical context. Thus, even as John Adams struggled for good civil law precedents in the case of the *Liberty, Sewall v. Hancock*, 1768–1769, "[a]n ensuing riot drove the customs commissioners to Castle William in Boston Harbor, where they remained until the troops which they had urgently requested were garrisoned in Boston." See L. Kinvin Wroth, "The Massachusetts Vice-Admiralty Court" in *Law and Authority in Colonial America*, George A. Billias ed., 53.

[7] See John M. Murrin, "The Legal Transformation: The Bench and Bar of Eighteenth-Century Massachusetts," 446–448.

[8] Morton J. Horwitz, *Transformation of American Law*, 4–9.

[9] "And while Americans always insisted on the right to receive only those common law principles which accorded with colonial conditions, most of the basic departures were accomplished not by judicial decision but by local statute. . . ." Ibid., 5. Mas-

change occurred only after the Revolution, with the breakdown of the "eighteenth century conception of law" and the emergence of an "instrumental conception of law," in which courts undertook, for the first time, to narrow the province of the jury and to undertake an "innovative and transforming role."[1]

Central to all discussions in this area have been the research and analysis of William E. Nelson. A pioneer in the use of unpublished court records—as opposed to relying exclusively on statutes and reported decisions and treatises—Nelson has concentrated on Massachusetts. His central thesis emphasizes the roles of judges and juries in the trial of cases. Nelson argues, in contrast to Murrin, that the pre-Revolutionary period saw the increasing power of juries, both in fact-finding and law-finding, the de-emphasis of special pleading, a limited role for judges, and a strong sense of local indigenous justice. The Revolution brought fundamental change in the form of new aspirations and a new focus on equality and freedom.

Massachusetts, in short, had been transformed from a society where men with stable places in the economy concentrated on pursuing ethical ends to a society where economic place was uncertain and many men used their wealth chiefly for the purpose of acquiring even greater wealth. The pre-revolutionary legal system, in which community was the primary social value, had largely been destroyed. A new system emphasizing rugged individualism . . . had begun to take its place.[2]

This important thesis, announced in Nelson's *Americanization of the*

sachusetts statutory policy during the Second Charter period remains a great area for future research. See above, xlv.

[1] According to Horwitz, ". . . American judges before the nineteenth century rarely analyzed common law rules functionally or purposively, and they almost never self-consciously employed the common law as a creative instrument for directing men's energies toward social change." Morton J. Horwitz, *The Transformation of American Law*, 1.

[2] William E. Nelson, *Americanization of the Common Law: The Impact of Legal Change on Massachusetts Society, 1760–1830* (Cambridge, Mass., 1975), 143. As to Murrin's thesis of "Anglicization," Nelson states: "[O]ne cannot explain developments in Massachusetts law . . . as a consequence of adherence to English law. . . . [B]y the last third of the eighteenth century each society was pursuing its own independent course even on those occasions when the courses seemed superficially to be parallel." Ibid., 10. See also William E. Nelson, "The Legal Restraint of Power in Pre-Revolutionary America: Massachusetts as a Case Study, 1760–1775," *American Journal of Legal History*, XVIII (1974), 1, 13–26, 32.

Common Law: The Impact of Legal Change on Massachusetts So-
ciety, 1760–1830 (Cambridge, Mass., 1975), emphasizes that the
change was in the social values of the people, as reflected in the legal
system, as well as in the convictions of judges as to the nature of
common law and the proper role of the courts and juries. Although
Horwitz stresses "instrumentalism" and Nelson, "centralization,"
both agree that the attitude of lawyers and judges changed in a
fundamental way, and both agree that economic factors played a
central role in this change. Nelson, however, also emphasizes a factor that could be totally unrelated to economics, but highly important — namely, personal freedom on a private, individual basis,
including freedom of religion.

Since his first book, Nelson has developed his thesis further in a
second important book, *Dispute and Conflict Resolution in Plymouth*
County, Massachusetts 1725–1825 (Chapel Hill, 1981), again making unprecedented use of original materials. This book also establishes an enviable standard for the use of court records — and its
boldness and originality will inspire other scholars to test Nelson's
conclusions about the social role of colonial law and the ultimate
focus of change.[3]

Nelson's conference paper, "The American Revolution and the
Emergence of Modern Doctrines of Federalism and Conflict of
Laws," continues to break important new ground in understanding
the legal effects of the Revolution. Nelson tackles a problem central
to any federation of sovereign states — how conflicts in legal doctrine
are to be resolved. "[T]he logical solution both for federal-state and
for interstate conflicts was that conceived by the framers — to place a
Supreme Court administering a supreme law atop the national judi-

---

[3] The research in *Dispute and Conflict Resolution* is based on the Plymouth Court
Records project, edited by David T. Konig and described above, note 7, xxiv.
Nelson's critics, predictably, argue that there was more "rugged individualism"
in pre-Revolutionary colonial society than he represents and less communal bliss,
and that Nelson exaggerates the changes wrought by the Revolution. See David
Flaherty's review of *Americanization of the Common Law* in the *University of*
Toronto Law Review (1976), 110–113, in which Flaherty also criticizes Michael
Zuckerman's *Peaceable Kingdoms: New England Towns in the Eighteenth Century*
(1970). Much more work is obviously required, of the type undertaken by David T.
Konig in the Essex records and by Nelson himself in the Plymouth records, before
any of these questions will be finally answered. See David T. Konig, *Law and So-*
ciety in Puritan Massachusetts, Essex County, 1629–1692 (Chapel Hill, 1979).

cial structure with a mandate to resolve all intercourt conflicts."[4]
This "logical" system was also related to the English doctrine. In
England, choice-of-court normally meant choice-of-law, and jurisdictional disputes between competing courts were, ideally, resolved by
the supervising jurisdiction of the King's Bench which, as Blackstone
explained, applied "one uniform rule" which kept "all inferior jurisdictions within the bounds of their authority."[5]

But this solution was not adopted. Instead, the power to resolve
conflict of laws questions became vested in the state courts. Nelson
believes that this rather surprising result occurred because of other
features of colonial law. "British North America possessed no unifying institutions resting atop a hierarchy of local institutions: the common law, which was at the top of the hierarchy and therefore curbed
local independence in England, was at the bottom of the hierarchy
and thereby had potentially the opposite effect in America."[6] Nelson's thesis, brilliantly developed by analysis of all known early conflicts cases, has many implications in explaining the nature of legal
change after the Revolution—and the ultimate triumph of American localism which "continues by an inertia to influence [the doctrine
of conflict of laws] today."[7]

I regard the three conference essays on the revolutionary period—
McKirdy's, Nelson's, and my own—as illustrating the complemen-
tary function of empirical professional research, ideological studies,
and doctrinal analysis. Taken together, particularly in the context of
interpreting original records, these methods offer much toward a
better understanding of the effects of the Revolution on American
law.[8]

---

[4] William E. Nelson, below, 467.

[5] Ibid., 428. William Blackstone, *Commentaries on the Laws of England* (Oxford,
1765–1769), III, *87, *42.

[6] William E. Nelson, below, 433.

[7] Ibid., 467.

[8] As Robert W. Gordon astutely suggests: "One of the aims of the recent work of
Morton Horwitz, William Nelson, and John Reid has been to identify the characteristics of 'modern' law . . . by reference to what they see as the 'pre-modern' law of
the eighteenth century. But reconstruction might do more for us than that: it might
demonstrate an actual continuity between the old system and our own." "Historicism
in Legal Scholarship," *Yale Law Journal*, XC (1981), 1049–1050. See also David H.
Flaherty, "Review," *University of Toronto Law Journal* (1976), 110, 115–117.

There is still a tremendous amount to learn. In particular, all of the leading scholarly theories about the effect of the Revolution on the legal system depend on assumptions about the prior colonial system, including aspects of the Second Charter period about which we know almost nothing. There are thousands of essentially unexamined records, and, again, even the important statutes of the Second Charter period have never been thoroughly analyzed.[9] Further, the dramatic religious changes of Second Charter society — both inside and outside the established church — have not been adequately examined for their impact on the ideal of community and on legal change.[1] Nor has the legal profession been studied in connection with such serious post-Revolutionary upheavals as Shays' Rebellion — which directly involved the courts and the law. But the essays in this book should point the way.

V. *Conclusion: "The Countenance of Authoritie"*

There is a true story about that much abused royal governor and amateur historian, Thomas Hutchinson. The manuscript papers of his big historical project, *The History of the Colony and Province of Massachusetts-Bay*, were pulled from the mud after a devastating home "visit" in 1765 by a ransacking mob. In 1769 he wrote: "He who rescues from oblivion interesting historical facts is beneficial to posterity as well as his contemporaries and the prospect thereof to a benevolent mind causes that employment to be agreeable and pleas-

---

At the very least, "[w]e should know more than we currently do about 'stable, preindustrial communities' in order to comprehend the distinctiveness of 'modern' legal systems; that is, we must know what modern law is *not.*" Stanley N. Katz, "The Problem of a Colonial Legal History," 481, 482.

[9] This suggestion, as with so many helpful comments, comes from Russell K. Osgood. Katz also points out that "we have never clearly worked out the process by which legislation and adjudication became distinguishable activities in the colonial period." Ibid., 482.

[1] Not only was there the trauma of the "Great Awakening" in the early 1740's, but also the local religious setting became far more diverse. In a critique of Michael Zuckerman's *Peaceable Kingdoms, supra,* John Murrin calculated that "by 1760, fifty-four percent of the total population of Massachusetts . . . lived in towns possessing permanent dissenting congregations of Anglicans, Quakers, Baptists or Separates." John Murrin, "Review Essay," *History and Theory,* XI (1972), 245–272. See also David Flaherty, "Review," *University of Toronto Law Journal* (1970), 111, 113; and William Nelson's fascinating description of "Hanover and Pembroke: The Quaker Towns" in *Dispute and Conflict Resolution in Plymouth County,* 58–68.

ant which otherwise would be irksome and painful."[2] Hutchinson, a
veteran of many bitter controversies, was doubtless unaware that he
was joining yet another—the incessant debate over the purpose of
history.[3]

"Legal" history has always been the special subject of controversy.
Indeed, renaissance lawyers can make claim to the dubious distinction
of inventing the "historicist fallacy," the idea that scientific study of
the past can discover first principles "which will not only explain the
present but reveal the future."[4] This notion stands in direct opposition to the idea that the study of history must be just an end unto itself, an idea tagged as "pure antiquarianism" by its detractors.

Lawyers have traditionally had a "pervasive fear of antiquarianism," probably because it appears to be—practically speaking—a
waste of time.[5] On the other hand, it has been said that lawyers are
especially susceptible to the "historicist fallacy" because they are in
the business of predicting outcomes and legitimizing them. A rejection of *both* the "historicist fallacy" and pure "antiquarianism"
leaves legal historians with an interesting problem of how to justify
their existence, particularly to the legal community. As Felix Gilbert
put it: "But what is our situation, for we believe neither in history as
a means of teaching ethical values nor in the possibility of discovering
laws to determine the process of world history?"[6]

[2] Preface, "An abstract of the Laws of New England" in Governor Thomas Hutchinson, *A Collection of Original Papers Relative to the History of the Colony of
Massachusetts-Bay* (Boston, 1769). As to the violent sack of Hutchinson's Boston
mansion, see Bernard Bailyn, *The Ordeal of Thomas Hutchinson* (Cambridge,
Mass., 1974), 35.

[3] See Frank E. Manuel, *Shapes of Philosophical History* (Stanford, 1965), 137;
Arthur Marwick, *The Nature of History* (New York, 1970), 227–279; Edward H.
Carr, *What Is History?* (New York, 1961), 3–35; W. H. Walsh, *An Introduction
to Philosophy of History* (Atlantic Highlands, N.J., 1951), 169–187.

[4] Grant Gilmore, "The Age of Antiquarius: On Legal History in the Time of
Troubles," *University of Chicago Law Review*, XXXIX (1972), 484. As to the "in-
vention" of legal history and "historical" schools of jurisprudence, see Donald R.
Kelley, "Guillaume Budé and the First Historical School of Law," *The American
Historical Review*, LXXII (1967), 833–834; Donald R. Kelley, *Foundations of
Modern Historical Scholarship: Language, Law, and History in the French Renais-
sance* (New York, 1970), 53–148; T. G. A. Pocock, *The Ancient Constitution and
the Feudal Law* (Cambridge, 1957), 8–17.

[5] Stephen M. Fuller, "Some Contemporary Approaches to the Study of Legal History and Jurisprudence," *Tulsa Law Journal*, X (1975), 576.

[6] Felix Gilbert, *History: Choice and Commitment* (Cambridge, Mass., 1977), 452.

I would like to suggest two answers to this dilemma, both well illustrated by this book. First, to the extent that the study of history is regarded as an end unto itself, there has been too little attention paid to the impact of legal ideas and legal institutions on the course of political, social, and economic events. The colonial history of Massachusetts is a prime example, and the essays in this book demonstrate the kind of benefits to be realized. Of course, as Michael S. Hindus has emphasized, not all power is "legal," nor can an isolated study of legal doctrine give a complete picture of anything, much less an operational legal system.[7] But, as this book illustrates, the old shibboleths dividing legal history from social history, political history, intellectual history, and economic history are crumbling, and cross-disciplinary cooperation is beginning to yield new insights into the past as it was.

But I am unwilling to stop with this relatively safe, limited answer. The reason is that I believe, and believe deeply, that the relationship between legal history and modern legal scholarship is a "special relationship" and, like most "special relationships," it is full of passion and danger. First, there is the relationship of historicism to modern legal scholarship and professional education. In particular, as Robert Gordon has brilliantly explained, any profession that attempts to legitimize existing procedures or rules will be tempted to demonstrate that such systems are inevitable, or are justified by "universal rationalizing principles."[8] Christopher Columbus Langdell, who established the model of "scientific" legal education that has dominated generations of American law students, was probably sitting in the front row of the audience when Oliver Wendell Holmes, Jr., warned that "[t]he life of the law has not been logic, it has been experience."[9]

Holmes was not just warning Langdell. He was warning all of

---

[7] See Michael S. Hindus, *Prison and Plantation: Crime, Justice, and Authority in Massachusetts and South Carolina,* 1767–1878 (Chapel Hill, 1980), 34–37. See also Hiller B. Zobel, "Law Under Pressure," 203–205.

[8] See Robert W. Gordon, "Historicism in Legal Scholarship," *Yale Law Journal,* XC (1981), 1018–1024; Morton J. Horwitz, "The Historical Contingency of the Role of History," ibid., 1057.

[9] O. W. Holmes, Jr., *The Common Law,* M. Howe ed. (Boston, 1963), 5. See Grant Gilmore, "The Age of Antiquarius," 480–481.

us that our attempts to rationalize legal rules are "contingent" on the particular social and historical conditions of the times.[1] Gordon has suggested that lawyers and legal scholars avoid a frank recognition of this fact, as it threatens to expose the ideological and political assumptions of the law, and to weaken what John Winthrop would call the "Countenance of Authoritie."[2] But authority in a free society should be able to tolerate such scrutiny, and defend its legitimacy.

This second point gets me to my "bottom line." The major task of history is to make us aware of the character of our own times by seeing it in comparison and by contrast with others. This is especially true of the character of our law and legal system, *our* "Countenance of Authoritie." As Gilmore puts it:

[T]he historian who shows us that what in fact happened need not have happened the way it did or need not have happened at all enriches our understanding of the past and, consequently, puts us in a position where we can deal more rationally with the infinitely complex problems which confront us. The argument that historical study which has no direct and immediate relevance to our present condition is "mere antiquarianism" is simply another aspect of the historicist fallacy.[3]

[1] Morton J. Horwitz, "The Historical Contingency," 1057. Erich Auerbach defines this insight as "[W]hen people realize that epochs and societies are not to be judged in terms of a pattern concept of what is desirable absolutely but rather in every case in terms of their own premises; when people reckon among such premises not only natural factors like climate and soil but also the intellectual and historical factors; when, in other words, they came to develop a sense of historical dynamics . . . when, finally, they accept the conviction that the meaning of events cannot be grasped in abstract and general forms of cognition. . . ."
Erich Auerbach, *Mimesis, the Representation of Reality in Western Literature* (W. Trask, Trans, Princeton, 1953), 391. See also Donald R. Kelley, *Foundations of Modern Historical Scholarship*, 301–309.

[2] Robert W. Gordon, "Historicism," 1017. See Darret B. Rutman, "The Mirror of Puritan Authority," *Law and Authority in Colonial America*, George A. Billias ed., 149–152.

[3] Grant Gilmore, "The Age of Antiquarius, 487. "If legal history does not tell us how things ought to be, it can at least tell us that they need not be the way they are." Adam J. Hirsch, "Pillory to Penitentiary," 1269. Arthur Marwick and Felix Gilbert have expressed the same idea in a broader context. "We cannot escape from history, our lives are governed by what happened in the past, our decisions by what we believe to have happened." Arthur Marwick, *The Nature of History* (New York, 1970), 319. "But, after all reservations have been made, we ought to remain aware that the man who acted and was acted upon in the past is the same man who acts in the present, and that the past is one way—and not the worst way—of acquiring the right and the criteria to judge the present. Our willingness to see the past as a

This has been demonstrated again and again by the insights of the contributors to this book. Whether the context be early professional history, lay judges, the use of the law to control the poor and provide welfare, early criminal law, the rights of defendants, the ideological background of lawyers approaching a revolution, or how an "illogical" doctrine developed to resolve conflict of laws, the benefits are better perspectives on our own hidden agendas and assumptions.

Clifford Shipton has observed that "Massachusetts in her first century and a half was an ideal proving ground for the principles on which our democratic way of life rests."[4] This is not to say the picture was always pretty, or progressive—the ghosts of the Antinomians, of Anne Hutchinson, of Mary Dyer, of the "strolling poor," of the victims of "spectral testimony," of the enslaved, of the dead on the streets of Boston and on the Green at Lexington—these do not represent triumphs of scientific jurisprudence or of human understanding. Yet, throughout all, a dominant theme of the colony's development was a pursuit of, and adherence to, ideals of lawful authority. The traditions of local government, of lay justice, of legal representation, of social innovation through legal forms, of faith in the law—these things are more than part of our past—they are what Holmes would call our "experience," the experience which remains at the very heart of what our law has become.[5] To understand these failures and triumphs, to see them clearly and understand, remains important.

Debts Owed

This volume was an obvious team effort. The editors, first and foremost, owe a great debt to the contributors. Their patience and effort, under what could be severe provocation, would be an inspiration to Job. This is not just true of the conference papers, but of the

whole, our willingness to take a stand, constitutes our card of identity." Felix Gilbert, *History: Choice and Commitment* (Cambridge, Mass., 1977), 453.

[4] Clifford K. Shipton, "The Locus of Authority in Colonial Massachusetts," in *Law and Authority in Colonial America*, 147.

[5] "Our recent preoccupation with the relation of law to the interests (primarily the material interests) of individuals and groups has led us to overlook the significance of legal institutions for the nature of man and his quest for a moral order." Daniel J. Boorstin, "The Humane Study of Law," *Yale Law Journal*, LVII (1948), 960, 975.

invaluable "sources" essays, which make this book of particular use to future scholars.

The conference behind the book was quite an event. The magic of the Bulfinch rooms and the beautiful fall weather on Beacon Hill, together with a truly civilized and distinguished audience, made it a "life-time" experience. All this, and the full support for the volume's production, is a tribute to the generosity of the Colonial Society of Massachusetts. Very special mention is due to Sinclair H. Hitchings, an extraordinary friend, who organized the conference and the hospitality in every detail, down to the first true use of Beacon Hill's largest silver wine cooler in at least a generation, and to William H. Bond and Lawrence Coolidge, whose leadership and generosity were vital. John Cushing and the Massachusetts Historical Society put on a splendid exhibition for the occasion. My tireless Harvard research assistant, John Monsky, was also of much assistance.

This conference could not have been held except for the pioneering record preservation efforts of the Supreme Judicial Court of Massachusetts, the oldest court with a continuous history in the United States. This is particularly due to the foresight of Chief Justice Edward F. Hennessey, for which he should be forgiven for occupying a position which, for nearly a third of its history, was entirely royal. His formation of the Massachusetts Judicial Records Committee, established in cooperation with that other extraordinary and historic institution, the Social Law Library, is making colonial record preservation a reality and not a dream.

It is no accident that two individuals at the heart of this "archival revolution" have also been absolutely essential to this book. Of course I am referring to the Assistant Editors, Catherine S. Menand, Chief Archivist of the Supreme Judicial Court, and Robert J. Brink, Special Projects Director of the Social Law Library, Director of the Colonial Court Records Project, and Secretary to the Judicial Records Committee. Their many acts of friendship have made working with them a most rewarding personal experience, and their expertise, their unflagging labor and their keen understanding of the colonial period have left their touch on every page of this book. I owe them the deepest thanks.

Finally, there is Frederick S. Allis, Jr., the Editor of Publications.

Every recent Colonial Society volume—but especially this one—is a tribute to his experience, wisdom, and dedication. Endless hours together in the majestic, but chilly, offices of the Colonial Society have left me in genuine awe of his energy and patience, and deeply in his debt. He is a great teacher and a true friend. I can now understand fully why generations of Andover students love and respect this man.

Personally, special thanks are always due to Anna, Sophia, Julia and, most of all, Judith.

DANIEL R. COQUILLETTE

Sodalitas

John Adams referred to the Sodalitas, the study group formed by Jeremiah Gridley in 1765 to discuss the law, as "A Clubb of Friends" and added that "I hope and expect to see . . . in consequence of this Sodality, a Purity, an Elegance, and a Spirit, surpassing any Thing that ever appeared in America."

The essayists, editors, and conference participants represented in this volume are, in spirit, descendants of Adams' and Gridley's Sodalitas. In November 1981, this "Clubb of Friends" from around the country convened at the Colonial Society in Boston and engaged, with "Purity," "Elegance," and "Spirit," in a lively exchange of ideas exploring colonial law in Massachusetts. In the long publication process which followed, editors and authors labored together to distill the essence of law in the colonial period, its personalities, procedures, and history.

As editors, we wish to express our deep appreciation to all the authors with whom we worked and, in particular, to Frederick S. Allis, Jr., the Editor of Publications for the Colonial Society.

But it is as members of the "Clubb of Friends" that we wish to record how much we enjoyed the editing of this volume under the direction of Daniel R. Coquillette. A man of wit and intellect, learned in the law, Dan is generous as well. He shared the pleasures of this book, structuring the work of editing so that we felt satisfaction and success as each phase of its production was completed. If he never spared us, shouting encouragement as he drove the project forward, he spared himself least of all. This volume is testimony to

Dan's unfailing attention to every detail and to his persistent sensitivity to the highest ideals of scholarship.

In the spirit of Sodalitas, we all hope that the substantive essays, combined with the guidance of the practical articles on sources, will help to stimulate further scholarship on colonial law "surpassing any Thing that ever appeared in America."

CATHERINE S. MENAND
ROBERT J. BRINK
Assistant Editors

Biographical Notes on Contributors

NEAL W. ALLEN, John Bigelow Professor of History at Union College, is a graduate of Bowdoin with a doctorate in history from Harvard, and has taught English and American constitutional and legal history for more than thirty years. He was the editor of Volumes IV and V of *Maine Province and Court Records,* and collaborated with the late Robert E. Moody in editing Volume VI in that series. He has been a visiting lecturer at Aberdeen University in Scotland and a fellow in law and history at the Harvard Law School.

THOMAS G. BARNES, a graduate of Harvard with a doctorate from Oxford, has since 1974 been Professor of History and Law at the University of California at Berkeley. A former Guggenheim Fellow and the winner of a number of prizes in history and in law, he has written several outstanding books on English legal history. His interest in early Massachusetts law and legal institutions is an outgrowth of his long-term research and writing on the Star Chamber, one facet of which is litigation and lawyers in the early seventeenth century.

BARBARA A. BLACK, a graduate of Brooklyn College, with a law degree from Columbia and a doctorate in history from Yale, has taught history at Yale and is presently Associate Professor of Law at the Yale Law School, teaching Contracts, Commercial Law, and Legal History. She has been visiting lecturer at both the Harvard and the Columbia Law Schools. Her main research interest is the adjudicative record of the General Court of Massachusetts in the seventeenth century, and she has written many scholarly articles.

ROBERT J. BRINK, a graduate of Boston University with a law degree from Northeastern, is Director of Special Projects at the Social Law Library in Boston. He also serves as Secretary and Treasurer of the Judicial Records Committee of the Supreme Judicial Court of Massachusetts. From 1976 to 1981 he directed a project to conserve the colonial court files of Suffolk County—a project which has since become the official state-wide program of the Supreme Judicial Court—and has written a number of articles on subjects in his field.

MORRIS L. COHEN is a graduate of the University of Chicago with a law degree from Columbia and a degree in Library Science from Pratt Institute. After several years in law practice he began a career as a law librarian

lxv

and has served at Rutgers, Columbia, S.U.N.Y. at Buffalo, the University of Pennsylvania, and Harvard. He is presently Librarian and Professor of Law at the Yale Law School. He has published a number of books and articles on legal research and has for almost twenty years been working on a comprehensive multi-volume work entitled *Bibliography of Early American Law*, to be published in 1985–1986.

DANIEL R. COQUILLETTE, a graduate of Williams, went as a Fulbright Scholar to Oxford, where he studied legal history and took a law degree. On his return to this country he graduated from the Harvard Law School. He then served as law clerk to the Hon. Robert Braucher of the Massachusetts Supreme Judicial Court and later as law clerk to the Hon. Warren E. Burger, Chief Justice of the United States. He is currently a partner in the law firm of Palmer and Dodge in Boston, and has been Visiting Professor from Practice at the Harvard and the Cornell Law Schools. He is the author of a number of articles on legal history.

JOHN D. CUSHING received his doctorate from Clark University and taught constitutional history and law at Norwich, Clark, and Boston Universities before joining the staff of the Massachusetts Historical Society, where he has been Librarian since 1963. He was the compiler of *A Bibliography of the Laws and Resolves of the Massachusetts Bay, 1642–1780* and of a facsimile edition of *The Laws and Liberties of Massachusetts, 1641–1691*, and is the author of several major articles on Massachusetts legal history. He was director of the Plymouth Court Record Project and has served on a number of boards concerned with the preservation of court records and the organization of archives.

DAVID H. FLAHERTY, a graduate of McGill University with a doctorate in history from Columbia, taught at Princeton and the University of Virginia before assuming his present position as Professor of History and Law at the University of Western Ontario in London, Canada. He has been a visiting fellow at Magdalen College, Oxford, and a fellow in law and history at the Harvard Law School. He is the author of *Privacy in Colonial New England* and the editor of *Essays in the History of Early American Law* and *Essays in the History of Canadian Law* (Vols. 1, 2) and has written a number of articles on early American colonial and legal history.

GEORGE L. HASKINS, a graduate of Harvard and the Harvard Law School, is currently the Algernon Sydney Biddle Professor at the Law School of the University of Pennsylvania. He was a Guggenheim Fellow and worked for the United Nations during its early years. Today, he is widely acknowledged as the dean of American colonial legal historians. His best-known work, of many, is the classic *Law and Authority in Early Massachusetts*. He is a Fellow of the Royal Historical Society and past President of the American Society for Legal History.

EDITH G. HENDERSON, a graduate of Swarthmore with both an LL.B. and an S.J.D. from the Harvard Law School, is currently Curator of the Treasure Room at the Harvard Law School Library. She has written and edited a number of articles and books on English legal history, including *Foundations of English Administrative Law* and a pending Selden Society volume.

MICHAEL S. HINDUS has a law degree from Harvard and a doctorate in history from the University of California at Berkeley. He has taught at the University of Minnesota and the Stanford Law School and from 1977 to 1979 was Project Director for the Judicial Records Committee of the Massachusetts Supreme Judicial Court. He is currently a practicing attorney in San Francisco. He is the author of *Prison and Plantation: Crime, Justice, and Authority in Massachusetts and South Carolina, 1767–1878* and *The Files of the Massachusetts Superior Court*.

DOUGLAS L. JONES is a graduate of Duke University with a master's degree from the University of Texas in Austin, a doctorate from Brandeis, and a law degree from Harvard. He has been a Research Fellow at The Charles Warren Center at Harvard and has taught at Tufts. He is the author of *Village and Seaport: Migration and Society in Eighteenth-Century Massachusetts* and has written several articles on American colonial and legal history.

CHARLES R. McKIRDY is a graduate of the State University of New York at Buffalo with a doctorate in history from Northwestern University and a law degree from Northwestern Law School. He has taught at the University of Illinois, Chicago Circle, and the Kent Law School. He is currently a litigation partner with the law firm of Pope, Ballard, Shepard and Fowle of Chicago. He has authored several articles concerning colonial lawyers, as well as articles on substantive and procedural aspects of the law.

KATHLEEN A. MAJOR taught American History at the high-school level for five years before joining the staff of the American Antiquarian Society in 1976 as a manuscripts cataloguer. In 1979 she became Assistant Curator of Manuscripts and is now Keeper of Manuscripts.

CATHERINE S. MENAND received her A.B. from Vassar College and then did graduate work at Columbia. She has been a Research Fellow at Wellesley College. She is currently Chief Archivist of the Massachusetts Supreme Judicial Court. Her most recent publication is "Politics, Passions and the Law: Otis v. Robinson 1769."

WILLIAM E. NELSON, a graduate of Hamilton with a law degree from New York University and a doctorate in history from Harvard, is one of the country's most distinguished legal scholars. He has been a law clerk to Associate Justice Byron R. White of the United States Supreme Court, a Teaching Fellow at Harvard, and has been a law professor at the University of Pennsylvania and Yale before assuming his present position as Professor of Law at New York University. He has written widely in his field, two of his most important books being *The Americanization of the Common Law: The Impact of Change on Massachusetts Society, 1760–1830* and *Dispute and Conflict Resolution in Plymouth County, Massachusetts, 1725–1825.*

RUSSELL K. OSGOOD, a graduate of Yale and of the Yale Law School, is currently Professor of Law at the Cornell Law School. He is the editor with Lloyd Bonfield of *Law and History Review,* published jointly by the Cornell Law School and the American Society for Legal History. He has written several leading articles on tax law and American legal history, and is the author of a major treatise on pensions and profit sharing.

CAROLINE PRESTON, a graduate of Dartmouth with a master's degree from Brown, served as Archivist for the Rhode Island Historical Society before joining the staff of the Essex Institute, Salem, Massachusetts, where she holds the position of Manuscript Librarian.

Law in Colonial Massachusetts

1630-1800

THOMAS G. BARNES

Thomas Lechford and the Earliest Lawyering in Massachusetts, 1638–1641

IN the Augustan rooms of this august society, my use of the ugly term "lawyering" must appear as a breach of *dulia* if not of *latria*. The *genii loci* of the Colonial Society of Massachusetts— those distinguished nineteenth-century founders, masters of elegant prose and measured elegiac rhetoric—wince to hear it, and perhaps find only cold comfort in noticing that it falls from the lips of one who can be called a frontiersman! My apologies to them, and to you, but I found it at best anomalous, at worst misleading, to use a more acceptable and less grating term such as "earliest legal practice." Those few whom we know or suspect were engaged in providing legal services for a fee in the first two decades of the Bay Colony did not fit the contemporary understanding of a "practicer" of the law: that is, they were neither barristers nor attorneys-at-law, either in Old England or New. The first of these, and the most learned, interesting, and important of them, was Thomas Lechford. He only once arrogated to himself a more impressive title than "scriptoris hujus" (his scribe) of the client. William Aspinwall described himself simply as "Notarie & Tabellion pub[lic]"; and such shadowy figures as Robert Saltonstall, Edward Colcord, George Keyser, and Robert Lord were apparently attorneys-in-fact, not in-law, though they were probably fee'd.[1] Nevertheless, if by contemporary canons there were no "learned practicers" in early Massachusetts, there were men engaged in lawyering. Though not formally "learned," they were not innocent of learning; though not technically "practicers," their

---

[1] *Note-Book kept by Thomas Lechford, Esq., Lawyer*, Archaeologia Americana, VII (Cambridge, Mass., 1885) [hereafter, *Note-Book*], 155; *Aspinwall Notarial Records* (Boston, 1903), 5; *Records of the Governor and Company of the Massachusetts Bay in New England*, N. B. Shurtleff, ed. (Boston, 1853) [hereafter, *Massachusetts Records*], II, 232; *Records and Files of the Quarterly Courts of Essex County Massachusetts* (Salem, 1911), I, 37, 89, 101 *et passim*. I am grateful to my colleague, James H. Kettner, for his helpful criticism of this paper and for many kindnesses in guiding my feet in "right paths."

practices were far from negligible. These men filled a real need for legal services in the routine conduct of legal business and litigation in a colonial society which had as high a regard for law, as perfectly developed a penchant for litigation, and almost as sophisticated, albeit less complicated and more condensed, a judicial arena as did Old England. They deserve a large place in our annals, for they founded the legal profession in Massachusetts, and from their small beginnings grew the company of those later and better known practicers who will engage our attention during the remainder of this conference.

The origins of the legal profession in Massachusetts are bedevilled by the conventional wisdom that Puritans had an inbred animus toward all lawyers. Recently a sizable literature on the demand for law reform in Old England during the rule of the Saints has lent emphasis, and perhaps undue credence, to this proposition.[2] Interestingly, recent legal-historical scholarship on Massachusetts has tended to stress less animus against lawyers for the slowness of a recognized legal profession to evolve in the colony than the fact that the colony's courts were more analogous to the local customary courts of England, notably the leet, than to the central courts at Westminster. The latest commentator, David Grayson Allen, argues that

Most men in England in the seventeenth century still lived in rural areas away from the influence of or need for the national court system. They seldom required the services of trained lawyers, and they were not likely to carry disputes beyond the manor or borough, or hundred or county courts. Life in Massachusetts was little different.[3]

The vague "most men" is misleading insofar as this is a description of the non-recourse of rural Englishmen to Westminster. In fact, a great many rural Englishmen of cognate status to their cousins in

---

[2] See especially S. E. Prall, *The Agitation for Law Reform during the Puritan Revolution, 1640–1660* (The Hague, 1966) and D. Veall, *The Popular Movement for Law Reform, 1640–1660* (Oxford, 1970).

[3] David Grayson Allen, *In English Ways: The Movement of Societies and the Transferal of English Local Law and Custom to Massachusetts Bay in the Seventeenth Century* (Chapel Hill, 1981), 209. George Lee Haskins, in his *Law and Authority in Early Massachusetts: A Study in Tradition and Design* (New York, 1960), especially Chapter X, 163–188, first emphasized the English local dimension in early Massachusetts law.

Massachusetts were involved in civil disputes in Westminster and all too familiar with the activities of "trained lawyers," barristers, and attorneys. Moreover, the English origins of a great many of the Bay immigrants were not that impeccably rural: about ten percent came from London and Middlesex, and a large proportion of the rest came from boroughs, especially in East Anglia and the Home Counties, with very sophisticated borough jurisdictions served by numerous local attorneys. I have argued elsewhere that the Massachusetts General Court *cum* Court of Assistants asserted and exercised as broad a jurisdiction and as deep a cognizance of matters as all the courts of England combined, including Chancery and Star Chamber.[4] Whatever longing there might have been for arcadian simplicity in the doing of law, realities dictated that within two decades of the Bay Colony's founding a legal profession would emerge. That does not appear to have surprised anyone save the magistrates, who resisted the development; neither does the lawyer appear to have been a novelty in the colonists' experience.

Yet the emergence of a legal profession was relatively slow in coming. An explanation for this slowness based upon rusticity and a lack of sophistication on the part of the colonists is hardly more satisfying than the older notion of "Puritan animus." In any event, there is merit in putting that animus in proper perspective. The most commonly cited evidence of the animus is clause 26 of Nathaniel Ward's "Body of Liberties" of 1641:

Every man that findeth himselfe unfit to plead his owne cause in any Court shall have Libertie to imploy any man against whom the Court doth not except, to helpe him, Provided he give him noe fee or reward for his paines. This shall not exempt the partie him selfe from Answering such Questions in person as the Court shall thinke meete to demand of him.[5]

---

[4] T. G. Barnes, "Law and Liberty (and Order) in Early Massachusetts," *The English Legal System: Carryover to the Colonies* (Clark Library, Los Angeles, 1975), 63–89. Lechford appreciated the breadth of that jurisdiction: "And they themselves say, that in the generall and quarter Courts, they have the power of Parliament, Kings Bench, Common Pleas, Chancery, High Commission, and Star-chamber, and all other Courts of England...." *Plain Dealing: or Newes from New-England* (London, 1642) (Wing L810) [hereafter, *Plain Dealing*], 26.

[5] *The Colonial Laws of Massachusetts*, W. H. Whitmore, ed. (Boston, 1889) [hereafter, Whitmore], 39.

Ward was one of only three men in the early years of the Colony who had been called to the English bar.[6] He was hardly a much-practiced barrister; within a few years of his call by Lincoln's Inn in 1615, he gave up the long robe for the severe gown of a Puritan parson. By 1641 he was far from Lincoln's Inn, his spiritual and intellectual as well as physical migration having taken him to a chaplaincy to English traders in a Hanse city, to the rectory of Stondon Massey in Essex, to deprivation by Archbishop Laud, and to the ministry of the gathered church in Ipswich, Massachusetts. In 1638 he gave up even the latter, and John Winthrop noted opprobriously that he was "now no minister by the received determination of our churches."[7] We do not know whether Ward's "Body of Liberties" had the force of law. Certainly clause 26 appears to have obtained in practice. However, though the *Lawes and Libertyes* of 1648 picked up all but nine of the "Body's" ninety-six substantive clauses, clause 26 was one of those omitted.[8] Whatever strength the "Puritan animus" had once possessed, by 1648 it had waned considerably.

We must also distinguish from "Body of Liberties" clause 26 that round condemnation by a former Attorney of Wards and Liveries of the "multitude of Atturnies ... [who] take out processe against their neighbors upon very light occasions...."[9] John Winthrop referred to the attorneys of Common Pleas, King's Bench, the Guildhall of London, and other lesser courts. Those who stuck to their last in the court upon whose rolls their names were entered and of which they were considered "clerks," those who did not "solicit" actions in other courts as "common solicitors of causes," would have escaped Winthrop's strictures. Certainly, those genuine officers of English-bill courts, such as the three attorneys of Wards and Liveries of whom he had once been one, who did not solicit causes but merely

---

[6] The other two were Richard Bellingham (Lincoln's Inn, no date of call, but was recorder of Boston, Lincolnshire) and John Humphrey (Lincoln's Inn, called 1623); both were Assistants, or magistrates, in Massachusetts.

[7] *Winthrop's Journal*, J. K. Hosmer, ed. (New York, 1908) [hereafter, Winthrop], II, 36.

[8] *The Book of the General Lawes and Libertyes Concerning the Inhabitants of the Massachusets*, T. G. Barnes, ed. (San Marino, Calif., 1975) [hereafter, *Lawes and Libertyes*]. Introduction, 10, note 15.

[9] Quoted in Darrett B. Rutman, *Winthrop's Boston: Portrait of a Puritan Town 1630–1649* (Chapel Hill, 1965) [hereafter, Rutman], 233.

handled the paperwork, appearances, and motions of the litigants who retained them in the particular court, were not the butt of Winthrop's scorn.[1] There was no hypocrisy in Winthrop's condemnation, only snobbery. More characteristic of the Puritan genre was the Reverend John Cotton's blast out of Zion at those "unconscionable Advocates" bolstering a "bad case by quirks of wit, and tricks and quillets of Law . . . ," who "use their tongues as weapons of unrighteousnesse . . . to plead in corrupt Causes."[2] If there were indeed a prejudice against lawyers in the Bay Colony, it appears to have been directed primarily at those thought responsible for barratry — the stirring up of unnecessary and unwarrantable suits in law — and at advocates whose forensic skills were looked upon with deep suspicion as instruments of deceit and obfuscation.

The explanation for the slowness of a legal profession to emerge in the Bay probably had more to do with the failure of a City Upon a Hill in a wilderness to attract lawyers than anything else. It demanded unusual devotion to the enterprise of the Godly Commonwealth to persuade even a moderately successful barrister or attorney to give up what was still in the 1630's the most lucrative vocation providing the greatest upward social mobility open to talent in England. Very few men — even the great many who can be identified as basically well-disposed to the cause, both from religious sentiment and political predilection — were prepared to give up so much for so little. Those who did found ready acceptance at the top level of colonial society. They became the accepted leaders — most of them were among the founders — of the Colony, as befitted their social status in England as lawyers. When the *quondam* recorder of Boston, Lincolnshire, Richard Bellingham, and his talents were needed on the bench as an Assistant, he was more usefully employed there than as advocate at its bar.

Something else was at work to discourage the emergence of a legal profession. When legal talent did not pour into the Colony voluntarily, the founders felt no compulsion to recruit it. The magistrates were understandably reluctant to nurture a profession which would

---

[1] H. E. Bell, *An Introduction to the History and Records of the Court of Wards and Liveries* (Cambridge, 1953), 30–31.

[2] Quoted in Rutman, 233–234.

4. John Winthrop (1587/88–1649), Governor, Chief Magistrate, Member of the Court of Assistants. Member, Gray's Inn and Inner Temple. Admitted, Court of Wards and Liveries. Courtesy, Massachusetts Historical Society, from a copy of a portrait painted in England before 1630.

at least make their lives more complicated and could challenge their control of the law and legal institutions upon which ultimately depended their leadership of the Godly enterprise. In common with the mother country's judges, upon whom they modeled their activities, the magistrates took seriously Chief Justice Coke's admonition that the bench look out for the interests of one accused of crime precisely because at common law an accused felon had no right to counsel at his trial.[3] In those civil suits and the administrative matters in which the common law allowed counsel to the parties, the magistrates sought to preserve the law in as rudimentary a state as possible, in order to obviate the need for learned assistance. The professional lawyer posed a threat to judicial control; even the most deferential and well-disposed advocate could not be relied upon to be taken into court! Magistrates such as Winthrop, Dudley, Downing, Pynchon, Humphrey (a barrister), Richard Saltonstall, and Bellingham had enough legal learning and judicial experience to appreciate the threat. What they could not do was steadfastly exclude lawyers from the courts. No matter how annoying the profession might be, it was an integral part of the legal system of Old England and could not forever be kept out of New.

Just as lawyers could not be excluded from the courts, neither could the magistrates long keep the laws a closed preserve, maintaining indefinitely their monopoly of knowledge of the law. Within five years of the Bay's settlement, the freemen began to agitate for a compendium of the Colony's laws that would limit the discretion of the magistrates by making available to everyone knowledge of the positive laws by which order was preserved, rights and liberties assured, and good governance effected. This agitation bore its first fruit in the collection of fundamental laws drawn up by Nathaniel Ward in 1641, the "Body of Liberties." The "Body of Liberties" was almost too fundamental: it did not limit sufficiently the magistrates' discretion because it was not a comprehensive collection of the criminal and public law of the Colony, which was growing rapidly by the legislation of the General Court. With the increasing prominence in the 1640's of the non-magistrate town Deputies as members

---

[3] *The Lord Coke his Speech and Charge* (London, 1607) (STC 5491).

of successive committees "for the laws," the effectual steps were taken that resulted in the printing in 1648 of six-hundred copies of *The Book of the General Lawes and Libertyes Concerning the Inhabitants of the Massachusets*.[4] While most, though, as we noted above, significantly not all, of the "Liberties" of 1641 found their way into the 1648 compendium, the bulk of it was legislation — the "General Lawes" rather than "Libertyes" — which constituted the largest portion of the positive law of the Colony. For three shillings anyone could have the entire public law, much of the criminal law, and the most important and uniquely Massachusetts part of the civil law in his hands.

The conversion of the magistrates to the notion that the laws should be available to all was a long and painful process. The first, and ultimately the most effective, convert was Richard Bellingham. He had come early to a realization that there was no way in which free-born Englishmen of the mid-seventeenth century could be prevented from knowing the laws by which they were governed, indeed, by which they governed themselves through the legislation of the General Court in its non-magisterial element, the Deputies. Bellingham was also enough of a realist, and quintessentially the counsellor-at-law, to recognize that people who placed such a premium on the enjoyment of their rights and liberties could not be denied professional assistance in litigating them. Clearly, the agitation that produced the printed laws also stimulated the development of a legal profession in Massachusetts. The uncomplicated law in the minds and from the mouths of the magistrates, when set down in cold print, had become complicated and voluminous. That law demanded professional involvement in its implementation. Ironically, while the printed laws might have made of every man his own lawyer, instead they drove every man to seek professional help. That the earliest clear emergence of a legal profession in the Colony dates from about 1650 indicates a connection with the circumstances surrounding and an impact on the law following the publication of the *Lawes and Libertyes* in 1648 that was more than coincidental.

---

[4] *Lawes and Libertyes*, Introduction, 5.

I. Thomas Lechford of Clement's Inn

The career of the first man known to undertake "lawyering" for fee in Massachusetts substantiates the observations set out above as to the reasons for the slowness of the legal profession to emerge in the Colony. Thomas Lechford of London was neither barrister nor attorney, neither esquire nor gentleman. He was in fact a "common solicitor of causes," one who would have certainly been included within John Winthrop's strictures. He came to Boston in 1638, not from religious sentiment, or political predilection, but rather from necessity. He had fallen foul of Archbishop Laud, the most powerful man in England, had been committed for contempt of court, and had decided that any further promotion in the legal profession was closed to him in consequence. Not only did he lack the learning and the social station that would have made him a magistrate in New England; he also lacked the visible piety of a Visible Saint that would have brought membership in the gathered church in Boston, and hence have made him free of the Colony and eligible for public office befitting his talents. In his three years in Boston, from this arrival on 27 June 1638 until his departure for England on 3 August 1641, he exercised his calling as a lawyer with continuous assiduity and considerable success, despite contretemps, growing isolation from the community, and some experience of that "Puritan animus," which, if it did not make life impossible for him, surely made it difficult.

Of his family background, nothing is known. J. Hammond Trumbull speculated in the introduction to the 1885 edition of the Lechford's *Note-Book* that Lechford was a descendant of Sir Richard Lechford of Shelwood, Surrey (*obiit* 1611) and therefore closely related to Sir Richard's grandson and heir, a knight of the same name and Gentleman Pensioner, who was a notorious Roman Catholic at the court of Charles I until put from his place in 1634 for attempting to send two of his daughters to nunneries in Europe.[5] This is unprovable. That Thomas Lechford first set down — and then struck

[5] *Note-Book*, vii–ix; Trumbull's introduction to a new edition of *Plain Dealing* (Boston, 1867), xi–xiii. Even if Thomas was no relation to Sir Richard Lechford, that the latter's name is indifferently spelled Lechford or Leechford indicates that Thomas's name should be pronounced with a long "e."

out — the self-ascription "late of Clements Inn in the county of Middlesex Gent" in a petition to the General Court in 1639, wherein he was attempting to clear himself of a charge of jury-embracery, proves only that he had been a member of that Inn of Chancery before coming to Massachusetts.[6] If descended from a knight whose arms had been confirmed in 1605 by Garter,[7] he would have been a gentleman by right; but as a member of one of the inferior Inns he might have arrogated to himself the status of "gent," which by common acceptance then would have been warranted only by one who was also an attorney-at-law. In fact, while discretion may have dictated deleting the self-ascription, the General Court never accorded Lechford gentle status by the honorable form of address, "Mr."

Equally speculative was Trumbull's conclusion from two ambiguous allusions — one by Lechford and the other by his New England nemesis, the Reverend John Cotton — that Lechford had been driven from England for assisting William Prynne's cause in the Star Chamber in 1637, when Prynne, Dr. John Bastwick, and the Reverend Henry Burton were prosecuted by the Attorney-General for seditious libel. Lechford wrote in 1642:

I suffered imprisonment, and a kind of banishment out of this good Land [England], for some acts construed to oppose, as tending to subvert Episcopacie, and the setled Ecclesiasticall government of England.[8]

Cotton, in 1648, stated that Lechford had left England because he had "witnessed" against the bishops "in soliciting the cause of Mr. Prynne. . . ."[9] It is possible that Lechford was involved in that Puritan *cause célèbre*, but there is absolutely no trace of Lechford to be found in the masses of documentation on the case.[1] Rather, there is direct evidence, apparently unknown to Trumbull, that provides a better explanation of these passages, albeit one not quite so emphati-

---

[6] *Note-Book*, 182.

[7] *Miscellanea Genealogica et Heraldica*, J. J. Howard, ed. (London, 1868), I, 54–55.

[8] *Plain Dealing*, Proheme.

[9] John Cotton, *The Way of Congregational Churches Cleared* (London, 1648) (Wing C6469), 71.

[1] The author, who has spent a quarter-century studying the Star Chamber from 1596 to 1641, has had access to all known, extant materials on the Case of Prynne, Bastwick, and Burton.

cally redounding to Lechford's reputation as a martyr to Laudian persecution.

One charge in the impeachment of William Laud, Archbishop of Canterbury, before the Lords in March 1644 was that he had interfered with the course of justice in suits brought by Ferdinando Adams, a churchwarden of St. Mary-at-Tower, Ipswich, Suffolk, against Henry Dade, the metropolitan's commissary and surrogate of Laud's vicar-general. St. Mary's was a hot-bed of Puritanism, and in 1635 Dade held his ecclesiastical court in the church in furtherance of Laud's injunctions to remove seats in the east end of the chancel and to put in their place a railed-in communion table on a north-south axis. When Dade took his commissarial seat in the church, he discovered that Adams had scrawled in large letters over it a somewhat less than indifferent passage from Scripture, Matthew 20.13, "'My house shall be called the house of prayer; but ye have made it a den of thieves.'"[2] Adams refused both to remove the offending passage and to take down the seats and replace them with the table, and Dade excommunicated him.[3] Adams retaliated by suing Dade in King's Bench in an action on the case, and also in Exchequer.

Ferdinando Adams's counsel was none other than William Prynne. Adams's solicitor was Thomas Lechford. Cotton's recalling, more than a decade later, that Lechford had solicited "the cause of Mr. Prynne" might have been a human slip for "the cause *for* Mr. Prynne," as Adams's solicitor in the cause in conjunction with Prynne. Lechford certainly did suffer "imprisonment": he was committed by Justice Jones of the King's Bench until Adams dropped his case in that court. At Laud's trial, Prynne testified that "'he [Prynne] advised Adams to an action of the case; that he blamed Lechford for deserting the suit; and that he advised him [Adams] to go to Mr. Attorney.'"[4] Attorney-General Bankes's principal clerk, John Cockshutt, took up the case on relation and had Dade and other officials served with process to appear in Star Chamber. Laud then expostu-

[2] William Laud, *Works* (Oxford, 1854) [hereafter, Laud], IV, 130.

[3] William Prynne, *Canterburies Doome* (London, 1646) (Wing P3917), 101. Peter Heylyn, Laud's chaplain, who is usually a good corrective to Prynne's animus towards Laud, agrees substantially with him on this, and adds some details. *Cyprianus Anglicanus* (London, 1668) (Wing H1699), 295.

[4] Laud, IV, 132.

lated with Bankes for "lending his name in such a scandalous cause," and Bankes withdrew before putting in an information.[5] Adams was left to prosecute on his own behalf, and in Easter Term 1636 his bill against Dade *et alios* was, as the course demanded upon a demurrer or plea-in-bar, referred to a judge, George Croke, JKB.[6] Croke's report obviously went against Adams. In Hilary term 1637, Star Chamber ordered: "Let the shoemaker [Adams] appeare heere in person in open court before the defendants be compelled to answeare" his bill, because the actions by Adams in King's Bench and Exchequer had been found "unfitt," the Attorney-General had refused to put in an information, Adams had "Opposed the Bishops coming into church" and was excommunicated.[7] At the hearing for the order, Laud, as Privy Councillor, made a slighting reference to Adams's "conscience" not admitting him to take the oath to give evidence in the matter. At this point, Adams fled to the Bay Colony, where he was admitted free in May 1640, having settled at Dedham.[8]

Perhaps Adams's flight moved Lechford to follow suit. Lechford stated that he was "thrown out of my station in England."[9] This leads to an inference that his "kind of banishment out of this good Land" was not a matter of being driven into exile to escape retribution, as much as it was a matter of finding employment. He claimed to have been offered a place in the court of Prince George I Rakoczy of Transylvania, and that "the Lords of Providence offered me place of preferment with them which I will not name."[1] In the event he did not avail himself of either of these exotic opportunities, if opportunities they were, for he referred to them while patently trying to impress the Reverend Hugh Peters in hopes of obtaining Peters's help in getting admitted to the church in Boston.

[5] Ibid., 131.

[6] Star Chamber registrar's rough book of orders and decrees, Bodleian Library: MS. Rawlinson C. 827, f.6v.

[7] Ibid., f.39.

[8] Laud, IV, 131; *Massachusetts Records*, I, 377. C. E. Banks, *Topographical Dictionary of 2885 English Emigrants to New England, 1620–1650* (Philadelphia, 1937), 39 and 103, lists a Ferdinando Adams of Barking, Essex, and one of the same name of St. Katherine's parish, London; both settled in Dedham, Mass.

[9] *Note-Book*, 47, Lechford to the Reverend Hugh Peters, 3 January 1639.

[1] Ibid., 48.

Lechford's movements between the conclusion of the Adams Case in March 1637 and his arrival in Boston at the end of June 1638 are obscure. He left England sometime between November 1637 and January 1638.[2] Allowing for a ten-week westward passage, a period as long as November 1637 to mid-April 1638 is unaccounted for between his leaving Old England and embarking for New. In July 1640 he wrote to an English friend that he looked to the prospect of leaving the Bay and being so

happy as to arrive in Ireland, there at leaste to follow my old profession, and where I have hope of some friendship, since I was last there with my Lord Deputy Wentworth now lord lieutenant-general.[3]

It was possible that Lechford's Irish sojourn pre-dated his Adams's Case troubles, but it was more likely that he tried to make a start in Dublin, with no success, before leaving for New England. A cursory search of Wentworth's letter-books for the 1630's has failed to turn up any reference to Lechford.[4]

It would be well now to consider what a "solicitor" in early seventeenth-century England did. There can be no doubt that Lechford was a solicitor in name and function both before and after his Massachusetts sojourn. His involvement in Adams's Case makes that clear; Cotton's reference supports it; the Boston court of Assistants long after he left the Bay referred to him as "an ordinary solicitor in England."[5] In 1639 Lechford described himself as "late of Clements Inn in the county of Middlesex Gent," and in 1642 as a gentleman of that same society.[6]

Clement's Inn was one of nine Inns of Chancery dependent upon and controlled by the four Inns of Court, in the case of Clement's, by the Inner Temple. The Inns of Court had gained a monopoly of call to the bar; only those who had completed the exercises of one

---

[2] Trumbull makes the case for this in his introduction, *Note-Book,* xiii.

[3] *Note-Book,* 275.

[4] Sheffield City Library: Wentworth-Woodhouse MSS., Letter-books, 5–11. I am grateful to Dr. David Postles, the Sheffield City Library Archivist, for his search—in vain—of the card-index to the Wentworth Letters, post-1631, for Lechford's name.

[5] *Massachusetts Records,* II, 206, 11 November 1647.

[6] *Note-Book,* 182; *Plain Dealing,* Title page.

of those four Inns had right of audience in the courts as "barristers,"[7] (hence the name). Indeed, in Common Pleas only those barristers who had received letters patent calling them to the order of Serjeants-at-Law (upon which they removed to Serjeants' Inn, which they shared with the common-law court judges, former Serjeants) had the right of audience. The Inns of Chancery, so called because the writ office for beginning common-law actions was in Chancery, were associated with the writ and clerical side of the law. Originally, a man bent on a legal career would pass some time at an Inn of Chancery learning the writ system before going on to an Inn of Court to become a barrister. By the beginning of the seventeenth century the Inns of Court seldom admitted aspirants from the inferior Inns. The Inns of Chancery became almost entirely working chambers for attorneys, court-clerks, and solicitors.

An attorney, though he could not plead or advocate at the bar of a court, was recognized by the court as being empowered to act for a principal by making appearance, directing the issue of process, and authorizing entries on the court's record. He was an officer of the court and was often referred to as a "clerk of court." The numbers of attorneys of Common Pleas and King's Bench were such that by the early seventeenth century neither court was certain exactly how many such "officers" it had.[8] These attorneys were recognized in all other common-law courts: Exchequer, the London courts, assizes, quarter sessions, and the like.

The English-bill courts—Chancery, Star Chamber, Requests, and Duchy of Lancaster — limited the number of attorneys to six or less, and they were truly officers of the court. This stringency stimulated

[7] Wilfrid R. Prest, in *The Inns of Court under Elizabeth I and the Early Stuarts, 1590–1640* (London, 1972) has dealt extensively with the development of "barristers"; see also, his "The English Bar, 1550–1700," in *Lawyers in Early Modern Europe and America*, W. R. Prest, ed. (New York, 1981), 65–85. See also, J. H. Baker, "Counsellors and Barristers," *Cambridge Law Journal*, XXVII (November 1969), 205–229; W. C. Richardson, *A History of the Inns of Court* (Baton Rouge, 1977); and E. W. Ives, *The Common Lawyers of Pre-Reformation England* (Cambridge, 1983), 36–89.

[8] C. W. Brooks, "Litigants and Attorneys in the King's Bench and Common Pleas, 1560–1640," *Legal Records and the Historian*, J. H. Baker, ed. (London, 1978), 53, and C. W. Brooks, "The Common Lawyers in England, c. 1558–1642," *Lawyers in Early Modern Europe and America*, W. R. Prest, ed. (New York, 1981), 42–64.

the growth of a class of practicers called solicitors[9] who were neither barristers nor attorneys and who did not yet enjoy the professional status of either. The office of solicitor was not a new phenomenon: it was at least as old as the fifteenth century. By the early seventeenth century the solicitor had become an indispensable agent in the conduct of litigation in the English-bill courts and a useful one in actions in common-law courts. Agent is the proper term, for he provided the nexus between client and counsel and counsel and attorney in the course of an action. Though the client "instructed" counsel directly, and counsel dealt with the attorney, the solicitor served as the messenger tying all together. The solicitor was in the most intimate contact with the client, at his beck and call in a way that neither barrister nor attorney was. Certainly a number of attorneys served as solicitors, especially in English-bill litigation, young men in the Inns of Court on their way to the bar "solicited" for principals, and some solicitors were really estate-agents and innocent of much, if any, legal learning.[1]

Thomas Lechford was none of these. His name will not be found on warrants of attorney in the records of the Common Pleas or King's Bench. He was never admitted to one of the four Inns of Court. He probably was not anyone's estate-agent, though this is not susceptible of proof. Indeed, we know nothing certain about Lechford's practice from Clement's Inn, beyond his misfortune in being the plaintiff's solicitor in *Adams v. Dade*.

There is one piece of evidence that will support some inferences about Lechford's English practice and training. At the end of Lechford's scrivener's book from his Massachusetts sojourn, preserved in the American Antiquarian Society in Worcester, Massachusetts, are forty-six pages in a neat hand that was not Lechford's[2] containing extracts from sixty-five legal instruments. Eight of these instruments

[9] J. H. Baker, "Solicitors and the Law of Maintenance 1590–1640," *Cambridge Law Journal*, XXXII (April, 1973), 56–80.

[1] T. G. Barnes, "Star Chamber Litigants and their Counsel, 1596–1641," *Legal Records and the Historian*, J. H. Baker, ed. (London, 1978), 25.

[2] The author is grateful to Marcus A. McCorison, Director and Librarian of the American Antiquarian Society, for making a xerox copy of the entire Lechford MS. available to him. J. Hammond Trumbull's choice of title, *Note-Book*, was unfortunate. The MS. makes very clear that "scrivener's entry book" would have been more appropriate; save that the instruments are given *in extenso*, it resembles

were conditions for obligations, releases, a warrant of attorney, a letter of attorney, and a defeasance upon judgment. Fifty-seven were extracts from written pleadings, some *ex parte* the plaintiff, the bulk special pleadings in defence. All these pleadings are in Latin, a clear sign that they were extracted from plea rolls of common-law courts. All were in civil suits, principally debt, trespass, and action on the case—the latter almost all assumpsit. Insofar as it is possible to determine jurisdiction and time, the suits were in the London Guildhall and date from the early 1630's. That is, they were in the court of the Lord Mayor of London or the Sheriffs' Court of London. The dominance of assumpsit helps confirm the jurisdiction, if we note the point made by a contemporary lawyer's handbook as to the popularity of assumpsit in the London courts.[3] Moreover, since written pleadings enrolled of record in a court usually gave the name of the attorney making the enrollment, we are furnished with an important clue. Almost sixty per cent of the pleadings were entered by one John Hatt.[4] Hatt was a well-known Guildhall attorney, and one who was to become notorious as a leading London radical in the turmoil surrounding the breakdown of Charles I's regime and the onset of revolution.[5]

Our clue—it is no more than that—suggests that Lechford had, as a solicitor, worked closely with Hatt, and conceivably with a

with respect to entries and fees three scrivener's waste-books of Robert Glover, 1611–1617, in the Public Record Office: Wards 9/351. Trumbull's and the other editors' transcription in the 1885 edition leaves something to be desired, both with respect to canons of transcription and accuracy; a comparison of their text on 46–47 with the plate below (the passport for the *Sparrow*) will indicate that "Virtute litterarum" in the MS. has been rendered—quite impossibly—as "Virtute harum." That the editors gave no indication in the 1885 edition of the existence of extracts at the rear of the MS. was inexcusable. The author intends to undertake a critical edition of the MS. at some future time, with an apparatus dealing with the legal matter in it.

[3] Thomas Powell, *The Attourneys Academy* (London, 1623) (STC 20163), 170.

[4] Of the 57 pleadings, Hatt is named in 4 *ex parte* the plaintiff and 29 *ex parte* the defendant; other named attorneys accounted for 5 plaintiff and 11 defendant; pleadings in which no attorney was named, 1 plaintiff and 7 defendant.

[5] British Library: Addition MSS. 31116 (Whitaker's diary of the Long Parliament) f.128, petition of the city of London to the Commons, 20 July 1643. Hatt was the son of Giles Hatt of Leckhampstead, Berks., and was admitted to Gray's Inn in 1629, but not called to the bar; his son, also John, was called in 1651, *Register of Admissions to Gray's Inn, 1521–1889*, J. Foster, ed. (London, 1889), 188 and 238; *The Pension Book of Gray's Inn, 1569–1669*, R. J. Fletcher, ed. (London, 1901), 381; *Four Visitations of Berkshire*, W. Harry Rylands, ed. (London, 1908), II, 142.

couple of the other attorneys whose names we have from these pleadings. Because the status of a solicitor was professionally so inchoate,
it was possible for an attorney and a solicitor to work together so
closely that the solicitor was in fact less a free agent than a subordinate
to the attorney, assisting the latter in his practice and perhaps undertaking clerical work, copying and the like. In Lechford's case, if he
did have such a relationship with an attorney, he might well have
done a considerable amount of drafting of instruments also. In his
submission to the Boston quarter court in December 1640 for having
meddled in religious controversies, Lechford confessed:

I am no pleader by nature. Oratory I have little, and if I had never so
expert a faculty that way I should not now use it to make any full defence
in my matters; and as for that other part of pleading which consisteth in
chirography wherein I had some little skill I do not desire neither to use
any of that.[6]

In short, Lechford was admittedly skilled in written pleadings,
precisely the kind of pleading that was by his time almost entirely
the province of an attorney, unless the matter was so unusual or so
complicated as to demand drafting by a barrister. Such skill in written
pleadings was acquired either in a clerical capacity in a court — and
there is no evidence that Lechford had ever so served — or in an
attorney's chambers. This would support the supposition that Lechford had had a clerical relationship with an attorney, probably Hatt.

Because Lechford supported himself primarily as a scrivener during his three years in the Bay Colony, the possibility that he had been
a scrivener by métier before departure from England cannot be
entirely ruled out. Some scriveners did in fact also act as "common
solicitors." Again, the inchoate professional status of the solicitor
permitted such activity. Moreover, in the Colony Lechford aspired
to the office of notary, and scrivener was synonymous with notary
public. Lechford was not, though, a member of the Company of
Scriveners of London.[7] Though not all scriveners in England were,
those in and around London found it difficult to prosper or even to
practice if they were not. Perhaps the best evidence to indicate that

[6] Note-Book, 441.

[7] Scriveners' Company Common Paper, 1357–1628, with a Continuation to 1678,
F. W. Steer, ed., London Record Society (London, 1968), 4.

Lechford was not a scrivener is to be found in his manuscript scrivener's book from his Massachusetts practice. He wrote a clear secretarial hand, but one lacking the formality of a scrivener's hand. The leaf separating Lechford's entries from the extracts from legal instruments contains some practice lines in a law-hand—one the royal style of Charles I as it would have been on a writ to the sheriff of Lincolnshire—and the law-hand signature of "William Laver."[8] Who the latter was is unknown; anyway, there is no reason to suppose that any of this part of the book was *written* by Lechford, though its provenance as being Lechford's is likely enough. We can accept the fact that Lechford was skilled in "chirography"—not to be taken too narrowly to mean the writing of an indenture counterparted, but rather, the drafting of a formal document—without expecting him to have the manual talent for formal engrossing which the scrivener's craft demanded.

II. Lechford in Massachusetts

In the Massachusetts Bay Colony Lechford could practice as a scrivener despite a want of engrossing dexterity. He was the proverbial cyclops in the land of the blind. There were few with scribal skills, and they were apparently largely employed in official capacities. The most notable were Simon Bradstreet and Increase Nowell, successively Secretary to the General Court during Lechford's sojourn, neither of whose hands quite deserves the sniff of copperplate disapproval that came from Dr. Shurtleff's nostrils![9] Moreover, Lechford alone in the Bay Colony had the legal training that made him a great deal more than a mere scribe.

Lechford landed at Boston on Wednesday, 27 June 1638. His first professional act was to draw a mortgage for John Jolliffe and William Chesebrough for a house and lot in Boston "next Mr. Cottons" to four Yorkshiremen—who may have been fellow-passengers with Lechford—as mortgagors, for one shilling paid by the mortgagees.[1] The instrument was not dated in Lechford's book, but it could not have been too long after his arrival. It was certainly before mid-

---

[8] AAS: Lechford's MS. scrivener's book, 241.

[9] *Massachusetts Records*, I, vii.

[1] *Note-Book*, 1.

October 1638. Lechford's last act before leaving the Colony was the drafting of articles of apprenticeship for Paul Allestree with Valentine Hill of Boston, merchant, 19 July 1641.[2] In all, during his three years of active practice in the Bay Colony, Lechford drew over 650 instruments. These included written pleadings, but the bulk were letters of attorney, articles (apprenticeship, factorage, copartnership, future bargain and sale, and the like), assignments, acquittances, releases, receipts, promissory notes, bonds, recognizances, mortgages, bills (of lading, exchange, good health for a vessel clearing), charter-parties, inventories, wills, affidavits, depositions, certificates under seal of the Colony, petitions, awards of arbitrators, statements of account, conveyances, exemplifications and copies, and business letters. The range is staggering.

The volume is no less remarkable. Assuming that Lechford had the Sabbath off, but allowing him no holidays—of which the Bay had few enough anyway—or vacations or even the luxury of illness, he drew and, if necessary, engrossed three instruments every four days on an average during a six-day working week. This was substantial even by English standards, whether the practicer was an attorney or solicitor drafting or merely a clerk or scrivener copying. In fact, as was the case with his English counterparts, Lechford's work came in spurts. It was particularly heavy in the form of pleadings and other instruments related to litigation around the times of the quarterly sittings of the court of Assistants. It was always heaviest, unlike in England, in the summer months, for a reason peculiar to the Bay: these were the months in which shipping to Old England was most available, and the colonists needed to get their conveyances, letters of attorney, business letters, and so forth, aboard ship against the resumption of the English legal year in Michaelmas Term. For example, of the fifty-four instruments drawn in July 1639, thirty-five were destined for Old England of the sort one would expect, including a certificate, under the seal by Governor Winthrop to the Exchequer, of an affidavit in a customs matter.[3]

There was a genuine need for Lechford's services as a legal draftsman and scrivener. The first month for which we have dated instru-

[2] Ibid., 437.
[3] Ibid., 119.

5. Passport for the *Sparrow*, 20 December 1638, from Thomas Lechford's Scrivener's Book page 29. Courtesy, American Antiquarian Society.

ments in his book, October 1638, he produced thirty-nine pieces, including a good number of conveyances and bonds to keep covenants. This represented a backlog of legal work that was literally awaiting a lawyer's advent. For the next few months his practice was much less spectacular, but picked up rapidly in the spring of 1639 to a crescendo in July. By the end of July 1639 he had drawn 178 instruments. Henceforth, his practice grew steadily, albeit with the spurts already indicated.

How good a draftsman was Thomas Lechford? Certainly he was better than anyone else in the Colony. But was he really competent in comparison to his counterparts in Old England? The answer must be an unqualified affirmative. To be sure, the formulary books of the age, particularly West's *Symboleography*, would supply most of what he would need, and we can safely surmise that he had these with him.[4] The eight non-pleadings precedents copied in the rear of his own book and probably dating from his English days were helpful. He demonstrated, though, an improvisational command of real property law usually associated with a barrister-conveyancer rather than with a mere scrivener.

Nowhere did Lechford better manifest his skill as conveyancer than in an early deed drawn by him, 18 October 1638, of a messuage with orchard and garden in Wokingham, Berkshire.[5] The parties were both resident in Massachusetts. Lechford used Francis Moore's brilliant device of lease-and-release with attornment to enable a new world vendor to convey to a new world purchaser real property in the old world without the complicated and costly expedients of retaining attorneys in the Common Pleas to execute a fine, or either to appear before a Berkshire JP and the clerk of the peace or else to move entry on the Chancery close roll to record a bargain and sale of freehold. Though the Statute of Enrollments (1536) required a record of conveyance by bargain and sale of freehold as effectual as the ancient conveyance by fine recorded in the feet of fines, a conveyance that did not require such record was an enormous help to parties fourteen hundred leagues from the Common Pleas office, the

---

[4] *Symboleography*, first published in one part in 1590 (Beal T500a), was very popular; Lechford would probably have possessed it, possibly the last edition of both parts bound in one volume, printed in 1622 (STC 25275).

[5] *Note-Book*, 74, Augustin Clement to John Tinker.

Rolls Chapel, and Berkshire. Moore's lease-and-release with attornment, originally created to make possible secret conveyances, was here used for the perfectly legitimate end of simplifying a conveyance otherwise physically almost impossible or else unnecessarily costly. A reader of the Inner Temple would have done no better than this *quondam* solicitor of Clement's Inn.

Neither West nor any other formulary would have provided the model for the passport and licence to trade, in Latin, granted under the Colony's seal by Governor John Winthrop for his son Stephen and the master of the ship *Sparrow* for a voyage to Bermuda. The instrument is economical, the Latin is as good as the age produced, and the diplomatic is very sophisticated—even if the engrossing, assuming it was no better than the entry, was not very elegantly executed.[6] Such a document was no job for an amateur scribbler, with French, Spanish, Dutch, and English sea-hawks poised to fall upon the poor little *Sparrow*. An English historian notices that the royal style is too much abbreviated and subsumed under the "&c"— "Angliae" should have been completed with "Scotiae, Franciae, et Hiberniae, Fidei Defensor, &c."[7] And he is a little surprised that the instrument is merely dated by the year Anno Domini and not by the regnal year of Charles I as well, both dates being appropriate for a passport. But then, this might merely indicate how sophisticated Lechford's diplomatic was. The Bay Colony studiously eschewed any regal notes in its documentation. It only grudgingly included the royal style in such a document as this, where it could not very well be avoided since it was for foreign rather than domestic consumption. Even Visible Saints needed to implore regal protection when launched upon a sea of potential troubles.

Unusual also, and testifying to the range of Lechford's learning, was the letter of attorney and proctorship for a testamentary matter in an English ecclesiastical court *ex parte* Mr. John Cogan.[8] Such a

[6] *Note-Book*, 46–47 and AAS: Lechford's MS. scrivener's book, 29. See illustration on page 22.

[7] AAS: Lechford's MSS., 241, has an entry-example of the proper style. It was possible that the engrossed instrument carried the full style; it was also possible that the Massachusetts Governor preferred to omit the red-flag of "Franciae" against the *Sparrow* encountering a French warship.

[8] *Note-Book*, 85.

document was more in the professional purview of an ecclesiastical notary or commissary's officer than a common-law solicitor. Yet this is very characteristic of Lechford's grasp. All of the instruments in his book indicate a sureness in drafting and a skill in diplomatic that goes beyond the merely clerical copying of models from formulary books.

Lechford complained bitterly, after a couple of years in the Colony, that he was "forced to get my living by writing petty things, which scarce finds me bread."[9] Whatever little his hyperbole proves about Lechford's prosperity or lack of it, clearly he hoped for a bigger and a different practice from that more appropriate to a scrivener, no matter how learned that scrivener was. In fact, he did act upon a greater stage. His greatest contribution to the Bay Colony and to the development of its legal profession arose from an activity that technically was not only beyond the competence of a scrivener, but beyond that of a solicitor: pleading.

By Lechford's day written pleadings had been in use for over a century. They had long since replaced the oral presentations of medieval counters which occasionally attained those heights of forensic brilliance revealed in the Year Books. Where once the oral pleadings had been the essence and almost the whole of the barrister's task in court, written pleadings had become merely the beginning of the process of litigation, and a task requiring little learning and no forensic skill. Once pleadings were set down in writing, in Latin as entries on the plea rolls, for the vast majority of actions the standard pleadings to issue could be drawn by attorneys rather than by counsel.[1] Increasingly, attorneys did just that. For Lechford's generation, the illustrious Coke's *A Booke of Entries* (1614) supplied a plethora of models for common-law pleadings, arranged alphabetically by actions, requiring little more than a command of Latin to be used effectively.[2] The ambitious attorney—or solicitor—made his own

[9] *Plain Dealing*, 69.

[1] The handiest, most learned, and historically most accurate brief introduction to the sixteenth and seventeenth centuries' developments in pleading is J. H. Baker, *An Introduction to English Legal History*, 2nd. ed. (London, 1979), 71–74.

[2] Edward Coke, *A Booke of Entries* (London, 1614) (STC 5488) was a great advance over the older printed literature of this sort, which began with William Rastell's *Collection of Entries*, first published in 1566 (Beal T448) with numerous

extracts for pleadings models; those in the rear of Lechford's book are good examples of such.

The fact that Lechford troubled to have these with him indicates that he had a use for them. He did. During his three years in practice in Massachusetts, he drew pleadings in thirty-five cases, in all but five of them, counts *ex parte* the plaintiff. Twenty-six of the cases were at common-law, eight were in equity, and the one remaining can be described only as a hybrid action in equity for account which depended upon Statute of Westminster II, c.11, and which was tried by a jury.[3] In two of the clear equity cases and in the hybrid case Lechford acted *ex parte* the defendant. The common-law causes were overwhelmingly those contemporaneously popular actions on the case of the kind that John Hatt made his living by in the London Guildhall: action on the case for assumpsit (10), conversion (2), words (3), negligence (1), enticing away an apprentice (1). The older forms of action were less numerous, notably account (3 — not including the hybrid) and debt (3). There were only two common-law real actions, and one of those was mixed.

From his first declaration for a plaintiff in the mixed action in June 1639 to his last in an action on the case for conversion in June 1641,[4] Lechford demonstrated a terseness and straightforwardness in common-law pleading that contrast favorably with the overly ornate and even architectonic structures one encounters on the plea rolls of the English common-law courts. In the one real action, *Hett v. Tose*, in June 1639, which was a collateral suit to an action on the case for assumpsit, *Hett v. Shave*, brought at the same quarter court, Lechford managed to make a perfect case to issue in about one hundred words.[5] Even his longer declarations avoided prolixity and art. Since his book does not contain a single replication or rejoinder, there is clear evidence that the worst features of English pleading were not

---

editions to 1670. It was probably Coke's *Entries* which the Massachusetts General Court ordered purchased in two copies, along with other law books, to "have the better light for making & proceeding about lawes . . . ," *Massachusetts Records*, 11, 212, 11 November 1647. The *Second Part* of West's *Symboleography* (Beal T500b, T500d, T500e) — usually bound up with the *First* — supplied a great many pleadings in English-bill, for Chancery, Star Chamber, and the like.

[3] *Woodcock v. Davis* (Lechford *ex parte* defendant), *Note-Book*, 367–372.

[4] *Cockerell v. Cockerham* and *Jones v. Leeke*, respectively, *Note-Book*, 80 and 427.

[5] *Note-Book*, 82–83.

encouraged in the Bay. Yet, pleading beyond the first declaration of a plaintiff's case and the plea in answer of the defendant could be avoided only if those pleas went to a simple issue and drew the issue clearly enough to be put to the jury. Lechford's pointed declarations managed to do just that.

The actions in equity are particularly interesting, in part because equity was the arena in which the English solicitor was best studied and most used, and in part because three of the eight actions in equity in which Lechford drew pleadings were in foreign jurisdictions. *Rucke v. Hatch*, September 1639, was Lechford's first equity case, and his bill for the plaintiff was to the Plymouth Colony's Governor and Assistants. The case was that Rucke, Hatch, and one Meriam became joint undertakers in a ship bringing cargo from England to Charlestown. Rucke and Meriam were Bay Colony men; Hatch was from Scituate in Plymouth Colony. Hatch undertook the management of the enterprise. Rucke sued Hatch for overcharging him for his goods carried in the vessel and for charging Rucke for goods shipped by others, and for failing to account and pay upon the same. Rucke's bill contained the usual equitable allegation that he could not prove the particulars as law required, and prayed that Hatch be enjoined to answer upon oath in writing and abide such "order & decree" as to the court seemed to stand "with equity and good conscience."[6] This bill was sent to the clerk of the Plymouth court on 26 August 1639. What is fascinating is that with it went a declaration in an action on the case for assumpsit *ex parte* Meriam against Hatch, in which Meriam claimed damages of £11 10s. for Hatch's failure to account in the same venture. This plea was accompanied by an affidavit by Rucke testifying that he had seen in Hatch's handwriting an acknowledgment that he owed Meriam £15 14s. in the venture.[7] On 3 September 1639 the Plymouth court upon verdict of a jury awarded Meriam £5 14s. 2d. damages, plus costs, against Hatch.[8] There is not a word in the records of the court about the bill in equity of *Rucke v. Hatch*. Perhaps the action in equity was pri-

---

[6] Ibid., 163–166.

[7] Ibid., 166–168.

[8] *Records of the Colony of New Plymouth: Judicial Acts, 1636–1692*, N. B. Shurtleff, ed. (Boston, 1857), 13.

marily a shoring and discovery action to the case in assumpsit, with considerable nuisance value against Hatch. Conceivably, the Plymouth court, while it was quite prepared to go ahead with a suit in law, was not prepared to buy an action in equity by English-bill.

In the other two foreign actions Lechford drew the bill in one and answered for the defendant in another. In December 1640 he prepared the bill of a Salem gentleman against his uncle in Virginia for detaining property due the plaintiff as a testator and executor. This case, *Stratton v. Stratton,* was before the Governor and Captain-General of Virginia.[9] The bill contained the usual allegations and prayers. The action in which Lechford answered, *Foxwill v. Cogan,* was before the Commissioners for the Province of Maine, also in December 1640. The plaintiff alleged that Cogan had forced him to enter an obligation.[1] The answer contained the usual saving of the advantages of exception to the uncertainties and insufficiencies of the bill, and prayed that the obligation might stand, that he, the defendant, receive £15 for his loss, and that the plaintiff's bill be dismissed with costs.

In all three of these foreign cases the pleadings that Lechford drafted were indistinguishable from such in the English Chancery, with all of the usual allegations and savings. Yet, interestingly enough, the five equity cases before the Bay Colony court were not always so formal: in one bill the usual allegation and reference to equity and good conscience were absent, and in an answer in another action there was no saving of exceptions.[2] Lechford might well have been sensitive to a certain informality in the Bay's courts, but unwilling to risk the slightest suspicion of irregularity in pleading in foreign courts.

In his equity pleading Lechford demonstrated the same terseness and pointedness that he did in common-law pleading—a welcome relief to one who has for decades struggled through overlong, multi-issue, English-bill pleadings. The question remains, though, how good a pleader was this solicitor become "counter"? Plaintiff's decla-

---

[9] *Note-Book,* 339.

[1] Ibid., 356.

[2] *Lang v. Upham et al.* and *Winslow v. Askew,* respectively, *Note-Book,* 338 and 365.

rations were not much of a test: as long as they met the requirements of certainty and sufficiency, were properly ordered, went to issue, and were appropriate to the action, they were soundly crafted. Lechford's were. So, too, were his pleadings in English-bill, which were somewhat more of a test for a pleader. Save for a certain informality noted above, they left nothing to be desired.

The contemporary mark of a good pleader was, however, how good he was as a special pleader *ex parte* the defendant. Our evidence for Lechford may be slim, but it is sufficient. In *Butters v. Stoughton*, an action on the case for assumpsit in the Boston "small causes" court in October 1639, he executed a very neat confession-and-avoidance.[3] But the real gem was a special plea that can only be described as brilliant and one worthy of the ablest barrister. In *Bacheller v. Brocke*, an action on the case for words, Lechford acted as the defendant's "Attorney." He drew a demurrer for the Boston quarter court of 3 September 1639 pleading that his client

ought not to be compelled nor is he any wayes bound to answere unto the pl[ain]t[iff] in this Court because the pl[ain]t[iff] hath not put in his declarac[i]on in writing to remaine upon Record.[4]

On 8 June previously, Lechford had submitted, "upon request," five proposals for the better keeping of the records of the courts—and seeking in the process to be appointed notary public for the Colony. Lechford's second proposition was

That every accion be declared in writing and the Defend[an]ts answer general or speciall as the case shall require be put in writing by a Public Notary before the cause be heard.[5]

Lechford's demurrer for Brocke was from the heart! Yet it was struck out by Lechford in his book, indicating it was never submitted. The reason is not hard to find. At the General Court six days after the quarter court, the Colony's recording system was decreed: *inter alia*, all judgments with "all the evidence" in the cases were to be recorded.[6] However, no explicit provision was made for entering writ-

[3] *Note-Book*, 215.

[4] Ibid., 179.

[5] Ibid., 88.

[6] *Massachusetts Records*, I, 275–276.

ten pleadings such as Bacheller's declaration. Lechford was probably already aware, when Bacheller's Case came on, that Brocke's demurrer would not fly.

The same Boston quarter court of 3 September 1639 threatened to put Lechford out of the business of pleading altogether. Among the last orders of that sitting was the following:

Mr. Thomas Lechford, for going to the iewry & pleading with them out of Court, is debarred from pleading any mans cause hearafter, vnlesse his owne, & admonished not to presume to meddle beyond what hee shalbee called to by the Courte.[7]

Lechford acknowledged that he had, in the case of William Cole and his wife, having been "retained" in the matter, spoken to the jury without the court's leave, and conceded that this was "not to be done by the law of England." But he argued it was not embracery, for he received no reward for it. And he pleaded extenuation because of "one or two seeming approbations of the like which he hath observed in other Causes here." He also noted—pointedly—that "Some speeches of his, specially some involuntary and of sudden [interruptions?] ... and zeal of speaking for his matters, may seem to offend such as have not been accustomed much to publique pleadings of advocates."[8] Here he touched the magistrates' raw nerve. For it was precisely such advocacy, rather than anything said to the jury "without leave," that brought down the court's wrath.

The magistrates were indeed not "accustomed much to publique pleadings of advocates," and they had no intention of becoming so. Significantly, the Reverend Nathaniel Ward's stricture against paid advocates in clause 26 of the "Body of Liberties" of 1641 was an advance over the thinking of the magistrates on the matter of legal assistance to litigants, even involving advocacy. Ward at the invitation of the freemen, not the Governor and Assistants, preached at the General Court of 2 June 1641. He spoke vehemently against magistrates giving "private advice" in civil cases. Some of the magistrates, Winthrop tells us, opposed Ward's stand for the commendable reason that the magistrates might be able to settle the dispute before

[7] Ibid., 270.
[8] *Note-Book*, 182–183.

it came to litigation, diverting the case if it was unjust or directing it in the right course if it was good. But they also opposed it "because we must then provide lawyers to direct men in their causes"; and "private advice" prevented "many difficulties and tediousness to the court to understand the cause aright (no advocate being allowed, and the parties being not able, for the most part, to open the cause fully and clearly, especially in public)."[9]

In this light clause 26 appears to have been a compromise between the magistrates' strenuous opposition to allowing legal assistance in party-and-party litigation and the felt need for such assistance. Clause 26 permitted an *unpaid* advocate to one who "findeth himselfe unfit to plead his owne cause . . ." so long as the principal was present to answer "such Questions in person as the Court shall thinke meete to demand of him. . . ."[1] Behind the magistrates' concern was a two-fold rationale. The first was that each man should plead his own *causa*, present his own case standing at bar. This was very much in keeping with the Puritan ideal of the responsibility of the individual to God, and its corollary, the individual's responsibility to the civil authority. The second was that over-sophistication threatened the arcadian simplicity of the City Upon a Hill, which would be destructive of the commonweal by introducing not only irresponsibility but also the errors of meddling with things beyond the intellectual and spiritual capacities of the ordinary man of ordinary calling. Such meddling, in challenging the civil authority, challenged God, from whom the civil authority was derived and in whose service it was to be exercised.

The magistrates were fighting a losing battle, as the publication of *Lawes and Libertyes* in 1648 confirmed. Within a decade of the "Body of Liberties," social and political realities had caught up with them, striking down Ward's compromise clause 26 and, predictably, challenging the arcadian simplicity of the commonwealth and its magistratical order. Lechford was ahead of his time. He was also alone in possessing skills that not only seemed to challenge the simple order, but gave an unfair advantage to those whom he represented. It was questionable whether the magistrates' solution — by which

---

[9] Winthrop, II, 37–38.

[1] Whitmore, 39.

each magistrate might easily find himself in the untenable position of private advocate — was any improvement.

Yet the effect of silencing Lechford was not to deny him his practice, but rather to turn that practice into another, and ultimately much more beneficial, channel. Henceforth, Lechford's clients pleaded by submission of written pleadings, filed in court and perhaps read out by the client. A score of Lechford's written pleadings post-date his so-called "disbarment."

How effective the unheard voice — but very visible hand — of Lechford could be is indicated by a written motion prepared for a client a year after the September 1639 contretemps. In *Wolcot v. Lymon* he drew a motion in arrest of judgment.[2] What is riveting about this was that such a motion post-verdict and judgment was the real task of the barrister in English practice. There was no reason, however, why the client could not speak the words and file the motion himself. We do not know whether Henry Lymon's plea, to stay judgment and execution "till he can produce his witnesses" then in England exonerating him upon the assumpsit, worked or not, but the motion was perfectly judiciable. Lechford's clients could still enjoy the advantage of his advocacy without his saying a word in court. All hopes of arcadian simplicity were dashed. Any lawyer could do the same. Thomas Lechford was, for his day, a voice crying in the wilderness, but he showed the way to the development of a legal profession in the Bay Colony. Practice by written pleadings, economical and shorn of ornate invention, in English, not tied to the writ system — in short, the "reformed procedure" that did not come to full fruition in England until the nineteenth century — was introduced in a learned and professional way at the very outset in Massachusetts, thanks to Thomas Lechford.

III. Lechford's Return to Old England

The 1639 "disbarment" of Lechford has led to the quite erroneous conclusion that he had no future in legal practice in Massachusetts. This is hard to reconcile with the fact that he remained the only man patently engaged in "lawyering" for fee for almost two more years, with his best year yet to come. The court's reproof did not

[2] *Note-Book*, 325.

help his *causa* to become the Colony's notary—an office not created until 1644 with the appointment of William Aspinwall, who was neither lawyer nor scrivener. But it did not hinder his doing what he had done before as both writer and pleader, and indeed his public employment by the General Court and the magistrates for writing postdates the court's reproof. Ironically, one of those tasks was to transcribe "certain Breviats of Propositions delivered to the generall Court, for the establishing a body of Lawes . . ." which became the "Body of Liberties" of 1641.[3]

We should also be suspicious of any explanation for Lechford's return to England in 1641 based upon the notion that he could not make a living in his practice. Trumbull takes too much at face value Lechford's continuous keening about his financial position.[4] The one note that rings true is in a letter to an unknown friend in England of 28 July 1640 stating that he was "kept from all place of preferment in the Common-wealth. . . ."[5] But Lechford's further lament that he was "forced to get my living by writing petty things, which scarce finds me bread . . ." is correct only in how he made his living, not how well he made it. His income from "writing petty things" alone brought him, over the three years of his practice, more than £86, or an average of £28 14s. per annum. This is cash only; it does not include goods or services given in lieu of cash. His best year, January to December 1640, produced £37 in fees. He averaged almost exactly 2s. 6d. per instrument drawn, which was comparable to what he would have made in Old England. Moreover, his volume of business, at three instruments every four working days on an average, was also good by English standards.[6] Since his rented quarters from September 1639 to September 1640 cost him £5 per annum (about

---

[3] *Plain Dealing*, 31. See also, *Note-Book*, 227, 231, 237–238, and 256.

[4] *Note-Book*, xx. Whitmore, 21, says Lechford was "starved into returning to England."

[5] *Plain Dealing*, 69.

[6] In the suit in equity by Lechford for the plaintiffs, *William and Elizabeth Cole v. Francis Doughty* (September 1639), for relief upon a bond as surety and for other testamentary matters, Lechford noted the following fees and charges: 6s. 8d. for the bill (it is a big one); copy, 3s. 4d; copy of the deed in question, 4d.; entering the action, 1s. 6d.: total 11s. 10d. plus a fee of 6s. more, for a grand total of 17s. 10d., upon which he received 7s. with 10s. remaining (apparently, he was willing to forego 10d.). AAS: Lechford's Ms., 110.

one-sixth of his income), his "bread" was rather better than an oc-casional weevily crust![7] He and his wife, who apparently joined him in 1639, had a maid and ate the "best suger." He sported a "silver laced coate and a gold wrought cap" and his wife a "tuft holland" waistcoat in 1639 and a new gown in 1640. There was beer for his table, and he smoked Spanish tobacco from Venezuela, the most ex-pensive at the time.[8] Moreover, in September 1640 he was able to buy a house and garden in Boston from a tailor who removed to Connecticut. Whatever Lechford's status before, he was no longer, as Trumbull erred in supposing, "not even a householder; in the eye of the law . . . merely a 'transient.'"[9] In view of the fact that the Dedham schoolmaster's salary at the time was £20 per annum and Henry Dunster's salary as "Professor" at Harvard was £50,[1] Lech-ford's average annual cash income of almost £29 was well above subsistence. True, he along with everyone else in the Bay felt the tight-money pinch of the famous crash of 1641: his cash income from January through July—the latter, his last month, was light because he was winding down business—was only a little over £8. In com-mon with his neighbors he increasingly took his fees in truck rather than cash from late 1640 to his departure in August 1641. Over all, Lechford appears to have been a true rarity, a lawyer who disproved the Marysville Theorem, as we call it in California, that if there are two lawyers in town they are both millionaires, if one, he is a pauper![2]

Neither should we conclude that Lechford's growing disenchant-ment with the rule of Visible Saints, his forthright public statements

[7] *Note-Book*, 234.

[8] Ibid., 67, 102, 127, 236, and 237. For Spanish tobacco, see Jacob M. Price, *France and the Chesapeake* (Ann Arbor, 1973), I, 4 and 182.

[9] *Note-Book*, 317 and xxiv. It should be noted that just after Lechford complained in July 1640 of no preferment, "writing petty things," and so forth, and also of having "not yet here an house of my owne to put my head in, or any stock going" (*Plain Dealing*, 69), he purchased his Boston house.

[1] Margery S. Foster, *"Out of Smalle Beginings . . ."* *An Economic History of Harvard College in the Puritan Period* (Cambridge, Mass., 1962), 54 and 88.

[2] The author will not stake his scholarly reputation on the origins of the Theorem, beyond noting that in 1849 two of the earliest Gold Rush lawyers were one Mulford and Stephen J. Field in Marysville, Yuba County, California. If neither made a million—and Field was very nearly gunned-down by an irate judge—at least Field ended up on the United States Supreme Court.

orally and in writing to the magistrates and the ministers that the only correct ecclesiastical polity was rule by bishops in the Apostolic Succession — "I disclaime *Parker*, And encline to *Hooker, Iewel*, as to government"[3] — loosed upon him a torrent of persecution that washed him out of New England. Lechford as ecclesiologist is another study in itself, and one well worth doing, but it cannot be done here. Suffice it to say, that in every scrape he had with civil and ecclesiastical authority in religious matters, he came away without official condemnation and even with heightened respect in the eyes of some of his adversaries. In September 1640 he stood into great danger. He put three questions to the church elders in Boston that went to the roots of congregational polity and orders.[4] At the December quarter court he was summoned to appear and admonished not to meddle with religious controversies but to "attend his calling," the law.[5] Lechford's account of what happened at that court indicates that his honesty and conscientiousness disarmed wrath:

I never intended openly to oppose the godly here in any thing I thought they mistooke, but I was lately taken at advantage, and brought before the Magistrates, before whom, giving a quiet and peaceable answer, I was dismissed with favour, and respect promised me by some of the chiefe for the future.[6]

Lechford was genuinely irenic. This attribute was evident even in his stout criticism of the Colony for its anti-monarchical sentiment and anti-episcopalian polity levelled in his pamphlet, *Plain Dealing: or News from New-England,* published a few months after his return to England. There is no bitterness in the tract; there is a handsome compliment paid to the founding-fathers of the Massachusetts Bay Colony:

And I think that wiser men then they, going into a wildernesse to set up

---

[3] *Plain Dealing*, 37. Lechford wrote this in a disquisition in May 1640 intended for, but perhaps never given to, John Winthrop, stressing *inter alia* the importance of converting the natives, which he argued could only be done by a church the polity of which was wider than a congregation.

[4] *Plain Dealing*, 55.

[5] *Massachusetts Records*, I, 310.

[6] *Plain Dealing*, 77.

another strange government differing from the setled government here, might have falne into greater errors then they have done.[7]

Trumbull found it difficult to explain why it was that Lechford was suffered to remain in New England once it became clear how disaffected he was to the ecclesiastical order so important to the magistrates and ministers. If Trumbull detected signs "that the founders of Massachusetts were not incapable of the exercise of toleration, even though they might not give it a place among the virtues," he was too quick to credit that as explanation.[8] That Lechford was endured at all had less to do with any genuine sentiment for "toleration" by magistrates and ministers than with the fact that, if he was "obnoxious" to the elders, as Trumbull correctly noted, he was *not* to the magistrates, as Trumbull erroneously surmised. It was not that Lechford's "calling" — the law — made him "unwelcome." Rather, it was his calling that persuaded the magistrates to tolerate him. Lechford remarked that though the General Court was willing to bestow employment on him, the magistrates told him "they could not doe it for feare of offending the Churches, because of my opinions."[9] The magistrates recognized and appreciated the value of Lechford's legal services and were loath to lose them merely because Lechford's opinions affronted the ministers. The episcopalian solicitor was not the only bone of contention over which magistrates and elders snapped at each other in these years.

What the civil authority could not do was to make Lechford a freeman and hence eligible for office, as notary public. The churches denied him the Sacrament, and therefore being no churchman he could not be made free of the godly commonwealth. Yet it was not the economic consequences of not being a churchman that drove Lechford home. It was the spiritual consequences of being denied the Sacrament that effected his departure. Lechford was a profoundly religious man, a devoted adherent of the Anglican Church. There is a poignant note in *Plain Dealing* in Lechford's description of the administration of the Sacrament in the Boston church:

[7] Ibid., Proheme.

[8] *Note-Book*, xxiv.

[9] Ibid., 89, June 1639.

Once I stood without one of the doores, and looked in, and saw the administration: Besides, I have had credible relation of all the particulars
from some of the members.[1]

He was excluded from the exercise of faith, though he piously desired it. Writing to an unknown English friend in December 1640,
immediately after the magistrate had "dismissed" him "with favour," he said:

Never since I saw you have I received the Sacrament of the Lords supper.
I have disputed in writing, though to my great hinderance, in regard of
outward things, yet blessed be the Lord, to my better satisfaction at the
last.[2]

Having achieved "better satisfaction at the last," Lechford took
ship for home on 3 August 1641. He was convinced that the gathered
churches in the Bay Colony were in deep error because they lacked
the authority of a ministry in the Apostolic Succession, that they were
in anarchy and confusion. Surely these were not his tenets when he
came in 1638. But his "slender" observations, queries, and experiments had brought him to a vigorous episcopalian and monarchical
position which would not permit him to remain in Massachusetts.[3]
Perhaps he was like some people of our day who, enamored of
"people's democracy," have passed a sojourn behind the Iron Cur-
tain only to return to the United States convinced of its superiority,
rightness, and even righteousness.

He was not, however, unique in his own day in his own right. The
1640's were a time that tried men's souls and their loyalties. By
November 1641, when he arrived in England, episcopacy was under
hot attack in the Commons, John Pym's grasping for control of the
King's power to control the executive and the army had converted
episcopalians to royalists, and the Commons was in process of passing
its revolutionary Grand Remonstrance, which carried in the House
on 22 November by a mere eleven votes. By the time Lechford dated
the proheme of *Plain Dealing* from Clement's Inn, 17 January 1642,
Pym's Parliamentarians were only a month away from excluding

[1] *Plain Dealing*, 17.

[2] Ibid., 77.

[3] Ibid., Proheme.

the bishops from the Lords and gaining control of the militia, and the King from preparing to regain the fortress at Hull from Parliamentarian supporters. Civil war was inevitable. Thomas Lechford, solicitor, found himself in that goodly company of those who henceforth would be called royalists.

Though the Royalists would meet the Saints on the fields of Edgehill, Marston Moor, and Naseby, Lechford would not be among them. He died shortly after publication of *Plain Dealing*. The Reverend John Cotton's uncharitable and canting obituary of Lechford proclaimed a sad truth:

but see the wise hand of God disappointing his [Lechford's] ends; When he came to *England* the Bishops were falling, so that he lost his friends, and hopes both in *Old-England* and *New* . . .[4]

A more appropriate epitaph, both more just and more charitable, would be that Lechford had left his mark, along with his hopes, in New England as its first lawyer.

---

[4] John Cotton, *The Way of Congregational Churches Cleared* (London, 1648), 71. We have only Cotton's word for when Lechford died: this quotation is completed by "yet put out his Book (such as it is) and soon after dyed." This would point to a death date in late 1642 or perhaps 1643. A search of the Prerogative Court of Canterbury wills (Public Record Office, Probate) failed to turn up a will probated there, which would indicate that he either died intestate or devised only a modest personal estate. Time did not permit a search of PCC act books (for administration on an intestacy), other probate jurisdictions, or parish registers.

GEORGE L. HASKINS

Lay Judges:
Magistrates and Justices in Early Massachusetts

SO accustomed have we become to professionalism in the law, and to the standards which that concept implies, that we tend to forget that in many civilized societies much of the administration of the law has been and still is performed by laymen. Today we expect our judges to be learned in the law and to pass the scrutiny of bar associations before they take their places on the bench. We expect our lawyers to have graduated from college and an approved law school, to have passed rigorous tests administered by bar examiners, and to have received certification as to character and experience. Even administrative officers and members of governmental commissions are expected to have some professional experience, often legal experience.

But the time is not far back—certainly in my recent professional lifetime—when a person could be certified for legal practice by having read law in the office of a well-known lawyer. If one goes back somewhat further, into the nineteenth century, such training was even more customary,[1] and professionalism was absent to the point that laymen such as artisans and day laborers could be found sitting on the higher courts of our states.[2] No doubt such men would be lost in the intricacies of modern tax or corporate practice; perhaps they were deficient in knowledge of the technicalities of pleadings, demurrers, and special motions. But in their time—especially in New England—they were highly competent. I once knew a justice of the

[1] A. H. Chroust, *The Rise of the Legal Profession in America* (Norman, Oklahoma, 1965), II, 220–221, 224ff.

[2] Ibid., 39–41. This practice, which began in the nineteenth century, still persists in Vermont today in the Superior Courts, where two of the three judges can be laymen. See *Boston Globe*, 18 July 1982, 32; 21 August 1983, 65. See also David Margolick, "Vermonters Consider the Case of Laymen Judges," New York *Times* for 27 October 1983, A24. In the assize courts in Italy today six of the eight judges are laymen. M. Cappelletti *et al.*, *The Italian Legal System* (Stanford, 1967), 79ff.

peace in my adoptive home town in Maine who, at 75, was more conversant with contracts and criminal law than are most present-day law school students. He could spot a defect in a deed or an option as readily as he could a lame cow. He was a farmer, who had little formal education beyond elementary high school, and his example leads me back to the seventeenth century.

When, twenty years ago, Professor John Dawson attempted to define "professionalism" in connection with lay lawyers and judges, he turned to such general tests as specialized training and the application of a "substantial part of [one's] time and energy ... to the task at hand," usually on a paid basis.[3] The professional judge he contrasts with the "lay" judge, who takes part in the judicial process irregularly and as a sideline, with unplanned regularity, so that training in legal techniques is not a qualification for his work.[4]

These general distinctions provide at least a background which has relevance for the beginnings of the legal profession in Massachusetts. In the 1630's and 1640's the colonists had no great liking for lawyers, that is, for professionals. Thomas Lechford, who came to the Bay Colony in 1638, partly to find clients, was formally rebuked for "pleading" with a jury "out of court."[5] At one time it was supposed that lawyers were not needed in the colony because its law was "rude, untechnical ... popular,"[6] but the drafting of documents and pleadings by Lechford reveals a heavy reliance on English legal devices, techniques, and forms of conveyancing.[7] Thus we know that the Bible was not the "infallible guide" for judge and legislator, as some have supposed.[8] We now know that the enacted laws of the colony were, in many areas, highly sophisticated and far more temperate and "modern" than contemporary seventeenth-century law in England. In some directions the colonists relied on common-law

[3] J. P. Dawson, *A History of Lay Judges* (Cambridge, Mass., 1960), 3.

[4] Ibid., 4.

[5] See T. Barnes' essay "Thomas Lechford and the Earliest Lawyering in Massachusetts, 1638–1641," in this volume, above, 3–38.

[6] P. S. Reinsch, "The English Common Law in the Early American Colonies," *Select Essays in Anglo-American Legal History* (Boston, 1907), I, 370.

[7] Barnes, "Thomas Lechford," 17–29.

[8] C. J. Hilkey, "Legal Development in Colonial Massachusetts," *Columbia Studies in History, Economics and Public Law*, xxxvii (1910), 68.

rules, on English statutes, on local customs; in other directions they were distinctly innovative, especially in areas involving civil liberties, and their attitudes about punishments were far more lenient than many have believed. One has only to go through the provisions of the Code of 1648 to find extensive adoption of English law and practices—to say nothing of technical terminology such as barratry, escheat, nonsuit, reversions, and remainders. But in doing so, one must bear in mind that this Code—though drafted and supervised by men who had had experience in the law and its administration— was basically the product of laymen working on committees of the General Court towards particular ends and purposes, namely, a compilation of existing laws and the reasons therefor.

Undoubtedly there was a dislike of the professional lawyer in the colony, but it may be suggested that it had little to do with Puritanism or Congregationalism. To those first colonists the aversion and distrust were in large measure an English importation, like so much other intellectual and practical baggage they brought with them. Their social and intellectual backgrounds continue to have special significance for our understanding of the beginnings of an indigenous American law.

The opposition to professionals—judges as well as lawyers—became intensified in England during the Puritan-dominated Interregnum that followed the execution of Charles I in 1649. That there had grown up a skepticism concerning the legal procedures even before the Civil War is illustrated by considerable evidence. For example, there was the important tract of Francis Bacon, written shortly before the 1630 emigration and proposing law reform to the end that uncertainties, varieties of opinion, delays, and evasions in the law might be removed.[9] John Winthrop, while still in England, had drafted a bill for presentation to Parliament requesting a reduction in the number of practicing attorneys.[1] In England, neither existing legal procedures nor professional lawyers had been entirely successful in providing men with needed protection against the arbitrary power of the Crown, and that fact was not forgotten—indeed

[9] F. Bacon, *Law Tracts* (London, 1741), 3, 9.

[1] For this and other bills drafted, see *Winthrop Papers* (Massachusetts Historical Society, Boston, 1929–1947), I, 295–310, 371–374, 418–419.

was to be emphasized—when the colonists reached Massachusetts and began to press for a code of laws and a bill of rights.

It was against such a background, particularly preceding the English Civil War, that the early colonists were copying to a great extent the types and forms of law and institutions with which they were familiar, and which they and their leaders had found appropriate to the New World. The habit of mind of most colonists remained emphatically hostile to the legal profession.[2] Thus John Cotton, the Boston minister, referred to lawyers as unconscionable advocates who "bolster out a bad case by quirks of wit and tricks and quillets of law."[3] Moreover, under Article 26 of the Body of Liberties of 1641, attorneys were permitted to plead causes other than their own, but all fees or rewards were disallowed.[4] Instead, it was a common practice for litigants who needed advice to consult privately with one of the magistrates.

In early Massachusetts Bay, as Professor Thomas Barnes has demonstrated, there were among the leaders of the colony men trained professionally in more than one area of the law, even persons admitted to the Inns of Court in London—for example John Winthrop, the Governor, and his son, as well as three of the first Assistants: namely, Isaac Johnson, John Humfry, and Roger Ludlow.[5] Others, like Richard Bellingham, who had held the important legal office of Recorder of Boston in Old England, had studied law;[6] and Nathaniel Ward, who drafted the first American bill of rights, known as the Body of Liberties of 1641, and who had been admitted to one of the Inns of Court before taking holy orders, stated that he had "read almost all the Common Law of *England*, and some Statutes."[7] A few colonists owned copies of manuals for justices of

[2] See Barnes, "Thomas Lechford," above, 5–7. See also G. L. Haskins, *Law and Authority in Early Massachusetts* (New York, 1960, 1977), 186.

[3] Quoted in J. H. Smith, *Colonial Justice in Western Massachusetts* (Cambridge, Mass., 1961), 199.

[4] *The Colonial Laws of Massachusetts*, ed. W. H. Whitmore (Boston, 1889), 39.

[5] Barnes, "Thomas Lechford," above, 6–7. See also summaries in Haskins, *Law and Authority*, 106, and footnotes 69–72.

[6] *Winthrop Papers*, II, 55, note.

[7] N. Ward, "The Simple Cobbler of Agawam," *Publications of the Ipswich Historical Society*, XIV (1905), 66.

the peace, such as that of Dalton; others had abridgements of the English statutes.[8]

The chief leaders of the colony, including those just named, were among the members of the Court of Assistants of the Massachusetts Bay Company as it had been in London. The company was similar to other English trading companies of the time. Analogous to a modern business corporation, it was a joint stock company headed by a Governor, a Deputy-Governor, and a board of eighteen Assistants. All were elected by the stockholders of the Company, known as "freemen." It was prescribed by the Company charter that the officers and board-members, together with freemen, were to meet annually in what was called the General Court for purposes of elections, for admitting new freemen, and for enacting ordinances both for the Company and for the colony which it was authorized to establish. Each month, or more often if necessary, the officers and the Assistants were expected to meet in executive session of the Court of Assistants to take care of routines and on-going business, much like the directors of the modern corporation.[9]

That the Massachusetts Company, like other trading companies of its day, was an association for commercial purposes is clear. It had been organized for profit and expected to send out colonists and planters to the New World and to be governed from England by the officers and shareholders. Nevertheless, the Massachusetts enterprise had attracted a number of well-to-do Puritans who had broader and more significant objectives in mind—political and religious—which soon displaced the commercial purposes of colonization. By a deft maneuver it was decided to transfer the management of the Company from London to New England and there to merge it with the government of the colony.[1] This was voted at a meeting of the General Court in 1629, and John Winthrop was elected Governor of both the Company and of the overseas colony, which had been sanctioned by royal charter. Hence, when the Governor, the Deputy-Governor,

---

[8] Haskins, *Law and Authority*, 278–279, notes 90–92.

[9] See generally, *Records of the Governor and Company of Massachusetts Bay*, ed. N. B. Shurtleff (Boston, 1853–1854), I, 3–20; F. Rose-Troup, *The Massachusetts Bay Company and its Predecessors* (New York, 1930); Haskins, *Law and Authority*, 9.

[1] *Massachusetts Bay Records*, I, 51–52.

and ten of the Assistants arrived in New England, they constituted not only the governing members of the Company but of the colony as well. They were legally in charge of the enterprise, its settlement, and its administrative structure. Indeed, until the admission of a large group of freemen in 1631, they were co-equal with the General Court, in the sense that on these shores the membership of both bodies was identical.[2] In spite of their broad powers, one of their most important acts — one which is vital for this discussion — was a declaration at their first meeting, on 23 August 1630, that six of their ten members be given powers of English justices of the peace.[3]

The declaration of 23 August 1630 was one of the first tangible steps in the deliberate transformation of what had been a chartered trading company in England, into a body politic in Massachusetts Bay — a transformation which began soon after arrival on these shores, when familiar English institutions were introduced as part of the framework of government. At least three of the Assistants had been justices of the peace in England — notably, John Winthrop, the Governor, and formerly Lord of the Manor of Groton in Sussex. Few could be more aware than he of the legal and administrative importance of the justices of the peace in England.[4] Initially, however, the power of an Assistant (now also called a magistrate, at least while he held office), was far greater than that of an English justice of the peace. When they sat singly, the parallel is very clear. But when they sat together as the Court of Assistants, these magistrates — for the first five or six years — exercised judicial powers "as broad as those of the three great English common-law courts, as well as of Chancery, the High Commission, and the Court of Star Chamber."[5]

After the General Court was technically separated from the Court of Assistants as a result of the admission of new freemen in 1631, its powers were not noticeably different from those held previously, except that it again became responsible for electing the Assistants as well as the Governor and Deputy-Governor. However, the General

---

[2] Haskins, *Law and Authority*, 28–29.

[3] *Massachusetts Bay Records*, I, 74.

[4] See *Winthrop Papers*, 178, 195, 207.

[5] Quoted from Haskins, *Law and Authority*, 32.

Court's membership, insofar as freemen were concerned, was restricted to those who had been formally admitted to one of the colony churches, with the result that there was now a drastic limitation on the franchise. When in 1634, as a result of the famous Watertown protest over taxes,[6] the General Court not only became a wholly elective body but, resuming the powers granted it under the charter, became again the chief organ of government, its business included what today we would refer to as legislative, along with judicial and administrative functions. Thus the General Court enacted laws and ordinances for the colony, answered petitions, authorized licenses, and supervised as well as made grants of land. Yet many of these matters were also dealt with, and normally in the first instance, by the Assistants, meeting separately as a court or as an executive board during the recesses of the General Court. Hence the magistrates continued to be virtually, and sometimes solely, involved in the enactment of laws and in the decision of cases, while they also performed most of the practical administrative work of the colony. Professor Herbert Osgood has written that the "continuous executive work of the colony was done as fully by the governor and assistants . . . as it was by the King and council in England."[7] After 1636, however, the powers of the Court of Assistants—but *not* the powers of the Assistants themselves—were narrowed by the creation of new courts of first instances—the county courts—so that the Court of Assistants had original jurisdiction primarily in civil suits involving more than £10, in cases of divorce, and in all capital and criminal cases extending to life, member, and banishment.[8] The Court of Assistants also heard appeals from the new county courts.[9]

It was in the new county courts that the weight of the magistrates' authority was particularly felt. Frequently joined with them were other "lay" judges, less experienced but dependable freemen who were designated *pro tem* by the General Court. By the end of the 1640's the jurisdiction of these two groups of lay judges sitting to-

[6] This episode is discussed in ibid., 29–30.

[7] H. L. Osgood, *The American Colonies in the Seventeenth Century* (New York, 1904), I, 177.

[8] Haskins, *Law and Authority*, 32–33, and footnote references.

[9] *Massachusetts Bay Records*, I, 169, 325–326.

gether in the county courts extended to all criminal and civil causes not expressly reserved to the Court of Assistants. Typically, what came before the county courts were actions for assault, battery, debt, defamation, drunkenness, fornication, Sabbath-breaking, theft, and trespass.[1] Another feature also stands out insofar as these lay judges were concerned. Like the English justices of the peace, whose example set precedents, the county courts also had extensive administrative jurisdiction which can be summarized as follows:

They appointed persons to lay out highways. They confirmed the nomination of military officers and apportioned charges for the repair for bridges. They ordered removal of obstruction on highways. They licensed innkeepers and others. They punished idle persons; they determined prices and wages when necessity required regulation. They fixed the allowances of ministers and saw that they were paid—and they oversaw the education of Indians as well as their relations in trade and otherwise with the colonists.[2]

Thus the ruling group of magistrates that comprised the Assistants were not only lay judges but were, for the most part, persons of practical experience and capacity as well. As indicated, most of them had been born or trained to responsibilities of administration or business, and several had served in positions which gave them knowledge of local customs as well as of the law of the special or national courts in England. Hence, in addition to their new positions as magistrates, set apart by divine law as "Gods vpon earthe," they came from backgrounds which placed them in a position similar in many respects to that of the English gentry, to whom deference was customarily paid. The majority of freemen—and most other inhabitants as well—likewise accepted, for the most part, the "due forme of Goverment" under which they lived.

One among several reasons for that acceptance was that the leaders of the colony did little violence to inherited traditions with which the inhabitants were familiar. Moreover, nearly all the colonists, and especially those from rural areas in England, had experienced self-government at the command of the Crown, enforced chiefly through local justices of the peace. The repairing of highways and bridges

[1] Haskins, *Laws and Authority*, 33.

[2] Summarized in ibid., 33.

and the scouring of ditches were among the endless duties which they had been expected to perform. Misdemeanors and failures to perform required duties — even the elastic concept of nuisance — were regulated in detail, so that enforcement by criminal process, conformable to what they had known, was readily accepted. It was only when the magistrates progressively introduced discretionary penalties for major offences, when the certainty of English practice appeared undermined, and when traditionally accepted sentiments were disregarded that the judicial work of the magistrates evoked strong criticism. Hence followed not only the well-known episode culminating in Winthrop's treatise on arbitrary government,[3] but the continued pressure for the preparation of the bill of rights known as "The Body of Liberties" (1641),[4] and eventually the carefully drafted and unique code, known as the *Lawes and Libertyes* of 1648.[5]

What occurred in this period was a remarkable change in attitude, one that needs special emphasis because the change seems to have escaped the attention of most scholars. Whereas in contemporary England efforts to protect civil liberties and individual rights from the usurpations or overbearing acts of the Crown were based upon so-called immutable concepts embodied in the traditions of the common law, in the colony the protection of individual rights through the rule of law was guaranteed by legislative enactments, as in the "Body of Liberties" of 1641 and in the Code of 1648. In part, the reason probably lies in the colonists' respect for the written customs of Old England, but even more in their early recourse to lay and church covenants. English statutes of the Elizabethan and Stuart periods rarely had such protective purposes but, instead, were typically harsh and largely regulatory, even when they affected individual rights of the poor and the wayward. Lord Coke's magnificent efforts had failed, judges had been manipulated, and Parliament was eventually prorogued. Yet in the colony the recognition and growth of a rule of law were the result of laymen whose legal experience was, at best, narrow and specialized. Much as the colonists revered the rule of law, as had their forebears, only infrequently did they become em-

---

[3] *Winthrop Papers*, IV, 468ff.
[4] *Colonial Laws of Massachusetts*.
[5] Edited by M. Farrand (Cambridge, Mass., 1929).

battled over the relationship between government and the individual. And when questions about excessive power of government did arise in the colony, there was no recourse to professional lawyers (persons comparable to Coke), but rather to compromise and debate among persons who were laymen and who produced the statutory solutions referred to.

As earlier stated, it was at the first meeting of the Court of Assistants held on these shores, on 23 August 1630—only a few weeks after their arrival—that six of the ten members of that body were given "like powers that justices of the peace hath in England for reformacion of abuses and punishing of offenders." [6] Two men, the Governor and the Deputy-Governor—at the time, respectively Winthrop and Thomas Dudley—were "alwais" to be justices; the other four only "for the present tyme." [7] The latter four were Sir Richard Saltonstall, nephew of the Lord Mayor of London and reputedly a former justice of the peace; Isaac Johnson, a wealthy landowner in Rutland and a son-in-law of the Earl of Lincoln; John Endicott, former governor of the plantation that had preceded the arrival of Winthrop's group and Roger Ludlow, who had been admitted to the Inner Temple and who, later, had led the emigrating contingent from the West of England. [8] The basis for the selection of the six is not clear, since, as indicated, the remaining four were well-known and competent persons. [9]

In any event these ten Assistants, as well as others later elected to that office, were all denominated "magistrates," which was an alternative title for justices of the peace in England, and they soon were serving as judges at all levels of the Colony's judicial system. [1] Many had had genuine—though specialized—legal experience. [2] Governor

[6] *Massachusetts Bay Records*, I, 74.

[7] Ibid.

[8] For Ludlow's position, see *Winthrop Papers*, II, 264; also, *Dictionary of National Biography*.

[9] E. g. Simon Bradstreet, who had served as Steward to the Earl of Lincoln, and William Pynchon, one of the original Assistants and known as a competent administrator. On the latter, see Smith, *Colonial Justice in Western Massachusetts*, 7–8, 10; Haskins, *Law and Authority*, 260, footnote 71.

[1] Haskins, *Law and Authority*, 27–28.

[2] That is, apart from training and experience as a justice of the peace, as explained in the instances cited in the following footnotes.

6. John Endicott (1589–1665), Governor, Magistrate, Member of the Court
of Assistants. From a portrait by an unknown artist. Courtesy, Massachusetts
Historical Society.

7. Simon Bradstreet (1603–1697), Governor, Member of the Court of Assistants, Member of the Council for the Safety of the People and the Conservation of the Peace. From a portrait by an unknown artist. Courtesy, Commonwealth of Massachusetts.

Winthrop had served in the Court of Wards and Liveries and had been admitted to Gray's Inn.[3] Dudley is said to have "learned much skill in the law."[4] Bellingham had been Recorder of Boston in England and is said also to have been a justice of the peace.[5] John Humfry was a member of Lincoln's Inn and had been an attorney in the Court of Wards and Liveries.[6] Isaac Johnson, a Cambridge graduate, was a member of Gray's Inn.[7] Roger Ludlow, Oxford educated, had been admitted to the Inner Temple, as already noted.[8]

It was one thing to bring from England a system of nonprofessional judges; it was another thing to retain it, enlarge it, and thus keep its principles. The latter would not have occurred unless the system had worked and had been acceptable to the colonists. What is remarkable is not that lay judges were able to perform their judicial, administrative, and legislative tasks but — to reverse Dr. Johnson's remark about the talking dog — that they performed them so well. Further, it should be emphasized that those Assistants who were "lay" judges, and whose powers were far broader than those of English justices of the peace, were *elected*, not appointed. We know how much of the English legal tradition was cast aside in favor of innovative practices and ideas that looked towards the new horizons which could nurture an indigenous local law. In other words, we know how, through the process of reason, logic, and evaluation of experience, the magistrates — and the electorate as well — were able to free themselves from the fetters of tradition.[9] Yet in doing so the magistrates, in particular, have been criticized for entrenching the kind of oligarchy they purportedly wished to move away from.

Entrenched they were, and it is a curious and singular feature of

[3] *Winthrop Papers*, II, 3; G. W. Robinson, *John Winthrop as Attorney* (Cambridge, Mass., 1930).

[4] A. Jones, *The Life and Work of Thomas Dudley* (Boston, 1899), 25.

[5] *Winthrop Papers*, II, 55, note; R. E. Wall, *Massachusetts Bay: The Crucial Decade* (New Haven, 1972), 31–32.

[6] A. P. Newton, *The Colonizing Activities of the English Puritans* (New Haven, 1914), 45; F. Rose-Troup, "John Humfry," *Essex Institute Historical Collections*, LXV (1929), 293.

[7] Johnson was also a wealthy landowner in Rutland, England, and was a brother-in-law of the Earl of Lincoln.

[8] See above, 42, footnote 5.

[9] Haskins, *Law and Authority*, chapter 11, and especially 220–221.

the early Massachusetts judicial system that so much control was exercised by the magistrates who dominated nearly every court of the colony. Yet to establish themselves in this way was one aspect of their overriding concern to create through their own activities the "Citty vpon a Hill" which had been the goal of emigration and settlement. However one may wish to characterize these leaders as a group, they were comparable to the ruling class of Virginia after the Revolution—in the words of Henry Adams "equal to any standard of excellence known to history. Their range was narrow but within it they were supreme."[1]

Another interesting and important feature of the system should be noted. In England it would have been unusual, except in a case reserved for the full bench, for a judge of that time to sit on one court to hear a case and on another court to hear an appeal from what he had already decided. Yet in the early years in Massachusetts Bay this is exactly what could and did happen. A magistrate sitting on a county court might hear a case for the first or second time, then again on appeal as a member of the Court of Assistants, and finally on appeal to the General Court. This type of rehearing was one of the issues in the Negative Vote conflict between deputies and magistrates in the 1640's, but the magistrates won out.[2] It has been a continuous subject of criticism until the present day, both because it seems "elitist" and oligarchical to some, and also, perhaps, because it does not comport with our customary appeals practices in state and federal courts. Nevertheless, despite occasional flare-ups between 1630 and 1650, the practice—an offshoot of the lay judges concept—not only persisted but thrived for the rest of the century, presumably because it accorded with the general sentiments of the community. Why?

When one looks at the record of continual reelection of almost the same slate of magistrates to office year after year—an office which made them available for judicial service as single magistrates, in the county courts, in the Court of Assistants, and in the General Court—one is bound to appreciate that the electorate placed trust in the judgment of these men, whether laymen or persons having

---

[1] H. Adams, *History of the United States of America* (New York, 1889), I, 133.
[2] The episode is discussed in Haskins, *Law and Authority*.

some basic learning in the law.[3] The colonists approved of the system. The same is substantially true of those freemen, regularly appointed upon nomination of the towns, to sit alone on commissioners' courts,[4] with full powers of magistrates when they sat with the Assistants as regular lay judges in the county courts. It is unlikely that, in the latter situation, the colonists failed to understand the importance of using non-professional laymen to provide and enlarge the magistrates' corps of experienced personnel, especially for the lower and trial courts. Uniformity of administration, with attendant discouragement of judicial separatism, was thereby fostered. The existence of that interlocking hierarchy, Joseph Smith has observed, was responsible for the "many common attributes ... found in the administration of justice in the purlieus of Boston, in the forests of York, and on the banks of the Connecticut."[5]

To involve laymen in the judicial system, men who were responsible not only to the electorate but to the communities they served, provided further cohesion within the colony beyond that fostered by the churches and by the general "due forme of Goverment."[6] To the seventeenth century there was little new about this form of self-government at the King's command. In various aspects it had been in operation for hundreds of years. From at least the early thirteenth century it had become usual to associate, by special commissions and on a regular basis, two royal judges with four knights of the shire — the latter, of course, laymen — to hold the possessory assizes.[7] In his *Memoranda de Parliamento of 1305* Maitland estimates that only a very small number of the judges who served throughout England

---

[3] The relevant elected lists are printed in W. H. Whitmore, *The Massachusetts Civil List* (Albany, 1870), 21–22.

[4] Commissioners' courts were established in 1638 for the settling of small cases by appointed freemen in communities where no magistrate resided. See Haskins, *Law and Authority*, 34, especially footnote 67. Also *Massachusetts Bay Records*, I, 239, 317; II, 208, 279.

[5] Smith, *Colonial Justice in Western Massachusetts*, 200.

[6] This expression is frequently used to describe the early government of Massachusetts. It first appears as a term of John Winthrop. See *Winthrop Papers*, II, 293. See also Haskins, *Law and Authority*, chapter 4.

[7] A. B. White, *Self-Government at the King's Command* (Minneapolis, 1933) *passim*; G. L. Haskins, *The Growth of English Representative Government* (Philadelphia, 1948), chapter 3.

at that time were royal judges from the central courts.[8] For minor crimes, misdemeanors, and administrative duties, generation after generation of local gentry had been deliberately used and received greater and greater practical training. Far more striking was the heavy burden placed upon the county gentry, especially with the expansion of the duties of justices of the peace in statute after statute under Elizabeth.[9] Moreover, since the later Middle Ages the House of Commons had begun to object to professionalized lawyers, and demands in Parliament seem to have led to an increase in the power of lay judges so that local affairs would be handled by local and nonprofessional men.[1] Hence new duties were continually being heaped upon these lay judges. Single justices of the peace were given specific powers for small causes and minor misdemeanors, as was the case with commissioners in the colony; sitting as a quorum of two or more they had far more extensive powers on criminal matters in Quarter Sessions based on their presumed superior knowledge of the law.[2] It is extraordinary how much of English local government could be, and was, carried on through the forms of criminal trial — not only offences which were designated as crimes, but misdeeds, malfeasances, and nonfeasances of local officers and communities.[3] The parallel to practices in the Bay Colony is striking and deserving of detailed comparisons.

In the *Collected Papers* of Maitland is a telling and relevant passage which illumines not only the work of the lay judges referred to, but the English habit of mind formed by close familiarity with that work. In his essay on "The Shadows and Silences of Real Life," he wrote:[4]

... Englishmen have trusted the laws; it were hardly too much to say that they have loved the law; but they have not loved and do not love lawyers, and the law that they have loved they did not think of as lawyers' law. The

[8] F. W. Maitland, *Memoranda de Parliamento* (London, 1893), xcix.

[9] E. P. Cheyney, *A History of England* (New York, 1926), II, chapters 37–41.

[1] See W. Notestein, *The English People on the Eve of Colonization* (New York, 1954), chapters 19, 20.

[2] Haskins, *Law and Authority*, 76.

[3] S. and B. Webb, *English Local Government* (London, 1906–1908), I, 308; Haskins, *Law and Authority*, 76, 174–178.

[4] F. W. Maitland, *Collected Papers* (Cambridge, 1911), I, 476–477.

most learned barrister ... will find it hard to get so high a reputation among country folk for speaking with the voice of the law, as that which has been enjoyed by many a country squire whose only *juristic attainment* [emphasis supplied] was the possession of a clerk who could find the appropriate page in [a manual for justices of the peace].

If this were true of the period of which Maitland was writing [1888], it was especially so of men in seventeenth-century England, and even more of those early colonists who adopted English traditions of lay judges to govern them and to preside over the judicial system of Massachusetts Bay.

Byfield beneath in peaceful slumber lies;
Byfield the good, the active and the wise;
His manly frame contained an equal mind;
Faithful to God, and generous to mankind;
High in his Country's Honors long he stood,
Succored distress and gave the hungry food;
In justice steady, in devotion warm,
A loyal subject, and a Patriot, firm;
Through every age his dauntless soul was tried;
Great while he lived, but greater when he died.

Epitaph, composed by Rev. Mather Byles[1]

[1] See, James P. Lane, *Historical Sketches of the First Congregational Church, Bristol, R.I., 1689–1872* (Providence, 1872), 37–38.

BARBARA A. BLACK

Nathaniel Byfield, 1653–1733

AS I explored various areas of eighteenth-century Massachusetts legal history, I ran into Nathaniel Byfield at every turn. It was this continual encountering of the man in the course of investigation of what I consider to be significant themes in the colony's legal history that piqued my curiosity about him. "Byfield the ubiquitous" he seemed to me, with the paradoxical consequence that although the world of legal history has hardly been impoverished by Byfield's absence, it may be enriched by his presence. To use a modern expression, Byfield was where the action was. Thus, however little that action owed to Byfield—he was, for example, certainly nothing so grand as a catalyst—still, if we follow *him* we arrive at *it*. And the journey is, or has been for me, most enjoyable. Were this essay not to be published by a Learned Society, I would say that I have had a helluva good time with Nathaniel Byfield. Under the circumstances, let us just say that it has been a most rewarding experience.

Nathaniel Byfield is a man mentioned by many, known, so far as I can tell, to none. History as written has not exactly ignored him,[2] but it tends to touch him lightly, glance off, and settle on men believed, apparently, more worthy of the historian's attention. This of course may be said of many figures in the past, and no doubt some of those richly deserve the obscurity they enjoy. And indeed, the

[2] See, e.g., Lane, *Historical Sketches;* Francis Baylies, *An Historical Memoir of the Colony of New Plymouth,* 2 vols., 4 parts (Boston, 1830); Emory Washburn, *Sketches of the Judicial History of Massachusetts From 1630 to the Revolution in 1775* (Boston, 1840); Wilfred H. Munro, *The History of Bristol, R.I.: The Story of the Mount Hope Lands, From the Visit of the Northmen to the Present Time* (Providence, 1880); *Celebration of the Two-Hundredth Anniversary of the Settlement of the Town of Bristol, Rhode Island, Sept. 24th ... 1880 ...,* compiler William J. Miller (Providence, 1881) (hereafter *Bicentennial*); Mark A. DeW. Howe, *Bristol, Rhode Island: A Town Biography* (Cambridge, 1930); George L. Howe, *Mount Hope: A New England Chronicle* (New York, 1959).

Facing page: portrait of Nathaniel Byfield painted by John Smibert, collection of Mr. and Mrs. S. Vagnino. Photo courtesy of R. H. Love Galleries, Inc., Chicago.

historian who does concentrate on Nathaniel Byfield will wonder whether that should be her final verdict on him. For example, I intended at first to title this essay "Nathaniel Byfield, a Remarkable Unknown," but feared for a time that the only effect of investigation would be to convert the man into an unremarkable known. But if that is the verdict, the fact is itself of considerable interest, for Byfield was a man of prominence and eminence in his time, as you will see from a brief sketch of his life.

I quote first from the obituary notice which appeared in the *Weekly News-letter,* 14 June 1733:

His immediate descent was from the Rev. Mr. Richard Byfield, the laborious, faithful pastor of Long-Ditton in Surrey, one of the Divines in the famous Westminster Assembly. His mother being of the noted family of the Juxons. He was the youngest of one and twenty children, and one of the sixteen that have sometimes followed their pious father to the Place of publick Worship. He was born in 1653, arrived at Boston in New England in 1674, and conceiving a Love to this Country, resolved to settle here;—and accordingly married the following year, Mrs. Deborah Clark, by whom he had five children, three whereof died in infancy; the other two lived to be married,—the youngest to the late Honourable Lieutenant-Governor Tailer, who quickly departed, without issue; the other to Edward Lyde, Esq., by whom she had five children, two of whom dying young, three only are now surviving, a son and two daughters.

He lived with the Wife of his Youth till 1717, upwards of forty years; and the following year married Mrs. Sarah Leverett, youngest daughter of the Honourable Governor Leverett, with whom he lived till 1730, when he was again left a sorrowful Widower. He has left his grandson, Byfield Lyde, Esq. (son-in-law to His Excellency Governor Belcher) Heir to the Bulk of his Estate.[3]

*   *   *   *

He was formerly a noted *Merchant* in this Place; and soon after PHILLIP's *War,* had the Honour to be One of the *Four* Proprietors, and the Principal Settler of the Town of *Bristol;* where he lived their Head & Glory 'till the year 1724; when his advancing Age put him upon return-

---

[3] "An Account of the Deceased," *Weekly News-Letter* No. 1533, With Amendment, Boston, 14 June 1733. This account is endlessly repeated, sometimes mis-quoted, but nowhere improved upon. Lane, *Historical Sketches,* 38–40, has some additional material on Byfield's wives. See also, *The Heraldic Journal,* 4 vols. (Boston, 1865–1868), II, 126–127.

ing back to BOSTON, the Place of his first Settlement; and where he remain'd 'till he died.[4]

Byfield died on 6 June 1733. A funeral sermon, preached by the Reverend Charles Chauncey, was afterward printed in a volume which includes a preface by the Reverend Thomas Foxcroft, and a copy of the newspaper obituary notice.[5] He was buried in the Granary Burial Ground, Boston.[6]

Byfield, who attained the rank of colonel, was elected a representative to the General Courts of Plymouth and of Massachusetts for several years, last in 1698, and served as Speaker of the House in Massachusetts.[7] He was chosen for the Massachusetts Council twenty-one times from 1699 to 1728 and negatived six times, by Dudley, Shute, and Dummer.[8] He served on the Court of Common

[4] The "Bristol" of which Byfield was "Principal Settler" has been since 1747 Bristol, Rhode Island. Byfield took the oath of freemanship in Plymouth on 5 June 1684, Records of the Colony of New Plymouth in New England, 1620–1692, 12 vols. ed. Nathaniel B. Shurtleff (Boston, 1855–1861), VI, 130. His name does not appear in the Index of Freemen in the volume of the Massachusetts Records where it should be if he had become a freeman of the Bay Colony between 1674 and 1684. See Records of the Governor and Company of the Massachusetts Bay in New England, 1628–1686, ed. Nathaniel B. Shurtleff, 5 vols. in 6 (Boston, 1854), V (1674–1686), 611–616 (hereafter Massachusetts Records). He is recorded as having taken the oath of allegiance in Boston in 1678. See Records of the Suffolk County Court, 1671–1680, with Introduction by Zechariah Chafee, Colonial Society of Massachusetts, Publications, XXIX–XXX (1933), II, 962.

[5] Charles Chauncy, Nathanael's character display'd. A sermon preach'd the Lord's Day after the funeral of the Honourable Nathanael Byfield, esq; late judge of the vice-admiralty, and one of His Majesty's council for this province. Who died at his house in Boston, on the 6th of June, 1733. In the 80th year of his age. (Boston [?] 1733).

[6] Munro, History of Bristol, 66; Lane, Historical Sketches, 37. The tombstone, no longer discoverable, bore the Byfield arms, with the name "Lyde," below, 105, and the Byles epitaph, above, 56, note 1, Lane, Historical Sketches, 37.

[7] In 1689 he was elected to the Plymouth General Court, but did not take his seat, Baylies, Historical Memoir, II:IV, 101. He was elected representative from Bristol to the Massachusetts General Court in 1693 and 1694, but was ineligible to serve in the latter year. See below, 67, on the non-residency law of 1693. In 1696, 1697, and 1698, he was elected representative from Boston. He was chosen speaker in 1693, and again in 1698, Acts and Resolves of the Province of Massachusetts Bay, 21 vols. (Boston, 1869–1922), VII (Resolves, Etc., 1692–1702), 21, 29, 45, 104, 148, 180 (hereafter Acts and Resolves). See, Records of the General Court, 68 vols. (1628–1833). (Archives of the Commonwealth, Boston, Massachusetts), VI (1689–1698), 338–339 (hereafter Court Records).

[8] See William Henry Whitmore, The Massachusetts Civil List For the Colonial and Provincial Periods, 1630–1774; being a list of the names and dates of appointment

Pleas, Bristol, for about nineteen years, on and off, from 1701 to 1724.[9] He was Judge of Probate for Bristol for some twenty-two years.[1] He was on the Court of Common Pleas for Suffolk County for the last couple of years of his life,[2] and a justice of the peace for Suffolk.[3] Last, and most important, he held a commission as Judge of Vice-Admiralty for approximately seventeen years.[4] And his portrait was painted, not once but at least three times, by John Smibert. A man of prominence and eminence.[5]

of all the civil officers constituted by authority of the charters, or the local government (Baltimore, 1969), 47, 48, 50, 51, 52, 53 (hereafter *Civil List*). Byfield was chosen for the Council 1699–1702, 1704, 1714–1728, and negatived in 1714, 1715, 1720, 1721, 1722, 1723.

[9] For facts (and fiction) about Byfield's position and tenure on the Bristol Court of Common Pleas, see below, 64–65, note 6.

[1] Whitmore, *Civil List*, 102. Records of the Governor and Council (Archives of the Commonwealth, Boston, Massachusetts), III (1698–1703), 378 (23 October 1702) (hereafter, Council Records). See Court Files, Suffolk County (Office of the Clerk, Supreme Judicial Court, Suffolk County, Boston) #5538 (hereafter Suffolk Files), for Byfield's commission as Judge of Probate, Bristol, 26 October 1702. It is signed by Dudley "by and with the advice of the Council," and it appears that the word "consent" was crossed out, and "advice" substituted, an interesting but mystifying datum. Byfield was off Probate from 1710 to 1715, then back on until 1729. See below, 102.

[2] Whitmore, *Civil List*, 78. He was appointed by Belcher, whose daughter married Byfield's grandson.

[3] Whitmore, *Civil List*, 127. He was appointed by Burnet on 19 December 1728, and presumably remained on the commission of the peace until his death. He was a J.P. for Suffolk in 1700, 1701 and 1702, possibly until 1706, Records of the Court of General Sessions of the Peace, Suffolk County (Office of the Clerk, Supreme Judicial Court, Suffolk County, Boston), I (July, 1702–July, 1712), 136–138; Massachusetts Archives, 328 vols. (Archives of the Commonwealth, Boston, Massachusetts), XL (Judicial, 1683–1724), 641, 642, Massachusetts Archives, VIII (Depositions, 1662–1776), 102 (hereafter Massachusetts Archives). Byfield was also, on occasion, appointed a special justice of the Superior Court for a particular cause, Whitmore, *Civil List*, 71–72. See also, Suffolk Files, #34664.

[4] See below, 64–65, note 6, 102.

[5] At least three Smibert portraits of Byfield survive. One authority believes, however, that all three may be Smibert copies of a lost Smibert original. The surviving paintings are standard bust length (30 x 25), while the fee recorded by Smibert was that amount which he would have charged for a ¾ length (50 x 40) painting. Nor would it have been unusual for Smibert to do bust length replicas of larger portraits. Richard H. Saunders, "John Smibert (1688–1741): Anglo-American Portrait Painter" (unpublished dissertation, Yale University, 1979) (conversation with author). One of the three surviving Byfield portraits (#1) is in the Metropolitan Museum of Art, another (#2) at the Vose Gallery, Boston, and the third (#3) privately owned. The portrait reproduced at the start of this article is #3. There is also a copy, by Jane Stuart, which is now at the Bristol, R.I., Historical

On Byfield the man opinions have always differed. Baylies, the first historian to offer an assessment of Byfield's character, had this to say:

The character of Colonel Byefield was not so elevated as to command the veneration of the people, or so low as to incur their contempt.[6] Generally honest, he was capable of duplicity; his ambition was overweening, and his resentments implacable. Sometimes he exhibited the appearance of public spirit, and seemed to feel its impulse, although his frugality bordered on meanness. Of imposing manners, respectable talents, ardent passions, and an enterprising disposition, he always contrived to preserve a large share of the public respect, . . .[7]

The natural pietism felt toward a town's "principal founder" by his descendant, and by the town's historians and celebrants, has produced a very different character, one in which integrity of purpose, uprightness of spirit, benevolence, courage, honesty, patriotism, lack of affectation, devoutness, and the like are inevitably dominant.[8] But this accent on the positive does not quite succeed in eliminating the negative, and it is plain, if only from the defensive tone of these accounts, that for one who would bestow unqualified praise on this man, the going is heavy. This unhappy truth emerges even from the sermon preached on Byfield's death. It has been said that "when his long and useful life was ended, his character and public services called forth unqualified eulogium." That is true of the *Weekly News-Letter*'s obituary notice and Foxcroft's preface to Chauncey's

Society. Smibert's notebook records the date of the painting as June 1729. The Metropolitan copy, marked "Aetatis 78, 1730," is reputed to have come down from the Pepperrell family, who are said to have believed for some time that it was a portrait of Jonathan Belcher. Portrait #2 was once owned by Byfield descendant George Lyde, of New York, and was given by him in 1825 to Byfield parish. Portrait #3 was once owned by Byfield descendant Francis Brinley, who, delivering the Byfield address at the Bristol Bicentennial ceremonies, explained that a daughter of Byfield's daughter Mrs. Lyde married Colonel Francis Brinley of Roxbury, the speaker's great-grandfather, *Bicentennial*, 114. See Henry W. Foote, *John Smibert, Painter, with a descriptive catalogue of portraits, and notes on the work of Nathaniel Smibert* (Cambridge, 1950), 140–141; John Smibert, *The Notebook of John Smibert with Essays by Sir David Evans, John Kerslake, and Andrew Oliver, and with notes relating to Smibert's American portraits, by Andrew Oliver* (Boston, 1969), 88.

[6] Howe, *Mount Hope*, 64, labels this "about as faint praise as ever damned a man."

[7] Baylies, *Historical Memoir*, II:IV, 55–57.

[8] See the works cited above, 56–57, notes 1 and 2.

funeral sermon. It is not true of the sermon itself, a fact I find both remarkable and sad. Chauncey took for his text John 1, 47 "Jesus saw Nathanael coming to him and saith of him, Behold an Israelite indeed, in whom is no guile," and after some exegesis turned to Byfield, thus:

> IT would be a great incongruity, just after a solemn discourse against guile and insincerity, if I shou'd allow my self, in saying any thing, either to flatter the dead, or deceive the living:
>
> *   *   *   *
>
> I do not speak of Him, as free from infirmities. For who among men can Pretend to be without fault?

Byfield was, Chauncey continued, "an Israelite indeed," without guile, free from "flattery and deceit." He was, as well, of exemplary piety "which he discovered in a flaming zeal for his [Byfield's, presumably] honour," as well as in strict ritual "observance of *all* the institutions of the LORD JESUS."

> But I have no need to insist here, not doubting, your tho'ts were upon *our* NATHANAEL, while I was representing the *Character* in the *Text:* the application was so easie and obvious; and I would hope, unexceptionable: having carefully avoided saying any thing, but what I tho't in justice belong'd to him.
>
> BUT tho' his open temper, and sincerely plain and undisguised manner of life, was that wherein he excelled: yet were there other things in him, which ought not to be passed over in silence.

Chauncey went on to the other things and managed a moderate amount of real praise, but even in this warmer half of the sermon there is a decided guardedness and, at one point, something very close to censure:

> HE was upon principle, a man of charity; . . . constantly paying . . . such a proportion out of his estate; which whatever it was ordinarily, it once happened, within *my knowledge,* in the course of one year, to amount to some hundreds of pounds. . . . *'Twas his principle to do what he did, this way, in the time of his life; and therefore if he has not by his last will, made many charitable donations, he herein only acted according to his known settled Judgment.* [last italics added][9]

---

[9] In Byfield, it appears, frugality warred with generosity, and there is substantial evidence of both in the records and in the histories: Jeremiah Dummer to Dr. Cole-

As Byfield's defenders point out with justice, people active in public affairs are likely to make enemies and therefore unlikely to escape calumny.[1] According to Munro, "for his career outside the limits of his adopted town, we have to rely mainly upon the records left by his political enemies."[2] That may be so; heaven knows he had enough enemies.[3] But one wonders why his political, or for that matter, personal friends should not have left some records as well. The logical possibilities are, it would seem, historical accident and paucity of friends, I suspect the latter. I certainly wonder about the author of his epitaph, who saw fit to conclude with that most equivocal line: "Great while he lived, but greater when he died."

Munro suggests an interesting contrast. For Byfield's career beyond Bristol we have only the reports of his enemies; but "of Mr. Byfield's course in Bristol, we have our own records to testify, and in them he always appears as an upright, public-spirited citizen, generous in his gifts to the town, an efficient friend and supporter of

man: "his [Byfield's] frugality makes him sick of coach hire, fees to officers and door-keepers, and other expenses . . . ," quoted in Baylies, *Historical Memoir*, II:IV, 55–56, note; see, Washburn, *Judicial History*, 183; Lane, *Historical Sketches*, 32–33, 36–37 ("His servants were remembered [in his will] with Christian affection and counsel. . . ." He did, however, free and provide for one "favorite servant," possibly a slave. According to Howe, *Mount Hope*, 103, "Byfield kept ten bonded whites and one slave.")

[1] Munro, *History of Bristol*, 67; Lane, *Historical Sketches*, 34; Washburn, *Judicial History*, 182.

[2] Munro, *History of Bristol*, 67.

[3] Probably including, at one time or another, Jeremiah Dummer, Cotton Mather, Increase Mather, Joseph Dudley, William Phips, Samuel Shute, William Dummer, John Saffin, Nathaniel Blagrove, Sir William Ashurst, and Samuel Sewall. I am baffled by Munro's apparent inclusion of Baylies in the ranks of Byfield's enemies. Baylies, as we have seen, wielded his pen as candidly as Smibert did his brush, and to much the same unflattering conclusion, but he seems to have been quite concerned to give a balanced account. At one point, indeed, he cautions us against swallowing whole the words of one of Byfield's enemies, on the ground that the detractor himself was a man not to be trusted. And, in addition to warning us about Jeremiah Dummer, Baylies says "Colonel Byefield much to his honor, resisted the insane fanaticism of the people during their delusion on the subject of witchcraft, and condemned the conduct of the Court with much severity," Baylies, *Historical Memoir*, II:IV, 55, note. (This is repeated by all, but I do not know its source in original records.) Munro, however, damns Baylies' account as "evidently much biased by personal prejudice," Munro, *History of Bristol*, 67. And Lane, mentioning "the detractions of prejudiced or ill-informed historians who came after him" (Lane, *Historical Sketches*, 34), probably means Baylies, as well.

religion and education. . . ."[4] The conclusion that Munro would like us to draw is, of course, that Byfield was in all likelihood the paragon outside Bristol that he was within the town. It is, however, also a possible deduction that Byfield was a kind of house (town) angel, street (province) devil. And then there is the dispiriting truth, which is simply that the Bristol town records merely skim the surface of life in Bristol. As we shall see, there is an abundance of evidence in other records that "Mr. Byfield's course in Bristol" was quite as uneven as his course in the wide world beyond the town he founded.

Disagreement among historians extends beyond assessment of Byfield's character to such matters as where he lived at a given time[5] and the dates of his judicial service.[6] And in truth the bare and basic

[4] Munro, *History of Bristol*, 67.

[5] Hutchinson and Baylies have him emigrating to America several years late, "about 1680" and "1680," respectively, Thomas Hutchinson, *The History of the Colony and Province of Massachusetts Bay*, ed. Lawrence S. Mayo, 3 vols. (Cambridge, 1936); Baylies, *Historical Memoir*, II:IV, 53. And most accounts follow the *Weekly News-Letter* in placing Byfield firmly in Bristol from about 1680 until 1724, Munro, *History of Bristol*, 66; Lane, *Historical Sketches*, 31; *Bicentennial*, 44; Washburn (who sends him back to Boston only in 1731), *Judicial History*, 178. But as Mark Howe points out, "The big-wig founders of the town . . . belonged somewhat to the class of absentee landlords. . . ." Howe, *Bristol*, 10. Byfield, says Howe, was the "least absentee of the quartette," Howe, *Bristol*, 17. Still, it is well known to historians that in 1693 and 1694 Byfield was one of the *Bostonian* representatives of "country towns" (Bristol in his case) at whom the non-residency act of 1693 was aimed, and in 1694 he was rejected on grounds of non-residency. See below. And in 1696, 1697, and 1698, with that act in force, Byfield was representative from Boston. Moreover, in 1700 he was Moderator and Overseer of the Poor for Boston, Robert F. Seybolt, *The Town Officials of Colonial Boston, 1634–1775* (Cambridge, 1939), 77. He was a justice of the peace for Suffolk County in 1700 and 1701; see above, 60, note 3. From all that I have seen, the residence story appears to be:

1674–1680	Boston
1680–ca. 1692	Bristol
ca. 1692–ca. 1702	Boston
ca. 1702–1724	Bristol
1724–1733	Boston

[6] The major confusion has to do with Byfield's tenure and position on the Court of Common Pleas for Bristol, and it originates in the statement in his obituary, unfortunately relied upon ever after, that Byfield:

sat CHIEF thirty-eight years in the court of general sessions of the peace, and common pleas for the county of Bristol, as afterwards he did two years for the county of Suffolk.

So far as I have been able to ascertain the facts concerning Byfield and the Bristol Court of Common Pleas, they are:

facts about Byfield's life are devilishly hard to pin down; as the material in the footnotes will reveal, I have not yet altogether succeeded in the pinning. As to Byfield's political predilections and

a. Chief Justice *under Andros,* probably from about 1687 to 1689, Baylies, *Historical Memoir,* II:IV, 98.
b. 1689–1701: not on any such court.
c. August 1701: Appointed (judge, *not Chief Justice*): Council Records, III, 232. Whitmore, *Civil List,* 99.
d. June 1710: Suspended, Whitmore, *Civil List,* 99.
e. December 1715: Re-appointed, Whitmore, *Civil List,* 99.
f. November or December 1724: Resigned, Whitmore, *Civil List,* 100.

So, the Dominion of New England aside, he was on the Court of Common Pleas, Bristol, for just under 18 years, not 38, nor was he Chief Justice (except under Andros) for the very good reason that there was no Chief Justice of Common Pleas. As to General Sessions: in the Province period, that was a court held by justices of the peace for the county. And, although I find this hard to credit, according to the *Civil List* Byfield was not a J.P. for Bristol *at all.*

As to Admiralty, as Kinvin Wroth has said of the early admiralty courts: "For seven years the new courts existed in a state of political conflict so confusing that no historian has succeeded in unraveling it completely." L. Kinvin Wroth, "The Massachusetts Vice Admiralty Court and the Federal Admiralty Jurisdiction," *American Journal of Legal History,* VI (1962), 259. The confusion extends to the dates of the judges' commissions. The actual Admiralty story for Byfield, so far as I can determine: Commission shown in Council, 21 March 1697/8, but taking of oath delayed. Took oath as Judge of Admiralty, 9 June 1699, only to be superseded almost immediately by Wait Winthrop. Appointed again, July 1703. After some confusion, recommissioned in 1704; sworn in April 1704. Sat until 1714 or 1715. Sitting again October 1728; sworn before Governor and Council, 10 April 1729. See Council Records, II (1686–1687, 1692–1698), 527; Council Records, III, 52, 59, 264; Wroth, "The Massachusetts Vice Admiralty Court," 259, 261; Richard S. Dunn, *Puritans and Yankees: The Winthrop Dynasty of New England 1630–1717* (New York, 1971), 271, 272; John G. Palfrey, *History of New England,* 5 vols. (Boston, 1859–1890), IV, 255, note 1; Charles M. Andrews, "Vice-Admiralty Courts in the Colonies," Introduction to *Records of the Vice-Admiralty Court of Rhode Island 1716–1752,* ed. Dorothy S. Towle (Washington, D.C., 1936), 14, note 4, 86–87; Marguerite Appleton, "Rhode Island's First Court of Admiralty," *New England Quarterly,* V (1932), 156 (quoting *Boston Newsletter,* 1 May 1704); Massachusetts Court of Admiralty Records, 3 vols. (Office of the Clerk, Supreme Judicial Court, Suffolk County, Boston), III (1726–1733), 52, 59–60 (hereafter Admiralty Records).

In his obituary notice it was said of Byfield as judge of admiralty that:

He was the *first* judge under our present charter; and never once had a decree revers'd upon an appeal home.

In Lane, *Historical Sketches,* 34, we read:

The wisdom and justice of Mr. Byfield's acts as a Civil Judge, are apparent from the remarkable fact that in no case were his decisions ever reversed on appeal to higher powers.

The context makes it clear that Lane, an ecclesiastical historian, intends by "Civil" not an opposition to "Admiralty" but merely "secular." Thus are legends made. See also, Munro, *History of Bristol,* 66, and *Bicentennial,* 117.

position on public issues, contrariety of opinion among historians was just about inevitable. The widest disparity is found in accounts of, and assumptions about, Byfield's attitude toward royal government and the tightening of imperial control from the last days of the old charter through the first decades of the Province. Where did Byfield stand on charter revocation, on the Andros regime, on the Revolution of 1689? Where should we place him in the major political opposition of the early provincial years? Does he belong in the Dudley or Cooke faction? Depending upon whom you read, you may get a picture of Byfield as a member of the "charter party"[7]—I like that label for an admiralty judge! —or a Randolph/Andros man,[8] a Cooke ally,[9] or a Dudley friend.[1]

The chief, though not only,[2] explanation for the tendency to place Byfield in all camps and on both sides of all questions is that, as my grandmother used to say, everybody is right. Byfield was

[7] See G. B. Warden, *Boston, 1689–1776* (Boston, 1970), 51.

[8] Wroth, "The Massachusetts Vice Admiralty Court," 258–259; Dunn, *Puritans and Yankees,* 271.

[9] Warden, *Boston,* 46, 48, 51.

[1] Everett Kimball, *The Public Life of Joseph Dudley: A Study of the Colonial Policy of the Stuarts in New England* (New York, 1911), 66, note 2; Howard M. Chapin, *Privateer Ships and Sailors, 1625–1725* (Toulon, 1926), 178 (Dudley's "servile agent Byfield"); Dunn, *Puritans and Yankees,* 268–271.

[2] There is a fascinating, if minor, bibliographic muddle which has almost certainly done its bit to produce confusion, and probably inaccuracy. On 29 April 1689, Byfield wrote a letter of introduction to a Declaration written by the revolutionaries who seized power from Andros. The letter, non-committal in the extreme, in itself enables neither contemporary nor historian to gather the political sentiments of the author. But Byfield's authorship of this innocuous if not helpful document has resulted in quite baseless attribution to him variously of two other documents— one on each side of the great political controversy. See, "An Account of the Late Revolution in New-England. Together with the Declaration of the Gentlemen, Merchants, and Inhabitants of Boston, and the Country adjacent. April 18, 1689. Written by Mr. Nathanael Byfield, a Merchant of Bristol in New-England to his friends in London." (Printed for Ric. Chiswell, 1689 at the Rose and Crown in St. Paul's Church-Yard.) The Declaration appears to have been written by Cotton Mather, see Palfrey, *History of New England,* III, 579 note 1; "An Account of the Late Revolutions in New England; In a Letter (Published at Boston by Benjamin Harris, and Sold at the London-Coffee, House there, June 6, 1689.) Signed "A.B." ("Frequently confused with a pamphlet by Nathaniel Byfield," Card Catalogue, John Carter Brown Library, Brown University, Providence, Rhode Island); "Seasonable Motives To our Duty and Allegiance (by a Lover of the Peace of New-England) offered to the Consideration of his Neighbors & Country-men." (Philadelphia, printed by William Bradford, 1689.) Signed "A.B." (Attributed to Byfield, Evans Catalogue #463.)

unquestionably all over the lot. To see what that means, let us take a look at the 1690's. Byfield was at that time undoubtedly of the Cooke faction, anti-Mather and anti-Phips. Thus, when it was enacted, in 1693, that no person might represent in the General Court a town in which he did not live,[3] this measure was aimed at eliminating certain men who were, in Palfrey's phrase, "friends to the old charter, *or for other causes unfriendly to Governor Phips.*"[4] That last clause is important; Byfield, a Bostonian representing Bristol, was hostile to Phips. And on Byfield's re-election in 1694, Phips properly refused to swear him in because of his non-residency in Bristol.[5] But Byfield's hostility to Phips, and for that matter, his alliance with Cooke, seem to have been "for other causes" than attachment to the old charter. According to Baylies, "It was the fortune of Colonel Byfield to have been accidentally" brought into political partnership with the Cookes, whose principled, patriotic aims happened to serve his goals: office and revenge.[6] Certainly I see no evidence that Byfield cared a hoot for the old charter, much less that he was a charter member of the old charter party.

Byfield's early and long service as judge of admiralty must warn us that he was hardly likely to have been as hostile to imperial control, to royal government, as his relationship with the Cookes suggests. And it is in the record of his appointments to that post that one finds confirmed a suspicion that Byfield, though an ally of the Cookes, was no Cooke. Byfield was originally Randolph's nominee.[7] Commissioned in March 1697/8, he took his oath in June 1699.[8] But the newly arrived Governor, Bellomont, possibly more in sympathy with the old charter party than with Randolph, replaced Byfield immediately with Wait Winthrop.[9] Bellomont, who died in

[3] *Acts and Resolves,* I (*Acts, 1692–1714*), 147. See objection by Byfield and others to the act, Massachusetts Archives, XLVIII (Legislature, 1643–1732), 224.

[4] Palfrey, *History of New England,* IV, 143 [emphasis added]; see Warden, *Boston,* 46.

[5] *Court Records,* VI, 338.

[6] Baylies, *Historical Memoir,* II:IV, 55–56, note; Washburn agrees, *Judicial History,* 180.

[7] Dunn, *Puritans and Yankees,* 271.

[8] See above, 65, footnote 6.

[9] See Wroth, "The Massachusetts Vice Admiralty Court," 259; cf. Dunn, *Puritans and Yankees,* 271–272.

1701, was succeeded by Joseph Dudley, arch-enemy of the Cookes and still anathema to the old charter party. And Dudley labored mightily, and successfully, for the reappointment of Nathaniel Byfield.[1] As well he might, since Byfield had supported him for Governor.[2] Dudley in 1702 also appointed Byfield to the Court of Common Pleas and made him Judge of Probate for Bristol. In short, although certainly a Cooke ally in the 1690's and forward, Byfield was also for much of that time on good terms with Dudley. Relations with Dudley deteriorated and in 1715 we find Byfield in London, trying, among other things, to have Governor Dudley removed,[3] but in and around 1700, Byfield and Dudley were in alliance, mutually supportive of each in the other's self-seeking endeavors.

In Byfield's performance as Judge of Admiralty, we see much the same historiographic pattern. That is to say, one can conclude from the secondary literature either that he was a staunch upholder of the admiralty jurisdiction against popular attempts to destroy this prerogative court, or a subverter of efforts to enforce imperial legislation in admiralty. There is an interesting apparent contradiction, or at least inconsistency, in two accounts of Byfield as judge of admiralty: the first in John Schutz' study of William Shirley[4] and the second in Joseph Malone's book *Pine Trees and Politics*,[5] a witty, absorbing account, which deserves to be far better known than it is, of the enforcement of the White Pine Acts. Schutz has Byfield a conscientious admiralty judge, "the scarred veteran of countless disputes with Boston seamen," whose activities against smugglers brought him much trouble in the form of personal actions entered against him in the civil courts. In particular, Schutz has Elisha Cooke, Jr., "self-appointed champion of the Boston smugglers," harassing

---

[1] Wroth, "The Massachusetts Vice Admiralty Court," 261, quoting Dudley: "I have now a second commission for Mr. Byfield. . . ."

[2] As a letter from Byfield to Dudley makes clear, quoted by Kimball, *Dudley*, 66, note 2.

[3] See below, 102, note 3.

[4] John A. Schutz, *William Shirley, King's Governor of Massachusetts* (Chapel Hill, 1961).

[5] Joseph J. Malone, *Pine Trees and Politics: The Naval Stores and Forest Policy in Colonial New England 1691–1775* (Seattle, 1964).

Byfield, and securing "several crippling judgments" against him.[6] Malone, on the other hand, documents Byfield's subversion of imperial enforcement of the White Pine Acts, including his practice of assessing court costs against the Surveyor-General in sterling, while accepting payment of fines in successful actions in devalued New England currency.[7] As Malone points out, Byfield "was in more ways than one ill-suited to play the role of a defender of the royal prerogative, being a partner in land speculation with Dr. Elisha Cooke, the Samuel Adams of his day."[8] Again, everybody is more or less right. Byfield was apparently a land speculator,[9] but not, so far as the records disclose, a smuggler; thus, he could be the terror of smugglers, His Majesty's most conscientious and devoted judicial servant, while working hard to nullify the legislation — the White Pine Acts — which stood athwart his personal path to riches.

My own investigation of Byfield's Admiralty career is unfortunately incomplete. As to the White Pine Acts, what I have seen supports Malone's position;[1] my evidence is slim, but then again it is supererogatory since Malone's account is very convincing in itself. On the question of Byfield's having been harassed by common law actions brought against him personally by smugglers, I have come across only one such case in the records thus far examined, and indeed Schutz cites only this one case.[2] Cases involving the Acts of Trade go both ways, customs seizures being upheld in some cases, dismissed in others, but there is a fair amount of evidence that Byfield was, in this as opposed to the White Pine cases, a sturdy de-

---

[6] Schutz, *William Shirley*, 8.

[7] Malone, *Pine Trees and Politics*, 71, 93, 106–109.

[8] Malone, *Pine Trees and Politics*, 71. Malone calls Byfield "a timber merchant and sawmill owner," ibid.

[9] He had, on his death, extensive land holdings in Maine and Vermont, Lane, *Historical Sketches*, 36.

[1] Admiralty Records, III, 108–109, 105, 132–133, 74–81.

[2] *Swazey v. Byfield*, Suffolk Files #35758, Writ of execution, 16 March 1732/3. Judgment for Swazey in Superior Court, Boston. [Reverse of document: Judgment satisfied, £23.4.0, 15 August 1733. This was after Byfield's death.] Schutz, noting that Byfield had hired Shirley to represent him in this matter, says of Shirley's appeal to the Privy Council, "The Council's ruling was inclusive." Schutz, *William Shirley*, 8.

fender of the royal prerogative; in 1732, for example, he complained
of the Province judges' indifference to Act of Trade violations and
of their "incroaching proceedings."[3]

As a man who occupied high judicial office for many years, Byfield
would presumably be of some slight interest to legal historians without more. But there is more, though a somewhat oblique more. The
author of Byfield's epitaph gives us a clue in his characterization of
the recently departed as "the active." Byfield was ceaselessly, relentlessly active. And since he was, pre-eminently, a man of law, his
activity involved him in a significant segment of the legal history of
his time. His being a "man of law" had two dimensions. The more
obvious, his career as a judge, is perhaps the less important. More
importantly, he was law-minded: that is, when circumstances involved him in controversy, or difficulty of almost any variety, his
mind turned immediately to thoughts of legal action. And since he
was also bloody-minded, he spent a good part of his life suing and
being sued.[4]

Byfield, as noted, was a founder of the town of Bristol. He and
three other men purchased a tract of land called Mount Hope from
Plymouth Colony in 1680; Byfield's partners in the original purchase were John Walley, Nathaniel Oliver, and Stephen Burton.
Byfield and Walley proceeded to develop the area, Oliver having
sold out to one Nathan Hayman immediately, and Burton being
relatively inactive. In 1685 Plymouth Colony was divided into three
counties, one of them Bristol, with Mount Hope, now the town of
Bristol, as the shire town. If we peer behind the facade, the work-a-
day facts of Bristol's beginnings, we find stark drama: Feuding, fighting and fussing, allegation, recrimination, vituperation, neighbor
against neighbor, undying enmity. If there was no blood shed, and
none appears in the records, we may see this as a testimonial to the
at least minimal efficacy of the legal system, a system put to the

---

[3] Suffolk Files #30398. See John Noble, "A Few Notes on Admiralty Jurisdiction
in the Colony and in the Province of Massachusetts Bay," Colonial Society of Massachusetts, *Publications*, VIII (1906), 168.

[4] I have discovered records of twenty-seven actions, civil or criminal, in which Byfield or his executor was a party, in a few of them as executor. As we shall see,
some of these stretched on for many years, through a number of courts, and in some
cases arbitration as well.

test again and again by the contentious inhabitants of Bristol.[5]

The main Bristol conflict, at its vital center, pitted Nathaniel Byfield and his partners against John Saffin and friends. Saffin is a figure of considerable interest to any who study Nathaniel Byfield. Although far better known than Byfield, he too is a man whose prominence in his own day is not reflected in the treatment accorded him by historians. Like Byfield, Saffin was judge, representative, councillor, and leading citizen. Again, like Byfield, he is an historical personage of no great personal appeal: self-seeking, avaricious, quarrelsome. The resemblance is striking.[6] The feud seems to have begun almost immediately; perhaps there was a pre-Bristol history to it. The first sign I have found of rancor between Saffin and Byfield was in 1681. Byfield was one of the men appointed "rater," that is tax assessor, of Bristol for that year. Saffin's land was rated at £12.16.1; Saffin refused to pay, and after this and that, landed in "his majesties gayle att Plymouth." In October 1683, Saffin brought an unsuccessful action "of the case" in Plymouth General Court against Byfield, Church, and Cary, the raters, alleging that "the said raters did . . . contrary to law and the liberty of an English subject, most unjustly and unreasonably rate or assess" his estate.[7] Mean-

[5] The inhabitants of Bristol were embroiled in controversy among themselves from virtually the moment of settlement. They squabbled, and sued, over rates and roads, mills and ministers, over land and water. Simple-minded though this may be, I believe the trouble to be in part traceable to the character and temperament of particular individuals—Nathaniel Byfield for one. One historian, taking a somewhat broader view, says of those men who followed the original proprietors, and who were induced to settle in Bristol by land grants: "Like most men who get something for nothing, the first sixty were malcontents." It will be seen that Bristol is a problem for any historian who might care to advance the thesis that New England was, in this era, harmonious. Perhaps the situation in Bristol supports the thesis that with a shift in societal focus from religion to commerce came disunity and strife. Bristol was, as its celebrants somewhat apologetically record, a commercial enterprise, in the words of the original deed to Byfield et al., "a town for trade." No Puritan Eden this. Or perhaps the Bristol story points up what we ought in any event to know by dead reckoning, that is, that times of settlement are likely to be times of confusion, therefore of conflict. Or perhaps Bristol was unique. Or perhaps New England was not particularly harmonious.

[6] On Saffin see Munro, *History of Bristol*, 87–90, Baylies, *Historical Memoir*, II:IV, 57–62, Washburn, *Judicial History*, 268–270.

[7] Plymouth Records, VI, 116–119, VII, 269. See also VII, 270. At the same time that Saffin sought justice against the tax assessors, he also took up a separate grievance against one of them. He brought an action of the case against Benjamin Church, alleging that by damming up a "certain watercourse, stream or creeke," Church had

while, at this same October 1683 General Court, the real opposing forces lined up. The original proprietors, Byfield, Walley, Burton, and Oliver brought and won an action against Saffin for maintaining a fence on land which, they alleged, was theirs.[8] This, however, was only one of many points in contention between the parties and, no doubt in the hope of settling everything at once, the parties abandoned more formal legal process and resorted to arbitration. In late 1683 or early 1684 Saffin on the one hand, and Byfield *et al.* on the other, submitted to arbitration "divers controversys differences and debates . . . touching and concerning the bounds between the meadows of the one party and the upland of the other party, and also concerning ways, stoppage of a water course erecting of a mill dam, tithe of land, removing of a fence exchange or sale of land or meadows for each partys convenience & Divers other matters & causes yet undertermined."[9] The parties gave bond "in the Penall sum of one thousand pounds in currant money of New England," the condition of the bond being compliance with the arbitration award.[1]

Although the arbitrators sought to reconcile differences and parties, rather than to select a winner, Saffin appears to have been to a considerable extent vindicated.[2] He had, however, perhaps more satisfaction from the arbitrators than from his adversaries. For in *1695*—that is, well over eleven years later—Saffin brought against Byfield *et al.* an action of debt on the 1683 penal bond, alleging failure to perform "according to their obligation and the Award of the said Arbitrator which is to the damage of the plaintiff five hundred pounds. . . ."[3] This action, entered in the Court of Common

flooded Saffin's land and deprived him of free access thereto. The jury, finding for Saffin, awarded him £3 and costs. He had asked £80 "with other due damages." Plymouth Records, VII, 270.

[8] Plymouth Records, VII, 270–271. They also brought an action against one Robert Skiff for withholding land belonging to them, apparently land sold to Skiff by Saffin. Plymouth Records, VII, 271.

[9] Massachusetts Archives, XL, 383. In ibid., XL, 382, is Saffin's bill of particulars, presented to the arbitrators in February 1683/4. The arbitrators were Thomas Hinckley, William Stoughton, Joseph Dudley, and Nathaniel Thomas.

[1] The bond given to Walley, Byfield, and Burton is at Massachusetts Archives, XL, 384, dated 9 February 1683/4. Saffin's bond, on the same date, is in ibid., XL, 383.

[2] The arbitration award, dated 13 February 1683/4, is in ibid., XL, 385.

[3] Ibid., 395.

Pleas for Bristol County, was not prosecuted, the parties instead having recourse once again to arbitration. Saffin detailed the respects in which his opponents had, as he believed, failed to comply with the arbitrators' directions.[4] Byfield had a ready and spirited answer to all charges, and a few counter-charges of his own.[5] The arbitrators once again seem to have split the difference, as it were, although this time, apparently, rather more in favor of Byfield and Walley than was the case in 1684.[6] But by this time the particular matters in controversy between Saffin and Byfield *et al.* were the least of it; they were overshadowed by a nasty conflict over the general state and management of affairs in Bristol.

In 1695 Saffin wrote and distributed a tract called "The Original of the Town of Bristol, or a true narrative of the first settlement of Mount Hope Neck."[7] The Narrative is a sustained vitriolic attack on the original purchasers of Mount Hope, who were charged with, as Byfield later put it, "Promoteing of [their] owne interest to the irreparable Detriment (if not ruine) of the place."[8] Byfield's answer, submitted to the second set of arbitrators, contained his defence, not only to his alleged failure to comply with the first arbitration award, but to the wide-ranging charges in Saffin's Narrative.[9] Byfield had a few colorful remarks to make about Saffin: "(in my opinion) he hath forfeited his Honor & Justice (if any he had)"[1] ... "nor have I ever had any Reason to have any good apprehension of him; but the contrary; and did always fear his comeing there would Ruine the place"[2]; "he quarrels with us because we did not make it a sheep pasture for the whole Towne, & so? have taken him in a partner with us; & one Reason why we Did not, was because we Remembered that ould (but true saying) that one scabby sheep will spoile a whole flocke."[3] "This gentleman dus also suggest, as if

[4] Ibid., 396.

[5] This is a lengthy document, appearing in ibid., 397–412.

[6] Ibid., 376–378, contains the arbitration award, dated 6 July 1696.

[7] Ibid., 413, is Saffin's summary of his Narrative.

[8] Ibid., 412.

[9] Ibid., 397–412.

[1] Ibid., 397.

[2] Ibid., 399.

[3] Ibid., 405.

we were not capiable of paying our purchase without selling of Land; which he had little Reason to mention had it bin true when it is more then probable when he marryed Madam Lidgett, he was not worth one hundred pounds in the world."[4] Madam Lidgett, we may assume, was a wealthy widow.

It is not wrong to say, as Munro did, that judgment was in By-field's favor: At least the arbitrators found that Saffin "had un-groundedly and very unchristianly reflected upon and recrimi-nated the said Major Walley, Captain Byfield and others the first purchasers of the said Mount Hope Neck," and ordered that Saffin make and deliver to Walley or Byfield "A Retraction and Acknowledgement."[5]

Saffin's "Retraction" was lengthy, and from first to last of this tenor:

Whereas I . . . am enjoyned by an award of arbitration to make a re-traction and acknowledgment in writing under my hand of supposed ill treatment, wrong and injury, offered to Major John Walley and Cap-tain Nathaniel Byfield, by sundry reflections in a manuscript . . . which was made in behalf of the inhabitants of said town, who for divers years have complained and groaned under the grievances therein mentioned.

Now, in order thereunto, I do hereby own and declare unto all man-kind, that if breach of promise to a person or people, in a matter of great concernment be no evil; if the chopping and changing of the town com-mons to the great prejudice of the town; obstructing and stopping up several ways leading to men's lands (some of them that have been enjoyed above thirty years without molestation or disturbance.) to be tolerable and not a nuisance strictly prohibited by the laws of our nation, then I am exceedingly to blame in charging with evil in so doing.[6]

Would "handsome" be the *mot juste?* Surviving documents make it clear that Saffin was not alone in his judgment. We cannot know how pervasive these sentiments were, but we do know that some

---

[4] Ibid., 408. Saffin was married three times, Baylies, *Historical Memoir*, II:IV, 62; Munro, *History of Bristol*, 88, although *not* "to a daughter of Colonel Byfield," as Washburn—tripping over some awkward footnoting in Baylies, I suspect—says. See Washburn, *Judicial History*, 270, Baylies, *Historical Memoir*, II:IV, 53.

[5] Massachusetts Archives, XL, 377.

[6] The Retraction is reprinted by both Baylies, *Historical Memoir*, II:IV, 58–61, and Munro, *History of Bristol*, 89–90; see also, Massachusetts Archives, XL, 320.

number of Bristol men considered Byfield and the others "cheats and worse" who failed to abide by their original agreement with Plymouth, who lured prospective settlers with promises never to be kept, who took the best for themselves without a thought for their fellows or their town.[7] Byfield's obituary, wherein it is said that having founded the town, "he lived their Head & Glory 'till the year 1724," must have sent not a few Bristol eyebrows skyward.

Understandably, Byfield felt it necessary to account for the unpleasant fact that a number of townsmen had subscribed to Saffin's Narrative. Some, no doubt, could be dismissed as "Saffin's creatures," but some others were less easily explained away. If we are to believe Nathaniel Byfield, Saffin persuaded "so maney as Seaven to signe his intollerable pampflett"[8] by a mix of more or less unsavory means, including:

(which is worst of all) he went to Richard Smith the fryday before he went to the generall court in February last; who for some months had bin confined with a consumption; & when I was there in January last was given over by most as past Recovery, and watched with every night; to this man in this condition he applyed himselfe to have him sett his hand to his booke, who refused many times and said he was a dyeing man and desired to dye in peace with all men; that he had no reason to signe to any thing that did reflect upon the first purchasers; nameing Major Walley, & myselfe, that he persisted in the denyall till he was spent whereupon Mr Saffin proceeded to Read a subpeony to him; in that condition upon which the poor man being thus constrained signed the Booke & Dyed on Satterday night the 29th day of February,[9]

It is reported by one Bristol historian that Byfield "acquired title to Hog Island, which Richard Smith had bought from King Philip, by

---

[7] Two statements in support of Saffin survive: (1) Nathaniel Reynolds, Massachusetts Archives, XL, 414, and (2) William Hoar, ibid., 414–419. Hoar asserts that he has "heard [Byfield and Walley] called cheats and worse terms to their faces at a Tavern in Bristol whilst they dwelt there. And at my house I have heard a near relation of Major Walley's call him a cheat and curse him, for he said that the Major had wheadled him out of a fair estate at Road Island to come & settle in Bristol, and there dealt as falsely with him in not performing what he pretended to him which promise was the very inducement to cause him to settle in Bristol."

[8] Ibid., 410.

[9] Ibid., 411.

seizing Smith and threatening him with death." Smith obviously just could not win.[1]

Independent assessment of the merits of this major controversy over the settling and management of Bristol is beyond me. Nor have I yet been able to discover its ultimate disposition; there are a number of separate strands which would have to be traced and woven together before we had a complete picture, and that is not the present task. What I do know is that the controversy continued for some years after the 1696 arbitration award in Byfield's favor. In particular, in 1702 one Bristol townsman petitioned the General Court for appointment of a committee "to make inquiry into the settlement of the said tract of land call'd Mount Hope, and how far the first purchasers have complied with their articles and agreements." The petitioner, John Wilkins, alleged that the town had not been settled, nor the land divided, according to the articles entered into by the first purchasers.[2] This action would have been something of an embarrassment to Byfield and Walley, for Wilkins was neither creature nor dupe of John Saffin, nor the victim of Saffin-applied duress. On the contrary, John Wilkins had himself been embroiled in a lengthy, involved battle with the Saffin faction, a battle which saw Wilkins hand-in-glove with Byfield and Walley. But the aspect of the Wilkins matter to which I wish to draw your attention at the moment is the involvement of the Massachusetts General Court. In fact, Wilkins turned to that body not only in 1702, when his complaint was against Walley and Byfield, but in 1696, when he stood with them against the Saffin bloc. To repeat, my interest in Nathaniel Byfield arose from the fact that in investigation of certain themes in the constitutional history of early Massachusetts, I tripped over the man at every step. One of those themes is the separation of powers, in particular, as central to that concept, the role of the General Court as an adjudicatory tribunal, the practice of bringing matters which we think of as "judicial" to the institution we tend to regard as a "legislature." Under the first royal charter, the General Court of Massachusetts functioned as an omnicompetent body, a *General*

---

[1] Howe, *Mount Hope*, 63–64.

[2] *Acts and Resolves*, VII, 351, 726; Massachusetts Archives, XLV (Lands, 1622–1726), 286–287; Court Records, VII (1699–1703), 324.

Court indeed.[3] Particularly to the point for present purposes, it was the "Supreame Court" of the colony. And even during the Provincial period, although not the active judicial body that it had been until 1686, the General Court did not go out of the business of adjudicating entirely. And the name Nathaniel Byfield keeps cropping up in this connection, as in so many. Here he is in the background of the two Wilkins matters; we shall find him a few years later a party in another action brought to the General Court.

The first Wilkins petition to the General Court is of special interest for a number of reasons, not least the probability that Byfield had a hand in its drafting. The background of the case is as follows:[4]

In 1695 certain Bristol selectmen whom Byfield chose to characterize as Saffin's creatures[5] levied a tax upon the inhabitants. Certain of those inhabitants, objecting to the tax as illegal, refused to pay it, upon which the selectmen seized some sheep. Wilkins then rescued the sheep and was for this brought before Quarter Sessions on a warrant issued by Saffin. Wilkins' request for a jury was denied, and he was convicted by the bench on which Saffin and others sat. Wilkins decided to turn to the General Court. Both the language and the strategy of his petition are extremely interesting. Although the petition complains of judicial proceedings in the regular courts, it employs the language of grievance, rather than of appeal: "Articles" are "laid against" the judges, and that not for error below but for deprivation of the liberties of an English subject. What Wilkins did was to invoke the grievance machinery rather than the appellate process.

Before the revocation of the first Massachusetts charter, the laws of the colony provided that any person who felt that justice had not

---

[3] This was of course true of most early colonial "legislatures," that of Plymouth, for example. As we have seen, the disputes which arose in Bristol, before the assimilation of Plymouth into Massachusetts in 1692, had been brought to the Plymouth General Court, where, by the way, trial was by jury, not ever the case in the Massachusetts General Court.

[4] The documents in the case are in Massachusetts Archives, XL, 352, 353, 354, 356, 357, 358, 359, 360, 361, 362, 363, 364, 365, 366, 367, 368, 369, 371, 372, 393, 414, 421, 422, 423; *Court Records*, VI, 460, 476, 477, 480. Just a few of the documents are printed in *Acts and Resolves*, VII, 110–111, 491–493.

[5] Massachusetts Archives, XL, 409. The selectmen were Nathaniel Blagrove (to whom we will return), John Rogers, and Thomas Walker.

been done him in the regular courts of first instance and appeal might turn to the General Court.[6] And people did turn to that institution in some numbers. Like Wilkins, they approached the court by way of petition, but these petitions were framed in the appellate mode, so to speak; the relief sought and, in meritorious cases granted, was reversal of the judgment below.

We do find the appellate-style petition in the Provincial period. But the revocation of the first charter had brought to a close the good old days when the General Court was unabashedly the "Supreame Court." Under the second charter it was at least doubtful whether the General Court was to enjoy any adjudicatory role, and fairly clear that royal government would frown upon the exercise of judicial power by the House of Representatives, the popular branch of the now properly called "legislature." Wilkins' strategy was brilliantly, whether or not deliberately, contrived to get around this hurdle. The appellate machinery at this level might be creaky, even moribund; it might be less and less promising to address petitions to the General Court as the ultimate *judicial* body, less and less likely that one would procure in that institution an overturning of judicial action below. But the grievance machinery is quite another matter. A "grievance" is of course properly addressed to the representatives of the people. And those representatives need not hesitate to act on a petition for redress of grievances. Nor, indeed, did they hesitate. The House, voting "that the denial of a jury to any of his majesty's subjects . . . is a grievance which ought to be animadverted on and redressed,"[7] heard the whole matter and ordered finally: "That the said justices present at the denial of a Jury, be admonished by His Honor the Lt. Governor in the face of this whole Court and shall repay the charge that the withinnamed Wilkins sustained by their Judgment, and reimburse him his Costs in prosecuting this Cause at this Court. . . ."[8]

---

[6] *The Colonial Laws of Massachusetts, Reprinted From the Edition of 1660 With the Supplements to 1686*, ed. William H. Whitmore (Boston, 1889), 41 ("The Body of Liberties," Sec. 36, 1641); 122 (*The Book of the General Lawes and Libertyes*, Sec. "appeal," 1660).

[7] Massachusetts Archives, XL, 352.

[8] Ibid., 353. See *Acts and Resolves*, VII, 493. Nonconcurred, Massachusetts Archives, XL, 353; *Acts and Resolves*, VII, 494.

In studying the history of separation of powers in Massachusetts, I have been impressed by the importance of the right to petition. The right to petition the representatives of the people for redress of grievances is close cousin to a right to appeal to those representatives for relief from injustice suffered in ordinary judicial tribunals. And what error cannot be viewed as injustice by a disappointed litigant! Thus, so long at least as the right to petition remains usefully ill-defined, it is the natural enemy of separation of powers. My conclusion from the records of adjudication in the General Court has been that the full implementation or flowering of the theory of separation of powers was retarded by the existence of an amorphous right to petition.

What we see in the Wilkins petition is the possibility of exploiting the ambiguity between the right to petition, in its classic political sense, and a right to appeal, in the classic judicial sense, to such an institution as the General Court. A subterfuge, in short, was available if needed, and it was needed more and more, as royal government made clear its disapproval of legislative justice. What we also see in the Wilkins petition is irony, for both the language and the strategy of the petition are irresistibly reminiscent of the Glorious Revolution and of the deep impulse to representative government which lay behind that Revolution. That impulse existed in Massachusetts as well as in England, and had from the start. And it was reinforced, in Massachusetts, by the events of 1688–1689 in England. And yet the kind of subterfuge we see in the Wilkins petition, the strategy of grievance, the language of liberties of an English subject, was necessary only because, in the era of the Glorious Revolution, Massachusetts saw not expansion, but restriction of representative government. The people may still have wished to have the General Court serve as Supreme Court, but it was not to be. From the perspective of popular government, the second charter was a disaster, a defeat from which the people were a long time recovering. They did recover, and adapt, this time. When, in the 1760's and 1770's, the people of Massachusetts believed that, once again, restrictions were being imposed upon popular government, they chose to rebel. The differences between the earlier and later periods are many and deep — although some would have chosen rebellion even in the first — but the Wilkins petition may serve to remind us of one unquestionably significant difference. "Liberties of an English subject," and similar phrases, although of course in use for a long time, were quite newly in vogue in the 1690's. As the eighteenth century wore on and imperial authorities chose to impress English ways upon the colonists, such language more and more became common coin. The language, as always, both reflected and reinforced attitudes, and by the 1770's those English subjects who resided in Massachusetts were in no mood to tolerate anything short of the full measure of what they chose to consider their liberties.

The arbitrators of 1696 ordered Saffin to "endeavor the suppressing and calling in any copy or copys" of the Narrative.[9] Saffin agreed to do this and to "cease all Animosityes . . . provided they allso will doe the like by them and live in Love and peace as Christians ought to doe."[1] The parties, however, seem not to have lived even "in peace," much less "in Love," for so much as ten minutes. In, I believe, late 1696, hostilities by way of legal process broke out.[2] By 1699 Byfield had been a party in *three* lawsuits with his Bristol foes: He recovered judgment against John Saffin and against Saffin ally Captain Nathaniel Reynolds; I do not know the nature of the litigation in either case.[3] The third suit was brought by the archetypical "Saffin creature," one Nathaniel Blagrove. From this time Blagrove becomes chief antagonist, and the Byfield-Blagrove feud occupies center stage, providing the dramatic interest for the period 1698–1710 which had been supplied by the Byfield-Saffin feud for the years from 1683 to 1696.

Blagrove was one of the selectmen who levied the rate so ob-

---

[9] Massachusetts Archives, XL, 377.

[1] Ibid., 421.

[2] In January 1696/7, an appeal was heard in the Superior Court, from a judgment in the Inferior Court, for Nathaniel Blagrove, executor of Nathan Hayman, against Jabez Goram, as tenant to Byfield; presumably the action was begun in late 1696. Records of the Superior Court of Judicature (Office of the Clerk, Supreme Judicial Court, Suffolk County, Boston) (1686–1700), 169. (Hereafter Superior Court Records.)

[3] Saffin and Reynolds appealed to the Superior Court, but withdrew their actions, "Mr. John Sparhawk of Bristol who was subpoenaed not being there." Byfield was awarded costs. Superior Court Records (1686–1700), 239. For Reynolds' deposition supporting Saffin in the controversy over the settling and management of Bristol, see Massachusetts Archives, XL, 414.

noxious to John Wilkins. More significantly, he married the widow of one Nathan Hayman and became administrator of Hayman's estate. Hayman was the man who bought Nathaniel Oliver's interest in Bristol shortly after the original purchase of Mount Hope, and he is listed in the earliest town meeting records as one of the four proprietors. Blagrove, in this representative capacity, was to play a major role in Byfield's life.

The beginnings are discernible in the great feud over affairs in Bristol. One of the charges levelled by Saffin and company was that Walley permitted the town's water mill, of which he was major owner, to lie idle, and thus brought suffering upon the townsfolk, who needed its services. In Byfield's response we see the involvement of Nathaniel Blagrove:

and now he [Saffin] quotes Mr. Blagrove to be an owner of the said mill; who then had nothing to doe with Capt Nathan Haymans estate for he tooke Administration But in February last & how farr an Administrator? may acte in such affaires I leave to the Gentlemen that understand the law. . . .[4]

Byfield's modest disclaimer of legal expertise sufficient to justify comment on the duties of an administrator is heavy-handedly ironic. Given the identity of the administrator concerned, and later events, there is real irony here.

At this moment, that is, May 1696, quite another dispute was ripening between Byfield and Hayman's administrator.[5] Two years later it was in the courts. In 1698, in his capacity as Hayman's administrator, Blagrove sued Byfield on a mortgage given by Byfield to Hayman on 27 July 1687, to secure a debt of £310. The mortgage set out a schedule of payment, viz.:

£100 on 20 November 1688
£100 on 20 November 1689
£110 on 20 November 1690.

[4] Ibid., XL, 406–407.

[5] The papers in this case, *Blagrove, Administrator of the Estate of Nathan Hayman v. Byfield*, are at:
  Suffolk Files, #4038 (17 papers, f. 129–146).
  Suffolk Files, #162489.
  Suffolk Files, #162509.
Superior Court Records (1686–1700), 169, 239, 242–245, 248–249.

According to Byfield, when he offered Hayman the first £100 on 20 November 1688, Hayman would take no more than £20, saying that he would accept the £80 remaining when he and Byfield met, as they were expecting to do, in Boston sometime later. There is no explanation offered for this bizarre behavior, but, so far as I can tell, no challenge to Byfield's account of it. In any case, Hayman and Byfield were fated never to meet in Boston; Hayman died on 27 July 1689, the second anniversary of his having taken the mortgage from Byfield, though I do not suppose that that is what killed him. There then appears to have been a lull, a period of some years during which Byfield stood pat. As he later explained, he did not come forward with the £80 remainder of the first payment, or indeed with the second and third payments as they came due, because there was nobody legally capable of receiving them. Hayman's children were all minors; he had died intestate and no administrator was appointed for several years. When the eldest Hayman child, Nathan, Jr., reached his majority, Byfield tendered him the full amount owing, but he refused it. Then, when Blagrove took administration of the estate on his marriage to the widow, in 1695 or 1696, Byfield made the same tender to him; Blagrove, too, refused the money.

There is of course nothing bizarre about *these* refusals to accept payment. Blagrove and young Hayman were after bigger game. They were in a position to claim that Byfield was in default, thus to foreclose and force a forfeiture of the mortgaged land, worth far more than a few hundred pounds. Blagrove, bringing suit in the Superior Court in 1698, was awarded judgment. The Superior Court evidently found Byfield in default. But why did that mean forfeiture? Was there no equity of redemption in Massachusetts in the eighteenth century? Apparently there was, for, some months after Blagrove's victory in the Superior Court, Byfield returned to that Court with a bill in equity begging to be allowed the equity of redemption, and succeeded. Blagrove sought a review of this decision, but the review did not change matters, and in the end Blagrove was compelled to accept Byfield's payment of the underlying obligation, and to surrender all claim to the land. Now the mystery must be why, if the Superior Court was going to allow Byfield to redeem the land, it did not do so in the first place. Why a judgment of forfeiture and then, months later, a judgment of no forfeiture? The answer is *not* that common law and equity were administered in separate courts. There was no Court of Chancery in Massachusetts, and such equitable relief as might be obtained was available in the common law courts. Nor, in the ordinary course, did a litigant seeking such relief as the equity of redemption, or chancering of a penal bond, have to exhibit a separate bill in equity; the point of equity would be decided by the bench immediately after the decision of the common law issue, and without additional process. But here we have judgment of forfeiture in the Superior Court, with the land awarded to the mortgagee, and then a separate bill in equity brought later in the same Court. What happened? Did Byfield forget about the equity of redemption for a few months?

What happened goes far to explain behavior in years to come, on the part of Nathaniel Byfield, which is otherwise mystifying in the extreme. As Byfield put it:

the said Nathaniel Blagrove, having married the widdow, and having obtained the Administration of the estate of the said Nathan Hayman the elder and designing to defraud and defeat your Complainant of the Estate so mortgaged as aforesaid, well knowing the same to be of far greater value than the Debt or money due thereon *and that there was then no Court of Equity to relieve your Complainant against the Strict Rules and Severity of the Common-Law* has commenced several actions and suites. . . .[6]

When Byfield says "there was then no Court of Equity," he does not refer merely to lack of a separate court, but to absolute unavailability of equitable relief of any kind, in any court, for a defaulting mortgagor. In the history of Massachusetts from the 1640's to the Revolution, equitable relief from penalties and forfeitures was available to debtors in default on bonds and mortgages at every moment, at all times, *except for one brief period*. While the early Massachusetts attitude toward equity in the large is somewhat cloudy, there is no doubt whatever about this one aspect of equity; this society, as Colony *and* Province, expressed its abhorrence of pen-

[6] Suffolk Files #4038, 6th paper.

alties and forfeitures and provided machinery for the avoidance thereof.[7] There was, nevertheless, a period during which the availability of equitable relief for mortgagors was uncertain, at best. The confusion of the inter-charter period and of the first years under the Province charter took its toll. From 1686 to 1698 first the President, then the Governor and Council, exercised equity powers. Thus relief from penalties and forfeitures was available, but considerably more difficult to procure than it had been before revocation of the first charter, when the court that heard the common law action was empowered to give such relief on the spot. The attempt to revest this power in the common law courts under the Province charter was hampered and delayed by successive royal disallowances.[8] We can detect the mischievous consequence for mortgagors of all this in the law which was enacted 10 December 1698, to remedy the mischief: By "An Act for Hearing and Determining of Cases in Equity," the General Court accomplished two things:

1) It provided prospectively that defaulting mortgagors were to be allowed to redeem their land, and

2) It provided that in any case tried *since April, 1686,* wherein a mortgagee, recovering an estate, entered into or obtained possession, the party to whom the right of redemption belonged might bring suit, by 10 December 1701, in the Superior Court or in an Inferior Court of Common Pleas. The Court, in such an action, was instructed to enter judgment agreeable to equity and good conscience, that is, in the usual case to allow the equity of redemption, and the mortgagee was required to take tender of the amount owing and to execute a deed of release and quit-claim.[9]

It would surprise me not at all to learn that Nathaniel Byfield engineered the passage of this act. It was certainly, for him, in the nick of time. At the time that Blagrove brought his action, default

---

[7] Massachusetts Records, II (1642–1649), 21 (1642); *Acts and Resolves,* I, 75, 144–145, 285, 356–357, 373.

[8] Horace Gray, "Note," Josiah Quincy, Jr., *Reports of Cases Argued and Adjudged in the Superior Court of Judicature of the Province of Massachusetts Bay between 1716 and 1722,* ed. Samuel M. Quincy (Boston, 1865).

[9] *Acts and Resolves,* I, 356–357.

having been found, the mortgagee might take the land; and indeed Blagrove did enter into possession of the mortgaged land. Then came this remarkably convenient statute, and redemption for Byfield—or at least for his land.

But the significant fact about this enactment is that it did remedy a mischief, or, more precisely, that it eliminated something perceived as mischievous. The unavailability of the equity of redemption was anomalous in this society, contrary to the prevailing sense of justice. Equity and good conscience demanded that a mortgagor in default be allowed to redeem his property; that much was, and had been from the beginning, accepted. Thus in equity and good conscience Blagrove should have accepted Byfield's payment of the underlying obligation. From Byfield's perspective, Blagrove's behavior was villainous, an unconscionable attempt to take improper advantage of accidental circumstances to impose the full rigor of the common law. Byfield may be said to have been the victor in this matter, since he did not contest the underlying debt, and the only real issue was forfeiture. But victory could only have deepened his conviction of Blagrove's villainy, by confirming the unconscionability of his actions. The upshot was that victory no less than defeat left Byfield determined to "get" Blagrove. Two could play at the game of taking full advantage of the rigor of the common law, of blocking any equitable softening thereof. Byfield surely lay in wait for his opportunity; he may, indeed, have manufactured it. In any event, he had to wait only until 23 October 1702, when he was appointed Judge of Probate for Bristol County.

Judicial appointments in the Province of Massachusetts Bay were in the control of the Governor, with the advice and consent of the Council. The Governor, newly appointed in 1702, was Joseph Dudley. Byfield and Dudley were, as we have seen, in alliance at this period, with Byfield a supporter of Dudley for the governorship. Dudley in turn boosted Byfield for the vice-admiralty and appointed him to the Court of Common Pleas and, of special interest to us just now, Judge of Probate, Bristol. While Byfield loved all office and could never feel a surfeit of appointments, I cannot but feel that he yearned for this one particularly. For in this office he succeeded our friend John Saffin and was now in a position to take revenge on that worthy as well as on Blagrove. We have come to what I will call *the affair Blagrove*.[1]

Blagrove's account of his administration of Hayman's estate had been allowed by Saffin in June 1702. One of the six Hayman children, Mary, claimed that Blagrove had failed to settle on her the amount to which she was entitled, and in January 1704/5 she petitioned the new Probate Judge—Byfield—for an order directing Blagrove to settle her portion of the estate on her. On 17 March 1704/5 Byfield issued an order in which he noted that distribution to Mary "cannot be done until you have rendered an account of your administration. . . ." He ordered Blagrove to appear before him on 24 March and render such an account. Blagrove had, of course, accounted once, before Saffin, but when he appeared on 24 March, Byfield specified the respect in which he found the first account, allowed by Saffin, to be deficient: viz, that it failed to account for proceeds and improvement of the estate since Hayman's death, consisting, apparently, of interest (£1010), rents and profits of houses and lands, and earnings and produce of vessels. Blagrove, given time to prepare his answer, was ordered to reappear before Byfield on 7 May 1705.

Correspondence between Blagrove and William Brattle, husband of Elizabeth, another Hayman daughter, thus Mary's brother-in-law, confirms that as of March 1704/5 Blagrove had not distributed Mary's portion to her, and more than suggests that he would have some difficulty coming up with the full amount immediately. Blagrove complains of Mary's "snappish" (?) manner toward him, and of her behavior in the whole matter, but he does not claim to have paid her what was due. Brattle, answering Blagrove, quotes Mary as saying "that whenever she asked you for her money you made her

---

[1] The documents in the case are:

Suffolk Files #7796 (14 papers, f. 110–119).

Superior Court Records (1700–1714), 187–188.

Council Records:

IV (1703–1708), 76, 154, 403–404, 406, 490, 410, 411, 428–431, 443, 447, 449, 533–534.

V (1708–1712), 132, 219–220, 234–236, 241–242, 243.

VII (1723–1727), 267.

Massachusetts Archives, XL, 884, 887–891.

Some of the documents, with narrative and analysis will be found in *Acts and Resolves*, VIII (*Resolves, 1703–1707*), 206–207, 650–657.

cry. . . ." Brattle notes also that he has retained Paul Dudley, well-known lawyer and son of the Governor, "to serve in the thing [for Mary] if there should be any need."

Blagrove did not appear before Byfield in May, and, so far as I can tell, did nothing. Byfield, of his own motion, brought an action of debt on the administration bond, in the Inferior Court of Common Pleas for Bristol, for the amount of the bond, £6,000; this was, of course, a penal bond, and the £6,000 was the penalty rather than the debt. The obligation of the bond was to John Saffin or his successor in the office of Probate. Byfield assigned as breach of the bond that Blagrove had not rendered an account according to law; Blagrove entered a number of pleas in abatement *and* a plea of performance of the condition, that is, that he had not breached.

The case was heard by jury, and a verdict returned for the plaintiff for £6,000 and costs. The Court, finding against Blagrove on the pleas in abatement, entered judgment for that amount. Blagrove appealed to the Superior Court of Judicature, on which appeal, after six pleas in abatement, he reached the merits, as follows:

that he hath allready accounted for his administracon &c: to John Saffin Esqr, . . . who Examind allowed and approved of the said account and order'd the same to be registred as of record appears, and the law of the Province fol: 6: directs that any person aggrieved at any sentence order &c. may have an appeal to the Governor & Council[2]

To which Paul Dudley, now attorney for Byfield, answered, in part:

. . . 2: whatever the Judge of probate will Doe or have an administrator to doe yet the Administrator must look to it that he administer according to law and If he dos not t'will not Exscuse him or his Bond to say that what he did was by the opinion & Consent of the Judge of probate &—for the Judge gives no security for his office But the Administrator must give Bond : & 3. the Common law is not to be Controwled By the proceedings of the Court of Probate of wills &c[3]

What you must note here is Blagrove's attempt to get this matter before the Governor and Council. That body was invested by the Province charter with jurisdiction over Probate;[4] by statute it sat

[2] Suffolk Files #7796, 6th paper.
[3] Suffolk Files #7796, 7th paper.
[4] *Acts and Resolves*, I, 15.

only on appeal from rulings of the County Probate judges.[5] Bla-grove, aware that only a common law action of debt on the bond could result in enforcement of the penalty, insisted that the proper procedure here was appeal, by anyone aggrieved by Saffin's ruling — that is, his allowance of Blagrove's account — to the Governor and Council. Dudley's response was a defense of common-law jurisdic-tion, a defense, really, of the supremacy of the common law, which "is not to be Controwled by the proceedings of the Court of Probate of wills. . . ."

It is not clear from surviving documents whether any Hayman children were behind the move for a second account by Blagrove. As Samuel Sewall caustically pointed out to Byfield, four of the Hay-man children were satisfied with Blagrove's administration of the estate.[6] And Mary's original complaint was simply that Blagrove had failed to distribute her portion to her, not that he had im-properly accounted, not, that is, that her portion was actually greater than, by Blagrove's reckoning, it appeared to be.[7] Perhaps it was Paul Dudley, acting first for Mary, then for Byfield, who thought of the new strategy; or perhaps it was Nathaniel Byfield. In any event, a splendid technique of harassment had been hit upon.

The case went to the Superior Court jury, who brought in a con-firmation of the judgment below; the bench, evidently ruling against Blagrove on the pleas in abatement, entered judgment for Byfield. Blagrove, now under the crushing burden of a judgment for £6,000, plus costs, moved that the bond "be Chancered down to Its Just debt & damage." The Superior Court denied this motion, and, on 23 October 1706, issued execution for the full penalty. The winning argument on the point of equity appears to have been that the Court

---

[5] *Acts and Resolves*, I, 43–45, 251–252, 430–431.

[6] "Your Apearance for Orphans is made something dim, by reason that Four of the Six, by Instrument under their hands, disavowed the Action; and declard them-selvs very well satisfied with the Management of Mr. Nathanl Blagrove their Father-in-Law." Sewall to Byfield, *Acts and Resolves*, VIII, 656, citing Sewall Letter Book, I, 318. The instruments referred to are in Suffolk Files #7796. See also Council Records, V, 132 (in November 1709, the Council heard a complaint by Nathan and Grace Hayman against Byfield's division of the real estate, and awarded £12 to Nathan, £30 to Grace).

[7] Although by May 1707 both Mary and her sister Elizabeth Brattle appear to have had complaints about the substance of the accounting, Council Records, IV (1703–1708), 403–404, 406, 409, 410, 411, 429–431.

had no power to chancer a bond to "the just debt and damages" but only to a sum certain; what we have here, it seems, is the distinction between the money bond and the performance bond. In the former, the bond secures an obligation to pay a sum certain, a debt. Thus, when equity stepped in to chancer the bond, it was in no doubt of the amount to which the bond was to be chancered. However, in the case of a bond securing some performance other than payment of a debt — building a house or administering a decedent's estate — a court of equity had no way to determine the sum to which the bond might be chancered and no recourse but to enforce the penalty.

Now in England by Lord Nottingham's time (in the mid 1670's) this difficulty had been largely obviated; what chancery did, in the case of the performance bond, was simply to relieve against the penalty on condition that the defaulting party pay damages, *to be assessed by a jury*, either on issue (*quantum damnificatus*) joined in an action on the case, or on writ in covenant for damages.[8] There might, of course, still be cases in which damages were impossible of ascertainment; there always are such cases, and recovery in any contract action may be defeated, or severely limited, by the incalculability of damages. But in most cases a jury will be able to assess damages, to arrive at a more-or-less compensatory figure. And, by the latter part of the seventeenth century, where compensation was possible, equity would intervene to prevent the imposition of a penalty. As a result, in England by Lord Nottingham's time (and in his words) "a penal bond to secure the performance of covenants is not much better security than a mere covenant, as equity now orders the matter." This was, *a fortiori*, true of the penal bond to secure payment of a debt.

For the latter, that is the money bond, by the mid 1670's relief against penalties might be had in the *common law* courts; defendant was granted a perpetual imparlance unless the plaintiff would accept a tender of principal, interest, and costs. Apparently the common law did not go so far as to relieve against penalties on a performance

---

[8] The account in the text of the English background is taken from A. W. B. Simpson, *A History of the Common Law of Contract: The Rise of the Action of Assumpsit* (Oxford, 1975), 120–122, and *Lord Nottingham's "Manual of Chancery and Practice" and "Prolegomena of Chancery and Equity,"* ed. D. E. C. Yale (Cambridge, 1965), 275.

bond, but in 1696–1697 a statute stepped in to do the job: It was enacted that after plaintiff in such a case alleged the breach, or breaches, the jury was to assess the damages for each breach; judgment might be entered for the whole penalty, but on payment of the damages found by the jury and costs the action was to be stayed (4 and 5 Anne, c. 3). An act of 1705 addressed the money bond penalty problem, allowing the court to discharge an obligor who paid principal, interest, and costs (8 and 9 Will. III, c. 11).

As we have seen, the common law courts in Massachusetts did enjoy the power to chancer penal bonds, and this was a power exercised regularly, but I do not know whether it was done in the case of performance bonds. And in any event, the *administration* bond adds a new dimension and an additional obstacle. In the ordinary performance bond, there would seem to be no reason why the court might not send the damage issue, by one mechanism or another, to the jury. But in the case of the administration bond such a course might well involve serious encroachment upon the jurisdiction of the Probate Courts. There might be, and indeed there was in Massachusetts, a case in which all that was necessary for the calculation of damages had been done in Probate: that is to say, what was left to be done was mechanical.[9] But Blagrove's refusal to account blocked such a determination by Byfield, and I suspect that the Superior Court was loathe to hand over to a common law jury that which was properly a matter for a court of probate. On this point, Blagrove did try to take advantage of the fact that Byfield had brought suit before a jury, arguing that either damages were readily ascertainable, the issue "having pass'ed the consideration of the Jury," or if they were not, it was only because the loss had not yet occurred. If the former, chancering of the bond was appropriate; if the latter, the suit was premature. Nevertheless, and despite Blagrove's cry that if administration bonds were not to be chancered, few would care to take on the duties of an administrator, the Superior Court, "of the opinion that the Bond would not Admitt of a Chancery," denied the motion.[1]

Ah! sweet revenge. Byfield seems to have gone Blagrove one

[9] *Addington v. Griggs*, described in *Acts and Resolves*, VIII, 657.
[1] Suffolk Files #7796, 6th paper.

better, trapping him in the jaws of the common law in a fully functioning system, where such equitable relief as the Provincial lawmakers thought appropriate was available, without the kind of undue, adventitious advantage Blagrove had earlier attempted to capitalize on. But appearances here may be deceptive. It is true that Byfield did not have the advantage that Blagrove had of legal suspension of equity; but Byfield may have had his own way of suspending the rules. While it is possible that the Superior Court's refusal to chancer the bond was fairly and squarely based on a rule that performance, or at least administration, bonds cannot be chancered, it really seems to have been a highly partial, improperly based ruling in Byfield's favor by Byfield's friends. Three judges sat on the Superior Court in this case: Byfield's great friend, John Walley, Byfield's friend and nephew-in-law to be, John Leverett,[2] and Samuel Sewall. Walley and Leverett voted to let the penalty stand. Sewall thought it should be chancered. Thus one suspects that the theoretical "availability" of equitable relief to Blagrove was illusory, that even if "the rules" supported chancering of administration bonds, as a practical matter Blagrove was not more likely to have his bond chancered than Byfield had been to obtain the equity of redemption in 1698 from courts which were not empowered to grant it. The suspicion of partiality must deepen on discovery that opinion in Massachusetts overwhelmingly supported the chancering of administration bonds. The House of Representatives was prepared to adopt the rule either judicially or legislatively; the Council believed it to be law.[3] Byfield and his friends stood alone.

Byfield, not one to overlook a slight, took offense at Sewall's conduct of the case, and wrote to him in this vein:

by all which it seems very apparent that the said Admin is guilty of Perjury: and yet nothing was said to him in Court, of his having done amiss:

---

[2] There are two interesting 1714 letters to John Leverett at the Massachusetts Historical Society. Byfield apologizes for not going to see Leverett in Cambridge while he was in Boston: "... I understood by a Friend of yours, that you were somewhat Timorus [?], and I being a neggatived person, and observed in all my motions, I was afraid my going might prove a disservice ...," Nathaniel Byfield to John Leverett, 1714, Folio XI-M, Saltonstall Papers, Massachusetts Historical Society.

[3] See Sewall on this point, *Acts and Resolves*, VIII, 657.

but my self (who as Judge of the Probat of Wills &c. in the behalf of Orphans, and in pursuance of the Law, and my Oath, appeared there to Answer the Apeal) was very much discountenanced by your Hon, to my great dissatisfaction,'[4]

What we see from Sewall's answering letter, in which he defends himself against this "groundless and injurious charge," is the intensity and implacability of Byfield's hatred of Blagrove, and his desire not merely to win the case but to destroy his adversary:

As to not speaking to Mr. Blagrove of his Perjury, he was not in Court to such purpose. You might have pursud him Criminally, if you had pleasd, But he was in Court as an Apellant in a Civil Action, to be Tried by a Jury; . . . . And I am of the Opinion, it was no Extravagant favour granted Mr. Blagrove, who is now Representative for Bristol that he was admitted to speak a few words to clear his Credit. Which proceeded not from the Court, but his almost irresistible Importunity. If an Indictment of Forgery has been found against him by the Grand Jury; yet Mr. Brattle's Letter ought not to have been read once, much less left upon File; it containing only Hearsay, and insinuating a very hainous Crime. Madam Brattle should have been present face to face. And therefore it seemd unreasonable to have the Letter read over agen whenas no Release was produced in Court; nor that Sum chargd in the Account.[5]

Equity could not, or would not, relieve Blagrove from the rigor of the common law; did he have no option then but to hand £6000 (plus) over to Byfield? It might seem that two jury trials of the issues of fact, consideration by two separate benches of the issues of law, and a hearing of the point of equity would qualify as due and full process, one's day in court, and then some. But Blagrove's tenacity was not inferior to that of his adversary; he persevered, and

---

[4] *Acts and Resolves,* VIII, 656.

[5] Ibid. Blagrove's petition to the General Court makes the same point:
    And May it Please this Hononrd Court
    Such is the hast & Severity of yor Petitionrs Enemys, that without any regard to Equall Justice, or to Yor Petitionrs being a Member of the Honourble House of represents, Execution is already actually taken Out against him, for the whole 6000£. Even while the Houss was sitting, thereby to Overawe, & keep him in Continuall dread, to Augmt & put him to unreasonable, & unnecessary charges (the first Step, at least is 40li or 50li fees to ye Sheriff) so that no less can be aim'd at or Intended then his utter ruin

for almost three more years the affair dragged on, occupying the time and attention of the Province's lawmakers and executive officials. Blagrove turned first to the General Court; he petitioned that body in November 1706, reciting his grievances and praying that "the Law mentioned (as he Humbly conceives) being sufficient to relieve him; the writt of Execution may forthwith be superceded, and the Judges of the Superiour Court be Ordered at their Next sitting to Chauncer the said Bond to the Just debt and damages, before another Execution issue; or that some other Effectual Care be taken without delay That Your Petitioner may be Judged according to the rules of Equity & good Conscience, and not by the Utmost rigour and Severity of the Common Law."[6]

The House of Representatives acted favorably on the petition, and sent to the Council, for concurrence, an order superseding the execution and commanding the Judges of the Superior Court to chancer the bond.[7] The Council, in its capacity as upper house of the legislature, non-concurred,[8] and the House tried first one, and then another, slightly different tack, the Council again refusing to go along.[9] Agreement was finally reached on 2 December 1706 on an order that execution be suspended to 31 May 1707, and that Blagrove meanwhile account to Byfield. Should Byfield approve the account, he was to acknowledge satisfaction of the judgment for £6,000. Should Byfield refuse to allow the account, Blagrove was to appeal to the Governor and Council and on their settlement of the case, which was to operate as a discharge of the judgment, Byfield was to acknowledge satisfaction.[1]

The Blagrove affair brings us yet again to the subject of adjudication by the General Court; as an instance of legislative adjudication, it was unique. The particular twist was that the matter involved Probate. As we have seen, anyone aggrieved by an order of a Judge

---

[6] Massachusetts Archives, XL, 890.

[7] Ibid., 891.

[8] Court Records, VIII (1703–1709), 254, 260.

[9] The House wanted to suspend judgment pending enactment of a law for the chancering of administration bonds, Massachusetts Archives, XL, 889, but the Council thought "the Law already Sufficient in that respect," Court Records, VIII, 265. See also Massachusetts Archives, XL, 888, 889.

[1] *Acts and Resolves,* VIII, 206–207.

of Probate might appeal to the Governor and Council — but such an order there must be! Blagrove had failed earlier to force his adversaries to take that route; now he himself could not take it, for he was aggrieved not by an order of a Judge of Probate, but by the verdict of a common law jury and the ruling of a common law court on a motion for equitable relief. Blagrove, looking upward from a final ruling of the Superior Court, thus had to turn to *the General Court*, not to the Governor and Council in its executive capacity. And, while the Governor and Council, along with, it appears, everybody but Byfield and friends, were in sympathy with Blagrove, the Governor and Council were not very happy about adjudication by the General Court — that is to say, they did not, by and large, approve of the interference of the lower, popular branch in the administration of justice.[2] And the first order which the House of Representatives sent up for concurrence was at the extreme of such interference. There were instances in which the General Court intervened in judicial matters without actually adjudicating.[3] But in ordering the Superior Court to chancer the bond, the House was certainly adjudicating. The Council's reluctance to go along with this is exactly what, having studied the history of this subject, I would expect. Now consider the order that the Council did find acceptable. Indeed it originated as a Council order and went down to the House for concurrence. Blagrove was to account to Byfield, who might either

(1) approve the account and acknowledge satisfaction of the judgment for £6,000, thus bringing the dispute to an end, or
(2) refuse to allow the account, thus issuing an order in Probate from which the aggrieved party could appeal to the Governor and Council.

This was, from the Council's perspective, a happy solution, since it promised to relieve Blagrove without involving the Council in approval of adjudication by the lower house. But, as perhaps you have by now realized, there was a catch. As we follow the story to its conclusion, we see that, in the end, whatever the desires, even commands, of the Council, Byfield's cooperation was essential. And

[2] This statement is based on incomplete but not inconsiderable study of the subject.

[3] That is, where, by lifting some bar (e.g., statute of limitations), it merely enabled a litigant to proceed in the regular courts.

Byfield was unlikely to cooperate in a scheme to save the man he had determined to destroy.

Let us see what actually happened. Blagrove did account; when, predictably, Byfield refused to allow the account, Blagrove appealed to Governor and Council. The matter was considered fully, at numerous Council meetings in May and June 1707, all interested parties being heard. The Council, taking into consideration certain items that they felt Blagrove should have accounted for, and on the other hand, outlays for which he should receive credit, made the necessary calculations and appropriate adjustment and arrived at a sum owed the estate; they ordered Blagrove to distribute that amount to Hayman's children. Blagrove was also to pay Byfield £5.6.0 for his own expenses. Byfield, for his part, was ordered to discharge the £6,000 judgment, and to acknowledge satisfaction thereof in writing upon Blagrove's compliance with the conciliar directive. Blagrove did as he was told. But Byfield dug his heels in; he would neither accept the £5.6.0 from Blagrove nor acknowledge satisfaction of the £6,000 judgment. And for good measure he levied execution on Blagrove's land. Now what?

On 14 June the Council ordered that a letter be sent to Byfield "to acquaint him of the just resentment of the Board of his refusal to observe and perform the said Decree and Order of the Supream Ordinary, and that they expect and require him forwith to pay due observance thereto as he ought without further excuse or delay."[4] On 23 June Byfield, who happened to be present before the Council, asked to be heard on the Blagrove matter. He was heard, as was Blagrove. We get the flavor of the proceedings from this item, entered in the Council Records on the following day:

Upon consideration of the unmannerly & rude behaviour of Nathaniel Byfield, Esquire, yesterday to his Excellency the Governor & the Board & his peremtory refusal to obey their order to him directed as Judge of Probate

Advised that his Excy be desired to suspend the said Nathaniel Byfield Esquire from the exercise of those civil offices that he holds under this Government.[5]

[4] Council Records, v (1708–1712), 235–236.
[5] Council Records, v, 243.

Byfield went off the Court of Common Pleas, and of Probate. But he was still Judge of Admiralty; indeed, his presence in the Council Chamber on 23 June was for the purpose of presenting the Queen's Commission for that post.[6] One could wish one had been there, too, to see Byfield taking the oath of office as Judge of Admiralty, and then, from this height, turning the full measure of his arrogant scorn on the Governor and Council for their attempt to get him to cease his harassment of Blagrove.

The Blagrove affair thus brings us to another theme in the constitutional history of Massachusetts, that is, the independence of the judiciary. Byfield was removed from office for refusing to obey an order of Council. The question would be whether this removal is appropriately to be considered, in the jargon of judicial independence, "arbitrary," as opposed to "for cause," and thus accounted an instance of executive interference with judicial independence. There were Council orders and Council orders; some no judge would be obliged to heed, others would be binding. In the Land Bank controversy of the 1740's, the Governor and Council issued an order to all judges that they refuse to receive Land Bank bills in judicial proceedings. A number of justices of the peace, refusing to obey, were removed from office. But, as one of them hotly insisted, surely this was an arbitrary removal, for executive proclamation of this sort was no law that the judges must follow.[7] Similarly, in 1772, Joseph Greenleaf was removed from the office of J.P. for ignoring a Council order to appear before that body and to answer charges laid against him. In this case, since the Governor and Council did have the power to remove judicial officers, it would seem that Greenleaf's refusal to appear constituted cause for removal—unless perhaps, as Greenleaf argued, he was not obliged to obey because there was no complaint laid against him and certified in a legal manner by Governor and Council, for anything done in his official capacity contrary to duty or injurious to the subject.[8] Byfield's case is, however, *sui*

[6] Council Records, v, 241–242.

[7] On the Land Bank dismissals, see Council Records, X (1735–1742), 463, 466, 476, 471, 473, 475, 479, 506, 508, 519.

[8] See, *Boston Gazette*, 16 December 1771, 6 January 1772, 13 January 1772; *Massachusetts Gazette*, 2 January 1772. The Greenleaf case was first brought to my attention by Catherine Menand.

generis, for Byfield was in the position of a lower court judge refusing to obey an order of the higher court issued in the exercise of its appellate jurisdiction, an order of "the Supream Ordinary." A removal for this would not appear to be arbitrary, or, therefore, in violation of the independence of the judiciary. Or would it? Obviously this is a complex issue.

No records have been discovered which reveal the final disposition of Byfield's action on the administration bond; we are left assuming that Blagrove did, after all, have to pay the £6,000. However, it should be stated that, despite appearances, it cannot be that Byfield was out to pocket a large sum of money to which he was not, on any conceivable respectable theory, entitled. The disposition of the sum awarded, the £6,000, was certainly a problem, and one that Blagrove made argumentative use of:

That Judgment could not in the case at barr be Enter'd up for more than was due; for that the children Could only claime their severall equal parts of their fathers Estate, and the Judge could distribute no more, that as for the Judge himself he neither had, nor ought to pttend to any benefitt by ye penalty, who was but the medium or Instrumt of the suit, what then was to be done with the surplus, or exorbitant part of this penal 6000£? [9]

What, indeed? But I cannot think that even Byfield thought it should go to Byfield, save in trust for the Hayman children. Then again, who knows what evil lurks in the hearts of men?

Byfield's story features repeated instances of the use of law by persons whose aim it was not so much to settle a particular dispute as to injure an enemy. But unless this impurity of motivation itself taints the process, only when we get to the Byfield-Blagrove matters, do we begin to think we may have to do with abuse, rather than use, of law. The question that the Byfield-Blagrove feud raises, in this context, is whether it may be an abuse, or perversion, of law merely to insist on its benefit. Since we begin, appropriately enough, with mortgage foreclosure, consider the classic villain of the screen serial as, twirling his mustaches, he forecloses on the widow and orphans: a moral leper to be sure, but surely not an abuser of the law. When society, through its law, approves the morally outrageous, then it is no perversion of the law to take advantage of it.

[9] Massachusetts Archives, XL, 890.

Blagrove's case is perhaps more doubtful, since, but for accidental circumstances, the law he took advantage of would not have been the law. What he attempted to do was condemned by society not only through moral consensus, but through law, or it had been, before external forces threw the world out of joint, and it would be again as soon as the society, still leaping hurdles placed by those same external forces, could put the world right. Does one abuse the law of the society of which one is a member by seeking the law's benefit at a moment when one knows the law to be the very opposite of that which the society thinks the law should be?

In the particulars, the Blagrove-Byfield mortgage situation was aberrational in the extreme; more abstractly, however, it is very like the situation arising every day in a system which features the institutional as well as theoretical separation of law and equity. And it points up just how bizarre the separation of law and equity is. The founders of the Bay Colony integrated law and equity, that is, granted equitable power to the judges of the common law courts. Explanations of this innovation tend to point us rather vaguely in the direction of simplification (at times with overtones of "simple" as in "primitive," or, occasionally, "simpleton"). That is not wrong, and there were other, prudential reasons for the move.[1] But I would suggest that the real question is why on earth any people who had experience with the separation of law and equity, finding themselves with the opportunity to integrate them, would not do so. Separation is understandable historically, but is it something one would adopt full-blown if one were creating a legal system from the ground up? Practical considerations aside, who would deliberately institute a system in which something called "the law" is authoritatively declared inequitable and unconscionable?

Among other things, the separation of law and equity must teach curious lessons; how can it fail, for a start, to engender some contempt for a "law" which, in its enforcement of rights and redress of wrongs, is understood to have no interest in right and wrong? I would like to suggest that this effect is a function of the transformation of equity from a means of affording relief where general rules

[1] That is, for *not* setting up a separate Court of Chancery, arguably outside the powers granted by the original royal charter and certain to be frowned upon by imperial authority.

work special hardship in particular cases, to a system of general rules. All people may understand the need for generality in law; considerations not only of efficiency but of fairness exert pressure in that direction. Tensions with the concern for justice in the hardship case are inevitable, but acceptable, and equitable relief in such cases will not bring the law into disrepute. Imperfect it may be, but some imperfection is inevitable when legitimate goals compete. Once equity has, however, developed rules no less general — or fixed and determinate — than those of "the law," distinguished from the latter *only* by the essential fairness of the equitable rules, we have quite another situation. We now have, whatever we call them, two systems of law side by side, one good, one bad. Equity is no longer merely saying that, for example, a given litigant whose illness kept him from appearing in court may have another chance; it is saying that mortgagors whom "the law" has found in default may redeem their land by payment within a certain time of the underlying obligation. If that is a good thing to say, why does the law not say it? If it is a good rule, why is it not a rule of law? And what do we think of a law that pronounces a forfeiture of the land?

The separation of law and equity has as well some potential for affecting negatively the relations between parties to a lawsuit. It is desirable that a legal system go beyond the classic, but minimal, goals of peace-keeping and resolution of particular controversies, that it operate if possible to dissipate or at least to reduce the tensions and animosities which threaten the peace and produce controversies. If law cannot guarantee that people will "Live in Love ... as Christians ought to doe," it might play a part in advancing society toward that goal. Judging by our (atypical?) sample, Massachusetts law was conspicuously unsuccessful in this respect. Particular issues were usually settled, and disputants dissuaded from mayhem, but that was it. Interestingly, arbitration was not, in this, superior to formal court proceedings; both failed utterly to soar above lowest-level effectiveness. But the system was at its least successful, actually counterproductive, sowing seeds of bitterness and of future conflict, when it gave one party the opportunity to insist upon the full measure of a law which society had stamped "against equity and good conscience."

In order to keep the concept usefully meaningful, we should probably conclude that what Blagrove did was not an abuse of law. On the other hand, if my suspicions about Byfield are correct, that is, if Walley and Leverett refused to chancer Blagrove's administration bond only because they were Byfield's friends, then we have here a clear case of abuse of law. It is most interesting that the method was the same in both cases, that is, denial of equitable relief. Blagrove, I have said, was able to do what he did because the world was out of joint. But Byfield's action was in 1704, after the world had been put right. Byfield's success may be thought of as a fluke; in almost every case involving a penal bond, chancering would be automatic. The administration bond just happened to be the one case doubtful enough so that Byfield's friends on the bench could, without bringing open disgrace upon themselves, refuse the chancery. But I think there was more to the matter than just a fluke, that it made a difference that Massachusetts' integration of law and equity was administrative rather than conceptual. In an analogous situation today, a court will refuse to enforce a liquidated damages clause in a contract which amounts to a penalty. That is the law. But the law in Massachusetts enforced a bond according to its terms, penalty and all. Only equity, although administered in the same proceeding, could reduce the judgment to "the just debt and damages." It was, however routinely granted, conceptually *special* relief, and as such inevitably precarious. The administrative integration would have avoided the phenomenon discussed earlier, of contempt for law bred by having to turn to a separate system to find equitable, conscionable treatment. But the lingering of a conceptual separation would have made it likely enough that on occasion, the law would operate in all its by this time anomalous and anachronistic rigor. Byfield struck on just such an occasion.

For obvious reasons the law/equity problem in Massachusetts did not present the aspect of rivalry between two systems that it wore in England. Students of Massachusetts history have assumed that the only such jurisdictional rivalry in the Province was that between the common law and Admiralty, a natural assumption since that is the only one we ever hear of. In this rivalry Byfield, so many years Judge of Admiralty, played an important part. And now we see in the Byfield materials another jurisdictional clash, or something very like it, between the common law and probate. The common law won.

As we saw in the matter of Hayman's estate, Blagrove's insistence from the first that the appropriate forum was probate was un-availing. There was no mechanism by which he could keep Byfield from bringing a common law action of debt on the administration bond. Moreover, as Paul Dudley argued for Byfield, it mattered not at all to the common law that a Judge of Probate had approved the administrator's actions. Given a failure to live up to obligations imposed by the common law, the approbation of a Judge of Probate was meaningless. Dudley proclaimed the supremacy of the common law, and that supremacy was vindicated by the later proceedings be-fore the Council. This "Supreame Ordinary," with unquestioned jurisdiction over Blagrove's appeal from Byfield's refusal to accept his final account, was nonetheless powerless in the face of the com-mon law judgment for £6,000. The Council could itself allow By-field's account, but only Byfield could acknowledge satisfaction of the judgment. When, ordered to do so, he refused, the Council was impotent; its petulant, foot-stamping response, dismissal of Byfield from office, was more degrading to the Council than injurious to Byfield, and certainly not very helpful to Blagrove. On the other hand, it should be noted that the Council did *not* take the one course of action which would have helped Blagrove, that is, concurrence in an order of the House of Representatives commanding the Justices of the Superior Court to chancer the administration bond. The Council's opposition to lower house adjudication may be viewed cynically as an attempt to retain the administration of justice as an aristocratic preserve. But it also reflected a concern for the integrity of the common law, to a degree because this was thought to be identi-cal with its administration by men of "the better sort."

One consequence of *the affair Blagrove* may have been an end to the alliance between Joseph Dudley and Nathaniel Byfield. Cer-tainly Byfield came to view his once-friend, the Governor, as an enemy. It has been said, rather vaguely, that this was owing to Byfield's having been "reproved" by Dudley in Council; one source seems to locate the reproof in the Hayman proceedings.[2] And from

[2] Hutchinson, *History*, 158 note; Baylies, *Historical Memoir*, II:IV, 55; Munro, *History of Bristol*, 70, note, suggests that the quarrel with Dudley was about Bla-grove's administration of Hayman's estate.

what we have seen, it is not unlikely that Dudley did retort sharply to Byfield's "rude and unmannerly behavior." But that was 1710, and the evidence we have of active Byfield-Dudley hostility comes from 1714–1715. In those years Byfield, having been chosen for the Council, was negatived by Governor Dudley. And in 1715 Byfield went to England to urge Dudley's removal from the governorship, and, it is said, to procure that office for himself.[3] Still, *the affair Blagrove* may well have marked the beginning of the end of good relations between Byfield and Dudley.[4]

If the break with Dudley was a consequence of the Blagrove matter, it must, I think, be accounted the major consequence. Byfield's loss of office, although not a trivial matter, and for such a man, and in the circumstances, embittering, was nevertheless short-lived. William Tailer, taking over as acting governor in November 1715, in December appointed Byfield Judge of the Inferior Court of Common Pleas, Bristol, and of Probate, Bristol. Byfield resigned from Common Pleas in 1724, and (I think) as Judge of Probate only in 1729, to be succeeded by, of all people, Nathaniel Blagrove! But in 1728 he was put on the Commission of the Peace for Suffolk and once again commissioned Judge of Admiralty. And then, in 1731, Governor Jonathan Belcher appointed Byfield to the Suffolk Court of Common Pleas. All these posts he held until his death. So Byfield did not suffer over-much in the great cause of destroying Nathaniel Blagrove. Massachusetts was, after all, a society in which merit was assured recognition. Part of Byfield's merit was that he trained his descendants to marry the right people. Governor Tailer was Byfield's son-in-law, and Governor Belcher the father-in-law of Byfield's grandson. If Governor Burnet was linked to Byfield by ties of kinship, the ties have not yet come to light.

[3] Hutchinson, *History*, II, 177; Baylies, *Historical Memoir*, II:IV, 55 note; Warden, *Boston*, 92; Washburn, *Judicial History*, 180–181; Howe, *Bristol*, 17. All of these mention Byfield's desire to procure the governorship for himself. While I do not doubt that he was ambitious enough for this, or anything, I have seen no contemporary support. Byfield's journey was also aimed at procuring royal approval for the private bank scheme of which he was a promoter, Warden, *Boston*, 92; Palfrey, *History of New England*, IV, 334–335.

[4] Although Malone, *Pine Trees and Politics*, 30, seems to be saying that in *1705*, when Sir Henry Ashurst worked in London for Dudley's removal, it was "with enthusiastic support in Boston led by Nathaniel Byfield. . . ." If this is the case, Byfield was acting more duplicitously than was in character for him.

If age slowed Nathaniel Byfield, the records fail to reveal the fact; assuredly it did not mellow him. Thus the records of the last decades of his life show him suing and being sued, presented by the grand jury for imposing extortionate fees as Judge of Admiralty, making life miserable for those of His Majesty's officers who attempted to enforce the White Pine Acts, and generally being the fellow we have come to know, if not more so. In fact, the record of contention continues beyond his life-time; the last case was brought against Byfield's executors in 1740, six and a half years after his death.[5] That action, in covenant, arose out the marriage contract between Nathaniel Byfield and Sarah Leverett, by which Byfield had agreed that his wife-to-be might dispose testamentarily of property worth a stated sum, and that in the event of her dying intestate, he, Byfield, would bequeath that sum to Sarah's Leverett kin. Sarah having died intestate, Byfield naturally made no such bequest. Byfield's executors, by their attorney Robert Auchmuty, pleaded tender of the sum before the date of the writ, therefore no breach. And the tender appears, in fact, under threat of suit to have been made; it was, however, made in Province bills, while plaintiffs claimed, successfully, that the sum was owed in sterling. Execution issued on a judgment against Byfield's executors in March 1740/41; with satisfaction of the judgment recorded, in August 1741—eight years after his death—the law closes its books on Nathaniel Byfield.

Notoriously, the biographer falls victim to the attractions of her subject, and objectivity suffers. The danger for Byfield's biographer is somewhat special, for the lure of the man is in his rascality; one becomes interested, then engaged, finally enthralled, by the defects rather than the excellences of one's subject. The peril then resides in the temptation to exaggerate those defects, to play up the lurid; it lies in the likelihood that one will present a distortedly negative, rather than affirmative, portrait. In Baylies' judicious words, "The character of Colonel Byfield was not so elevated as to command the veneration of the people, or so low as to incur their contempt."[6] While I cannot revise that estimate upward so to speak, not for the

[5] The documents are at Suffolk File #50704, 51460, 52419, 52859, 53172, 53980 (2 papers, f. 134–135), 54555.
[6] Baylies, *Historical Memoir*, II:IV, 55–57.

world would I convey the impression that it is too high, too mild an indictment. Nathaniel Byfield, obviously no saint, was not a bad man; his faults rather leap to the eye, but my experience is that the more one knows the more inclined one is to think of Byfield as merely, if substantially, flawed. This is conspicuously true of *the affair Blagrove*. To one who knows the details, but not the background, of that incident, Byfield will appear in the worst light; in particular, without knowing of the Byfield-Blagrove feud, and especially of Blagrove's suit on the mortgage in 1698, one will not understand that it was Blagrove, rather than £6,000, that Byfield was after. It may seem hardly a favor to Byfield to portray him as vengeful rather than venal. But at least, having identified revenge as the motive, we can go on to note that there was considerable justification for Byfield's thirst for revenge. Blagrove had, as it were, asked for it. In short, we do justice to our subject, and that is more rather than less important with a subject who needs all the justice he can get.

Once upon a time historians of Massachusetts exhibited a tendency to concentrate on the beginning and the end, according short shrift to the middle. Founding and Revolution hypnotized us, and we leaped merrily from John Winthrop to John Adams. There were a lot of other people named John—or Nathaniel—in between of whom nobody ever heard. The tendency was entirely understandable, not only because of the obvious powerful attraction of those dramatic eras, but because Massachusetts history, from 1629 to 1776, does legitimately present itself as two histories: there was a sharp break between colony and province. The break was nothing like absolute of course. A heritage is never entirely lost. Moreover, we have yet to explore, much less understand, the workings of historical memory in this setting. Nevertheless, it is reasonably consonant with the history itself, therefore not inappropriate, to focus on one period as if the other had never been. And of course, historians being people, the bulk of attention will go to the more exciting years of each period.

In consequence Massachusetts had its Dark Age. Moreover, continuities were missed which might have had important explanatory potential. Today, of course, the general history of this period is brightly illuminated. But the legal history is not. There the Age remains Dim, if not Dark. Byfield, in a small but not derisory way, helps by having lived a long time at, as it were, the right time. He was also a ceaselessly, relentlessly active man of law, in both the saddle and the ring to his last moment. Not even for his besotted biographer does Nathaniel Byfield assume the proportions of a major figure, but he is legitimately *a* figure in Massachusetts legal history.

And indeed, for all who enjoy seeing illustrated the sweep of history and the seamlessness of the historical web, Byfield's story seems made to order. When we first meet him, he is suing and being sued in the old County Courts, and the Court of Assistants, that judicial stronghold of the early colonial magistracy. In the last action, that against his executors in 1739, suit was brought by Andrew and Peter Oliver. John Winthrop meet John Adams! To His Majesty's Surveyors of the Woods, desperate for a Judge of Admiralty inclined to aid them in enforcing the White Pine Acts, it was maddening that Byfield "had discovered the Fountain of Youth."[7] But how nice for the rest of us.

Byfield

---

[7] The phrase is Malone's, *Pine Trees and Politics,* 109, note 107. Dunbar, the Surveyor-General, called Byfield a "poor Superannuated Gentleman near 80 years old, who had already distinguished himself very partial to the Country," Malone, *Pine Trees and Politics,* 108, note 103.

RUSSELL K. OSGOOD

John Clark, Esq., Justice of the Peace, 1667–1728

> For us in America, even more than in England itself, the
> courts of common law have become the guardians of constitu-
> tionalism. Its source, far more than we have realized, may be
> found in another kind of court — the courts of neighbors, the
> "little commonwealths," which preserved an ancient experience
> that most Englishmen had shared.
>
> John P. Dawson[1]

THE *Boston Weekly News-Letter* for the week ending 12
December 1728 reported:

On Thursday Night of the 5th of this instant December, died here after
long indisposition the Honorable John Clark Esq. about 61 Years old; he
was made a Justice of Peace June 7, 1700, sometime since was Elected
One of His Majesties Council of this Province and is to be interred on
Saturday next the 14th.[2]

Apart from his will,[3] which was proved before Samuel Sewall on
23 December 1728, very little remains of the record of the life of
John Clark. The will is suitably, but not emphatically, pious. The
estate's account, submitted on 3 May 1731, discloses property worth
well over £6000, including a large number of modest debts owed
Clark.

There are a few other facts to be gleaned from surviving records.
Clark graduated from Harvard in 1687; his senior oration was entitled, "An Morborum Sedes Sit Anima Sensitiva."[4] Both his grand-

[1] J. P. Dawson, *A History of Lay Judges* (Cambridge: Harvard University Press,
1960), 303.

[2] The *Weekly Newsletter* is included in The Early American Newspaper Series
(1704–1820) of the microform cards of the Readex Microprint Corporation on
the microform for the *Newsletter* for 28 November 1728 to 1 May 1729.

[3] The will and executors' account for John Clark's estate are maintained in the
Suffolk County Registry of Probate.

[4] J. L. Sibley, *Biographical Sketches of Graduates of Harvard University* (Cambridge: C. W. Sever, 1873–1975), III (1885), 368–369 and 375–379.

father and father were physicians, an occupation which John Clark, Esq., also followed, although the extent of his medical activities is unclear. In his will he left to his son John "all my Instruments and utensills of surgery." Samuel Sewall, a prominent figure in Massachusetts legal affairs, reported in his diary that on 23 January 1718/19 Dr. Clark came to treat his daughter Hannah's swollen ankle.[5] Hannah recovered six months later.[6]

John Clark's life was very much like, and yet contrasts with, that of a close contemporary, Cotton Mather. Mather lived from 1663 until 23 February 1727/8, almost exactly the same lifespan as John Clark. They both resided in the north end of Boston, and John Clark belonged to Cotton Mather's church, the North Meetinghouse. Mather mentioned Clark in his diary occasionally. He was identified as being on several special committees having to do with repairing the meetinghouse.[7] Sewall, by contrast, recounted numerous meetings with Clark on ceremonial occasions and referred to Clark at death as his "beloved Physician."[8]

The major element of contrast, evident in the *Journal of the House of Representatives of Massachusetts*,[9] is that as Mather's political power receded, Clark's grew, along with that of the group of people with whom he was identified politically, primarily the Elisha Cookes, father and later son. David Levin has argued that Cotton Mather lost his power because of the witchcraft episode and his family's identification with the Charter of 1691, which Increase Mather obtained from King William.[1] Clark apparently joined what

---

[5] *Diary of Samuel Sewall* (3rd vol.), Massachusetts Historical Society, *Collections*, XVII (1882), 210. [Hereinafter cited as *Sewall Diary*.] For an account of the early colonial medical practices, including those of Clark's relatives, see *Medicine in Colonial Massachusetts*, Colonial Society of Massachusetts, *Publications*, LVII, 122.

[6] Ibid., 227.

[7] *Diary of Cotton Mather*, Massachusetts Historical Society, *Collections*, LXVII, 189, and LXVIII, 299. [Hereinafter cited as *Mather Diary*.]

[8] Sibley, *Harvard Graduates*, III, 377.

[9] *Journals of the House of Representatives of Massachusetts* (1919). [Hereinafter cited as *Journal*.] Volumes one through eight cover 1715 to 1730. The printing of the journal was initiated after a quarrel with Governor Dudley.

[1] D. Levin, *Cotton Mather: The Young Life of the Lord's Remembrancer, 1663–1703* (Cambridge: Harvard University Press, 1978). My only criticism of this thoughtful book is that in his effort to be sympathetic Levin may have missed the obvious point that Cotton Mather lost power because he was a hypocrite and a wind-

has been called the "popular party"[2] in the House, a loose grouping of representatives characterized by opposition to the royal governors under the Charter of 1691 in general, and opposition to provincial taxation in particular.

Once Clark's rise to political prominence was achieved, it continued nearly to the end of his life. He was named a justice of the peace on 7 June 1700.[3] First elected representative to the General Court from Boston in 1708,[4] he served until he was elected to the Governor's Council by the General Court in May 1715.[5] He remained on the Council until the Royal Governor, Samuel Shute, rejected his re-selection in 1720.[6] Clark was promptly returned as a member for Boston and immediately elected Speaker,[7] being re-elected in 1721,[8] 1722,[9] and 1723.[1] Elisha Cooke, the son, replaced Clark temporarily in 1722 on account of Clark having an "indisposition."[2] He was re-elected to the Council and accepted by the Governor in 1724,[3] serving there until his final illness.[4]

bag. There are two good examples of Mather's obvious failing. He had the motto "Be Short" inscribed over his study door and yet was notoriously unable to be short about anything. Mather's feverish defense of his father went well beyond that required, even of a dutiful Puritan son. Perry Miller described Cotton Mather's obsequiousness as an "unction which infects even his most worthy actions...." P. Miller, *The New England Mind: From Colony to Province* (Cambridge: Harvard University Press, 1953), 194.

[2] Sibley, *Harvard Graduates*, III, 375–376.

[3] Ibid., 376. The Charter of 1691 gave the Governor the right to appoint justices of the peace. *Acts & Resolves of the Province of Massachusetts Bay*, I (1867), 12. [Hereinafter cited as *Acts & Resolves*.]

[4] *A Report of the Record Commissioners containing the Boston Records from 1700 to 1728*, 55 (Report #8:1883). [Hereinafter cited as *Report #8 (1883): The Boston Records from 1700 to 1728*.]

[5] *Journal*, I, 2.

[6] *Journal*, II, 232.

[7] *Journal*, III, 3–4.

[8] Ibid., 86.

[9] *Journal*, IV, 1–2.

[1] *Journal*, V, 4.

[2] Ibid., 27, 130.

[3] *Journal*, VI, 6. William Dummer was acting governor at the time, having succeeded Samuel Shute, who fled in January of 1723. P. Miller, *The New England Mind*, 457.

[4] See, e.g., *Journal*, VI, 217. *Journal*, VII, 6, note 9.

Clark's political position in the ongoing fights between the Governor and the House of Representatives of this period is shown by the *Journal* report of Clark's election as Speaker after Shute's rejection of him as a councillor:

A Message from his Excellency by Mr. Secretary, in the words following, Viz I Accept the Choice of John Clarke Esqr as Speaker of the House of Representatives.

August 23d 1721 Samuel Shute *Ordered* That the said Message be Returned by Mr. John Fortes, and that he inform his Excellency, that this House, when they sent up to Acquaint his Excellency, and the Honorable Board [Council], with the Choice of a Speaker, they did it for Information only, and not Approbation.[5]

Not surprisingly, the first Amendment to the Second Charter, included in King George's Explanatory Charter of 1726, provided that a Speaker chosen by the General Court must be presented to the Governor "for his Approbation."[6]

There are other bits of evidence which demonstrate Clark's adherence to the "popular party." Clark and Cooke were frequently elected together and Cooke succeeded Clark as Speaker. Clark is identified as being a member of the numerous committees appointed by the General Court to audit the province's financial affairs, including the validity of muster rolls.[7] His service on these committees occurred at a time of constant, but not savage, conflict between the General Court and the royal governors over financial affairs. In his years as Speaker, Clark had to speak officially for the General Court on such matters. In a letter to Governor Shute, dated 1 September 1721, he defended the House vigorously, but not disrespectfully, for adjourning in a prior session without the Governor's permission.[8] The second Amendment included in King George's Explanatory Charter decreed that the General Court could not adjourn itself for more than two consecutive days "without leave from the Governor."[9]

[5] *Journal,* III, 87.

[6] *Acts & Resolves,* I, 22.

[7] See, e.g., *Journal,* II, 69, 117.

[8] *Journal,* III, 96–101.

[9] *Acts & Resolves,* I, 23.

These facts and the will were all we previously knew about John Clark. But, by great good fortune, it has recently been discovered that Clark also left a 269-page judicial book, still in private hands, which contains 1,379 entries describing his actions as a justice of the peace from July 1700 until December 1726. The book may be akin to an official record, for it does not contain a single personal comment or reference. The litigants' names are listed first; the dispute described; the disposition entered; moneys received are noted; and occasionally the legal issue applied in a case is adumbrated. The book appears to have been kept chronologically and contemporaneously; only an occasional entry is out of order.[1] Later notations are made on earlier entries in the event of the issuance of a writ of execution, but such notations are separately dated.[2]

After spending considerable time with a book such as Clark's, one is tempted to overrate its importance. As a record describing the activities of a busy justice of the peace in the fairly stable, legally speaking, period of the second charter, it is unique. It permits some evaluation of social developments in Massachusetts in the provincial period. Finally, it is a document which allows one to assess, probably as well as any eighteenth-century legal materials, the performance of a true lay judge. Clark was a physician, a commercial figure, the owner of several parcels of real estate, and, as just described, a politician of some eminence. He was not a lawyer, and there is no evidence that he had any legal training or access to any legal materials, such as a copy of Lambard's *Eirenarcha: or of the Office of the Justice of Peace* or Dalton's *The Countrey Justice*.[3]

---

[1] For instance, on the third and fourth page of the book the entries proceed: March 6, March 4 and March 10. The book will be cited henceforth as *Book*, date of entry, unless the text states it, and a page number, assigned by this author.

[2] See, e.g., *Book*, 4 March 1700/01, 3. John Clark dated events within the first three months of the year using the 1700/01 format used in this note. This convention will be observed in this paper.

[3] Joseph H. Smith has written that William Pynchon (1590–1651) "had some familiarity with . . . Dalton's *The Countrey Justice.* . . ." *Colonial Justice in Western Massachusetts 1639–1702*, J. H. Smith ed. (Cambridge: Harvard University Press, 1961), 157–158. When compiling the *Laws & Liberties* in 1648, the General Court ordered two copies of *The Countrey Justice*. G. L. Haskins, *Law and Authority in Early Massachusetts* (New York: Macmillan, 1960), 135. The inventory of Clark's estate disappointingly included the following cryptic entry: "222 Old Books £30." This is a large number of books for any colonial person.

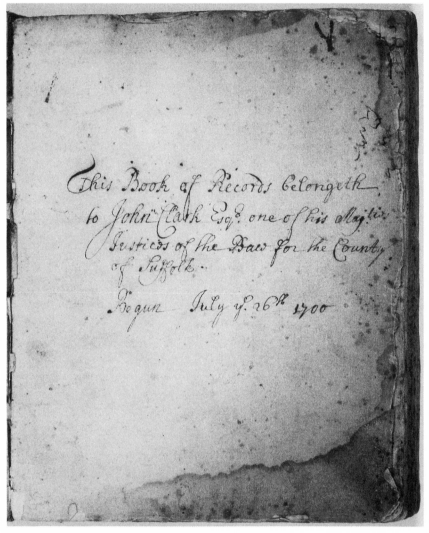

10. Title Page, Book of Records belonging to John Clark (1667–1728), Justice of the Peace, Suffolk. Courtesy, Collection of James A. Henderson, Jr.

A. *A Justice of the Peace*

Those who have read the judicial book[4] of the various Pynchon family judges will easily grasp the main difference between it and Clark's book. Clark's book is a formal, tightly controlled record of the proceedings before him. It may be that the organization, discipline, consistent format, and flavor of doctrinal stability found in the Clark book are attributable to the author. It seems more likely, however, that these characteristics are due to the fact that a justice of the peace in Boston around 1700 was dealing with fewer legal uncertainties than the Pynchons. In addition, Clark did not have to establish the credibility of his judicial office in a quasi-frontier context. Thus, unfortunately, Clark was less likely to be as fully descriptive as the Pynchons in recording various matters.

Justices of the peace, like John Clark, were selected by the royal governor. Although there is no direct evidence on Clark's appointment, the Governor presumably acted on the advice of his council in judicial appointment matters, as provided in the Charter.[5] The oath required of a justice of the peace was established by statute[6] and followed closely the oath current in England at that time.[7]

The large number of matters handled by John Clark, particularly in the years 1710 to 1720, in relation to the Boston population which Carl Bridenbaugh has estimated at 9,000 in 1710 and 12,000 in 1720,[8] raises the question of the number of justices in Boston and their level of activity. The Boston selectmen's records provide some

---

[4] See *Colonial Justice in Western Massachusetts*. See also *The Pynchon Papers*, The Colonial Society of Massachusetts, *Publications*, LX.

[5] Originally, Massachusetts did not have judges called justices of the peace; instead, they were "magistrates." Since individuals frequently became magistrates by virtue of holding another office and/or their social status, Massachusetts did not have much experience in the appointment of judges until the period of the Second Charter. See Haskins, *Law and Authority*, 173–178.

[6] *Acts & Resolves*, I, 78 (Chapter 35 of the Acts of 1692–3).

[7] M. Dalton (and one of the Masters of Chancery), *The Countrey Justice* (London: W. Rawlins & S. Roycroft, 1705 ed.), 13. The statutory origin of the precise words of the English oath were unclear according to 1705 edition of Dalton's. The Massachusetts oath differed in that certain references to the King and institutions not physically present in Massachusetts were eliminated. "The oath concerning this office seemeth to be by force of the Statute made 13 R.2.c.7." Ibid., 12.

[8] C. Bridenbaugh, *Cities in the Wilderness: The First Century of Urban Life in America 1625–1742*, 2d ed. (New York: Knopf, 1955), 143.

evidence on this matter. The selectmen met frequently with the justices and occasionally with the justices and the overseers of the poor. The three groups jointly appointed deputies to perform certain extra-judicial functions. In this period the number of justices who met with the selectmen averaged ten.[9] The core of this group in the early years included Clark, Elisha Cooke, Sr., Jeremiah Dummer, Elisha Hutchinson, Edward Bromfield, Penn Townsend, and Isaac Addington.[1] Judging from the records of joint meetings of the justices, selectmen, and overseers, there must have been sixteen or seventeen justices actually holding office.[2] It is not possible to estimate how many of this number were active.

Being a justice of the peace may not have been the road to wealth in colonial Boston, but the fact that it did produce income can not be ignored. A justice of the peace seems to have derived income primarily from his issuance of "process-type" papers. Chapter 18 of the Province Laws, passed on 22 October 1694, provided that a justice should receive a fee of one shilling for issuing a writ in any

---

[9] See, e.g., *Report #11 (1884): Records of Boston Selectmen, 1701 to 1715*, 18. This report for 16 March 1702 is typical:

> March 16.
> At a meeting of the Justices of y[e] Peace & Select men within the Town of Boston viz[t]. John Foster, Esq., Elisha Cook, Esq[r]., Eliak[m] Hutchinson, Esq, Sam[ll] Sewall Esq[r]., Jer. Dummer Esq[r]., Elisha Hutchinson Esq[r]., 2[d] Edw[d] Brumfield Esq[r]., Penn Townsend Esq[r]., John Clark, Esq[r]., Isaac Addington Esq[r].
>
> The Select men then present were
> m[rs]. Rob[t] Gibbs   Rich Draper
>   Timothy Clark   Joseph Prout
>   Gyles Dyer   John Barnet
>
> It was then by the Said Justices & Select men Agreed That the Bakehouse belonging to the Rev[d] M[r]. James Allen being on the Back side of the Town, and the Grainary belonging to M[r]. Arthur Mason butting on the Common or Training field and the ware house belonging to John Foster Esq[r]. Night unto the great Still house at the north end of Boston be the Houses at present improved for the Lodging of Gunpowder in until Other & better provision be made for the Same.
>
> And that Cap[t] John Fairwether be treated with about his takeing care to receive in and deliver out S[d] powder.
>
> At a meeting of y[e] Select men March 23[d]. M[r]. John Stevens his Petition for a Timb[r] building was approved.

[1] Ibid.

[2] At the meeting on 27 January 1706/07 the three groups appointed sixteen individuals labelled "Esq.," including the ten or so regulars, to "Visit the Families of the Town on Wednesday the 5th of February next." Ibid., 55–56.

case to be tried before a justice.[3] John Clark's book does not account for the receipt of such sums even though he was careful to show payments of fines. The notation of each fine received, at least early in the diary, was accompanied by a pointed reference to its belonging to King William.[4]

Chapter 21 of the Province Laws of 1700–1701 required a justice to account for and pay over all the King's fines to the receiver-general of the province once every six months. The penalty for failure to file this account in a timely fashion was five pounds.[5] The clerk of the peace, who performed such duties for the justices in session, was not responsible for the activities of a single justice.[6] Thus justices of the peace may have appropriated to themselves extra income by failing to report receipt of fines or by holding such fines for periods before turning them over to the proper authorities. Since at his death the inventory of Clark's estate showed a large number of small debts, it is reasonable to infer that he had a ready supply of cash which he was lending out. It is possible that the King's fines provided some or all of that cash.

When finally paid, not all fines were awarded to the King. For instance, upon conviction of a single offense of profane cursing or swearing, an individual had to pay a fine of five shillings to the "poor of the town" or sit in the stocks.[7] Clark regularly fined profaners for the benefit of the poor.[8] People convicted of selling alcohol without a license were fined substantial sums, four pounds[9] or six pounds,[1] to be applied to "the use of the free school" in Boston and paid to the town treasurer. All fines due to a town or county for the use of the poor or whatever had to be reported and paid biannually.

Another source of revenue for a justice of the peace was his per-

[3] *Acts & Resolves*, I, 185.

[4] See, e.g., *Book*, 26 July 1700, 1.

[5] *Acts & Resolves*, I, 449.

[6] Ibid.

[7] Ibid., 51 (chapter 18 of the Acts of 1692–3). Punishment in the stocks was added by chapter 9 of the Acts of 1693. Ibid., 122–123. Drunkenness fines also went to the poor. See, e.g., *Book*, 10 December 1706, 44.

[8] See, e.g., *Book*, 7 September 1701, 7.

[9] Ibid., 28 October 1700, 2.

[1] *Acts & Resolves*, I, 681 (Chapter 6 of the Acts of 1711–12).

formance of certain functions which were not likely to be recorded. Chapter 21 of the Province Laws of 1697 provided that a deed "be signed and sealed . . . and acknowledged . . . before a justice of the peace. . . ."[2] The statute set no fee, but something was presumably paid for this accommodation. Few matters of this sort are included in Clark's book. On 8 July 1701 Clark wrote, "Joseph Richards and Anna Carver both of Weymouth personally appearing before me John Clark one of his Majesty's Justices of the Peace for the County of Suffolk producing a certificate of their publishment according to law were married."[3] Significantly no payment for performing the marriage is mentioned, supporting the view that the diary noted only receipt of sums due to the Crown or local governments.[4] Also significantly, no other marriage was recorded in the remainder of the book.

It is probable that some of John Clark's activities as a justice were uncompensated. For instance, he recorded on 21 March 1701 the swearing of Benjamin Frame of Boston as a constable.[5] Justices performed numerous other such duties, discussed later in this paper, which revolved around their status as quasi-municipal officials and which were uncompensated. For instance, Chapter 6 of the Province Laws of 1692–1693[6] sets no fee for the service of a justice in swearing a surveyor of highways. On the other hand, not all ancillary functions were unpaid. In 13 March 1704-1705 Clark ordered one John Tedman, who was found after a search pursuant to a warrant to have Peter Paity's missing copper kettle, to pay "the Charge of [Paity's] Warrant."[7]

In sum, although the financial dimensions of being a justice of the peace are not completely clear, the position seems to have provided an opportunity for earning some income. Some income might have

---

[2] Ibid., 298.

[3] See, e.g., *Book*, 6.

[4] Chapter 25 of the Acts of Second Session of 1692–3 gave a justice of the peace, within his county, and an ordained minister, within his town, the power to solemnize marriages, but only after publication by way of posting or saying of the banns. The statute set a fee of three shillings for this service. *Acts & Resolves*, I, 61.

[5] *Book*, 4.

[6] *Acts & Resolves*, I, 136.

[7] *Book*, 23–24.

been direct and legal, like fees for services. Other income might have
been attributable to "borrowing" or using fines due the Crown or
local authorities until such time as they had to be accounted for.

B. *Crime*

The English justice of the peace was primarily associated with
criminal justice. Books of authority contemporaneous with John
Clark's activities, such as W. Nelson's *Office and Authority of a
Justice of Peace* (1721), J. Shaw's *The Practical Justice of Peace*
(1728), or Dalton's are mainly concerned with crime and what is
labeled below as regulatory offenses.

John Clark's book, by contrast, indicates that his activities were
largely civil. In his twenty-six years as justice of the peace, he reported 264 criminal matters and 455 civil matters.[8] There were also
fifty-six prosecutions noted of "special" ordinances of a local character in the third category of "regulatory" offenses.

Even though Clark's activities involved primarily civil matters,
his criminal jurisdiction was nonetheless important. As a justice of
the peace, Clark tried and decided the merits of four major classes
of offenses: (i) theft and receipt of stolen goods, (ii) breach of the
peace, (iii) speaking profanely, and (iv) libel or false reporting. In
addition, he handled four other classes of offenders in his capacity
as an officer empowered to grant recognizances: (i) sexual offenders,
including fornication and bastardy, (ii) suspicious or threatening individuals, (iii) Sabbath breakers and other blasphemers, and (iv)
people indicted by the Suffolk County grand jury.

Theft accounted for approximately one-tenth of Clark's criminal
business. As a single justice of the peace, he was authorized to decide
a theft if the "damage" caused did not exceed forty shillings.[9] Damage, as applied by Clark, meant the value of the goods purloined. As
punishment for a theft, John Clark invariably ordered that the de-

---

[8] Different people would no doubt tally the sometimes ambiguous entries differently.
Chart A of the Appendix shows aggregate figures for the book. The proportion of
criminal matters is significantly higher than Richard Gaskins found in similar
books for Connecticut for later periods. Gaskins, "Changes in the Criminal Law in
Eighteenth Century Connecticut," *American Journal of Legal History*, xxv (1981),
309.

[9] *Acts & Resolves*, I, 52 (Chapter 18 of the Acts of 1692–3, 2d Sess.).

fendant pay to the victim three times the value of the goods stolen.[1] He would give a credit of up to one-third of this amount if the stolen property was returned.[2] Colonial law appears to have permitted a justice to impose on a thief a fine for the Crown in addition to the trebling. John Clark fined thieves five to fifteen shillings,[3] and if they were unable to pay the fine, they were whipped. The book noted receipt of the Crown's fine in almost every case, but does not account for the payment to the victim.

Peace offenses comprised over half of Clark's criminal jurisdiction. The range was large, from "rioting" to family quarrels, with one-on-one assaults being the norm. One of the more serious "peace" cases in the book[4] involved a riot and fight among four lodgers at Atkeson's house in the north end of Boston at two in the morning. Clark and another justice, Jeremiah Duncan, fined the rioters five shillings each and required them to make recognizances for future good behavior.

Various punishments were available in peace cases,[5] including fines, the stocks, whipping, or placing the wrongdoer in a cage. Fines predominated, and of the alternatives whipping was used the most, particularly where Clark appeared to doubt the defendant's ability to pay a fine. One case involved a punishment for a battery committed by Timon, a black servant to Mr. Samuel Dummer.[6]

A modest proportion of the peace offenses was related to drunkenness, technically a separate crime from breach of the peace.[7] Historians of the criminal law have found it difficult to distinguish these crimes. Thus, although Clark occasionally dealt with drunkenness offenses,[8] one cannot confidently separate these few instances from the general category of peace offenses.

Convictions for profane cursing or swearing constituted the second largest number of criminal matters, 79 out of 264. Chapter 18

[1] See, e.g., *Book*, 1 March 1705/06, 34.

[2] See, e.g., *Book*, 10 January 1709/10, 70.

[3] Ibid.

[4] Ibid., 7 May 1711, 90.

[5] *Acts & Resolves*, I, 122–123 (Chapter 9 of the Acts of 1693).

[6] See, e.g., *Book*, 20 May 1726, 268.

[7] *Acts & Resolves*, I, 51 (chapter 18 of the Acts of 1692–3, 2d Sess.).

[8] See, e.g., *Book*, 10 December 1706, 44.

of the Province Laws of 1692–1693,[9] as amended by Chapter 9 of 1693,[1] authorized a five-shilling fine for the first swear or curse and twelve pence for every additional profanity spoken on the same occasion, all fines to be applied for the relief of the poor. If a profaner could not pay the fine, the stocks and lash were available. A profaner could be convicted by his own confession, the testimony of a single justice of the peace, or the testimony of two other witnesses. If a profanation offense was not reported within thirty days, it was not actionable. One of the early entries in the book is typical of profanity matters:

Sept. 7 [1701] William Cavet resident in Boston Mariner convicted before me John Clark Justice of the Peace of prophane cursing and swearing five times. Ordered to pay nine shillings as a fine to the use of the poor of the town of Boston or to set in the stocks two hours received 9s.[2]

This entry shows that Clark adhered to the rules on the fines, but it does not reveal by which evidentiary method Cavet was convicted. The "before me" referred to the conviction, not hearing the actual profanation. Clark's failure to describe the method of proof contrasts with his care in reciting the basis of proof in a civil debt and contract matter, to be discussed later, in which a defendant failed to appear.

Knowledge of the incidence of profanation offenses in Massachusetts in the period of turbulent economic growth from 1700 to 1730 would be very interesting to a social historian. One might expect concern with such matters to diminish during the period of Clark's book. Unfortunately, no sure conclusion based on the book alone is possible. Since the book trails off beginning in 1721, as Clark's political and other activities took perhaps more of his time, it would be impossible even to guess about the frequency of profanation prosecutions. There is always the possibility that Clark might personally have held a particular position on the crime itself, favoring or disfavoring it by his issuance of process papers. In spite of these *caveats*, the book does give the reader the impression that profanity was receding as a social concern.

[9] *Acts & Resolves*, I, 51 (Chapter 18 of the Acts of 1692–3, 2d Sess.).

[1] Ibid., 122–123 (Chapter 9 of the Acts of 1693).

[2] *Book*, 7.

Section 7 of Chapter 18 of the Province Laws of 1692–1693 made it a crime for "any person . . . of the age of discretion (. . . fourteen years or upwards) wittingly and willingly [to] make or publish any lye or libel, tending to the defamation or damage of any particular person . . . , [or] make or spread any false news or reports with intent to abuse and deceive others."[3] John Clark heard a number of defamation matters. If convicted, an offender was fined five shillings and Clark also made him present "sureties for good behaviour"[4] until he appeared at the next general sessions of the peace.

One sensitive libel case[5] shows that Clark would occasionally act without explicit authority. On 30 August 1706 Clark had James Robes and Jonathan Woodman before him for "publishing a base, abusive and scandalous lying report concerning his Excellency Joseph Dudley, Esq." Dudley was an unpopular governor. Clark did not hear the merits of the case but required the defendants to find sureties and be recognized in the startling sum of £100. A libel action of this sort seems to have been within Clark's statutory jurisdiction. It may be that "serious" matters, even if within a single justice's jurisdiction, were sent to the general sessions of the peace.[6]

A Massachusetts justice of the peace was more than a trial judge for petty criminal and small civil actions. He handled the equivalent of bail hearings for individuals charged with crimes beyond his jurisdiction. Although technically within Clark's jurisdiction, the case involving Governor Dudley, just mentioned, is an example. More often, a justice usually determined a bail equivalent on matters clearly placed by statute beyond his jurisdiction. Sexual crimes comprised

---

[3] *Acts & Resolves*, I, 53.

[4] The punishments were prescribed in Section 7, as well. Ibid. For a typical case, see *Book*, 30 August 1710, 77. Ester (sic) Flag was convicted for "publishing a false report . . . by saying that . . . Catherine was drunk at a burial. . . ." Mrs. Flag was fined five shillings and required to find two sureties five pounds each to guarantee her appearance at the next sessions.

[5] *Book*, 40.

[6] A similar legal phenomenon is discussed in Dalton, *Countrey Justice*, 71–73, note 34. Many felonies were technically triable by English justices of the peace, but were dealt by binding over the accused to some other court. Blackstone, writing some sixty years after Clark, noted a similar reluctance of English justices of the peace, sitting as the court of general sessions, to tackle serious criminal matters even if within their jurisdiction. W. Blackstone, *Commentaries* (Oxford: Clarendon Press, 1st ed. 1769), IV, 268–269.

the largest class of criminal cases in which John Clark had to obtain security for the appearance of an accused person in another court. Massachusetts law placed fornication and bastardy within the jurisdiction of the general sessions of the justices of the peace.[7]

A typical case[8] involved Alice Cook of Needham, who confessed on 15 July 1712 to fornicating with Henry Dewin of Needham and that she "now goeth withall" pregnant by him. Clark ordered Alice to find sureties in the amount of four pounds to guarantee her appearance before the general sessions for the following October. He also issued a warrant for the apprehension of Henry Dewin. On 17 July Henry made his own recognizance[9] before Clark, in the amount of five pounds to appear before the sessions and was ordered to "not depart [from Boston] without license."

A second class of isolated recognizances, those not linked to appeals of matters previously decided by John Clark, involved people thought to be suspicious or threatening. Modern police practice is not as aggressive as that of colonial Massachusetts in this regard. On several occasions citizens brought before Clark individuals who, they alleged, had been threatening people. In each case Clark would require the accused to find sureties in a significant amount. For instance, on 24 July 1706 Joseph Callender, a Boston tailor, sought protection from Thomas Hunt, a Boston turner.[1] Clark ordered Hunt to find a surety and be recognized in the amount of fifty pounds for his appearance at the next general sessions of the peace. Entries like this one were not annotated in any way that would reveal what happened at the general session.

The ability to bind over a defendant indefinitely and without a specific accusation was linked to a justice's right to issue the ancient recognizance of the peace. The author of the 1705 edition of Dalton's explained in twenty-three pages[2] that the recognizance of the peace, existing by implication rather than express grant, lasted for the lifetime of the defendant and could be lifted only by the sessions with

---

[7] *Acts & Resolves*, I, 52.

[8] *Book*, 108.

[9] Ibid., 109.

[1] Ibid., 38.

[2] Dalton, *Countrey Justice*, 275ff.

the consent of the victim or victims of the original offense.[3] It was distinguishable from the various recognizances requiring an appearance to answer a charge in that it was equivalent to a suspended sentence or probation. Clark used the recognizance of the peace occasionally, as in the case of the four lodgers mentioned earlier.[4]

The third class of recognizances involved Sabbath breaking and other actions which bordered on blasphemy. Early on, Massachusetts made blasphemy a capital crime.[5] The Privy Council disallowed a statute under the second charter which had maintained it as a capital offense.[6] The disallowed statute was replaced in 1697 with one that made blasphemy punishable by six months imprisonment or various forms of torture or humiliation.[7] Lesser crimes of this type also existed. For example, a person convicted of Sabbath breaking could be fined twenty shillings.[8] A single justice of the peace could decide such cases. That only a few trials of these latter offenses were reported in Clark's book,[9] and all in the early 1700's, suggest that minor religious offenses were not prosecuted in Boston during this period.

Finally, recognizances were imposed to guarantee appearances to answer various presentments by the grand jury. By far the largest number of grand jury presentments which led to recognitions before Clark involved the unlicensed selling of alcoholic beverages. These will be discussed in the next section as part of the regulatory responsibilities of the justice of the peace. Another significant group of presentments involved allegations of fairly serious religious deviance. John Green, a Boston schoolmaster, was brought before Clark and Samuel Sewall, another justice, to post security to appear and

---

[3] Ibid., 278–279. The use of this punishment as an instrument of social control is discussed briefly in A. H. Manchester, *Modern Legal History* (London: Butterworths, 1980), 194–198.

[4] See above, 118, text accompanying footnote 4.

[5] M. Farrand, *The Laws and Liberties of Massachusetts*, reprint of 1648 edition (Cambridge: Harvard University Press, 1929), 5.

[6] *Acts & Resolves*, I, 55 (Chapter 19 of the Acts of 1692–3, 2d Sess.).

[7] Ibid., 297 (Chapter 20 of the Acts of 1697, 3d Sess.).

[8] Ibid., 58–59 (Chapter 22 of the Acts of 1692–3, 2d Sess.).

[9] See, e.g., *Book*, 6 June 1701, 6.

answer a charge of "composing and publishing a mock sermon full of monstrous prophaness and obscenity. . . ."[1] Green was fined and required to recognize a surety in the sum of fifty pounds. He produced Ephraim Savage, identified as a "Gentleman" in Clark's book, as his surety.

Sewall reported in his diary for 22 and 23 February 1711–12 that the case against Green had commenced when a Mr. Pemberton complained to him. Sewall went to "Dr. Clark's" the next morning because "his house [was] amidst the people concerned." Together Sewall and Clark "stop'd Green's Lying mouth."[2] It is not clear whether there is any relation, but a month later the General Court passed a law which fixed as a punishment for "composing any filthy, obscene or prophane . . . mock-sermon, . . . a fine to her majesty not exceeding twenty pounds, or by standing in the pillory once, or oftener, with an inscription of his crime, in capital letters, affixed on his head. . . ."[3]

Although it is not possible to learn a great deal about the grand jury in Boston from the recognizances in Clark's book, a few observations can be made. First, since Clark's book shows thirty-five recognizances generated by grand jury presentments, it seems reasonable to conclude that the grand jury was active in Boston during this period. Second, the grand jury seems to have acted on noncapital matters only if they involved cases outside the jurisdiction of a single justice of the peace. Third, some matters, like fornication, which could be formally initiated by a summons, sometimes commenced with a presentment. There is no explanation why some commenced one way and others did not.[4]

This third description is illustrated by the case of Eliza Faulkner, a Boston widow, who was required on 23 June 1707 to make a recognizance and find a surety to answer before the general sessions "a presentment of the Grand Inquest for . . . the County of Suffolk

---

[1] *Book,* 23 February 1711/12, 101.

[2] *Sewall Diary,* 336–337.

[3] *Acts & Resolves,* I, 682 (Chapter 6 of the Acts of 1711–12, 6th Sess.).

[4] Chapter 11, Article 7 of the Acts of 1692–3, 2d Sess., attempted to establish the "grand inquest" in all capital cases as one of the "rights and liberties of the people." *Acts & Resolves,* I, 40. The Privy Council disallowed this statute.

for being guilty of uncleaness with Dr. Hewes at the House of the widow Midwinter of Boston."[5] On 16 July 1707 the widow, Provided Midwinter, also made a recognizance "to answer to a presentment of the grand inquest for . . . the county of Suffolk for keeping a bawdy house."[6] It is not surprising that these offenses went to the sessions, but it is hard to find any principle which separates Eliza Faulkner's matter from the non-grand jury cases of fornication which Clark regularly bound over to the sessions without a presentment. It may be that Eliza Faulkner's companion was married and that the more serious, but still non-capital,[7] punishment for adultery required the grand jury's attention.

To summarize, John Clark's criminal business was about one-half the magnitude of his civil business. The majority of the crimes were theft and peace offenses, and the rest a mixture of religious and morality offenses. In addition to trials, Clark acted to secure the appearance of individuals charged with more significant crimes either upon a private complaint or a grand jury presentment.

As anyone familiar with modern criminal law will attest, the substantive criminal law is only one part of any system for identifying and punishing crime. A source of great modern concern has been pre-trial and trial procedure. Unfortunately we can glean very little about these matters from Clark's book. One thing is clear; justices of the peace relied heavily on local constables to operate their courts. Clark fined two people for resisting a constable[8] and two other people for refusing to cooperate with a constable.[9] In only one case is the office of the sheriff mentioned;[1] three sailors were fined ten shillings for "affronting the Deputy Sheriff in his attempts to secure" the peace. This heavy reliance on the constabulary perhaps explains the

[5] *Book*, 48.

[6] Ibid., 16 July 1707, 49.

[7] *Acts & Resolves*, I, 171 (Chapter 5 of the Acts of 1694–5, 1st Sess.) established a variety of savage, but non-deadly, punishments for adultery. Polygamy remained a capital offense.

[8] *Book*, 4 May 1705, 25, and 17 April 1706, 36.

[9] Ibid., 3 February 1710/11, 84–85 and 24 February 1710/11, 86–87.

[1] Ibid., 13 January 1712/13, 123.

large number of people who declined election to that office, according to Boston's records, during this period.[2]

Justices of the peace were authorized to grant warrants to search for stolen or illegally imported goods.[3] There is no way to evaluate the basis on which warrants were issued; indeed, the use of a warrant is mentioned in only one of Clark's cases.[4] Peter Paity procured from Clark a warrant directing a constable to search for a copper kettle. Constable Gardner found the kettle in the shop of a brazier named John Tedman, who claimed his wife had recently purchased it. Clark gave Tedman's wife the chance to produce her vendors. She apparently failed to do so, whereas Paity had witnesses who testified to his ownership of the kettle. Clark ordered Tedman to return the kettle and pay Paity the "charge of the warrant. . . ."

John Clark's book provides more insight into the disposition of cases than pre-conviction procedure. One fact is startling by modern standards: every criminal case reported in the book ended in a conviction. Since Clark did report the occasional victory by a defendant in a civil matter, it is possible that the absence of findings of innocence may indicate that each person charged criminally was convicted. On the other hand, it may have been a record-keeping convention not to enter findings of innocence since there were no fines to be reported and thus they had no record-keeping significance.[5]

In the vast majority of cases the defendants were punished with fines. The size of the fines depended on the relevant statutes. Clark

[2] See, e.g., *Report #8 (1883): The Boston Records from 1700 to 1728.* At the freeholders meeting of 9 March 1701/02 all four people elected constable, including Adam Winthrop, refused to serve and had to be replaced. Chapter 28 of the Acts of 1692–3 (2d Sess.) imposed a fine of £5 for refusing to serve as constable of any community other than Boston or Salem and £10 for refusing to serve in the latter two communities. *Acts & Resolves,* I, 67.

[3] *Acts & Resolves,* I, 345 (chapter 16 of the Acts of 1698 [1st Sess.]).

[4] *Book,* 13 March 1704/05, 23–24.

[5] It is interesting that article 3 of the act, which purported to recognize "the rights and liberties of the people," only protected a person from being "twice sentenced for one and the same crime, offense or trespass." *Acts & Resolves,* I, 40 (Chapter 11 of the Acts of 1692–3, 2d Sess.). This act was disapproved by the Privy Council on 22 August 1695. William Nelson has stated that protection against double jeopardy in something like its modern form was in existence in early nineteenth century Massachusetts. W. E. Nelson, *Americanization of the Common Law: The Impact of Legal Change on Massachusetts Society, 1760–1830* (Cambridge: Harvard University Press, 1975), 99, note 141.

seems to have imposed fairly low fines, viewed from the allowable limit. This may help explain the startlingly low level of criminal appeals.

In the rare instance in which a defendant could not pay his fine, Clark would substitute, depending on the case, a whipping, a night in jail, or some other punishment of public humiliation. There are only two cases in the book in which Clark ordered a whipping without mentioning a fine; one involved an Indian defendant[6] and the other a black.[7] The case of John Tunagain is illustrative:

John Tunagain Indian convicted of drunkeness and prophane cursing three times the last night ordered to pay five shillings for cursing or to be whipt publicly ten stripes and to pay costs of prosecution. Standing committed till the sentence be performed.[8]

A number of convicted individuals were committed to jail pending payment of their fines, but in most cases John Clark's book notes receipt of the fine assessed. "Costs" are occasionally assessed in criminal matters, as in the Tunagain case, but the elements and amount are not specified.

It has been noted that Clark tended to fine in the lower ranges of what the law permitted. On one occasion when Clark imposed the maximum fine, a case of selling liquor without a license, he wrote that it was Margaret Johnson's "second conviction."[9] Apart from this one comment there is little information on what influenced Clark in sentencing. He treated seamen specially. For instance, he lifted the recognizance of the peace imposed on Thomas Lonyon, a mariner, "upon [his] going to sea."[1] In another case Lieutenant William Skye of a company of Marines was asked to guarantee the appearance of Thomas Turland, a seaman, "upon the return of the ship Saphire from her present cruise."[2]

A criminal defendant aggrieved by the decision of a single justice of the peace could appeal for a new trial to all the justices gathered

[6] Book, 11 October 1715, 200.

[7] Ibid., 20 May 1726, 268.

[8] Ibid., 2 June 1712, 106.

[9] Ibid., 17 February, 1706/07, 46.

[1] Ibid., 16 July 1703, 17.

[2] Ibid., 26 May 1712, 106.

at the general session.[3] Only five people made recognizances to appeal from Clark's criminal judgments.[4] This is a small number of the over 260 criminal convictions during the period of the book, but probably not atypical.

The deeper social facts about the jurisdiction of a single justice of the peace are hard to learn from Clark's book. Who was involved in Clark's court and what was the geographic and sociological domain of his criminal litigants? As mentioned previously, Clark lived in the north end of Boston. If a Massachusetts justice of the peace of this period was a truly local figure, then one might suppose that Clark handled cases with a locus in the north end. There is some support for this in the book. All of the precise geographic locations within Boston mentioned in the book were near Clark's home. Scarlet's Wharf is mentioned in two cases;[5] a riot occurred on Prince Street;[6] two servants scuffled in the new North Meetinghouse one Sunday.[7]

Unfortunately the precise location of most crimes is not mentioned and all that can be confidently stated is that the defendants and victims were overwhelmingly from Boston.[8] Thus the issue of how people came to Clark as a justice, whether because of geographic proximity or, as seems more likely, the result of a decision made at some point in the issuance or return of original process cannot be established from the book. The sharp decline in the number of cases during the last ten years of the book suggests that either Clark or the litigants could control the number of cases which he was to hear and that there was, within Boston, no rule requiring a litigant to use the nearest justice of the peace.

Somewhat more can be said about the social status of those who were involved in Clark's criminal jurisdiction. In general, the book seems to support the notion that criminal defendants either had no profession or occupied what can easily be identified as lower status

---

[3] *Acts & Resolves*, I, 368 (Chapter 1 of the Acts of 1699, 1st Sess.).

[4] See, e.g., *Book*, 25 October 1701, 10.

[5] Ibid., 13 April 1716, 213 and 24 February 1710/11, 86–87.

[6] Ibid., 26 December 1718, 272.

[7] Ibid., 15 December 1715, 204.

[8] See Chart B, which classifies all matters during the period from 1 January 1713/14 until 31 December 1714.

positions, like mariners or laborers.[9] By contrast, and this will be discussed later, civil litigants seemed to be predominantly shop-keepers and small-business people.[1]

In addition to being overwhelmingly of low occupational status a number of criminal defendants were black; some were identified as freemen, most were referred to as servants, and one was called a "slave." Most of the matters involving blacks were theft offenses and, as mentioned earlier, Clark's punishments seemed harsh.[2] In all cases involving blacks, the possibility of a whipping was noted, whereas with whites it was rarely mentioned. The record indicates at several points that the master or mistress of a black servant inter-vened to pay the fine or provide security for the servant's good behavior.[3]

One of the well-known local policies from the earliest settlement of colonial Massachusetts was the prevention of idleness.[4] Chapter 8 of the Province Laws of 1699–1700 gave to a single justice of the peace, or the general sessions, the right to commit persons to a county house of correction—a workhouse supervised by the justices:

all rogues, vagabonds and idle persons going about in any town or county begging or persons using any subtle craft, juggling or unlawful games or plays, or feigning themselves to have knowledge of physiognomy, palm-estry, or pretending that they can tell destinies, fortunes or discover where lost or stolen goods may be found, common pipers, fidlers, runaways, stub-born servants or children, common drunkards, common nightwalkers, pilferers, wanton and lascivious persons, either in speech or behavior, com-mon jailers or brawlers, such as neglect their callings, mispend what they earn, and do not provide for themselves or the support for their families.[5]

In one case John Clark committed Lucy, a black servant of a Mrs. Moor of Boston, to the house of correction for fortune telling.[6]

[9] Ibid.

[1] See below, 150–151.

[2] See above, 117–118, text accompanying notes 2 and 3.

[3] *Book*, 19 March 1707/08, 54.

[4] See, e.g., *The Laws and Liberties of Massachusetts*, 25.

[5] *Acts & Resolves*, I, 378. Both the abhorrence of idleness and the institution of a house of correction, by the justices in session, were directly imported from England. See Dalton, *Countrey Justice*, 112–113.

[6] *Book*, 19 March 1707/08, 54.

Her mistress made a recognizance sufficient to secure Lucy's freedom until the next general sessions. In another case,[7] John Endicott, identified as a Boston cooper, turned his black servant over to Clark for commitment to the house of correction because of ungovernability and stubbornness. The servant attempted to escape and Clark ordered that he be whipped. Apparently Endicott and his servant were reconciled, for three weeks later Endicott made a recognizance[8] after appealing a new conviction of his servant for publishing a lie concerning Jonathan Wardell, a carpenter.

Blacks were occasionally identified as victims before Clark. In five cases[9] Clark convicted a non-black of assaulting a black. One master, John Peak, a Boston sawyer, was required to make a forty-pound recognizance guaranteeing his appearance at the next general sessions to answer for "cruel treatment towards his Negroman Primus and that he shall carry it well toward his said Negro in the meanwhile."[1]

The two largest racial minorities in Boston in 1700 were blacks and Indians. Only a few of Clark's criminal cases involved Indians. They were mostly peace matters and one interesting theft case:

Dick an Indian man servant to Mrs. Leach convicted of stealing cabbages from Captain James Grant at the north end of Boston the cabbage being returned with which said Grant being satisfied. Ordered that the said Dick be whipt ten stripes at the public whipping post in Boston.[2]

This is the only entry in the book in which Clark mentioned that he meted out a punishment greater than what had been sought.

Beyond the foregoing, there is not much which can be confidently said about the status of the criminal litigants. There is one case[3] in which a minor was the defendant. Occasionally white servants appeared and, as implied previously, virtually no matters involving people of high status. Family violence cases do stand out in the

[7] Ibid., 6 August 1705, 26.

[8] Ibid., 27 August 1705, 29.

[9] Ibid., 30 August 1706, 41; 16 September 1706, 41; 13 November 1708, 60; 5 October 1713, 147, and 29 February 1715/16, 211.

[1] Ibid., 23 February 1715/16, 210.

[2] Ibid., 11 October 1715, 200.

[3] Ibid., 6 May 1715, 191.

record, not because of their great number but because of the apparent severity of Clark's punishments. John Allum, a currier, was required to make a recognizance with sureties in the amount of £100 for "beating and bruising his wife."[4] Job Bull was also required to make a £100 recognizance with sureties for having an altercation with his wife.[5] George Burrel had to make a £20 recognizance for fighting with his wife,[6] and Thomas Atkins made a recognizance for £30 for "abusing his mother-in-law."[7] It is unclear why Clark did not try to convict these defendants under the assault language in the breach of the peace statute.[8] It may have been that these assaults were considered so serious that the probable punishment was beyond the power of a single justice, like Clark.

C. *Regulatory Offenses*

A Massachusetts justice of the peace was not just a judge. As a magistrate, he performed numerous executive functions. The records of Boston's selectmen for the years of John Clark's justiceship refer to numerous meetings among Boston's justices of the peace in session and the selectmen. William E. Nelson has written that a county's sessions court "was, in effect, the county government."[9] Frequent meetings were called to agree on how and when the justices, selectmen, and overseers of the poor would share the duty of taking nightly walks "to Supress disorders for the Space of Eight weeks...."[1]

The records of the selectmen list the justices who attended and,

[4] Ibid., 31 July 1718, 237.

[5] Ibid., 19 May 1715, 192. Bull, a victualler, who surely lived near Clark, appears in the book on over two dozen occasions. He was a civil plaintiff, civil defendant, and criminal defendant at various times.

[6] Ibid., 4 October 1712, 116.

[7] Ibid., 28 May 1711, 91.

[8] *Acts & Resolves*, I, 52–53 (Chapter 18 of the Acts of 1692–3, 2d Sess.). An assault on a woman in any "fields, streets, or lanes" was cognizable at the general sessions or when out of sessions before two justices of the peace. Ibid., 673–674 (chapter 2 of the Acts of 1711–12 [1st Sess.]). It may have been that these offenses lacked any public "peace" aspect.

[9] W. E. Nelson, *Americanization of the Common Law*, 15.

[1] See, e.g., *Report #13 (1885): Records of Boston Selectmen, 1716 to 1736*, 25 (7 August 1717).

Suffolk ss. Records 1711.

May 7th & Continued to ye 14th & thence to ye 18th Currt

Samuel Grice of Boston Mason plt: verss
Thomas Atkins of sd Boston Mason Deft —

J give Judgmt that ye Deft pay to the Plt
ye Sum of forty shillt sued for & Costs of
Suit. From which Judgmt ye Deft hath
Appealed.

14th Thomas Atkins of Boston Mason as principall & John
Neeland of Boston aforesd mason as Surety
Recognized to Saml Grice in the Sum of four
pounds on Condition that ye sd Tho: Atkins
Shall prosecute to Effect his Appeal at ye
next Inferior Court of Judicature to be
holden at Boston for ye County of Suffolk
on ye first tuesday of July next & abide ye
Order & determination of sd Court.

18. Thomas Atkins of Boston Mason Convicted
of abusing his mother in Law Ordered to find
Sureties in Sum of thirty pounds for his good
Behaviour & keeping the peace towards all her
Majesties Leige people espec: his mother in law
untill next Session

11. Entries, 7 May to 14 May 1711, Book of Records belonging to John Clark,
Justice of the Peace, Suffolk. Courtesy, Collection of James A. Henderson, Jr.

as compared with Samuel Sewall and others, Clark came infrequently. Some of Clark's appearances seem attributable to his position as a physician rather than his justiceship, but one cannot be sure. For instance, the selectmen asked that:

> John Clark, Esq. . . . goe on board his majesties Ship Seahorse and Report in what State of health or sickness the Ships Company are in, Especially with respect to Smal Pox or other Contagious Sickness.[2]

A later entry disclosed[3] that the *Seahorse* was so badly infected with smallpox that outsiders had to pilot it down to Bird Island to put the risk of infection further from the city. At first glance this might appear to have been an occasion on which the selectmen were relying on Clark's medical expertise. The General Court had attempted to give justices of the peace the power to fine sailors who disembarked from quarantined vessels not yet licensed by the health officials to land.[4] The Privy Council rejected this statute on the ground that the royal governor could control this problem by rules.[5] In any event it is not always easy to determine in what capacity the selectmen called upon a particular person who might be a justice of the peace.

The primary executive role of the justice was to act on, or participate in, the administration of various matters of a regulatory nature. For instance, the justices and selectmen agreed on 31 January 1723/4 that various of them, including John Clark, Esq., inspect within their assigned parts of town on 14 February "Disorderly Persons new Comers the Circomstances of the Poor and Education of their Children etc. and to meet at the hour of five of the Clock of the Evening. . . ."[6]

These regular inspections involved the justices directly. They were less directly involved in the licensing of innholders to serve strong drink. The selectmen did this at least annually,[7] and their

[2] Ibid., 81 (8 May 1721).

[3] Ibid., 82 (12 May 1721).

[4] *Acts & Resolves*, I, 377 (Chapter 7 of the Acts of 1699–1700, 1st Sess.).

[5] Ibid.

[6] *Report #13 1885: Records of Boston Selectmen, 1716 to 1736*, 122.

[7] Ibid., 154–155 (11 July 1726). The power of licensure was given to the Selectmen and to the justices in session in certain situations. *Acts & Resolves*, I, 56 (Chapter 20 of the Acts of 1692–3, 2d Sess.) and at 475–478 (Chapter 15 of the Acts of 1701–02, 1st Sess.).

records suggest that it was a function of some significance. Clark bound over all licensing offenders indicted by the grand jury, sixteen in the twenty-six years, to the general sessions. These represent the largest single classification of presentments handled by Clark. The level of the recognizance amount was typically low if compared to the criminal recognizances. The following case is illustrative:

Rebeccah Philpot recognized in the sum of five pounds on condition that she shall appear before her majesties Justices of the Peace at their next sessions by adjournment on the last Monday of this current August to answer to a presentment of the Grand Jury for selling drink by retail without license.[8]

Clark decided a number of liquor sales cases generated by informations[9] rather than grand jury presentments. Statutes provided that conviction for unlicensed sale subjected a person to a fine by a single justice or the justices in session of forty shillings; one-half to go to an informer and the other half to the poor of the town.[1] In cases of this sort, Clark would mention that an informer provided the information,[2] as in the case of John Buttley. On 7 August 1710 Clark noted, "I paid the informer 40s," which was one-half the fine he imposed.[3] Richard Pullen "informed against himself,"[4] perhaps hoping to reduce the fine, and Mary Smith appealed her conviction to the general sessions.[5]

Justices of the peace were supposed to work with local officials to ensure that a ready militia, composed of companies organized around individual officers, was maintained. Chapter 3 of the Province Laws of 1693–1694 established an elaborate system for raising the militia,[6] giving a single justice the power to fine a person who failed to par-

---

[8] *Book*, 14 August 1706, 39.

[9] Although this term is never used in the Book, Dalton does use it to refer to prosecutions of this type. Dalton, *Countrey Justice*, 525–526.

[1] *Acts & Resolves*, I, 56 (Chapter 20 of the Acts of 1692–3, 2d Sess.) and at 475–478 (Chapter 15 of the Acts of 1701–02, 1st Sess.).

[2] *Book*, 30 May 1709, 67.

[3] Ibid., 7 August 1710, 76.

[4] Ibid., 10 March 1706/07, 47.

[5] Ibid., 6 February 1701/02, 11–12.

[6] *Acts & Resolves*, I, 128 (1st Sess.).

ticipate. John Clark fined one Henry Wright ten shillings, as provided in Chapter 3, for failing to appear for muster.[7] Clark bound over to the general sessions an individual "impressed in her majesties name" into the company of Lieutenant-Colonel Adam Winthrop.[8] Although Clark's book contains relatively few entries of this type, the simultaneous records of the selectmen reveal a constant concern with military matters. On 16 March 1702, for instance, the selectmen and justices, including John Clark, Esq., met to agree on places for the "Lodging of Gunpowder."[9]

Several matters which are quite significant in the records of the selectmen and the separate records of the town have no analogue in Clark's book. A frequent topic of concern with the town was the arrival of people likely to need poor relief.[1] The names and circumstances of such arrivals were referred by town officials to the general sessions. Except for a few illegitimacy cases which had a flavor of this, Clark had no cases of this kind as a single justice.

Another set of issues frequently discussed by the justices with the selectmen at their joint meetings, but not reflected in Clark's book, are those involving highways, town property ownership, and boundary matters. Thus the decision made by the justices together with the selectmen on how to compensate people whose homes were blown up to stop an advancing fire on 9 October 1710 had no single-justice aspect.[2] Also, the many decisions on road, path, and wharf matters are not reflected in litigation before a single justice.

Clark handled some purely ceremonial municipal matters. He swore in an occasional municipal officer: John Brockus, as military clerk of Colonel Samuel Checkley's company,[3] and Josiah Winchester as Town Clerk of Brooklyn [sic].[4]

---

[7] *Book*, 3 October 1715, 200.

[8] Ibid., 28 December 1709, 70. Adam Winthrop, it will be recalled, refused to serve as a constable for Boston. See above, 124–125, note 2.

[9] *Report #11 (1884): Records of Boston Selectmen 1701 to 1715*, 19 (16 March 1702/03).

[1] Ibid., 101 (23 January 1709). The formal structures for control and support of the poor resemble those of Elizabethan England. See Dalton, *Countrey Justice*, 146–173.

[2] Ibid., 151 (10 December 1710).

[3] *Book*, 2 January 1710/11 at 82.

[4] Ibid., 30 July 1713 at 139.

The remaining regulatory matters recorded by Clark constituted violations of numerous petty municipal ordinances. John Prichard was fined twenty shillings for buying a turkey on Boston Neck on 7 January 1714/15.[5] Samuel Burrel was fined twenty shillings for having a black servant sweep his chimney "without the approbation of the selectmen of Boston."[6] William Robie paid twenty shillings after being convicted of cutting wood "not measured by a sworn corder nor viewed and found measured by the officers appointed for that end by the selectmen."[7]

D. *Civil Matters*

The civil jurisdiction of a Massachusetts justice of the peace was stable and substantial throughout the period of John Clark's justiceship. It extended to "all manner of debts, trespasses and other matters not exceeding the value of forty shillings (wherein the title of land is not concerned)."[8] Civil cases in the book outnumbered criminal by two to one. The vast majority of the civil cases concerned collection of a debt or contract-type damages. Since a large number of these cases involved claims for thirty-nine or forty shillings,[9] it would appear that people sought out justices of the peace in general[1] or John Clark in particular.

The first major class of civil matters involved confessions of judgment:

March 24 [1701] John Tuckerman of Boston Cordwainer acknowledged Judgment against his person and estate for the sum of twenty-one shillings due to John Coomer Junior of Boston Pewterer.

April 15th Execution Granted.[2]

The book contains sixty-three such acknowledgments, nine of

---

[5] Ibid., 181.

[6] Ibid., 3 March 1715/16, 211.

[7] Ibid., 6 September 1712, 113.

[8] *Acts & Resolves*, I, 282–283 (Chapter 8 of the Acts of 1697, 1st Sess.).

[9] See, e.g., *Book*, 2 March 1701/02, 13.

[1] Some slight support for this may be found in the fact that in the 1780's agrarian reformers obtained an enlargement of the jurisdictional amount in single justice civil matters. See W. E. Nelson, *Americanization of the Common Law*, 70.

[2] *Book*, 3.

which have subsequent executions noted, like Tuckerman's. Not much can be gleaned from the confessions except that their number suggests that creditors knew enough of the English practice to understand that a confessed judgment provided a quicker and surer remedy than a regular law suit.[3]

By contrast, civil proceedings for the collection of a debt or contract-type damages reveal a good deal of interesting legal information. In supporting the prosecution of a number of these cases, bills of exchange or notes were introduced as evidence. The existence of a bill or note was usually revealed in cases which threatened to go by default.[4] John Clark would not enter judgment in a defaulted debt or contract proceeding without a showing of proof beyond the plaintiff's bare allegation:

January 2. Christopher Webb of Boston Tailor plaintiff versus John Wakefield of Boston Shipright defendant. Default. The defendant not appearing the plaintiff produced a bill for 40 shillings endorsed accepted by the defendant. Whereupon I give judgment that the defendant pay to the plaintiff the sum of 40 shillings money sued for and cost of suits 6/. Execution issued January 4.[5]

In one of the defaulted bill of exchange cases, Clark noted that the defendant had been "thrice called."[6] Most entries do not indicate that defendants were called, and there is no explanation why in that particular case and a few others Clark mentioned that the defendant had been summonsed three times. English common law had from the earliest time abhorred and avoided default judgments.[7] Thus John Clark's occasional references to a defendant being called three times are perhaps merely an example of how general notions of fairness derived from the common law may have seeped, without explicit adoption, into the law of Massachusetts. Such a generalization does

---

[3] William Nelson seems to suggest that executions on confessions of judgment without a law suit were not possible until the Confession Act of 1782. W. E. Nelson, *Americanization of the Common Law*, 148. Clark's book does not support this suggestion.

[4] See, e.g., *Book*, 15 December 1712, 121.

[5] Ibid., 2 January 1715/16, 207.

[6] Ibid., 8 December 1707, 52.

[7] J. H. Baker, *An Introduction to English Legal History*, 2d ed. (London: Butterworths, 1979), 56.

not explain why some people got the benefit of the three-times rule and others apparently did not. A clue may be found in Chapter 20 of the Province Laws of 1700–1701[8], which provided that in a suit in which goods or other property were attached the defendant, if "not an inhabitant *or* [who was a] soujourner within the province, ... or [who was to] be absent out of the same at the time of the commencing such suit, and shall not return before the time for trial," could not be defaulted until he had been summonsed on three separate occasions. In the case mentioned at the beginning of this paragraph, the defendant was a mariner and it may have been that John Clark applied something like the rule in attachment cases.[9]

In most debt or contract-type matters there was nothing as damning against the defendant as a signed note or bill. If the defendant failed to appear, the plaintiff generally would produce and swear to a "book" or account. An entry for 11 September 1701 is illustrative:

Elijah Doubleday of Boston Butcher petitioner versus John Chadwick of said Boston sailor defendant in a plea of the case for the value of eighteen shillings and six pence due by book for meat sold him and the defendants not appearing at the time and the petitioner making oath to his book Judgment is granted by Default for 18s and 6d and costs of suit.[1]

In some cases this pattern varied slightly; the wife of the petitioner[2] or a servant[3] might swear to the book or account. In one entry Clark wrote that the account was annexed to the writ[4] commencing the litigation. Finally, one Sarah Horton, not having a book to swear to, made her case in the face of the defendant's default by the testimony of two witnesses.[5]

Evidence in Clark's book suggests that books and accounts formed the evidentiary basis for most contract and debt-type proceedings,

[8] *Acts & Resolves*, I, 447–448 (2d Sess.).
[9] Another case which mentions the three times rule involved a Thomas West of Martha's Vineyard. *Book*, 15 May 1710, 74.
[1] Ibid., 8.
[2] Ibid., 3 January 1714/15, 181.
[3] Ibid., 1 October 1705, 31.
[4] Ibid., 14 April 1718, 235.
[5] Ibid., 8 October 1711, 94.

not just defaulted cases. Thus, in a contested case,[6] Thomas Webber's wife testified that she had kept a running account of John Pitts' debt on a wall partition but had removed the partition and transcribed the figures into a book, the accuracy of which she then affirmed. Clark entered judgment for Webber in the amount of thirty-eight shillings based on his wife's testimony and the defendant appealed.

A number of civil matters involved collection of contract damages. Several cases reveal that the petitioners would estimate the liquidated value of performance in a contract case and sue for that amount. Clark, on several occasions, ordered payment of the liquidated sum or, as an alternative, partial or complete performance.[7] Samual Parrot, a tailor who apparently failed to do his job, was ordered to pay the petitioner thirty-six shillings or return "so much of the materials as were taken up for the jacket and breeches mentioned in the attachment."[8] Isaac Spencer, a gunsmith, was forced to return the "fusee or musket sued for" or pay thirty shillings and costs.[9] Nathan Millet of Gloucester, a boatman, was to "fulfill the bargain and deliver" some lumber at the promised price or pay the petitioner six shillings and costs.[1] Finally, the irrepressible Job Bull was to give over a ring sued for—perhaps by a disappointed fiancée —or pay twenty-six shillings money "in lieu thereof."[2]

The most enduring debate about colonial legal history has been over the extent of, and methodology by which, English common law was received in Massachusetts. A few tantalizing references in Clark's civil cases seem to show that Clark and his litigants were familiar with some common law terminology. A number of the contract-type actions were referred to as a "plea of the case."[3] It does not appear that this usage or its absence implied anything particular in a civil action. In some cases it referred to an action to recover on a

[6] Ibid., 18 August 1705, 26.

[7] Dalton has a lengthy entry on relief in the form of restitution in the context of the crime of forcible entry and detainer. Dalton, *Countrey Justice*, 312–319.

[8] *Book*, 22 May 1702, 14.

[9] Ibid., 28 April 1703, 17.

[1] Ibid., 21 March 1714/15, 187.

[2] Ibid., 23 January 1715/16, 207.

[3] Ibid., undated, 3.

bargain,[4] but in others it was employed in an action to collect a money debt.[5] Another common law reference, although an isolated one, occurred when William Jephson brought an action of replevin to obtain two of his cows which were "wrongfully and illegally impound[ed]...."[6]

Justices of the peace could hear actions in trespass "wherein the title of land [was] not concerned."[7] The Province Laws provided[8] that if a litigant demurred to a single justice's jurisdiction on the basis of a claim of title, then he would have to make a recognizance guaranteeing that he would prosecute his claim of title at the next session of the inferior court of common pleas for the county in which the trespass occurred. Only four actions are identified by Clark as "trespass," and in all of them the defendants demurred based on a claim of title.[9] Case actions are not referred to as trespass actions.

Clark's book does not give much insight into the dynamics of civil litigation. He seems to have had a liberal attitude to adjournments and continuances. Some may have been involuntary, because of the defendants' absences, but others seem to have been at the request of the parties, perhaps while they tried to settle.[1] One trial device which Clark used in contested contract cases was reference to auditors:

John Pedley of Boston Joiner plaintiff versus Joseph Essex of Boston aforesaid Watchmaker defendant. The defendant pleads that the work is not worth half the money that the plaintiff sues for whereupon by the agreement of both parties Mr. Frogley and Mr. Whittemore are appointed to view and appraise the work and make their report to me.[2]

Clark's judgments were usually in a form whereby the defendant

[4] Ibid., 4 January 1701, 3.

[5] Ibid., undated, 2.

[6] Ibid., 24 October 1709, 68.

[7] Acts & Resolves, I, 282–283 (Chapter 8 of the Acts of 1697, 1st Sess.).

[8] Ibid., 324–325 (Chapter 7 of the Acts of 1698, 1st Sess.).

[9] Book, 1 December 1702, 16; 27 April 1713, 131; 18 September 1713, 145; and 31 October 1715, 202.

[1] Book, 15 May 1710, 74.

[2] Ibid., 29 June 1711, 135. See also 23 March 1718/19, 245.

was ordered to pay the plaintiff the money sued for. Occasionally the defendant won. No matter what party eventually prevailed, Clark seems to have assessed costs, in an unspecified amount, on the loser. On rare occasions Clark found for the plaintiff but reduced the amount sought.[3] This was perhaps a result of his own evaluation of the evidence introduced in cases in which the right sought to be enforced was not a simple money debt.[4]

Litigants could appeal Clark's determination of the merits to the inferior court of common pleas.[5] Twenty-seven parties sought such appeals by making recognizances to Clark, usually in a fairly modest amount, which secured their promise to appeal. One case involving Job Bull suggests that appeals were discouraged. On 29 June 1713 Bull lost by default an action to collect thirty-three shillings, six pence.[6] Clark recorded Bull's recognizance one day later but subsequently wrote in the margin:

Memorandum. The appeal being granted after the court was risen and the plaintiff was gone the law not allowing such liberty. It considered further and upon the plaintiff['s] instance issued out an execution July 7th.[7]

Justices of the peace depended on the effectiveness of writs of execution in view of the large number of defaulted civil actions. Clark's book reveals that nine cognovits resulted in executions and ninety executions issued on regular judgments. On very few of the execution entries is there a subsequent notation. In one case Clark noted "Returned Satisfied Costs 5s Oct. 1" on a judgment made on 5 May 1712.[8] On an execution of 20 July 1714 he wrote, "Not paid the while."[9] No inference as to the efficacy of such executions is possible in view of the incompleteness of the record. One prevailing

---

[3] Ibid., undated, 2.

[4] Ibid., 17 August 1713, 141, and 13 January 1715/16, 206.

[5] *Acts & Resolves*, I, 282–283 (Chapter 8 of the Acts of 1697, 1st Sess.).

[6] *Book*, 136.

[7] Ibid.

[8] Ibid., 104. The meaning of the term "costs" is unclear, but it may have included the prevailer's reasonable attorney's fees.

[9] Ibid., 14 December 1713, 150.

plaintiff refreshingly relinquished his judgment because he suspected that his writ was "false laid."[1]

The geographic and social status of the civil litigants before Clark is a little clearer than that of the criminal litigants. Chart B of the Appendix includes all cases recorded for the year 1 January 1713/14 to 31 December 1714 and shows that the contestants were overwhelmingly from Boston.[2] Because debts do not occur on a street corner, unlike assaults, there is less evidence to tie the civil cases to a particular part of Boston, like the north end. Several names, particularly Job Bull's, recur in civil matters. Chart B also shows that small shopkeepers and manufacturers, cordwainers, victuallers, and innholders, who might be expected to have had numerous modest-sized debts, used Clark's justice court frequently. They also tended to prevail. By contrast, people of lower status occupations, unknown occupations, mariners, and carpenters tended to be the defendants and tended to lose.

Occasional bits of additional information are of interest. As compared with Clark's criminal cases, only one civil case involved a black or Indian as plaintiff. Several legal representatives of decedents' estates[3] sued; one trustee sued[4] and one gentleman was sued. The entry concerning the gentleman may suggest the power of high social status before a local justice of the peace like Clark.

May 22 [1710] Mary Baker Widow Relict and administratrix of Nathaniel Baker of Boston, Baker deceased. Plaintiff versus John Harris of Ipswich in the County of Essex gentleman Defendant. The plaintiff and defendant both appearing and the plaintiff refusing to enter the action the defendant prayes his costs of suit which is accordingly granted him.[5]

E. *Miscellaneous*

Two striking facts about the legal system revealed in Clark's book merit discussion apart from the relationship to the substantive law—the absence of attorneys and the heavy reliance on recognizances.

---

[1] Ibid., 9 November 1713, 148.

[2] Chart B is included in the appendix.

[3] See, e.g., *Book*, 1 October 1705, 31.

[4] Ibid., 3 May 1714, 161.

[5] Ibid., 75.

John Winthrop's dislike[6] for common law lawyers had given way to statutory toleration by the time John Clark started his book. Chapter 7 of Province Laws of 1701–1702[7] permitted an attorney to appear "in any suit" if he took the prescribed oath. Legal fees were limited in Superior and Inferior Court actions, but no fee was set for appearing in an action in a court of a justice of the peace. The statute also provided that "none but such as are allowed and sworn attorneys as aforesaid shall have any fee taxed for them in bills of costs," implying that fee awards were paid by losing litigants.

The word attorney appears in John Clark's book on merely ten occasions. The only person identified as an "Attorney at Law" was one Ralph Lyndery of Boston,[8] who was convicted of stealing some neckcloth and a pair of worsted stockings. Five of the occasions involved the appearance of a near relative, a son or wife, to perform a task in the court for an absent litigant:

[September 10, 1711] Thomas Hitchburn of Boston Joiner, Plaintiff, versus Mary Daftorn of Boston aforesaid Widow defendant in a plea of the case for not paying to the plaintiff the sum of forty shillings due according to attachment. The defendant appeared by her son Isaac Daftorn of Boston Cooper by a power of attorney who pleaded that the defendant owed nothing as set forth in the writ. Whereupon the plaintiff made oath to the account in his book and the evidences in the case being heard I give judgment that the defendant pay the petitioner the sum of forty shillings sued for and costs of suit. From which judgment the defendant hath appealed.[9]

On two of these occasions the family member confessed a judgment.[1]

In only four cases does the designation "attorney" appear for a party in which no familial relationship is mentioned. A Mr. Gee appeared to make out a debt on behalf of the petitioner, one Nathaniel Gookin of Sherborn.[2] Joseph Billings was "admitted at-

---

[6] Winthrop's attitude was attributable in part to his experience with the decaying Court of Wards in England. E. S. Morgan, *The Puritan Dilemma: The Story of John Winthrop*, edited by Oscar Handlin (Boston: Little Brown Co., 1958), 22–26.

[7] *Acts & Resolves*, I, 467 (1st Sess.).

[8] *Book*, 6 September 1705, 25.

[9] Ibid., 93.

[1] Ibid., 17 October 1701, 10, and 28 April 1706/07, 47.

[2] Ibid., 18 February 1711/12, 99.

torney for the defendant" and won a case of undeterminable subject matter.[3] An attorney appeared for William Coffin, a mariner, to make out his debt against a non-appearing defendant.[4] The conclusion to be drawn from the foregoing is that, while Clark was familiar with the concept of an attorney, no attorneys at law, as such, appeared in his court.

Equally striking to a modern reader is Clark's almost exclusive reliance on recognizances to guarantee that individuals perform something—prosecute appeals to the Inferior Court of Common Pleas,[5] appear as witnesses,[6] or leave others alone. The recognizance was in a money amount with a surety for performance. Not a single recognizance given with a surety is executed upon in Clark's book. In one case,[7] William Thomas, a mariner, did not produce a surety so he was "recognized to his majesty King George in the sum of 20 pounds to be levied on his goods and chattels land and tenements [and] in what thereof on his person" if he defaulted. The book noted a later sale of some goods on this pledge. Whether this lone example of an enforcement of a pledge proves that all the others worked is perhaps too speculative a matter, but Clark's book does give the impression that the recognizance system worked reasonably well.

F. *The Significance of the Book of John Clark, Esq.*

A single record or book covering the period 1700 to 1726 cannot be safely used to characterize Massachusetts society, its legal culture, major intellectual developments in law, or even the institution of the single justice of the peace. Clark's book is evidence which must be fitted into a larger picture.

English law provides a perspective by which to assess the significance of Clark's book. Although there have been few English local histories focused on a single justice and even fewer editions of justice

---

[3] Ibid., 7 June 1708, 55.

[4] Ibid., 18 May 1719, 246.

[5] Ibid., 14 January 1716/17, 225.

[6] Ibid.

[7] Ibid., 8 August 1718, 238.

of the peace records,[8] the impression that one gets from Clark's book is of a judicial world not far from that depicted in the 1705 edition of Dalton's *The Countrey Justice* or the other contemporaneous English justice of the peace handbooks. Clark's criminal and regulatory jurisdiction, both as a trial judge and magistrate, are consistent with the broad outlines of Dalton's. The two worlds diverged in that Clark's civil jurisdiction was much more robust than that of an average English justice of the peace.

Another perspective on Clark's book is Massachusetts legal history. In recent years two somewhat polar positions have been staked out on the development of Massachusetts Bay law from 1630 to 1700. David Konig[9] has argued that the earlier settlers possessed a communal ideal, which led them to de-emphasize the formal dispute settlement procedures of English law in favor of community accommodation mechanisms. Konig believes that the substance of the law began to change, and these procedures dropped away, when the original ideal ceased to be widely held. The law reflected this change, but also helped to advance it.

Konig's thesis is based on the belief that a good deal of English law and institutions came along with the communal ideal, and, in particular, that the magistrate central to the *Lawes and Libertyes* of 1648 was patterned on the English justice of the peace. The popularity of the office of justice of the peace with the Puritans in England and Massachusetts sprang from its local identification and the occasional refusals of English justices to enforce central policy. The justice of the peace was installed in Massachusetts because he was a local figure, but, as Massachusetts moved away from the communal ideal, the institution of the justice was left to increase its power and judicial business.

William E. Nelson's latest book[1] describes a similar pattern of change in Plymouth County from communal dispute resolution to

[8] The best recent book on the institution has been a purely institutional study. J. H. Gleason, *The Justices of the Peace in England 1558 to 1640* (Oxford: Clarendon Press, 1969).

[9] D. T. Konig, *Law and Society in Puritan Massachusetts: Essex County, 1629–1692* (Chapel Hill: University of North Carolina Press, 1979).

[1] W. E. Nelson, *Dispute and Conflict Resolution in Plymouth County, Massachusetts, 1725–1825* (Chapel Hill: University of North Carolina Press, 1981).

reliance on formal legal structures. Nelson's book places that change in the century from 1725 to 1825, and, but for this dating, it seems to agree with the Konig model, which may itself have been generated by Nelson's first book.[2] This is not to say that Nelson has necessarily endorsed Konig's view on the extent of importation of English law into Massachusetts.

At the other pole from Konig are the innovationists: scholars like Barbara Black[3] who think that the Konig approach misses the extent of legal innovation in Massachusetts. Professor Black has written that Konig's thesis on the magistrate's equivalency with the English justice of the peace ignores the source of the magistrate's power — and the essence of his office — his position as an assistant.[4]

The professionalism of the Clark book, and the number and detail of statutes passed regulating justices of the peace after the granting of the second charter in 1691, indicate that the justice of the peace was well established in Massachusetts in 1700. The book also shows that a single justice was in no sense concerned with the whole "community" of Boston. High status people are missing; perhaps they used other justices, but this is doubtful. Thus, while the justice courts may have been small scale, they did not handle randomly matters which concerned the entire community.

These conclusions would seem to support Konig's view that the office of the justice of the peace was congenial to the Puritans and therefore was quickly and solidly established in the magistrate analogue. They would also seem to raise questions about whether the pattern which William Nelson notes in Plymouth was even close to that in urban Boston. Nelson, of course, had no justice records comparable to Clark's for Plymouth during the 1725 to 1825 period.[5]

The evidence of the social status of the litigants in the Clark book should lead the participants in the debate to rethink the meanings of

---

[2] D. T. Konig, *Law and Society in Puritan Massachusetts*, xvi.

[3] Black, Book Review, *Yale Law Journal*, XC (1980), 232, reviewing Konig's book.

[4] An assistant was originally an enfranchised member of the Massachusetts Bay Company. "The Charter of the Colony of the Massachusetts Bay in New England 1628–29," reprinted in *The Founding of Massachusetts*, E. S. Morgan, ed. (Indianapolis, Bobbs-Merrill, 1964), 314.

[5] W. E. Nelson, *Dispute and Conflict Resolution*, 22–23.

the words "communal" and "community." If Boston was several economic communities or clusters in 1700, was it really one cohesive group in 1650? Was Plymouth ethically unified in 1725? The justice of the peace in England was more a local figure than a representative of some communal or medieval ideal. The strength of this institution in England, and then in Massachusetts, may have been in the familiarity of its officials and the surroundings of justice, in the scale of its grandeur and the modest size of most issues confronted. The economic divisions of the judicial system, shown in Clark's book, may indicate that there was never a "communal" ideal, because there was no single community.

A third perspective on Clark's book is how it fits into theories about the development of the criminal law in eighteenth-century America. The dominant insight, which others have modified or refined but for the most accepted, has been William E. Nelson's claim that the criminal law evolved from a religiously oriented construct at the beginning of the eighteenth century to a property oriented one at the beginning of the nineteenth. In his first book Nelson placed this change near the end of the eighteenth century.[6] In a recent article[7] Richard Gaskins has argued that the change occurred earlier in Connecticut. Nelson did not have much data on justice of the peace records; Gaskins relies on them.

The Nelson thesis can be challenged on three grounds. First, the data on eighteenth-century criminal law is so incomplete that major generalizations are not possible. Even if one can discover changes in the numbers or type of prosecutions, it is dangerous to derive grand interpretations from them. John Clark's book provides at least more data, but a long study of it makes one even less willing to contemplate making grand generalizations based on an aggregate of similar materials. Clark's book, like all such records, while fascinating, is *sui generis*. As any criminal sociologist will attest, records, even if excellently kept, are only evidence of convictions which may represent an unreliable indication of the purposes and impact of the criminal law.

[6] See W. E. Nelson, *The Americanization of the Common Law: The Impact of Legal Change on Massachusetts Society*, 1760–1830, 133–152.

[7] Gaskins, "Changes in the Criminal Law in Eighteenth Century Connecticut," 310.

A second possible challenge to the Nelson thesis begins with a concession that "religious-type" offenses probably diminished in number and property offenses increased in the eighteenth century. Such a change does not necessarily show an alteration of an ethical consensus about the purposes of the criminal law. It may instead show something quite different. If one accepts that the criminal law is in large part designed to define and control deviance, as Kai Erikson has argued,[8] it may be that the substantive content of the rules applied is less significant than Nelson and others have supposed. Why then did Massachusetts judges seem to apply moral law as opposed to property law more frequently at the beginning of the eighteenth century? There are several explanations, none of which is refuted by Nelson's data. For instance, it may be that property type offenses were rarer in an absolute sense in the early part of the century. With the Revolution and the post-Revolutionary economic problems, property offenses might have become more common and deviance control was being performed adequately by the property offenses.

A third possible challenge has been put forward by Robert Gordon in an excellent review[9] of Nelson's first book. Does the law immediately reflect changes in underlying social values? Do social values change quickly? Law and legal institutions seem resistant to such changes. John Clark's book reinforces this notion. A comparison of the book with Dalton and other justice of the peace manuals from England shows great similarities. The justice of the peace is a solid, local community figure who administers quick justice to the lower classes of the population. The major modification in Massachusetts is that John Clark is handling a large volume of civil cases in which he is acting as a debt collector for small shopkeepers. This may have been done by others in England, but it seems to fit in with his position in Massachusetts.

In sum, John Clark's book does not support or refute any of the great claims made in the latest scholarship on eighteenth-century legal history. A generation ago, John Dawson noted that a major divergence between English and French law was English tenacity or

[8] K. T. Erikson, *Wayward Puritans: A Study in the Sociology of Deviance* (1966).
[9] R. W. Gordon, Book Review, *New York University Law Review*, LI (1976), 686.

luck in holding onto local institutions charged with enforcing the law. Whether he was correct that these institutions and their longevity were an important part of the creed of "constitutionalism" is beyond the scope of this paper. Nonetheless, Professor Dawson was surely right when he observed that as these local institutions "evolved they left larger room than was provided elsewhere in Europe for wide participation by untrained people — not only in the process of judging disputes but in all the processes of government that clustered around that vital center. There was wisdom, no doubt, in retaining them and in letting their meanings unfold."[1]

CHART A—CUMULATIVE

Recognizances

Grand Jury presentments—

Illegitimacy	3
Miscellaneous	10
Selling liquor without license	16
Uncleanness	2
Bawdy house	1
Neglect of worship	1
Building with wood	1
Man and Wife fornicating	1

For Appeals—

Court of Common Pleas	27
General Sessions	5

To sue at Court of Common Pleas	5
General Sessions matters	108
To present a criminal complaint	10
To appear as a witness	3

Civil Matters

Trespass	4
Contract and debt	388
Default by defendant	242
Executions on judgment	90
Cognovit	63
Executions	9

[1] J. P. Dawson, *A History of Lay Judges*, 299.

Criminal Matters

Libel	16
Breach of peace	127
Theft	30
Profane cursing	39
Profane swearing	40
Profaning the Sabbath	5
Receiving stolen goods	2
Sentence to House of Correction (suspicion)	5

Administrative

Violating a municipal ordinance	44
Swearing in a clerk	9
Desertion from a ship	2
Marriage	1

Unknown Actions	63
Unclassifiable	7

CHART B

Entries in John Clark, Esq.'s Book from 1 January 1713/14
to 31 December 1714

A. *Matters* 87
  (Civil & Criminal)

B. *Civil Actions*
  1. *Residence*
    Plaintiff residence

Salem	5	Unknown	4
Boston	60		

Defendant residence

Boston	57	Dorchester	3
Salem	2	Unknown	5

  2. *Disposition*

Heard the case	18
Cognovit	2
Continuance	7
Appealed	6
Defaults	45

Nonsuit   1
Disposition not revealed   9
No won/lost disposition   1
Recognizance   9
Auditors empaneled   2
[Executed later per entry]   2
[Later judgment per entry]   2
Execution ordered or noted   6

3. *Prevailer*
   a. *Residence*

Salem	2	Unknown	4
Boston	51	Charlestown	1

   b. *Plaintiff or Defendant*

Plaintiff	57	Defendant	1

   c. *Occupation*

Innholder	6	Haywright	1
Sailmaker	1	Blacksmith	1
Shipwright	4	Joiner	1
Cordwainer	9	Fence Viewer	1
Wharfinger	3	Housewright	3
Mariner	2	Clothier	1
Unknown	4	Merchant	1
Widow	5	Glover	1
Victualler	8	Tailor	1
Barber	1	Pewterer	1
Retailer	3	Shipkeeper	1

4. *Civil Loser*
   a. *Residence*

Boston	49	Dorchester	3
Salem	1	Roxbury	1
Unknown	5		

   b. *Plaintiff or Defendant*

Defendant	58	Plaintiff	1

   c. *Occupation*

Wigmaker	1	Mariner	5
Bricklayer	4	Cordwainer	1
Innholder	3	Sadler	2
Joiner	5	Ship carpenter	1
Cooper	2	Carter	2

Blacksmith	2	Sailmaker	4
Unknown	7	Widow	2
Shipwright	5	Housewright	2
Laborer	3	Varnisher	1
Tailor	4	Fisherman	1
Husbandman	1	Blacks (occupation	
Mason	1	not given)	2

C. *Criminal*

   1. *Victim Residence*

Noodle Island	1
Boston	4
No victim	6
Unknown	4

   2. *Offense*

Profane cursing	1
Profane swearing	1
Breach of peace	5
Theft	1
False report	1

   3. *Victim Occupation*

Servant	1	Wife of a mariner	1
Tailor	1	Mariner (by his Captain)	1
Unspecified	4	Joiner	1
		Merchant	1

   4. *Defendant Residence*

Boston	7	Unknown	7

   5. *Defendant Occupation*

Butcher	1	Merchant	2
Singleman	1	Captain	1
Surgeon	1	Joiner	1
Unknown	5	Sailor	1

   6. *Conviction Appealed by a Recognizance*   2

   7. *Committed to Perform*   1

DOUGLAS LAMAR JONES

The Transformation of the Law of Poverty in Eighteenth-Century Massachusetts

URING the middle decades of the eighteenth century, people in Massachusetts experienced poverty in a way that they had not known it before. The numbers of poor and dependent people increased sharply both in the countryside and in the seaport towns; transiency became more common as "strolling poor" people moved from town to town in search of work and poor relief; almshouses and workhouses appeared not only in the large seaports of Boston and Salem, but also in some towns in the countryside; and town officials and ministers alike warned of poverty as the economic and social costs of poor relief began to rise.[1]

Three factors coincided to contribute to the rise of poverty in pre-Revolutionary Massachusetts. First, sustained population growth, especially in the eastern farming towns, led to a decline of land relative to the population; the result was constricted economic opportunities, stratification, migration, and unemployment.[2] Second, the

Financial support for this research was provided by the National Endowment for the Humanities, the Charles Warren Center of Harvard University, and Tufts University. The author wishes to thank Virginia Drachman and the editors of this volume for suggested revisions, and Edward Hanson and Dane Morrison for their research assistance.

[1] For example, see Douglas Lamar Jones, "The Strolling Poor: Transiency in Eighteenth-Century Massachusetts," *Journal of Social History*, VIII (1975), 28–54; Allan Kulikoff, "The Progress of Inequality in Revolutionary Boston," *William and Mary Quarterly*, XVIII (1971), 375–412; Gary B. Nash, "Urban Wealth and Poverty in Pre-Revolutionary America," *Journal of Interdisciplinary History*, VI (1976), 545–584; Gary B. Nash, *The Urban Crucible: Social Change, Political Consciousness, and the Origins of the American Revolution* (Cambridge, Mass., 1979), especially chapters seven, eight, and nine; Steven Wiberley, "Four Cities: Public Poor Relief in Urban America, 1700–1775," unpublished Ph.D. dissertation, Yale University, 1975; David J. Rothman, *The Discovery of the Asylum: Social Order and Disorder in the New Republic* (New York, 1971), chapters one through three.

[2] Douglas Lamar Jones, *Village and Seaport: Migration and Society in Eighteenth-Century Massachusetts* (Hanover, 1981); Kenneth A. Lockridge, *A New England*

series of eighteenth-century wars, especially the French and Indian War, disrupted the Massachusetts economy, displacing soldiers and their families.[3] Third, inflation during the early eighteenth century caused prices to rise while wages either declined or remained the same, resulting in both unemployment and a loss of income for those at the bottom of the economic ladder.[4] Taken together, these demographic, political, and economic changes posed significant challenges to the system of social welfare, and ultimately to the eighteenth-century legal system.

English in heritage but American in their social origins, the Massachusetts poor laws underwent a dramatic transformation in the eighteenth century.[5] Confronted with a growing class of paupers and transients, selectmen, overseers of the poor, town meetings, and the General Court redefined what I have termed here the "law of poverty." In the seventeenth century, the law of poverty reflected the fact that relatively few people fell into overt pauperism; with full employment, a generous supply of land, and minimal inflation, poverty simply was not the social problem that it became in the eighteenth century. Private charity through the churches and individuals combined with public relief to meet the needs of the desti-

---

Town: The First Hundred Years (New York, 1970); Philip J. Greven, Jr., *Four Generations: Population, Land and Family in Colonial Andover, Massachusetts* (Ithaca, 1970); Kulikoff, "The Progress of Inequality"; Robert A. Gross, *The Minutemen and Their World* (New York, 1976).

[3] Nash, *Urban Crucible*, chapters three, six, seven, and nine.

[4] Ruth Crandall, "Wholesale Commodity Prices in Boston during the Eighteenth Century," *Review of Economic Statistics*, XVI (1934), 117–128; Arthur Harrison Cole, *Wholesale Commodity Prices in the United States, 1700–1861* (Cambridge, Mass., 1938), Appendix A; Andrew McFarland Davis, *Currency and Banking in the Province of the Massachusetts-Bay*, 2 vols. (New York, 1900–1901), I. 172–173, 378–379; Carl Bridenbaugh, "The High Cost of Living in Boston, 1728," *New England Quarterly*, V (1932), 800–811.

[5] Scholars have tended to view the emergence of poor laws in colonial America as essentially a replication of the English poor laws. This essay suggests that the actual process of adaptation of poor laws in colonial Massachusetts arose from the particular economic and social conditions of eighteenth-century American life as much as from the inherited legal tradition of English poor relief policies and practices. Compare Caleb Foote, "Vagrancy-Type Law and its Administration," *University of Pennsylvania Law Review*, CIV (1956), 603, 615–617 and William B. Chambliss, "A Sociological Analysis of the Law of Vagrancy," *Social Problems*, XII (1964), 67–77.

tute, resulting in a minimal system of poor laws.[6] By the beginning of the eighteenth century, however, the transformation of the law of poverty began to occur. Social welfare programs in the towns became more common as the number of paupers increased; institutions of welfare appeared throughout Massachusetts; settlement laws began to clarify more specifically those who were entitled to benefits; and the warning-out system became the primary mechanism for detecting the presence of the transient poor. Taken together, these programs of welfare and control comprised the core of the transformation of the law of poverty.

Yet the law of poverty in eighteenth-century Massachusetts represented a tension between the material needs of the destitute and the needs of the larger society to control the costs of relief as well as the movements of the poor themselves. On the one side, compassion and humanitarianism demanded that the destitute receive at least a minimal level of subsistence; on the other, fears of "great disorder and idleness" and "great Public Expense" prompted the call for containment and control.[7] Yet neither compassion nor control, alone, is sufficient explanation for the transformation of the law of poverty in early Massachusetts.[8] This essay argues that the transformation was characterized by the gradual emergence of legal limitations on the towns and town officials who provided public relief *and* on the rights of the poor to social welfare. Rather than

[6] See Stephen Foster, *Their Solitary Way: The Puritan Social Ethic in the First Century of Settlement in New England* (New Haven, 1971), chapter five.

[7] The quoted passages are from the Petition of Daniel Giddinge and others, 1760, Record Book, vol. 1749–1763, Essex County Court of General Sessions of the Peace, 301, hereafter cited as Essex Sessions. These records are now located in the Essex Institute, Salem, MA.

[8] Historians have tended to view colonial systems of social welfare and social control as mutually exclusive. For the former, see Walter I. Trattner, *From Poor Law to Welfare State: A History of Social Welfare in America* (New York, 1974), chapters two and three; William E. Nelson, *Americanization of the Common Law: The Impact of Legal Change on Massachusetts Society, 1760–1830* (Cambridge, Mass., 1975), 48; and Gerald Grob, *Mental Institutions in America* (New York, 1973), chapter one. The social control perspective is more pervasive in the literature; for example, see Jones, "The Strolling Poor"; Rothman, *Discovery of the Asylum*; Nash, *Urban Crucible*; David H. Flaherty, "Crime and Social Control in Provincial Massachusetts," *The Historical Journal*, XXIV (1981), 339–360; Julius Goebel, Jr., and T. Raymond Naughton, *Law Enforcement in Colonial New York* (Montclair, 1970), 101, 107–108; and John K. Alexander, *Render Them Submissive: Responses to Poverty in Philadelphia, 1760–1800* (Amherst, 1980).

portraying the law of poverty as either compassionate or controlling, this essay seeks to demonstrate that welfare and control were intrinsically related parts of the administration and enforcement of the poor laws. Ultimately, the law of poverty in eighteenth-century Massachusetts gained a new legitimacy as the poor laws embraced both the needs of the poor and the economic and social interests of the townspeople who provided public relief.[9]

I.

The origins of the laws providing for public poor relief in colonial Massachusetts extend far back into the history of the colony's early settlement. The seventeenth-century laws continued the English tradition of public poor relief, but reflected in their application a society with relatively little poverty. In 1639, the General Court provided that either the Court itself or any two of its members could resolve any dispute concerning relief for poor inhabitants.[1] The General Court did not delineate guidelines or rules for resolving such disputes; rather, it relied on the discretion and wisdom of its members. Only six years later, however, the General Court appointed a committee to reconsider the existing poor law. Apparently two problems existed: one, the towns wanted a more predictable system of poor relief in order to plan their town budgets; and two, the General Court sought to "prevent multiplying of petitions" presented to the Court.[2] The General Court responded quickly, giving every town the power to present "idle and unprofitable persons, and all children, who are not diligently [employed] by their parents" to the quarterly courts to be disposed of both for their own welfare and for the common good.[3]

While relatively simple in its language, the poor law of 1646

[9] Useful theoretical perspectives which bear on the issue of legitimacy include Eugene D. Genovese, *Roll, Jordan, Roll: The World the Slaves Made* (New York, 1974); E. P. Thompson, *Whigs and Hunters: The Origins of the Black Act* (New York, 1975); and Douglas Hay, "Property, Authority and the Criminal Law," *Albion's Fatal Tree: Crime and Society in Eighteenth-Century England*, ed. Douglas Hay et al. (New York, 1975), 17–63.

[1] *Records of the Governor and Company of the Massachusetts Bay in New England*, 5 vols., ed. Nathaniel B. Shurtleff, M.D. (Boston, 1853), I. 264.

[2] *Ibid.*, III. 15.

[3] *Ibid.*, II. 180.

defined the categories of public poor relief in colonial Massachusetts. Moreover, the 1646 law provided for the dual authority of town officials and justices of the quarterly courts, a feature that would become even more important in the eighteenth century. The final cornerstone of the eighteenth-century poor laws was established with the passage of the 1659 poor law. That law, passed after years of discontent over the presence of "strangers," required a three-month residency for entitlement to poor relief.[4]

The relatively simple and straightforward poor laws of colonial Massachusetts gave way in the eighteenth century to more specific statutes regarding the recipients of poor relief, the powers of town officials under the laws, and the duty of care owed to the poor. Under the Second Charter of Massachusetts in 1692, poor relief laws provided that selectmen, overseers of the poor, and county courts of general sessions of the peace focus on three groups of paupers: the destitute, children, and the able but unemployed. Initially, the Provincial poor laws rarely provided for how town officials would care for paupers; the laws usually required only "care" or "effectual care."[5] As with the colonial laws, the Provincial statutes permitted poor relief officials to use their discretion in providing care. Indeed, it is difficult to state with certainty what the duties of selectmen and overseers of the poor actually were in the early eighteenth century. Still, this discretion accorded to public officials made perfect sense; public relief was paternalistic. It was public charity that was given by the towns, so it was assumed that benevolent motives would inform the poor relief decisions of town officials.

By the 1730's and 1740's abuses had crept into the poor relief system to such an extent that the General Court began to define more specifically the rights of the poor and the responsibilities of the selectmen and overseers of the poor. In a law passed in 1743 the preamble to the statute stated that "it has sometimes happened ... that persons who are poor ... have and may greatly suffer by reason of the neglect of overseers of the town ...," either because of legal disputes over liability for relief or "supposition or pretence that

[4] *Ibid.*, IV. Part 1, 365. For the concern over "strangers," see *ibid.*, I. 192, 241, 264; III. 376.

[5] *Acts and Resolves*, I (1692–93), ch. 28, 67; (1703–04), ch. 14, 538–539; (1693–94), ch. 19, 151–152.

condition and circumstances of such poor persons are not . . . necessitous. . . ." To remedy these abuses the 1743 law provided more precise duties of overseers and selectmen towards the poor. They became subject to a forty-shilling fine if they denied relief to someone entitled to it; towns were required to tax themselves to provide adequate poor relief; and the justices of the courts of general sessions of the peace were empowered to resolve disputed residency cases as well as to collect taxes if the towns failed to do so.[6] While the 1743 law did not fully eliminate the element of discretion from poor relief decisions by town officials, it did attempt to limit that power.

Once the overseers of the poor or selectmen in the towns determined that a pauper needed and was entitled to assistance, they typically turned to local families to provide care. In both seventeenth- and eighteenth-century Massachusetts, the care of paupers generally remained with the family—the basic economic and social unit that could provide housing, food, clothing, education, and nursing in the event of illness.[7] But in the eighteenth century, family care began to assume a different quality, becoming more custodial as it was linked legally to the public poor relief system. Town officials employed families to care for the aged, poor widows, and orphans. While the town officials turned naturally to the family to resolve problems of poverty, the custodial families undoubtedly benefitted from the cash paid by the town as well as the labor of the working poor.

Agreements between town officials and custodial families were remarkably uniform; the towns paid a fee, usually for a year's duration, for a resident to provide food, housing, and clothing for a pauper. If the pauper was physically able, the agreement would stipulate that he or she would perform labor. Similarly, the town usually agreed to provide the costs of medical care. These contracts for custodial care usually lasted one year. At the end of the year paupers often found themselves placed in another family. Ezekiel Day of Wenham, for example, lived with seven different families

[6] *Acts and Resolves*, III (1742–43), ch. 18, 37–38; quote at 37.

[7] For the seventeenth-century practices, see John Demos, *A Little Commonwealth: Family Life in Plymouth Colony* (New York, 1970); and Edmund S. Morgan, *The Puritan Family: Religion and Domestic Relations in Seventeenth-Century New England* (New York, 1966).

between 1757 and 1764.[8] But widow Elizabeth McLane, a pauper from Northampton, remained with Samuel Clapp at the town expense between 1746 and 1760.[9] Obviously a mutually satisfying relationship existed between Samuel Clapp and widow McLane for the town to continue support for fourteen years. Similarly, the Selectmen of Littleton employed John Bridges to care for John and Margaret Barret, two of the town poor, for nearly ten years. Bridges took the Barrets into his home in 1755, receiving four pounds for one year of care. When Margaret Barret died in 1761, Bridges buried her at a cost of twelve shillings to the town. Two years later, Bridges moved to Groton, and John Barret went with him "at the Desire and Request of the Selectmen of Littleton." While living in Groton, the Littleton Selectmen paid Bridges ten pounds for Barret's support. After twelve months, however, the Littleton Selectmen refused to pay maintenance costs for Barret, arguing that both Bridges and Barret had become residents of Groton. The Groton Selectmen, however, refused to support the eighty-five-year-old Barret. The sessions court resolved the dispute, holding that Littleton was legally responsible for Barret.[1]

The duration of time in which paupers lived with custodial families indicates that those who cared for the poor did so from a variety of motives. Clearly, there was a financial benefit in taking in a pauper, for the annual supplements paid by the selectmen were welcome cash income for farm families. Becoming a custodial family meant that the family income could be augmented, not only by cash, but also by the casual labor some paupers could perform. Although paupers were often aged men and women, or young mothers with children, not all were bedridden. Richard Dodge, Jr., for example, a Wenham farmer, contracted with the Selectmen "to keep Elisabeth Senie and her youngest Child . . . for the Consideration of twenty shillings and what Labour She can do During the Sd Term."[2] In addition to the

[8] *Wenham Town Records*, 4 vols. (Wenham, 1940), III, 163, 166–171, 174, 179, 182, 187, 190.

[9] Judd Manuscript, Northampton, vol. 3, 56. Taken from Northampton Treasurer's Papers, Forbes Library, Northampton, MA.

[1] John Bridges Petition, File Papers, 1764–1765, Middlesex Sessions; located in the Middlesex County Court House, Cambridge, MA.

[2] *Wenham Town Records*, III. 212.

economic motives of taking in a pauper, the cases of John Barret and Elizabeth McLane suggest the possibility of strong emotional attachments between some paupers and caretakers. Custodial care of paupers was more than social welfare; it represented a direct extension of family life and the family economy. Just as adults took in their aging parents, so too did custodial families take in the aged, even though unrelated. Similarly, poor children became apprentices, supplementing the labor supply on the farms.[3]

Indeed, a persistent arena of tension between town officials and paupers was over the failure of family members to care for their poor relatives. Under the 1692 poor law and its successors a pauper was entitled to poor relief by a town "unless the relations of such poor, impotent person in the line or degree of father or grandfather, mother or grandmother, children or grandchildren be of sufficient ability to provide relief."[4] Relief of the poor was primarily the responsibility of the lineal family, extending through three generations. This responsibility depended on a line of descent (or ascent) which relied on the obligations of parents to children, children to parents, and grandchildren to grandparents. Laterally-extended relatives such as brothers, sisters, aunts, and uncles were not legally responsible for their poor kin; it was the lineal family that was the legal link to the pauper. Town officials had an economic interest in maintaining the family responsibilities of relatives of the poor. If children failed to care for their aged parents, then their poor relief costs fell on the town. Town officials typically petitioned the sessions courts to order families to care for their members. For example, the sessions court of Hampshire County ordered the Selectmen of Suffield to care for widow Priscilla Froe; the support,

---

[3] Apprenticing of poor and orphaned children occurred not only in Boston but in the country towns as well. Indeed, substantial numbers of Boston's poor apprentices were sent to country towns; see Lawrence W. Towner, "The Indentures of Boston's Poor Apprentices: 1734–1805," Colonial Society of Massachusetts, *Publications*, XLIII (1966), 417–468; and W. Graham Millar, "The Poor Apprentices of Boston: Indentures of Poor Children Bound by the Overseers of the Poor of Boston, 1734–1776," unpublished M.A. thesis, College of William and Mary, 1958, Appendix B, Table 2, 69–71.

[4] *Acts and Resolves*, I (1692), ch. 28, 67. For a more general discussion of the distinctions between lineally- and laterally-extended families in early New England, see James H. Henretta, "Families and Farms: *Mentalité* in Pre-Industrial America," *William and Mary Quarterly*, XXXV (1978), 3–32.

however, was to be provided by the widow's four grandchildren.[5]

In addition, aged widows and married couples also petitioned the sessions courts directly to gain support from their children. William King, a yeoman from Great Barrington, with his wife, Esther, petitioned the Berkshire County Sessions Court for relief because their children failed to provide support. King and his wife were both old and indisposed, and unable to support themselves, in part, because King had "conveyed his Estate to his three Eldest Children; relying on their generosity and filial Duty for Support in case he or his Consort should live to want it."[6] Similarly, John Cooper of Cambridge refused to aid his poor parents but was forced to do so by the Middlesex County Sessions Court.[7] Generally, the sessions courts held in favor of the aged in their petitions against their children, upholding the standard of family care when it was not fulfilled voluntarily.

But with town officials trying to minimize poor relief costs and some family members shirking their responsibilities, some of the poor were truly unwanted and neglected. It was often up to the sessions courts to resolve any disputes among these groups. Mary Stephens of Marblehead, for example, plaintively asked the Essex County Sessions Court to "give orders for me to have support. Either from my sons or from the town of Marblehead . . . ," since neither wanted to support her.[8] And Amos George, a boy of fifteen years, was "weakly and Infirm, without a father, and whose mother could not support him," was refused assistance by his grandparents. But the Selectmen of Haverhill succesfully took their case against the grandparents to the sessions court.[9]

[5] Case of Widow Froe, Record Book, 1724, Hampshire Sessions, 215; located in the Hampden County Court House, Springfield, MA. For similar cases, see Petition of the Town of Rowley, File Papers, 1769, Essex Sessions; Petition of Tho. Rowell, Etc. for Mary Flanders, File Papers, 1759, Essex Files; and Petition of H. Long, File Papers, 1757, Essex Sessions.

[6] Petition of William King and Wife, File Papers, 1764, Berkshire Sessions; located in Berkshire County Court House, Pittsfield, MA.

[7] Benj. Crackbone's Petition, File Papers, 1759, Middlesex Sessions; also see Case of Thomas Farmer, File Papers, 1756, Middlesex Sessions.

[8] Petition of Mary Stephens, File Papers, 1752, Essex Sessions.

[9] Petition of Selectmen of Haverhill, File Papers, 1765, Essex Sessions; Record Book, 1749–1777, 55, Essex Sessions.

As the sessions courts became more involved in the administration and enforcement of the poor laws in the eighteenth century, their role as mediator among competing groups (selectmen, paupers, and their families) became more important. A detailed record of the conflicts among these participants in the legal system occurred in the case of Sarah Moor in 1765.[1] In that year Sarah Moor of Rowley gave birth to twin boys fathered by Amos Jewett, Jr. This normally happy event was marred by the fact that Sarah and Amos were not married. Sarah became the twenty-one-year-old mother of illegitimate twin boys; Amos became the convicted father of two bastard children and legally responsible for five shillings per week in child support payments. Within the first two years of the birth of these children, both Sarah and Amos felt the weight of the law on their shoulders as they became involved with the Rowley Selectmen and the Essex County Sessions Court.

Sarah's early years and family origins are uncertain. Except for her birth in Rowley in 1743 and her baptism in Newbury, she rarely appears in the public records of Essex County. Her parents probably migrated to Rowley early in the eighteenth century. When Sarah moved to Newbury, she was legally warned out and probably returned to Rowley. There she met Amos Jewett, Jr., a member of a prominent Rowley family. Six months after the birth of the twins, Amos married Ann Noyes and settled in Rowley. Sarah's pregnancy and subsequent illegitimate births were not unusual for mid-eighteenth-century Massachusetts; pre-marital pregnancies had increased sharply, and contributed to the rising poor costs.[2] What was unusual was that the Rowley Selectmen tried to use the poor relief system to take Sarah's children away from her and bind them into service.

The Rowley Selectmen officially interjected themselves into the affairs of Sarah Moor in 1767, when Amos Jewett, Jr., went to debtors' prison because he could not keep up his child support payments. Amos appealed to the Selectmen for financial assistance, and

---

[1] The following discussion is drawn from Rowley v. Sarah Moor, File Papers, 1767, Essex Sessions; Record Book, 1765–1777, March 1765, Essex Sessions for the fornication prosecution; *Early Settlers of Rowley, Massachusetts*, comp. George Brainard Blodgette and ed. Amos Everett Jewett (Rowley, 1933), 207.

[2] Daniel Scott Smith and Michael S. Hindus, "Pre-Marital Pregnancy in America, 1640–1966: An Overview and Interpretation," *Journal of Interdisciplinary History*, VI (1975), 537–571.

they agreed to give security for his support payments. In return, Amos turned his property over to the town for an indemnity. The Selectmen were eager to keep Amos out of prison because the town would have to absorb the costs of raising Sarah's children. Still, since Amos could not keep up with the payments, the Selectmen petitioned the sessions court to release Amos from his weekly payments and to permit them to bind out the twins, who were now two years of age.

For her part, Sarah proved to be a resourceful protector of her children. She resisted the Selectmen's informal attempts to persuade her to bind out her children, and once in court, became an articulate and forceful defender of her rights. In a written document to the sessions court Sarah argued that it was not customary to permit local officials to take illegitimate children away from their mothers when they had a good home.[3] She stated that she was fortunate to have found a man who had been willing to take in both children as well as Sarah, herself, and that she planned to apprentice her children to this man when they reached the age of seven years. Further, she argued that her children, at the age of two, were too young to be taken from her. In contrast, the Rowley Selectmen wanted to take her children from her and place them elsewhere only because it would be a little cheaper. She felt that this other family was "not so good a place nor [in] no ways to be compared with" the family with whom she now lived. Simply put, Sarah argued that the Selectmen were insensitive to her wishes as well as the best interests of her children. She also alleged that the Selectmen had been cruel towards her, had threatened her, and did not agree that her children were an economic burden. The justices of the sessions court agreed with Sarah; they dismissed the petition and ordered Amos to continue his support payments.[4] While the Selectmen made their case primarily on economic grounds, the justices saw the issue as one of the rights of a mother to be with her children. In this way the justices preserved the rights of paupers and prevented extreme though possibly legal actions by town officials.

The case of Sarah Moor, though fascinating for its rich detail, also symbolizes the growing tension between welfare and control. By

[3] Sarah Moor, Answer to Rowley Petition, File Papers, 1767, Essex Sessions.

[4] Record Book, 1749–1777, 1767, 136, Essex Sessions.

accepting Sarah's argument that the Rowley Selectmen had over-stepped their authority under the poor laws, the Essex County Sessions Court placed boundaries on the discretionary power of town officials. Of course, not all town officials lacked compassion or acted incorrectly; one cannot weigh acts of compassion against those of control. But the law of poverty in the eighteenth century did begin to recognize that abuses did occur, and that the moral force of the community, through the sessions courts, sought to uphold both standards of fairness and appropriate custodial care.

II.

The alternative to custodial family care—formal institutionalization—emerged as a distinct and important part of the social welfare system in eighteenth-century Massachusetts. Large-scale almshouses and workhouses flourished primarily in Boston and Salem in the eighteenth century, but the problems of poverty forced some country towns to build or to consider building almshouses. The result was intense interest in institutional forms of care for paupers during the middle decades of the eighteenth century.

In the countryside small-scale poorhouses were occasionally built in order to provide housing and employment for the poor. Usually a dwelling house was converted into an almshouse, but new houses were built as well. Northampton, for example, voted to build a poorhouse in 1705, while Ipswich actually built one in 1719.[5] It was described as an "almshouse," and was a log house, forty feet long, sixteen feet wide, six feet high, with a slat roof. Ipswich used the house as an almshouse until 1734, when the town returned to maintenance of the poor in custodial families but with supervised employment by the overseers of the poor.[6]

Following this early interest in almshouses, concern over the poor led to more extensive debate over the feasibility of poorhouses in the 1740's and the 1760's. Braintree residents debated the merits of building or renting a house "for the Entertaining or Imploying such poor persons as the Town are obliged to take care of" in 1740, but took no action at that time. In 1747 the town agreed to build a house

[5] Judd Manuscript, Northampton, I, 232.

[6] Thomas Franklin Waters, *Ipswich in the Massachusetts Bay Colony*, 2 vols. (Ipswich, 1917), II. 396–397.

for the poor which was approximately the same size as the one built in Ipswich in 1719. But two months later the town rejected the poorhouse concept, returning to the custodial family practice.[7] Braintree's interest in a poorhouse undoubtedly was part of a general concern in Massachusetts over the rising costs of relief. Boston had built a new workhouse in the 1730's, and probably influenced other towns to consider similar approaches.[8]

By the 1760's small farming towns like Wenham debated the merits of a poorhouse, while neighboring Manchester voted to hire a house for the poor in 1765. Ultimately, Manchester decided not to build a poorhouse, choosing instead to place the poor in custodial families "as in years past." Northampton voted to hire a house for the poor in 1767, as well.[9] It is difficult to know how these country poorhouses actually operated. Some were converted dwelling houses, while others were built specifically for the poor. Still, these country almshouses were small-scale, absorbing only the town poor and unemployed. But the very existence of these poorhouses in the country towns reveals their shared concerns with seaports like Boston and Salem: inexpensive poor relief, employment of idle persons, and the rationalization of poor relief administration.

In Boston and Salem the demands of urban poverty prompted the use of almshouses, workhouses, outdoor relief through cash payments, and custodial families.[1] This blending of a variety of types of social welfare, however, was overshadowed as the almshouse and

[7] *Records of the Town of Braintree, 1740–1793*, ed. Samuel A. Bates (Randolph, 1886), 236, 281–282, 285, 531, 573.

[8] Nash, *Urban Crucible*, 126–127.

[9] *Wenham Town Records*, III, 188; *Town Records of Manchester, 1718–1769*, 2 vols. (Salem, 1891), II, 105, 114, 126, 129, and Judd Manuscript, Northampton, III, 72.

[1] On the Boston almshouse and workhouse, the most recent studies include Nash, *Urban Crucible, passim;* and Wiberley, "Four Cities." There is no complete study of the Salem almshouse and workhouse in the eighteenth century. For useful and suggestive studies, see Anne Farnam, "Uncle Venner's Farm: Refuge or Workhouse for Salem's Poor?" *Essex Institute Historical Collections*, CIX (1973), 60–86, which looks at the early nineteenth-century developments; see also Joseph B. Felt, *Annals of Salem*, 2 vols. (Salem, 1849), II. 396–408. The research reported here relies primarily on this author's analysis of materials in the Massachusetts Historical Society and the Rare Books and Manuscripts Room, Boston Public Library, for the Boston experiences with poverty. For Salem, the Essex Institute contains a substantial collection of materials on the eighteenth-century workhouse.

workhouse emerged in the eighteenth century as the dominant forms of public poor relief. These eighteenth-century urban institutions of care represented a transition between the custodial family of the countryside and the truly large-scale institutions that emerged in early nineteenth-century America.[2] On the one hand the almshouse and the workhouse of Boston and Salem were modeled after the family: they provided discipline for the unemployed; they gave unmarried but pregnant women a home in which to give birth; they put people to work; and they eased the pain of the aged and the dying.[3] The urban almshouse and workhouse were analogous to the custodial family of the countryside, providing many of the same functions, for they were tailored to the needs of the urban wage economy. But they were more impersonal, housing large numbers of paupers together. The living arrangements in the Boston almshouse, for example, resembled an urban boarding house. Its thirty-three rooms housed some one hundred thirty-three paupers; men and women shared whatever rooms were available; and there usually was more than one person in a bed.[4] Fewer people lived in the Salem workhouse, but the conditions of life were the same. Because these institutions were intended to reduce the costs of poor relief, there was inherent in them the tension between compassion and control.

Both Boston and Salem had separate almshouses in the seventeenth century, but with the growing numbers and costs of the poor in the 1730's and 1740's, formal institutionalization of the workhouse became popular in each town. Boston led the way in 1735, when the General Court granted the town the right to organize a

[2] For an analysis of this transition, see Rothman, *Discovery of the Asylum*, 30–78, 130–179.

[3] The almshouse and the workhouse co-existed in the middle of the eighteenth century; the former was primarily for the destitute who were unable to care for themselves, while the latter was intended to reform the poor and to reduce poor relief costs through a pauper work program. See Boston Overseers of the Poor, Admissions, 1760–1812, Massachusetts Historical Society. My analysis of all admissions between 1763 and 1769 reveals that twenty-seven percent of the paupers were men, forty-seven percent were women (of all ages), and twenty-six percent were children. Typically, about twenty-five people died in the Boston Almshouse each year, though the variability in urban mortality rates revealed more deaths in some years. In 1764, for example, sixty-one people died, including adults as well as infant children.

[4] "A List of Persons, Beds . . . in the Almshouse Aug. 1756," Boston Indentures, vol. 1 (1734–1751), Rare Books and Manuscripts, Boston Public Library.

workhouse.[5] Other towns followed the lead of Boston, most notably Salem, by building a workhouse in 1749.[6] Earlier, in 1743, the General Court extended the right to build a workhouse to all the towns, permitting them to erect workhouses for both the idle and the indigent.[7] This law provided that the overseers of the poor, not the town selectmen, were to be the legally responsible officials for running the workhouse. The overseers were given broad powers of both oversight and regulation of the workhouse, while the town was required to provide the essentials for running the workhouse (furniture and implements for work, for example).

With the creation of public institutions of poor relief, overseers of the poor gained both new responsibilities towards paupers as well as new problems in the administration of social welfare. Given the large expenditures of town funds needed to build a workhouse, the Selectmen of Salem, for example, directed the Overseers "not to make any allowance this year to any Poor Persons that are out of [the] Work-House, saving in cases of [the] utmost necessity, [and] then but a small sum."[8] To some extent, the town poor in Salem were coerced into entering the workhouse, since they were threatened with the loss of support. Eventually, twenty men and women entered the new Salem workhouse when it opened in December of 1749.[9]

Prescriptive rules governed the lives of paupers who lived in the workhouses of Boston and Salem.[1] (In fact, Salem's Overseers

[5] *Acts and Resolves*, II (1735–36), ch. 4, 756–758.

[6] Salem Town Records, 10 May 1749, 22–23. The overlapping perceptions of the almshouse and the workhouse may be seen vividly in the Salem committee report: the members recommended "the building an Almshouse and Work-House for the Reception and Employment of the Idle and Poor of the Towne." The quotation is from ibid., 22. The source here is the handwritten copy of the Salem Town Records, Box 4 (1748–1775), Folder 1, Essex Institute, Salem, MA.

[7] *Acts and Resolves*, III (1743–44), ch. 12, 108–111.

[8] Salem Town Records, 12 March 1750, 87.

[9] Rules and Orders for the Management of the Workhouse … 1749–1798, vol. 14, Public Welfare Department, Salem, MA, Essex Institute.

[1] [1749 Rules for the Salem Workhouse], Rules and Orders for the Management of the Workhouse … 1749–1798; for the rules of the Boston Workhouse, see Boston Town Records, 1739, 234–240, in vol. 12, *Boston Records Commission* (Boston, 1885). The rules adopted by Salem are identical to those of Boston except for slight modifications. For example, Salem struck out the provision of the removal of the sick poor from the workhouse to the almshouse, since Salem did not have a separate almshouse. Citations to the following rules will be taken from those of Salem.

adopted the identical rules set forth by the Boston Overseers.) Life in the workhouse was intended to reform the idle worker and to care for the destitute. A range of punishments awaited the "disobedient poor," including the denial of a meal and loss of a day's allowance of food. More severe infractions resulted in strict punishments, such as wearing a wooden collar around one's neck, standing in a public place "with a Paper fixed on their Breasts denoting their Crime in Capitals for the space of one Hour," and being placed in the dungeon for forty-eight hours with bread and water.[2] If an inmate escaped from the workhouses of Boston or Salem and was recaptured, the master of the workhouse was permitted to attach a wooden clog to the person's leg to inhibit his mobility.[3]

The exact frequency with which these punishments were meted out is simply not clear. What the rules suggest, however, is that the townspeople, through their overseers of the poor, sought to do more than administer social welfare; they were determined to enforce institutionalized care. This combination of welfare with control in the workhouses may be seen vividly in the rules and experiences of the town of Springfield, which opened a workhouse in 1802. The Overseers of that town believed that they, too, had to coerce the paupers because of threatening behavior, drinking, and disobedience. Having decided that "punishment must be resorted to," the Springfield Overseers erected stocks ("the punishment is infamous painful") and a cell above the barn of the workhouse. The Overseers found that forty-eight hours "has generally been sufficient to create a dread of it." Clearly, control was a conscious element involved in running a workhouse, given the dual functions of the house to reduce poor relief costs and effect moral reform.[4] In addition, the very existence of a workhouse or almshouse actually deterred the poor from seeking public relief; they did not want to subject themselves to harsh treatment. For example, William Bentley, the Salem minister, expressed concern about the problem of poorly run workhouses and almshouses. He observed that Marblehead provided only a "house"

[2] [1749 Rules . . .], 4.

[3] Ibid., 5.

[4] Zibina Stibbins to Capt. William Edwards, Springfield, 17 May 1805, Northampton Town Records, reel 143, Forbes Library, Northampton, MA.

for their poor, which "makes the poor reluctant to return, [and] Overseers of other Towns unwilling to send [the poor back there]...."[5] Finally, some of the paupers of the Boston and Salem workhouses took matters into their own hands and simply "went away" or "ran away."[6]

Standing between the paupers and the overseers of the poor were the justices of the sessions courts, who attempted to enforce standards of fairness on the overseers as well as to insure that only legally entitled paupers received relief. A vivid example of the conflicting relationships that occasionally developed among town officials, paupers, and sessions justices occurred in Berkshire County in 1769. Barnet and Sarah Campbell, an aging couple who lived in Great Barrington, applied to the town for poor relief. Barnet had been a tailor, but because of old age, ill health, and poverty, he and his wife were unable to support themselves. Sarah Campbell, according to five matrons who examined her for the local physician, William Whiting, had "Sores, Bruises and other [female] Disorders not proper for us to mention..., [so] we judge her at present Extremely unfit for Labor."[7] When the Campbells applied for relief, they expected to receive outdoor relief from the town; that is, monetary payments to provide the basics for living. Instead, the Overseers of the Poor ordered them to the workhouse.[8]

Barnet Campbell was unwilling to accept such treatment. Placement in the workhouse, to Barnet Campbell, was in itself inhumane treatment. He believed that "instead of that Kindness and tenderness which Old Age, and impaired health require and that provision and support which Human nature Demands, [he and his wife] have been treated with ... Roughness, threatened with the workhouse, whips and chains ..., and left without any support." Instead of being able to rely on public poor relief, the Campbells survived on the

---

[5] *The Diary of William Bentley*, 3 vols. (Gloucester, 1962), II. 81.

[6] For example, on 18 April 1764 Mary Tufts was admitted to the Boston Almshouse. On 10 July she "Jumpt the fence and went off from ye house...." See Boston Admissions, 1763–1768, for numerous examples.

[7] Letter of William Whiting, Physician, File Papers, 1769, Berkshire Sessions.

[8] Overseers of the Workhouse in Great Barrington to Barnet and Sarah Cammel [Campbell], 10 April 1769, File Papers, 1769, Berkshire Sessions.

charity of "a few good people."[9] Campbell believed that the work-house was for those who would not work, not those who could not work. Campbell's perception of the workhouse echoed the views of William Bentley that the poor tried to avoid the workhouse or the almshouse, but Campbell suggested a new point: he and his wife were too respectable to be placed in the workhouse. Although the statute of 1743, which enabled towns to create workhouses, intended them for both the indigent and the idle, Campbell's perception was probably the typical one.

Campbell took his problem to the Berkshire County sessions court, where he petitioned the court to intervene in his behalf and to force the Overseers of Great Barrington to provide outdoor relief. To prove that he was not one of the idle poor, Campbell obtained the support of friends where he had lived for nearly twenty years in Albany County, New York. Twenty-three persons testified by deposition to his good moral character and his "Industrious and frugal manner."[1]

The justices of the sessions court agreed with Barnet Campbell and held that the Campbells did not belong in the Great Barrington workhouse.[2] Reviewing the statutory basis for confinement to the workhouse, the justices said that the act applied only to idle persons or persons who refused to work and were able to work; it did not include "persons which providence has rendered unable for Service in this manner." Still, the justices remained conciliatory towards the overseers, recommending that they "put those old persons into some more Eligible and Easy circumstances than a work house." One of the justices, Timothy Woodbridge, expressed deep concern for the Campbells to his fellow justices: "I must commiserate the case of the poor helpless old people and could heartily wish some other Expedient might be found for their relief Then sending Them to a House of Correction."[3]

But the Overseers were persistent. One day after the justices or-

---

[9] Petition of Barnet Campbell and Wife, File Papers, 1769, Berkshire Sessions.

[1] County of Albany, Witnesses, File Papers, 1769, Berkshire Sessions.

[2] Findings of Justices of the Peace in Case of Barnet Campbell, 8 May 1769, File Papers, 1769, Berkshire Sessions.

[3] Timothy Woodbridge to Gentlemen, File Papers, 1769, Berkshire Sessions.

dered the Overseers to provide outdoor relief for the Campbells, the Overseers again threatened to put Sarah and Barnet in the work-house. Israel Dewey, one of the Overseers, informed the Campbells that the Overseers voted to take them into the workhouse, rejecting the advice of the justices. Moreover, Dewey said that the master of the workhouse waited for the Campbells with two pairs of iron fetters "If you can be found in Town Next Week."[4] Again the sessions justices stepped in, but this time summoning the Selectmen to appear.[5] Unfortunately, the resolution of this case is unclear, since the records remain silent after 1772. It is possible that the Campbells found some private way to resolve their economic problems. What is clear, though, is that the Overseers of Great Barrington exercised their power over these paupers in the face of a court order. The power of the Berkshire Sessions Court was apparently insufficient to persuade the Overseers to provide outdoor relief. In the case of Barnet and Sarah Campbell, the balance between compassion and control weighed heavily on the side of control. As long as the eighteenth-century almshouse and workhouse offered the hope of relief from increasing poor relief costs, there remained the possibility of coercion. To be sure, these institutions also provided needed care for the absolutely destitute, especially in Boston and Salem. But control mixed readily with compassion as overseers, selectmen, and justices of the peace sought to administer and enforce the law of poverty.

III.

Perhaps no area of the law of poverty in eighteenth-century Massachusetts was as important as the law of settlement. Since paupers qualified for social welfare primarily by establishing legal residency, the law of settlement gradually became an arena of conflict between town officials and transient paupers, mediated by the justices of the sessions courts. With the increased mobility of the people of Massachusetts during the eighteenth century, the law of settlement was at the very heart of the transformation of the law of poverty.

From the very outset of colonization in the seventeenth century

---

[4] Israel Dewey to Bernard Camble, File Papers, 1769, Berkshire Sessions.

[5] Summons to the Selectmen of Great Barrington, File Papers, 1772, Berkshire Sessions.

the English settlers of Massachusetts attempted to control the process of settlement in order to protect their Puritan ideals. Both the General Court and individual towns monitored the movement of newcomers. In 1637, the General Court ordered that no town or person could "receive any stranger ... [with] intent to reside" in the colony more than three weeks except by permission of the Council or two magistrates.[6] Similarly, Ipswich admitted newcomers into their "meeting" only if they agreed to "the like orders and penalties that we the freemen of the Towne have established for our own peace and comfort...."[7] Braintree regulated the sale of houses and land, permitting it first to be offered to current inhabitants, and only later to outsiders who were properly approved by the townsmen.[8]

As the populations of the towns became more settled, the townsmen of the Puritan villages began to monitor newcomers with a slightly different eye: they were alert to potential paupers. Cambridge, Salem, Braintree, and Topsfield all banished unwanted transients in the middle decades of the seventeenth century, though the number of people was small.[9] Topsfield, a small farming town, excluded a transient about every other year during the 1680's, while Salem did so at least every year. The Salem Selectmen took particular care to exclude both "menacing" and poor transients. The Selectmen did not permit Indians in the town except during daylight hours and instructed the constables to watch for suspicious "nightwalkers."[1] Banishment, in these cases, served to maintain control before the creation of police forces. No less important was the control of potential paupers; some towns sought security bonds from transients in case they became ill, while other towns admitted migrants only if they had jobs.[2] Employment defused the threat of poor relief.

[6] Shurtleff, I, 196; also see I, 264.

[7] Waters, *Ipswich*, II. 386.

[8] *Records of the Town of Braintree*, 2.

[9] *The Records of the Town of Cambridge, 1630–1703* (Cambridge, Mass., 1901), 24, 108, 155, 190; *Town Records of Salem, Massachusetts, 1659–1680* (Salem, 1913), 6, 7, 61, 112; *Town Records of Topsfield, Massachusetts, 1659–1739* (Topsfield, 1917), 22, 35, 41; *Records of the Town of Braintree*, 19–20.

[1] *Town Records of Salem*, 303–304.

[2] Waters, *Ipswich*, II, 392–393; *Wenham Town Records*, 4 vols. (Wenham, 1930), I, 5; *Town Records of Salem*, 50.

But as the numbers of transients increased dramatically in the eighteenth century, the law of settlement was transformed. In Essex County the number of transients approximately doubled every decade between the 1730's and the 1760's. On the western frontier of Massachusetts the number of transients increased over five times between the 1740's and the 1760's.[3] A similar pattern of increasing numbers of transients also occurred in Boston during the middle decades of the eighteenth century, with the peak also occurring in the 1760's.[4] The primary solution to the problem of transiency came in the form of revised settlement laws. The General Court hoped to minimize poor relief costs on the towns in two ways: one, by extending the length of residence required for a legal inhabitancy; and two, by placing the burden of disclosure of transients on the migrants themselves, and increasingly away from the towns' officials.

The basic form of the eighteenth-century settlement law may be traced, in part, to the seventeenth century. Under the poor law of 1659, the General Court for the first time required that a person was entitled to poor relief if he or his family had been a resident of the town for more than three months. The town could avoid relief only if its constable or one of its selectmen had given notice that the "poore person" was not welcome to remain. Additionally, the selectmen were required to notify the county court of their intention not to provide relief.[5] The central elements of this 1659 law—a residency requirement, a warning by the constable or selectman, and notification of the county court—became the core of the law of settlement for over one hundred years in Massachusetts. But social conditions in the eighteenth century, affected by increasing poverty and

---

[3] The exact numbers of the transient heads of households in Essex and Hampshire Counties, by decade, are reported below:

	1730–39	1740–49	1750–59	1760–69	1770–79	1780–89
Essex	206	419	939	1707	64	101
Hampshire	—	131	202	634	109	100

The sources for this evidence include the Record Books of the Courts of General Sessions of the Peace, Essex and Hampshire Counties, Massachusetts, 1730–1789. See Douglas Lamar Jones, "Poverty and Vagabondage: The Process of Survival in Eighteenth-Century Massachusetts," *The New England Historical and Genealogical Register*, CXXXIII (1979), 253, Table 1.

[4] Unpublished data on all transients warned-out of Boston were kindly provided by Allan Kulikoff to the author.

[5] Shurtleff, IV, Part 1, 365.

transiency, gave the law of settlement heightened importance.

Between 1692 and 1701 the General Court continued to permit a legal residency to be established for purposes of poor relief if a person was not legally warned to leave a town within three months.[6] The exception to this rule was that lineal family members had to care for their poor relatives.[7] The 1692 statute was a more elaborate statement of the 1659 law. It made more explicit the town's burden of discovering the presence of transients, and their legal liability for either detecting unwanted migrants or providing relief for them if they established legal inhabitancies. Also, the law made clear the fact that towns had an obligation to return a "warning" or "caution" to the county court of general sessions of the peace as proof that the town had warned the transient to leave. The purpose of the warning was to protect the town against poor relief costs of nonresidents; moreover, it also provided a method of excluding unwanted persons. These procedures, including the discovery of transients and their legal warning, became functions of both the towns and the sessions courts. In most towns populations were small and transients were easily identified. But in the more populated towns like Salem and Boston, detection of transients required more than the customary reliance on casual encounters. Such towns often hired men to inquire about strangers, although the task eventually fell to the constables.[8]

Commencing with the 1701 settlement law the General Court began to make inhabitancy more difficult to obtain. Apparently in response to the difficulties of identifying all strangers within three months, the General Court extended the residency requirement to twelve months in 1701, a standard that lasted until 1767.[9]

The settlement laws applied not only to transients with legal residences in some town of Massachusetts; they also embraced foreign immigrants. For purposes of the settlement law an immigrant's port of entry became his legal residence. To protect the seaports from excessive poor relief costs, however, the law provided that masters of ships provide the selectmen of seaports with lists of passengers, their

---

[6] *Acts and Resolves*, I (1692–93), ch. 28, 64–68.

[7] Ibid., esp. 67–68.

[8] For example, see *Town Records of Salem*, 112.

[9] *Acts and Resolves*, I (1700–01), ch. 23, 451–453.

estimated worth and possessions, and a bond for potential poor relief costs.[1] Passed in 1723, this law anticipated one of the central problems with the regulation of transients: migrants who entered Massachusetts from other parts of New England as well as Europe.

During the 1720's and 1730's, the General Court altered the settlement law by shifting the burden of identifying transients from the towns to the local inhabitants who provided them with food and shelter. Called "entertainment" laws, these statutes provided that transients could not remain in a town longer than twenty days without special permission from the selectmen.[2] Inhabitants who housed transients had to submit written descriptions of the transients' personal characteristics, or be subject to a forty-shilling fine for noncompliance. One half of this fine, appropriately enough, was to be used for the town poor.[3] The "entertainment" laws provided an additional source of indemnity against poor relief costs. Not only could the towns warn out transients, but they could also hold their own town residents responsible for encouraging mobility among the poor. While casual workers, such as seasonal migrants, might still work for a few days at harvest and planting time, these laws discouraged labor mobility. This eighteenth-century Massachusetts policy stood in marked contrast to the English settlement laws, which explicitly encouraged the distribution of workers to towns which held better opportunities.[4]

Throughout the eighteenth century, the law of settlement in Massachusetts affirmed that migrants could gain legal residences only with the consent of the town. There could be no presumption of residence; payment of taxes, for example, did not entitle an indi-

---

[1] *Acts and Resolves*, II (1722–23), ch. 5, 244–245. The Boston Selectmen used this law in 1729, bringing suit against Captain John Nimeno for a poor spinster, Sarah Bell, who entered Boston from Ireland. Petition of the Selectmen of Boston to the Suffolk County Sessions Court, 27 October 1729, Rare Books and Manuscripts Room, Boston Public Library.

[2] *Acts and Resolves*, II (1715–41), ch. 6, 386; ch. 8, 616; ch. 9, 994–995; ch. 16, 835–836.

[3] *Acts and Resolves*, II (1731–32), ch. 8, 616; (1736–37), ch. 16, 835–836; (1739–40), ch. 9, 994–995.

[4] James Stephen Taylor, "The Impact of Pauper Settlement, 1691–1834," *Past and Present*, LXXIII (1976), 42–74; E. J. Hobsbawm, *Labouring Men: Studies in the History of Labour* (New York, 1967), 41–72.

vidual to poor relief.[5] The General Court was particularly clear on this point: legal inhabitancy could be obtained only with the "approbation of the town, at a meeting of the inhabitants . . . , or the approbation of the selectmen. . . ."[6] Practically speaking, this right to select town members in mid-eighteenth-century Massachusetts was the power to exclude the transient poor. The warning-out system— the enforcement arm of the settlement law—became the focal point for town officials and migrants alike, as transiency and poor relief became identified with each other.

IV.

The chain of legal steps in the warning-out system began when the selectmen of a town ordered one of its constables to warn out a transient. For example, in 1766, the Selectmen of Newburyport directed Constable Francis Hodgkins "to warn and give Notice to the Several Persons hereafter named (who have lately come here to dwell and not being duly admitted Inhabitants) to depart and leave this Town immediately."[7] Similarly, the Selectmen of Egremont, in Berkshire County, expressed concern about transient poor people in their warnings-out warrant: "Whereas Sundry Persons in May Last have Entered and Inhabit in the District of Egremont . . . contrary to the Laws of this Province and whereas Sd Persons appear to be Needy and Indigent . . . ," they should be warned out.[8] Following such directions from their selectmen, constables attempted to locate the people named by the selectmen and orally inform them that they were warned out. Constables did not locate every transient, however. Some undoubtedly moved on, while others tried to avoid being warned out. But some constables were persistent, and reported that they "made diligent inquiry" even if a transient was not found.[9] For those transients who were found, the constables gathered the names of all of the family members, ascertained their date of arrival into town, and determined the transient's "circumstances," or eco-

[5] *Acts and Resolves*, II (1739–40), ch. 9, 994–995.

[6] Ibid.

[7] Newburyport Warnings, File Papers, 1766, Essex Sessions.

[8] Egremont Warnings, Record Book, 1764, vol. 1762–1764, unpaginated, Berkshire Sessions.

[9] Record Book, 1766, vol. 1766–1771, 111, 115, Hampshire Sessions.

Boston ss: To Mr. ____ Sweetser ____ of Boston Greeting

In his Majesties Name you are required to Warn
Elisabeth Parson: Danial Buckle ____
Susanah Best: meatthew Dodg: Elisabeth
Dodg: Sarah Dodg & Sisters: Epham
Stilman: Lyda Right: Ramsel Kimelton
New Genly: Thomas Wickers & wife
Rachel: Elisabeth Jadeson:

To Depart this Town in a fourteen Days or give security
to the Selectmen of Boston to indemnify said Town from
all Charges that may arise by their Means during
their Abode here, & you are to make return thereof with
your doings herein to the Clerk of the Sessions of the
Peace togeather with a Certificate of the Place of their
last Abode and Time of their residence he as the Law
directs ____

By Order of the Selectmen

Boston June 1. 1765 ____   William Cooper Town Clerk

12. Boston Selectmen to Constable, "Warning Out" dated 1 June 1765, Court
of General Sessions of the Peace, Suffolk. Courtesy, Supreme Judicial Court.

Boston June 1: 1765 By
vertue of the with in warrant of haue
warnd ye within Named Elisabeth Parson
from medsoed: June 3: 1765 + Danial
Buckle from Halafax: June 8 1765
+ Susanah Best from Hingam: June 11
1765 jonatthew Dodg Elisabeth Dodg —
Sarah Dodg & Sisters from wesford —
June 21 1765: Ephraham Stilman
from Dartmouth: June 21: 1765
Lyda Right from willenton: June
26 1765 Ganesel Kemelton from Kitry
June 28 1765: Hew Finly from Roxsbery
June 28 1765 Thomas vickers & wife
Rachil from Etait: June 29 1765
Elisabeth Pedeson from Sheepscutt — —
      Theas Pasons warnd out a
   Town By one John Sweetsor

13. Return dated 3 June 1765, on "Warning Out" dated 1 June 1765; Court of General Sessions of the Peace, Suffolk. Courtesy, Supreme Judicial Court.

nomic status. Some constables reported that particular transients had "little or no estate" or "no estate that I know of."[1] Although the office of constable had little enforcement power in and of itself, the warning-out system appears to have been one area of law enforcement in which the constables, when acting on behalf of the selectmen, had a measure of power.[2]

Having warned the transients, constables reported back to the selectmen, attesting that a verbal warning had been given. The selectmen then sent the warrant of the warnings-out to be filed with the court of general sessions of the peace of the county. Acting primarily in an administrative capacity, the sessions courts entered the names of the transients warned and the respective towns into its records, retaining the warrants from the town selectmen on file. Yet the justices did not treat the warning-out process lightly. As the warning-out system began to be used more frequently in the early eighteenth century, the sessions justices examined the warrants to insure that the selectmen followed the intent of the settlement law. For example, the justices of the Essex County Sessions Court reviewed the warnings filed with the court in the 1720's and 1730's with extreme care, often rejecting warnings because they were not filed according to the law.[3] Some selectmen failed to state a transient's length of residence prior to being warned, while others did not name each transient individually. Even as late as the 1770's, Hampshire County sessions justices rejected warnings out because the constable failed to provide evidence of a face-to-face encounter with the transient.[4] The sessions justices provided an important legal check on the accuracy and honesty of town officials.

In general, the selectmen, the constables, and the justices developed the warnings-out process into a fairly routine system during the eighteenth century. The critical factor, aside from accurate in-

[1] Record Book, 1770, vol. 1766–1771, 165, Hampshire Sessions.

[2] For a more pessimistic assessment of the constables' law enforcement powers and effectiveness, see Michael Zuckerman, *Peaceable Kingdoms: New England Towns in the Eighteenth Century* (New York, 1970), 85–88.

[3] Numerous examples occurred. See Beverly Warnings, Boxford Warnings, Record Book, 1732, vol. 1726–1744, 232; Haverhill Warnings, Record Book, 1737, vol. 1726–1744, 522, Essex Sessions.

[4] Colerain Warnings, Greenwich Warnings, Record Book, 1772, vol. 13, 28, 35, Hampshire Sessions.

formation by the selectmen, was for the warrant of warnings to reach the sessions court within the prescribed twelve months. Some towns either advertently or inadvertently circumvented the letter of the law and warned out transients up to twenty months after the date they entered town. Similarly, justices occasionally overlooked this delay and accepted the warrants. More typically, selectmen brought their warnings to the courts with efficiency and reasonable speed. In both Essex and Hampshire Counties selectmen delivered almost ninety-five percent of the warnings to the sessions courts within the prescribed time period.[5] Moreover, the selectmen maintained a steady, watchful eye over transients, warning them out in a consistent manner throughout the year. Three-fourths of the transients in both Essex and Hampshire Counties were identified by the selectmen, warned out by the constables, and presented to the sessions courts within ten months of the transients' entrance into the towns.

Some town selectmen were more efficient than others. Seaport towns like Salem, Marblehead, and Gloucester averaged only about five months between the time a transient appeared in town and the month of the warning in court. In contrast, the farming towns of Essex County averaged nearly eight months before entering a warrant in court. Even in Hampshire County, the three largest towns of Springfield, Northampton, and Westfield were more efficient in warning out transients than the smaller farming towns. Location was an important factor in processing a warning-out warrant. Seaports in Essex County were conveniently located to the towns where the sessions courts met, while rural constables probably made fewer trips to court. Moreover, the farming towns tended to have fewer transients than the large towns and seaports. By 1735 poverty and transiency had become so widespread in Boston that the General Court permitted the Overseers of the Poor to warn out transients "in the same manner, and with as full power as the selectmen."[6]

By the middle of the eighteenth century, both the substantive pro-

[5] These conclusions, and those in the following paragraph, are based on a quantitative analysis of all transient heads of households warned out of Essex and Hampshire Counties. In order to gather this information, I coded every transient with available data on household size, economic characteristics, and residential history in Essex and Hampshire. This evidence was then keypunched and analyzed by computer, and is still in my possession.

[6] *Acts and Resolves*, II (1735–36), ch. 4, 756–758.

visions of the settlement laws and the procedures of the warning-out system restricted the availability of public poor relief for transients. To qualify for poor relief, one had to establish a legal residence; the relevant test was primarily a twelve-month residency without a warning, and formal acceptance by the town. In addition, marriage, birth, or parentage could also establish a legal residency. But the warning-out system was directed primarily at poor transients, not marriages between people of two different towns.[7] Cases of disputed settlement based on marriage, for example, seemed to occur if the transient in question had already been identified as a pauper.[8]

The settlement laws and the warning-out system apparently were intended to identify actual or potential paupers, not simply to exclude all migrants. Since the settlement laws did not provide economic standards for identifying such transients, constables and selectmen evolved their own categories for deciding who was to be warned out. A transient might have been lower-class, poor or indigent, unemployed, unemployable, idle, single, sickly, or travelling alone with young children. If a transient had one or several of these characteristics, or even potentially might have them, he or she could be excluded from legal inhabitancy by being warned out. Since the mid-eighteenth-century settlement laws were based primarily on the geography of legal residency—not economic or social class—these attributes of poverty were left to the discretion of town officials. Only in the late eighteenth century did wealth become an explicit criterion for inhabitancy.

A case of contested residency of a transient family litigated by Waltham and Weston in 1763 dramatically reveals the consciousness of the poor laws among both the transients and town officials. Together with their five children, Elisha and Anna Cox moved from Waltham to Weston in 1752. Weston town officials warned them out of town and physically removed them to Waltham. As a result Waltham initiated a case of contested residency before the Middlesex County Sessions Court. Ultimately, the court held that, while the warning out of the Cox family by Weston was legal, the legal re-

[7] On the prevalence of marital migration, see Jones, *Village and Seaport*, 70–85.

[8] For example, see Bradford v. Andover, Record Book, 1767, 136, Essex Sessions, which involved both the legality of a pauper marriage as well as legal residence.

sponsibility for these transients still fell on Weston. When the Cox family thought they were living on the Waltham border of Weston, in fact they were living on the Weston border of Waltham and were legal residents of Weston.[9]

More importantly, testimony in this case revealed the intensity of the enforcement of the settlement laws by town officials. Josiah Allen, a Weston selectman, testified that he was conscious of the Cox family's presence in town and believed that "it would not be safe for the town to admit [Cox and his family] to be Inhabitants...." He further testified that he "thought it my Duty to Take particular care to Inform myself of the Time of their coming into Town and also to take care that they were warned out within a year...."[1] Allen's vigilance in identifying and learning the "circumstances" of the Cox family was repeated in town after town in the middle of the eighteenth century in Massachusetts.

While the warning-out system relied on the discretion of town officials for its enforcement, and the sessions justices held selectmen to procedural accuracy, the transients themselves were also aware of the warning-out law. They certainly were aware that selectmen and constables were anxious to warn them out. Some transients probably did not care, since they would move on again soon anyway. Others, like the Cox family, tried to avoid being warned out. One of Elisha Cox's neighbors in Weston, Mehetabel Warren, testified that she had discussed the warning out with Elisha's wife. Warren said that she "asked [Elisha's wife] whether she was warned out of Weston, and she said she was not," to which Warren replied, "if it was not done in a little time, it would be too late...."[2] Later Elisha's wife told Mehetabel Warren that she had been warned out. Interestingly, Warren inquired as to the time and place of the warning, suggesting that it was done one day past the required one year. This comment suggests both a consciousness of the warning-out law and the possibility that some transients circumvented that law. While the Cox family remained residents of Weston because of a disputed boundary

[9] Waltham v. Weston, File Papers, 1762–1763, Middlesex Sessions.

[1] Quotations are from the Deposition [of Josiah Allen], File Papers, 1762–1763, Middlesex Sessions.

[2] Quotations are from the Deposition of Mehetabel Warren, File Papers, 1762–1763, Middlesex Sessions.

line, the evidence of Mehetabel Warren reveals that transients did not necessarily have to rely on the sessions judges to look out after their interests.

Only a very few transients were so bold as to challenge overtly the town officials and justices. If transients were warned out but returned to a town, they could be prosecuted as vagabonds.[3] Justices of the peace heard alleged cases of vagabondage, brought usually by town selectmen against recalcitrant or threatening transients. In 1700 the General Court of Massachusetts ordered that each county was to build a house of correction to be used to punish "rogues, vagabonds and idle persons going about in any town or county" for a variety of crimes such as begging, "using any subtle craft," running away, being "railers or brawlers," and neglecting their callings and families. Under the law, vagabonds were to be put back to work, whipped moderately (only ten stripes), or fettered and shackled.[4] Despite the apparent severity of the law, few convictions for vagabondage occurred. In 1700 vagabonds encompassed a broad range of undesirables: gamblers, fortune-tellers, runaways, and those who did not work. By 1756 the law of vagabondage became substantially broader, reaching not only the penniless, but also those who had some property and failed to improve it. Under this law selectmen were empowered to "inspect" people who lived idly, misspent their time and money, and lived dissolute lives—"as if they were poor, indigent, and impotent persons"—and could bind their children, with the assent of two justices, into "orderly families."[5]

Yet enforcement of these statutes was not widespread. An occasional fragment of evidence appears in the sessions records which suggests that vagabonds were convicted, such as Constable Benjamin Smith's commission of Betsy Travis, "a vagrant person," to the Ipswich gaol.[6] But the lack of enforcement is more striking than the statutory power to commit vagabonds to houses of correction. One reason behind a lack of enforcement of this law was economic. Towns were responsible for the daily support of any person convicted as

---

[3] *Acts and Resolves*, I (1700–1701), ch. 23, 453.

[4] *Acts and Resolves*, I (1699–1700), ch. 8, 378–381.

[5] *Acts and Resolves*, III (1755–1756), ch. 43, 926–928.

[6] Benj. Smith's Petition, File Papers, 1763, Essex Sessions.

a vagabond, a fact which could militate against strenuous enforcement. Moreover, even though people felt threatened by vagabonds, many counties did not even build houses of correction. By 1770 the General Court gave the court of general sessions, or one or more of the justices of the court, the power either to send vagabonds to houses of correction or to put them into stocks.[7]

Nevertheless, the law of vagabondage was important to town officials because it was a deterrent to be used if necessary; a few cases, strictly enforced, could powerfully illustrate the firmness of the law. The Selectmen of Northampton, for example, used the law of vagabondage in 1767 and 1768 to control the behavior of a transient, mulatto laborer named Philemon Lee.[8] The Selectmen warned Lee out of Northampton; he refused to leave and the constables removed him to the nearby town of Simsbury in 1766. Lee was persistent and returned to Northampton. The Selectmen then brought Lee before Eleazer Porter, a justice of the peace, who found him guilty of vagabondage. Porter committed Lee to the Hampshire County house of correction, where he remained for about two weeks until he promised never to return to Northampton. But Lee was soon walking the streets of Northampton, whereupon the Selectmen brought him before the sessions court and he again was convicted of vagabondage and was indefinitely confined to the house of correction. Lee remained there for about six months, until the sessions justices thought that "Philemon is reduced to a better state of mind. . . ." Lee's case is important, though probably unique; it is an example of the failure of the warning-out system as well as the employment of the little-used deterrent of the law of vagabondage to control transients.

More typically, for the first two thirds of the eighteenth-century Massachusetts towns monitored transients by using the warning-out system to avoid poor relief costs and by excluding unwanted persons. Suddenly, in 1767, the General Court transformed the law of settlement. Under this new statute the General Court removed the burden of the identification of transients from the towns and placed it on the

[7] *Acts and Resolves*, v (1769–1770), ch. 19, 46.

[8] Selectmen of Northampton v. Philemon Lee, Record Book, 1767, vol. 1766–1771, 69–70, 80, Hampshire Sessions.

H-df-n's SPEECH from the Pillory.

WHAT mean thefe Crouds, this Noife and Roar!
 Did ye ne'er fee a *Rogue* before?
Are *Villains* then a Sight fo rare,
To make you prefs and gape and ftare?
Come forward all who look fo fine,
With Gain as illy got as mine:
Step up———you'l foon reverfe the Show;
The *Croud* above, and *few* below.

 Well—for my Roguery here I ftand,
A Spectacle to all the Land:
High elevated on this Stage,
The *greateft Villain* of the Age.
My Crimes have been both great and many,
Equal'd by very few, if any:
And for the Mifchiefs I have done
I put this *wooden Neckcloth* on.

 There *HOW* his brawny Back is ftripping,
Quite callous grown with often whipping.
In vain you wear your *Whip-Cord* out,
You'l ne'er reclaim that *Rogue fo ftout.*
To make him honeft, take my Word,
You muft apply a *bigger Cord.*

 Now all ye who behold this Sight,
That ye may get fome profit by't,
Keep always in your Mind, I pray,
Thefe few Words that I have to fay.
Follow my Steps and you may be
In Time, perhaps, advanc'd like me;
Or, like my fellow Lab'rer *HOW,*
You'l get at leaft a *Poft* below.

Sold by N, HURD, near the Exchange, and at the *Heart* and *Crown* in Cornhill, *Bofton.*

14. Broadside depicting the confinement in the pillory, the whipping, and public confessional of a "rogue," Seth Hudson, in Boston, 1762. Courtesy, Boston Public Library.

transients themselves. Instead of relying on constables and selectmen to warn transients through the sessions courts, the 1767 statute required all transients to inform the selectmen of their presence as they entered a town.[9] Responsibility for being a transient came to rest with each migrant. Selectmen no longer had to search out transients; rather, transients gained legal residence only upon direct application to the selectmen. This statute reversed the relationship between the towns and the migrants: transiency was decriminalized as the warning-out process was discarded.

The most striking aspect of the 1767 law was its effect on the warning-out system, the primary mechanism for enforcing the settlement laws as they applied to paupers. The end of the warning-out system was particularly swift in Essex County. In 1766 the towns warned out over three hundred different families; two years later they warned only sixteen transient families. With this law of 1767 the General Court began to change the assumptions of settlement and poor relief law in Massachusetts quite radically, for the law now presumed that transients might well remain in the towns.

Still, aspects of the old settlement and warning-out laws remained. Transients who failed to gain legal residences were still liable to physical removal by the constable upon application to a justice of the peace. Transients were to pay for their own removal if they possessed some estate; otherwise the town of legal residence bore the expense. The General Court agreed to bear the costs of removal of transients who were not residents of Massachusetts, solving the persistent problem of immigrants.

The rationale behind this 1767 law is difficult to explain. The journals of the House of Representatives of Massachusetts remain silent on the bill. However, the preamble to the act cites the unfairness of other settlement laws which failed to account for persons who had no legal residences in Massachusetts. This question of fairness undoubtedly was important, particularly among the seaport towns like Boston that were major ports of entry into Massachusetts. A second factor was the growing organizational problems of an expanding number of warnings out. The decade of the 1760's represented the peak in the number of warnings processed by the sessions courts

---

[9] *Acts and Resolves*, IV (1766–1767), ch. 17, 911–912.

in the eighteenth century, with no immediate alleviation in sight. Under the 1767 statute the sessions courts no longer had to spend time on this quasi-administrative procedure. In addition, litigation among the towns over poor relief costs also flooded the courts in the 1760's, costing considerable sums of money and, again, taking the time of the court.[1] Finally, a social explanation may be in order: the General Court, for whatever reasons, began to perceive that the warning-out system, with its premises of residential stability, no longer fit the needs of Massachusetts. Migrants, transients or not, had to be free to move about and find jobs.

Following passage of the act, towns in Essex and Hampshire Counties generally obeyed the intent of the law and did not warn out transients. The eastern Massachusetts county of Essex integrated this new law more fully than the western county of Hampshire. Between 1768 and 1778 towns in Essex filed only seventy-two warnings with the sessions court, and none appeared again until 1786. In Hampshire the towns filed one hundred twenty-eight warnings between 1768 and 1774, and none again until 1779. Still, in both counties the sessions courts permitted warnings to be filed by towns if they chose to do so, reflecting some confusion over the change in the law itself.

During the American Revolution, the General Court did not alter the law of poverty; it simply renewed acts concerning the poor which had been in use earlier in the eighteenth century. In particular, the General Court provided that towns were to use the most "convenient" means for relieving the poor and for the assistance of families of soldiers who were involved in the war.[2] Just following the Revolution, however, there was a general resurgence of the use of warnings as the towns fell back on familiar ways to cope with the poverty-stricken transients displaced by the war.[3] But for the Revolu-

---

[1] For example, the General Court construed the 1767 poor law to provide that any justice of the peace could authorize removal of a transient if the justice lived in the same town from which the transient was sent; see *Acts and Resolves*, v (1772–1773), ch. 4, 198. For the background of this statute, see "Brookline v. Roxbury, 1767–1772," *The Adams Papers: Legal Papers of John Adams*, ed. L. Kinvin Wroth and Hiller B. Zobel, 3 vols. (Boston, 1965), I, 299–319.

[2] *Acts and Resolves*, v (1777–78), ch. 20, 774–775; also see ibid., v (1775–76), ch. 14, 457–462; and v (1778–79), ch. 17, 903–905.

[3] See above, page 173, footnote 3 for the warnings out in the 1770's and the 1780's in Essex and Hampshire Counties.

tion, the warning-out system probably would have passed into disuse as the towns began to rely on removal of transients rather than the constant vigilance of the warnings. But the 1767 law remains important, for it represents a step towards a new conceptualization of the law of poverty.

V.

The prelude to the new conception of the law of poverty came in the immediate post-Revolutionary years. Although the General Court had maintained the eighteenth-century poor laws by statutory renewal, the end of the war and its social and economic dislocation brought about a heightened concern over both poverty and transiency—and who was to pay for social welfare. The result was a temporary overlap between the traditional methods of welfare and control and a shift towards newer practices. Boston, for example, passed a town order placing the burden of poor relief costs on town residents who might "admit or entertain in any of their houses or tenements" any "stranger or new-comer" who had not been admitted by the Selectmen.[4] Boston had, in effect, re-enacted the early eighteenth-century entertainment laws that shifted the burden of relief directly onto the townspeople. Similarly, a settlement law passed by the General Court in 1789 reinstituted a version of the warning-out system.[5] Under this law selectmen administered the warnings to nonresidents and maintained their own records in the "Town Book," not with the sessions court.[6] The law returned the concept of indemnification against poor relief costs but added a new factor: a transient could become a legal resident after two years without being warned out, not the one year that prevailed during most of the eighteenth century.[7]

While the 1789 settlement law included traditional methods of identifying and limiting poor relief, it also stated new premises for determining legal residency. For the first time a Massachusetts settlement law contained an explicit test of residence based on wealth. In

[4] *The By-Laws and Town-Orders of The Town of Boston, 1785 and 1786* (Boston, 1786), 108–109.

[5] *Acts and Resolves* (1789), ch. 14, 408–410.

[6] Ibid., 409–410.

[7] Ibid., 409.

addition to the usual methods of gaining legal residence by approbation of the town, birth, or marriage, the law provided two standards of residence based on property ownership.[8] First, the 1789 law provided that those "seized of an estate freehold . . . of the clear annual income of *three pounds*," and who lived continuously in a town for two years could become legal residents. Second, a person twenty-one years of age who resided in a town and paid taxes for five consecutive years could also become a legal inhabitant. This concern over a newcomer's wealth, long implicit in the laws of the early and middle eighteenth century, was finally made explicit. Even the legal forms appended to the 1789 statute revealed the concern over the poverty of transients: constables were directed to "warn, and give notice unto *A. B.* of   in the County of   labourer, (or a transient as the case may be). . . ."[9] Towns complied with this new law and began to warn out transients again. Salem, for example, warned out both domestic and foreign transients in its town lists of 1791.[1]

But the 1789 settlement law, with its almost virtual return to the status quo of the 1760's, almost immediately became anachronistic. In 1794 the General Court enacted a sweeping revision of the poor laws that finally laid the warning-out system to rest, and, in the process, sought to strike a balance between the pauper's need for public welfare and the society's need for control.[2] The 1794 poor law specifically ended the warning-out system, substituting a detailed procedure for the return of paupers who might fall onto the poor relief rolls.[3] The element of control of both poor transients and of town expenses for welfare was preserved in the 1794 law. But at the same time the law required each town to provide care and immediate poor relief for all persons, regardless of their legal residence, for a period up to three months.[4] The burden of responsibility of care for the poor finally came to rest on the towns as paupers were recognized

---

[8] Ibid., 408, for the standards based on wealth.

[9] Ibid., 410.

[1] "Salem Warnings, 1791," *Essex Institute Historical Collections*, XLIII (1907), 345–352.

[2] *Laws and Resolves* (1793), ch. 59, 479–493. The act was approved on 26 February 1794, so I refer to it as the law of 1794, rather than the one of 1793.

[3] Ibid., 485–486.

[4] Ibid., 485.

as a part of everyday life. The towns were given two courses of action in case they had to provide for a transient pauper: one, they could sue the pauper's town of legal residence in a civil action to recover their costs; and two, the towns could sue for costs on a complaint in the court of common pleas, subject to a two-year statute of limitations after the case arose.[5] While transients were still subject to removal, they gained both short-term poor relief as well as procedural protections such as an appeal to the court of common pleas.[6] Underlying the 1794 law was the resolution of a long history of tension over the allocation of economic resources for poor relief and the control of transients.

The transformation of the law of poverty in eighteenth-century Massachusetts was symbolized by the law of 1794. This transformation was born of the unique social, economic, and demographic forces of the eighteenth century; it was nurtured by a variety of experiments with the law of settlement, the warning-out system, and custodial and institutional forms of poor relief. This new conception of poverty, one that integrated the necessity of poor relief with the desire for control, was more a product of the early and middle eighteenth century than of the Revolution itself. Banishment of transients and the warning-out system, rejected first in 1767, utimately pointed to the revised poor law of 1794 that guaranteed at least temporary care for all of the poor *and* the allocation of legal responsibilities for that care among the towns. In the end, the 1794 poor law gained its legitimacy because it explicitly recognized the needs of the poor and the economic interests of the towns.

---

[5] Ibid., 485, 489.
[6] Ibid., 488.

DAVID H. FLAHERTY

Criminal Practice in Provincial Massachusetts

URING the twentieth century Americans have been fasci-
nated by the careers of prominent criminal lawyers.[1] One
might easily presume that lawyers specializing in criminal
law have always dominated criminal trials. Yet, at least in one early
American jurisdiction, lawyers only gradually became involved in
criminal practice and then only to a limited extent compared to their
role in the civil courts. This essay began as an effort to discover what
could be learned about the practice of criminal law in Massachusetts.
The results are both disappointing and revealing. Although a surprising amount of information exists about the practice of criminal
law, a great deal remains elusive, especially because of the limitations of the available evidence.

It is now reasonably well established that the first half of the eighteenth century witnessed the first flowering of the Massachusetts
legal profession.[2] Yet a great deal remains unknown about the nature
of legal practice and the actual role of counsel during the provincial
era. One cannot simply assume that attorneys did for their clients
what their successors do today, especially in criminal as opposed to
civil practice. Nor can one simply look to eighteenth-century England
for relevant models, since lawyers played almost no role in English
criminal trials for felonies until well into the second half of the
eighteenth century.[3] Nevertheless, the existence of voluminous court

---

[1] The most recent example is Alan M. Dershowitz's popular book *The Best Defense*
(New York, 1982).

[2] See John M. Murrin, "The Legal Transformation: The Bench and Bar of Eighteenth-Century Massachusetts," in Stanley N. Katz, ed., *Colonial America. Essays in
Politics and Social Development* (1st ed., Boston, 1971), 415–449; Gerard W.
Gawalt, *The Promise of Power. The Emergence of the Legal Profession in Massachusetts 1760–1840* (Westport, Conn., 1979), 7–35. The use of the word "profession" here is very loose and implies none of the trappings of twentieth-century
professionalism. See McKirdy's "Massachusetts Lawyers on the Eve of the American Revolution: The State of the Profession," below, 313–316.

[3] John H. Langbein, "The Criminal Trial before the Lawyers," *University of
Chicago Law Review*, XLV (1978), 263–316.

records for Massachusetts does make it possible to shed some light on the nature of criminal practice during the provincial era.

Beginning in 1692 the Superior Court of Judicature, the Court of Assizes and General Gaol Delivery, exercised jurisdiction over the most serious crimes tried in Massachusetts courts. It was overwhelmingly a court that handled civil disputes, which, as will be seen, may have influenced criminal practice. It is likely that the emerging role of defense counsel was largely a spillover from practices and roles accepted in civil litigation. The Assizes or criminal side was largely a court of first instance for serious crimes, meeting at least once a year in and for each county in the colony. It also heard appeals from county courts of General Sessions of the Peace. There were 1,461 criminal prosecutions before the Assizes between 1693 and 1769, 1,192 based on original jurisdiction (81.6 percent), and 269 appeals (18.4 percent).[4] Whether an appeal was based on a matter of law or fact was largely irrelevant, because the appellant in fact received a new trial in almost every case before new judges and a new jury. Although the amount of serious crime tried before the court was comparably modest because of an effective system of social control at work in society, most sittings of the Assizes, especially in the largest counties, heard at least one criminal case.[5]

Criminal prosecutions at the Assizes, as revealed by the extensive records of cases tried before the court between 1692 and 1770, provide several interesting perspectives on colonial legal practice. The first section of this essay will identify those attorneys who most prominently appeared in the records as defense counsel. The second section suggests general ways in which the presence of lawyers was to the advantage of defendants. It also explores general evidence which indicates an increased presence, as well as an improved proficiency, of defense counsel. There is also evidence which helps to explain the interplay between civil and criminal practice.

The final section shows how scattered cases can be pieced together to illustrate the activities of attorneys at particular stages in criminal proceedings. As will be seen, lawyers during the provincial period

---

[4] David H. Flaherty, "Crime and Social Control in Provincial Massachusetts," *The Historical Journal*, XXIV (1981), 357.

[5] Ibid., 339–360.

represented clients at bail and plea bargaining proceedings; they attempted to quash indictments; they argued the facts and legal merits of cases at first instance and on appeal; they were even sometimes involved in sentencing and pardons. From the first to the last stages of the legal process, the beginnings of the so-called "professionalization" of the American criminal trial are evident in the early eighteenth century.

The Leading Criminal Lawyers

The use of lawyers at the Assizes depended in large part on the development of the legal profession through the gradual appearance of trained lawyers in the province. Those accustomed to reading about the surplus of lawyers today must adjust to the small numbers of the provincial era. Gerard Gawalt concludes that there were fifteen practicing lawyers in 1740, twenty-five who attained the newly created rank of barrister in 1762, and seventy-one in 1775.[6] The paucity of highly trained professional attorneys during the first generation of the Superior Court's existence (1692–1710) may have contributed to the infrequent appearances of lawyers at criminal trials. This characterization must be made with caution. Although research for this essay has uncovered evidence that was previously unknown, concrete conclusions about the presence of attorneys and their role in criminal cases for this early period must be reserved, because of the character of the surviving records. After the creation of the Superior Court, a small number of lawyers were seemingly present at each session, and they were definitely employed in at least a few criminal cases on behalf of defendants. A major enactment in 1701 pertaining to "attorneys" repeated the common Massachusetts stipulation that any plaintiff or defendant in any civil suit could represent himself or employ the assistance of any other person.[7] It provided for the formal admission of attorneys to practice before particular courts upon the administration of an oath which made the lawyer an officer of the court with a responsible role to play in the

[6] Gawalt, *Promise of Power*, 14, 17.

[7] *The Acts and Resolves, Public and Private, of the Province of the Massachusetts Bay*, ed. A. C. Goodell (Boston, 1869–1922), I, 75, 287, 374, 467. Hereafter cited as *Acts and Resolves*.

administration of justice.[8] The records of the Superior Court occasionally refer to the admission of attorneys in subsequent years. The statute of 1701 limited a party to one sworn attorney in a civil case; this limit was raised to two in 1708.[9] The subsequent increase suggests what other evidence indicates, that more lawyers were available by the end of the first decade of the eighteenth century. Yet the 1701 enactment clearly presumes that civil cases would be the main business of attorneys.

A handful of lawyers appear to have been the leading practitioners in criminal cases at the Assizes in the first half of the eighteenth century. Since they have been elusive figures in the pages of history, this essay will first introduce the leaders among them: Thomas Newton, John Valentine, John Read, Robert Auchmuty, and John Overing.

The legal profession that was beginning to emerge in the 1710's and 1720's could furnish clients with specialized assistance in criminal prosecutions. At least eleven new attorneys were admitted to practice by the Superior Court during these decades.[1] Thomas Newton (1660–1721) and John Valentine (1653–1724) stand out as the two leaders of the Massachusetts bar during the first two decades of the eighteenth century. Newton was one of the most active lawyers before the Superior Court in the early eighteenth century, especially in criminal cases. He was born in England in 1660. As a newcomer to Boston, he took the oath as an attorney before Samuel Sewall in 1688. The latter subsequently served as a justice of the Superior Court from 1692 to 1728. Newton, who presumably had received some legal education in England, became a justice of the peace in

---

[8] Neal Allen has pointed out that the form of this oath was nearly identical with the English equivalent. See Charles T. Libby, Robert E. Moody, and Neal W. Allen, Jr., eds., *Province and Court Records of Maine* (Portland, Maine, 1928–), IV, lxiii. Hereafter cited as *Maine Court Records*.

[9] See the admission of Benjamin Lynde (1701) and Jonathan Remington (1710), Superior Court of Judicature, Court of Assize and General Gaol Delivery Records, 1700–1714, 50, 246, Suffolk County Court House, Boston, hereafter cited as Superior Court Records; and ibid., 467, 622–623.

[1] The list included: Jonathan Remington (1710); Joseph Hiller (1718); Joseph Gooch and Edward Shove (1724); William Bollan (1726); Addington Davenport, Jr., Elisha Bisbee, Silvanus Bourn, and Elkanah Leonard (1728); and Joseph Marion and Andrew Lane (1729). Superior Court Records, 1710–1714, 246; ibid., 1715–1721, 258; ibid., 1721–1725, 195, 223; ibid., 1725–1729, 58, 297; and ibid., 1725–1730, 183, 226.

1715. He served as a deputy-judge of the Admiralty Court in Massachusetts and was elected Attorney General in July 1720 and served to his death on 28 May 1721. In 1707 he began a royal appointment as comptroller of the customs in Boston, which he also held until his death.[2] The newspaper report of his death described him as for "many Years one of the chief Lawyers of this Place. A Gentleman very much belov'd who carried himself handsomely and well in every Post, of a Circumspect and inoffensive Walk and Conversation, of strict Devotion towards God and Humanity to his Fellow Creatures, a Lover of all Good Men, much Lamented by all that knew him."[3]

John Valentine was the other notably prominent lawyer during the early decades of the eighteenth century. The son of a Lancashire merchant, he probably immigrated to Boston with his father in the early 1670's. A "well-trained lawyer," he served both as Attorney General (1718–1720) and Advocate General. At times during his distinguished career, he combined his considerable talents with those of Thomas Newton, defending persons accused of illegal trade and also prosecuting pirates.[4] On 1 February 1724 John Valentine committed suicide. A coroner's inquest of eighteen persons viewed the body as it hung in his own house. Justice Sewall noted that "Some Justices and many Attorneys were present. The jury returned that he was *Non Compos*."[5] The bearers at his public funeral were John Read, Robert Auchmuty, John Overing, John Nelson, and Robert Robinson. Valentine died a wealthy man with a total estate worth more than four thousand pounds. His books alone were worth more than one hundred pounds, and he also owned three slaves.

The passing of Newton and Valentine left two relative newcomers, John Read and Robert Auchmuty, as the leaders of the Massachu-

[2] Massachusetts Council Records, IV, 469–470, Massachusetts Archives, Boston. Hereafter cited as Council Records.

[3] Boston *News Letter*, 22–29 May 1721.

[4] Council Records, IV, 105.

[5] *The Saltonstall Papers, 1607–1815*, edited by Robert E. Moody, Massachusetts Historical Society *Collections*, Vols. LXXX–LXXXI (Boston, 1972–1974), I, 330; Murrin, "Legal Transformation," 422; and M. Halsey Thomas, ed., *The Diary of Samuel Sewall 1674–1729* (New York, 1973), 1012. Hereafter cited as *Sewall Diary*.

15. Paul Dudley (1675–1751) by an unknown artist (*circa* 1720).
Chief Justice, Superior Court of Judicature; Attorney General.
Courtesy, Supreme Judicial Court.

setts bar in the 1720's and 1730's. Read had an extraordinary career. Born in Connecticut in 1680 and graduated from Harvard in the class of 1697, he served until 1707 as a Congregational minister in various Connecticut towns. His conversion to the Church of England led to his resignation in 1707 from the Stratford pulpit. Sometime between 1708 and 1711, Read settled in New Milford, Connecticut, where, as Clifford K. Shipton describes it, "possessing much spare time, a keen mind, and pressing legal disputes over land, he naturally turned to the law."[6] He became self-trained in the law. In a letter to President John Leverett of Harvard seeking legal advice about disputes over some of his own land in June 1708, Read described himself as an abdicated clergyman, who had "fallen out with the times." Although he claimed that he knew "little in the Law never making it my Study but sometimes a little for diversion," the tenor of the letter and his analysis of his own legal problems suggest that he was learning quickly.[7] In the fall of 1708 he became the sixth attorney admitted to practice in Connecticut under a system of admission begun the preceding May. During the next several years his career did not prosper. He even found himself cited for contempt of court before the Court of Assistants and temporarily suspended from practice.

Read's legal career finally began to flourish. In December 1719 he evidently travelled to Salem, Massachusetts, to represent Governor Gurdon Saltonstall of Connecticut. In December 1718 the latter had written a letter of introduction for Read to President Leverett, explaining that Read would appear for him "upon Mr. [Paul] Dudleys Remove, and being unavoidably hindred from attending there my Self." Saltonstall asked Leverett to lend his "old Law Book" to Read and to direct him to a 1695 statute on intestacy.[8] In 1720 he

[6] See generally, Clifford K. Shipton, *Sibley's Harvard Graduates: Biographical Sketches of Those Who Attended Harvard College....* (Boston, 1873–), IV, 367–378; hereafter cited as Shipton, *Sibley's Harvard Graduates; Saltonstall Papers,* I, 286; and Richard B. Morris, "John Read," *Dictionary of American Biography,* XV (New York, 1935), 425–427.

[7] *Saltonstall Papers,* I, 282–284.

[8] *Saltonstall Papers,* I, 327. Paul Dudley was trained at the Inns of Court, but his only involvement with criminal practice was in the important role of Attorney General or chief prosecutor from 1702 to 1718. He had become a Superior Court judge the previous November. Appointment as Attorney General normally prevented a lawyer, such as Valentine, Newton, Read, or Overing, from practicing as a defense lawyer in criminal cases. Only fifteen residents of Massachusetts went to the Inns of

travelled to Boston as one of the commissioners from the New England colonies to discuss currency problems. This experience may have convinced Read to move to the metropolis of Boston in 1721 at the age of forty-one. From 1723 to 1728 he served as the elected Attorney General of the province, which made him the chief prosecutor at the Assizes. His activities during this decade began to distinguish him as the outstanding New England lawyer of his generation. Chief Justice Sewall recognized his abilities on 28 August 1727 when he gave Read "a General Retaining Fee to plead any Cause I might have." In the late 1720's the General Court retained him to defend a sheriff sued for false arrest in a criminal case.[9]

Robert Auchmuty, who also came to Massachusetts from a different jurisdiction, is another example of an English-trained lawyer who made successful use of his advantages in the New World. He was born in Scotland, admitted to the Middle Temple in 1705, and called to the bar in England in 1711. The last point suggests that he had taken his legal education seriously and actually managed to learn some law at the Inns of Court, which were primarily dining and social clubs.[1] Nothing further is known about the beginnings of Auchmuty's legal career in England. However, given the fact that criminal defense work hardly existed there, a lawyer from the mother country brought no specialized knowledge of the practice of criminal law to the colonies, except perhaps for handling misdemeanors.

Auchmuty must have made the acquaintance of Samuel Shute, because he seems to have accompanied the new governor to Boston in the fall of 1716. On 22 October 1716 Sewall reported that "the new Lawyer" Auchmuty and John Valentine pleaded at the proving of an individual's will. Sewall seems to have initially been suspicious of the newcomer. On 20 December 1716 he made clear his dislike of

Court for their legal education before the Revolution. Alan M. Smith, "Virginia Lawyers, 1680–1776: The Birth of an American Profession," unpublished Ph.D. dissertation, Johns Hopkins University, 1967, 141–142.

[9] *Sewall Diary*, 1054. *Journals of the House of Representatives of Massachusetts* (Boston, 1919–), VIII, 180, 182. Hereafter cited as *Massachusetts House Journals*.

[1] Paul Lucas has written that "after the Restoration, a greater spirit of 'professionalism' reigned in the Inns, for a larger proportion of students were called to the bar than ever before: whereas one out of fourteen had been called to the bar in the period 1615–1625, during 1702–1713, the proportion was two out of five." See "Blackstone and the Reform of the Legal Profession," *English Historical Review*, LXXVII (1962), 465.

Auchmuty's bantering about matrimony with a minister at a dinner they attended together. Four days later he, perhaps enviously, recorded seeing the lawyer with Governor Shute. But by the spring of 1717 Sewall had begun to admire Auchmuty's legal abilities. He attended a hearing between Cambridge and Charlestown about the location of the county seat: "Mr. Auchmooty pleaded very well for Charlestown: His first Discourse was very well worth Hearing."[2]

Auchmuty's entrance into the practicing bar was successful. Judging from the surviving records of arguments prepared for their clients, he and Read were the most popular and sophisticated criminal lawyers in the province during the 1720's. John Read's continued service as Attorney General during the middle of this decade left the role of defense counsel to Auchmuty on a great many occasions.

Surprisingly little is known about Auchmuty's private and personal life through the 1720's and thereafter. The matter is of some interest because he was a defendant before the General Sessions in Boston in 1722 in a peculiar prosecution. He and a woman were indicted for living together for four months as husband and wife although unmarried. When first presented in January, his several pleas on his own behalf to quash the indictment were overruled. He then pleaded not guilty and the case was continued until the April sessions, when Auchmuty withdrew the former pleas and stated that he was now married. He defended his previous behavior by claiming that he and the woman had been married privately at an earlier date, but not in conformity with Massachusetts law. The couple were fined five pounds each and costs.[3]

Another leading practitioner in terms of frequency of appearances and positions held was John Overing (1694–1748) who was born in England, and brought to Boston that same year. He began to practice law in Boston about 1720 and did so until his death on 29 November 1748. Overing may have studied law with Auchmuty; his marriage to the eldest Auchmuty daughter suggests a close associa-

[2] *Sewall Diary*, 836, 839–841, 855–856; see also Murrin, "Legal Transformation," 426.

[3] Suffolk County Court of General Sessions of the Peace, 1719–1725, 125, Suffolk County Court House, Boston.

tion with the family.[4] During almost all of the 1730's and 1740's, Overing enjoyed gubernatorial appointments as Attorney General, which made him the chief criminal prosecutor in the province. He continued to engage in civil practice during these years, especially since his official position brought him to public notice and furnished increased opportunities for clients.

By the 1730's and 1740's the normal process of legal education in Massachusetts involved attendance at Harvard College and practical apprenticeship in the office of an established lawyer or judge. John Murrin has noted that "the Harvard and Yale classes of 1730 through 1738 contributed seventeen lawyers to Massachusetts. The next nine classes, caught up by the Great Awakening, added only nine."[5] He argues that the leading lawyers of the 1730's were still Englishmen and outsiders in Massachusetts, although it seems difficult to apply such terms to attorneys like John Read, Robert Auchmuty, and William Bollan, who had been residents in the province for some time. Murrin suggests that most Massachusetts recruits to the new profession of law came from undistinguished families and, like Read, had had a negative response to a career in the church.[6]

The increased incidence of talented young Massachusetts men professionally associating themselves with the bar instead of the Bible suggests that the attractions outweighed any of the disadvantages sometimes associated with the legal profession. During this generation there were relatively few published attacks on lawyers. The newspapers reported an attorney who absconded from his creditors, another convicted of forgery, and one attacked while a candidate at election time, but two of these three episodes occurred in England.[7] A Boston newspaper even printed an adulatory poem about "the

---

[4] Details are from A. Townsend, *The Auchmuty Family of Scotland and America* (New York, 1932).

[5] John M. Murrin, "Anglicizing an American Colony: The Transformation of Provincial Massachusetts," unpublished Ph.D. dissertation, Yale University, 1966, 221–222.

[6] Ibid., 214–215.

[7] Boston *News Letter*, 19–26 April 1733; Boston *Evening Post*, 26 January 1741; 11–18 June 1741.

Portion of a Just Lawyer."[8] Knowledgeable persons nevertheless associated certain traits with members of the bar, such as those described in a private letter from Jonathan Sewall of Charlestown to Thomas Robie in Marblehead on 15 April 1757: "for I cannot conceive it possible for you to triumph over such a strict Inquisition, without the help of Equivocation, Evasion, Unintelligible Jargon, Impudence, etc. in short, without being compleat Master of the Art of disguising Truth." Robie had allegedly displayed such characteristics in warding off attempts to discover the identity of Lindamira, a pen name used by Sewall and himself in some correspondence.[9]

The leaders of the Massachusetts bar during the 1730's and 1740's were Auchmuty, William Bollan, Overing, Read, and William Shirley.[1] Auchmuty maintained his reputation as the leading criminal lawyer of his generation in terms of recorded appearances at the Assizes and was probably the leading lawyer in the province as well, since John Read had reached a venerable age. Auchmuty was also a prominent man of affairs in Massachusetts, which was not unusual for a leading member of the bar. For example, the province selected him to assist in the New Hampshire-Massachusetts boundary dispute in the 1730's. He was also a judge of the Massachusetts Vice-Admiralty Court from September 1733 to 1747.

Auchmuty was a friend of Governor Jonathan Belcher until the pair had a falling out in the fall of 1739. In the mid-1730's Belcher in a letter to his son in England had referred to Auchmuty and William Shirley as "two of the most eminent of the long robe here."[2] Belcher's compliments changed to contempt in a letter to a prominent friend in New Hampshire in September 1739, which reported that the naval officer in New Hampshire had "made a valuable seizure, and a good one, worth 4 or 5000£. The Irish Judge [Auchmuty] is a villain, and the Advocate [William Shirley] a greater, so it may be lost without good advice and assistance. The Judge and Advocate

---

[8] Boston *Gazette*, 2–9 June 1740.

[9] Jonathan Sewall Letterbook, 10, Massachusetts Historical Society, Boston.

[1] William Shirley arrived in Boston from England in 1731 and quickly established a distinguished law practice. He represented clients at the Assizes during ten years of active practice before he became governor in 1741.

[2] *The Belcher Papers*, Massachusetts Historical Society, *Collections*, Series 6, VI–VII, VII, 54–55, 97–98, 142–143.

will clear the ship and cargo, if they can, but I think in this case it's hardly possible."[3] It took less than two months for the impossible to happen in Vice-Admiralty Court. By November the Governor wrote concerning Auchmuty that "I don't thank him, nor forgive him, nor can I ever again allow myself any acquaintance with so uncommon a rascal." He believed Judge Auchmuty hardly ever made a decision in favor of the king, because he was bribed to the contrary: "I suppose there's not a more finisht villain than the former in Christendom." Belcher was, of course, primarily concerned about losing his own share in the Admiralty proceedings, and by November 1740 he was even denouncing Auchmuty in letters to his son in England, whose education on Auchmuty's character had now come full circle.[4]

Auchmuty's friend and ally in the Admiralty Court, Shirley, became governor in 1741 and sent him to London in the early 1740's to conduct an appeal in the Rhode Island boundary case. On 4 May 1742 Shirley informed the Duke of Newcastle of Auchmuty's presence in England as a colonial agent and of the governor's awareness that Auchmuty was scheming to have the secretary of the province replaced.[5] Auchmuty spent most of the years 1742, 1743, and 1744 in England.[6]

John Read remained the elder patriarch of the New England bar through the 1730's and 1740's, even though his presence in criminal matters at the Assizes is less evident than that of Auchmuty, who was younger than Read but who had begun to practice in Boston about five years earlier. The editors of the *Legal Papers of John Adams* have called Read the "leading Massachusetts lawyer of the first half of the eighteenth century."[7] Other lawyers such as James

---

[3] *Belcher Papers*, VII, 203.

[4] *Belcher Papers*, VII, 493, 495, 523.

[5] Charles H. Lincoln, ed., *Correspondence of William Shirley* (New York, 1912), I, 86.

[6] *Massachusetts House Journals*, XVI, 126–143; ibid., XIX, 162–165; ibid., XXI, 145–146.

[7] L. Kinvin Wroth and Hiller B. Zobel, eds., *Legal Papers of John Adams* (Cambridge, Mass., 1965), I, cvii–cviii. For valuable information about the practicing lawyers of the immediate pre-Revolutionary period, see "The Massachusetts Bench and Bar: A Biographical Register of John Adams' Contemporaries," in ibid., I, xcv–cxiv.

16. Ezekiel Goldthwait (1710–1782) by John Singleton Copley (1771).
Registrar of Deeds, Suffolk; Clerk, Inferior Court of Common Pleas,
Suffolk; Clerk, City of Boston. Courtesy, Museum of Fine Arts, Boston.

Otis, Sr., and the much younger John Adams had the highest opinion of Read. Thomas Hutchinson called him "a very eminent lawyer and, which is more, a person of great integrity and firmness of mind."[8] Read was kept busy as a senior legal advisor to the province in Admiralty proceedings and in the boundary commissions with Rhode Island and New Hampshire.[9] He also enjoyed the distinction of being the first lawyer from Boston elected to the House of Representatives in 1738 and to the Council in 1741 and 1742. In January 1739 and July 1741 his colleagues appointed him to committees to prepare substantially new editions of statutes.[1] Read also continued to represent persons at the General Sessions in Boston.[2] He was one of the bail bondsmen for two accused persons in 1740, suggesting the multiple roles of provincial lawyers, especially when it came to supplementing their incomes.[3] As late in his life as 1749, he served as acting Attorney General at the Assizes in Suffolk, Bristol, and Essex counties.[4] He also was involved in a considerable amount of civil business at Inferior Courts of Common Pleas and the Superior Court of Judicature. When Read died in Boston on 7 February 1749, he owned more than fifty volumes of legal works, about half of which were law reports.[5]

The Use of Defense Counsel

Evidence derived from the assize records of 1693 to 1709 indicates that fewer than a half dozen attorneys were practicing criminal law in Massachusetts. There is a problem evaluating the extent

[8] Thomas Hutchinson, *The History of the Colony and Province of Massachusetts-Bay*, ed. Lawrence Shaw Mayo (Cambridge, Mass., 1936), II, 285. The best sketch of Read's career is in Shipton, *Sibley's Harvard Graduates*, IV, 369–378, from which portions of these paragraphs are drawn.

[9] See *Massachusetts House Journals*, XVI, 117–118; ibid., XVIII, 194; ibid., XIX, 172; ibid., XXII, 175; *Belcher Papers*, VII, 306–307.

[1] *Massachusetts House Journals*, XVI, 245; ibid., XIX, 45.

[2] See Suffolk General Sessions, 26 January 1747.

[3] Early Files in the Office of the Clerk of the Supreme Judicial Court, Nos. 52030, 49885: 2, Suffolk County Court House, Boston. Hereafter cited as Suffolk Court Files.

[4] Superior Court Records, 1747–1750, 188, 227, 231.

[5] The inventory of law books can be found in George B. Reed, *Sketch of the Life of the Honorable John Read* (Boston, 1879), 17–18.

of legal representation, since court files rarely specify that attorneys have appeared on behalf of defendants. The most common evidence is found in cases appealed to the Assizes, since attorneys normally signed their names to reasons of appeal. In some unusual prosecutions in 1708–1709 for illegal trade with the enemy the records reveal that defendants asked the court for permission to be represented by Valentine and Newton; it is not clear whether such petitions were normally necessary, and the wording of the records suggests that the requests were pro forma.[6] In a few other cases before 1710 the bill of costs submitted to the province included a twelve shilling fee for an attorney, thereby indicating the presence of a defense lawyer.[7]

Massachusetts defendants enjoyed the right to employ counsel in any type of criminal case, which was a marked departure from the English rule of allowing counsel as a matter of right only in misdemeanor cases, but not for felonies, which covered most serious and many not-so-serious crimes.[8] Blackstone stated that it was a settled rule that no prisoner could have a lawyer in a felony trial, "unless some point of law shall arise proper to be debated." The theory was that the judge served as counsel on matters of fact for the prisoner charged with a felony, whose innocence would emerge spontaneously during the trial without the assistance of a hired "mouthpiece." Since this practice was so much at odds with the existing right to counsel in trials for misdemeanors, Blackstone wrote in the middle of the eighteenth century that it was the custom of judges "to allow a prisoner counsel to stand by him at the bar, and instruct him what questions to ask, or even to ask questions for him, with respect to matters of fact: for as to matters of law, arising on the trial, they are *intitled* to

---

[6] Superior Court Records, 1700–1714, 230.

[7] See ibid., 253; Suffolk Court Files: 8148. The name of the attorney is not given at this Bristol Assizes in 1710. By statute only sworn attorneys enjoyed the privilege of a fee, which was fixed by law at twelve shillings per case at the Superior Court. A June 1707 statute, which may have been in effect for only three years, required attorneys to assist a party to a civil suit seeking their aid at an established fee. See *Acts and Resolves*, I, 467 (1701), 622.

[8] See the valuable discussion of the theory and practice of using defense counsel in eighteenth-century England, especially at the Old Bailey in London, in Langbein, "Criminal Trial Before the Lawyers," 307–313.

the assistance of counsel."[9] Yet the use of defense lawyers in England remained exceptional; the privilege of counsel in all cases of felony did not exist until 1836.[1] Massachusetts did not use the English distinction between felony and misdemeanor in either theory or practice. Most of the approximately 1,200 original prosecutions between 1693 and 1769 were for what can usefully be described as serious crimes, even if the term felony would not be appropriate, in part because the province had less than a dozen capital offenses and sentenced an average of less than one person a year to death. The appellate jurisdiction of the Assizes, which averaged less than 20 percent of the total number of prosecutions, comprised a variety of charges that often approximated misdemeanors.

Massachusetts moved closer than the English during the first half of the eighteenth century to the modern form of lawyer-dominated criminal trial, since normally the prosecution and sometimes the defense were represented by lawyers. This encouraged the pursuit of justice at least to the extent that experienced lawyers were regularly available at the Assizes, thereby promoting such standards as fairness in decisions and regularity in procedure. Lawyers in the province could meddle at will with questions of law and fact during trials. The growing presence of lawyers in the Massachusetts courtroom thus put at least some limits on the influence of the bench at the General Sessions and the Assizes. James Cockburn has pointed out that the English judiciary opposed the increased use of counsel in the late eighteenth century, at least in part because they challenged the "constant and pervasive influence of judicial interference" in criminal trials.[2] Massachusetts judges had to accept the role of lawyers in their courtrooms as a fact of life; both English and Massachusetts

[9] William Blackstone, *Commentaries on the Laws of England* (Oxford, 1765–1769; Chicago, 1979), IV, 349–350. The province of New York followed the English rules on legal representation in misdemeanors and felonies, which again emphasizes the extent of the Massachusetts innovation. See Julius Goebel, Jr., and T. Raymond Naughton, *Law Enforcement in Colonial New York. A Study in Criminal Procedure, 1664–1776* (New York, 1944), 573–575.

[1] See J. S. Cockburn, *A History of English Assizes 1558–1714* (Cambridge, Eng., 1972), 121–122, 141.

[2] J. S. Cockburn, ed., *Somerset Assize Orders 1640–1659*, Somerset Record Society, LXXI (Frome, Eng., 1971), 16–17; and Cockburn, *History of English Assizes*, 122.

judges had to live with the juries that made the ultimate decisions about guilt in most cases.

Contemporary recognition of the gradual development of the legal profession in provincial Massachusetts is illustrated by the lofty conception of lawyers set forth by the distinguished Puritan minister, Cotton Mather. His *Bonifacius. An Essay upon the Good*, published in 1710, somewhat surprisingly included several pages of positive advice for lawyers. One of Mather's first prescriptions is that they be skillful and learned in the law through extensive study and reading.[3] A lawyer should be a scholar and be wise in order to do good:

A *lawyer* must shun all those *indirect ways* of *making haste to be rich*, in which a man cannot be *innocent:* . . . Sir, be prevailed withal, to keep constantly a *court of chancery* in your own breast; and scorn and fear to do anything, but what your *conscience* will pronounce, consistent with, yea, conducting to, *glory to God in the highest, on earth peace, good will towards men.* . . .
This piety must operate very particularly, in the *pleading of causes.* You will abhor, Sir, to appear in a *dirty cause.* If you discern, that your *client* has an *unjust cause*, you will faithfully advise him of it. . . . You will be sincerely desirous, *Truth* and *Right* may take place. You will speak nothing that shall be to the prejudice of *either.* You will abominate the use of all unfair arts, to confound *evidences*, to browbeat *testimonies*, to suppress what may give light in the case.[4]

The surprising element in Mather's characterization of lawyers and their obligations is the positive tone he adopts; the anti-lawyer sentiments alleged to have been so common in the previous century seem to have dissipated, even though Mather seems well aware of the less attractive possibilities of legal practice.[5] At the opening of the new courthouse in Boston in 1713, Justice Samuel Sewall of the Superior Court further characterized the appropriate role for law-

[3] Cotton Mather, *Bonifacius. An Essay upon the Good*, ed. David Levin (Cambridge, Mass., 1966), 122–131.

[4] Ibid., 127.

[5] It would appear that few trained lawyers practiced as attorneys in the colony of Massachusetts Bay in the seventeenth century. See the useful comments of Zechariah Chafee, Jr., in Samuel E. Morison, ed. *Records of the Suffolk County Court, 1671–1680*, Colonial Society of Massachusetts, *Collections*, vols. XXIX–XXX (Boston, 1933), XXIX, xxiii–xxvii.

17. Samuel Sewall (1652–1730) by John Smibert (1729). Chief Justice, Superior Court of Judicature; Judge of the Probate Court, Suffolk. Courtesy, Museum of Fine Arts, Boston.

yers: "Let this large, transparent, costly Glass serve to oblige the Attornys always to set Things in a True Light, And let the Character of none of them be *Impar sibi* [unequal to himself]; Let them Remember they are to advise the Court, as well as plead for their clients."[6]

At the very least these statements by Mather and Sewall acknowledge the presence of attorneys. Before discussing the actual roles of lawyers at various stages of criminal proceedings, including appeals, several general observations are germane. First, the evidence suggests that the special skills of attorneys helped defendants. For instance, at the Middlesex Assizes in July 1723 the crown brought a perjury prosecution against two gentlemen, Joseph Buckminster and Thomas Smith. When the grand jury returned a true bill, Attorney General Read added this note to the indictment: "Joseph Buckminster being sick made a Motion by his Attorny John Valentine Esq. that the said Valentine might be allowd to plead against the indictment." The judges then permitted Valentine and Read to debate the pleas in open court before quashing the indictment "for the Insufficiency thereof."[7]

A petition presented to the Superior Court for Hampshire County in September 1721 revealed a belief in the utility of an attorney for a person accused of a serious crime, which probably reflected commonly-held views. Ovid Rushbrook, a convicted counterfeiter, who was facing another prosecution in Springfield, reminded the justices that he had freely given evidence for the crown and was pleading guilty, "tho' he is advis'd by some to deny it and they will Ingage him a Lawyer in Court that shall stand By him there, But such advice your petitioner minds not."[8] The 1723 trial of Daniel Tuttle of Wallingford, Connecticut, for uttering a counterfeit bill in Boston, specifically illustrated the actual benefits of legal assistance. The jury returned a special verdict on the issue of what constituted an uttering under provincial law: "Upon which Special Verdict the Kings Attorney General as well as the said Daniel Tuttle by his

---

[6] *Sewall Diary*, 714. Since trained lawyers were relatively new in the province, it seems likely that the comment of Mather and Sewall reflected popular English tradition about lawyers rather than their own local experience.

[7] Suffolk Court Files: 17087: 1; Superior Court Records, 1721–1725, 135.

[8] Ibid., 202; Suffolk Court Files: 15426: 9.

Council were fully heard and after Mature Advisement thereon" the court found Tuttle not guilty.[9] Most accused would have found it impossible to match wits with Attorney General Read on such an issue.

A second general observation is that lawyers' skills seem to become more sophisticated throughout the first half of the eighteenth century. There are many indications that attorneys became more legally adroit. For example, in the spring of 1723 Joseph Woodsum of Berwick appealed a conviction in a paternity prosecution to the York Assizes. His attorney argued that contrary to established practice the mother did not accuse Woodsum during childbirth and that therefore her oath was not adequate to convict him. The bench at the Assizes reheard both parties and affirmed the lower court sentence.[1] The result was different in an identical appeal to the Plymouth Assizes in April 1728, in which a woman's oath had been enough to convict the appellant at General Sessions. This time Robert Auchmuty had prepared the reasons of appeal in an expansive and sophisticated form. He stated that the mother had not followed the proper accusatory procedures established by provincial law. An accusation by a single person had to be done during childbirth: "This being a penall Statute and altering the Common Law as to the Mode of Evidence must by the Rules of Law be Expounded Litterally and strictly and therefore no other Mode of proof will be Sufficient or Equal to the Manner of proof required by the Law in these cases."[2] A modern expert has pointed out that in England "the eighteenth century witnessed the growth of a presumption in favour of a strict construction of criminal statutes which persists to this day."[3] Overall, Auchmuty presented one of the most persuasive series of reasons of appeal extant for the 1720's. The Assizes accepted the argument of counsel and reversed the decision of the lower court, despite testimony that the

[9] Superior Court Records, 1721–1725, 162. Tuttle's lawyer is not identified. In a special verdict the trial jury set out its findings of fact in the case and left the judges to determine ultimate guilt or innocence on the basis of a determination of the correct law.

[1] Suffolk Court Files: 15983; Superior Court Records, 1721–1725, 121–122.

[2] Suffolk Court Files: 21442: 2.

[3] Rupert Cross, *Statutory Interpretation* (London, 1976), 10.

appellant had threatened to murder the mother, if she accused him during childbirth.[4]

It seems most likely that the evolving practices of lawyers in civil suits influenced this increased sophistication in criminal practice. Such a process reflected the fact that the legal profession gradually emerged in the early eighteenth century in response to the commercialization and maturation of society. Thus Boston remained the headquarters for the leading lawyers attracted there during the provincial era. All practicing lawyers had far greater opportunities to earn income from civil actions, which were much more voluminous than criminal prosecutions at the Superior Court of Judicature. In the provincial era civil business always comprised the vast bulk of a lawyer's work.[5] The small annual number of criminal prosecutions, coupled with regulated fees, made the Assizes no source for a criminal lawyer to earn a decent living. The extremely low rate of recidivism also meant that there was no regular, returning clientele for the most part. It seems likely, however, that a reputation in criminal work helped to attract the necessary volume of civil business at all superior and inferior courts. The low fees and the low rates of recidivism also were bound to encourage the use of defense counsel by defendants, who were almost always personally inexperienced as objects of criminal prosecutions.

The participation of lawyers in civil suits is also easier to document. The records of civil cases display lawyers' attempts at introducing various innovations, which probably led to comparable efforts in criminal practice. A major study of criminal procedure in colonial New York noted "a tendency, perceptible also in England, for rules used in civil litigation to be applied in criminal cases where the pressure of analogy made the precedents persuasive, and where counsel was on hand to use the advantage."[6] At Suffolk Superior Court in 1715, for example, the crown, in a civil case, appealed an adverse decision about money due to the crown. After losing again, Thomas

---

[4] Superior Court Records, 1725–1730, 135; Suffolk Court Files: 21444: 4.

[5] See Gawalt, *Promise of Power*, 7–35; Charles R. McKirdy, "Before the Storm: The Working Lawyer in Pre-Revolutionary Massachusetts," *Suffolk University Law Review*, XI (1976–1977), 52–53; and Goebel and Naughton, *Law Enforcement in Colonial New York*, 744.

[6] Goebel and Naughton, *Law Enforcement in Colonial New York*, 633.

Newton moved an appeal to the King and Council in England on behalf of the crown: "The Court are of Oppinion that no Appeal lyes in this Case."[7] A comparable attempt at innovation occurred at Salem on 16 December 1718, when John Read from Connecticut appeared on behalf of the Saltonstall interests. "After long Pleadings on both sides; Mr. John Read offered a Demurrer in a sheet written which the Court look'd upon as an Innovation, and inconvenient to be introduced, Especially because the Defendant refus'd to join in the Demurrer, being just now offer'd; and not seen before. And therefore 'twas unanimously Rejected."[8] Since only two of the five members of the court at the time had had formal legal training, the bench may have been generally suspicious of the "new tricks" of lawyers. The presence of trained lawyers in court contributed to the growing professionalization of the Superior Court itself during the first half of the eighteenth century.

Legal assistance was also helpful to a defendant if civil litigation for damages paralleled a criminal case. Pleas in civil cases were, by the nature of the problems that arose in litigation, more sophisticated than in criminal prosecutions. Read and Auchmuty were among the ablest pleaders during the 1720's. Read demonstrated his abilities at the Charlestown Superior Court in January 1729, when he was first successful in quashing for insufficiency the presentment of ten men for riotously assembling with axes and clubs and cutting down some fence belonging to David Gold of Stoneham. Read then represented one of the same defendants, Timothy Sprague, in an appeal from a decision of Middlesex Common Pleas the previous month. Gold had successfully sued Sprague for damages to his crops after the destruction of the fence.[9]

Firm evidence about the activities of lawyers before trials at the

[7] Dominus Rex v James Blin *et al.*, Superior Court Records, 1715–1721, 59.

[8] Samuel Sewall, "Journal from August 1, 1717 to July 26, 1726," 4b, Massachusetts Historical Society, Boston. Hereafter cited as Sewall, "Court Journal." In this bound volume Chief Justice Sewall made notes on cases at various sittings of the Superior Court of Judicature from 28 April 1718 to 26 July 1726. I am most grateful to the late Robert E. Moody for referring me to this important source and for allowing me to consult his transcription.

[9] Superior Court Records, 1725–1730, 195; Suffolk Court Files: 23833: 1. The fate of Read's reserved pleas at the Superior Court is unclear. It should be noted that the Superior Court tried both civil and criminal cases at the same sittings.

Assizes appears in written reasons of appeal filed by attorneys on behalf of appellants from criminal convictions, which again had no real English equivalents. In Massachusetts the sense of justice was very tolerant of appeals in criminal cases, normally from courts of general sessions to the Superior Court of Judicature, but the burden of additional court costs on appellants kept the number of such appeals from becoming excessive. An analysis of these reasons of appeal sheds additional light on the general nature of criminal practice, particularly the benefits counsel offered clients, and exhibits improved legal competency. Reasons of appeal were rarely sophisticated legal efforts: they mainly deny the facts charged and question the adequacy of the evidence for conviction. For example, when stating the reasons of appeal for a Boston baker, Lately Gee, appealing a conviction for altering a bond, Robert Auchmuty first asserted that his client should have been found not guilty. Secondly, he argued, "that the proofs in the Case are not Sufficient in the Law to Support the said Indictment and to Convict the Appellant." The third point was more novel: "by the very proofs in the Case it Evidently appears nothing Criminaliter [creating criminal liability] in the Law wuld or ought to have Charged or fastened on the Appellant." At the trial Auchmuty must have elaborated on these simple points in a persuasive manner, since the jury acquitted his client.[1]

The reasons of appeal asserted by Christopher Jacob Lawton for his client, Matthew Copley, Jr., a Suffield "bloomer" accused of assaulting a deputy sheriff of Hampshire County in 1729, claimed that the "Facts Charged in the Complaint on which the Appellant received his Tryal as aforesaid was not proved by any such Evidenc as the Law should or Can Own."[2] Lawton sent these reasons to the clerk of the Superior Court in Hampshire, appending a note: "If you see anything amiss in the above please to alter and you will highly oblige your servant." Such a rare request suggests the attorney, in fact, lacked formal legal training. Attorney General John Overing wasted little time in denying the force of these reasons of appeal, charging that the evidence was sufficient to convict, "and as it satisfyed the former Jury we have great reason to pray confirma-

[1] Suffolk Court Files: 15181: 2; Superior Court Records, 1715–1721, 359.
[2] Suffolk Court Files: 23358: 3.

tion and costs." At the Assizes the jury proved Overing was a good prophet by finding Copley guilty.[3]

Still, the preparation of reasons of appeal benefited from the advice of counsel, who contributed to the development of the law by proposing more and varied rationales for quashing or reversal. The list of reasons furnished the bench and/or the jury with plausible alternatives, especially in cases where the weight of popular sentiment lay with appellants. An appeal by three yeomen from Falmouth in Barnstable County to the Assizes in 1726 illustrates this process at work. The trio were convicted at Edgartown in Dukes County for riotously seizing Thomas Tupper. John Otis, Jr., the attorney who prepared and filed the reasons of appeal, first asserted that the jury should not have found his clients guilty, "there being no evidence of the facts set forth in the Inditement only the complainant who was not bound by Recognizance to prosecute your Appellants." Secondly, he pointed out that Tupper did not have a house but only a small hut on the island in dispute and had himself indeed evicted the appellants, who at the time Tupper erected his cottage "had been Quietly and Peaceably in Possession of Island of Nonamosett [Nonamesset] for more than Three Years as Tenants to John Winthrop Esq. of New London." Thirdly, "the Appellants further say said Judgment was wrong by reason The Inditement was Joint and Your Appellants Jointly tryed and the Judgment is Severall; viz; each to pay a fine of Four Pounds." The judges seized on a fourth reason of appeal to reverse the conviction. Otis pointed out that his clients were convicted at a general session held by adjournment on the last Tuesday of October, but that this was illegal since the law required a new session to begin on that day.[4] Laymen could not have produced such a varied list on their own.

Persons who used legal assistance on appeal had probably employed the same lawyers at the General Sessions. Robert Sturgeon, a Watertown gentleman, illustrated the possibilities by employing both Robert Auchmuty and Robert Robinson to represent him at the General Sessions in Middlesex County, where he was tried for con-

---

[3] Ibid.: 23358: 5; Superior Court Records, 1725–1730, 255. An appeal to the Assizes in fact resulted in a trial *de novo*, a most un-English form of practice.

[4] Ibid., 38; Suffolk Court Files: 19285.

tempt of the General Court for continuing to preach in a local church although forbidden to do so. At the Middlesex General Sessions his attorneys made several pleas to quash the indictment, which Attorney General Overing successfully opposed. The bench also overruled the claim that Sturgeon had a right to preach but permitted him, with the approval of the Attorney General, to have the full benefit of the plea at the next assizes. Auchmuty prepared the reasons of appeal, including several references to English cases. At the Superior Court of Judicature, Sturgeon's lawyers succeeded in obtaining a special verdict from the jury, but the bench found against him after advising on the verdict for approximately six months.[5]

It is a measure of John Read's special talents that his reasons of appeal in criminal cases were the most elaborate and sophisticated of any of those still extant from the 1720's.[6] His defenses more frequently moved beyond simple denial of guilt or of certain facts into substantive or procedural issues. In 1729 two New Hampshire laborers were charged with leading a group of Irishmen in an assault on some "English people" in a dispute over land ownership. At the Essex General Sessions Read first argued that the Massachusetts court had no jurisdiction since the alleged assault and battery took place in New Hampshire. Secondly, he argued that the presentment should be quashed for the duplicity of its contents, since it did not charge both defendants with the same offenses. Read next asserted that the defendants had acted lawfully by virtue of a warrant from a justice of the peace. When it came time to file reasons of appeal, Read essentially repeated these same oral arguments. The text of the reasons ran to a full page, which was much lengthier than most such papers. But the effort was wasted. For some unknown reason Read's clients failed to appear in court to prosecute their appeal, which was not uncommon. After the judgment against the pair was affirmed, they were taxed the substantial amount of £38.10.6 in court costs.[7]

---

[5] Ibid.: 17428: 10; ibid.: 17428: 2, 3, 4; Superior Court Records, 1721–1725, 165–166.

[6] Read's defense of John Checkley in a criminal libel trial is discussed below, 232.

[7] Suffolk Court Files: 23647: 2, 4; Superior Court Records, 1725–1730, 267.

Overall, the use of defense counsel was well established by the 1720's at the latest, although the problems of proving this statistically are immense because of the unreliability of the surviving evidence. Efforts to produce statistical tables about the presence of attorneys are doomed to failure for such reasons. The hard evidence concerning the presence of attorneys is as follows. There is direct proof of the presence of defense counsel in 5 (4.5 percent) of 110 cases in the period 1700–1710, 34 (18.9 percent) of 181 cases in the 1720's, and 26 (12.9 percent) of 202 cases in the 1740's. Lawyers appeared in all counties and in cases from appeals of minor convictions to trials of capital offences. The crucial point is that this is the minimum proof available; there is every expectation that much more defense work occurred, especially by the 1720's. The evidence above is based only on those decades for which a search for every file paper in a particular case was made, since it is most often the file papers, especially reasons of appeal, that indicate the presence of defense lawyers. But there are very few file papers for any cases in the first decade of the eighteenth century. There are no file papers available, for example, for seven of a total of twenty-four prosecutions for theft during the 1720's. It is rare for the formal entries of the trial to refer to attorneys, except when the record specifies that the prisoner was heard by his counsel on a point, but sometimes the clerk of court's entry states the prisoner's defense was heard without specifying whether or not the accused presented his own case or had representation. In certain grouped prosecutions against the same persons at the assizes, a defense lawyer participated in the appeal, but there is no evidence of his likely participation in defense of the original prosecutions as well. The overall numbers listed above also include cases that are counted in the overall totals, but in which there was no role for defense counsel, such as a situation in which the grand jury returned an ignoramus and no trial ensued, or a prosecution against an individual for failure to appear to prosecute an appeal to the assizes. Finally, there are cases in which pleas for benefit of clergy or to challenge indictments, for example, are recorded in the court records without any definite proof that, as seems likely, an attorney entered such pleas for the defendant.

The Role of Defense Counsel at the Assizes

Lawyers were unlikely to be employed to assist defendants in pre-liminary examinations before justices of the peace and were not per-mitted to be present when the Attorney General or a local prosecu-tor was privately setting forth the grounds for proceeding with a prosecution before a grand jury at either the general sessions or the assizes.

An episode in 1723 at a court of general sessions raised the issue of the specific stage in a prosecution when an individual could employ counsel. Daniel Clark refused to respond to a presentment for selling liquor without a license unless he was permitted a lawyer. The Essex county bench told Clark he could have counsel after he pleaded. When Clark continued to demand legal advice at once, the general sessions dropped the presentment and proceeded to convict him on an earlier plea before a justice of the peace.[8]

One of the few instances before the actual start of a trial when a lawyer could formally help a client was in preparing a petition for bail or appearing at a hearing on petition for bail. A major episode that indirectly sheds light on this point occurred in December 1705, after two carters, Thomas Trowbridge and John Winchester, Jr., refused to give way to a carriage carrying Governor Joseph Dudley. The pair were committed to prison at the insistence of the Governor. His son Paul, the Attorney General of the province and a lawyer trained in England, opposed the granting of bail. It took almost a week for the justices of the Superior Court of Judicature to allow it. The important point for our purposes is that the two prisoners had no attorneys at the hearing, nor, according to Justice Sewall, could they procure any in this politically sensitive case. Not surprisingly, the few lawyers in Boston who practiced criminal law were unwilling to take a stand against the Governor and the Attorney General. At least Sewall's account implies that one could be represented by coun-sel in a hearing for bail.[9]

Records of bail hearings remain rare in subsequent years, in part because it was uncommon for defendants to be held in jail pending a

[8] Ibid., 1721–1725, 29; Suffolk Court Files: 17820, 17516: 3. The complicated issues in this case led to appeals.

[9] Information from *Sewall Diary*, 532–537.

trial. On at least two occasions Robert Auchmuty brought petitions for bail to the assizes on behalf of his clients. John Taggart was in Cambridge jail for assaulting Robert Butterfield during the sitting of the Suffolk Assizes in August 1739. He applied for a writ of habeas corpus to be moved to the Boston jail, so that he "might be admitted to give Bail, and to be proceeded with as to Law and Justice appertains." Auchmuty apparently prepared a separate petition for bail for Taggart, which the court granted. He reported that Butterfield had now recovered from his wounds, and since his client's trial was not scheduled until January 1740, he would have to spend a long time in jail during the winter. The system of bail did not work well initially in this episode, because both Patrick Taggart, a co-assailant who was not jailed, and John Taggart required much prompting, including the issuance of writs of *scire facias*, before finally appearing in court for their trials. This caused problems for Auchmuty, who was evidently operating a private system of bail bonding and had stood surety for the pair.[1] Auchmuty also acted for David Doughty of York County in February 1747 when he prepared a petition to the Suffolk Assizes for a writ of habeas corpus. Doughty was in jail on suspicion of murder, but his attorney claimed that the inquest had showed the victim did not die from a murderous act and that prison was hurting his client's health.[2]

These two isolated episodes in 1739 and 1747 are unlikely to represent a new trend in criminal practice. Incomplete record-keeping seems a better explanation for the absence of materials showing the role of lawyers in bail hearings. Moreover, the speediness with which trials occurred in the provincial era, especially for serious crimes tried at the Assizes, meant that the accused rarely spent much time in jail awaiting trial. Finally, bail was in fact granted fairly easily, except for persons charged with capital offenses.

A person indicted by a grand jury came before the Assizes for trial by jury, unless he or she pleaded guilty. Arraignment involved entering a plea after a reading of the indictment, and at this point a lawyer could really begin to help his client.

It was probably only after being indicted that most individuals ac-

[1] Suffolk Court Files: 49885, 49960, 50733, 52030, 54806.

[2] The records do not indicate whether or not this petition succeeded. Ibid.: 62856.

quired counsel. There is evidence of the court's appointing counsel, as in 1702–1703, when the Superior Court assigned John Newton as the attorney for Adam, a Negro, during a dispute in civil and criminal courts with the prominent John Saffin over Adam's freedom.[3] Also, a suspect at Hampshire General Sessions on 20 January 1736, who moved for counsel when he was required to plead to an indictment for fornication, had an attorney assigned to him.[4]

At the Worcester Assizes in September 1768 the court appointed John Adams to defend Samuel Quinn, who was accused of rape. Adams' own record suggests that Quinn had asked for him to be appointed.[5] After Quinn's acquittal, he was remanded to jail on another indictment for assault with intent to ravish. Adams continues the story: "When he had returned to Prison, he broke out of his own Accord — God bless Mr. Adams. God bless his Soul I am not to be hanged, and I dont care what else they do to me." Writing in his diary in June 1770, Adams recalled his pleasure then: "Here was his Blessing and his Transport which gave me more Pleasure, when I first heard the Relation and when I have recollected it since, than any fee would have done. This was a worthless fellow, but nihil humanum, alienum. His joy, which I had in some sense been instrumental in procuring, and his Blessings and good Wishes, occasioned very agreable Emotions in the Heart."[6] Adams' client subsequently pleaded guilty and was severely punished with whippings and a twelve-month imprisonment.

At least in theory, and sometimes in practice, a lawyer could engage in plea bargaining, attempt to quash an indictment, advise his client about pleading guilty or not guilty, and assist his client during trial by jury. The overwhelming majority of suspects in original prosecutions pleaded not guilty. Even some of those who initially admitted their guilt at a preliminary examination pleaded not guilty

---

[3] Superior Court Records, 1700–1714, 84–85.

[4] Hampshire County Court of General Sessions of the Peace, Book B, No. 3, 1735–1740, 51, Court House, Northampton.

[5] L. H. Butterfield, ed., *Diary and Autobiography of John Adams* (New York, 1964), I, 353. Hiller Zobel and Kinvin Wroth suggest that the appointment of counsel was "apparently an established practice, although it is not yet clear whether the practice was limited to capital cases." *Legal Papers of John Adams*, I, li.

[6] Butterfield, ed., *Diary and Autobiography of John Adams*, I, 353–354.

upon subsequent arraignment and were ultimately acquitted. When Daniel Tuttle of Wallingford, Connecticut, was in jail in Boston in the early 1720's charged with the much-feared crime of counterfeiting, he fully confessed his crime and was promised that he could furnish evidence for the crown. Yet Tuttle then pleaded not guilty and was acquitted by the justices after a special verdict.[7] The important difference for Tuttle was that he had a lawyer at his trial, who may well have encouraged his plea of not guilty and helped to persuade the jury to return a special verdict. The judges of the assizes permitted this lawyer to argue before them on the special verdict.

The evidence for plea bargaining in general and for the role of lawyers therein is indirect and elusive.[8] There was one specific episode in Boston in February 1749 where persons charged with burglary pleaded guilty to theft only after the Attorney General declared that he would not prosecute them for burglary.[9] It is possible that the Attorney General had simply reconsidered the strength of his case or, perhaps, personal factors may have played a decisive part in the plea bargaining decision. It is interesting that Robert Auchmuty was the acting Attorney General. As a leading criminal lawyer who never served full time in that prosecutorial post, he may have been personally amenable to such an accommodating arrangement. This episode, brought out in open court, evidently received the approbation of the judges. Although this episode is the only concrete evidence found on plea bargaining, the suspicion remains that the practice was more common than the formal records indicate, especially when multiple charges of counterfeiting against the same individual or prosecutions for burglary (a capital offense) were actually tried as simple thefts. If attorneys wished to plea bargain for their clients, the professional climate in Massachusetts was favorable. The leading lawyers travelled and lived together on circuit with the Superior Court and knew each other intimately. The Attorney General was

[7] Suffolk Court Files: 17418: 3; Superior Court Records, 1721–1725, 162.

[8] John H. Langbein discusses the history of plea bargaining in "Understanding the Short History of Plea Bargaining," *Law & Society Review*, XIII (1979), 261–272. A useful by-product of his article is its illustration of how different eighteenth-century English criminal trials were from the system described in this essay.

[9] Superior Court Records, 1747–1750, 224.

someone who might return shortly to a defense practice. An Attorney General *pro hac vice* may have been even easier to deal with because of the temporary nature of his elevation to represent the crown at one specific sitting.

Pleas by lawyers to quash indictments are the most commonly-documented episodes involving counsel in the surviving records of the assizes that I have examined. In an early case in November 1708 involving illegal trade, John Borland, a prominent Boston merchant, and William Rouse, a Charlestown sea captain, both used attorneys, with the court's permission, to try to quash indictments. Thomas Newton and John Valentine initially pleaded that the court did not have jurisdiction over the offense, an argument which the court rejected. They then argued that Borland was an accessory rather than a principal and further that "there is no Month, day or year Mentioned when the Goods were Sold." After the court overruled all of the motions to quash, Borland pleaded not guilty and a jury acquitted him. Captain Rouse had better luck in attempts to quash his indictment for illegal trade. His lawyers were overruled in questioning the jurisdiction of the court, but succeeded on the grounds that there was no mention of the county where he lived.[1] The nature of the arguments advanced clearly illustrates the important role of defense counsel in a controversial and highly visible case.

By the 1720's attorneys were making several types of special pleas to quash indictments. These were a seeming novelty in the 1720's, and another reflection of the development of the legal profession since 1710. Reasons of appeal often included a plea to quash an indictment that had served as the basis for prosecution at the general sessions. A person who failed to quash an indictment below could reserve such a plea for consideration at the assizes. Since reasons of appeal tended to include every possible ground for winning a case, the typical arguments did not distinguish between attempts to quash an indictment and efforts to defeat the prosecution on a legal issue or

---

[1] Ibid., 1700–1714, 230. Newton and Valentine successfully defended a third client in this series of prosecutions, but a fourth client was found guilty. John Langbein has pointed out to me that the English rule denied the accused a copy of the indictment; the issues in this 1708 Massachusetts case are ones on which counsel had always been allowed in England.

on a factual basis. As was evident in an earlier discussion, lawyers adopted a multiple approach to drafting reasons of appeal, hoping that one of their points would strike home. Such a pattern also characterized reasons of appeal in civil cases, which may have inspired the use of written reasons in criminal cases as well.[2] The prosecution of Daniel Clark, a Topsfield innholder, for swearing and for striking one Jesse Dorman, illustrates the use of reserved pleas. In the fall of 1723 an Essex county grand jury indicted Clark at the General Sessions. The defendant employed John Overing, who had completed a one-year term as Attorney General in June, to prepare his pleas. He pointed out the failure to include the time and place of the alleged offense, the abode of the defendant, and the name of the county: "The presentment ought to be Quashed for that 2 Crimes of Different Nature are Joined in same presentment." The General Sessions ignored these assertions of error and convicted Clark but permitted an appeal. The Essex Assizes in May 1724 swiftly quashed the presentment on the basis of the reserved pleas.[3]

The uncertainty of a presentment was a major reason to reverse a conviction on appeal.[4] It is a reminder that, unlike England, Massachusetts lacked a corps of trained persons to serve as justices of the peace and court clerks, especially at the sittings of the general sessions, and on-the-job training in the province occasionally was of questionable quality.

It appears, however, that the assizes were not always hospitable to procedural pleas and that the judges preferred to try a case on its merits whenever possible. They were probably resistant to seeming

[2] The character of reasons of appeal in civil cases can be reviewed easily in *Maine Court Records*, IV, passim.

[3] Suffolk Court Files: 17516: 3; Superior Court Records, 1721–1725, 202.

[4] After Philip English, Sr., a Salem merchant, was convicted at the Salem General Sessions in 1722 for words "vilifying and reproaching to the Church of Christ in saying that they were the Devils Church or Members," he hired Robert Auchmuty to prepare an appeal, another illustration of the wise use of counsel in cases involving public controversy. The first of two brief reasons simply asserted that "the Presentment is so Uncertain that in the Law no Judgment or Sentence can or ought to be given thereupon." Although the bench did not grant this plea, but convicted English again, it quashed the second prosecution against English on appeal because the presentment was "uncertain." This was in line with Auchmuty's argument in the second case, which involved allegations going back to the 1692 witchcraft episode. Suffolk Court Files: 16251: 3, 4; Superior Court Records, 1721–1725, 80.

quibbles raised by lawyers. The proof underlying this observation is that most original prosecutions and appeals went to trial. After 1724 the judges could refer to legislative authority. In late November the General Court decided it was devoting too much time to fashioning relief for parties and criminal defendants that had lost appeals "through some error or mistake in the party, or his attorney, and sometimes of the clerk of the court, in misreciting the parties or judgement, or misnaming the courts appeal'd to or from, or otherwise." The legislation directed the Superior Court judges to "order an amendment of such defective or mistaken reasons of appeal, and to proceed to tryal of the cause, as though no such error had been committed."[5]

A case involving a group of appellants from Dedham, who were convicted of interrupting a town meeting, demonstrates a reluctance of the high court justices to accept technical pleas to quash indictments. The second reason of appeal filed by attorney Robert Robinson argued that the indictment should have been quashed because provincial law had appointed another mode of redress in the event that the defendants had indeed disturbed the meeting. They could only have been fined five shillings if the facts alleged were true.[6] In answering these reasons of appeal in preparation for the Suffolk Assizes in August 1728, the newly-elected Attorney General Joseph Hiller, perhaps overzealous in the first few days of his brief term in office, not only denied the force of Robinson's argument but offered him an elementary legal lesson. He argued that the indictment was good, "but if not the appellant Council should have pleaded to quash it at the Court below, and he would have served his Clyents better than he will be able to do now by putting the reason for quashing it into their Reasons of Appeal." The justices apparently agreed with

[5] *Acts and Resolves*, II, 331. Even if this directive had been specifically for civil litigation, it would have had a spill-over effect on reasons of appeal in criminal cases because of the similarity between the intent and character of reasons in either type of case. The same high court and the same five judges heard both civil and criminal cases.

[6] Suffolk Court Files: 21901: 2. I have learned nothing about the life of Robert Robinson, who appears as defense counsel a number of times in the 1720's. Sewall's diary identifies him as a lawyer in 1716 and as on circuit with the Superior Court in 1719 and 1725. *Sewall Diary*, 814, 936, 1031–1032.

the Attorney General, since they permitted the appellants to be tried by a jury, which convicted them.[7]

There were at least two cases on appeal before the Assizes during the 1720's in which errors in the indictments and presentments prepared at the General Sessions led to a quashing of the prosecution. No indictment drafted at the Assizes, however, was found insufficient, which suggests that the Attorney General either did these himself or supervised the work of clerks more carefully because of the seriousness of the charges.[8] One appeal involved a husband and wife convicted at Northampton in March 1721 of fornication before marriage. The attorney for the couple, who is not named, filed substantial reasons of appeal that nevertheless missed the essential technicality on which the prosecution foundered at the assizes. The original indictment simply said: "We the Grand jury do Present Eben Dickenson and Sarah Dickenson his wife of Hadley for the sinn of fornication." The justices reversed the sentence "for that the presentment of the Grand Jury does not alledge the Fornication to be Committed before Marriage and no time laid in the presentment when the Fact was committed."[9] Such prosecutions were common at the general sessions, but they were rarely appealed, which suggests that recourse to defense counsel was worthwhile when individuals felt particularly aroused or aggrieved by a charge or conviction. An accused at the general sessions had limited incentive to spend money on a lawyer until conviction, since an appeal to the assizes was a matter of right and led to another trial before new judges and a new jury. The risk of incurring high costs of court at the assizes created a countervailing pressure.

The issue of errors in presentments and indictments was again a factor at the Suffolk Assizes in November 1723 in an appeal of a conviction for selling strong drink without a license. At general

[7] Suffolk Court Files: 21901: 3; Superior Court Records, 1725–1730, 182.

[8] It also seems unlikely that the Attorney General attended General Sessions in each county to direct prosecutions. Since the Attorney General, as well as the leading lawyers and a majority of the Superior Court justices, normally resided in Boston, he would have been readily available for consultation about events in Suffolk General Sessions, where, however, most cases involved trivial matters. Flaherty, "Crime and Social Control," 341.

[9] Suffolk Court Files: 15419: 1, 3; Superior Court Records, 1721–1725, 27–28.

sessions the indictment asserted that Henry Whitton of Boston had sold strong drink without a license "within three months last past." Most persons accused of this common crime simply paid their fines; Whitton was obviously aroused enough to take on the financial burden of hiring a lawyer to represent him at the general sessions and later on appeal. In September 1723 Robert Robinson tried to quash this presentment at the general sessions: "The Defendant pleads that the Presentment doth not set forth any certain Day when he sold the Drink mentioned in the presentment without Licence wherefore it is uncertain for the Defendant to know how to make Answer thereto and ought therefore to be quashed for want of Certainty." After the general sessions overruled this plea and a jury found Whitton guilty, Robinson repeated his earlier plea in written reasons of appeal to the Assizes. In responding to these arguments, the Attorney General argued that the fact of Whitton's selling drink without a license was plainly proved "by one witness to three severall facts at severall times for selling drink without License which being soo notorious the Jury made noe hesitation but found the Appellant guilty of the same." The assize judges followed Robinson and quashed the indictment "for the uncertainty thereof, there being no day therein laid when the Drink was Sold."[1]

Since pleas to quash indictments were not recorded in the formal court records, there are problems exploring the degree of legal sophistication of such pleadings. It seems likely that the types of objections raised in the material just treated were comparable to those recorded in reasons of appeal discussed earlier. It is clear that the bench quashed indictments in a relatively few instances, such as at the Suffolk Assizes in February 1743 when the court quashed two or three indictments against Mary Barry for counterfeiting, "upon the pleas made by her Attorney Benjamin Kent for Quashing the same."[2]

Once an accused person had pleaded not guilty and the trial had actually begun, the role of defense counsel was one of argumentation,

[1] Suffolk Court Files: 17167: 3; 17379: 1, 6, 2; Superior Court Records, 1721–1725, 162.

[2] Superior Court Records, Minute Book 45. Kent (1707–1788) was admitted to Superior Court practice in 1739. See Shipton, *Sibley's Harvard Graduates*, VIII, 220–230.

mostly over facts, but sometimes over the law. The latter point must be made with a great deal of caution, since there are no trial transcripts in the modern sense for provincial Massachusetts. The only "law report" for colonial Massachusetts comprises notes taken in court by Josiah Quincy, Jr., between 1761 and 1772. Although he reported only four criminal cases, defense lawyers definitely appeared in three of them. Quincy noted that the trial at the Suffolk Assizes of Jemima Mangent for infanticide lasted from 10 A.M. to 8 P.M., "during which Time neither Judges or Jury departed. It turned chiefly on Matters of Fact." Despite this focus, the defense cited a long list of legal authorities, including English statutes, treatises, and law reports.[3]

Although legal authorities were cited during trials, as the Mangent case demonstrates, an analysis of this issue requires two prefatory points. First, most trials seem to have involved disputes over facts rather than laws. Thorny issues of substantive or procedural law were less likely to emerge in criminal cases than in civil litigation, especially in the first half of the eighteenth century, when lawyers were only beginning to make their presence felt. Statutes defining the elements of criminal behavior in the province were simple and straightforward. The central issue was whether the accused had committed the act charged in the indictment. Secondly, the absence of transcripts for trials limits awareness of the extent of recourse to legal authority by defendants and their attorneys. Knowledge of this issue depends heavily on the written reasons filed by appellants. In the early eighteenth century these documents tended to be very factual in nature, as the appellants primarily sought to rebut the Crown's version of the facts in a case.[4] Occasionally, attorneys made semi-legal

[3] Josiah Quincy, Jr., *Reports of Cases Argued and Adjudged in the Superior Court of Judicature of the Province of Massachusetts Bay, Between 1761 and 1772* (Reprint, New York, 1969), 162–163.

[4] See *Maine Court Records*, IV, lxix, passim. Paternity suits by unwed mothers for child support were fruitful sources of appeals. Usually the defense attorney pointed out that the mother had failed to follow the statutory procedures for accusing the father during the time of her travail. See the appeal of Joseph Woodsum, Superior Court Records, 1721–1725, 121–122; Suffolk Court Files: 15983. James Jeffrey was the lawyer in this case. His reasons of appeal are printed in *Maine Court Records*, VI, 71–72. Jeffrey quoted provincial law to the court. This was his only recorded appearance in a York County case from 1719 to 1727.

points as part of the reasons of appeal.[5] But there was little evident legal sophistication either in the argumentation or in the issues at stake in trials. Most matters in dispute had a factual basis, which either had to be established or undermined in what was essentially a new trial at the Assizes.

The wording of indictments indicates that the primary task of the Assizes was to enforce the province's criminal statutes.[6] The recorded instances of references to such laws at actual trials, at least during the 1720's, occurred in reasons of appeal. At Bristol in 1721 Robert Auchmuty, the attorney for three Freetown assessors appealing a conviction for neglect of duty, referred to a specific statute requiring towns to support ministers. This task was the burden of the select-men, who alone should be bothered when problems arose. Auchmuty perhaps unwisely added that "the Wisdome of no Court is above the Law." In an additional reason of appeal Auchmuty discussed an-other statutory provision: "If it should be pretended that the said Judgment or Sentence is grounded upon the Province Law page 175 there likewise the Appellants Conceive the said Judgment or Sen-tence is wrong and Erronious for that Enables the Court of quarter sessions in case of a Delinquencie of selectmen or Assessors to appoint three or more sufficient freeholders within the County to assess or apportion the same etc all which the said judgment has not allowed neither were there any grounds or reasons for such a proceeding." Auchmuty's reasoning was in vain, since the full bench affirmed the judgment below against the assessors.[7]

Judges and lawyers used English statutes when they proved rele-vant, especially if there was no comparable provision in provincial law. In one of the few explicit references to English statutes found in the records of the assizes, John Read in the 1720's cited laws con-

---

[5] Such a procedure occurred at the Bristol Assizes in the fall of 1793, when Thomas Newton drafted reasons of appeal for Adam, a Negro, who wanted freedom from his master, the prominent John Saffin. Newton's arguments moved beyond factual issues to question the implications of the absence in the instrument of indenture of a pro-vision covering what would happen if Adam did not serve his master faithfully. Suffolk Court Files: 5941: 2.

[6] Chief Justice Thomas Hutchinson stated in a charge to a grand jury in 1767 that: "The principal Crown-Law of this Province is grounded on our provincial Laws: where these fail, the Common Law of England is the Rule." Quincy, *Reports*, 235.

[7] Suffolk Court Files: 15379: 1; Superior Court Records, 1721–1725, 20.

cerning misbehavior on the Sabbath enacted under Edward III and Queen Mary in 1376 and 1553 respectively.[8] Read also cited a case from *12 Coke's Reports*. The records of the Suffolk Assizes for 1725 contain an undated summary of the laws of England concerning the escape of prisoners.[9] During this period the assizes presided over the prosecution of Lieutenant John Lane, a gentleman from York, on a charge of escaping from the Boston jail.[1] This summary was perhaps prepared for the use of the judges or submitted to them by attorneys involved in the case.

Citation of English cases from printed reports, which constituted the true backbone of the common law, was more restricted than reference to English statutes. Although English decisions could be cited in Massachusetts courts, colonial judges and lawyers probably had limited access to such material. The unsophisticated nature of legal argumentation in criminal cases in the first half of the eighteenth century may have been due in part to a general paucity of treatises and law reports to which reference could be made. An English authority noted that in the seventeenth century "Coke's Third Institute was the principal authority as to the criminal law, and the little which he says on the subject is fragmentary and incomplete."[2] Sewall owned this treatise, first published in 1644, which he referred to as Coke's *Pleas of the Crown*. He read passages in open court and at hearings on several occasions.[3] Sir Matthew Hale's brief and methodical summary of the *Pleas of the Crown* appeared posthumously in 1678 as a manual for circuit riders, and his major two-volume *History of the Pleas of the Crown,* written in 1676, did not appear in print until 1736. Hale's two books became, in succession, the leading English authorities on the criminal law. Since several judges attending the Charlestown Assizes in 1705 discussed one of Hale's religious tracts of 1677 over dinner, it seems possible that

[8] Petition of John Doan and Josiah Oakes, Suffolk Court Files: 21440: 1.

[9] Ibid.: 26631.

[1] Superior Court Records, 1721–1725, 264.

[2] James Fitzjames Stephen, *A History of the Criminal Law of England* (London, 1883), I, 359. See the valuable critique of English primary sources in L. A. Knafla, "Crime and Criminal Justice: A Critical Bibliography," in J. S. Cockburn, ed., *Crime in England 1550–1800* (London, 1977), 286–298.

[3] *Sewall Diary,* 537; Sewall, "Court Journal," 7a.

they knew his *Pleas of the Crown* as well. The contents of the 1736 volumes seem particularly sophisticated in comparison to the kinds of legal arguments that were recorded in Massachusetts court-rooms.[4]

The basic handbook for justices of the peace commonly used in the American colonies was Michael Dalton's *Countrey Justice* (1618), which went through numerous seventeenth- and eighteenth-century editions. At the Ipswich Assizes in 1702 the crown's answer to reasons of appeal cited Dalton on a particular point.[5] At a 1705 meeting of the provincial council both Sewall and Governor Dudley cited Dalton in discussing how to handle a petition from George Lawson, whose home had been attacked by a mob because of an adulterous affair.[6]

Knowledge is lacking about English legal materials held in public and private hands in provincial Massachusetts. Only random information is currently available. Anthony Stoddard, for example, was a justice of the peace in Boston after 1715 and a judge of the Inferior Court of Common Pleas for Suffolk County after 1733. When he died in 1748, he owned Hawkins' *Pleas of the Crown,* justice of the peace handbooks by Dalton and Nelson, and Lilly's *Abridgement of English Law.*[7] There is no reason to think that such holdings were unusual for a lower-court judge. Sewall built his own library, and it stands to reason that other Superior Court justices did so as well. In Boston in 1686 a person left three books for Sewall: "one is Michael Dalton, the second is Gilberts Presidents, the third is the office of clerk of Assise, and Clerk of the Peace. . . ."[8] It seems especially

---

[4] *Sewall Diary,* 518; M. Hale, *Historia Placitorum Coronae: The History of the Pleas of the Crown* (2 vols., London, 1736).

[5] Suffolk Court Files: 5417.

[6] *Sewall Diary,* 520, 521.

[7] Shipton, *Sibley's Harvard Graduates,* IV, 387. The library was sold at auction, Boston *News Letter,* 11 August 1748. The titles of the volumes in question are: William Hawkins, *A Treatise of the Pleas of the Crown* (2 vols., London, 1716–1721); Michael Dalton, *The Countrey Justice* (London, 1618); William Nelson, *The Office and Authority of a Justice of Peace* (London, 1704); John Lilly, *The Practical Register: or, A General Abridgment of the Law* (2 vols., London, 1718). One cannot readily tell which editions Stoddart owned.

[8] "Letter-Book of Samuel Sewall," Massachusetts Historical Society *Collections,* 6th series, I and II (Boston, 1886–1888), I, 40. Hereafter cited as "Sewall Letterbook." I have been unable to identify the volume by Gilbert.

significant for the subsequent history of the Massachusetts Assizes that Sewall owned or at least had read the 1676 or 1682 editions of the standard handbook for operating such a court.[9] After Thomas Newton died in 1721, his library was advertised for sale as "the greatest and best collection of law books that ever was exposed to sale in the country."[1] John Read had more than fifty volumes of English treatises and law reports when he died in 1749. The Harvard College library had fifty-seven law books in 1723, about 2 percent of its total holdings.[2]

Newspaper advertisements during the 1740's offered for sale such items as Coke's *Institutes* and *Reports,* law dictionaries, and guides for justices of the peace. The only volumes of English law reports listed by name are Lord Coke's.[3] The estates of such varying personages as Lieutenant Governor Spencer Phips, who was a justice of the peace for Middlesex County, and Daniel How, a yeoman in Shrewsbury, revealed ownership of statute books, guides for justices of the peace, and legal dictionaries. Nahum Ward, a justice of the peace who died in Shrewsbury in 1754, divided his law books between two sons. Artemas Ward, Harvard College, class of 1748, became a justice of the peace himself in 1750 at the age of twenty-three.[4] When John Adams was studying law in Worcester in the mid-1750's, he read Hawkins' *Pleas of the Crown.* Benjamin Prat (1711–1763), who began to practice with great success in Boston about 1745, used to bring lawbooks to court to argue various points.[5] This was probably typical.

The general attitude of the Superior Court toward English legal opinions seems evident in 1712 when Justice Sewall himself sought

[9] *The Office of the Clerk of Assize . . . Together with the Office of the Peace* (London, 1676; 2nd edition, revised and enlarged, London, 1682).

[1] Boston *News Letter,* 11–18 September 1721.

[2] Lawrence Cremin, *American Education. The Colonial Experience 1607–1783* (New York, 1970), 397.

[3] See Boston *Evening Post,* 14 May to 11 June 1744, 21 December 1747; Boston *News Letter,* 17 March 1748.

[4] Shipton, *Sibley's Harvard Graduates,* V, 234; Artemas Ward Mss., I, Massachusetts Historical Society.

[5] Wroth and Zobel, eds., *Adams Legal Papers,* I, liv; Shipton, *Sibley's Harvard Graduates,* X, 229. On Prat's career, see ibid., X, 226–239.

English legal advice on a case pending before the assizes. In a letter to the Massachusetts agent Jeremiah Dummer on 22 April 1712 Sewall enclosed a memorandum on a case, "upon which I intreat you humbly to ask the Advice of my Lord Chief Justice Parker, or Sir Peter King; or of whom you shall think most convenient; and send the resolution by the first opportunity."[6] Parker was Lord Chief Justice of the Queen's Bench and King was Recorder of London. The case involved Hittee, an Indian girl, found guilty of arson by a jury. At her sentencing it was suggested that she was under sixteen years of age. Sewall wondered whether the issue of her age could be determinative at this stage of the proceedings, since the age had not been included in the jury's verdict. Dummer did obtain advice for Sewall, but its nature is unclear.[7] The practical solution was to try Hittee again for the same offense at the Plymouth Assizes in March 1713. This time the indictment specifically stated that she was a full sixteen years of age in June 1711 when the alleged offense occurred. A jury then acquitted her.[8] The probability that she had already been in a prison for almost two years must have strongly inclined the jury to have mercy on this Indian girl.

Concrete evidence of the citation of specific English treatises and reported cases at the Assizes is infrequent. On occasion there was a vague general reference to a practice that was against the common law. A reason of appeal from a fornication prosecution in Hampshire County is unusual in that it stated the law of England concerning legitimate births and referred the court to Sir Edward Coke's *First Institutes* (London, 1628) for substantiation.[9] Robert Auchmuty cited specific English cases on behalf of several defendants in the 1720's. In July 1723 at an appeal at Cambridge by Robert Sturgeon, a gentleman from Watertown, of a conviction for continuing to preach although forbidden to do so by the authorities, Auchmuty argued in one of his reasons of appeal that "the verdict is uncertain and ambiguous and by many Cases in the Law no Judgment can be made thereupon." Another lawyer might simply have made this

---

[6] "Sewall Letterbook," I, 423–424.

[7] Ibid., II, 14.

[8] Superior Court Records, 1700–1714, 282.

[9] Case of Ebenezer and Sarah Dickenson, Suffolk Court Files: 15419: 1.

assertion, but Auchmuty added specific page references to law reports and treatises.[1]

One of the most outstanding recorded displays of legal argumentation in the provincial period occurred at the Suffolk Assizes in the fall of 1724, when Attorney General John Read relinquished his prosecutor's role and defended John Checkley on a charge of criminal libel, an exceptional offense with political overtones. The notes used by Read in defense of his client appear in detail in his own hand in the records of the Assizes.[2] Although full records of this sort are extremely unusual, Read's arguments demonstrate that the leading attorneys had the ability to rise to the occasion in major prosecutions. He quoted at least ten English cases in the course of presentation of arguments for reversal of his client's conviction. Most of the citations are from Salkeld's *King Bench Reports* and Shower's *Kings Bench Reports*. But Read did not simply use the cases as windowdressing. He discussed each situation and distinguished it from the case at hand. His performance demonstrates a belief that English precedents could be of value in convincing a court, even if on this occasion he lost after a special verdict by the jury, which effectively permitted the judges to decide whether or not the contents of the book published by Checkley in defense of episcopacy were libelous. This action by the jury was surprising in such a sensitive and sensational case, although it did acquit Checkley on one part of the indictment. Read had argued that the judges did not have the power to decide whether or not the book was a libel; only a jury could do this.[3] In this instance the bench found Checkley guilty of publishing and selling "a false and scandalous Libel."

Various English legal sources were evidently more readily available in Massachusetts after the middle of the eighteenth century, as the *Legal Papers of John Adams* amply demonstrate. Chief Justice Hutchinson, who was appointed in 1760, told a grand jury in 1768 that for the previous seven or eight years he had made it his "constant Practice to read every Book upon the Crown-Law I could meet

[1] Ibid.: 17428: 2, 3. Auchmuty may have been making pleas in arrest of judgment at the Assizes rather than stating reasons of appeal.

[2] Ibid.: 18112: 1.

[3] Superior Court Records, 1721–1725, 236–237; Suffolk Court Files: 18112.

with."[4] At the Suffolk Assizes in August 1763 James Otis, Jr., quoted Hawkins's *Pleas of the Crown* during his successful defense of a husbandman accused of assaulting a deputy sheriff.[5] At the same Assizes in August 1764 Benjamin Kent made a legal argument on the acceptability of a convicted woman as witness for the defense, quoting various authorities, while successfully defending a man and woman charged with theft.[6]

The first recorded special verdicts at the Assizes occurred in the early 1720's. Their use suggests that the jurors were acting on their own initiative or at the suggestion of experienced lawyers rather than simply on the instruction of the judges. Jurors probably carried over the practice from civil cases. For example, at Plymouth Superior Court on 1 May 1719, the full bench heard arguments from Auchmuty, Read, Valentine, and Robinson on a special verdict by the jury in William Thomas' case of entail. At issue was the status of Plymouth laws after Plymouth ceased to be a separate colony in 1691. The bench advised for one whole term before reaching a decision in April 1720 in favor of Thomas, with Justice Lynde alone in the minority.[7]

Special verdicts in criminal cases during the 1720's were of two kinds: those in which special verdicts identified legal problems of some moment and those in which juries appear to have abdicated decision-making powers in controversial cases. At the trial of Daniel Tuttle for counterfeiting at Boston in 1723, the special verdict revolved around the legal definition of "uttering" a bill of credit that was counterfeit. When the accused offered the bill in payment for some goods, he specifically encouraged the recipient to verify its genuineness if she so desired. When the woman found the bill to be counterfeit, the purchase fell through. The judges had to decide whether the "Producing, Offering and putting the aforesaid bill into the hands of Mrs. Ellis by the said Daniel Tuttle be Deemed an Uttering by the Law of this Province upon which he stands In-

[4] Wroth and Zobel, eds., *Legal Papers of John Adams*, passim; Quincy, *Reports*, 263. See also Herbert A. Johnson, *Imported Eighteenth-Century Law Treatises in the American Libraries, 1700–1799* (Knoxville, 1978).

[5] Quincy, *Reports*, 92; Superior Court Records, 1763–1764, 132.

[6] Quincy, *Reports*, 104–106; Superior Court Records, 1764–1765, 123–124.

[7] Sewall, "Court Journal," 10a–11a, 13b.

dicted."[8] The bench heard legal argument from both the Attorney General and counsel for the accused, who is not identified, before acquitting Tuttle. Although the judges may have been pressuring juries to return special verdicts, and thus occasionally transferring the power of conviction or acquittal into their hands, it is equally possible that lawyers for the accused were persuading juries to reach special verdicts under certain circumstances and then trying to use legal arguments to persuade the judges of the merits of their clients' cases.

If a client was acquitted, a lawyer might congratulate himself on a job well done and then set about the occasionally difficult task of attempting to collect his fees, which were fixed by law at a relatively modest amount. A statutory fee of ten or twelve shillings in a criminal case must have limited the scope of a lawyer's contributions to the defense, especially with respect to the extent of pre-trial preparation.[9] If a client was convicted, the imposition of sentence was a relatively mechanical task of the judges applying the relevant statutory provisions. Yet some lawyers entered motions in arrest of judgment and also pleas to obtain benefit of clergy for their clients.

An early case at the Plymouth Assizes in March 1712 demonstrates the role that a lawyer could play for a client at the time of sentencing, although a professional was not, in fact, involved. In a case discussed above, a jury had found Hittee, an Indian girl, guilty of burning the home of her master, Isaac Little, a Marshfield gentleman. When the court asked her what she had to say about whether or not she should be condemned to death, "Her Master pleaded, that she was under the Age of Sixteen years, and therefore not within our Act."[1] It is noteworthy that in this capital case the Indian girl did not have a trained lawyer, but was depending on her master,

---

[8] Superior Court Records, 1721–1725, 162. John Langbein informs me that there were special verdicts at the Old Bailey in cases of legal difficulty.

[9] Four enactments between 1694 and 1701 confirmed that an attorney's fee was twelve shillings at Superior Court and ten shillings in inferior courts, *Acts and Resolves*, I, 185, 287, 374, 467. An unknown attorney's fee in a defendant's bill of costs at York General Sessions in July 1725 was ten shillings, *Maine Court Records*, VI, 175. On the continuance of low fee scales, see *Legal Papers of John Adams*, I, lxix–lxx.

[1] See Sewall's account in "Sewall Letterbook," I, 423–424; *Sewall Diary*, 683–684.

whose house she had burned, to plead at least this part of her case. Her master raised a good point, since the statute against arson applied only to persons aged sixteen years and upward.[2]

Making motions in arrest of judgment, usually with the assistance of an attorney, was the one way to seize the initiative at the time of sentencing. Such motions are known to have been made in only a half dozen cases during the 1730's and 1740's indicating that this was a relatively unknown, or at least an unrecorded, procedure in previous decades. However, at the sentencing of Jeremiah Phenix for murder at the Boston Assizes in May 1717, he "Moved some Exceptions to the Indictment for Arresting of Judgment," probably with the help of a lawyer, but the court overruled the motions, presumably on substantive grounds.[3] In two other episodes, lawyers succeeded in freeing their clients after juries had found them guilty. At Bristol in September 1736 William Bollan moved in arrest of judgment against Jonathan Chapman for selling liquor without a license. The court postponed consideration of the motions because one of the judges was absent. After several continuations, the judges dismissed the conviction in September 1738 at Bollan's request.[4] At Charlestown in January 1745 the bench stayed judgments against Phineas Blood and Samuel Blood in appeals of theft convictions, after separate juries had convicted them again. In Phineas' case the court may have been exercising clemency because there were two other convictions against him at the same court, and he had been sick recently.[5] It does seem surprising for judges to be accepting motions after conviction that they had presumably rejected during pleas to the indictment. There is at least a possibility that judges were nullifying jury verdicts that they did not approve. On the other hand, such a procedure allowed a verdict on the facts.[6] If a case survived because of a jury verdict, the judges could then deliberate on a close question of law or take counsel with others.

---

[2] *Acts and Resolves*, I, 577; also see the discussion above, 231.

[3] Superior Court Records, 1715–1721, 182.

[4] Ibid., Minute Book, 31. Bollan studied law in Boston around 1720 with Auchmuty. He later became the son-in-law of William Shirley and served as the province's London agent from 1745–1762.

[5] Ibid., 1740–1745, 182–183, 186.

[6] I credit John H. Langbein for this observation.

In the 1740's the attorney of a person convicted of a capital offense normally made motions in arrest of judgment at the time of sentencing. At the sentencings of Margaret Fennison in 1743 and Edward Fitzpatrick in 1744, the judges simply overruled their motions.[7] At the 1746 trials of those involved in impressment murders in Boston, the attorney for John Fowles moved in arrest of judgment because the indictment did not specifically set forth the day of the wounding, and did not charge him with the stroke that killed the victim, nor state that he was even present at the time. These motions resulted in "a full hearing of the Council for the prisoner, and the Kings Attorney in answer thereto, on two several Days assign'd for that purpose." The judges then decided there was sufficient matter in the second part of the motion to arrest the judgment.[8] Fowles's fellow prisoner, John Warren, then successfully moved the same motions with the result that the Attorney General quashed the indictment with respect to all other persons charged therein. The judges may have found it easier to arrest these judgments because they knew by the time of decision that the pair had been convicted in one and perhaps two other capital cases.

Lawyers probably were responsible for introducing claims for benefit of clergy on behalf of those convicted of a variety of offenses at the assizes, although, as usual, concrete evidence of the role of lawyers is lacking. William Shirley arrived in Boston from the Inns of Court in 1731, and it is tempting to suggest that he was responsible for encouraging this practice. The first recorded claim during the provincial era was at the trial of William Wheeler, Jr., for murder in Boston in 1732. After the jury found him guilty of manslaughter on 18 February, Wheeler sought and received benefit of clergy.[9] On 24 February the Council sent down a bill to remove benefit of clergy, which suggests a direct response to his claim. On

[7] Superior Court Records, 1740–1742, 264; ibid., 1743–1747, 119. Such motions were also possible in England. See J. H. Baker, "Criminal Courts and Procedure at Common Law 1550–1800," in Cockburn, ed., *Crime in England 1550–1800*, 42.

[8] Superior Court Records, 1740–1745, 266. The defense lawyer is not identified. The jury trials lasted ten to eleven hours. Boston *Evening Post*, 24 March 1746; *Pennsylvania Gazette*, 3 April 1746.

[9] Superior Court Records, Minute Book 19. There were several recorded pleas for benefit of clergy in 1686 and 1687 during the Dominion of New England. See ibid., 1686–1700, I, 12, 17–20.

25 February the House gave first reading to an "Act for taking away the Benefit of Clergy from Criminals in all Cases." On 25 February there was a debate on second reading. The House read the bill for the third time on 2 March but refused to pass it for engrossment.[1] Benefit of clergy thus had been implicitly accepted in the province.

At the Assizes on Nantucket in June 1732 Simon Hue stood convicted of manslaughter for killing a fellow Indian: "Whereupon he prayed the Court, that he might have the Privilege or benefit of the Law of England that Englishmen have in the Case of Manslaughter, i.e., the Benefit of Clergy. It's therefore Considered and ordered by the Court, that the said Simon Hue be branded in the Brawn of the Thumb in his left hand with a hot Iron with the letter T and pays Costs of prosecution. . . . NB on the Sixteenth of June 1732 The said Sentence was put in Execution in open Court."[2] Hue could hardly have discovered this plea by himself. The legislature further recognized the existence of benefit of clergy by removing it in January 1736 from capital convictions for counterfeiting Massachusetts bills of credit and from a third conviction for theft.[3]

From 1733 to 1739 persons successfully pleaded their clergy on at least five more occasions. At Barnstable in April 1733 James Otis moved benefit of clergy for Jeremiah Ralph, Jr., in a manslaughter case.[4] In April 1739 at Barnstable David Stevens received his clergy for the same offense, as did Silas Holmes at Bristol in October.[5] At York in June 1736 Auchmuty became responsible for a further innovation by obtaining benefit of clergy for John MacDonald, who was convicted of counterfeiting. In this instance, however, the court sentenced him to six months in prison.[6] Although counterfeiting the bills of credit of any province was a capital offense, the 1736 enactment had removed benefit of clergy from a conviction for counterfeiting Massachusetts money. At Salem in November 1739 Joseph

[1] *Massachusetts House Journals*, x, 32–43.

[2] Superior Court Records, 1730–1733, 175.

[3] *Acts and Resolves*, II, 785, 838.

[4] Superior Court Records, Minute Book, 23, 5.

[5] Ibid., 1739–1740, 47; ibid., Minute Book 35, Bristol Assizes, October 1739.

[6] Ibid., Minute Book, 22, 56.

Parker also successfully pleaded his clergy for counterfeiting.[7]

During the 1740's convicted persons sought to plead benefit of clergy in at least seven more cases. There were two straightforward episodes following the convictions for manslaughter of Sack Cut, a black person, in 1745 and David Doughty in 1747.[8] On at least three occasions counterfeiters successfully pleaded their clergy. At Salem in November 1742 Eleazer Lyndsey had counterfeited Rhode Island bills. In a separate conviction at the same court Robert Neal, a Salem mariner, was found guilty of counterfeiting some Rhode Island bills: "He produced a pardon granted him by his Excellency the Governor [Shirley] whereby the burning in the hand was remitted him, which pardon was allowed by the Court."[9] Governor Shirley's unusual leniency seems astonishing, given the major scale of Neal's operation and the fact that the Attorney General had to enter a *nolle prosequi* on five other indictments against him for counterfeiting. In fact, another counterfeiter imitated Neal after a conviction at the February term of the Suffolk Assizes in 1746. Gideon Rice was first indicted in August 1744 and a special verdict found in August 1745. When the bench decided he was guilty in 1746, the Attorney General moved for sentence of death, but Rice pleaded his clergy. On 28 March Rice had with admirable foresight petitioned Governor Shirley for mercy and release from the punishment of burning in the hand.[1] When granted his clergy, he simply produced a "Charter of Pardon" from the governor and had only to pay costs. Once again the governor's leniency seems surprising, since there was evidence of Rice's confederacy with a group of old offenders in Essex County.[2] Perhaps Shirley felt Rice had suffered enough by being imprisoned from August 1744 till after the court upheld his conviction. Although the evidence is scanty, it is possible that attorneys helped to obtain such pardons from the governor.

[7] Ibid., Minute Book, 24, 51.

[8] Ibid., 1743–1747, 158; ibid., Minute Book, 33.

[9] Ibid., 1740–1742, 253–254.

[1] Ibid., 1740–1745, 243; Suffolk Court Files: 61167.

[2] On 15 June 1748 Governor Shirley pardoned an English mariner unable to pay his fine after a conviction for participation in impressment riots. The application to the governor was dated 8 March. See John Lax and William Pencak, "The Knowles Riot and the Crisis of the 1740's in Massachusetts," *Perspectives in American History*, X (1976), 200.

In two instances during the 1740's the justices deliberated at length before making a decision on benefit of clergy. At the Assizes at York in June 1739 a jury found George Necho, an Indian laborer from Wells, guilty of raping a three-year-old white girl. When Necho's attorney moved for benefit of clergy, the court delayed judgment until June 1740, when it heard his attorney Matthew Livermore, who argued "that the facts which the Jury have found against the said George were not felony of Death at the Common Law (with Respect to a woman Child of about three years old) but made so by an act of the Great and General Court."[3] He further argued "that by the aforesaid Act the benefit of Clergy is not taken away that in all Cases where any Crime is made felony of Death by a statute that was not felony of Death at the Common Law and benefit of Clergy is not taken away by such Statute, the benefit of clergy is pleadable and by Law ought to be allowed." Despite this persuasive argument, which was supported in English law by Blackstone's *Commentaries*, the justices followed the more established English law on rape by denying Necho his clergy and sentencing him to death.[4] In another case, a conviction against Medad, a Negro, for arson at the Springfield Assizes in September 1747, the justices deliberated for two years before deciding that Medad could have his clergy.[5] The continuation of the case from September 1748 to September 1749 suggests a divided court. Medad was also represented by counsel at his trial. Perhaps it was easier to be merciful in 1749, after the slave had spent almost three years in jail.

Conclusion

Under normal circumstances a lawyer was unable to be of much direct assistance to his client until a trial had actually begun and pleas had to be entered on an indictment. It is likely that a suspect in an original prosecution did not even engage an attorney until he appeared at a sitting of the assizes or general sessions to be tried for an alleged crime. Thus a lawyer hardly had time to prepare an

---

[3] Suffolk Court Files: 49240: 1.

[4] Superior Court Records, 1739–1740, 225; Blackstone, *Commentaries on the Laws of England*, IV, 366.

[5] Superior Court Records, Minute Books, 54, 59.

extensive defense after being retained, unless the case was on appeal. The assizes at least on occasion helped an accused to obtain a lawyer. There is some evidence that persons accused of capital offenses found themselves in the hands of court-appointed counsel when this proved necessary.[6]

Government regulation of the fees of attorneys meant that most defendants at the assizes, except for the most indigent, probably could afford to retain defense counsel. The fines imposed on convicted persons were usually much higher than the basic twelve-shilling fee of an attorney, and it was a rare defendant who was unable to pay such fines. Even in those days an indicted person faced the arcane language, procedures, rituals, and mystique of the courtroom; it was not difficult to conclude that the assistance of counsel was desirable, especially since the low rate of serious crime meant it was most unusual for any person to be prosecuted at the assizes. The decision was even easier for those with financial means, prior experience as a defendant, or prior involvement in a controversial case.

The contributions of attorneys to the defense of their clients have been illustrated in some detail in the preceding pages. Lawyers were a source of considerable assistance for those accused of serious crimes, but given the prevalence of jury trials and the presence of strong men as judges, attorneys were not in a position to make it too easy for the guilty to escape unscathed. Juries made the final decisions on innocence or guilt in most original prosecutions, acquitting an average of almost 44 percent of defendants between 1693 and 1769.[7]

Although lack of information about the involvement of attorneys in cases makes it impossible to answer many questions about their activities with precision, especially their work during trials, some evidence suggests that they could be of assistance in furnishing the accused with the best possible defense both on legal and factual grounds. Suspects were wise to depend on the practical experience and technical knowledge of a trial lawyer. At the assizes the lawyer could counterbalance the prosecutorial efforts of the Attorney General and the presence of five experienced justices on the bench. He

[6] William E. Nelson, *Americanization of the Common Law. The Impact of Legal Change on Massachusetts Society, 1760–1830* (Cambridge, Mass., 1975), 226–227.

[7] Flaherty, "Crime and Social Control," 357. The acquittal rates per decade ranged from a low of nineteen percent to a high of seventy-two percent.

could attack an insufficient indictment and move to quash the proceedings. During the presentation of evidence for the crown at trial, at least at the assizes, the average defendant was not skilled in doing verbal battle with witnesses and the Attorney General. An indicted person without a lawyer at the Assizes was hardly in a good position to conduct a high-quality defense, which helps to explain why defendants seem to have made increased use of defense counsel once a number of trained lawyers became available in Massachusetts. An attorney could attack the quality of proof offered by the crown both as to the facts and the law. An attorney also knew how to make a closing argument to the jury for his client, which was not allowed in England. A colonial lawyer could discuss both the law and the facts in his address to a jury, whereas the twentieth-century lawyer has to leave matters of law solely to the judges.[8] The closing argument of an attorney could have a powerful influence on a jury of largely inexperienced laymen.

By the middle of the eighteenth century persons in Massachusetts accused of a serious crime were in the fortunate position of having talented defense counsel available. The contrast with the plight of those tried for witchcraft in 1692 and 1693 is evident.[9] The innovation of allowing unrestricted use of defense counsel obviously reflected the prevailing conception of justice in a society in which serious crime was not a significant problem. It stands to reason that criminal lawyers promoted at least the accused's sense of obtaining justice.

Acknowledgments

John H. Langbein and John M. Beattie have helped me greatly by furnishing comparative insights into the English practice and making critical comments on my text. I also owe a special type of gratitude to my

[8] Hiller B. Zobel, *The Boston Massacre* (New York, 1970), 224–225.

[9] Edwin Powers has written that "in the witchcraft trials of 1692 none of the defendants had the benefit of a lawyer, and every accused witch who was tried was found guilty. Perhaps a competent lawyer could have attacked the jurisdiction of the special tribunal set up for the purpose of trying witches or, at the least, could have prevented the introduction of damaging 'specter evidence.'" Edwin Powers, *Crime and Punishment in Early Massachusetts 1620–1692. A Documentary History* (Boston, 1966), 438. On the other hand, leading lawyers Thomas Newton and Anthony Checkley were the successive crown prosecutors during the same trials, ibid., 477. Checkley served as the province's first Attorney General; Paul Dudley succeeded him from 1702–1718, *Sewall Diary*, 606 note.

colleagues in the United States history seminar at the University of Western Ontario. They treated me in our accustomed manner and encouraged me to try to do a number of things I would have liked to have avoided. Special thanks to Jack S. Blocker, Jr., George N. Emery, Robert A. Hohner, Fred H. and Jean V. Matthews, Peter E. Russell, Craig M. Simpson, and Carl E. Swanson. Mention of any of these names is not intended to make them in any way responsible for the final product.

A Note on Sources

My research has included reading and codifying the formal court record of every criminal case tried at the assizes between 1693 and the end of 1769. In the essay I have emphasized the pre-1750 material because of its novelty and because of the fact that more is known about the work of lawyers during the years immediately preceding the Revolution. The formal records of criminal cases are interspersed in bound volumes among the civil cases tried at the Superior Court of Judicature. In some instances criminal cases can be found only in the eighteen volumes of rough Minute Books. The surviving file papers associated with a prosecution are mounted and indexed in 1,289 volumes at the Suffolk County Court House in Boston. Each piece of paper is numbered, but the indexing system is somewhat mysterious and chaotic. I have tried to examine the file papers for cases during three complete decades: 1700–1709, 1720–1729, and 1740–1749. Since file papers alone reveal the presence of lawyers, the evidence presented in this essay is inevitably sparse on the overall role of defense lawyers, especially for other years during the provincial era. Moreover, there are more surviving file papers for the 1720's than for the other two decades. Finally, there are no file papers for a significant number of cases during the decades studied. The ravages of time, plus a suspicion of the destruction of some sexually-explicit material by the late nineteenth-century compilers of these records, probably explains this situation. I have presented the work of the assizes in tabular form in David H. Flaherty, "Crime and Social Control in Provincial Massachusetts," *The Historical Journal*, XXIV (1981), 357–360, and described the court records in Flaherty, "A Select Guide to the Manuscript Court Records of Colonial New England," *American Journal of Legal History*, XI (1967), 108–110.

MORRIS L. COHEN

Legal Literature in Colonial Massachusetts

A LMOST every substantial discussion of law or lawyers in colonial America includes some reference, at least in passing, to the paucity of lawbooks throughout the colonies and the lack of any significant local law publishing. No American court reports were published until 1789; no major treatises from any source were issued here until the publication of Blackstone's *Commentaries* in Philadelphia in 1771–1772; and there was virtually no writing on technical legal doctrine until the controversies over the adoption of the federal constitution.

Lawrence Friedman's conclusions in *A History of American Law* are typical:

In one sense, colonial legal literature is quickly disposed of: there was no such thing worthy of the name before 1776. Law libraries were scarce, small, and scattered. What they contained was English law, with perhaps a collection of local statutes. Native law books were few and utterly insignificant. No substantial body of case law was in print until after the Revolution.[1]

Charles Warren in *A History of the American Bar*,[2] Anton-Hermann Chroust in *The Rise of the Legal Profession in America*,[3] and Paul Hamlin in *Legal Education in Colonial New York*[4] all comment on that lack of legal writing and publishing and on the general scarcity of lawbooks in the colonies.

Considerably more information has now been provided by Herbert Johnson's careful analysis of the library inventories and catalogs of some twenty-two colonial lawyers and judges in his study, *Imported Eighteenth Century Law Treatises in American Libraries*

[1] New York, 1973, 88.
[2] Cambridge, Mass., 1911, 157–161.
[3] Two vols., Norman, Okla., 1965, I, 18–19.
[4] New York, 1939, 66, 73.

1700–1799.[5] From his listings of these relatively extensive collections, we get a much fuller view of what *English* lawbooks were held here. The earlier publication of law library lists by Edwin Wolf, II,[6] and Paul Hamlin[7] had indicated that the distinguished collections of John Adams, William Byrd, II, and Thomas Jefferson were not as exceptional as had been assumed. Johnson has shown us the breadth, depth, and sophistication of these early law libraries. But the inventories on which his work is based tend to confirm the absence of a domestic legal literature of traditional texts.

In 1934 Eldon R. James, then Librarian at the Harvard Law School, compiled the first substantial list of "legal treatises printed in the British Colonies and American States before 1801."[8] That list, largely drawn from Charles Evans' *American Bibliography*,[9] records only two treatises published here in the seventeenth century and a total of only fifty treatises through the year 1776. James prefaces his bibliography with the following comment: "In the hundred years between the publication in 1687 of William Penn's gleanings from Lord Coke and the issuance of the American editions of Buller's Nisi Prius and Gilbert's Evidence in 1788, not a single book that could be called a treatise intended for the use of professional lawyers was published in the British Colonies and the American States."[1] That conclusion rests, of course, on James' restricted concern with *treatises* and on his limiting qualification "for the use of professional lawyers." Professional lawyers, it should be recalled,

[5] Knoxville, Tenn., 1978.

[6] "The Library of Ralph Assheton: The Book Background of a Colonial Philadelphia Lawyer," *Papers of the Bibliographical Society of America*, LVIII (1964), 345–379; and "The Library of a Philadelphia Judge, 1708," *Pennsylvania Magazine of History and Biography*, LXXXIII (1959), 180–191.

[7] See Appendix VII, Hamlin, *Legal Education*, 171–196. See also, as to the apparently extensive libraries of John Valentine and John Read, D. Flaherty, "Criminal Practice in Provincial Massachusetts," above, 195, 204.

[8] "A List of Treatises Printed in the British Colonies and the American States before 1801," in *Harvard Legal Essays Written in Honor of and Presented to Joseph Henry Beale and Samuel Williston* . . . (Cambridge, 1934).

[9] *American Bibliography; A Chronological Dictionary of All Books, Pamphlets and Periodical Publications Printed in the United States of America from the Genesis of Printing in 1639 down to and including the year 1800; with Bibliographical and Biographical Notes* (Chicago, 1903–1959), 14 vols. (reprinted New York, 1941–1967).

[1] James, "A List of Treatises," 159.

were a very small group in Massachusetts in the seventeenth and well into the eighteenth centuries.[2]

If, however, we define legal literature more broadly as including any publication which reflected and influenced the law and the legal system operating in the colonies, we can identify a larger body of material. This literature would include publications of the founding charters; the early seventeenth-century legal codes; the statutes enacted by colonial legislatures and the proceedings of such bodies; formbooks and practical guides designed to assist the lay judiciary and the public in the conduct of their legal business; religious works, sermons, and tracts on legal issues; reports of important trials and legal proceedings; treaties and reports of treaty conferences between the colonists and local tribes of native Americans; and colonial reprints of English legal texts and accounts of legal developments in the colonies found in political pamphlets, personal memoirs, and histories published here and in England.

Zechariah Chafee, Jr., in his 1969 analysis of three theories of American colonial law, published in "Colonial Courts and the Common Law,"[3] called for a fuller study of colonial lawbooks:

> Since law is a function of lawbooks . . . scholars need more information about books on English law which were owned in the Colonies. Carlyle defined a university as a great collection of books, and the same may be said of a system of case-law and detailed doctrines. Until very many books were available to colonial courts and lawyers, the common law must have mainly stayed a body of general principles. The law grew as law libraries grew.

Thanks to Professor Johnson, we now have a comprehensive study of imported English legal treatises in the major colonial libraries owned by lawyers and judges. We still need, however, an integrated survey of the total literature of and on the law which was published in the colonies. Eldon James' list is a beginning, but too limited in

---

[2] Estimates of the actual number of lawyers vary widely, but are usually less than twenty. Gerard W. Gawalt, *The Promise of Power, the Legal Profession in Massachusetts 1760–1840* (Westport, Conn., 1979), 13–14, indicates that as late as 1740 there were only fifteen "trained" lawyers in Massachusetts.

[3] In *Proceedings of the Massachusetts Historical Society*, LXVIII (1952), 132–159; reprinted in David H. Flaherty, *Essays in the History of Early American Law* (Chapel Hill, 1969), 53–82.

scope. The statutory material has been well listed,[4] but in isolation from other legal publications. Although the traditional wisdom of a meager legal output may not be seriously refuted by a broader view of domestic literature, such a view is long overdue and may suggest new insights into colonial legal history. For this conference on law in colonial Massachusetts, I will offer a brief survey of the legal literature produced in Massachusetts before Independence. The publications referred to in each category are not meant to constitute an exhaustive listing, but are, rather, merely illustrative of the various types of law-related material which were published here. The bibliography of American law up to 1860 which Balfour Halevy and I have been preparing will, in the near future, we hope, offer a much fuller picture.[5] Since the focus of this paper is on works printed in Massachusetts, it should be noted that some of the Massachusetts authors were published in the other American colonies or in London and that many of the lawbooks printed in the other colonies were widely circulated in Massachusetts. This, therefore, is not intended to provide a comprehensive survey of the legal literature produced by, or used in, the Bay Colony.

The Beginnings

The first printing in the American colonies was from the press established at Cambridge, Massachusetts, in 1639. Presses were then set up in Boston in 1675; in Jamestown, Virginia, in 1682; in Maryland in 1685; in Philadelphia in 1685; and in New York in 1693.[6] It has been estimated, however, that by 1755 there were only twenty-four presses operating in fifteen towns of ten of the American colonies.[7] Specialized law publishing did not develop in America until Stephen Gould, who had started a printing business and bookshop in

[4] See, for example, State Library of Massachusetts, *Hand-List of Legislative Sessions and Session Laws, Statutory Revisions, Compilations, Codes, etc.* ... (Boston, 1912); Lawrence Keitt, *An Annotated Bibliography of Bibliographies of Statutory Materials of the United States* (Cambridge, 1934); Meira G. Pimsleur, *Checklists of Basic American Legal Publications*, 2 vols. (South Hackensack, N.J., 1962, loose-leaf).

[5] *Bibliography of Early American Law*, projected for publication in 1985 by Kraus-Thomson, N.Y.

[6] Lawrence C. Wroth, *The Colonial Printer* (New York, 1931), 15.

[7] Lawrence C. Wroth, *An American Bookshelf 1755* (Philadelphia, 1934), 3.

New York City in 1790,[8] began in 1803 to concentrate on legal publications.

Virtually every significant colonial printer, beginning with the first press in the colonies—that of Steven Day in Cambridge—published lawbooks or books related to law. The presses of Massachusetts were, into the early eighteenth century, the most active legal printers in the colonies. Of the seven volumes listed by Charles Warren as the first seven lawbooks printed in the American colonies,[9] six were published in Boston. Although both Philadelphia and New York overtook Boston by the middle of the eighteenth century as the leading centers of law printing, an examination of the production of the Massachusetts presses reveals the wide range of law-related publishing before Independence. Considering the size of the population in colonial Massachusetts and the difficulties of establishing a life here, the volume of domestic printing, and of legal publication in particular, seems appropriate to local needs. It has been said "that, throughout the seventeenth century at least, printing and bookmaking in the American colonies were of much the same character as in the English 'provinces' at home."[1]

The extent of printing in the colonies before Independence can be measured most easily by the entries in Charles Evans' *American Bibliography*, although the actual volume of printing is now considered to be much larger than that recorded by Evans.[2] When the first volumes of the *American Bibliography* were published in 1903, they included a total of 14,638 titles for the period up to 1776. Of that number 967 were issued through 1700. In 1903, Evans predicted, in the preface to his first volume, that, even with later discoveries, the number of imprints through 1700 was unlikely to exceed one thousand. Nevertheless, Roger Bristol's supplement to Evans,[3] published in 1970, added 4,175 titles to Evans for the period

---

[8] John Tebbel, *A History of Book Publishing in the United States* (New York, 1972), I, 163, 457.

[9] *A History of the American Bar*, 158–159.

[1] Henry W. Boynton, *Annals of American Bookselling 1638–1850* (New York, 1932), 4.

[2] Wroth, *The Colonial Printer*, 184–186.

[3] *Supplement to Charles Evans' American Bibliography* (Charlottesville, 1970).

up to 1776, of which two hundred and fifteen were issued before 1701.

Thus, from 1639 to 1776, using Evans *and* Bristol, we find a total of 18,813 imprints from the presses in the British colonies which are now part of the United States. Of that number 1,182 were published before 1701. Reviewing those 1,182 imprints from their bibliographic entries, I find approximately four hundred, or over one-third, are of legal import or significance.[4] That count *includes* government proclamations, single acts and orders of general application, and law-related sermons, but it *excludes* advertisements, single legal forms, and commissions or instruments of limited application. Of these four hundred printings prior to 1701, two hundred and eighty-five, or about 70%, were issued in Massachusetts. With the spread of printing throughout the colonies after 1700, we can assume that the proportion of Massachusetts publishing to the total in America before Independence was much lower. Still, these figures indicate the importance of the Massachusetts presses in what can be considered the period of American incunabula, particularly with regard to *legal* printing.

The story of the first press in America has been told often, but remains a curiosity of American printing history.[5] The Reverend Josse Glover, bringing the press to Massachusetts on the good ship *John* in 1638, died during the voyage. He had been accompanied by Mrs. Glover, their five children, and a locksmith named Steven Day, who was to operate the press. The press was set up in Cambridge by the widow and printing began. Two years later Mrs. Glover married Henry Dunster, president of Harvard College, thereby giving him an important role in the control of the press.

The first publication of the Glover-Day press was a broadside containing a civic oath, which has come to be called *The Oath of a Free-*

----

[4] For the period from 1639 to 1763 another researcher has calculated that law represented 19.5 percent of the press output in all of the American colonies and political science represented 6.5 percent. See Hellmut Lehmann-Haupt, *The Book in America* (New York, 1939), 31. A more recent analysis, using Evans' indexes, shows lower estimates for law in the period from 1764 to 1783. See G. T. Tanselle, "Some Statistics on American Printing, 1764–1783," in B. Bailyn and J. Hench, *The Press and the American Revolution* (Worcester, 1980).

[5] See for example, George P. Winship, *The Cambridge Press 1638–1692* (Philadelphia, 1945).

Man.[6] The oath was required for citizenship in the colony from every resident over twenty years of age who had been a householder for at least six months. A typical formulary of the time, it was based on a 1634 text adopted by the General Court and contained some variations from the contemporary English versions which shed light on political attitudes in the Massachusetts Bay colony. No copy of the

---

THE OATH OF A FREE-MAN.

I *(A.B.)* being by Gods providence, an Inhabitant, and Freeman, within the Jurifdiction of this Commonwealth; do freely acknowledge my felf to be fubject to the Government thereof: And therefore do here fwear by the great and dreadful Name of the Ever-living God, that *I* will be true and faithfull to the fame, and will accordingly yield affiftance & fupport thereunto, with my perfon and eftate, as in equity *I* am bound; and will alfo truly endeavour to maintain and preferve all the liberties and priviledges thereof, fubmitting my felf to the wholefome Lawes & Orders made and eftablifhed by the fame. And further, that *I* will not plot or practice any evill againft it, or confent to any that fhall fo do; but will timely difcover and reveal the fame to lawfull Authority now here eftablifhed, for the fpeedy preventing thereof.

Moreover, *I* doe folemnly bind my felf in the fight of God, that when *I* fhal be called to give my voyce touching any fuch matter of this State, in which Freemen are to deal, *I* will give my vote and fuffrage as *I* fhall judge in mine own confcience may beft conduce and tend to the publike weal of the body, without refpect of perfons, or favour of any man. So help me God in the Lord Jefus Chrift.

---

18. Reconstruction of the content and typography of the first printing (1639) of the Glover-Day Press in Cambridge, Massachusetts, *The Oath of a Free-Man*. Courtesy of The Press of the Woolly Whale Collection, Beinecke Rare Book and Manuscript Library, Yale University.

broadside is known to survive, but John Winthrop's earlier manuscript draft, possibly dating from 1631, is at the Boston Public Library. The text was reprinted in London in 1647 in John Child's controversial pamphlet, *New-Englands Jonas East up at London.*

Charles Evans has traced the history of the text and reconstructed

---

[6] Lawrence C. Wroth, *The Oath of a Free-Man* (New York, 1939).

the probable 1639 version, which included a rather nice closing addition to the usual form of such oaths:

... when I shall be called to give my voice touching any such matter of this State, in which Freemen are to deal, I will give my vote and suffrage as I shall judge in mine own conscience may best conduce and tend to the public weal of the body, without respect of persons, or favor of any man.[7]

John Winthrop recorded the first printing of the Day press in his Journal in March 1639 as follows:

A printing house was begun at Cambridge by one Daye, at the charge of Mr. Glover, who died on seas hitherward. The first thing which was printed was the freeman's oath; ...[8]

It is significant that printing began in Massachusetts with a document of legal interest — not a lawbook certainly, but a dramatic prologue for what follows.

Codes and Statutes

Clearly, the most numerous legal publications of the colony were statutory in nature, beginning with the early codes, printed in London and Massachusetts. William Whitmore's *Bibliographical Sketch of the Laws of the Massachusetts Colony from 1630 to 1686*[9] provides useful detail on the texts, but the early printing history of the codes is still unsettled.

The first effort at printing codes was made by John Cotton for the General Court in 1636 and called *Moses His Judicials* because of its biblical basis.[1] That text, however, was not enacted and in 1639 Nathaniel Ward prepared another draft, "The Body of Liberties." Both the Cotton and Ward statements were strongly biblical in derivation, but Ward — with his legal training and experience in England — produced a more acceptable draft, which was adopted by the General Court in 1641. Nevertheless, it was apparently not then printed. A passage in the preface to John Child's *New-Englands*

---

[7] Charles Evans, "Oaths of Allegiance in Colonial New England," *Proceedings of the American Antiquarian Society*, New Series, XXXI, 395. See ibid., 377–438.

[8] Winship, *Cambridge Press*, 1.

[9] Boston, 1890.

[1] Samuel E. Morison, *Builders of the Bay Colony* (Boston, 1930), 227–230.

Jonas . . . suggests the existence of a Cambridge printing of Ward's code, but references in the records of the General Court to the preparation and distribution of manuscript copies seem to belie such a printing.[2] John Cotton's draft, on the other hand, *was* published in London in 1641, probably on the mistaken assumption there that it *had* been adopted in the colony.[3] Although rejected in Massachusetts Bay, Cotton's text was taken to Connecticut, where it served as the basis of the fundamental law and frame of government for the New Haven colony.

The first statutory compilation printed in the colony, *The Book Of The General Lawes And Libertyes,* included eighty-six out of the one hundred clauses of Ward's "Body of Liberties." The Ward material constituted less than a fifth of the whole work. The compilation was published in 1648 by Matthew Day, Steven's son and successor, and carried the following title:

The Book Of The General Lawes And Libertyes Concerning The Inhabitants Of The Massachusets Collected Out Of The Records Of The General Court For The Several Years Wherein They Were Made And Established, And now revised by the same Court and disposed into an Alphabetical order and published by the same Authoritie in the General Court held at Boston the fourteenth of the first month Anno 1647....[4]

The only copy known to have survived was found in Rye, England, in 1906. It is now at the Huntington Library and has been reprinted in several facsimile editions.[5] The records of the General Court indicate that each copy of the original printing took seventeen sheets;

[2] Whitmore, *Bibliographical Sketch,* 9.

[3] *An Abstract or the Lawes of New England, As they are now established* (London: Printed for F. Coules, and W. Ley, 1641).

[4] For discussion of its origin, contents, and significance, see Thorp L. Wolford, "The Laws and Liberties of 1648," *Boston University Law Review,* XXVIII (1948), 426–463, reprinted in D. H. Flaherty, ed., *Essays in the History of Early American Law* (Chapel Hill, 1969). See also George L. Haskins, "Codification of the Law in Colonial Massachusetts . . . ," *Indiana Law Journal,* XXX (1954), 1–17.

[5] *The Laws and Liberties of Massachusetts,* with an Introduction by Max Farrand (Cambridge, Mass., 1929); *The Book of the General Lawes and Liberties concerning the Inhabitants of the Massachusetts,* edited with an introduction by Thomas G. Barnes (San Marino, Calif., 1975). Barnes' introduction describes the relationship between Ward's "Body of Liberties" and *The Book of the General Lawes and Liberties* and argues persuasively against the designation "code" for these early statutory compilations.

THE
BOOK OF THE GENERAL

LAUUES AND LIBERTYES

CONCERNING THE INHABITANTS OF THE MASSACHUSETS
COLLECTED OUT OF THE RECORDS OF THE GENERAL COURT
FOR THE SEVERAL YEARS WHERIN THEY WERE MADE
AND ESTABLISHED,

And now revised by the same Court and disposed into an Alphabetical order
and published by the same Authorit.e in the General Court
held at *Boston* the fourteenth of the
first month *Anno*
1647.

―――――――――――

VVhosoever therefore resisteth the power, resisteth the ordinance of God,
and they that resist receive to themselves damnation. *Romanes* 13. 2.

―――――――――――

❊❊❊❊❊
❊   ❊
❊   ❊
❊❊❊❊❊

―――――――――――

CAMBRIDGE.
Printed according to order of the *GENERAL COURT.*
1648.

―――――――――――

And are to be solde at the shop of *Hezekiah Usher*
in *Boston.*

19. Title Page of Matthew Day's printing of *The Book of the General Lawes and Libertyes* (Cambridge, 1648), now at the Huntington Library, San Marino, California. Courtesy, Huntington Library.

that six hundred copies were made, using twenty-one reams of paper; and that each copy sold for seventeen pence. The printing cost £15 16s 3d and the paper £5 5s.[6]

The Days were succeeded as Dunster's printer by Samuel Green in 1649. The press passed to Harvard College some time before 1658, and a second press was set up in Cambridge in 1659. Bartholomew Green, Samuel's son, opened another press in Boston in 1690. He soon became the dominant printer in the area. Statutory publications by these presses were numerous and included three supplements to the *General Lawes And Libertyes* (Cambridge, 1650, 1654, and 1657), *The Book Of The General Lawes* (Cambridge, Samuel Green, 1660), and *The General Laws And Liberties ... Revised & Reprinted* by Edward Rawson (Cambridge, Samuel Green for John Usher, 1672).

The Cambridge and Boston presses also printed legal materials for other colonies. Compilations for the Plymouth Colony were issued in 1672 (*Book of the General Laws of ... New-Plymouth ...*, Cambridge, Samuel Green) and in 1685 (*Book of the General Laws ...*, Boston, Samuel Green); for the Connecticut Colony in 1673 (*Book of the General Laws For the People within the Jurisdiction of Connecticut ...*, Cambridge, Samuel Green); and for the New Hampshire Province in 1699 (*Acts and Laws, Passed by the General Court or Assembly of ... New-Hampshire ...*, Boston, Bartholomew Green, and John Allen).

Laws And Orders of the General Court for the Massachusetts Bay Colony were issued regularly beginning in 1661, with fifty-five separate issues for the years 1661 to 1691; one hundred and forty-six separate issues for the period of the Province from 1692 to 1742; and two hundred and eight issues of *Acts and Laws* from November 1742 to 1775. Most of these were publications of only a few sheets, but they indicate a regular pattern of the printing of laws shortly after enactment. Government printing was an established practice in the colony. Virtually all of it was legal in nature.[7]

The Charters of Massachusetts were printed in Boston in 1689,

[6] Winship, *Cambridge Press*, 108.

[7] Rollo G. Silver, *Government Printing in Massachusetts-Bay, 1700–1750* (Worcester, 1958, reprinted from the *Proceedings of the American Antiquarian Society* for April 1958).

1692, 1699, 1725, 1742, 1759, and 1775; compilations of the *Charter, Acts and Laws* ... in 1699, 1714, 1726, 1742, and 1759; and collections of *Temporary Acts and Laws* ... in 1742, 1755, and 1763. Proclamations, resolutions, and orders of the Council, Governor, Lieutenant Governor, and the General Court were regularly printed, usually as single sheets. Such broadsides were the usual form of publicizing governmental actions and announcements. The Journal of the House of Representatives was regularly published from 1715 to 1774 and totalled over one hundred and fifty separate issues during that period.

Legal Manuals

Lay judges, peace officers, and other local officials, as well as the educated public, needed instruction in the proper use of legal procedures and the standard forms required by such procedures. That need led to the publication of numerous manuals and formbooks in England prior to the settlement of America. It was to be expected that similar guides would be needed in the colonies, where access to professional assistance was more difficult and opposition to the legal profession so strong. Probably the most popular of the American manuals was *Conductor Generalis* ..., first published in New York by William and Andrew Bradford in 1711[8] and reissued in at least seven editions before Independence—all outside of Massachusetts. Although *Conductor Generalis* ... was never printed in Massachusetts, another comparable guide *was* published here: *An Abridgment of Burn's Justice of the Peace and Parish Officer* (Boston, Joseph Greenleaf, 1773). Similar works were also published in Virginia (*The Office and Authority of a Justice of Peace,* Williamsburg, William Parks, 1736); South Carolina (*The Practical Justice of the Peace and Parish-Officer* ..., Charlestown, Robert Wells, 1761); New York (*Every Man His Own Lawyer* ..., New York, Hugh Gaine, 1768); and North Carolina (*The Office and Authority of a Justice of Peace,* Newbern, James Davis, 1774).

It seems surprising that no substantial legal manuals were pub-

[8] *Conductor Generalis; or a Guide for Justices of the Peace, And Coroners, Constables, Jury-Men, Over-seers of the Poor, Surveyors of High-ways, Governors of Fairs, Gaolers, etc. A Treatise Briefly showing the Extent and Latitude of the several Officers Therein. To which is Added Copies of Warrant, Mittimusses, Recognizances, and other Necessary Instruments.*

lished in Massachusetts until the appearance of Joseph Greenleaf's *Abridgment of Burn's Justice of the Peace* in 1773. This may have been due to the availability of English editions of Burn's popular but massive work[9] and the wide distribution of *Conductor Generalis* throughout the colonies. Two earlier manuals—more modest in coverage than Greenleaf's abridgment—were also published in Massachusetts, both of which seem to have been prepared from local sources with little direct inclusion of English material. These were Nicholas Boone's *The Constables Pocket-Book* ... (1710),[1] and *The County and Town Officer* ... (1768).[2] Unlike *Conductor Generalis* and the *Abridgment of Burn's Justice of the Peace,* these guides, with their heavy Massachusetts emphasis, were not widely distributed in the other colonies. Boone was a Boston bookseller who had also served as a constable here. The author of *The County and Town Officer* is not known.

Joseph Greenleaf, who abridged and adapted *Burn's Justice,* was a Boston printer and a writer for the colonial cause. He had been a justice of the peace for Plymouth county, until he was dismissed by the Council in 1771 for his involvement with Isaiah Thomas in publishing the seditious *Massachusetts Spy* and for his failure to appear before the Council when summoned in that regard.[3] The growing movement for independence from England and its effect on local law may be inferred from the following statement in Greenleaf's preface to his *Abridgment of Burn's Justice of the Peace:*

... The circle of a justices business in those places [England and Scot-

[9] *Justice of the Peace, and Parish Officer.* 1st edition, London, 1755; 2d edition, London, 1756; 3rd edition, London, 1756; 4th edition, London, 1757, 3 vols. Greenleaf's *Abridgment* was based on the 4th edition.

[1] *The Constables Pocket-Book; or, A Dialogue Between an Old Constable & a New. Being a Guide, In their Keeping the Peace, &c, In Serving all Warrants. Observing Orders of Courts. Summoning Town-Officers and Town-Meetings. Collecting Rates and Assessments. Serving Writs, Summons, Executions. How to make Returns of all Writs and Warrants. Forms of Bail Bonds, &c. An Account of all Lawful Fees.* By N.B. a late Constable in the Town of Boston, N.E. (Boston: Printed for Eleazer Phillips, 1710).

[2] *The County and Town Officer: or, An Abridgment of the Laws of the Province of the Massachusetts-Bay, Relative to County and Town Officers. By a Gentleman* ... (Boston: Printed by T. and J. Fleet, 1768).

[3] Isaiah Thomas, *The History of Printing in America, with a Biography of Printers* ... 2d edition (Albany, 1874), II, 255–256.

land] is vastly extensive, and is founded chiefly on acts of the British parliament, which can never have any relation to this colony, such parts therefore are not taken into this abridgment. What we have rejected relates to acts made for the regulating their woolen manufactory, witchcraft, weights and measures, vagrants, treasure, transportation, torn, tobacco, tiles, titles, thames, stock in company, stamps, soldiers, shoemakers, servants, seamen, public worship, prophecies, players, plague, physicians, pewter and other mettles, peer, northern borders, old and new militia, linen cloth, leather, land tax, custos rotulorum, cottage, cole and cole pits, clergy, churchwardens, church and yard, black act, billets, and a number of articles, under other heads of no possible use or importance to use in America.

Reprints of English Texts

Despite the legal, political, and cultural ties between England and her American colonies, we find remarkably few English lawbooks reprinted here. The importation of English lawbooks and their wide dissemination throughout the colonies, particularly toward the middle of the eighteenth century, may partially explain the lack of local reprints. The small number of professional lawyers was undoubtedly another factor of significance, indicating a limited market. There was certainly very little reprinting of English books *in general* in seventeenth-century Massachusetts, and the number of lawbooks remained low until the 1770's. Robert Bell's Philadelphia edition of Blackstone's *Commentaries* in 1771–1772 was the first major undertaking of this type in the whole of colonial America.

Although the publication of technical and doctrinal legal treatises was substantial in England in this period, none was reissued in Massachusetts. In the early period of the Massachusetts Bay Colony this may have been in part a function of the Puritan cast of that legal system, its relatively simple economic base, and its borrowing from English local government law.[4] By the middle of the eighteenth century growing political contention with Britain and increased importation of English treatises by professional lawyers were also factors that may have discouraged reprints. A comparative study of the cost of imported books — data is easily available in Herbert Johnson's

---

[4] Julius Goebel, Jr., "King's Law and Local Custom in Seventeenth Century New England," *Columbia Law Review*, XXXI (1931), 416–448, reprinted in David H. Flaherty, *Essays in the History of Early American Law*.

study of such imports—and local printing costs here—available from a few surviving printer's records—might shed further light on this factor.

When reviewing those English works which were reprinted in Massachusetts, it is noteworthy that, except for Joseph Greenleaf's *Abridgment of Burn's Justice of the Peace*, they were virtually all books dealing with the rights and liberties of Englishmen and were originally issued in London during the political controversies of 1680–1682, following the "Popish Plot." Their later publication here was probably based more on their local political significance than on any great legal value. Bernard Bailyn has recognized the influence of the earlier English conflict on pre-revolutionary American political writing.[5] He does not, however, focus on the several reprints of English radical pamphlets discussed below.

The first American reprint of an English lawbook may have been that of Sir John Hawles' *The Englishman's Right: a dialogue between a barrister at law, and a jury-man. Plainly setting forth I. The antiquity II. The excellent designed use III. The office & just privileges of juries. By The laws of England* (Boston, Benjamin Harris, 1693). Although doubt has been raised about the existence of this 1693 edition,[6] an apparently unique copy at Yale's Beinecke Library now confirms its publication in Boston. Hawles was a Whig member of Parliament and served as Solicitor General from 1695 to 1702. Holdsworth has described this and another work on juries by Hawles as follows: "Though weak in their history, they give a clear description of the jury's rights and duties, and good advice as to the conduct of jurymen."[7] The local relevance of this text seems clear, and it was reprinted in Boston in 1772 and in Philadelphia in 1798 and in 1806.

Henry Care's *English Liberties, or the Free-Born Subject's Inheritance*, was first printed in London by George Larkin, for Ben-

[5] See Bernard Bailyn, *The Ideological Origins of the American Revolution* (Cambridge, 1967); and his *Pamphlets of the American Revolution* ... (Cambridge, 1965).

[6] C. K. Shipton and J. E. Mooney, *National Index of American Imprints through 1800, the Short-Title Evans* (Worcester, 1969). The authors state that that edition was "probably a ghost of a London edition arising from a book-seller's adv." (I, 348).

[7] William Holdsworth, *A History of English Law* (London, 1938), XII, 459.

jamin Harris, without an imprint date. Wing[8] suggests 1680 as the probable year of publication. Care was a political journalist and editor of the anti-Catholic paper, *Weekly Pacquet of Advice from Rome*. He was convicted of libel for attacks on the Church of England for its papist tendencies and for attacks on its members, including Chief Justice Scroggs, who presided at Care's trial.

Harris, another anti-Catholic radical, was a prominent participant in the "exposé" of the imaginary Popish Plot of 1678. He was forced to flee to America in 1686 in part for his publication of *English Liberties*, five thousand copies of which were seized by the authorities.[9] Harris made several trips back to England, but was one of the most active Boston printers and booksellers from 1687 to 1695. It is significant that he also published *The Englishman's Right* (above) and the first London edition of *The Triumphs Of Justice Over Unjust Judges* ... (below). He is perhaps best known, however, as the author and first publisher of the long-popular and frequently reprinted *New England Primer*.

English Liberties was reprinted in London in 1700, 1703, and 1719, and printed in Boston in 1721 by James Franklin and again in Providence in 1774. The appearance of imported editions in several colonial law libraries and the survival of many copies of the Boston and Providence editions confirm its considerable popularity here. As indicated by its full title,[1] *English Liberties* is a melange of historic English legal documents, a text on rights and liberties, and a manual

[8] Donald Wing, *Short-Title Catalog of Books Printed in England ... 1641–1700.* Second edition, revised and enlarged (New York, 1972), I, entry #C515.

[9] *Dictionary of American Biography* (New York, 1932), viii, 304.

[1] *English Liberties, or the Free-Born Subject's Inheritance; containing Magna Charta, Charta de Foresta, The Statute De Tallagio non concedendo, the Habeas Corpus Act, and several other Statutes; with Comments on each of them. Likewise the Proceedings in Appeals of Murder: Of Ship-Money; Of Tonnage and Poundage. Of Parliaments, and the Qualification and Choice of Members: Of the Three Estates, and Of the Settlement of the Crown by Parliament. Together with A short History of the Succession, not by any Hereditary Right: Also a Declaration of the Liberties of the Subject: And of the Oath of Allegiance and Supremacy. The Petition of Right; with a short but impartial relation of the Difference between K. Charles I. and the Long Parliament, concerning the Prerogative of the King, the Liberties of the Subject, and the Rise of the Civil Wars. Of Trials by Juries, and of the Qualifications of Jurors; their Punishment for Misbehavior, and of Challenges to them. Lastly, of Justices of the Peace, Coroners, Constables, Churchwardens, Overseers of the Poor, Surveyors of the Highways, etc. With many Law-Cases throughout the Whole.*

English Liberties,

OR THE
Free-born Subject's Inheritance;

CONTAINING

Magna Charta, Charta de Foresta, The Statute *De Tallagio non concedendo,* The *Habeas Corpus* Act, and several other Statutes; with Comments on each of them.

LIKEWISE

The Proceedings in Appeals of Murder: Of Ship-Money; Of Tonnage and Poundage. Of Parliaments, and the Qualification and Choice of Members: Of the Three Estates, and of the Settlement of the Crown by Parliament.

Together with

A short History of the Succession, not by any Hereditary Right: Also a Declaration of the Liberties of the Subject: And of the Oath of Allegiance and Supremacy. The Petition of Right; with a short but impartial Relation of the Difference between K. *Charles* I. and the Long Parliament, concerning the Prerogative of the King, the Liberties of the Subject, and the Rise of the Civil Wars. Of Trials by Juries, and of the Qualifications of Jurors; their Punishment for Misbehaviour, and of Challenges to them.

LASTLY,

Of Justices of the Peace, Coroners, Constables, Churchwardens, Overseers of the Poor, Surveyors of the High-ways, &c. With many Law-Cases throughout the Whole.

Compiled first by *HENRY CARE,* and continued, with large Additions, by *W. N.* of the *Middle-Temple,* Esq;

The FIFTH EDITION.

BOSTON: Printed by *J. Franklin,* for *N. Buttolph, B. Eliot,* and *D. Henchman,* and Sold at their Shops. 1721.

20. Title Page of Henry Care, *English Liberties*, from its first American edition, printed in Boston by James Franklin, 1712. Courtesy, Yale Law School.

for justices of the peace, various local officials, and peace officers. It was a lawbook of many uses for Americans. It has been described by Bernard Bailyn as "a combination casebook in law, guide to legal procedures, and Anglophile propaganda piece...."[2]

Another radical English legal and political tract was published in London by Benjamin Harris at about the same time as *English Liberties*. It too was reprinted in Boston, probably by Samuel Kneeland and Thomas Green in 1732. Its title, from the London edition, reveals something of both its content and rationale:

> *The Triumphs Of Justice Over Unjust Judges; Exhibiting, I. The Names and Crimes of Four and Forty Judges Hand'd in one Year in England, as Murderers for their corrupt Judgments. II. The Case of the Lord Chief Justice Tresilian, Hang'd at Tyburn, and all the rest of the Judges of England (save one) banisht in K. Rich. the 2ds Time. III. The Crimes of Empson and Dudley, Executed in K. Henry the 8th's Days. IV. The Proceedings of the Ship-money-Judges in the Reign of K. Charles the First. V. Diverse other Presidents both Antient and Modern. To which is added VI. The Judges Oath, and some Observations thereupon. Humbly Dedicated to the Lord Chief Justice Scroggs* ... London, Printed for Benjamin Harris, at the Stationers Arms, 1681.

Signed only with the pseudonym, "Philo-Dicaios," this work, with its timing, style, and ironic dedication to Justice Scroggs, suggests Harris or Care as the probable author, although a definite attribution has not been made. Scroggs had presided at Care's trial, as noted above, and at one of Harris's trials as well, both shortly before this publication.

Finally, we should note an Evans entry[3] for a doubtful Boston, 1720 edition of John Somers, *The Security of Englishmen's Lives, or the Trust, Power and Duty of the Grand Juries of England* ... (London, 1681). This text was listed by Charles Warren as one of the first seven lawbooks printed in America.[4] No copy of the Boston edition has been located, and Shipton and Mooney indicate "Title from Prince," but it is not listed in the *Catalogue Of The American Portion Of The Library Of The Rev. Thomas Prince*, by William H.

---

[2] *Pamphlets of the American revolution* ..., 743, footnote 9.

[3] *American Bibliography*, entry #2178.

[4] Warren, *History of the American Bar*, 158.

Whitmore.[5] It *was* reprinted in New York in 1773, by Hodge and Shober, for Noel and Hazard (Evans 13024). Subsequent to this work, Somers became Attorney General and then Lord Chancellor, and, according to the *Dictionary of National Biography*, this tract was "a vindication of the right of the grand jury to reject the bill of indictment against Lord Shaftesbury."[6] Somers' work reflects the same political attitudes as those of the previous pamphlets, as is indicated by the declaration on its title page that it had been "Published for the prevention of popish designs against the lives of many protestant lords and commoners, who stand firm to the religion and the ancient government of England."

Religious Writing on Legal Issues

Religious concerns were the reason why many of the early settlers of Massachusetts came, and religion continued to provide a central focus of their life and literature through most of the seventeenth century. Religion shaped the law and government of the colony[7] and influenced the social and personal conduct of the colonists. In the early years of settlement, religious and civic matters were often inseparable, and the leaders of the colony frequently functioned in both spheres.

It is, therefore, not surprising that most of the writing in seventeenth-century Massachusetts was religious in nature. Religious works constituted the largest single part of the published literature. Works by Increase and Cotton Mather alone accounted for approximately six hundred separate publications in Massachusetts in the seventeenth and first half of the eighteenth centuries, exclusive of later reprints and printings outside of Massachusetts.[8] Sermons,

---

[5] Boston, 1868.

[6] *Dictionary of National Biography* (New York and Boston, 1898), LIII, 228.

[7] Although earlier views of *great* religious influence—see, for example, Paul S. Reinsch, *English Common Law in the Early American Colonies* (Madison, Wis., 1899) and Charles J. Hilkey, *Legal Development in Colonial Massachusetts 1630–1686* (New York, 1910)—have been largely superseded, the important role of religion in seventeenth-century Massachusetts law is still acknowledged, as in George L. Haskins, *Law and Authority in Early Massachusetts . . .* (New York, 1960).

[8] Thomas J. Holmes, *Cotton Mather: A Bibliography Of His Works*, 3 vols. (Cambridge, Mass., 1940), and *Increase Mather: A Bibliography Of His Works*, 2 vols. (Cleveland, 1931).

tracts, and books of religious instruction and inspiration dominated the presses of Massachusetts through the seventeenth century and continued to represent a significant portion of the printing business in the eighteenth century. One researcher has estimated the proportion of religious writing in the output of all of the American presses for the period from 1639 to 1763 at 37%.[9]

In addition to the Puritan influences on the early legal codes and on the governance of the New England colonies, many of the religious leaders spoke out and wrote on legal issues. The number and range of such writings are beyond the scope of this paper, but the following few examples from the writings of Cotton Mather are illustrative of this literature. Their respective titles give some indication of content and legal relevance, but for fuller treatment see the entries in Thomas J. Holmes' bibliography of Cotton Mather, as cited.

A Faithful Monitor. Offering, An Abstract of the Lawes in the Province of the Massachusett-Bay, New-England, Against those Disorders, the Suppression whereof is desired and pursued by them that wish well to the worthy Designs of Reformation. With some Directions and Encouragements, to dispense due Rebukes, & Censures unto all Censurable Actions . . . (Boston, Printed and sold by Timothy Green, 1704.)[1]

Lex Mercatoria. Or, The Just Rules of Commerce Declared. And Offenses against the Rules of Justice in the Dealing of men with one another, Detected. With a Testimony Publicly given against all Dishonest Gain, in the Audience of the General Assembly of the Province of Massachuset-Bay, New-England. Nov. 9. 1704. (Boston, Printed and Sold by Timothy Green, 1705.)[2]

Fair Dealing between Debtor and Creditor. A very brief Essay Upon The Caution to be used, about coming in to Debt, and getting out of it. Offered at Boston-Lecture; 5.d.XI.m. 1715/16 . . . (Boston, Printed by B. Green, for Samuel Gerrish, 1716.)[3]

Bonifacius. An Essay Upon the Good, that is to be Devised and Designed,

[9] Lehmann-Haupt, *Book in America*, 31.

[1] Holmes, *Cotton Mather*, I, No. 124, 360–363.

[2] *Ibid.*, II, No. 205, 557–559.

[3] *Ibid.*, II, No. 117, 346–347.

By Those Who Desire to Answer the Great End of Life, and to Do Good While they Live. A Book Offered, First, in General, unto all Christians, in a Personal Capacity, or in a Relative. Then more Particularly, Unto Magistrates, unto Ministers, unto Physicians, unto Lawyers.... (Boston, Printed by B. Green, for Samuel Gerrish. 1710.)[4]

Mather's *Bonifacius ...,*[5] perhaps his most often reprinted work, included a section (No. 20) dealing with lawyers. Among his admonitions to lawyers were these:

A lawyer that is a knave deserves death more than a band of robbers; for he profanes the sanctuary of the distressed, and betrayes the liberties of the people. (160)

This piety must operate very particularly, in the pleading of causes. You will abhor, Sir, to appear in a dirty cause. If you discern, that your client has an unjust cause, you will faithfully advise him of it.... (161)

You will abominate the use of all unfair arts, to confound evidences, to browbeat testimonies, to suppress what may give light in the case.... (161)

In plain English: excessive fees must be disgorged by restitution.... (163)

Wealthy people going to make their wills, often ask your advice. You may take the opportunity to advise them, unto such liberalities upon pious uses, as may greatly advance the King of God in the world.... (164)

Is there nothing to be mended in the laws? Perhaps, you may discover many things yet wanting in the law; mischiefs in the execution and application of the laws, which ought to be provided against; mischiefs annoying of mankind, against which no laws are yet provided. The reformation of the law, and more law for the reformation of the world, is what is mightily called for.... (165)

Your learning often qualifies you to write excellent things, not only in your own profession, but also on all the entertaining and edifying themes in the work. The books that have been written by learned lawyers, would for number almost equal an Alexandrian library.... Sirs, you may plead the cause of religion, and of the reformation, by your well directed pens; and you may do innumerable services.... (165–166)

[4] *Ibid.,* I, Nos. 35-A, 35-B, and 112A to 112-R, 89–95, and 324–338.
[5] See the Boston edition of 1710, 155–167.

Many of the sermons delivered in colonial Massachusetts were subsequently printed and thus reached a larger audience and had impact far beyond their original auditors. In addition to their usual didactic function in the worship service, sermons were also an important feature of various public ceremonies and events. Among the most numerous of these were election sermons, usually delivered at the opening of a legislative session,[6] and execution sermons, delivered at the execution of convicted criminals or on the following Sabbath.[7] Approximately one hundred election sermons, and almost the same number of printings of about fifty execution sermons, were made in Massachusetts before Independence. Both types of sermons frequently contained material which described aspects of the legal system or commented on current legal concerns.

An example of an election sermon is Cotton Mather's *The Serviceable Man. A Discourse Made unto the General Court Of The Massachusets Colony* ... (Boston, Samuel Green, 1690).[8] The colony had deposed the Andros government, and the provisional government under Simon Bradstreet was temporarily in office, awaiting the charter which Increase Mather and others were seeking in London. Cotton Mather, comparing the restored colonial government to that of the Jews in Jerusalem under Nehemiah after the Babylonian captivity, focuses on a variety of local troubles, including several of legal import. He refers to the burdensome cost of the war with the French and the Indians, the poor trade conditions, the foreclosure of mortgages made at 12% interest, the former oppressions of the Andros government, the dangers posed by Quaker activity, the poor pay of teachers, and the need for more schools. More broadly, he

---

[6] R. W. G. Vail, *A Check List of New England Election Sermons* (Worcester, 1936).

[7] Daniel A. Cohen, *Pillars of Salt and Monuments of Grace—the Execution Literature of Colonial New England,* graduate research paper, Brandeis University, Department of the History of American Civilization, 1982; see also, Wayne C. Winnick, "The New England Execution Sermons, 1639–1800," *Speech Monographs,* xxxv (1968), 77–89; Ronald A. Bosco, "Lectures at the Pillory: the Early American Execution Sermon," *American Quarterly,* xxx (1978), 156–176; and Lawrence W. Towner, "True Confessions and Dying Warnings in Colonial New England," in *Sibley's Heir,* Colonial Society of Massachusetts, *Publications,* LIX (Boston, 1982), 523–539.

[8] Holmes, *Cotton Mather,* III, No. 351, 969–973.

calls upon the populace and its leaders to be public spirited and to support and obey the government of the colony.

Published execution sermons could contain more than the usual exhortations to the criminal and warnings to the youth of the community and the general public. They gradually began to include material relating to the life, misdeeds, and disposition of the condemned. These included short biographical or autobiographical narratives; brief summaries of the trial proceedings; the criminal's confession; and his or her last conversations or gallows speech. The careful researcher can learn much about crime, criminals, and their adjudication from these documents. The printed version of one such sermon, Cotton Mather's *Pillars of Salt*,[9] included brief accounts of eleven other executed criminals in addition to that of the immediate subject.

Sermons and religious tracts frequently reflected religious, legal, and political controversies in colonial Massachusetts. The list is a long one. Some of these disputes will be referred to in the next section of this survey, but we can note a number of examples: the suppression of the Antinomian movement, the Quakers, the Presbyterians, and other non-Congregationalists; the trial of Samuel Gorton; the remonstrance of Robert Child; the revocation of the Charter; the rebellion against Governor Andros; the quest for restoration of the Charter; the short-lived Dominion of New England; the Salem witchcraft trials; the struggle against Governor Joseph Dudley; the "heresies" of Jonathan Mayhew; and finally the series of crises leading to the American revolution.

Each of these disputes had serious legal implications, and all of them involved religious publications in Massachusetts, and often in London as well. Jonathan Mayhew's *Discourse Concerning Unlimited Submission And Non-Resistance To The Higher Powers* ... (Boston, D. Fowle, 1750), for example, has been described by Bailyn as "the most famous sermon preached in pre-Revolutionary America — illustrat[ing] dramatically the ultimate sources of American Revolutionary thought and the distinctive emphasis imparted

---

[9] *Pillars of Salt. An History Of Some Criminals Executed in this Land; for Capital Crimes. With some of their Dying Speeches; Collected and Published, for the Warning of such as Live in Destructive Courses of Ungodliness* ... (Boston: B. Green and J. Allen, 1699). See Holmes, *Cotton Mather*, II, Nos. 284-A and 284-B, 818, 822.

to them in the process of their transmission."[1] All of these controversies and their documentation merit fuller bibliographic description, but perhaps this brief mention will suffice to justify their
future consideration as a part of the legal literature of colonial
Massachusetts.

Trials

A variety of publications containing the proceedings or extracts
from English and American trials were printed and distributed in
colonial Massachusetts. Some were criminal trials of obviously sensational interest. Others were of religious concern, and yet others
clearly of political significance. The rationale for local publication in
a few cases is uncertain, but the interest in most of them is fairly
obvious. Here again, a full bibliography is beyond the scope of this
effort, but a few illustrations may be suggestive of the genre.

Piracy trials were of considerable popularity among the Boston
printers and their readers. The ports of Massachusetts were active,
and sailors, particularly prone to the temptations of that crime, were
frequent visitors. The accounts appealed to readers seeking robust
and often bloody adventure, and the warnings to seafarers were
clear from the inevitable execution descriptions. Among these local
publications were the following:[2]

*An Account of the Behavior and last Dying Speeches Of the Six Pirates,
that were Executed on Charles River, Boston side, on Friday June 30th
1704. . . .* (Boston, Nicholas Boone, 1704.)[3]

*The Trials Of Eight Persons Indited for Piracy etc. Of whom Two
were acquitted, and the rest found Guilty. At a Justiciary Court of Admiralty Assembled and Held in Boston within His Majesty's Province of*

---

[1] Bernard Bailyn, *Pamphlets of the American Revolution 1750–1776*, 204. Bailyn's
introduction to the *Discourse* (204–211), preceding its reprinting there, describes its
sources and impact.

[2] For cases in which murder was involved in the piracy, see Thomas M. McDade,
*Annals of Murder: a Bibliography of Books and Pamphlets on American Murders
from Colonial Times to 1900* (Norman, Okla., 1961).

[3] A full account of the trial in this case (*The Arraignment, trial, and condemnation of Capt. John Quelch, and others of his company for sundry piracies, robberies
and murders . . .*) was also supposed to have been printed by Boone in Boston in
1704. No copy has ever been located, and it is probably a bibliographic ghost based
on the London edition of 1705, with that title.

*the Massachusetts-Bay in New-England, on the 18th of October 1717.
. . .* (Boston, B. Green, 1718.)

*Tryals Of Thirty-Six Persons for Piracy . . . At a Court of Admiralty
for Tryal of Pirates, Held at Newport . . . Rhode Island. . . .* (Boston,
Samuel Kneeland, 1723.)

The tryals of sixteen persons for piracy, etc. at a Special Court of Admiralty Boston, July 4, 1726. (Boston, 1726.)

Several other British criminal trials, covering a range of crimes,
were published in Boston. A sampling includes:

*Some Account of the Trial of Samuel Goodere, for the murder of Sir
John Dinely Goodere, Bart. in Bristol* [England]. (Boston, 1741.)

*The Proceedings of the Court-Martial on the Trial of Admiral Byng,
Held on Board His Majesty's Ship St. George, in Portsmouth Harbour,
begun December 27, 1756. . . .* (Boston, Green & Russell, 1757.)

*An Authentick Account of the Proceedings Against John Wilkes, With
An Abstract of the Habeas Corpus Act . . . Addressed to all Lovers of
Liberty.* (Boston, Draper, Fleet, and Edes & Gill, 1763.)

*The Trial and defense of the Reverend John Allen, for forgery, held at
Justice-Hall in the Old Bailey, on . . . January 1769.* (Boston, Kneeland
and Davis, 1773.)

Publications of trial material relating to the witchcraft prosecutions and various religious controversies were numerous. Although
the prosecutions occurred in Massachusetts, more accounts of these
proceedings were published in London than here. The following
Boston imprints indicate the activity of local presses following the
witchcraft trials:[4]

Deodat Lawson, *A brief and true narrative of some remarkable passages
relating to sundry persons afflicted by Witchcraft, at Salem village. . . .*
(Boston, Benjamin Harris, 1692.)

[4] For later documentary compilations on the Salem trials, see W. E. Woodward,
Records of Salem Witchcraft Copied from the Original Documents, 2 vols. (Roxbury, Mass., 1864; reprinted New York, 1969); George L. Burr, *Narratives of the
Witchcraft Cases, 1648–1706* (New York, 1914; reprinted New York, 1968); and
Paul Boyer & Stephen Nissenbaum, *Salem-Village Witchcraft: a Documentary
Record of Local Conflict in Colonial New England* (Belmont, Calif., 1972).

Cotton Mather, *The Wonders of the Invisible World. Observations As well Historical as Theological, upon the Nature, the Number, and the Operations of the Devils. . . . and the Trials of some eminent Malefactors Executed upon occasion thereof. . . .* (Boston, Benjamin Harris, 1693.)[5]

Increase Mather, *Cases of Conscience Concerning evil Spirits Personating Men, Witchcrafts, Infallible Proofs of Guilt in such as are accused with that Crime. . . .* (Boston, Benjamin Harris, 1693.)

The suppression of religious dissenters in Massachusetts produced fewer local imprints, but the following London publications reflect some of the struggles raging here. The two Winthrop tracts relate the attacks on John Wheelwright and Anne Hutchinson which ultimately resulted in their banishment. Following that is Wheelwright's response to Thomas Weld, who is often considered the joint author of the Winthrop tracts:

John Winthrop, *Antinomians and Familists Condemned By the Synod of Elders in New-England: With The Proceedings of the Magistrates against them, And their Apology for the same. . . .* (London, Ralph Smith, 1644.)

John Winthrop, *A Short Story of the Rise, reign and ruin of the Antinomians, Familists & Libertines, that infected the Churches of New England: And how they were confuted by the Assembly of Ministers there: As also of the Magistrates Proceedings in Court against them. . . .* (London, Ralph Smith, 1644.)

John Wheelwright, *Mercurius Americanus, Mr. Welds his Antitype, or, Massachusetts great Apologie examined, Being Observations upon a Paper styled, A short story of the Rise, Reign, and Ruine of Familists . . .* etc. (London, 1645.)

The trials of Samuel Gorton and Robert Child in Boston in 1646–1647 produced similar exchanges of pamphlets in London in those years. The later persecution of the Quakers in London, Massachusetts, Bermuda, and other American colonies stimulated an extensive literature from both sides.[6]

[5] Holmes, *Cotton Mather*, III, No. 454, 1234–1266.

[6] For bibliographic treatment of the Quaker controversies, see four extensive bibliographies, all by Joseph Smith: *Descriptive Catalogue of Friends' books . . .* , 2 vols.

A reflection of the early New England concern over slavery and interest in abolition here is to be seen in the following Boston reprint of Francis Hargrave's argument in the landmark case of James Somerset, decided in London by Lord Mansfield:

An argument in the Case of James Sommersett A Negro Lately Determined by the Court of King's Bench; Wherein it is attempted to demonstrate The Present Unlawfulness of Domestic Slavery In England. . . . (Boston, E. Russell, 1774.)[7]

American court reports in series did not begin until 1789. Nevertheless, well before then, certain local civil cases were published separately in Boston. One was a defamation action in 1752 brought by William Fletcher against William Vassall. The plaintiff was awarded substantial damages—£2,000.[8] The other civil case reported was a commercial claim based on land investments, brought by Dr. Sylvester Gardiner against James Flagg, a merchant. The case was adjudicated by referees and then led to a series of pamphlets from 1767 to 1770.[9]

More dramatic than these civil cases were two celebrated trials resulting from the growing tensions between the colonies and Great Britain: the trial of John Peter Zenger in New York[1] and the trial of the British soldiers involved in the Boston Mas-

---

(London, 1867; reprinted New York, 1970); *Supplement* (London, 1893; reprinted New York, 1970); *Bibliotheca Anti-Quakeriana* . . . (London, 1873; reprinted New York, 1968); and *Bibliotheca Quakeristica* . . . (London, 1883).

[7] Another interesting publication relating to slavery is the following disputation at Harvard College: *A forensic dispute on the legality of enslaving the Africans, held at the public commencement in Cambridge, New England, July 21st, 1773, by two candidates for the bachelor's degree, Theodore Parsons and Eliphalet Pearson* (Boston: John Boyle, 1773).

[8] *The State of the Action Brought by William Fletcher against William Vassall, For Defaming him: tried In the Superiour Court at Boston, August Term, A.D. 1752. And Now Pending by Appeal to His Majesty in Council* (Boston, 1753).

[9] See Evans, *American Bibliography*, entry Nos. 10614, 10622–10627.

[1] For a bibliography of the trial, see Livingston Rutherford, *John Peter Zenger His Press, His Trial and a Bibliography of Zenger Imprints* (New York, 1904; reprinted New York, 1941, and Gloucester, Mass., 1963); for studies of the trial, see Stanley N. Katz's introduction to *A brief narrative of the case and tryal of John Peter Zenger* . . . (Cambridge, Mass., 1963), and Leonard W. Levy, *Freedom of Speech and Press in Early American History, Legacy of Suppression* (Cambridge, Mass., 1960; reprinted New York, 1963).

sacre.[2] The Zenger trial was published in several versions, the first major account being that often attributed to Andrew Hamilton, Zenger's counsel. It was probably extensively reworked, however, from Hamilton's rough draft by James Alexander, who had defended Zenger in the pre-trial proceedings and was then disbarred. The first edition was published by Zenger himself in New York:

A brief Narrative of the Case and Tryal of John Peter Zenger, Printer of the New-York Weekly Journal (New-York, Printed and sold by John Peter Zenger, 1736).

It was reprinted in Boston by Thomas Fleet in 1738 and again in 1799.

The trial for murder of William Wemms and the other British soldiers involved in the shooting of the Boston citizens on 5 March 1770 resulted in an acquittal, largely because of their skillful defense by John Adams and Josiah Quincy, Jr. Although the trial of the officer in charge, Captain Thomas Preston, also acquitted, was taken in shorthand and sent to England, it was not published. The Wemms trial was printed in Boston in 1770, 1807, and 1824; the first edition is as follows:

The trial of William Wemms, James Hartigan, William McCauley, Hugh White, Matthew Kilroy, William Warren, John Carrol, and Hugh Montgomery, soldiers in His Majesty's 29th regiment of foot, for the murder of Crispus Attucks, Samuel Gray, Samuel Maverick, James Caldwell, and Patrick Carr, on Monday-evening, the 5th of March 1770, at the Superior Court of Judicature, Court of Assize, and General Goal Delivery, held at Boston. . . . Published by permission of the Court. Taken in short-hand by John Hodgson. Boston: Printed by J. Fleming . . . 1770.

A considerable subsidiary literature of narratives, comments, and commemoration relating to those events continued in the years following them.

Histories

Considerable material relating to the early legal history of colonial Massachusetts can be found in the personal memoirs, diaries, and journals of individual participants. However, the most interest-

[2] Hiller B. Zobel's study, *The Boston Massacre* (New York, 1970) includes an extensive bibliography of the event.

ing of these — John Winthrop's *Journal*, William Bradford's *History of the Plymouth Colony*, Thomas Lechford's *Notebook*, and Samuel Sewall's *Diaries* — were not published until much later. During the colonial period several histories were published in London or Massachusetts which deserve mention in view of the insights they provide on various legal issues. Despite the well-known biases of their authors, we note the following works in this regard:

Cotton Mather, *Magnalia Christi Americana: Or, The Ecclesiastical History Of New-England, From Its First Planting in the Year 1620. unto the Year of our Lord, 1698....* (London, Thomas Parkhurst, 1702.)[3]

Thomas Hutchinson, *The History of the Colony of Massachusetts-Bay, From the First Settlement Thereof in 1628, Until its Incorporation With the Colony of Plimouth, Province of Main, etc. By the Charter of King William and Queen Mary, in 1691.* Vols. 1 & 2. (Boston, Thomas & John Fleet, 1764–1767.)[4]

Thomas Hutchinson, *A Collection of Original Papers Relative to the History of the Colony of Massachusetts-Bay.* (Boston, Thomas & John Fleet, 1769.)[5]

Israel Mauduit, *A Short View of the History of the Colony of Massachusetts Bay, With Respect to their original charter and constitution.* (London, J. Wilkie, 1769.)[6]

Conclusion

There are, of course, other types of law-related publications which have not been fully described here. The relations between the Massachusetts colonists and local tribes of native Americans produced a

---

[3] Holmes, *Cotton Mather*, II, No. 213, 573–596.

[4] The second volume covered the period 1691 to 1750, and a third volume was issued in London in 1828, covering the period from 1750 to 1774, edited by John Hutchinson, Thomas Hutchinson's grandson. The history was also continued by George Richards Minot, who published his *Continuation of the History of the Province of Massachusetts Bay ...*, in Boston, 1798.

[5] The Preface indicates: "Intended to ... elucidate the principal facts related in the first part of the History of Massachusetts-bay [1628–1691] and may serve as an appendix to it."

[6] Published anonymously, this was a British view designed to refute the colonists' claim that their charters made them independent of Parliament. It was revised, enlarged, and reissued in London several times between 1769 and 1776.

substantial religious literature, and also led to many publications of treaties and treaty conferences.[7] In addition, an extensive pamphlet literature developed around the various legal and political issues leading up to the American Revolution. Boston was a major printing center for these publications, many of which contain sophisticated legal arguments and reflections of legal conditions in colonial Massachusetts. Fortunately these have been well described in two annotated, scholarly bibliographies by Thomas R. Adams.[8] Additional sources of documentation for the study of the law of colonial Massachusetts are described in articles later in this volume.

It is hoped that this brief survey of colonial Massachusetts publications will broaden the general view of the relevant literature of this important time and place in American legal history. Although the number of actual legal treatises was very small, the printed literature directly or indirectly related to law was substantial and richly deserves further study.

[7] For a partial listing, see Henry F. DuPuy, *A Bibliography of the English Colonial Treaties with the American Indians Including a Synopsis of Each Treaty* (New York, 1917).

[8] For the American pamphlets, see Adams, *American Independence: The Growth of an Idea. A Bibliographical Study of the American Political Pamphlets Printed between 1764 and 1776 Dealing with the Dispute between Great Britain and Her Colonies* (Providence, 1965). For the British pamphlets, including those published here, see his *The American Controversy. A Bibliographical Study of the British Pamphlets about the American Disputes, 1764–1783*, 2 vols. (Providence, 1980).

NEAL W. ALLEN, JR.

Law and Authority to the Eastward:
Maine Courts, Magistrates, and Lawyers,
1690–1730

NO history of law in colonial Massachusetts would be complete without some examination of the administration of justice in that region which the authorities in Boston were accustomed to call "The Eastern Parts." Although Maine's earliest beginnings form a distinct chapter in the colonial American experience, the history of the State itself dates from the separation from Massachusetts in 1820. For more than a century and a half between those events, Maine was a part of The Colony, Province, and Commonwealth of Massachusetts. From 1651, with only brief interruptions, the laws enacted by the General Court had force east of the Piscataqua River, representatives of the Maine towns travelled up to Boston as deputies, and members of the area's leading families sat at the Council Board. County courts in Maine administered justice according to the same forms that governed judicial procedure in Suffolk or Essex or Hampshire Counties; and after 1692, from the days of Judge Samuel Sewall in 1700 to those of lawyer John Adams in the decade before the Revolution, the justices of the Superior Court, with their attendant lawyers, clerks, and servants, travelled the eastern circuit. The legal and institutional history of the old District of Maine is thus very much a part of Massachusetts legal and institutional history.[1]

---

[1] For the history of the successive changes of government, see W. D. Williamson, *The History of the State of Maine*, 2 vols. (Hallowell, 1839), I, 272–306, 334–357, 371–452, 554–603. Maine Court Records between 1636 and 1727 have been edited in six volumes, *Province and Court Records of Maine*, for the Maine Historical Society by Charles T. Libby (vols. I and II), Robert E. Moody (vol. III), and Neal W. Allen, Jr. (vols. IV–VI) (Portland: Maine Historical Society, 1928 ff.) The introductions to the first three volumes summarize the history of Maine and my own introduction to volume IV provides a detailed discussion of Maine courts, the records, background, court officers, and law and procedure.

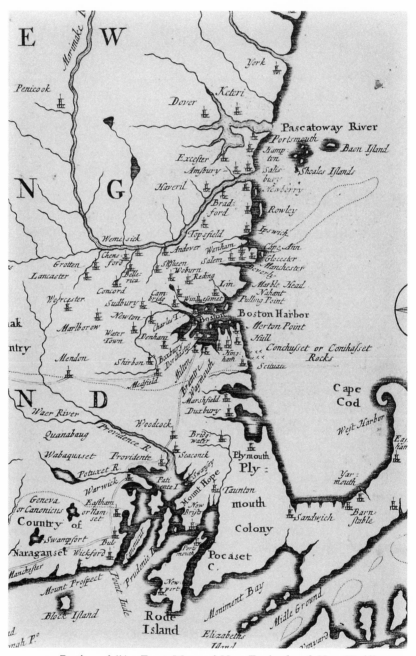

21. Portion of "An Exact Mapp of New England and New York" showing the "Pascatoway River" [Piscataqua] from Cotton Mather, *Magnalia Christi Americana* (1702).

Yet law and authority in Maine reflected differences that had early marked off this region from the Puritan colonies to the south. The proprietors of the Maine and New Hampshire lands had failed to establish direct, personal authority or a lasting scheme of government. Thus the planters and servants who had come over in the 1630's and 1640's to fulfill the plans of Gorges and Mason were soon left to their own devices. They found leaders from their own ranks, or from among those who were soon attracted to the "Eastern Parts" as dissenters from Puritan orthodoxy or economic opportunists. Most of these men adjusted readily to the changes that came with Massachusetts rule in the later seventeenth century, although the traditions of government by a few dominant families persisted.

The area was also more exposed. During the period on which this paper will focus, 1690 to 1730, Maine was, indeed, a kind of "eastern march" of the Province. An Act of March 1694/5, entitled "An Act to Prevent the Deserting of the Frontiers,"[2] indicates the concern of the government in Boston to stem the flow of refugees from Indian raids that threatened to weaken dangerously the fragile and extended defenses of the eastern settlements. Such a law only reenforced a pattern of authority that had existed from the earliest days of settlement, a pattern that saw, by 1690, the emergence of dominant families, whose members exercised exceptional authority and enjoyed a high degree of local prestige. These men and their descendants bore heavy responsibilities of both a civil and a military kind. They dominated the official life of the region during a large part of the eighteenth century, and established little dynasties of power. Their members for three or four generations were prominent in the affairs of church, town, and county, and as garrison holders and militia officers they were important to the security of the region.

During this period the history of the Maine settlements cannot be separated entirely from that of the neighboring province of New Hampshire, which lay directly across the Piscataqua River. Until Falmouth (later Portland) and the region from Casco Bay to the Kennebec began to equal Kittery, York, Wells, and Berwick in importance, the official life of this part of Massachusetts Bay over-

[2] *Massachusetts Acts and Resolves*, I, 194, 402.

laps that of New Hampshire. The ruling families of York County and adjoining Portsmouth, New Hampshire, constituted a Piscataqua establishment. The largely unprofessional lawyers who appeared in the Maine courts of the early eighteenth century were often from the west side of the river; and frequently enough the equally unprofessional judges of those courts were linked by both family and business ties to New Hampshire. In short, the historian of the region can discern a pattern of authority that seems to have endured well into the middle of the eighteenth century. Perhaps that keen observer, John Adams, writing home to Abigail from York in June 1774 on his final journey on the eastern circuit as a lawyer, is a good witness to the lasting importance attached to the magistrate's place and functions. "The Office of a Justice of the Peace," he wrote, "is a great acquisition in the Country, and such a Distinction to a Man among his Neighbours as is enough to purchase and corrupt allmost any Man."[3]

The Legal Profession in Maine

During the late fall and winter of 1707–1708, John Bridger, Queen Anne's Surveyor of Woods and Forests in America, set out to enforce the existing laws against the unlicensed cutting of mast timber in the great white pine stands of the Piscataqua region. With a small armed guard Bridger made at least two forays into the country just west of the small Maine and New Hampshire settlements. On the eastern (Maine) side of the river, about thirteen miles above Salmon Falls, Bridger found, in late November, four Kittery men in the process of cutting and felling "Six mast trees that would make Masts from twenty-eight to thirty-two inches Diameter." On 7 December he apprehended, near Exeter, New Hampshire, seven cutters at work. Bridger's information to the New Hampshire Court of Sessions the following March alleged that the woodsmen, employed by John Plaisted, "Did Cutt, fell and Destroy Nine white pine trees one of which was marked with a Broad Arrow."

Bridger's actions in that season bespeak a clear intention to give

---

[3] John Adams to Abigail Adams, 30 June 1774. *Adams Family Correspondence* (Cambridge, Mass., 1963), I, 116.

effect to his authority.[4] He moved as quickly as possible to prosecute offenders in both New Hampshire and Maine. He wished particularly to punish the powerful men who were the real culprits. He attempted to arrive at the Maine court—the Court of General Sessions of the Peace for the County of York—in time to lodge his information about the November cutting at its January sitting. But distance, the elements, and lack of cooperation thwarted him:

I then took up the workmen and bound them over to appear at the next Court, [he wrote to the Lords of Trade in March] which obliged me to go to Boston to take advice from the lawyers. This was in the extreamest cold weather as ever I knew. I froze my face and neck many times this winter. The snow and cold caused me to miss the Court at York by two hours, but the case was continued till Aprill.

He pleaded for support, both financial and moral: "These trialls will cost me a great sum," he complained, "and no lawyers but at Boston."[5] It would be tempting to dwell at greater length on Bridger's problems, for they are part of an episode that has its own interest. But it is Bridger's last point—"and no lawyers but at Boston"—which sets the theme here. The records seem to support Bridger's statement as essentially accurate for the first decade of the eighteenth century; it is hard to identify anyone in the Piscataqua region who, even by the most generous use of the word "profession," could be called a lawyer. Certainly no one was primarily earning his livelihood from the meager pickings that the law allowed those who acted as attorneys or advocates. But a number of readily identifiable men were providing their neighbors with practical legal advice, were drafting wills or drawing deeds, and were, as needed, appearing before the courts as advocates with some regularity. Thus, although Bridger was, strictly speaking, correct, to leave his statement as conclusive would be to miss an interesting and picturesque part of the history of the practice of law in colonial New England.

While the focus of this paper is on the decades between 1690 and 1730, it might be of some interest first to look briefly at the evidence for the presence and influence of lawyers during the age

---

[4] *Province and Court Records*, IV, 349–355.

[5] John Bridger to the Lords of Trade, 9 March 1707/8. *Calendar of State Papers Colonial*, XXIII, No. 1384, 697–699.

of beginnings—when Maine was Sir Ferdinando Gorges' Province, and not the "eastern March" of Puritan Massachusetts.

William Willis, in *A History of the Law, the Courts and the Lawyers of Maine* more than a century ago, noted that Thomas Gorges, a young cousin of the Proprietor, was the first educated lawyer in the region that later became the State of Maine.[6] There seems little reason to revise that view. When Gorges came over as Deputy Governor in 1640, he had been a law student for two years. Robert Moody's recent edition of Thomas Gorges' *Letters*[7] reveals a sensitive, thoughtful young man, who was certainly concerned not merely with the technicalities of current English practice. We glimpse in these too brief and incomplete copies of the letters that Thomas Gorges wrote home a man interested in the larger problems of government, one who was, in addition, sensitive to the liberties of the subject. "I could wish I had my law books, which I left in England," he wrote to his father shortly after he reached Maine, "for I studdy law and have more and more need to use it then ever I had."[8] He was still pressing to have the books sent over three months later. It would be a year before they reached him.

In response to a suggested prescription for a "way of government" from Sir Ferdinando, Thomas noted that "in my opinion [it] is conformable to the laws of England and suitable to the times heer," but he was quick to point out that the detailed provisions for the frequent sitting of Courts needed to be modified in light of the sparse population and the rigors of the climate.[9]

Even more striking are the evidences of Thomas's concern that the laws of the new plantation should reflect the reforming views of the age. "I think we should be very cautious for the punishing of theft with death," he wrote in the fall of 1641. "Sir. Tho: Moors Utopia

---

[6] William Willis, *A History of Law, the Courts and the Lawyers of Maine* ... (Portland, 1864), 14.

[7] *The Letters of Thomas Gorges, Deputy Governor of the Province of Maine 1640–1643*, Robert L. Moody, ed. (Portland: Maine Historical Society, 1978).

[8] Thomas Gorges to Henry Gorges, 19 July 1640. *Gorges Letters*, 2.

[9] Thomas Gorges to Sir Ferdinando Gorges, 29 June 1642. *Gorges Letters*, 113.

hath good rules for it."[1] On the matter of a religious establishment, he noted in the same letter:

We are in hopes of settling the ministers in the province but if you tye men strictly to the government of the Church of England all will goe to wracke. You must of necessity tolerate liberty of conscience in many particulars. Nothing hath hindered your parts but this, and want of government, and I wish that our Laws here will [en] able true men to undertake it.[2]

To an apparent suggestion from Sir Ferdinando that trial by jury be limited or repressed, Thomas wrote in cautious terms in December 1641: "Whether putting down Juries be not barringe the Subject of his liberty, I leave to your consideration."[3] And the next spring, speculating on the possible use of Negro slaves, he wondered if "theyr bodyes can agree with the coldness of the country." Though he tentatively thought that if so, "they would be excellent," he followed that with the interesting statement: ". . . I believe I could frame an argument against the lawfullness of taking them from theyr own country. . . ."[4]

Finally, this young man shows himself to have been a sensitive and informed student of the political theory of his age. In a letter of December 1641 he comments on the New Hampshire settlers' voluntary submission to the authority of Massachusetts, which had recently taken place. "The Bay have taken the South side of the Pascattaway river uppon the peoples request, for the want of good government; so they [the Massachusetts authorities] have done it partly by virtue of theyr love and partly by the peoples desires, supposing themselves bound to shelter those that looke to them by the law of nations and nature."[5]

[1] Thomas Gorges to Sir Ferdinando Gorges, September 1641. *Gorges Letters*, 55. See Thomas More, *Utopia* (Crofts Classics, H. V. S. Ogden, ed., New York, 1949), 13, 59–61. Gorges probably had in mind More's description in Book I of the law of theft in the mythical land of the Polyerites. There, those convicted of theft are required to perform acts of public service, but are neither imprisoned nor chained unless their crimes are heinous. The description of criminal sanctions in Utopia itself is less specific, but does emphasize servitude rather than capital punishment, few and simple laws, and the encouragement of virtue as a counterpart to punishment.

[2] Thomas Gorges to Sir Ferdinando Gorges, September 1641. *Gorges Letters*, 57.

[3] Thomas Gorges to Sir Ferdinando Gorges, 5 December 1641. *Gorges Letters*, 89.

[4] Thomas Gorges to Sir Ferdinando Gorges, 19 May 1642. *Gorges Letters*, 95.

[5] Thomas Gorges to Sir Ferdinando Gorges, 5 December 1641. *Gorges Letters*, 89.

Thomas Gorges was to be in Maine for a scant three years. In the decades after 1650 the struggling settlements offered small scope and less attraction for lawyers. Yet even in that period there was need for the practical management of both public and private business. In Maine, as elsewhere in the English colonies, the law ruled. Courts needed to be set up and staffed, a criminal justice system established, deeds executed and recorded, indentures drafted, and wills drawn. If in the circumstances of time and place these matters did not call for skilled or learned lawyers, they did require men of experience, energy, prudence, intelligence, and probity. An outstanding example of those who emerged to meet the needs of frontier law in seventeenth-century Maine was Edward Rishworth (1619–1690).[6] He was a member of the important and intellectually distinguished Hutchinson family, grandson of the matriarch Susannah Hutchinson and son-in-law of the Reverend John Wheelwright. Rishworth was Recorder of the Maine courts (in the clerical rather than judicial meaning of the title) from 1651 to 1686, save for two years. He served impartially under the successive governments of the period, and though Charles Thornton Libby wrote that he was termed a "turncoat," the charge seems too strong, and probably unfair. During much of that time he was also a sitting magistrate; as Libby continued, "the page was white under his pen until a sound judgment had been reached." Libby added, "While evidently not bred to the law, the urge in his nature to see things go right developed him . . . into a sound lawyer."[7] In addition to his public functions as clerk and judge, it is clear that Rishworth served also as a practical legal adviser and drafter of legal papers in private matters.[8] He was an outstanding early example of a type at its best that was to serve the region for two generations after 1690.

Who were the Maine magistrates of these years?[9] Neither time

[6] For Rishworth, see *Province and Court Records*, I, iv–v; II, xii–xv. Charles Thornton Libby expended an inordinate amount of space discussing Rishworth's orthography and speculating about his education; his career as public servant might still be more fully examined with profit.

[7] *Province and Court Records*, I, xiv.

[8] For example, Rishworth appeared in behalf of his relative, Edward Hutchinson, Jr., at a county court in October 1653. *Province and Court Records*, II, 20–21.

[9] *Province and Court Records*, IV, liii–lxii; V, xxi–xxxv.

nor space allows an extended discussion of the question, but a summary view is useful. In Kittery, three families dominated official life in the period: the William Pepperrells, father and son, merchant shipowners with their homes and businesses at Kittery Point; the Frosts, whose homestead at Sturgeon Creek in the upper part of the town had been settled by the immigrant Nicholas Frost by 1640 and was to remain in the family for over three centuries; and the Hammonds, neighbors and relatives of the Frosts, who by 1700 had already established a near monopoly of the office of Clerk of the Courts.

In Berwick, the Plaisteds dominated affairs. Active in lumbering and milling, the brothers Ichabod and John Plaisted were frequently willing to use high public office to further private ends. At a time when Ichabod was a deputy mast agent under the Crown, brother John was busy cutting white pine above the dimensions permitted by the charter provisions and was successfully defying authority. When, in 1708, John Bridger, the Queen's Surveyor-General of Woods, sought to prosecute four of Plaisted's men for unlawfully cutting mast timber, John and Ichabod were both members of the York County Court of General Sessions that tried the accused men. At one time John Plaisted was a magistrate in both Maine and New Hampshire, and the family had close ties, in business, in official life, and by marriage, to leading figures in New Hampshire.

In York the Prebles, descendants of Kentish yeomen, were leaders of the town in the later seventeenth century and on into the eighteenth. The first Abraham Preble, a carpenter, was in Maine by 1639 and established the family tradition of office-holding. His son, another Abraham, from the 1660's followed a typical colonial *cursus honorum*: constable, many times selectman, deputy to the General Court, militia officer, and a justice of the peace in the first commission under the second charter. His nephew of the same name carried on this tradition of public service until the nephew's death in 1724. The Prebles of this period were active, energetic men of affairs, but they did not achieve the social eminence or economic power of Pepperrells, Frosts, or Plaisteds.

In Wells, the preeminent governing family was that of the Wheelwrights. By 1643 the Reverend John Wheelwright had moved to that town from Exeter, New Hampshire. His son Samuel (d. 1700) and Samuel's son, Colonel John, were the squires of Wells until the latter's death in 1745. Since, from the 1680's until the end of Queen Anne's war, Wells was on the eastern edge of the Province, Colonel John Wheelwright's duties were correspondingly heavy and dangerous.

Marriage linked nearly all of these families, giving substance to the term "establishment." The Pepperrells and Frosts were closely bound; evidence from later in the eighteenth century suggests that this produced considerable family pride. Judge Simon Frost, writing to a friend in 1746, complained that "there were people who did not show him that respect which was his due, in regard to his Honorable and Worthy Ancestors." The Plaisteds formed marriage alliances on both sides of the Piscataqua; Ichabod's son, Samuel, was married to Hannah Wentworth, daughter of Lieutenant Governor John Wentworth of New Hampshire. Samuel's cousin, Elisha, son of John, married Hannah Wheelwright, the daughter of Colonel John. The Hammonds were, as noted, closely related to the Frosts; the first Joseph Hammond (d. 1711) had married Catherine, daughter of Nicholas Frost. Thus, the Frosts and Hammonds of the period under consideration here were cousins.

This kind of pattern might be expected in a small and relatively isolated society. What is perhaps more significant, and is certainly interesting in the context of this study, is the creation of family traditions of office. William Pepperrell, Jr., was serving as his father's clerk in court by his sixteenth birthday,[1] and as a young man, succeeded to judicial office. Joseph Hammond, Sr., and his son by the same name were clerks of the courts from 1694 to 1720. The elder Hammond had been "clerk of the writts" in Kittery since 1673, and the family tradition began even earlier when Joseph's father, William Hammond, the immigrant, was clerk of the writs in 1668 in

---

[1] Warrant issued over the signature of Colonel William Pepperrell, Sr., dated 11 September 1712, penned by W. P., Jr., then 16 years 3 months. *Province and Court Records*, V, 131.

Wells, where he had first settled.[2] Although other examples might be given, one striking instance of a family's domination of office will suffice. From 1724 until the Revolution, the High Sheriff of York County was a Moulton.[3]

During the period which followed the establishment of government under the second charter, at least three groups of persons can be identified as providers of legal services in Maine. First would be those who were admitted to practice in the courts in accordance with the provisions of the Massachusetts statute of 1701, "An Act Relating to Attorneys."[4] Their names are to be found in the York County court records; most of them, however, were not residents of Maine at all but of New Hampshire. Prominent were John Pickering of Portsmouth; Charles Story of New Castle, for many years secretary of the Province of New Hampshire; Benjamin Gambling, a Harvard graduate in the class of 1702 who had migrated to Portsmouth from his native Roxbury; and Thomas Phipps, another Harvard man, class of 1695, who had come down from Boston to Portsmouth as a schoolteacher the year after his graduation. A second group consisted of those Boston lawyers who frequently followed the Superior Court on its eastern circuit, and who sometimes served as counsel for Maine persons of large interests. Finally, one must in-

---

[2] A County Court held 7 July 1668 appointed "Clarkes of the writs" in the several towns to provide for a smooth administration of justice, "In prosedinges of Law. . . ." *Province and Court Records*, II, 164–165.

[3] William H. Whitmore, *The Massachusetts Civil List for the Colonial and Provincial Periods* (Albany, 1870), 110. Even well into the eighteenth century the isolated nature of the eastern frontier was a basis for the continuing importance of strong figures of authority. Thus, as the regions east of Wells were settled after the Treaty of Utrecht had brought an end to the first intercolonial war, law and authority in the "Eastern Parts" rested largely in the hands of resident magistrates.

[4] "An Act Relating to Attorneys," 1701–1702 Province Laws, chapter 7, *Massachusetts Acts and Resolves*, I, 467. The York court records contain the following list of persons who were admitted attorneys and took the oath:

> Charles Story of Portsmouth, October 1701.
> Richard Briar of Kittery, October 1701.
> Jarvis Ring of Salisbury, July 1702.
> Nicholas Gowen of Kittery, April 1703.
> Thomas Phipps of Portsmouth, October 1718.

The list is obviously incomplete. Apart from Boston lawyers such as Thomas Newton, Paul Dudley, and John Valentine, who argued Maine cases before the Superior Court, others in the Piscataqua region appeared in court and had doubtless been admitted and sworn. A clear example is the Portsmouth official, Benjamin Gambling.

clude residents of York County who, though not recorded as admitted to practice, nevertheless appeared as advocates or counsel in the courts.

Of the first group, John Pickering was over fifty years of age when he took the attorney's oath at the York court in January 1701/2. His career amply supports Jeremy Belknap's description of him as a man of "rough and adventurous spirit," and Page's later judgment is that he was a person of little education "though of much force." Pickering was a carpenter and miller with interests in mills in York, and was the owner of property there. His public career took him to the speakership of the New Hampshire Assembly and by 1700 to the position of Crown Attorney. He was holding the latter office at the time Bridger was prosecuting John Plaisted's mast cutters in 1708; but in the York court of April in that year, Pickering, who was Plaisted's father-in-law, appeared as counsel for the defendants. His answer to Bridger's information was shrewd, forceful, rough-hewn, and even by the standards of that somewhat casual age, replete with strange spellings.[5]

Charles Story had come to New Hampshire as Proprietor Samuel Allen's appointee for the posts of provincial Judge of Admiralty and Secretary. The first position he never filled, and the second he lost for a short time because he failed to deal tactfully with the Council. He had refused to attend a meeting called soon after he arrived from England, and had answered the Council's request to meet with them "with lofty indecent carriage." But he made his peace, adjusted to what was surely at first an uncomfortable environment, and became an established figure in the region. He was active in the courts on both sides of the river until his death in 1715. Story seems to have been familiar with English law, and as one who had been sent over to serve as an admiralty judge, may well have been trained in the civil law also. Bell, in a footnote in Volume II of *New Hampshire Provincial Papers* (670), suggested that Story might have studied at Doctors' Commons. In the records of the York courts, Story's performance bears out these necessarily somewhat tentative judgments.

---

[5] For Pickering, see *Province and Court Records*, IV, lxiv; E. L. Page, *Judicial Beginnings of New Hampshire* (Concord: New Hampshire Historical Society, 1959), 149.

He was at times a stickler for precision and technicality of process; and the reasons of appeal which he drafted often indicate some knowledge of substantive rules as well. In a case of 1705 (Mainwaring and Frost v. Shores in the Inferior Court of Common Pleas in York), Story, representing the appellants, argued closely for a reversal on the grounds that the action was brought as trespass on the case, whereas it should have been detinue since the action had been brought for the recovery of a chest and contents and one of the defendants at trial was the wife. "By the Common Law," Story urged, "the wife cannot be a detainer, but the Husband." Further, he pointed out, the appellee Shores had failed to state adequately and precisely the facts on which his claim had been based. The contents of the chest ("Cloathes") had not been particularly described nor had their value been stated, as law required; nor had Shores stated exactly when the detention had taken place.

Benjamin Gambling and Thomas Phipps took their places in New Hampshire official circles soon after 1700. They both married into the Portsmouth ruling group. Gambling's wife was Mary Penhallow, whose father, the historian of the Indian wars, sat on the Superior Court bench; and her brother John, the factor at Georgetown after 1715, became a York County justice of the peace in 1718. In Maine, Gambling was frequently counsel for appellants to the Superior Court, and his work as a drafter of reasons of appeal suggests acuity and at least some familiarity with the technicalities of the law.

Thomas Phipps had come down to Portsmouth in 1696, the year after his graduation from Harvard. He was lured by the town's decision to hire an "abell schollmaster," one "not visious in conversation." He too married well; his first wife was Eleanor Cutt, widow of a substantial merchant. By 1704 he was a justice of the peace in New Hampshire and became active in official life. Before 1712 his first wife had died, for in the spring of that year he married another widow, Mary (Plaisted) Hoddy; she was the daughter of John Plaisted. Phipps' rise from the schoolroom to high office was fairly impressive, but it did not take place without some troubles along the way. As sheriff, and later as King's attorney in New Hampshire, he was charged by his enemies with padding official expenses and neglecting his duties. When asked why, as King's Attorney, he had not seized a parcel of stolen masts, Phipps is said to have retorted that "Inasmuch as the King has commissionated an Officer to inspect the King's Woods . . . it appears to be his business and not mine. . . ." Phipps, like Gambling, was a knowledgeable, acute, but essentially self-educated lawyer.[6]

Less frequently present in the Maine courts, and then usually serving as advocates for appellants in important cases, were members of the still embryonic Suffolk County bar. Paul Dudley, Thomas Newton, John Valentine, and Addington Davenport, Jr., appeared in York from time to time when the Superior Court was travelling the eastern circuit.

Others who took the oath and were admitted to practice in Maine courts were residents of York County, but their effectiveness seems not to have been very great, nor their reputations such as to attract important clients, even in that simple society. A Kittery man, Lt. Richard Briar, took the oath in 1701. Of a social rank somewhat lower than that of the established families of the region, Briar appeared infrequently, and then not impressively, in the York courts. He probably served as his own lawyer in an almost Dickensian episode touching a pair of missing mittens in April 1704. Shortly after that, he had left Maine. Another local person, Nicholas Gowen, was admitted in 1703. One of his sons, James, was destined to sit on the York County Inferior Court bench later in the century, but Nicholas achieved no great eminence. He was a man of practical bent, a surveyor and scout, and a sometime deputy from Kittery to the General Court. Though connected to the Frosts, he was not highly regarded by some of that family. His uncle, Major Charles Frost, testified in January 1695–6 that Nicholas was accounted a "busy body" who concerned himself with matters that did not affect him. Although he lived until 1742, his role as a lawyer was, on the evidence, minimal.[7]

Still others acted as agents or attorneys or gave legal advice, even if they had not been formally admitted to practice in the courts. One who can be readily identified was the Kittery surveyor, William

[6] For Story, *Province and Court Records*, IV, lxiv–lxvi. For Gambling and Phipps, *Province and Court Records*, V, xxxvi; C. K. Shipton, *Sibley's Harvard Graduates*, IV, V (Cambridge: Harvard University Press, 1933, 1937).

[7] *Province and Court Records*, IV, 165–167, lxvi–lxvii.

Godsoe. He was frequently called on for advice in situations where title to land was at issue, or where rightful possession was challenged. The York files for the period contain many papers from his hand or references to his testimony in such cases. Not only did Godsoe often appear as a kind of expert witness in these matters; he was also the author of reasons of appeal, or answers to such reasons, in cases that were carried to the Superior Court. Thus, in 1717 Godsoe served as a *de facto* lawyer for a neighbor, John Shepard, who was the appellee in a bitterly contested case brought by Samuel Spinney. At trial Shepard had prevailed; but Spinney appealed, and Godsoe prepared Shepard's lengthy "answer" to Spinney's reasons of appeal. It is an interesting document and clear evidence of the existence of lay participation in the legal process. Godsoe's rambling, colorful argument also surely tells us something about courtroom exchanges; it is hard to escape the feeling that this was meant to be delivered aloud in court. In arguing Shepard's case, Godsoe invoked for authority Euclid (in defining a line); local gossip (as to Spinney's reputation for honesty); and the "Proverb first come first serv'd." The peroration embodied some powerful invective: Spinney is a frivolous litigant; "he acts the part of a Child that has been parted with a Ba[u]ble." He is a constant thorn in the side of his neighbors: "som Lands he snips att the ends and squesed others in the side . . . to screw out a few Poles of Land that people had Injoyed many years." Such documents are vivid echoes of grass-roots litigation.[8]

Finally, one should certainly include in this description of the legal world of colonial Maine examples of those more eminent men who, usually officeholders themselves, also served on the side as advisers, as drafters of legal papers, and as givers of legal opinions. Like Edward Rishworth earlier, the magistrates of the period after 1690 were often found in these roles. Joseph Hammond, Jr., clerk, county treasurer, and justice, frequently served as a lawyer in fact, if not in name. William Pepperrell, Jr., was the drafter of legal papers of a routine kind, as were the Frosts and Wheelwrights. These men needed to have a grasp of such law as defined their property interests and business engagements, and they often relied on

---

[8] For Godsoe, *Province and Court Records,* v, xxxviii, 80.

that knowledge to protect their own concerns or those of neighbors and friends.

How familiar with legal authorities were these frontier magistrates and lawyers? We have scant evidence. Certainly the Boston men, Newton and Dudley, had professional training. Dudley, with John Read, is said to have encouraged special pleading; and Washburn wrote that when Thomas Newton died in 1721, he had owned the largest and best collection of law books ever offered for sale in Massachusetts.[9] Charles Story, as has been noted, was probably an educated lawyer also.

But the York County justices and lay lawyers of the early eighteenth century were certainly self-educated and in varying degrees. Some, indeed, were concerned to attain as much competence and understanding as their remote stations and harsh life would allow. When the second Charles Frost was buried in 1724, the Reverend Jeremiah Wise eulogized him in this manner: he was, Wise said,

a Man of great natural Abilities and did excel in a clear Head, a solid Judgment and a very tenacious Memory. . . . He was considerably studied in Mathematicks, Natural Philosophy and History, but he did excel himself in the knowledge of English law, as did well become a Gentleman of his Character.[1]

It would be rash to read too much from this; yet Wise doubtless had some basis for his appraisal of Frost's knowledge and abilities. Circumstantially it seems certain that Charles Frost had acquired some law books beyond the current editions of Province Laws or Dalton's *Countrey Justice*. The inventory of his estate carries an item of £120 for "Books," a figure far larger than any other I have seen for that period in Maine. Unfortunately, the appraisers did not list titles, nor even indicate categories. We know that Frost's cousin, William Pepperrell, Jr., ordered law books from England when, in 1729, Governor Belcher named him chief judge of the York County Inferior Court of Common Pleas, and there are scattered references to

[9] Emory Washburn, *Judicial History of Massachusetts* (Boston, 1840), 205–206.
[1] Jeremiah Wise, "A Funeral Sermon Preached upon the Death of the Honourable Charles Frost, Esq. . . ." (Boston, 1725), 28–29.

collections of reports and treatises in pre-Revolutionary Maine.[2] But specific information is lacking, and only occasionally does a particular title appear. It is perhaps interesting that James Menzies, who was a lawyer in Essex County and appeared in the New Hampshire courts in the early eighteenth century, owned a copy of William Sheppard's well-known tract on the reform of the common law, *England's Balme*, published in 1653.[3] The Puritan zeal for law reform was not unknown in New England.

Not until the years just before the Revolution was there a Maine bar of any stature or consequence; even then, it had few members.[4] But to suggest that the unprofessional lay lawyers and justices who preceded them had any significant influence on these later developments would be asking too much of the evidence. Certainly men like Richard Briar, Nicholas Gowen, or William Godsoe fall into that group of "pettifoggers" who were castigated by the young John Adams.[5] And the Plaisteds of the time seem often to have regarded public office as a private convenience. But we should remember, too, men like Charles Story, Charles Frost, John Wheelwright, the two Joseph Hammonds, and the future Sir William Pepperell. Learned they were not, but as clerks, magistrates, or legal advisers and attorneys they were shrewd, experienced, and, on the evidence, fair.

In March 1708 Nathaniel Raynes of York, a Quaker, complained to Governor Dudley that the Inferior Court of Common Pleas at York had awarded judgment against him by default. Raynes had not appeared. He argued that he had been near the courtroom all the time, but had not been notified when his case was called. Joseph Hammond, Sr., who was the chief judge of the court, wrote to Dudley about the episode at length. Pointing out that the judges had delayed other business for some time while waiting for Raynes, Hammond added: "let him be what he will, he ought to have Justice

[2] Usher Parsons, *The Life of Sir William Pepperrell, Bart.* (Boston, 1855), 27.

[3] Menzies' inscribed copy of Sheppard's *England's Balme* is in the special collections of the Hawthorne-Longfellow Library of Bowdoin College.

[4] David Sewall of York; David Wyer of Falmouth; Theophilus Bradbury and the young Theophilus Parsons, Bradbury's student; the brothers John and James Sullivan—all were, for greater or lesser periods of time, active in the Maine courts. To discuss them at length would require a separate paper. They laid the groundwork for the substantial achievements of the early-nineteenth-century legal profession in Maine.

[5] Lawrence M. Friedman, *A History of American Law* (New York, 1972), 87.

done him. Cap't'n Wheelwright Informs me that they waited for him a great while after the Case was called & sent the officer into every roome in the house to enquire for him. . . . I believe theres not a man of the Court but are desirous it Should come to a fair tryall, that the Merit of the Case might be inquired into; undoubtedly Raines will be extreamely wronged if he Should pay so much as Judgment went against him for. . . ."[6] More than a century later Williamson would write that Hammond was a "man of great integrity and worth, whom the people held in high estimation. He left a son of the same name, the worthy heir of his virtues. . . ."[7] The York County records of the period would bear this out. Perhaps the Hammonds, who were simple husbandmen, should stand as the best representatives of law and authority in the "Eastern Parts."

A Day in Court: A Reconstruction of the Court of General Sessions of the Peace for York County, 6 July 1725

This survey of the early history of Maine magistrates and lawyers would not be complete, certainly not satisfactory, if it did not include a picture of what really took place when courts met and the rule of law—even in this simple society—was given effect. Fortunately the Maine court records are a rich source of information for the historian who would seek to fill out that picture.

On Monday afternoon, 5 July 1725 the frontier village of York in the Province of Massachusetts Bay would be beginning to fill up with all those whom official duty, stern coercion, or mere curiosity drew in for the quarterly sitting of the Court of General Sessions of the Peace, to be followed by the July session of the Court of Common Pleas. The larger events which must have dominated tavern talk in that summer of 1725 no doubt gave way to "discourse" about the cases pending before the courts. Temporarily at least the topics of conversation must have shifted from the recent defeat of Captain Lovewell's little force near Pigwacket village or the coming conference with the eastern Indians at St. George's, to speculation about the bitter litigation that was splitting loyalties in the Frost-Hammond-Leighton families in the upper part of Kittery; or to the

---

[6] Massachusetts Archives, XL, 913, 914, 915.

[7] W. D. Williamson, *A History of the State of Maine*, II, 75.

charges that had been brought against Daniel Morrison and Malachi Edwards for their "Threating Speeches" and "Contemptuous Manner" at the Wells town meeting two months earlier. What went on in the courts attracted a great deal of attention in a small community like York village, and except for those whose services were indispensable elsewhere, it is not difficult to imagine that virtually the whole population of York was attracted to the events surrounding the holding of the courts.

By evening as many as sixty or seventy persons would have come in to York.[8] The horses of those who had ridden overland would be in temporary stables or at pasture, and the vessels of people who had come by sea at their moorings in the harbor or in the broad reach of York River. Well before sunset on that long summer day the taverns would be filling up, and the houses of substantial townsmen (Prebles, Banes, Moultons, Simpsons, Cames) would be the scene of more genteel entertainment; for the families of this rural "establishment" were closely related, and the quarterly sittings of the two county courts afforded welcome opportunity for social gatherings. Perhaps the Reverend Samuel Moody was pondering the court-week lecture that he would be delivering the next morning, and doubtless the under-sheriff, Benjamin Stone, had installed the simple "platform" that transformed John Woodbridge's tavern parlor into a courtroom for His Majesty's justices. By early evening that same room, the adjoining hall and chambers, and the benches outside would become the noisy center of the informal preliminaries, for court days vied with ship launchings, militia musters — and Cambridge commencements — as occasions for large-scale and often turbulent celebration.

On this particular evening that was certainly true, and Woodbridge's tavern was the scene of a brawl that had its inevitable sequel the next morning. Nay, more; one of the principals in this picturesque episode was John Woodbridge himself. For neither the first nor the last time the court's host was to find himself in the slightly ridiculous position of standing charged with an offense in his

[8] A calculation based on the records of both courts (the Court of Sessions and the Inferior Court of Common Pleas) suggests that perhaps as many as sixty to seventy outsiders were in York for the courts. This would include four of the six justices, county and town officers, grand and trial jurors, informers, witnesses, and litigants.

own tavern parlor, before a company that included, besides the justices and other officials, a good number of his friends and neighbors. Although some details of the disturbance that broke out that evening of 5 July escape us, its main outlines are vivid enough. One of those who had come in to face charges at this court was John Smith, a fisherman suspected of uttering a counterfeit fifteen-shilling note. Smith was among the company at Woodbridge's, and for reasons that are not apparent in any of the records, was either carrying or sitting near a gun. He was also doubtless sitting close to the supply of drink: New England rum was clearly the catalyst that most often precipitated such events. Smith, according to the clerk's note of the matter the next day, was guilty of "Reveling & disorderly Carriage, in fireing of a gun in the house of Mr. John Woodbridge." The taverner himself seems to have over-reacted; records from other sittings indicate that he was perhaps too fond of his own staples of trade. At any rate, on this occasion a witness deposed that he saw Woodbridge "coller John Smith & [tell] sd Smith he would knock his brains out if he would not go out of his house." Smith stood his ground, and Woodbridge proceeded to carry out his threat; the witness testified that Woodbridge "let go his hold & caught up a gun & Strock sd Smith over the head. . . ."

The court records are silent about any other outbreaks that night. By eight o'clock the next morning, however, Smith was lodging a complaint against Woodbridge before one of the resident justices of the peace, Samuel Came. The innkeeper appeared; and Came, after hearing the charge and taking the depositions of two witnesses, bound him over to answer "before the Justices of the Court of Gen'l Sessions of the peace to be holden at York . . . on this day." It is permissible to hazard the guess that more than one of the participants at this early morning scene was nursing a sore head; gun barrels and rum, if applied with sufficient force or in enough volume, seem equally capable of producing unpleasant sensations. Thus, even before the solemnities of Quarter Sessions took place, the judicial machinery of the county was invoked to deal with this brawl, itself directly related to the gathering of persons for the sitting of the court.

Even in this remote corner of British North America, the authorities were not unmindful of the traditional ceremonies associated with

Quarter Sessions and Assizes. Thus, when the justices of the Superior Court came down from Boston in May, they were met at the county line, in this case the Piscataqua River, by the High Sheriff and his deputies, often attended by other gentlemen.[9] While the justices of the county courts would not have been accorded this particular dignity, they did vest their own proceedings with some of the ceremony that custom and the law manuals prescribed.[1] And so, shortly after Samuel Came had bound over John Woodbridge, the justices and other officers probably gathered on the common. To the tolling of a bell, perhaps to the beat of a drum, they marched in procession to the meetinghouse—the sheriff with his wand, the constables with their staffs of office, the justices in their finest clothes. For by a custom that in York County, at least, went back twenty years, the members of the courts would "wait on God in his House before they Entred on Court Business."[2] The weekly lecture, a fixture in any well-regulated Puritan community, was ordinarily held on Wednesday, but on the four occasions when the courts were meeting, the authorities moved it up to Tuesday morning. We may assume that the pastor at York, Samuel Moody, was the preacher on the occasion. "Frontier parson and fighting chaplain," he had already ministered to this exposed community since 1698; in July 1725 there still remained twenty-two years of his near half-century of service. What he said on that July morning we shall never know; conventionally such sermons were tailored to the occasion, and one might expect, therefore, that Moody dwelt on the doing of justice. But Samuel Moody was not a conventional parson; he was an eccentric, perfectly capable of startling his congregation with outrageously personal remarks, a spiritual dictator who thought nothing of shooing people out of the taverns or marching into a fellow townsman's home to "see about" a falling off

[9] On 9 May 1716 Samuel Sewall recorded in his diary: "Ferry'd over very pleasantly and were met by Sheriff Layton [Leighton] our Host, and his Wand...." *The Diary of Samuel Sewall, 1674–1729*, 3 vols. Massachusetts Historical Society, *Collections*, Series 5, Vols. V–VII, 1878–1882, II, 194.

[1] Michael Dalton, *The Countrey Justice* (many editions, 1618–1727); William Lambard, *Eirenarcha: or of The Office of the Justices of Peace* (many editions, 1581–1607); G. Jacob, *Court Keeper's Companion* (1717); T. W., *Clerk of Assize, Judges Marshall and Cryer* (1660).

[2] Nathaniel Raynes to the Governor and Council, January or February, 1708. Massachusetts Archives, XL, 913, and *Maine Province and Court Records*, IV, 217.

in family worship.[3] It is not inconceivable, therefore, that he spiced his remarks on 6 July 1725 with some pointed and explicit comments on the events of the preceding evening.

After the lecture the procession formed again and moved to Woodbridge's tavern. There, doubtless in the best parlor, six justices of the peace for York County took their places on the platform that had been prepared. In front of them, or to one side, quill sharpened, was the new Clerk of the Courts, young Charles Frost. Perhaps behind them on the wall was fixed that "Coat of the King's Arms" which, ten years later — when the County had its own courthouse at last — Samuel Came and Jeremiah Moulton were directed to purchase, if they could, from John Woodbridge.[4]

The court on that July morning consisted of six of the ten persons who were active in the Commission of the Peace for York County at that time.[5] The senior in point of service, and probably also in age, was John Wheelwright of Wells (c. 1664–1745), whose interesting gravestone portrait has been reproduced for this volume. The primitive quality of this likeness and the medium only enhance the powerful effect, and suggest the character of the man. Behind the conventional pose and popeyed stare, one glimpses the vigorous, forceful magistrate and soldier who for more than four decades was one of the two or three most influential figures on the exposed eastern frontier of the province. Perhaps Wheelwright had inherited from his grandfather, Winthrop's famous antagonist, both the strong frame and the sturdy spirit. The Wheelwrights of these years were a remarkable family.[6]

Equally well known to contemporaries was the next senior justice of the peace, Joseph Hammond of the "upper part" of Kittery, later the town of Eliot. He was the second bearer of that name to serve as

[3] Shipton, *Sibley's Harvard Graduates*, VI (1942), 356–365.

[4] An entry in York County Court Records, Volume X, for 1735.

[5] Absent were Lewis Bane (Bean), John Gray, Samuel Plaisted, and John Penhallow. Joseph Heath of Richmond may also have been a York justice of the peace by 1725, but the records do not clearly indicate this.

[6] Tradition has it that Oliver Cromwell once said of the first John Wheelwright, "I remember the time when I was more afraid of meeting Wheelwright at foot-ball, than I have since been of meeting an army in the field." They were fellow students at Cambridge. Colonel John's daughter, Esther, was captured in the great attack on Wells in August 1703; she became the Mother Superior of the Ursulines at Quebec.

22. Gravestone portrait of Colonel John Wheelwright of Wells (1745).

Clerk of Courts, Justice of the Peace, and Judge of the Inferior Court of Common Pleas. His grandfather, William Hammond, had been an early settler of Wells and clerk of the writs there in the seventeenth century. William's son, the first Joseph Hammond, had been a man of commanding abilities. The second Joseph, who sat down in Woodbridge's tavern with his fellow magistrates that July, was thus the heir to a long tradition of public service.

Up from Casco Bay had come Major Samuel Moody. Related distantly, if at all, to the York minister of the same name, Major Moody was the second founder of Falmouth, later Portland. A graduate of Harvard in the class of 1689, frontier preacher turned soldier-magistrate, Moody must have dominated the resettled regions north and east of the four old towns. That he was not accorded the fullest measure of loyal affection is unhappily clear, however. Two years after this court of July 1725, Moody was to lodge a sharp complaint against Benjamin Wright, a fellow-townsman. Wright, said the Major, had "abused and Scandilised him as a Justice of the Peace." When Lieutenant Governor William Dummer visited Falmouth earlier, Moody had sent out orders for a number of people, including Wright, to "Attend in Arms." Wright was quoted as saying "he was very ready to wait on his Hon'r but would not do it by Old Beelzebub's Ord'r."[7] Like his fellow magistrates John Penhallow at Arrowsic and Joseph Heath at Richmond, Moody was under a constant strain to maintain order over the still largely masculine, transitory, and rootless population of the region east of Wells.

Joseph Hill, brother of John Hill, who had served on this court briefly from 1711 to his death in 1713, was from Wells. Hill, like so many of his colleagues, was active in military affairs during these times. He first came on the court in April 1722. Though he was over fifty years of age in 1725, he had had less service in civil affairs than the other justices. John and Joseph Hill's father, Roger, had been an early settler of Saco. Indian troubles, probably, account for John's removal to Kittery and Joseph's to Wells after 1700. Joseph Hill, like his fellow townsman, John Wheelwright, had a special interest in two of those who were to come before the court this day. Daniel Morrison and Malachi Edwards had been charged by the two Wells

[7] *Province and Court Records*, VI, 267–268.

justices with disrupting the town meeting in that place two months before, and that disruption had included, on Edwards's part, open defiance of orders given by the magistrates.

Samuel Came we have already seen presiding as a resident justice of the peace over the hearing into the brawl at Woodbridge's tavern. In July 1725 he was already about fifty years of age; but very few of those present in York on that summer day — and those few could only have been young people or children — were destined to outlive him. Came's life spanned a major portion of Maine's pre-Revolutionary history, and he was an active participant in the public affairs of town, county, and province for over sixty years. He died 26 December 1768 in his ninety-fifth year.

The youngest member of the court was the bearer of the most distinguished name in Maine's colonial history. William Pepperrell, Jr., had just turned twenty-nine in July 1725; but since at least his sixteenth birthday he had been acting as clerk to his father, as papers in the York court files reveal, and he had served as clerk of the two county courts since January 1720–1721. He had been a justice of the peace and a member of the court since July 1724. Thus Pepperrell had combined the work of justice and clerk for a full year, for it was only at this July court that the younger Charles Frost took his place as clerk for the first time. Pepperrell's career as merchant-shipowner and later, as a military commander, Province Councilor, and judge, have obscured his long apprenticeship in public affairs, and particularly his activities as clerk and magistrate at the county level. Despite a busy life as heir to important commercial enterprises, Pepperrell, like his father, was an active and conscientious magistrate, as the records of these years make abundantly clear. In July 1725, too, he assumed his place as one of the four judges of the Inferior Court of Common Pleas.

The grand jurors took their places, perhaps on benches which at other times were occupied by Master Woodbridge's customers. Fifteen of them had been elected at the annual town meetings in March and in April had been sworn to office "for the year Ensuing." Thirteen of their number were present on 6 July.[8] The newly settled communities east of Wells had sent in one, or at most two, jurors to this

[8] Job Burnham and John Davis were absent.

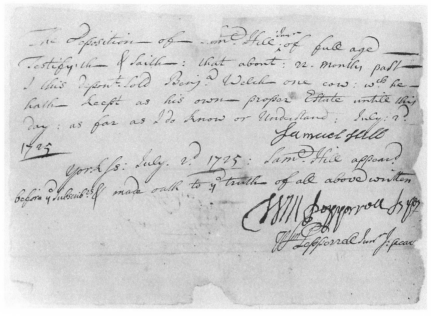

23. A deposition of 2 July 1725, York County Court Records. The body
of the deposition is in the hand of William Pepperrell, Jr. The signature of
the deponent, Samuel Hill, is attested by both William Pepperrells,
junior and senior.

court. But the four old towns were well represented: four from York,
including the foreman, Jonathan Bane; three, possibly four, from
Kittery; three from Wells, and probably two from Berwick.

Other officers were there, too; the High Sheriff, Jeremiah Moulton, who only a year before had been organizing his company of
militia for the great attack on Norridgewock; Daniel Simpson, the
new County Treasurer; the coroner, Joseph Curtis; and a cluster of
town constables, selectmen, informers, and lesser fry. The clerk's
record does not indicate that the members of the "Grand inquest"
were sworn to office again; presumably once, in April, was enough.
Nor is there mention of any grand jury charge by Justice Wheelwright, the senior member of the Court. Charges to the grand jury
were customary, however; they were a regular part of the formalities
of Superior Court sessions, and possibly, too, of the Sessions of the
Peace. We will not err greatly, then, if we re-create a scenario that

included a formal proclamation by the Clerk that the Court of General Sessions of the Peace, for and within the County of York, was now in session; and a brief, pointed charge to the grand jurors by John Wheelwright, that touched not only their duties in general, but pointed out particular matters that were to come before them.

Institutional history too often suffers from depersonalized treatment. We read of parliaments, assemblies, government departments, or courts as though statute book or manual could tell us how such bodies really functioned. Too rarely do we listen or observe. Of course, valid generalization must rest on a broad range of data; history is not written out of scattered anecdotes or random episodes. But in addition to studies based on a systematic and thoughtful distillation of representative evidence, we need occasionally to let the records speak to us directly. We may know much about how institutions or formal bodies were supposed to function; we can know what contemporary people experienced in such gatherings only if we look closely at the records of actual performances. It is with this in mind that we turn the pages of the ancient court book which Joseph Hammond, Jr., clerk from 1700 to 1720, William Pepperrell, Jr., clerk from 1720 to 1725, and Charles Frost, assuming the position in 1725, filled up between January 1719 and October 1727. Let us start at the point where Frost began his duties,[9] on this July day in 1725.

Charles Frost may have been nervous as he picked up his quill pen, though it was not in character for members of that prominent clan to betray such feelings. Yet Frost may have been aware that his kinsman, Justice Hammond, was figuratively—and perhaps literally—peering critically over his shoulder. For Hammond had served as clerk for twenty years, and it would be unusual if he did not have a proprietary feeling for the position. He knew all the details of that exacting job. So Clerk Frost consulted his notes and Captain William Pepperrell's record of the last court, and called for James Parker of Falmouth. Parker had been bound over a full year before by Samuel Moody, for selling liquor without license. Term after term he had defaulted, and most recently had failed to appear at April court. Now he was again absent and was declared to have forfeited his bonds of

---

[9] The following account is drawn from the records of the court that sat at York, 6 July 1725. *Maine Province and Court Records,* VI, 186–204.

yᵉ publick Worship of God

Hannah Stanford of Berwick for fornication

Sarah Hosum of Berwick for fornication

Mary Bragdon of York for fornication

Peter Mathews of York for not attending the
Worship of God

John Parsons of York for prophane Cursing

ught into Court By Nich° Cole foreman

Pepperrell is appointed Clerk of yᵉ Court of General
of yᵉ peace & Inferiod Court of Comon pleas for
ty & was Sworn in Court to yᵉ faithfull discharg
...

Attest Jos Hammond Cler

Anno Regni Regis Georgij Septimo

at of Genˡ Sessions of the peace holden at
for and within the county of York: January. 3. 1720/
John Wheelwright: Charls Frost Abraham
& Joseph Hammond Esqʳˢ

rand Inquest are as followeth: Vizᵗ

Impˢ: Nich° Cole Foreman   Sylvanus Wintwor
...onnoit   Depend° Littlefeald   Jorᵃᵈ Moulton
...illion   Alexsandʳ Junkings   Mallachi Edward
...ajor   Abiel Gooding   Joseph Sweat
Hambleton   Rich° Rogers   Wᵐ Gowel

twenty pounds; the clerk was directed to issue a warrant of distress for the bonds, and Parker was further saddled with costs of 35 shillings.

Turning next to presentments and orders from the April court, the justices first dealt with two matters that had been initiated then by the hard-pressed minister of Scarborough, Hugh Henry. Samuel Libby and Job Burnham, the selectmen of that town, appeared to answer Henry's complaint that they were "not Supporting him in the work of the Ministry there" — a sadly familiar complaint of ministers in the poorer towns of northern New England. The court, which was not always sympathetic to Henry's troubles, ordered the selectmen to assess "in due proportion" the town's ratable polls and estates, guarding the interest of those who had already paid their share and make up the sum of twenty pounds that constituted Mr. Henry's salary since June 1724. In making their order the justices recognized that Scarborough had been through hard times, reduced to "very low Circumstances" since "the late distroying warr." For reasons not apparent the justices were less agreeable to another complaint that Hugh Henry had entered with them in April; he had at that time accused Selectman Libby of non-attendance at public worship. This court acquitted Libby—though they did tax him with substantial costs of court.

Samuel Smith, the Biddeford constable, then appeared to be admonished for neglect of duty in not making return on a warrant for bringing in his fellow townsman John Stackpole to the April court. He had apparently made good at last, however, for Stackpole himself next came forward to answer his presentment "for breaking the peace in Striking." He was convicted and sentenced to pay a fine of five shillings and costs of twenty-five shillings. Smith and Stackpole were followed by another delinquent constable, Nathaniel Fernald of Kittery, and his prisoner, John Woodman of the same town. Fernald too was admonished, and paid ten shillings three pence in costs; Woodman, "for being drunk," was fined five shillings to be used for the poor of Kittery, and fourteen shillings for fees of court. Two grand jurors who had failed to appear in April were next brought up; apparently their unrecorded excuses were good, for they were both acquitted.

The Court of General Sessions of the Peace had a general competence to oversee nearly every aspect of local government. That authority was exercised by and through the judicial process, and the next piece of business illustrates this aspect of the justices' work. In April the town of Kittery had been found delinquent in not having "Standards" — that is, a set of officially approved scales, weights, and measures as required by law.[1] Now came forward John Dennett and John Thompson, selectmen of Kittery, to answer their town's presentment. They were ordered "to take Effectual care" that the town obtain the required standards.

There was perhaps a stir, and maybe some laughter, as the clerk next called up John Woodbridge to face the charge of "striking" John Smith. Samuel Came had bound him over, as we have seen; the papers in the case were now read, or at least summarized. Woodbridge's neighbor, John Adams, was surety for the innkeeper's appearance "this day . . . before the Justices of the Court of Gen'l Sessions of the Peace"; perhaps he stood with Woodbridge as the latter faced the court. Jonathan Johnson and William Rowse testified, swearing that their written "evidences" were true; and Woodbridge was fined the usual five shillings to the King; then he must have gone back to keep a watchful eye on those provisions that he had stocked for the entertainment of the court and the onlookers.

The next case came to nothing, but it is not uninteresting to the observer two centuries later and probably evoked some talk at the time. In April Captain Elisha Plaisted of Berwick had lodged a formal complaint against one James Turner, also of Berwick, before Justice Hammond. Plaisted was a member of the Piscataqua "establishment." John Wheelwright was his father-in-law, and his father and uncle had been prominent figures in both official and business circles in New Hampshire and Maine. Plaisted's accusation was that Turner had stolen an iron canting dog from him; the tool had been "lying at the door" of Plaisted's garrison house when Turner was alleged to have taken it. One witness, who testified at Hammond's hearing of the charge in early May, had been told that Turner had "offered it at the Tavern for Strong drink." But there were compli-

---

[1] "An Act for the Regulation of Weights and Measures," *Massachusetts Acts and Resolves*, I, 19–70. Amendments to that law of 1692 were passed in 1705 and 1731.

cations; other evidence hinted at an argument about the "dogg" between Plaisted and a Captain Oliver, who was commanding a detachment of soldiers in Berwick. Others besides Turner were also implicated, for Margaret Frost had said that "Edw'd Steward Offered to pawn an Iron Dogg for 20s" on 21 April; Turner, Michael Kelley, and Joseph Cross were in the house at the same time, and she heard Stewart and Cross say that "they would Stand by One Another in the Affair of the Dogg." Turner had refused bail in May, had been committed, and it is possible, though not at all certain, that he had thus spent two months in jail awaiting his appearance at the court in July. But the court ordered an acquittal, "no Evidence Appearing to Convict him." Acquittal did not free the accused of all obligations, however; the justices slapped a very heavy bill of costs on poor Turner. He was ordered to pay fees of court in the amount of £5:1:0.

In spite of that, James Turner went back to celebrate, perhaps. Equally fortunate was John Smith, the fisherman, who, still nursing a bruised head, now came forward to stand trial on the charge of uttering a counterfeit fifteen-shilling bill. Smith had been bound over by William Pepperrell, Jr., after what must have been a rather fascinating hearing in early May; at that time the offensive note was traced in a sequence of transactions back to Smith. A Portsmouth tavern keeper, Thomas Harvey, had spotted the counterfeit bill when it was offered him by John Neal; the latter said he had received it from Benjamin Lord, and Lord, in turn, traced it to one John Hooper. It was Hooper who implicated Smith. At the initial investigation, Smith, appearing before William Pepperrell, had refused "to make oath who he received sd bill of."

All of this was doubtless retold before the assembly in Woodbridge's tavern on that July day two months later, as Smith stood before the court. Then came the denouement; it may well have caused a mild sensation. John Smith, in court, "made Oath that the above sd fifteen Shilling bill w'ch he paid Jno Hupper he Receiv'd of Cap'tn Peter Nowel of York." Nowel was a respected member of the community, a builder, militia officer, and grand juror, and in July 1725 a selectman; he was just a few rungs down from the top of the social ladder. Why, or how, he had obtained the counterfeit bill, never came out; nor was any charge ever laid against him in the matter.

Things were warming up, and the onlookers were perhaps beginning to feel that court week was not disappointing their expectations. There was perhaps some talk — certainly there had been some earlier — when James McCartney of Kittery stepped up to be cleared of his bond. In June McCartney had been placed under obligation, in five pounds, with two sureties, to be of good behavior until this July court; Colonel Pepperrell had found him guilty of "making & publishing a false & Scandalous report of John Woodman." The latter, McCartney had said, "was a murdering old roge"; he had murdered two wives, and ". . . he was a wizard & had bewitcht Several people. . . ." How fully these lurid charges were repeated in July, we cannot know, but most of those in attendance must certainly have heard them.

The flow of business went on. The selectmen of York answered satisfactorily a presentment for "deficient high ways"; John Burrill was fined for "profain swearing"; and John Smith stepped forward once again, this time to face the music for his "Reveling & disorderly Carriage" of the night before; perhaps Woodbridge had lodged a formal complaint against him. It had been a busy day and night for Smith, all in all. On this charge he was convicted and fined the usual five shillings for breach of the peace.

The court, spurred on by Justice Hammond perhaps, next ordered the clerk once more to issue process for summoning Captain John Heard of Kittery to appear at the October Sessions. Heard had been stalling for three years. In July 1722 he had been convicted of abusive behavior on Hammond's complaint; he had stubbornly refused to pay the fine imposed then, and the court now rather testily said he must appear in October "to give his reason if any he have why he don't pay the fine & fees of Court. . . ." Nearly everyone present must have known that Heard's original conviction had stemmed from an unseemly altercation in the course of which he had repeatedly called Hammond "son of a whore."[2]

[2] *Province and Court Records*, VI, 97–99. The first Joseph Hammond and Catherine (Frost) Leighton were presented for fornication 5 July 1670. Hammond "owned the fact" and was fined; but this common slip hardly made Catherine a whore. *Province and Court Records*, II, 196.

Another absentee who had long defied authority was the object of the next order of the court. Daniel Grant was in constant trouble on the matter of attendance at public worship. He was perhaps an unbeliever, possibly a Quaker; certainly his record was one of consistent refusal to attend public worship in Berwick, where he resided. Now the justices ordered process for his appearance at the next sessions to answer for his breaking away from the constable, who had sought to enforce Grant's obedience to a sentence imposed in January 1723/24, more than a year earlier.

This court did not ordinarily concern itself with matters involving death; its jurisdiction did not, in practice, embrace capital crimes, nor did Quarter Sessions have competence in probate business. But it was the court to which the coroner reported, and the next entry on the docket reflects this. The entry also tells us, inferentially, of the dangers of that season and points up the fact that not all military casualties of the frontier stemmed directly from enemy action. In the winter of 1724–1725 William Welch was a soldier in Captain Jordan's company at Winter Harbor (Saco). In April he had overturned and drowned as he proceeded upriver in a canoe; his body was not recovered for five or six weeks, for the inquest was held on 3 June, when he was "Taken up Dead & Brought in to York." Now the coroner, Joseph Curtis, presented his record of the inquest *post mortem* and requested payment of three pounds, seventeen shillings. That sum represented what was still due, after Welch's back wages of one pound, ten shillings, and four pence had been paid by the Province Treasury.

Another request for payment followed, from Benjamin Stone, who presented his account "for ringing the bell & fitting a plattform for the Superior Court," which had convened in York the preceding May. Stone was paid twenty-seven shillings "In full discharge" of the account.

The county faced a more difficult and awkward problem as a result of the next matter to come before the justices. John Leighton, Joseph Hammond's half brother, had served as High Sheriff from 1715 until his death in 1724. Now the committee which had been named to examine his accounts reported "that there is due to his Maj'ty £12:14:0 which [Leighton] received for fines more than he paid." Leighton's successor, Jeremiah Moulton, was ordered to demand the amount due from Leighton's estate; the committee, William Pepperrell, Jr., and Samuel Came, were to receive eight shillings apiece for their trouble.

The July court was always an especially busy one, where such administrative orders were concerned. At least the clerk's records showed more business of that kind then, for it was also in July that the justices granted annual licenses for tavern keepers and retailers of liquor and levied an assessment on the several towns for the county's share of the Province tax. On this July day in 1725 the justices granted twenty-five licenses of one kind or the other, and in addition gave their host, John Woodbridge, leave to sell until the October court, he "having a Stock of drink by him." Because the clerk always listed licensees by their town of residence, the social historian can readily identify the number of lawful taverns and retailers of drink for county and township. There was, too, an interesting sociology of taverns in colonial Maine. Tavern keepers in the more settled towns were frequently quite respectable widows; at the time, for example, Mary Preble kept a public house in York Village. She was the relict of Abraham Preble, formerly a justice of the peace and a judge of the Inferior Court, County Treasurer, and a man active in civic, religious, and military affairs; on his gravestone in York Village, he is styled "Captain of the Town." Also employers were often licensed to retail liquor "out of doors." The Pepperrells usually exercised this right, and so did Elisha Plaisted, who was heir to an extensive lumbering business in Berwick and the Salmon Falls region. In the more remote outposts, places like Falmouth, Richmond, or Arrowsic, it was usually the leading man of the place who conducted tavern business. So at this court Major Samuel Moody was licensed to retail in Falmouth, and John Penhallow was as usual given authority to sell liquor and operate a tavern at Arrowsic.

The Court of General Sessions of the Peace also had as one of its most responsible administrative functions the allotment of the Province tax among the towns, and the justices turned now to that business. It is more than likely that Daniel Simpson, the County Treasurer, had done his homework before this; the allotment of the county's share of the Province tax involved a scrutiny of polls and estates and a pro-rated assessment of the total levy against each community, based upon the town assessments. So, now, the justices ordered an assessment against Kittery, York, Berwick, and Wells in amounts that give the historian a rough guide to the respective wealth of those towns; the total, set by the General Court, was one hundred pounds, half of which was payable on 1 October next following, and half on the first day of April 1726. It is to be noted that the newly settled towns east of Wells were not yet assessed. They had barely emerged as organized communities after nearly thirty years of war, and the 1720's had seen, of course, a recurrence of hostilities. By 1726 things were better, for Falmouth, Biddeford, and Arundel appeared in the assessment, though for very small amounts.

If the clerk's record accurately mirrors the sequence of events, the grand jurors may have been preparing their presentments while the justices considered the matter of liquor and tavern licenses; in the court book the list of presentments comes between the record of grants of licenses and the allotment of the Province tax. When Jonathan Bane of York, the foreman, stood up to hand in his report, the list of delinquents that he presented was perhaps a bit shorter than usual, though it was representative enough of the shortcomings of this colonial society: three presentments for "profain Cursing," three for fornication, and one — that of John Jordan of Kittery, "Shipwright" — for neglecting the public worship of God on the Lord's day.

It may have been the clerk's afterthought, or a prompting from Justice Hammond, who had originally dealt with the matter, that led to the next piece of business. In January Peter "Wittum" (Witham) and his wife of Kittery had been presented for neglecting public worship. Perhaps, like the Grants of Berwick, they were dissenters from orthodoxy, because no fewer than eight Withams had originally been accused. Peter and his wife were convicted and sentenced at the April court, but three months later she had not yet taken her punishment. Now the court ordered a warrant of distress against "Peter Withum Jun'r his wife" for the fine and accumulated costs; in default of payment of the fine she was to be placed in the stocks for an hour. On the reverse of the warrant is the endorsement of Nathaniel Fernald, the Kittery constable, dated the next 4 October, that he had "put the wife of Peter Withom Juner in the Stocks the full Speace of one oure" and had collected the court fees of eleven shillings.

Assuming that the court book actually reflects the true order of events, the three most complicated cases came up at the end. The grand jurors had done their work and had been dismissed. The court had disposed of the county business, which was its responsibility to direct. Now the justices took on three matters which, it may be supposed, were the most complex and sensitive cases of those they were to face. An examination of the records will suggest why this was so. The first two of these cases stemmed from the same episode: they emanated from charges lodged against Daniel Morrison and Malachi Edwards of Wells, who were participants in a serious disruption of a special town meeting the preceding May; both men were presented for flagrant defiance of authority. The particular issue at the town meeting seems to have involved the potentially explosive question of a contested vote on the ministry; and the charge of defiant behavior against Edwards was the more serious because he was at the time one of the town's constables. The third of these cases was also sensitive, for the defendants, seven residents of Kittery, had been accused of voting in the March town meeting, though not qualified.

Although Morrison and Edwards were tried separately, it is appropriate to look at the episode as a whole, for the accusations against them and the papers in the two cases give a single picture of the events which led to their troubles. The details of that turbulent affair were doubtless rehearsed before the company in Woodbridge's tavern; how, before the formal opening of Wells town meeting on 5 May, Morrison was the leader of "a Confused tumult or disorder" in which many people were trying to talk at once; how Morrison called out in a loud voice, "We will have our Vote for our Minister in Spite of you all"; how, when Justice Joseph Hill ordered Constable Edwards to keep order and take Morrison into custody, Edwards refused to obey; how, when John Wheelwright thereupon ordered him to remove Morrison and confine him, "Malachy" went up to Justice Hill "in a Contemptious Manner," pulled him by the sleeve of his coat and commanded him "in his Maj't's name to go and Stand guard over Morrison." We cannot recover all of the details of this crisis, nor have anything more than a surface feeling for the animosities that rent the town of Wells in the spring of 1725. What sentiments were stirred when Morrison and Edwards came into court in July, we cannot know. It is perhaps safe to say, however, that the bench felt the powerful emotions of pride and outrage; and that some, at least, of the spectators warmed to the plight of the two accused men. The court records of these years reflect more than once a pervasive "we-they" divisiveness of feeling.

Perhaps Justices Wheelwright and Hill did not take part in the trials; the York magistrates of these years seem to have been generally scrupulous—or perhaps cautious—about sitting in cases where they were interested parties. But if so, their brethren upheld the honor of the court. Morrison was fined ten shillings and ordered to give bonds for his good behavior. Edwards, whose offense was clearly more serious in the eyes of the court, was fined the considerable sum of ten pounds and was also bound to his good behavior in the amount of fifty pounds.

Before that result was reached, however, some important procedural moves had taken place. A belief that popular feeling was with them prompted Edwards, at least, to ask for a jury. This was denied. Was it perhaps because in the justices' view the two cases were seen as contempt of authority and, therefore, properly dealt with in a more summary fashion?

In addition, Edwards, and possibly Morrison, was almost certainly represented by counsel in the person of Benjamin Gambling, the Portsmouth attorney. It was Gambling who later drew up Edwards's reasons of appeal, and that document reveals a full awareness of the trial proceedings in the case. The prosecution was likewise in the hands of an advocate, for the bill of costs lists a chargeable expenditure of ten shillings to the "Kings Attorney."[3] In short, these two cases appear to have gone to trial in a real sense; so also did the case of the Kittery voters.

---

[3] The prosecutor's name is not given, either in the court book or in any of the file papers. If the court knew that a formal indictment was forthcoming, provision seems to have been made ahead of time. Thus at a sessions in 1727 the clerk noted that

That issue, too, was a lively product of political tendencies fostered by the institution of the New England town meeting. More particularly, the case at bar had come about when, at the Kittery town meeting on the preceding 22 March, ten residents of that place "did presume to vote in the sd meeting," though, it was alleged, they were not qualified by law. A reading of the record of the April court reveals that this was directly related to, or a cause of, bad blood between the Hammonds and their Frost kinsmen. The accused men had been "encouraged" to vote by Charles Frost, and Joseph Hammond had bound Frost over to the April court to answer that charge. Twenty-three of the defendants' more affluent fellow townsmen had presented a formal petition to the April Court of Sessions, challenging their pretensions to the franchise. At that time the justices had committed the papers in the case to the grand jury, who, after careful study and deliberation, had returned presentments against seven of the accused men. It is the most fully documented political case to be found in the Maine records of the period from 1700 to 1727. The papers include: the complaint; a full list of all those who voted; reports of the constables, who were charged with collecting rates; a number of interesting depositions brought in to show the true value of the estates of the challenged men; and the bills of costs.

Now in July the cause came on for trial. The accused men put themselves on trial by a jury "Specially appointed & Sworn for that purpose." The result was hardly calculated to give satisfaction or certainty. The jury returned a special verdict; the seven challenged men were found not guilty, "Except there be a Law that requires as voters Quallified to bring Evidence to the Town Meeting that he is Quallified." There was no law that actually said a voter must "bring Evidence" to town meetings of his right to vote; there was, of course, an authenticated list of those who were qualified, drawn up by the town's selectmen in their capacity as assessors. The accused men had been challenging this official list. The court's judgment was that,

inasmuch as it appears by the List of rates [i.e., the official list] they were not Quallified at that time by the Law directing the Quallification of voters

Addington Davenport, Jr., was appointed "King's Attorney in any Case that Shall come before this Court During the Setting of this Sessions." *Province and Court Records*, VI, 259.

in town affairs, & were So found by the grand jury upon their Oaths, Its Considered by the Court that they be Admonished to conform themselves Accordingly for the future. . . .

The defendants were ordered to pay costs of court of £3:17:0.

I think we can assume that these last three cases, which were clearly of some importance and were, additionally, highly sensitive, were taken up after all the lesser matters and administrative decisions had cleared the docket. Probably, as in most complex and serious matters, no one quite knew how long the proceedings against Morrison, Edwards, and the seven Kittery voters might take. More to the point, perhaps, counsel required time to prepare argument and marshal facts, for, as in the cases against Edwards and probably Morrison, so in the Kittery voters' case a defense attorney, Thomas Phipps, appears and doubtless someone representing the Kittery selectmen argued for the town, though the record is silent as to his identity.

It is not stretching fact to believe that these three "big" cases may have carried the court into the afternoon. The business of the Court of Sessions did not go over to Wednesday, however, for the depositions taken in the case of the voters bear the clerk's endorsement "Sworn in Court, July 6, 1725."

Well before sundown, then, the business of the Court of General Sessions of the Peace for the county of York was probably concluded. A few of those who had been fined or assessed costs of court might well have spent that night in the new prison that stood on a knoll opposite the meetinghouse and above the burial ground. Some who had no more business in York might already have gone home, but perhaps most of those who came in for court week stayed on. For the business of the Inferior Court of Common Pleas was still to be done and early the next morning, or even that afternoon, the civil side of the county's judicial business would have its own day in court.

There was, indeed, a postscript to this Quarter Sessions. Daniel Morrison, Malachi Edwards, and the seven Kittery voters all appealed their convictions to the next Superior Court of Judicature, Court of Assize and General Gaol Delivery. Morrison and Edwards were successful; in their cases the judges of the Superior Court reversed the judgments of the York Court of Sessions. The case of the Kittery voters ended, not with an appellate bang, but in a post-trial whimper. They, or Thomas Phipps, their attorney, must have had second thoughts. They paid in their costs of £3:20:0 to Sheriff Moulton and put in no appearance on the appeal.

But all of that took place almost a year later, in May 1726. By the evening of 6 July 1725 the participants of the day's events had retired from the field, each perhaps to find solace or celebrate a victory in his own way. Though doubtless for many rum was again the chosen medium, the records are silent as to any consequences. Perhaps even John Smith and John Woodbridge clinked a can together; at any rate, we hear no more — for this court, at least — of "Reveling and disorderly Carriage."

Vernon Parrington wrote that "[t]he undistinguished years of the early and middle eighteenth century, rude and drab in their insularity, were the creative spring-time of democratic America. . . ."[4] Perhaps this account of a court day in the shire town of the old county of York gives some meaning to the statement. Not all the participants of events on that day would have found appealing the idea of a future American democracy. But all shared in a legal tradition whose roots went deep. Unruly and "rude" they often appear in these records, but the institutional framework and the inherited traditions gave force and meaning to the idea that law ruled. "Let him be what he will, he ought to have Justice done him," wrote Joseph Hammond in 1708. And in April 1702 Joan Crafts, a widow who kept the tavern at Kittery Point, responded to a summons for her appearance, "For I desir as I live onder the Law to be guided by the Law. . . ."[5]

[4] Vernon L. Parrington, *Main Currents in American Thought: The Colonial Mind* (New York, 1927), I, 133.

[5] *Province and Court Records*, IV, 218, 274.

CHARLES R. McKIRDY

Massachusetts Lawyers on the Eve of the American Revolution: The State of the Profession

THE American Revolution placed American lawyers on a world stage. Their names include those of our most revered patriots. Twenty-five of the fifty-six Signers of the Declaration of Independence and thirty-one of the fifty-five members of the Federal Constitutional Convention were lawyers. In the First Congress, ten of twenty-nine Senators and seventeen of sixty-five Representatives were lawyers.[1] What of the profession itself? What stage of "professionalization" had American lawyers reached when their society was shaken by revolution?[2] This essay explores this question by scrutinizing the bar of Massachusetts in the ten years immediately prior to the American Revolution.

The concept of a "profession," with its aura of hierarchy and elitism, is an inherently difficult subject for objective study.[3] Only after subjective value judgments are put aside does the concept have value as a tool of analysis. Scholars disagree on practically everything relating to "professionalism." Nevertheless, most scholars share a rather loose consensus as to the salient traits associated with profes-

---

[1] C. Warren, *A History of the American Bar* (3d ed., Boston, 1966), 213.

[2] According to the *Oxford English Dictionary* (Micrographic ed. 1971), "profession" was first used *circa* 1747, and "professionalism" *circa* 1856. Ibid., 2316. For the importance of "professionalization" as "a pervasive feature of American cultural life in the late nineteenth century," see B. Bledstein, *The Culture of Professionalism: The Middle Class and the Development of Higher Education in America* (New York, 1978), as described by M. S. Hindus, "Crime and History," *Stanford Law Review*, XXXIV (1982), 927.

[3] As to usages of the term "profession," see *e.g.*, H. S. Becker, "The Nature of a Profession," in *Education for the Professions* (Manchester, England, 1962), 27–46. Undefined, the term evokes unreflective and romantic notions of power, prestige, and a positive evolution which may be unjustified by the actual record. See, *e.g.*, A.-H. Chroust, *The Rise of the Legal Profession in America* (Norman, Okla., 1965), I, 90–108; G. W. Gawalt, *The Promise of Power: The Emergence of the Legal Profession in Massachusetts, 1790–1840* (Westport, Conn., 1979), 7–35.

sions. Employing these traits as a starting point, one may gain valuable insights into the way that pre-Revolutionary Massachusetts lawyers viewed themselves and their society.

Perhaps the most obvious trait that has been suggested was that a profession be a full-time occupation providing the professional's principal source of income.[4] In eighteenth-century Massachusetts, most lawyers were actively engaged in pursuits outside the realm of law and some owed the bulk of their income to extracurricular interests.[5] There was also a sizable group of "amateur" lawyers, or "pettifoggers," who plied some other trade, but earned money from drafting documents and performing other legal functions.[6] Sometimes the difference between these practitioners and the recognized members of the bar was merely a question of degree. Thus, as far as a full-time commitment to an occupation is concerned, the colonial Massachusetts lawyers fell somewhat short of the "professional ideal."

Another criteria, which A. M. Carr-Saunders and P. A. Wilson

[4] W. E. Moore, *The Professions: Roles and Rules* (New York, 1970), 6–7. Much of the analysis in this essay relies on Moore's excellent study.

[5] Many lawyers turned to farming, both to supply their needs and for additional income. For example, John Worthington had a 340-acre farm in Monson, Hampshire County. R. Taylor, *Western Massachusetts in the Revolution* (Providence, 1954), 20. One young attorney, Stephen Fessenden, worked as a surveyor. J. L. Sibley and C. K. Shipton, *Biographical Sketches of Graduates of Harvard University* (Cambridge, Mass.), x, 169. Others were active in commerce. See J. Cushing, "A Revolutionary Conservative: The Public Life of William Cushing, 1732–1810," Unpublished Ph.D. Dissertation, Clark University, 1960, 55–57. Cushing engaged in the cargo trade between Maine and Massachusetts and lent money at interest.

By 1760, however, the law could be one of the most profitable professions in the colony. "Lawyers might earn ten times as much as did doctors and ministers, as much as all but the wealthiest merchants and planters, and less risk, and greater odds in favor of acquiring and retaining fortunes." J. Main, *The Social Structure of Revolutionary America* (Princeton, 1965), 101. Josiah Quincy noted in his journal that Charlestown lawyers made from £2,000 to £3,000 sterling annually, and Robert Treat Paine complained that his cost of living was high because "we lawyers are such big folks that no one will board us without paying top price...." Letter from Robert Treat Paine to Eunice Paine, 28 August 1758, Robert Treat Paine Papers, Massachusetts Historical Society. Of course not all of the lawyers in Massachusetts were reaping fortunes; many had difficulty making ends meet. See C. R. McKirdy, "Before the Storm: The Working Lawyer in Pre-Revolutionary Massachusetts," *Suffolk University Law Review*, xi (1976), 46.

[6] See C. R. McKirdy, "Lawyers in Crisis: The Massachusetts Legal Profession, 1760–1790," Unpublished Ph.D. Dissertation, Northwestern University, 1969, 22.

labeled as "the distinguishing mark of a profession," was that the occupation be founded in esoteric but useful theoretical knowledge and useful skills based upon formal education of exceptional duration and difficulty.[7] While some scholars stress that "professional" knowledge is essentially theoretical and systematized, they do not consider it necessary that it be scientific.[8] Such is the case with clergymen, who start with moral absolutes, and, more to the point, with lawyers, who must deal with man-made social norms and rules.

Much of the respect accorded a profession depends upon the esotericism of the profession's knowledge base and the society's appreciation of the specialized services it offers. The apprenticeship training that most colonial Massachusetts lawyers received did not cloak them with a mystique that impressed their lay contemporaries.[9] A practitioner such as Joseph Hawley might be known for his understanding of the mysteries of black letter law or his adroitness in the complexities of special pleading,[1] but such deference or respect was earned on an individual basis. The bar as a collective entity was not generally viewed as possessing mysterious and valued knowledge. This accounts, in part, for the colony's low fee schedules and relatively high threshold of professional legal services, that is, the willingness of such a notoriously litigious people to utilize amateurs to manage legal matters.[2]

[7] A. M. Carr-Saunders and P. A. Wilson, "Professions," in *Encyclopedia of the Social Sciences*, XII (1934), 476. See also Moore, "Professions," 10-11; E. Greenwood, "Attributes of a Profession," *Social Work*, II (1957), 44. T. Parsons, "Professions," *International Encyclopedia of the Social Sciences*, XII (1969), 536. W. Goode, "The Librarian: From Occupation to Profession," *Library Quarterly*, XXXI (1961), 306.

[8] See D. Rueschmeyer, "Doctors and Lawyers: A Comment on the Theory of Professions," *Canadian Review of Sociology & Anthropology*, I (1964), 17, 21; H. L. Wilensky, "The Professionalization of Everyone," *American Journal of Sociology*, LXX (1964-1965), 138.

[9] This may have been due to the fact that the average colonial, at least according to one observer, "almost qualified for a country-attorney in England." W. Douglass, *A Summary ... British Settlements in North America* (Boston, 1755), I, 520.

[1] J. Willard, "Address before the Members of the Bar of Worcester, Massachusetts, October 2, 1829," in *Addresses Before the Members of the Bar of Worcester, Massachusetts* (1879), 38; G. Bliss, "Address Delivered to the Gentlemen of Hampshire, Franklin, and Hampden Bars," *Connecticut Valley Historical Society Papers*, IV (1912), 1, 15.

[2] See Moore, "Professions," 88-91. Another indicator of the colony's ambivalence toward the value of legal training was its slow acceptance of the notion that a

A third criteria advanced for a profession was that its members identify with one another and with the profession as a whole.[3] Such identification involves the inculcation and acceptance of appropriate norms, standards, and values or, as Everett Hughes labels it, the profession's "culture."[4] It is this culture, composed of "comparatively clear and controlling group values, behavior norms, and symbols," which, according to Hughes and others, differentiates professional from non-professional occupations.[5] The professional culture involves the group's fundamental beliefs, especially the belief in the essential worth of the service that the profession renders the community and usually the belief in the need for a professional monopoly.

The establishment of professional group identity must be, at least in part, directly related to the homogeneity of the occupation in question. By 1760 most lawyers in Massachusetts shared a common educational experience as well as similar ethnic, religious, and social backgrounds. With few exceptions they came from the middle class.[6] After attending either Harvard or Yale, they underwent a period of apprenticeship during which they may have learned some or little about law, but probably much about being a lawyer.[7] From his men-

judge should be a lawyer. Most of the early judges of the Massachusetts Superior Court were laymen. See Appendix I: "Occupation and Education of Judges of the Massachusetts Superior Court, 1692–1774." After the appointment of Benjamin Lynde, a barrister, in 1712, the number of "professionally" trained judges increased, but lawyers certainly had no monopoly on judicial appointments. Ibid.

[3] Ibid., 8–9.

[4] E. C. Hughes, *Men and Their Work* (Westport, Conn., 1958), 40–41.

[5] Ibid. See E. Greenwood, "Attributes of a Profession," *Social Work*, II (1957), 44. See also E. C. Hughes, *Men and Their Work* (Westport, Conn., 1958), 40–41.

[6] For brief biographies of most of those lawyers practicing in Massachusetts in 1775, see Appendix IV, from C. R. McKirdy, "Lawyers in Crisis: The Massachusetts Legal Profession, 1760–1790," Unpublished Ph.D. Dissertation, Northwestern University, 1969, 238–256.

[7] See E. C. Hughes, *Men and Their Work*, 33, 119, for a discussion of this process in relation to medical training. See Appendix II, Table A: "Professional Choices of Harvard Graduates: 1642–1760" and Table B: "Professional Choices of Harvard Graduates: 1691–1760: Per Cent Per Five Year Period." For a detailed review of John Adams' legal training, see Coquillette, "Justinian in Braintree: John Adams, Civilian Learning, and Legal Elitism, 1758–1775," below, 362–376.

Out of 81 lawyers practicing in Massachusetts in 1775 and studied by the author, all but six attended either Harvard or Yale. While there is no way of determining

tor and his mentor's associates, the clerk learned the mores, the etiquette, and the technique of a lawyer's role. Equally important in forming group identity was the very drudgery of legal training. This drudgery, experienced by nearly every clerk, often spurred individual ambition, but also formed a bond or "fellowship of suffering" between members of the bar which provided a foundation for group identity.[8]

This basis for professional solidarity was strengthened to some extent by the nature of practice in eighteenth-century Massachusetts. As virtually all of the colony's lawyers were sole practitioners dependent upon fees from litigation, they were interested in representing as many clients as possible. This naturally bred competition detrimental to group identity, but the effect was mitigated because, as practitioners, the lawyers shared common experiences and problems. Appearing in court together day after day as allies or adversaries, facing the same judges, often sleeping at the same inns and sharing the same table, the lawyers had ample opportunity to get to know one another. While this familiarity did not always lead to esteem or

the exact number of lawyers in practice at this time, it generally is agreed that the number was approximately 100. For one estimate, see G. W. Gawalt, "Sources of Anti-Lawyer Sentiment in Massachusetts, 1740–1840," *American Journal of Legal History*, XIV (1970), 285. For more detailed descriptions of the 81 lawyers in the author's sample, see C. R. McKirdy, "Lawyers in Crisis: The Massachusetts Legal Profession, 1760–1790," Unpublished Ph.D. Dissertation, Northwestern University, 1969.

A college education was not required, and there were some lawyers who were respected without it, including James Otis, Sr., Elisha Bishee, and James Hovey. See below, 321–322, notes 4–8 and accompanying text. After 1750, however, such successes were rare, and the exceptions had to seek obscure corners of the province in which to practice. The three counties of Maine were a favorite place for untrained lawyers to begin practice. For example, James Sullivan, who eventually became a Superior Court Justice, began his legal career there. See *Legal Papers of John Adams*, L. Wroth and H. Zobel eds. (Cambridge, Mass., 1965), I, CX (hereinafter cited as *Adams' Legal Papers*). See Appendix III: "Geographical Distribution of the Three Classes of Massachusetts Lawyers [Superior Court Barrister, Superior Court Attorney, Inferior Court Attorney], as of 1775." Also included in Appendix III are "Loyalty Patterns of the Three Classes of Massachusetts Lawyers by Geographical Area: 1775" and "Loyalty Patterns of the Three Classes of Massachusetts Lawyers by Age: 1775." For John Adams' description of his apprenticeship, see *Diary and Autobiography of John Adams*, L. Butterfield, L. Faber and W. Garrett, eds. (Cambridge, Mass., 1961), I, 58–59.

[8] Moore, "Professions," 76–79.

even respect, it did lead to an awareness of shared experiences and difficulties.[9]

In the years immediately prior to the American Revolution, the lawyers of Massachusetts faced a variety of mutual problems, ranging from the unhappy quality of some of the inns on the judicial circuit to the bar's standing in the community. Foremost was the growing competition for clients. While realizing that competition was inevitable, some lawyers felt that it had gotten out of hand and were alarmed at the growing number of young men entering the profession. Furthermore, despite legislation and court orders designed to discourage them, unsworn practitioners carried on a flourishing legal business, taking clients away from regular attorneys and, as far as the bar was concerned, bringing dishonor on the profession.[1]

[9] See, e.g., Letter from Jonathan Sewall to John Adams, 5 October 1765, Robert Treat Paine Papers, Massachusetts Historical Society; Letter from John Adams to Abigail Adams, 5 July 1774, in Adams Family Correspondence, L. H. Butterfield ed. (Cambridge, Mass., 1963), I, 122, [hereinafter Adams Correspondence]; Benjamin Pratt's "Fairewell to the Bar," Boston Gazette, 26 October 1761. This emphasis on collegiality, while present in established professions, is more noticeable among those occupations attempting to gain acceptance as a profession. Moore, "Professions," 109.

For a daily account of a trip on one of the judicial circuits, see Adams, Diary, II, 35–45. See also Adams Legal Papers, I, lxvi–lxvii (reflections of difficulties in riding circuit). With a bar of not more than 100, it would have been very difficult for practitioners not to see many of their colleagues repeatedly. Indeed, there were cases in which father and son or brother and brother appeared as opposing counsel. See, e.g., Fletcher v. Vassall (Superior Court at Boston 1752) (James Otis, Sr. for plaintiff, James Otis, Jr. for defendant); Rex v. Preston et al. (The Boston Massacre Trial) (Superior Court of Judicature, Court of Assize and General Gaol Delivery, held at Boston 1770). (Josiah Quincy, Jr. appeared with John Adams for the defendants, and his older brother Samuel Quincy appeared with Robert Treat Paine for the prosecution.) See Adams Legal Papers, III, 1–45, and sources cited.

[1] For one lawyer's complaints about growing competition at the bar, see Adams, Diary, I, 55, 316, 320.

John Adams believed that there were too many lawyers in Massachusetts, and discouraged others from studying for the bar because "[T]here were such swarms of young ones. . . ." Diary, II, 52. Such anxiety still is strong among individual practitioners. See D. C. Lotte, "Laymen to Lawmen: Law School, Careers and Professional Socialization," Harvard Educational Review, XXIV (1959), 352, 356. Adams complained about "Deputy Sheriffs, petit Justices, and Pettifogging Meddlers" who "attempt to draw Writs, and draw them wrong oftener than they do right," Diary, I, 70. In 1720, the Massachusetts General Court had tried to provide some regulation of these men. It ordered that "if the plaintiff in any action suffer a nonsuit, through the default, negligence or omission of his attorney that drew the writ, . . . by mislaying the action or otherwise, such attorney shall draw a new writ without fee . . .", The Acts and Resolves, Public and Private of the Province of Massachusetts Bay, E. Ames, A. C. Goodell et al. eds. (Boston, 1869), I, [hereinafter Acts and Resolves].

Whether or not this fear of growing competition was exaggerated, it was doubtless the primary motive for the attack on unlicensed practitioners that took place in Suffolk County in the 1760's. In 1763 the Suffolk County bar proposed several rules to the Suffolk County Court of Common Pleas. The lawyers wanted the court to order: 1) that no general powers of attorney be granted; 2) that no attorney's fee be taxed, unless the declaration was drawn by the plaintiff or a sworn attorney; 3) that no attendance be taxed unless the plaintiff or a sworn attorney attended personally; and 4) that only sworn attorneys be permitted to practice before the court.[2] The plan failed when James Otis refused to support the motion, believing it to be illegal and unjust. This led the court to declare that it could do nothing unless the bar was unanimous.[3]

Otis' colleagues were outraged by his behavior, and the next year plans were afoot for a meeting of the Suffolk bar to "advise Proper Measures for the Supporte of the Honour of the Barr, and to Prevent Irregular admissions for the Future."[4] While there is no evidence that the projected meeting ever materialized, attorney James Hovey of Plymouth probably reflected the feeling of many of his colleagues when he proposed that all those recommended to the court as attorneys be graduates of a "Regular Course of Study," well versed in the law, and ready to "*Bare-hard*" (if need be) against the

As of 1760, the only formal requirements for practice in the various county courts were contained in very general court orders or bar agreements. The order of the Middlesex Court of Common Pleas was typical in this regard: "Ordered that no Person who has not been sworn as Attorney in this Court or in the Superior Court of Juda. etc. (altho sworn in any other inferr. Court in any other county) shall be entitled to the Fee of an attorney in this Court." Minute Book of the Middlesex Court of Common Pleas (December Term, 1748). The Worcester County Court of Common Pleas passed a similar rule in 1757 when Timothy Ruggles came to the bench. *Worcester Address*, 41. It should be remembered, of course, that the courts did not always require that sworn attorneys be educated.

[2] Adams, *Diary*, I, 235–236.

[3] When Jeremy Gridley read the proposed rules to the bench for approval, James Otis rose to his feet storming that he had never agreed "for any such Rules as these, for they were vs. the Province Law, vs. the Rights of Mankind, and he was amazed that so many wise Heads as that Bar was blessed with could think them practible...." "All schemes to surpress Pettyfoggers," he declared, "must rest on the Honor of the Bar." As the bar was not fully agreed on the proposal, the court could do nothing and the issue was temporarily dropped. Ibid., 236.

[4] Letter from James Hovey to Robert Treat Paine, 22 October 1764, Robert Treat Paine Papers, Massachusetts Historical Society.

25. James Otis, Jr. (1725–1783) by Joseph Blackburn (1755), from a photographic copy, courtesy of the Harvard Law School Art Collection.

Pettifogger Tribe in order to Suppress that Growing Evill."[5] Hovey argued that a lawyer should serve time in the lower courts before being admitted to practice before the Superior Court, and then only if he demonstrated proper character, comradeship, and the will to support the bar against all opposition.[6]

It was ironic that James Hovey advanced such proposals. In many ways he was the last of a breed. With no college degree, he had joined the labor force as a joiner, picked up enough scraps of law to initiate a practice, and risen to the position of barrister.[7] Safely within the fold, he sought to exclude others by requiring long periods of training and apprenticeship. Hovey was not blind to this irony and might honestly have desired to improve the character of the bar, but obviously stricter control of entry to the bar was bound to reduce the number of successful aspirants, and, consequently, aid the competitive position of those already within the chosen circle.[8]

During the next five years, there were more attempts to restrict the practice of law. In 1765 the lawyers obtained an order from the Superior Court that only attorneys admitted to practice before it could secure blank writs.[9] Two years later the lawyers of the York County Inferior Court, plagued by unsworn competitors, agreed not to enter, argue, or in any way assist in the prosecution of cases where

---

[5] Ibid.

[6] Ibid.

[7] E. Washburn, *Sketches of the Judicial History of Massachusetts from 1630 to the Revolution in 1775* (Boston, 1840), 238. Chief Justice Thomas Hutchinson decreed in 1762 that only "Barristers" could argue before the Superior Court of Judicature. See Adams, *Diary*, II, 276; Minute Book, Superior Court of Judicature, Suffolk, August 1762, August 1764. There is evidence that this restriction, if it had any clear meaning, was not always enforced. Josiah Quincy, Jr., although never appointed a "barrister," claims to have pleaded before the Superior Court on several occasions. See J. Quincy, Jr., *Reports . . . Superior Court of the Province of Massachusetts Bay, Between 1761 and 1772* (Boston, 1865), 317. Quincy appeared before the Court at the Boston Massacre Trial. See below, 350. See also C. R. McKirdy, Unpublished Ph.D. Dissertation, 47, and C. R. McKirdy, "A Bar Divided: The Lawyers of Massachusetts and the American Revolution," *American Journal of Legal History*, XVI (1972), 205.

[8] Hovey assured Robert Treat Paine that he, Hovey, made his suggestions with the knowledge that his qualifications were "very small" when compared to those of his colleagues. Letter of James Hovey to Robert Treat Paine, 22 October 1764, Robert Treat Paine Papers.

[9] G. W. Gawalt, *The Promise of Power: The Emergence of the Legal Profession in Massachusetts, 1760–1840* (Westport, Conn., 1979), 17.

the writs were written by persons not regularly admitted and sworn.[1] The Essex County lawyers agreed to a similar rule in March 1768.[2] In September 1769 they tightened their grip on access to the bar:

It is agreed that we will not take any young gentlemen to study with us, without previously having the consent of the bar of this county; that we will not recommend any persons to be admitted to the Inferior Court, as attorneys, who have not studied with some barrister three years at least, nor as attorneys to the Superior Court, who have not studied as aforesaid, and have been admitted at the Inferior Court, two years at least, nor recommend them as barristers till they have been through the preceding degrees and have been attorneys at the Superior Court two years at the least. . . .[3]

While it is true that the lawyers of Essex County drew up guidelines and apparently met on a regular basis, there is little evidence as to the nature of their organization. Consequently, the Suffolk County lawyers are credited with forming the first legal organization in Massachusetts. After a few false starts, and limited to attorneys and barristers of the Superior Court, this body first met at the Bunch of Grapes Tavern in Boston on the evening of 3 January 1770. The thirteen lawyers who attended the meeting voted that the oldest barrister present should preside, that John Adams should serve as secretary, and that all transactions of the society should be kept secret.[4]

Although the Suffolk Bar Society dealt with some questions relating to practice, its main concern was controlling admission to the profession. In 1771 the Suffolk bar accepted the educational requirements of the Essex bar with the added stipulation that no young gentleman could even begin legal study unless he had the consent of the bar taken at a general meeting and had a college education or "a liberal education equivalent in the judgment of the bar."[5] Realiz-

[1] W. Willis, *A History of the Law, the Courts and the Lawyers of Maine* (Portland, 1883), 83, 652.

[2] G. Dexter, ed., "Record Book of the Suffolk Bar," Massachusetts Historical Society, *Proceedings*, XIX (1881–1882), 149.

[3] Ibid.

[4] Ibid., 147.

[5] Ibid., 150. In addition to the required liberal arts education, the applicant had to serve a three-year apprenticeship with a recognized barrister before he could re-

ing that such measures would have only limited effect unless instituted throughout the colony, the Suffolk lawyers attempted to contact lawyers in other counties in order "to consult and advise together concerning the general affairs of the profession through the province. . . ."[6]

It is difficult to ascertain how much of the impulse in the organizing of the Suffolk Law Society was due to a mutual identification of distinctly occupational interests and commitment to a professional culture, and how much was merely an expression of the urge to socialize. Granting that the founding of the society evidences some professional identification, this identification apparently was, at best, sporadic. John Adams' minutes of the society's meetings record sixteen meetings in the five years before the hostilities at Lexington, seven of them in 1770.[7] Attendance probably never exceeded the thirteen present at the first organizational meeting, and twice Adams noted that the gathering was so "thin" that no business could be transacted.[8] While such figures are far from conclusive, they cast doubt on the idea that the formal organization of the Suffolk bar was a strong indication of professional identification. The Suffolk bar also failed to generate enthusiasm for organizing in other counties. With the exception of Essex and perhaps Hampshire there were no other bar associations in colonial Massachusetts.[9] There is no evidence that lawyers in other counties even responded to Suffolk's attempts at communication.

In fact, although lawyers often wrote to one another concerning specific cases, few of them wrote about the profession itself. When they did, it was usually little more than a passing reference.[1] Of course there were exceptions. James Hovey was one; John Adams,

quest the bar to recommend him to the Inferior Court as an attorney. Ibid. Once recognized at the bar of the County Court of Common Pleas, attorneys had to practice there for at least two years before the bar would recommend advancement to the status of attorney of the Superior Court. Two more years were required before a lawyer could hope to be named a barrister of the high court. Ibid.

[6] Ibid.

[7] Ibid., 147–152.

[8] Ibid., 148.

[9] *Worcester Address*, 41.

[1] See *e.g.*, Letter from Jonathan Sewall to Edward Winslow, 10 November 1773, Miscellaneous Manuscripts Bound, XIV, Massachusetts Historical Society.

another. Adams deserves special attention in this respect. Too often otherwise cautious historians represent him as a typical colonial lawyer with typical experiences and attitudes. No doubt much of the emphasis on Adams stems from the richness of the primary data relating to him and the general paucity of information that exists in this area, but one suspects that the reliance on Adams also reflects an unconscious urge to find in Adams the symbol of emerging professionalism. There are many weaknesses in such an approach. To depict Adams as a typical Massachusetts lawyer runs the same risks as depicting Jefferson as a typical Virginia planter, or Franklin as a typical Philadelphia printer. Obviously all three men had much in common with their colleagues, but they also differed from them in significant aspects. Adams' feeling of professional identity may be one of these aspects. It is highly likely that Adams had a professional commitment much deeper than that of most of his colleagues. Yet even his identification was far from complete. While most of his writing seems to indicate a strong devotion to his profession, he had his moments of disenchantment, moments when he was ready to abandon the law for other pursuits.[2]

Perhaps the most important aspect of any professional culture is what motivates its members. Ideally, a professional is "service oriented," which means that actions are based not on self-interest, but on the perceived needs of clients and the good of the community.[3] This service orientation should not be confused with altruism. Professionals seek personal gain as much as those of any other occupational group, but must operate in a different institutional setting.[4] They usually seek at least some professional monopoly and auton-

[2] See, e.g., Letter from John Adams to Abigail Adams, 29 June 1774, in Adams Correspondence, I, 113; Letter from John Adams to Abigail Adams, 1 July 1774, in Adams Correspondence, I, 119.

[3] Roscoe Pound contended that the "spirit of public service" was the essence of a profession. R. Pound, The Lawyer From Antiquity to Modern Times (St. Paul, 1953), 9–10. See also Moore, "Professions," 13–15; B. Barber, "Some Problems in the Sociology of the Professions," in the Professions in America, K. S. Lynn ed. (Cambridge, Mass., 1965), 18. In recent times, this orientation has often been formalized in a code of ethics which emphasizes the proper relations with colleagues, clients, and others outside the occupational group. E. C. Hughes, Men and Their Work, 46–47.

[4] T. Parsons, "The Professions and Social Structure," Social Forces, XVII (1939), 457–467.

omy, specifically sole rights to deliver specific services and rights to determine, at least in part, when, how, and by whom these services should be rendered. While their claim to such privileges could rest on their claim to sole possession of the requisite knowledge, this in itself is unlikely to achieve their desired status. Society must be convinced that the profession will not abuse its privileges. Thus professional altruism really represents a bargain between society and a profession. It is the price a profession must pay for monopoly.[5]

On the whole, the regular practitioners in Massachusetts seemed to grasp the idea that their position in society was directly dependent upon their maintaining certain standards of ethics and competence, but this recognition was by no means consistent or universal. Shady dealings by members of the bar were not unknown and two rather common practices did the bar no credit. Lawyers were in the habit of purchasing notes, usually at a discount, and then taking the debtor to court for satisfaction. Less frequent, but more odious, was the behavior of some lawyers in taking "hush money." After hiring the statutory maximum of two lawyers to present his case, a litigant would pay other prominent attorneys a retainer—"hush money"—not to take his opponent's case, thus depriving his adversary of his choice of legal counsel.[6]

While the members of the pre-Revolutionary Massachusetts bar did virtually nothing to check these abuses, they moved in other ways toward reinforcing the service ideal. Demands for strict educational requirements represent the greatest effort in this respect. Although such demands undoubtedly stemmed, in part, from a desire to reduce competition, they also may have resulted from a sincere

[5] In colonial Massachusetts, the practice which attorneys sought to monopolize largely involved routine actions for the collection of debts. *Superior Court Docket Books for Massachusetts Counties* (1757–1773), Massachusetts Historical Society. Disputes involving land constituted another significant portion of the lawyer's business. See *Adams Legal Papers*, I, li (nature of lawyer's business in eighteenth-century Massachusetts). See also E. Brown, *Joseph Hawley; Colonial Radical* (New York, 1931), 51 (description of Joseph Hawley's practice in western Massachusetts).

[6] See *Massachusetts Acts & Resolves*, I, ch. 3, 622 (1708–9). For an example of how the system worked, see Letter from John Adams to Josiah Quincy, October 1761, in Adams, *Diary*, I, 223. Adams refused to accept "hush money." Even William Cushing purchased notes at a discount. J. Cushing, "A Revolutionary Conservative: The Public Life of William Cushing 1732–1810," Unpublished Ph.D. Dissertation, Clark University, 1960, 55–57.

intention to improve the quality of the bar and thus, indirectly, to improve the position of individual practitioners.

The apprenticeship system of legal training was better than no training. Yet the apprenticeship stage of legal education may not have been as important in establishing the "character" of the bar as were the four years of required liberal education that preceded it. The liberal education that the few colonial colleges offered was designed to instill in their students the values of a gentleman, especially those of virtue and public service.[7] By restricting the supply of new lawyers to such a source, the colonial bar may have assumed that the

[7] S. E. Morison, *Three Centuries of Harvard, 1636–1936* (Cambridge, Mass., 1963), 22–25; G. C. Brauer, Jr., *The Education of a Gentleman: Theories of Gentlemanly Education in England, 1660–1775* (New Haven, 1959), 13–28, 34–42. There were several indications of an improving social position of the bar, one of which was the growing number of Harvard graduates choosing careers in law. Of the 741 Harvard men who took degrees from 1642 to 1720, over one-half followed clerical pursuits. During the same period forty-three became doctors, and only fourteen by any stretch of the imagination could be called lawyers. In the period from 1720 to 1760, while the clergy still represented the most popular professional choice, it represented approximately one-third of the graduates. During the same forty years, 121 men chose medicine and sixty-seven chose the law. Twenty-seven of these new lawyers graduated between 1751 and 1760. See Appendix II: "Professional Choices of Harvard Graduates: 1642–1760."

Of equal, if not more, significance was the fact that, by the late 1740's, the leading Bay Colony families no longer spurned the practice of law. By 1760 some of the most prominent names in Massachusetts—Winslow, Leonard, Dudley, Sewall, Quincy, and Willard—were listed on the roles of the legal profession, *i.e.*, Pelham Winslow (Harvard College, 1753), Daniel Leonard (H. C., 1760), George Leonard (H. C., 1743), Joseph Dudley (H. C., 1751), Jonathan Sewall (H. C., 1748), David Sewall (H. C., 1755), Samuel Quincy (H. C., 1754), and Abel Willard (H. C., 1752). The practice of law had gained a stature by 1760 which Adams, six years out of Harvard College, could only admire:

> For let the smart sayings of the gay, and the grave Satyrs, even of the wise and learned be what they will, I have for my own Part, and I thank God for it no bad Opinion of the Law, either as a science, or a Profession. . . .
> Multitudes of needless Matters and some that are nonsensical, it must be confessed have in the Course of Ages, crept into the Law. But I beg to know, what Art or Science can be found in the whole Circle, that has not been taught by silly, senseless, Pedants, and is not stuffed with their Crudities and Jargon. . . .
> But if the Grandeur and Importance of a subject, has any share in the Pleasure it communicates, I am sure that Law has by far the advantages of most other sciences.
> Nothing less that the Preservation of the Health and Properties, Lives and Tranquility, Moralls and Liberties of Millions of the human species, is the object and Designs of the Law, and a Comparision of Several Constitutions of Government, invented for those Purposes, an Examination of the great Causes of their Danger, as well as those of their safety, just be as Agreeable an Employment as can exercise the Mind. Adams, *Diary*, I, 196–197.

bar's character inevitably must improve. Such a faith in liberal education arguably did away with the need for a formal code of ethics for
the colonial Massachusetts bar. Establishing such formal rules would
have been tantamount to denying a lawyer's status as a gentleman.[8]

The attack on pettifoggers in the early 1760's, originating in part
from a desire to reduce competition, also represented a sincere effort
on the part of some lawyers to rid the colony of what they considered
a real evil. John Adams set the tone, blaming the "dirty, quacking
practice" for multiplying lawsuits, propagating a "brawling, wrangling Temper," and leading to the destruction of honest men.[9] The
bar's foray against pettifoggers, couched as it was in terms of public
service, was a justification for its claim to a monopoly of legal services
which it hoped would result.

Success was impossible unless individual lawyers united behind
the effort. Such unity was not forthcoming in the 1760's. James
Otis' violent opposition to the anti-pettifogger resolutions is a case
in point. According to John Adams' jaundiced view, Otis originated
the proposals in order to force some of the pettifoggers to work for
him and only opposed them to "save his popularity, with the Constables, Justices Story and Ruddock & Co. and Pettifoggers of the
town, and with pettifoggers that he uses as tools and Mirmidons in
the House."[1] If Otis did hope to use pettifoggers as "underworkers"
to help him in his practice, he was not alone. Several leading lights
of the bar apparently employed unsworn attorneys to assist with
their business.[2]

Unable to present a united front, the Massachusetts lawyers were
hamstrung in their pursuit of the "ultimate value for self-identified
members of an occupational category — autonomy in their own affairs."[3] Although they attempted to control education, admission to

---

[8] Moore, "Professions," 114.

[9] *Diary*, I, 137. Adams had little good to say about the "pettifoggers." See, *e.g.*,
Diary, I, 70, 132–133, 135–137.

[1] *Diary*, I, 236. As to Adams' motivation in attacking the pettifoggers, see R. Zemsky,
*Merchants, Farmers, and River Gods: An Essay on Eighteenth Century American
Politics* (Boston, 1971), 86–87. See Nathaniel Ames, *An Astronomical Diary: Or,
Almanack For The Year of our Lord Christ, 1765* (Boston, 1765), for a layman's
view of pettifoggers.

[2] Adams, *Diary*, I, 136.

[3] Moore, "Professions," 16.

practice, and the norms of practice, the bar found that it had to share this control with the provincial legislature and judiciary. The bar could set educational requirements, but the courts could and did swear in uneducated attorneys. The bar could recommend young men to practice, but the courts made the final decision. The court could disbar lawyers without the bar's consent.[4] The fee table was in the hands of the legislature.[5] By 1770 the Massachusetts bar had won a certain degree of autonomy in its own affairs, but this autonomy was tenuous at best and subject to strains and tensions.

The failure to gain autonomy, the uncertain struggles against the pettifoggers, and the halting movement toward better education and organization highlight the degree to which Massachusetts lawyers in the decades immediately prior to the American Revolution defy definition, at least as a collective body, in modern professional terms. Professional practices and attitudes were riddled with exceptions and qualifications. Too often the process of professionalization has been depicted as a professionally attuned leadership driving a less enlightened membership from one discernible professional plateau to another.[6] Whether or not this has been true in recent times, it simply was not the case in eighteenth-century Massachusetts. Not only was the professional impetus spread unevenly among Massachusetts lawyers, but certain individuals were more "professional" in some aspects of their business than in others. Leaders in some areas of professionalization were laggards in others. Otis, the erudite lawyer, allegedly encouraged uneducated amateurs as "underworkers." Benjamin Kent, who presided over meetings of the Suffolk bar, reputedly ignored the interest of his clients.[7] If these lawyers were part professionals, they also were part free-wheeling legal entrepreneurs.

[4] Joseph Hawley, for example, was disbarred for one year for attacking a Superior Court decision in the press. R. Taylor, *Western Massachusetts in the Revolution* (Providence, 1954), 55.

[5] *Acts and Resolves*, I, 374.

[6] See B. Bernard, "Some Problems in the Sociology of the Professions," in *The Professions in America*, K. S. Lynn *et al.*, eds., 22.

[7] J. L. Sibley and C. K. Shipton, *Biographical Sketches of Graduates of Harvard University* (Cambridge, Mass.), VIII (1951), 224–225. See also Adams, *Diary*, I, 160, where Adams claims that Richard Dana, another venerable member of the bar, put his interests before those of his clients.

APPENDIX I

OCCUPATION AND EDUCATION OF JUDGES OF THE MASSACHUSETTS
SUPERIOR COURT: 1692–1774

Name	Term	Education	Years on Inf. Ct.	Occupation
William Stoughton	C.J. 1692–1701	*H.C. (1650)		Minister
Thomas Danforth	J. 1692–1699			Gentleman
Waite Winthrop	J. 1692–1701 C.J. 1701 C.J. 1708–1717			Physician
John Richards	J. 1692–1694			Merchant
Samuel Sewall	J. 1692–1718 C.J. 1718–1728	H.C. (1671)		Minister
Elisha Cooke	J. 1695–1702 C.J. 1703–1708	H.C. (1657)		Physician
John Walley	J. 1700–1712			Soldier
John Saffin	J. 1701–1702			
Isaac Addington	C.J. 1702–1703		9 years	Physician
John Hawthorne	J. 1702–1712			
John Leverett	J. 1702–1708	H.C. (1680)		
Jonathan Curwin	J. 1708–1715		16 years	Merchant

* Harvard College and class hereafter represented as "H.C. (class year)."

Name	Term	Education	Years on Inf. Ct.	Occupation
Benjamin Lynde	J. 1712–1728 C.J. 1728–1745	H.C. (1686)		Barrister
Nathaniel Thomas	J. 1712–1718		10 years	
Addington Davenport	J. 1715–1736	H.C. (1689)		Barrister
Edmund Quincy	J. 1718–1745	H.C. (1699)		Gentleman
Paul Dudley	J. 1718–1745 C.J. 1745–1751	H.C. (1690)		Barrister
John Cushing	J. 1728–1733		26 years	
Jonathan Remington	J. 1733–1745	H.C. (1696)	18 years	Tavern-keeper; part-time lawyer
Richard Saltonstall	J. 1736–1756	H.C. (1722)		Gentleman
Thomas Graves	J. 1738–1739	H.C. (1703)	5 years	Physician
Stephen Sewall	J. 1739–1752 C.J. 1752–1760	H.C. (1721)		Tutor at H.C.
Nathaniel Hubbard	J. 1745–1747	H.C. (1698)	17 years	
Benjamin Lynde, Jr.	J. 1746–1771 C.J. 1771–1772	H.C. (1718)	7 years	Gentleman
John Cushing, Jr.	J. 1748–1771		8 years	
Chambers Russell	J. 1752–1766	H.C. (1731)	5 years	Gentleman

26. Stephen Sewall (1702–1760) by Benjamin Feke (*circa* 1755). Chief Justice, Superior Court of Judicature. Courtesy, Harvard Law School Art Collection.

Name	Term	Education	Years on Inf. Ct.	Occupation
Peter Oliver	J. 1756–1772 C.J. 1772–1775	H.C. (1730)	9 years	Merchant
Thomas Hutchinson	C.J. 1760–1771	H.C. (1727)	6 years	Merchant
Edmund Trowbridge	J. 1767–1775	H.C. (1728)		Lawyer
Foster Hutchinson	J. 1771–1775	H.C. (1743)	13 years	Merchant
Nathaniel Ropes	J. 1772–1774	H.C. (1745)	11 years	Merchant
William Browne	J. 1774–1775	H.C. (1775)	4 years	Gentleman
William Cushing	J. 1774–1775	H.C. (1751)		Lawyer

APPENDIX II

PROFESSIONAL CHOICES OF HARVARD GRADUATES: 1642–1760

TABLE A

Professional Choices of Harvard Graduates: 1642–1760

Year	Graduates	Law (%)	Medicine (%)	Ministry (%)
1642	9		2 (22.2)	4 (44.4)
1643	4			3 (75.0)
1644	None			
1645	7			4 (57.1)
1646	4		2 (50.0)	2 (50.0)
1647	7			5 (71.4)
1648	None			
1649	5			4 (80.0)
1650	9			5 (55.5)
1651	10			5 (50.0)
1652	1			1 (100.0)
1653	17			8 (47.1)
1654	1			
1655	2			1 (50.0)
1656	8		1 (12.5)	7 (87.5)
1657	7		1 (14.3)	5 (71.4)
1658	7	1 (14.3)		5 (71.4)
1659	10		1 (10.0)	6 (60.0)
1660	8			2 (25.0)
1661	12		2 (16.7)	4 (33.3)
1662	6		1 (16.7)	2 (33.3)
1663	6			3 (50.0)
1664	7		1 (14.3)	4 (57.1)
1665	8			3 (37.5)
1666	4		1 (25.0)	1 (25.0)
1667	7		1 (14.3)	4 (57.1)
1668	5			3 (60.0)
1669	10		1 (10.0)	7 (70.0)
1670	4			2 (50.0)
1671	11			7 (63.6)
1672	None			
1673	4			2 (50.0)
1674				

Year	Graduates	Law (%)	Medicine (%)	Ministry (%)
1675	9		1 (11.1)	6 (66.6)
1676	3			2 (66.6)
1677	6			4 (66.6)
1678	4			3 (75.0)
1679	4			2 (50.0)
1680	5		1 (20.0)	3 (60.0)
1681	9		1 (11.1)	4 (44.4)
1682	None			
1683	3			3 (100.0)
1684	9			7 (77.7)
1685	14	1 (7.1)		5 (35.7)
1686	7	1 (14.3)		2 (28.6)
1687	11		1 (9.1)	6 (54.5)
1688	None			
1689	14	1 (7.1)	1 (7.1)	6 (42.8)
1690	23	1 (4.3)		13 (56.5)
1691	8			5 (62.5)
1692	8			4 (50.0)
1693	16		2 (12.5)	11 (68.9)
1694	8			5 (62.5)
1695	23	2 (8.7)	3 (13.0)	9 (39.1)
1696	9	1 (11.1)	1 (11.1)	5 (55.5)
1697	14	1 (7.1)	1 (7.1)	10 (71.4)
1698	14		1 (7.1)	7 (50.0)
1699	12			7 (58.3)
1700	15		1 (6.7)	8 (53.3)
1701	19			9 (47.4)
1702	14			4 (28.6)
1703	14		1 (7.1)	9 (64.3)
1704	5	1 (20.0)	1 (20.0)	2 (40.0)
1705	11	1 (9.1)		6 (54.6)
1706	7		1 (14.3)	5 (71.4)
1707	19	1 (5.3)	1 (5.3)	11 (57.9)
1708	13		1 (7.7)	8 (61.5)
1709	10			6 (60.0)
1710	14	1 (7.1)		9 (64.3)
1711	12			5 (41.7)
1712	20		1 (5.0)	6 (30.0)
1713	6			2 (33.3)
1714	11		1 (9.1)	6 (54.6)

1715	20		1 (5.0)	9 (45.0)
1716	8		1 (12.5)	3 (37.5)
1717	17		1 (5.9)	10 (58.8)
1718	23	1 (4.3)	2 (8.7)	5 (21.7)
1719	27		2 (7.4)	15 (55.6)
1720	21	1 (4.8)	1 (4.8)	16 (76.2)
1721	31	1 (3.2)	3 (9.7)	19 (61.3)
1722	32	3 (9.3)	1 (3.1)	9 (28.1)
1723	43	1 (2.3)	1 (2.3)	18 (41.9)
1724	40		5 (12.5)	16 (40.0)
1725	49	1 (2.0)	7 (14.3)	20 (40.8)
1726	34	1 (2.9)	7 (20.6)	8 (23.5)
1727	37	1 (2.7)	1 (2.7)	6 (16.2)
1728	48	2 (4.2)	2 (4.2)	15 (31.3)
1729	28	1 (3.6)	2 (7.1)	12 (42.9)
1730	33	1 (3.0)	2 (6.1)	15 (45.5)
1731	34	5 (14.7)		13 (38.2)
1732	27	1 (3.7)	2 (7.4)	11 (40.7)
1733	39	2 (5.1)	1 (2.6)	17 (43.6)
1734	27	1 (3.7)	4 (14.8)	9 (33.3)
1735	38	2 (5.3)	4 (10.5)	12 (31.6)
1736	31		3 (9.7)	10 (32.3)
1737	32	2 (6.3)	5 (15.6)	17 (53.1)
1738	35	3 (8.6)	4 (11.4)	12 (34.3)
1739	32	2 (6.3)	5 (15.6)	9 (28.1)
1740	23			6 (26.1)
1741	25		2 (8.0)	12 (48.0)
1742	26		2 (7.7)	6 (23.1)
1743	31	3 (9.7)	4 (12.9)	11 (35.5)
1744	30		4 (13.3)	9 (30.0)
1745	24	1 (4.2)	1 (4.2)	6 (25.0)
1746	12	1 (8.3)	4 (33.3)	3 (25.0)
1747	29	1 (3.4)	7 (24.1)	10 (34.5)
1748	24	2 (8.3)	3 (12.5)	8 (33.3)
1749	22	1 (4.5)	3 (13.6)	7 (31.8)
1750	19	1 (5.3)	2 (10.5)	7 (36.8)
1751	35	7 (20.0)	3 (8.6)	10 (28.6)
1752	30	2 (6.7)	4 (13.3)	15 (50.0)
1753	17	1 (5.9)	1 (5.9)	7 (41.2)
1754	20	1 (5.0)	4 (20.0)	9 (45.0)
1755	24	3 (12.5)	2 (8.3)	9 (37.5)
1756	25	2 (8.0)	4 (16.0)	4 (16.0)
1757	26	4 (15.4)	4 (15.4)	6 (23.1)
1758	32	1 (3.1)	3 (9.3)	12 (37.5)

Year	Graduates	Law (%)	Medicine (%)	Ministry (%)
1759	35	2 (5.7)	4 (11.4)	15 (42.9)
1760	26	4 (15.4)	3 (11.5)	10 (38.5)

Source: Sibley and Shipton, *Harvard Graduates*, I–XIV.

TABLE B
Professional Choices of Harvard Graduates: 1696–1760
Percent Per Five Year Period

Years	Graduates	Law (%)	Medicine (%)	Ministry (%)
1696–1700	64	2 (3.1)	4 (6.3)	37 (57.8)
1701–1705	63	2 (3.2)	2 (3.2)	30 (47.6)
1706–1710	63	2 (3.2)	2 (3.2)	39 (61.9)
1711–1715	69		3 (4.3)	28 (40.6)
1716–1720	96	2 (2.1)	7 (7.3)	49 (51.0)
1721–1725	195	6 (3.1)	17 (8.7)	82 (42.1)
1726–1730	180	6 (3.3)	14 (7.8)	56 (31.1)
1731–1735	165	11 (6.7)	11 (6.7)	62 (37.6)
1736–1740	153	7 (4.6)	17 (11.1)	54 (35.3)
1741–1745	136	4 (2.9)	13 (9.6)	44 (32.3)
1746–1750	106	6 (5.7)	19 (17.9)	35 (33.0)
1751–1755	126	14 (11.1)	14 (11.1)	50 (39.7)
1756–1760	144	13 (9.0)	18 (12.5)	47 (32.6)

Source: Sibley and Shipton, *Harvard Graduates*, IV–XIV.

APPENDIX III

GEOGRAPHICAL DISTRIBUTION OF THE THREE CLASSES OF
MASSACHUSETTS LAWYERS IN 1775, TOGETHER WITH
LOYALTY PATTERNS BY GEOGRAPHICAL AREA AND AGE

For a detailed analysis, see McKirdy, "A Bar Divided: The Lawyers of Massachusetts and the American Revolution," *American Journal of Legal History*, XVI (1972), 205.

TABLE A

Geographical Distribution of the Three Classes of Massachusetts Lawyers

	Maine (12.3%)[a]	North (19.8%)	Suffolk (19.8%)	West (33.3%)	South (14.8%)
Sup. Ct. Bar.	5 (12.2)[b]	10 (24.4)	11 (26.8)	8 (19.5)	7 (17.1)
Sup. Ct. Att.	0	1 (10.0)[c]	1 (10.0)	6 (60.0)	2 (20.0)
Inf. Ct. Att.	5 (16.7)[d]	5 (16.7)	4 (13.3)	13 (43.3)	3 (10.0)

[a] Percent of total lawyers in Massachusetts in 1775 (taking 81 lawyers as 100%).
[b] Percent of total barristers in Massachusetts in 1775 (taking 41 as 100%).
[c] Percent of Superior Court attorneys in Massachusetts in 1775 (taking 10 as 100%).
[d] Percent of Inferior Court attorneys in Massachusetts in 1775 (taking 30 as 100%).

TABLE B

Loyalty Patterns of the Three Classes of Massachusetts Lawyers by Geographical Area: 1775

	Maine		North		Suffolk		West		South	
	T[a]	P	T	P	T	P	T	P	T	P
Sup. Ct. Bar.	1	4	7	3	6	5	5	3	2	4
Sup. Ct. Att.	0	0	0	0	0	1	4	2	0	2
Inf. Ct. Att.	0	4	1	3	0	4	5	4	0	1

[a] T represents those lawyers who were Loyalists; P represents those who were rebels. Neutral lawyers or those of unknown loyalty are not represented in the table.

TABLE C

Loyalty Patterns of the Three Classes of Massachusetts Lawyers
by Age: 1775

Age Group	25–35		36–45		46–55		56–65		Over 65	
Loyalty	Ta	P	T	P	T	P	T	P	T	P
Sup. Ct. Bar.	7	5	6	7	5	3	2	1	1	3
Sup. Ct. Att.	2	2	2	2	0	0	0	1	0	0
Inf. Ct. Att.	2	9	2	4	0	2	0	0	2	1

a Neutral lawyers or those of unknown loyalty are not represented in this table.

APPENDIX IV

BIOGRAPHICAL SKETCHES OF LAWYERS PRACTICING IN
MASSACHUSETTS IN 1775

Lawyers Practicing in Massachusetts in 1775

JOHN ADAMS (1735–1826). Born in Braintree (Suffolk Co.), the son of John Adams, a farmer. Harvard College (1755); ranked fourteenth in a class of twenty-five. Studied law in Worcester with James Putnam (later a Tory refugee) and taught Worcester school. Admitted to the Suffolk Bar in 1758; admitted barrister at Superior Court in 1762. In 1775, probably the leading lawyer in Massachusetts. Representative to General Court for Boston (1770). House chose him for Council in 1773 and 1774, but the Governor negatived him both times. Active whig in politics before the war. Elected Vice President (1788, 1792) and President (1796) of the United States. *Dictionary of American Biography*, I, 72–82. Patriot.

JONATHAN ALLEN (1734–1784). Born in Chilmark (Martha's Vineyard), the son of Colonel John Allen, Sheriff and lawyer. Harvard College (1757); ranked tenth in a class of twenty-nine. Practiced in Chilmark and farmed. Small practice. Representative to General Court for Chilmark (1761, 1767, 1769–1770, 1773). General Court appointed him a Justice of the Peace (1775), but he refused the commission. Sibley and Shipton, *Harvard Graduates*, XIV, 125. Neutral.

OAKES ANGIER (1745–1786). Harvard College (1764). Studied law in Boston with John Adams (Patriot) from about 1766–1768. Admitted as an attorney to the Superior Court (May 1771), as a barrister (August 1773). Practiced in Bridgewater (Plymouth County). Equivocal in his politics before the war. Representative to General Court for Bridgewater (1776, 1778–1779). *Adams Legal Papers*, I, xcvi. Reluctant Patriot.

JOHN ASHLEY (1709–1802). Born in Westfield (Hampshire County), the son of Colonel John Ashley, one of the proprietors of Great Barrington and Sheffield in Berkshire County. Yale College (1730). Practiced in Sheffield and rose to distinction as a lawyer. Colonel in the militia, a representative to the General Court, Judge of the Inferior Court of Common Pleas (1761–1781). Dexter, *Yale Graduates*, I, 405–406. Unknown.

ROBERT AUCHMUTY (ca. 1723–1788). Born in Boston, the son of Robert Auchmuty of the Middle Temple and Judge of the Admiralty. Admitted to Harvard College (1746), but never matriculated. Probably studied law with his father. Admitted as an attorney to the Superior Court (1752), as a barrister (1762). Practiced in Boston and was highly successful. Advocate General in

Admiralty (1762–1767), Judge of the Massachusetts Vice Admiralty Court (1767–1776), and a Justice of the Peace and Quorum (1769–1776). An addresser of Hutchinson in 1774. Proscribed (1778). Sibley and Shipton, *Harvard Graduates*, XII, 12–16; *Adams Legal Papers*, I, xcvi. Tory Refugee.

JONATHAN WILLIAMS AUSTIN (1751–1779). Born in Boston, the son of Benjamin Austin. Harvard College (1769). Studied law with John Adams (Patriot) in Boston. Admitted to Suffolk Bar (1772). Practiced in Chelmsford (Middlesex County). Major in the Massachusetts forces and Continental infantry (1775–1776). *Adams Legal Papers*, I, xcvi. Patriot.

SAMUEL BARRETT (1738/9–1798). Born in Boston, the son of Deacon Samuel Barrett. Harvard College (1757); ranked sixteenth in a class of twenty-nine. Turned to law after failure as a merchant with his father. Practiced in Boston. Law clerk to Justice Peter Oliver (ca. 1770). Justice of the Peace (1774). Town committees. Muster Master in Middlesex (1777). After the Revolution he was a Justice of the Peace and Quorum (1780–1798) and a judge of the Inferior Court of Common Pleas appointed in 1789. Sibley and Shipton, *Harvard Graduates*, XIV, 135–142. Patriot.

DANIEL BLISS (1739/40–1806). Born in Concord (Middlesex County), the son of the Reverend Daniel Bliss. Brother of Jonathan Bliss (Tory Refugee). Harvard College (1760); ranked eleventh in a class of twenty-seven. Studied law with Abel Willard of Worcester (Tory Refugee). Admitted to the Worcester Bar (1765), as an attorney of the Superior Court (1768), as a barrister (1772). Practiced first in Worcester; moved to Concord in 1772. Justice of the Peace (1767). An addresser of Hutchinson in 1774. Proscribed in 1778. Commissary in the British army during the Revolution. Later a member of the Council and Judge of the Court of Common Pleas in New Brunswick. Sibley and Shipton, *Harvard Graduates*, XIV, 563–566. Tory Refugee.

JONATHAN BLISS (1742–1822). Born in Concord, the son of the Reverend Daniel Bliss. Brother of Daniel Bliss (Tory Refugee). Harvard College (1763). Probably studied with Thomas Hutchinson. Practiced in Springfield (Hampshire County). Admitted to the Superior Court as an attorney (1768), as a barrister (1772). Representative to the General Court (1768–1769). One of the seventeen "Rescinders" who voted to withdraw resolutions protesting the Townshend Acts (1768). Appointed Justice of the Peace (1768). Proscribed in 1778. In 1785 appointed Attorney General of New Brunswick; Chief Justice there from 1809 to 1822. *Dictionary of American Biography*, II, 374–375. Tory Refugee.

MOSES BLISS (1736–1814). Born in Springfield, the son of Jedediah Bliss, a tanner. Yale College (1755); ranked sixteenth in a class of twenty-three. Studied theology and licensed to preach in 1757. Studied law with John Worthington (Tory) in Springfield. Admitted to the Hampshire Bar (1761) and as an attorney at the Superior Court (1763). Practiced in Springfield. Appointed a Justice of the Peace in 1769 and of the Quorum in 1771. Quit town offices out of lack of sympathy with the popular cause. After war represented Springfield in the General Court (1796–1797) and served as a Judge on the Inferior Court of Common Pleas (1798–1810). Dexter, *Yale Graduates*, I, 365–366. Tory Sympathizer.

SAMPSON SALTERS BLOWERS (1742–1842). Born in Boston. Harvard College (1763). Said to have read law with Thomas Hutchinson. Admitted to Suffolk Bar (1766), as an attorney to the Superior Court (1768), and as a barrister (1772). Practiced in Boston. Married to daughter of Benjamin Kent (Patriot). An addresser to Hutchinson in 1774. Served as a Judge of the Royal Court of Vice Admiralty in Rhode Island (1779): as Solicitor General of New York (1780–1783); and as Attorney General, Speaker of the House, Councilor, and, from 1797 to 1833, Chief Justice and President of the Council in Halifax, Nova Scotia. *Dictionary of American Biography*, II, 393–394. Tory Refugee.

SHEARJASHUB BOURNE (1746–1806). Born in Barnstable. Harvard College (1764). Admitted as an attorney to the Superior Court (1767), as a barrister (1772). Practiced in Barnstable County. Appointed a Justice of the Peace in 1773. Signed address to Hutchinson in 1774, but recanted. Represented Barnstable in the General Court (1782–1785, 1788–1790), United States Congress (1791–1795), and Chief Justice of the Suffolk County Inferior Court of Common Pleas (1799–1806). *Adams Legal Papers*, I, xcvii. Reluctant Patriot.

THEOPHILUS BRADBURY (1739–1803). Born in Newbury (Essex County), the son of Captain Theophilus Bradbury, a mariner. Harvard College (1757); ranked twenty-second in a class of twenty-nine. Taught Falmouth (Cumberland County, Maine) school until 1761. Admitted to Cumberland Bar (1762), as an attorney to the Superior Court (1765), and as a barrister (1767). Practiced in Falmouth. Justice of the Peace (1768). Protested radical meetings in Falmouth, but the British shelling of the town changed his mind. Attorney General of Cumberland County (1777–1779), state senator (1791–1792), United States Congress (1795–1796), appointed Justice of the Peace (1783), and sat on the Supreme Judicial Court of Massachusetts (1797–1803). Sibley and Shipton, *Harvard Graduates*, XIV, 143–146. Reluctant Patriot.

WILLIAM BRATTLE (1706–1776). Born in Cambridge (Middlesex County), the son of Parson William Brattle. Harvard College (1722); ranked first in a class of thirty-two. Tried preaching, medicine, then took up law. Practiced in Cambridge where he was elected selectman in 1729 and twenty times thereafter. Many times sent to General Court and Council (1755–1769). Appointed major in the militia (1729), Colonel, General (1758–1760), Brigadier (1762) and Major General (1773). Special justice of the Superior Court (1749). Appointed Justice of the Peace in 1729. Headed anti-Hutchinson group until about 1773 when he became a Tory. Signed address to Hutchinson in 1774. Sibley and Shipton, *Harvard Graduates*, VII, 10–23. Tory.

JOHN BROWN (1744–1780). Born in Haverhill (Essex County), the son of Daniel Brown. Yale College (1771). Studied law with his brother-in-law, Oliver Arnold, of Providence, Rhode Island. Practiced in Caughnawaga (Johnstown), New York where he was appointed King's attorney. Moved to Pittsfield (Berkshire County) in 1773. Delegate to First Provincial Congress (1774). Lieutenant Colonel under Benedict Arnold in Quebec campaign. Colonel in Berkshire militia. Representative to General Court (1778) and Judge of Common Pleas (1779). Killed in the war. Dexter, *Yale Graduates*, III, 404–406. Patriot.

ANDREW CAZNEAU (ca. 1734–1792). Brother-in-law of Daniel Leonard (Tory Refugee). Admitted as an attorney to the Superior Court in 1765 and as a barrister in 1767. Practiced in Boston. Addressed Hutchinson in 1774 and Gage in 1775. Fought with British in defense of New York. Proscribed in 1778. Marshal of the Rhode Island Vice Admiralty Court (1780), Judge of the Vice Admiralty Court and member of the Council, Bermuda (1780–1783). Returned to Boston in 1788. *John Adams Legal Papers*, I, xcviii. Tory Refugee.

NATHANIEL CHANDLER (1750–1801). Born in Worcester. A son of Colonel John Chandler and brother of Rufus Chandler (Tory). Harvard College (1768). Studied law with James Putnam (Tory Refugee) in Worcester. Admitted to Worcester Bar in 1771 and practiced in Petersham (Worcester County). Commanded a corps of volunteers in the British service during the Revolution. Returned to Petersham in 1784 as a merchant. A better lawyer than his brother. Willard, "Address to the Worcester Bar," 64. Tory.

RUFUS CHANDLER (1747–1823). Born in Worcester, the son of Colonel John Chandler and the brother of Nathaniel Chandler (Tory). Harvard College (1766). Studied law with James Putnam (Tory Refugee) in Worcester. Admitted to Worcester Bar in 1768 and as an attorney to the Superior Court in 1771. Left country during the war. Willard, "Address to the Worcester Bar," 62–63. Tory.

ROLAND CUSHING (1750–1788). Born in Scituate (Plymouth County), the son of John Cushing of the Superior Court and a brother of William Cushing (Patriot). Harvard College (1768). Studied law with his brother William in Pownalborough (Lincoln County, Maine). Practiced in Lincoln County, then York County. William Willis, *A History of the Law, the Courts, and the Lawyers of Maine, From its first Colonization to the Early Part of the Present Century* (Portland: Bailey & Noyes, 1863), 99. Hereinafter referred to as *Lawyers of Maine*.) Unknown.

WILLIAM CUSHING (1732/33–1810). Born in Scituate, the son of Justice John Cushing and the brother of Roland Cushing (Unknown). Harvard

College (1751); ranked third in a class of thirty-six. Taught Roxbury (Suffolk County) school in 1752. Studied law with Jeremiah Gridley. Admitted as an attorney in the Superior Court in 1758 and as a barrister in 1762. Practiced in Scituate (1755–1760) and in Pownalborough (1760–1772). Appointed a Justice of the Peace and Quorum (1761), Judge of Probate (1761), and Justice of the Superior Court (1772). Kept political views to himself, but would not take grant from the Crown. Appointed a Judge of the Superior Court (1772–1775, 1775–1777); Chief Justice, Supreme Judicial Court (1777–1789); Justice, Supreme Court of the United States (1789–1810). Sibley and Shipton, *Harvard Graduates*, XIII, 26–39. Patriot.

FRANCIS DANA (1743–1811). Born in Charlestown (Middlesex County), the son of Richard Dana, a lawyer and Justice of the Peace. Harvard College (1762). Studied law with his maternal uncle, Edmund Trowbridge (Tory) for five years. Admitted as an attorney of the Superior Court in 1768, as a barrister in 1772. Practiced in Cambridge. Although not a radical, became identified with Sons of Liberty because of his opposition to British policy. Served on Massachusetts Council (1776–1780), was a delegate to Continental Congress (1777–1779), secretary to John Adams' legation in France (1779–1780), and was the unrecognized minister of the United States to Russia (1781–1783). Appointed to Massachusetts Supreme Judicial Court (1785); named Chief Justice, Massachusetts Supreme Judicial Court (1791–1806). *Dictionary of American Biography*, v, 52–54. Patriot.

JUSTIN ELY (1739–1817). Born in West Springfield (Hampshire County), the son of Ensign John Ely. Harvard College (1759); ranked twenty-fifth in a class of forty-five. For a brief period he was a storekeeper. Admitted to the Hampshire Bar in 1771. Practiced in West Springfield. During the Revolution served eight years on the Massachusetts Committee of War Supplies. Representative to the General Court (1777, almost every year between 1780 and 1798). Justice of the Peace and Quorum (1788). Sibley and Shipton, *Harvard Graduates*, XIV, 422–423. Patriot.

DANIEL FARNHAM (1719–1776). Born in York (York County, Maine). Harvard College (1739); ranked twenty-fourth in a class of thirty-two. Studied law with Edmund Trowbridge (Tory). Admitted an attorney of the Superior Court in 1745, a barrister in 1762. Practiced in Newburyport (Essex County), a town he helped to found. A selectman and representative to the General Court. Appointed Attorney General of York County (1744) and a Justice of the Peace and Quorum in Essex County (1752). Made a good living from the law. At first boldly denounced the whigs, but later moderated his views. Sibley and Shipton, *Harvard Graduates*, x, 364–366. Tory Sympathizer.

SAMUEL FITCH (1724–1799). Born in Lebanon, Connecticut, the son of Joseph Fitch, a substantial farmer. Yale College (1742); ranked sixth in a class of seventeen. Admitted an attorney in the Superior Court in 1754, a barrister in 1762. Practiced in Boston; never did really well. Appointed a Captain in the militia (1746), Justice of the Peace (1762), Advocate General pro tempore of the Admiralty (1768–1770), Advocate General of the Admiralty (1770–1776) and a Deputy Judge of Admiralty (1768). Addressed Hutchinson (1774) and Gage (1775). Proscribed in 1778. Dexter, *Yale Graduates*, I, 706–707; Sibley and Shipton, *Harvard Graduates*, XI, 144–147. Tory Refugee.

ENOCH FREEMAN (1706–1788). Born in Eastham (Barnstable County), the son of Captain Samuel Freeman. Harvard College (1729); ranked seventeenth in a class of twenty-eight. Carried on trade as a merchant for a while. Practiced in Falmouth, Maine. Served in the General Court (1756– , 1774) and held many appointive positions including Judge of Common Pleas, Judge of Probate (1770), and Justice of the Peace. Organized the revolutionary movement in Cumberland County. Muster Master of Militia (1775). Sibley and Shipton, *Harvard Graduates*, VIII, 572–581. Patriot.

DAVID GORHAM (1712–1786). Born in Barnstable, the son of Colonel Shubael Gorham, who was a member of the Council. Harvard College (1733); ranked tenth in a class of thirty-nine. Tried whaling and trading before law. Admitted to the Superior Court as an attorney in 1766. Practiced in Barnstable. Appointed Register of Probate (1740) and Justice of the Peace and Quorum (1753). Signed address to Hutchinson, but mob forced him to recant. Held minor offices after the war, but denied a Commission as Justice of the Peace. Sibley and Shipton, *Harvard Graduates*, IX, 300–303. Reluctant Patriot.

BENJAMIN GRIDLEY (1732–before 1800). Harvard College (1751); ranked sixteenth in a class of thirty-six. A Commissary in the French and Indian War. Admitted as an attorney and barrister at the Superior Court (1762). Small practice in Boston. Appointed Justice of the Peace (1774) and Judge of the Court of Common Pleas (1775). Attacked whigs in newspapers (1765), as a J. P. acted against mobs, signed address to Hutchinson (1774) and Gage (1775). Served in Timothy Ruggles' Loyalist Corps. Sibley and Shipton. *Harvard Graduates*, XIII, 90–94. Tory Refugee.

JOSEPH HAWLEY (1723–1788). Born in Northampton (Hampshire County), the son of Lieutenant Joseph Hawley. Yale College (1742); ranked fourth in a class of seventeen. Served as a chaplain in the Louisburg expedition and studied theology with his cousin, Jonathan Edwards. Studied law with Phineas Lyman of Suffield (Hampshire County now part of Connecticut). Admitted as an attorney to the Superior Court in 1751, as a barrister in 1762. Practiced in Northampton where he was a selectman almost every year from 1747 to 1777. Appointed Justice of the Peace (1749) and of the Quorum (1762). A Major in the militia. Often stood for Northampton in the General Court where he was the most active whig from the west. Elected to Council in 1769. Urged independence early. Declined to serve in Continental Congress in 1774. Elected to General Court (1775–1777). A learned lawyer with a large practice, but after 1776 developing mental illness forced him to withdraw from professional and public life. Critic of Massachusetts Constitution of 1780, refused to serve in state senate because of religious test imposed. Dexter, *Yale Graduates*, I, 709–712. Patriot.

MARK HOPKINS (1739–1776). Born in Waterbury (Berkshire County), the son of Captain Timothy Hopkins. Yale College (1758); ranked fourteenth in a class of forty-three. Admitted to the Berkshire Bar in 1761, as a barrister in the Superior Court in 1765. Practiced in Great Barrington (Berkshire County) where he was the town clerk and the representative to the General Court (1773–1774). Appointed Register of Deeds (1761) and Justice of the Peace (1766). An early rebel, he served on the Committee of Correspondence. Major in the continental army; died in its service. Dexter, *Yale Graduates*, II, 536–537. Patriot.

JAMES HOVEY (1712–1781). Before he became a lawyer he was a joiner. Admitted as an attorney to the Superior Court in 1752, as a barrister in 1762. Practiced in Plymouth County. Appointed Justice of the Peace (1760) and of the Quorum (1764). Washburn, *Judicial Sketches*, 238; *Adams Legal Papers*, I, cii. Unknown.

DAVID INGERSOLL (1742–1796). Born in Great Barrington, the son of Captain David Ingersoll, a discredited businessman. Yale College (1765). Admitted to Berkshire Bar (1765) and as an attorney to the Superior Court (1768). Practiced in Great Barrington which sent him to the General Court. Appointed a Justice of the Peace in 1767. Signed address to Hutchinson (1774). Rebels tarred and feathered him. Proscribed in 1778. Dexter, *Yale Graduates*, II, 698–699. Tory Refugee.

BENJAMIN KENT (1708–1788). Born in Charlestown (Middlesex County), the son of Joseph Kent. Harvard College (1727); ranked thirty-sixth of thirty-seven. Taught Framingham school then turned to preaching as a Congregationalist minister. Dismissed by an ecclesiastical council after a heresy trial in 1735, but won a long civil suit for his back salary in 1737. Admitted as an attorney to the Superior Court in about 1739, as a barrister in 1762. Practiced in Boston where he reputedly handled "dirty" actions. Served on many town committees. A Son of Liberty and correspondent of John Wilkes. Called for independence very early. Appointed Attorney General (1776) and served as Attorney General for Suffolk County (1777–1785). Sibley and Shipton, *Harvard Graduates*, VIII, 220–230. Patriot.

TIMOTHY LANGDON (ca. 1746–1808). Harvard College (1765). Practiced in Wiscasset (then part of Pownalborough), Maine. Before the Revolution was a Crown Lawyer. Served in Provincial Congress (1776) and Admiralty Judge for Maine (1778). Willis, *Lawyers of Maine*, 98–99. Patriot.

DANIEL LEONARD (1740–1829). Born in Norton (Bristol County), the son of wealthy Colonel Ephraim Leonard. Harvard College (1760); ranked third in a class of twenty-seven. Studied law with Samuel White of Taunton (Bristol County). Married White's daughter and succeeded to his practice. Admitted an attorney to the Superior Court in 1765, a barrister in 1767. Practiced in Taunton. Representative to the General Court (1769–1772, 1773–1774). Appointed Justice of the Peace (1767) and King's Attorney for Bristol County (1769). Addresser of Hutchinson and Mandamus Councilor (1774). Author of Tory "Massachusettensis" papers. Appointed solicitor to the Customs Commissioners (1775). Proscribed in 1778. Admitted to Inner Temple in 1779. Chief Justice of Bermuda from 1782 to 1806 when he returned to practice in England where he was a leading barrister until his death. Sibley and Shipton, *Harvard Graduates*, xiv, 640–648. Tory Refugee.

GEORGE LEONARD (1729–1819). Born in Norton, son of the Honorable George Leonard, a wealthy ironmonger. Harvard College (1748); ranked third in a class of twenty-nine. Admitted to Bristol Bar; would not take cases that would take him away from home. Practiced in Norton where he served as town clerk, selectman, moderator, treasurer, and Representative to the General Court (1764–1768). Nominated to Council in 1770 and regularly thereafter. Appointed Register of Probate (1748), Justice of the Peace (1754) and Quorum (1762), and colonel in the militia (1772). At first supported Hutchinson, but then became a consistent whig. Elected to the first Congress of the United States and again in 1794. Served in the General Court (1801–1802). Appointed Judge of Probate Court (1785) and Judge of Inferior Court of Common Pleas (1787). Sibley and Shipton, *Harvard Graduates*, xii, 281–282. Patriot.

ZEPHANIAH LEONARD (1736–1814). Born in Raynham (Bristol County), the son of the Honorable Major Zephaniah Leonard. Yale College (1758); ranked ninth in a class of forty-three. Attorney of the Superior Court. Practiced in Raynham which sent him to the General Court (1768–1769, 1771, 1777–1778). Appointed a Justice of the Peace in 1768. Ardent rebel. Appointed High Sheriff of Bristol County in 1776 and served until 1808. Colonel in the militia. Dexter, *Yale Graduates*, ii, 545–546. Patriot.

WOODBRIDGE LITTLE (1740–1813). Born in Hartford, Connecticut, the son of Dr. Nathaniel Woodbridge. Yale College (1760). A licensed preacher, he quit the ministry for law and was admitted to the bar in 1764. Practiced in Pittsfield (Berkshire County). Appointed Justice of the Peace in 1770. Opposed the popular party; one of the tory leaders in the west. In 1775 fled to New York, but was captured. In 1777 took an oath to the United States and volunteered to serve in the army. Representative to the General Court (1788–1790). Dexter, *Yale Graduates*, ii, 664–666. Tory.

JONATHAN LORING (1719–1782). Born in Sudbury (Middlesex County), the son of the Reverend Israel Loring. Harvard College (1738);

ranked sixth in a class of thirty-five. Taught Sudbury school for a while. Admitted an attorney to the Superior Court in about 1740. Had a meager practice in Marlborough (Middlesex County). Refused to sign boycott of British goods in 1774, but had three sons who served in the revolutionary army. Sibley and Shipton, *Harvard Graduates*, x, 298–299. Unknown.

JOHN LOWELL (1743–1802). Born in Newbury (Essex County), the son of the Reverend John Lowell. Harvard College (1760); ranked seventh in a class of twenty-seven. Studied law with Oxenbridge Thacher in Boston. Admitted to bar (1763), as a Superior Court attorney (1765), and as a barrister (1767). Practiced in Newburyport until moved to Boston in 1776. Appointed Justice of the Peace (1769). Opposed those who opposed the Stamp Act (1765), refused to join embargo of British goods (1767), and signed address to Hutchinson (1774); recanted a few months later. Representative to General Court (1776, 1778, 1780), to Continental Congress (1782–1783), and to state senate (1784–1786). Appointed Justice of the Peace (1775) and Quorum (1780), Judge of the United States Admiralty Court of Appeals (1782), Judge of the United States District Court of Massachusetts (1789), and Chief Justice of the United States Court of the First Circuit (1801). Sibley and Shipton, *Harvard Graduates*, xiv, 650–661. Reluctant Patriot.

DAVID MITCHELL (1728–1796). Born in Pembroke (Plymouth County), the son of Deacon Jacob Mitchell. Harvard College (1751); ranked twenty-sixth in a class of thirty-six. Taught Falmouth school, preached for a while, and taught North Yarmouth (Cumberland County, Maine) school before turning to law. Never officially admitted to the bar, but practiced in North Yarmouth where he served as the town clerk from 1762 to his death. Appointed Justice of the Peace in 1764. Served on the local committee of correspondence, but not a firebrand. Provincial Congress (1775) and General Court (1791). Appointed Colonel of Militia (1775), Justice of the Peace (1775), Special Justice of the Cumberland Court of Common Pleas (1775), Judge of the Inferior Court of Common Pleas (1778), Chief Justice (1781), and a state senator (1791). Sibley and Shipton, *Harvard Graduates*, xiii, 116–118. Patriot.

PEREZ MORTON (1751–1837). Harvard College (1771). Studied law with Josiah Quincy (Patriot) in Boston. Practiced in Boston. One of few Massachusetts lawyers who supported Jefferson. State Attorney General (1810–1832). Warren, *History of the American Bar*, 318n. Patriot.

DANIEL MURRAY (ca. 1750–1830). Born in Rutland (Worcester County), the son of Colonel Murray. Harvard College (1771). Practiced in Rutland. Became Major in British dragoons when war broke out. Willard, "Address to Worcester Bar," 83n. Tory.

DAVID NOBLE (1744–1803). Born in New Milford, Connecticut. Yale College (1764). Probably read law with Woodbridge Little (Tory) in Pittsfield. Practiced in Williamstown (Berkshire County). Later became a merchant.

Appointed Judge of Common Pleas (1795). Dexter, *Yale Graduates*, III, 78. Unknown.

DANIEL OLIVER (1743–1826). A nephew of Chief Justice Peter Oliver. Harvard College (1762). Admitted to Suffolk Bar (1776), as an attorney at the Superior Court (1768), and as a barrister (1772). Practiced in Hardwick in Worcester County which he represented in the General Court in 1770 and 1771. Appointed Justice of the Peace in 1768. Addressed Hutchinson in 1774. Proscribed in 1778. Died in England. *Adams Legal Papers*, I, civ. Tory Refugee.

JAMES OTIS, SR. (1702–1778). Father of James Otis, Jr. (Patriot). Self-taught lawyer. Admitted as an attorney to the Superior Court in 1731, as a barrister in 1762. Practiced in Barnstable and Plymouth Counties. Appointed Justice of the Peace (1734) and Quorum (1748), Attorney General (1748), and Chief Justice of the Barnstable Inferior Court of Common Pleas and Judge of Probate Court (1764). Disappointed in his aspirations to sit on the Superior Court by the appointment of Thomas Hutchinson in 1760 which supposedly turned his son against the Crown. Represented Barnstable in the General Court (1745–1756), Speaker (1760–1761), Councilor (1762–1774; negatived, 1767–1769). First Revolutionary Council (1775–1776). *Adams Legal Papers*, I, cv. Patriot.

JAMES OTIS, JR. (1725–1783). Born in Barnstable, the son of James Otis (Patriot). Harvard College (1743); ranked thirteenth in a class of thirty-nine. Studied law with Jeremiah Gridley of Boston. Admitted a Superior Court attorney in 1750, a barrister in 1762. After 1749 practiced in Boston: one of the most able and successful lawyers of the period. Representative to General Court (1761–1769, 1771) and elected Speaker in 1766, but the Governor disallowed. One of the leaders of the Patriot party in the House. Appointed Justice of the Peace (1756) and Advocate General in Admiralty (ca. 1756). Turned against Crown in 1760 supposedly over Hutchinson's appointment as Chief Justice in preference to Otis' father. Resigned as Advocate General (1761). Argued famous writs of assistance case. His political dealings and the logic of his pamphlets often cast doubt on his loyalty to the Patriot cause. After attack on his person by Customs Commissioner John Robinson, Otis' madness, from which he had suffered periodically, grew worse and forced him into retirement. Killed by a bolt of lightning as he stood in his doorway watching a storm. Sibley and Shipton, *Harvard Graduates*, XI, 247–287. Patriot.

SETH PADDLEFORD (1751–1810). Born in Taunton. He practiced in Hardwick (Worcester County) until 1775 when he moved back to Taunton. Appointed Attorney General of Bristol County (1776), County Treasurer (1783), and Judge of Probate (1792). Dexter, *Yale Graduates*, III, 390–391. Unknown.

ROBERT TREAT PAINE (1731–1814). Born in Boston, the son of

Thomas Paine, a once-wealthy merchant. Harvard College (1749); ranked ninth in a class of twenty-six. From 1749 to 1757, variously schoolteacher, merchant, whaler, preacher, and law student. Studied law with Benjamin Prat. Admitted to Suffolk Bar in 1757, as an attorney to the Superior Court in 1758, and as a barrister in 1762. Practiced in Taunton and Boston. Appointed Justice of the Peace (1763). Represented Taunton in General Court (1773–1775, 1779); Speaker (1777–1778). A strong whig. Delegate to Continental Congress; signed Declaration of Independence. Declined seat on the Superior Court four times between 1775 and 1784. State Attorney General (1777–1790). Council (1775, 1780). Justice, Massachusetts Supreme Judicial Court (1790–1804). Sibley and Shipton, *Harvard Graduates*, XII, 462–482. Patriot.

THEOPHILUS PARSONS (1750–1813). Born in Byfield (Essex County), the son of the Reverend Moses Parsons. Harvard College (1769). Taught Falmouth school for a brief period. Studied law with Theophilus Bradbury (Reluctant Patriot) and Edmund Trowbridge (Tory Sympathizer). Admitted to the Cumberland Bar in 1774, as an attorney of the Superior Court in 1776, and as a barrister in about 1784. Practiced in Falmouth (1774–1775), Newburyport (1775–1800), and Boston. Leading lawyer of the post-war generation. Author of *Essex Result*, report of the Essex Convention in opposition to the proposed state Constitution of 1778. Representative to General Court (1779, 1787–1791, 1805) and Chief Justice of Massachusetts Supreme Judicial Court (1806–1813). *Dictionary of American Biography*, XIV, 271–273. Patriot.

TIMOTHY PICKERING (1745–1829). Born in Salem (Essex County), the son of Timothy Pickering. Harvard College (1763). Admitted to Essex Bar (1768), but never practiced in earnest or with much distinction. Practiced in Salem where he held town office and served as a representative to the General Court. Appointed a lieutenant in the militia (1766). An early advocate of the Revolution, he wrote pamphlets and served on various committees. Adjutant-General of the Continental Army (1777) and Quarter-master General (1780–1783). United States Senate (1803–1811) and House of Representatives (1813–1817). United States Post-master General (1791–1795), Secretary of War (1795), and Secretary of State (1795–1800). Massachusetts Executive Council (1812–1813). Before war had been Register of Deeds (1774) and Colonel in militia (1775). *Dictionary of American Biography*, XIV, 565–568. Patriot.

ELISHA PORTER (1742–1796). Harvard College (1761). Admitted to Hampshire Bar and practiced in Hampshire County. Colonel in Continental Army and present at Saratoga. High Sheriff of Hampshire County during and after war. Notes at the beginning of Elisha Porter Papers, Massachusetts Historical Society. Patriot.

SAMUEL PORTER (1743–1798). Harvard College (1763). Studied law with Daniel Farnham (Tory Sympathizer) in Newburyport. Admitted an attorney at the Superior Court in 1768 and as a barrister in 1772. Practiced in Essex County. Addressed Hutchinson (1774) and Gage (1775). Proscribed in 1778. *Adams Legal Papers*, I, cvi. Tory Refugee.

JAMES PUTNAM (1726–1789). Born in Danvers (Essex County), the son of James Putnam who owned a large farm. Harvard College (1746); ranked twelfth in a class of thirteen. Studied law with Edmund Trowbridge (Tory Sympathizer). Admitted to Worcester Bar (ca. 1748), as an attorney to the Superior Court (1749), and as a barrister (1762). Practiced in Worcester where held many town offices. Has been called ablest lawyer in America at this time. Appointed Lieutenant Colonel in militia (1756) and Justice of the Peace (1758) and Quorum (1762). Declined office of Attorney General (1768). Drew the Worcester protest against whig actions in 1774, signed addresses to Hutchinson (1774) and Gage (1775), and was considered an obdurate Tory. Appointed Attorney General (1775) by Gage. Captain in the Second Company of Loyal American Associates. Proscribed in 1778. Appointed Senior Judge and Member of Council of New Brunswick (1784). Sibley and Shipton, *Harvard Graduates*, XII, 57–66. Tory Refugee.

WILLIAM PYNCHON (1723–1789). Born in Springfield, the son of Colonel William Pynchon. Harvard College (1743); ranked fourth in a class of thirty-nine. Studied law with Mitchel Sewall, Clerk of Courts for Essex County. Admitted an attorney at Superior Court (1757) and a barrister (1762). Practiced in Salem and became the head of the Essex Bar. Justice of the Peace (1761). Signed address to Hutchinson (1774), but recanted. Addressed Gage (1775). Watched Revolution. Law partnership with William Wetmore (Reluctant Patriot) after war. Appointed Justice of Peace and Quorum (1786). Sibley and Shipton, *Harvard Graduates*, XI, 295–301. Tory.

JOSIAH QUINCY, JR. (1744–1775). Born in Boston, the son of Josiah Quincy who was a prosperous merchant. His brother was Samuel Quincy (Tory Refugee). Often called "the Patriot" to distinguish him from his father ("the Colonel") and his son ("the President"—of Harvard). Harvard College (1763). Studied law with Oxenbridge Thacher. Admitted to Suffolk Bar (1766) and as an attorney to the Superior Court (1768), but never called as a barrister perhaps because of political beliefs. Author of *Reports of Cases Argued and Adjudged in the Superior Court . . . 1761–1772* (Boston, 1865). Practiced in Boston and was a successful lawyer. Radical leader, newspaper writer, pamphleteer, and orator. Died returning from unsuccessful attempt to reconcile England and the colonies. *Dictionary of American Biography*, xv, 307–308. Patriot.

SAMUEL QUINCY (1734–1789). Born in Braintree (Suffolk County), the son of Josiah Quincy and the brother of Josiah Quincy, Jr. (Patriot). Harvard College (1754); ranked third in a class of twenty. Studied law with Benjamin Prat. Admitted to Suffolk Bar in 1758, as an attorney to Superior Court in 1761, and as a barrister in 1762. Appointed Justice of the Peace and Solicitor General in 1771. Addressed Hutchinson and Gage (1774). Proscribed in 1778. Customs officer and successful barrister in Antigua and elsewhere in West Indies (1779–1789). Sibley and Shipton, *Harvard Graduates*, XIII, 478–488. Tory Refugee.

WILLIAM READ (1710–1780). Son of John Read (1680–1749), the leading lawyer in Massachusetts in the first half of the eighteenth century. Probably studied law with his father. Admitted an attorney at the Superior Court in 1759, a barrister in 1762. Appointed Deputy Judge of the Vice Admiralty Court (1766), Judge of the Suffolk Inferior Court of Common Pleas (1770), and to the Superior Court (1775—declined). *Adams Legal Papers*, I, cviii. Reluctant Patriot.

JEREMIAH DUMMER ROGERS (ca. 1743–1784). Born in Littleton (Middlesex County). Harvard College (1762). Studied law with Robert Auchmuty (Tory Refugee). Admitted an attorney in the Superior Court (1769) and a barrister (1772). Practiced in Littleton. Appointed a Justice of the Peace in 1766. An addresser of Hutchinson in 1774. Served with Tory Corps in Boston. Proscribed in 1778. Became wine merchant in Halifax in 1776. *Adams Legal Papers*, I, cviii. Tory Refugee.

TIMOTHY RUGGLES (1711–1795). Born in Rochester (Plymouth County), the son of the Reverend Timothy Ruggles. Harvard College (1732); ranked ninth in a class of twenty-seven. Admitted to Plymouth Bar in 1733 where he was the great rival of James Otis, Sr. (Patriot). Also kept a tavern. Practiced in Rochester until 1737 when moved to Sandwich (Plymouth County). Moved to Hardwick (Worcester County) in 1753. Appointed Captain in the militia (1740), Colonel (1755), and Brigadier General (1758). Appointed a Justice of the Peace (1753), Judge of Inferior Court of Common Pleas (1757), Chief Justice of Inferior Court of Common Pleas (1762), and Surveyor of the King's Woods in New Hampshire (1770). Representative in General Court (1736, 1739–1740, 1743, 1746, 1751–1752, 1754–1771); Speaker (1762–1763) where he led the conservatives from 1766 to 1769. Delegate to Stamp Act Congress, but did not sign resolutions. Mandamus Councilor (1774). Raised a corps of tories (1775). Went to Nova Scotia (1783). Sibley and Shipton, *Harvard Graduates*, IX, 199–223. Tory.

NATHANIEL PEASELEE SARGEANT (1731–1791). Born in Methuen (Essex County), the son of Reverend Christopher Sargeant. Harvard College (1750); ranked tenth in a class of twenty-one. Taught Littleton school for a while. Admitted as an attorney at the Superior Court in 1764 and as a barrister in 1767. Practiced in Haverhill (Essex County). Justice of the Peace (1767). Delegate to the Second Provincial Congress (1775). General Court (1776). Appointed Justice of the Peace and Quorum (1775), to the Superior Court

(1776), and Chief Justice (1790). Sibley and Shipton, *Harvard Graduates*, XII, 574–580. Patriot.

THEODORE SEDGWICK (1746–1813). Born in West Hartford, Connecticut, the son of Benjamin Sedgwick who owned a small store. Yale College (1765). Studied law with his cousin, Mark Hopkins (Patriot) in Great Barrington. Admitted to Berkshire Bar in 1766, as an attorney to the Superior Court in 1771 and as a barrister after the war. Practiced in Great Barrington and Sheffield (Berkshire County) before the war; moved to Stockbridge in 1785. Early took an active part in opposition to Great Britain, but opposed independence as late as May, 1776. Served as military secretary to General John Thomas (1776). Representative to General Court (1780, 1782–1783, 1787–1788); Speaker (1788); a state senator (1784–1785); Continental Congress (1785–1788); United States Congress (1788–1796); United States Senate (1796–1799); Congress (1799–1801); and served on the Massachusetts Supreme Judicial Court (1802–1813). *Dictionary of American Biography*, XVI, 549–551. Patriot.

DAVID SEWALL (1735–1825). Born in York, Maine, the son of Samuel Sewall and cousin of Jonathan Sewall (Tory Refugee). Harvard College (1755); ranked tenth in a class of twenty-five. Studied law with Judge William Parker of Portsmouth, New Hampshire. Admitted a barrister at the Superior Court in 1763. Practiced in York where he was the only college-educated lawyer in the county. Appointed Register of Probate (1766) and Justice of the Peace (1767). Captain in the militia (1772). A timid whig. Appointed Register of Probate (1775), Justice of the Peace (1775), Judge of Superior Court (1777–1789), and Judge of the United States District Court for the District of Maine (1789–1818). Served on Council (1776–1777) and elected to General Court (1790), but was refused seat because of his judicial post. Sibley and Shipton, *Harvard Graduates*, 638–645. Reluctant Patriot.

JONATHAN SEWALL (1729–1796). Born in Boston, the son of Jonathan Sewall, a merchant who failed financially. Cousin of David Sewall. Harvard College (1748); ranked fifteenth in a class of twenty-nine. Kept various schools until 1756. Studied law with Judge Chambers Russell in Lincoln (Middlesex County). Admitted an attorney to the Superior Court in 1757, a barrister in 1762. Practiced in Charlestown (Middlesex County) where he held town offices. Appointed Justice of the Peace (1762); Solicitor General, Attorney General, and Advocate General in Admiralty (1767); and Judge of the new District Vice Admiralty Court to sit at Halifax (1769). An early friend of John Adams (Patriot), he was said to have turned to the Crown when a petition to clear the bankrupt estate of his uncle, the late Chief Justice Stephen Sewall, was rejected by the General Court after the Otises (Patriots) had promised to secure its passage. Defended Governor Bernard in newspapers (1766–1767), addressed

27. Theodore Sedgwick (1746–1813) by an unknown artist. Justice, Supreme Judicial Court. Courtesy, Harvard Law School Art Collection.

Hutchinson (1774) and Gage (1775), and served as one of Gage's chief advisors urging stronger methods. Still, never approved of British policies toward the colonies. Proscribed in 1778. Practiced law in New Brunswick (1787–1796), the Halifax Admiralty Court having been abolished. Sibley and Shipton, *Harvard Graduates*, xii, 306–324. Tory Refugee.

JOHN SPRAGUE (1740–1800). Born in Rochester. Harvard College (1765). Studied medicine and kept school in Roxbury (Suffolk County), but quit in 1766 to study law with James Putnam (Tory Refugee) in Worcester. Admitted to the Worcester Bar in 1768 and as an attorney at the Superior Court in 1771. Practiced in Rhode Island (1768–1769), New Hampshire (1769–1770), and finally settled in Lancaster (Worcester County) in 1770 where he went into partnership with Abel Willard (Tory Refugee). Only lawyer in Worcester County who was not a tory. Representative to the General Court for ten years and sat in the state senate in 1783 and 1785. Appointed a barrister (1784), legal advisor to General Lincoln in his expedition against Shays (1786), High Sheriff of Worcester County (1788–1792), and Chief Justice of the Inferior Court of Common Pleas (1798–1800). Willard, "Address to the Worcester Bar," 60–62. Patriot.

SOLOMON STODDARD (1736–   ). Born in Northampton. His father was an honorary colonel and cousin of Jonathan Edwards. Yale College (1756). Practiced in Northampton. Commissioned High Sheriff of Hampshire County (1768). Dexter, *Yale Graduates*, ii, 434–435. Tory Sympathizer.

CALEB STRONG (1745–1819). Born in Northampton, the son of Caleb Strong, a tanner. Harvard College (1764). Studied law with Joseph Hawley (Patriot) in Northampton. Practiced in Northampton where he was elected a Selectman in 1772. Served on the town committee of safety (1774–1783), as a Representative to the General Court (1776–1778), as a state senator (1780–1788), as United States Senator (1789–1796), and as Governor of Massachusetts (1800–1807, 1812–1816). *Dictionary of American Biography*, xviii, 144–146. Patriot.

SIMEON STRONG (1736–1805). Born in Northampton, the son of Nehemiah Strong. Yale College (1756). Preached for a while and then studied law with John Worthington (Tory) in Springfield. Admitted to the Worcester Bar in 1765, as an attorney to the Superior Court in 1765, and later as a barrister. Practiced in Amherst (Hampshire County). Representative to General Court (1767–1768, 1769–1770). Suspected of being a tory, he sat out the war, although probably he was not a tory, as indicated by his election to the Massachusetts Senate in 1793 and his appointment to the Supreme Judicial Court (1800–1805). Dexter, *Yale Graduates*, ii, 437–439. Patriot.

JAMES SULLIVAN (1744–1808). Born in Berwick (York County, Maine). Studied law with his brother, John Sullivan who was a general in the

Revolution and "President" of New Hampshire (1786–1787, 1789). Admitted as an attorney at the Superior Court in 1770, as a barrister in 1772. Practiced in York County until 1778 and thereafter in Groton (Middlesex County) and Boston. Appointed King's Attorney for York County and Justice of the Peace (1774). Served periodically in the Provincial Congress and the House (1775–1784). Judge of the Superior Court (1776–1782). Elected to Continental Congress (1783). One of few lawyers to become a Democrat early. State Attorney General (1790). Governor (1807, 1808). *Adams Legal Papers*, I, cx. Patriot.

SAMUEL SWIFT (1715–1775). Born in Milton (Suffolk County), the son of wealthy Colonel Samuel Swift. Harvard College (1735); ranked twenty-first in a class of forty. Studied for the ministry before taking up legal studies with Jeremy Gridley in Boston. Admitted an attorney to the Superior Court in 1761, a barrister in 1762. Practiced in Boston. Appointed Justice of the Peace in 1741, but not reappointed in 1760 when George III took the throne. A leading Son of Liberty, said to have been a manager of the Boston Tea Party. Served on Committee of Correspondence. Member of radical Possy Club. Handled many cases in court, but made little money. Died while under arrest by the British in Boston. Sibley and Shipton, *Harvard Graduates*, IX, 580–583. Patriot.

EZRA TAYLOR (ca. 1728–?). Practiced in Southborough (Worcester County) from about 1751 to the Revolution. Perhaps called to the bar, he carried on an extensive business preparing cases for other lawyers. Married Edmund Trowbridge's sister. Moved to Maine during the war and died there. Willard, "Address to the Worcester Bar," 54–55. Unknown.

EDMUND TROWBRIDGE (1709–1793). Raised by his uncle and guardian, Colonel Edmund Goffe of Cambridge whose name he used well into middle life. Harvard College (1728); ranked twenty-eighth in a class of forty-nine. Admitted an attorney to the Superior Court in 1732, a barrister in 1762. Practiced in Cambridge where he was a Selectman and served on many town committees. The master of the Middlesex and Worcester Bars who loved legal technicalities. Represented Cambridge in the General Court (1750–1752, 1755, 1763) and member of the Council (1764–1766) where he supported Crown policy. Appointed Justice of the Peace and of the Quorum (1739), Attorney General (1749–1767), and Judge of the Superior Court (1767–1775). Refused Royal salary grant in 1774 and remained neutral in the Revolution. Sibley and Shipton, *Harvard Graduates*, VIII, 507–520. Tory Sympathizer.

WILLIAM TUDOR (1750–1819). Son of Deacon John Tudor. Harvard College (1769). Studied law with John Adams (Patriot). Admitted to Suffolk Bar (1772). Judge Advocate of the Continental Army (1775–1778). Attorney of Supreme Judicial Court (1778) and barrister (1784). Practiced in Boston.

Justice of the Peace (1781), General Court (1779, 1791–1796), a state senator (1801–1803), Massachusetts Secretary of State (1809–1810), and Clerk of Supreme Judicial Court (1811–1819). *Adams Legal Papers*, I, cxii. Patriot.

JOSHUA UPHAM (1741–1808). Born in Brookfield (Worcester County), the son of Dr. Jabez Upham. Harvard College (1763). Admitted to Worcester Bar in 1765, as an attorney to the Superior Court in 1768, and as barrister in 1772. Practiced in Brookfield. Justice of the Peace (1769). Loyalist in sympathy, he recanted, but was proscribed in 1778. Appointed Advocate General of Rhode Island Admiralty Court (1779), but never served. Colonel in British Dragoons (1781–1782). Judge of Superior Court of New Brunswick and Councilor (ca. 1785–1808). *Adams Legal Papers*, I, cxiii. Tory Refugee.

EDWARD WALKER (1739–1801). Born in Boston, the son of Isaac Walker who was a merchant. Harvard College (1757); ranked fifteenth in a class of twenty-nine. Worked as a merchant with his father before studying law with Samuel Quincy (Tory Refugee). Admitted to Suffolk Bar (1775). Practiced in Boston where he held town offices although not very successful at the bar. Served as a Lieutenant in the Fourth Massachusetts Continentals (1777–1783). Practiced in Westfield (Hampshire County) from 1783 to 1793, in Blandford (Hampshire) from 1793 to 1796, in Pittsfield from 1796 to 1800, and in Lenox (Berkshire) from 1800 to 1801. Appointed Justice of the Peace in 1786, he was not reappointed when he moved to Berkshire County. His life after the war was one of hard times getting harder, and he died insolvent. Sibley and Shipton, *Harvard Graduates*, XIV, 233–234. Patriot.

WILLIAM WETMORE (1749–1830). Harvard College (1770). Studied with William Pynchon (Tory) in Salem. Admitted to Essex Bar in 1774. Practiced in Salem with Pynchon. Addressed Gage in 1774. General Court (1777). Admitted an attorney at the Superior Court (1776), a barrister in 1784. Chief Justice of Suffolk Inferior Court of Common Pleas and Associate Justice of the successor Massachusetts Court of Common Pleas (1807–1821). *Adams Legal Papers*, I, cxiii. Reluctant Patriot.

ABEL WILLARD (1732–1781). Born in Lancaster, the son of Colonel Samuel Willard who was a judge on the Court of Common Pleas. Harvard College (1752); ranked third in a class of thirty-two. Taught Lancaster School then studied with Benjamin Prat in Boston. Admitted to Worcester Bar in 1755 and as an attorney to the Superior Court in 1762. Practiced in Lancaster where he was elected a selectman and did much local business. Justice of the Peace and Quorum (1760). Addressed Hutchinson and Gage (1774). Proscribed in 1778. Died in England. Sibley and Shipton, *Harvard Graduates*, XIII, 301–303. Tory Refugee.

JONATHAN WILLIAMS (ca. 1751–1780). Son of John Williams who

was the Inspector General of the Customs. Harvard College (1772). Studied law with John Adams (Patriot). Admitted to Suffolk Bar (1775). Practiced in Worcester. Traveled to Europe for his health in 1779. Sibley and Shipton, *Harvard Graduate*, XII, 60–61 and *Adams Legal Papers*, I, cxiii. Unknown.

PELHAM WINSLOW (1737–1783). Born in Marshfield (Plymouth County), the son of Captain (later General) John Winslow of the British Army. Harvard College (1753); ranked second in a class of twenty. Studied law with James Otis, Jr. (Patriot). Admitted an attorney to the Superior Court in 1764, a barrister in 1767. Practiced in Plymouth where he held town office. Appointed Justice of the Peace in 1771. Addressed Hutchinson and Gage. In the Revolution was a British Major at Fort William, Deputy Commissary in New York (1777), and second-in-command of George Leonard's loyalist fleet (1779). Discouraged and embittered, he drank himself to death. Sibley and Shipton, *Harvard Graduates*, XIII, 374–377. Tory Refugee.

JOHN WORTHINGTON (1719–1800). Born in Springfield, the son of Lieutenant John Worthington. Yale College (1740); ranked thirteenth in a class of twenty-one. Studied theology and preached for a while. Studied law with Phineas Lyman of Suffield (then in Massachusetts, now in Connecticut). Admitted to Hampshire Bar in 1744, as attorney to the Superior Court in 1749, as a barrister in 1762. Practiced in Springfield where he was the leader of the Hampshire Bar. Representative to General Court (1747–1768, 1770–1774) and member of Council (1767–1768). King's Attorney, colonel in the militia (1754), Justice of the Peace (1748) and Quorum, and asked to serve as Attorney General and Justice of the Superior Court, but declined. Although approved of the Stamp Act Congress, he was never against the act. Appointed a Mandamus Councilor, but declined to serve. A tory, by 1778 he was reconciled and active again in politics and practice. Dexter, *Yale Graduates*, I, 658–660. Tory.

DAVID WYER (1741–1776). Born in Charlestown, the son of Captain David Wyer, a mariner. Harvard College (1758); ranked eighteenth in a class of thirty-seven. Kept school then studied with James Otis, Jr. (Patriot). Admitted to the Cumberland Bar in 1762, as an attorney to the Superior Court in 1765, and as a barrister in 1767. Practiced in Falmouth where he was one of the two lawyers in that county of Maine and did well. Often served as King's Attorney and was appointed Justice of the Peace in 1772. Sympathized with Hutchinson, although claimed not to be against the patriots' cause. Died in epidemic following the burning of Falmouth by the British. Others in his family were Tories. Sibley and Shipton, *Harvard Graduates*, XIV, 371–372. Tory Sympathizer.

JOHN WYETH (1743–1811). Born in Cambridge, the son of John Wyeth who was a selectman of that town. Harvard College (1760); ranked seventeenth in a class of twenty-seven. Tried the ministry, but was dismissed.

In 1773 he turned to the practice of law in his home town, but was untalented and only employed in humble suits. Had to keep a farm to make ends meet. Moved to Chelmsford in 1778; failed there and moved back to Cambridge. Generally regarded as a local character, although he was elected a Selectman. Sibley and Shipton, *Harvard Graduates*, xiv, 676–677. Unknown.

DANIEL R. COQUILLETTE

Justinian in Braintree: John Adams, Civilian Learning, and Legal Elitism, 1758–1775

> I have read about 10 pages in Justinian and Translated about
> 4 Pages into English. This is the whole of my Days Work. I
> have smoaked, chatted, trifled, loitered away this whole day
> almost. . . . But I am resolved to translate Justinian and his
> Commentators Notes by day light and read Gilberts Tenures
> by Night till I am master of both. . . . [*Diary*, 5 October 1758[1]]

> But, it is my Destiny to dig Treasures with my own fingers.
> No Body will lend me or sell me a Pick axe. [*Diary*, 18 De-
> cember 1758[2]]

I. INTRODUCTION: THE INFLUENCE OF CIVILIAN LEARNING
IN EARLY AMERICAN JURISPRUDENCE

WHAT influence did continental European jurisprudence, the civilian learning of the Roman-based civil law and of the European Enlightenment, have on the English colonies in America? Much ink has flowed on aspects of this topic, over issues as disparate as whether the characteristic American "district attorney" derived from the Dutch institution of the "schout" and whether Cicero was a "role model for early American lawyers."[3]

Note: To Professors Charles Donahue, Samuel Thorne, Harold Berman, and Andrew Kaufman at Harvard Law School, my teachers and friends, and to Catherine Menand, Theodore Chase, and Professor John Leubsdorf, who carefully examined this text, I owe a special debt.

[1] *Diary and Autobiography of John Adams*, L. H. Butterfield ed., 4 vols. (Cambridge, Mass., 1964), I, 45. (Hereafter cited as *Diary*.)

[2] Ibid., I, 63.

[3] See W. Scott Van Alstyne, Jr., "The District Attorney—A Historical Puzzle," *Wisconsin Law Review*, CXXV (1952); Stephen Botein, "Cicero as Role Model for Early American Lawyers: A Case Study in Classical 'Influence,'" *Classical Journal*, LXXIII (1977–1978), 313; Peter Stein, "The Attraction of the Civil Law in Post-Revolutionary America," *Virginia Law Review*, LII (1966), 403; Herbert A. Johnson, *The Law Merchant and Negotiable Instruments in Colonial New York 1664 to 1730* (Chicago, 1963).

Masterful studies have been done by Peter Stein on "The Attraction of Civil Law in Post-Revolutionary America" and by Herbert Alan Johnson on the law merchant in colonial New York. I certainly do not intend to make outrageous claims for civilian influence[4] or to populate the rural courthouses of America with Ulpians, Justinians, and home-spun Montesquieus. I put forward only one such "barn yard Justinian," and a very atypical one at that, John Adams.

Young Adams, sitting in Braintree as a neophyte lawyer in 1758, certainly saw himself as something of a classical Roman character. In his mind's eye an invisible toga often descended over his young shoulders, at least when he was not chasing the attractive Hannah Quincy in "Cupid's Grove."[5] Adjusting the imaginary folds of this toga, he wrote in his new diary: "Few of my Contemporary Beginners, in the Study of the Law, have the Resolution, to aim at much Knowledge in the Civil Law. Let me therefore distinguish my self from them, by the Study of the Civil Law, in its native languages, those of Greece and Rome."[6]

Adams was ever eager to put distance between his young self, humble in origin but Harvard educated, and what he perceived to be the rabble of "common" colonial lawyers, whom he characterized as "Petty foggers" and "dirty Dablers in the Law."[7] And he was ambitious. Even before he had met his role-models in the elite of the Boston bar, such as Jeremiah Gridley, James Otis, Benjamin Pratt, Benjamin Kent, and Oxenbridge Thacher, Adams felt the pressing need to be one of a select few.[8] A direct corollary, at least in his aspiring young mind, was the need to master the classics of both the civilian and the common law literature.

---

[4] Cf. Charles P. Sherman, *Roman Law in the Modern World*, I (Boston, 1937), 344–413.

[5] As to Adams' infatuation with Hannah Quincy, which occurred simultaneously with his first serious legal study, see *Diary*, I, 72–74. "And by Reason of my Inattention my mind is liable to be called off from Law, by a Girl. . . ." Ibid., I, 72. See also below, page 380, note 8.

[6] Ibid., I, 44–45.

[7] Ibid., I, 137–138.

[8] Ibid., I, 44–46, 54. See the helpful biographical register of Adams' contemporaries in *Legal Papers of John Adams*, L. K. Wroth and H. B. Zobel, eds. (Cambridge, Mass., 1965), I, xcv–cxiv, (hereafter cited as *Legal Papers*); and the useful biographical list of lawyers practicing in Massachusetts in 1775 attached as Appendix

28. John Adams (1735–1826) by Benjamin Blyth (*circa* 1766). The earliest portrait of Adams, painted after he had started his career as a lawyer. Courtesy, Massachusetts Historical Society.

Adams started out his legal career in rural Worcester. He had gone there after Harvard to teach school. Teaching school was one way to avoid the family pressure to become a minister, but Worcester was dull. The best source of intellectual and social excitement was the occasional visits of the circuit judges to the local courthouse.[9] In 1756 Adams signed up for the usual legal apprenticeship. His master was James Putnam, a Worcester attorney.

Life with Putnam was not all roses. Adams would later lament that "[n]ow I feel the Disadvantages of Putnams Insociability, and neglect of me. Had he given me now and then a few Hints concerning Practice, I should be able to judge better at this Hour than I can now."[1] Nevertheless, Putnam had a good library. It was, according to Adams, "not large: but he had all the most essential Law Books: immediately after I entered with him however he sent to England for a handsome Addition of Law Books and for Lord Bacons Works."[2] And Adams read. By his contemporary account he did, while at Worcester, read "Wood. Coke. 2 Vols. Lillies Ab[ridgemen]t. 2 Vols. Salk [eld's] Rep[orts]. Swinburne. Hawkins Pleas of the Crown. Fortescue. Fitzgibbons. Ten Volumes in folio I read, at Worcester, quite thro—besides Octavos and Lesser Volumes, and many others of all sizes that I consulted occasionally, without Reading in Course as Dictionaries, Reporters, Entries, and Abridgements, Etc."[3]

On completion of his Worcester apprenticeship, Adams returned to his native Braintree to seek his fortune in law practice. But he had a problem. His primary need was to gain admission to the Suffolk

IV to C. R. McKirdy's "Massachusetts Lawyers on the Eve of the American Revolution: The State of the Profession, above, 339–358.

[9] See *Legal Papers*, I, ii–liii. "Moreover, amidst rural boredom, the law was hardly an arid study but the principal entertainment after church-going. . . ." Ibid., liii. Braintree was hardly a "hot spot." As Adams wrote to his friend John Wentworth, "Here, no Idea of a Lady, of Diversions . . . or of Pleasure ever enters. . . . Old Roman Lawyers, and dutch Commentators are my constant Companions." *The Earliest Diary of John Adams*, L. H. Butterfield, ed. (Cambridge, Mass., 1966), 64. (Hereafter cited as *Earliest Diary*.)

[1] *Diary*, I, 63.

[2] *Diary*, III, 264. Adams recalls that he brought with him to Worcester "Lord Bolingbrokes Study and Use of History, and his Patriot King," which made Putnam "so well pleased" that they were added to Putnam's book seller order. Ibid., III, 264.

[3] Ibid., I, 173.

bar, and that would require being put forward by some influential Boston lawyers. What to do? His first act, the day after arriving from Worcester, was to go to the Harvard College Library and take out "Justinians Institutions with Arnold Vinnius's Notes."[4] Why? "I shall gain the Consideration and perhaps favour of Mr. Gridley and Mr. Pratt [patriarchs of the Boston bar] by this means."[5]

He was not far from the mark. In Adams' fateful call on Gridley three weeks later, to obtain Gridley's crucial support for his bar application, Gridley cross-examined him on his education, emphasizing the need to study the "civil Law, and natural Law, and Admiralty Law."[6] Adams particularly recalled being asked if he had read Grotius and Pufendorf, whom Gridley described as "great writers."[7] Adams had to make lame excuses. "I cannot say I have Sir. Mr. Putnam read them, when I was with him, and as his Book lay on the Desk in the office for the most part when he had it not in his hand, I had generally followed him in a cursory manner, so that I had some very imperfect Idea of their Contents. . . ."[8] "[B]ut," Adams hastily added, it was his "intention to read them both as soon as possible."

Fortunately, because of his cram efforts with Vinnius on his arrival from Worcester, Adams was better able to answer another question. What, Gridley inquired, had Adams "lately read" in Latin? Adams answered proudly, "Cicero's Orations and Epistles, and the last Latin I read was Justinians Institute with Vinnius's Notes."[9] Gridley, at that point, took Adams to his library and lent Adams a copy of Van Muyden's *Compendiosa Institutionum Justiniani Tractatio In Usum Collegiorum*.[1] In Gridley's opinion this text was better for Adams,

---

[4] *Diary*, I, 44. This was probably the Leyden 1730 edition. See ibid., I, 45, note 3.

[5] Ibid., I, 45.

[6] Ibid., I, 55.

[7] Ibid., III, 272.

[8] Ibid., III, 271–272. According to Adams' recollection in his *Autobiography*, he had been able to mention that he had read "Burlamaqui . . . and Heineccius in Turnbulls Translation, and Turnbulls Moral Phylosophy" as books "upon the Law of Nature and Nations." Ibid., III, 271. There are substantial differences between the *Diary* and the *Autobiography* accounts of the meeting with Gridley. Cf. ibid., I, 54–56; III, 270–272, but the emphasis on neoclassical learning was present in both accounts.

[9] Ibid., III, 271.

[1] Ibid., I, 56.

29. Purported to be Jeremiah Gridley (1701/1702–1767). Attorney General,
Justice of the Peace and of the Quorum. Courtesy,
Harvard Law School Art Collection.

JOHANNIS van MUYDEN *Jer. Gridley*

Jo: JCti & Antecessoris *Campbell*

COMPENDIOSA *J. Adams,*

INSTITUTIONUM

JUSTINIANI

TRACTATIO

In Usum

COLLEGIORUM.

Editio tertia prioribus Auctior & Emendatior.

ULTRAJECTI.

Ex Officina GUILIELMI vande WATER, Academiæ Typographi, cIɔ Iɔc ccvII

30. The Gridley-Adams copy of Johannis Van Muyden's *Compendiosa Institutionum Justiniani Tractatio* (Utrecht, 1707). This book was loaned by Jeremiah Gridley to John Adams in 1758 and bought by Adams from Gridley's estate after 1767. Courtesy, Boston Public Library.

Vinnius being "a Commentator more suitable for Persons, of more advanced Age and longer research, than yours."[2] Adams recalled, years later, how he was utterly dumbfounded by Gridley's "handsome library of the civil and Cannon Laws and Writers in the Law of Nature and Nations."

Adams next dutifully called on Benjamin Prat and James Otis. They also cross-examined Adams on his classical training and asked him why he had omitted being sworn in the Worcester Inferior Pleas Court and had failed to get the usual letter of recommendation from Putnam.[3] But, nevertheless, "Mr. Otis received me more like a Brother than a father, and began to descant on Homer and Horace and Latin and Greek Prosody."[4]

As a result of his efforts Adams was routinely sworn in at the Suffolk bar on 6 November 1758. He had no formal legal education and only a two years' apprenticeship in the countryside.[5] But he could talk about Cicero. As Gridley put it to the Court, on moving Adams' application, "I take it he is qualified to study the Law by his scholarship. . . ."[6]

So Cicero and Justinian helped Adams get sworn at the bar. But what practical use did civilian learning—the civil law jurisprudence of the neoclassicists and the European Enlightenment—have in Braintree or Boston in 1758? Was it just an elite affectation? Or was it a device for restricting practice to an educated few and controlling the "pettyfogger" competition? Could it have influenced, in

[2] Ibid., III, 271.

[3] Ibid., I, 56; III, 272–273.

[4] Ibid., III, 273.

[5] This was not atypical, although the "normal" education of colonial lawyers could reward further study. Some were educated at the Inns of Court in London, if a gentleman's life in those institutions in the eighteenth century could be described as a "formal legal education." See W. Holdsworth, *A History of English Law* (London, 1938), XII; C. R. McKirdy, "Massachusetts Lawyers on the Eve of the American Revolution: The State of the Profession," Appendix IV, "Biographical Sketches of Lawyers Practicing in Massachusetts in 1775," above, 339–358. Very few Massachusetts lawyers were educated in the Inns of Court after 1733. See G. W. Gawalt, *The Promise of Power: The Emergence of the Legal Profession in Massachusetts, 1760–1840* (Westport, Conn., 1979), 31–32, note 17; E. A. Jones, *American Members of the Inns of Court* (London, 1924), xviii–xx.

[6] *Diary*, I, 58. Gridley went on, "and that he has made a very considerable, a very great Proficiency in the Principles of the Law, and therefore that the Clients Interest may be safely intrusted in his Hands."

any demonstrable way, the fundamental jurisprudence of important colonial lawyers such as Adams?

One thing is certain. The civil law and Roman law books were here, and in surprising numbers. Recent research by Herbert Johnson and others has clearly established that.[7] But, as Maxwell Bloomfield has recently queried, were these books really read?[8] Did the

[7] See H. A. Johnson, *Imported Eighteenth Century Law Treatises in American Libraries 1700–1799* (Knoxville, Tenn., 1978), xxiii–xxiv. (Hereafter cited as Johnson, *Law Treatises.*) As to the substantial collection of books on Roman and civil law in the early Harvard catalogue, see J. Quincy, *The History of Harvard University* (Cambridge, Mass., 1840), II, 424–425, 586; A. Sutherland, *The Law at Harvard* (Cambridge, Mass., 1967), 68. As a result of the bequest of a New Orleans practitioner, Samuel Livermore, in 1833, Harvard Law School received a "whole library of foreign law, consisting of the works of leading civilians . . . amounting in numbers to upwards of three hundred costly volumes." J. Quincy, *History*, II, 425. See also ibid., I, 586. These books were actively used in a curriculum, as designed by Joseph Story and Nathan Dane, which emphasized "Law of Nature, the Law of Nations, Commercial and Maritime Law," II, 375. Quincy paid Story the compliment of describing him as an "eminent lawyer and civilian." Ibid., II, 377. In 1917 Roman law was still required for an advanced law degree at Harvard. See *The Centennial History of the Harvard Law School, 1817–1917* (Boston, 1918), 77.

[8] See M. Bloomfield, *Book Review, American Journal of Legal History*, XXV, 79 (1981). By 1756 the College of Philadelphia (now the University of Pennsylvania) was offering a course which included the "civil laws" and assigned Grotius' *De Jure Belli ac Pacis* and Pufendorf's *De jure Naturae et Gentium.* A-H Chroust, *The Rise of the Legal Profession in America* (Norman, Oklahoma, 1965), II, 176. See Johnson, *Law Treatises*, 27, 46. By 1763 both Grotius and Pufendorf were part of the fourth-year curriculum at King's College (Columbia). Johnson, *Law Treatises*, xxiv. But were they part of a professional legal education, or just thought of as treatises on ethics and philosophy? Much later, during the enthusiasm of the codification movement, anonymous writers in the *North American Review* would state that "The common, civil, and customary law of Europe have each precisely the same force with us in this branch [the law merchant and maritime law]. . . . [O]ur courts study them all, and adopt from them whatever is most applicable to our situation, and whatever is on the whole just and expedient, without considering either course obligatory. . . . In fact, all eminent lawyers in this country sooner or later find it necessary to study the law books of the continent. . . . [T]he continental law ought to be made an important, it might also be said the most important, branch of elementary legal education." Anonymous, *North American Review*, XL (October 1820), 412; *North American Review*, XXI (October 1825), 387–388; quoted in Chroust, *Rise of Legal Profession*, II, 55–56. "In our courts of justice the writings of the [French] civilians are referred to freely and fearlessly. The Institutes of Justinian and the commercial treatises of Pothier, Emerigon and Roccus are naturalized among us." Anonymous, *North American Review*, XXI (October 1825), 387–388, quoted in Chroust, *Rise of Legal Profession*, II, 55. As to the practical reality of these statements, which is more doubtful, see Peter Stein's article "The Attraction of Civil Law in Post Revolutionary America," *Virginia Law Review*, LII (1966), 403, and A. W. B. Simpson's "The Rise and Fall of the Legal Treatise Legal Principles and the Form of Legal Literature," *Chicago Law Review*, XLVIII (1981), 632. See also

serious study of continental jurisprudence and civilian learning pre-
date the Revolution? Was it part of the Revolution's background, or
was it a result of the Revolution? Or both? Was it applied in
practice? Any kind of complete answer is far beyond the scope of
this paper, but, fortunately, the tireless labors of the editors of the
Adams Papers, particularly the editors of *The Legal Papers of John
Adams*, Kinvin Wroth and Hiller Zobel, and the editors of the first
two volumes of the *Papers of John Adams*,[9] together with the work
of Julius Goebel, Jr. on *The Law Practice of Alexander Hamilton*[1]
have begun to shed some light on these problems. Most particularly,
we now can know more about the application of civilian learning in
early American legal practice and the influence of neoclassicism on
the self-image of the legal profession.[2]

Again, I intend to concentrate solely on the legal career of John
Adams from 1758 to 1775. Why? I certainly do not intend to imply
that Adams was a typical lawyer of the period, or that anything that
was true of his knowledge, his legal education, or his practice was
necessarily true for anyone else. But Adams was in at the beginning
of a formal structure for the Suffolk County bar in 1770 and at the
initiation of requirements for legal education in Massachusetts. His
extraordinary papers give us a "candid" view of the pre-revolution-

Alan Watson's illuminating *The Making of the Civil Law* (Cambridge, Mass.,
1981), 27–38.

[9] *Papers of John Adams*, R. J. Taylor, M. Kline, G. L. Lint, eds. (Cambridge, Mass.,
1977). (Hereafter cited as *Papers*.)

[1] See *The Law Practice of Alexander Hamilton*, J. Goebel, Jr., ed., 2 vols. (New
York, 1964, 1969). (Hereafter cited as *Law Practice*.)

[2] Hamilton was "profoundly" learned in the law, and this included "basic Roman
law texts" and contemporary civilian sources. See *Law Practice*, I, 6–7. Goebel's edition of Hamilton's legal papers provides detailed evidence of how European civil
law sources were used in maritime and law merchant cases during the early eighteenth
century in New York. Ibid., II, 48–231. These papers also show that questions of
"incorporation," ibid., II, 20–21, and "universal principles of custom," ibid., II,
1–28, were very much afoot, encouraged by the rapid expansion of New York trade
from 1775 to 1800. There were regular citations to the civilian law merchant
treatises, ibid., II, 215, 428, and to French law, ibid., II, 224–227. This evidence
backs up other contemporary documents stressing the value of civil law as it pertains
to *ius gentium*, including the lectures of President Stiles at Yale in 1777 on Montesquieu, Vattel, Pufendorf, and "modern continental civil law." See *The Literary
Diary of Ezra Stiles*, Dexter, ed. (New York, 1901), 166–168. See also the lectures
by Justice James Wilson in Philadelphia in 1790. *The Works of James Wilson*, R. C.
McCloskey, ed. (Cambridge, Mass., 1967), I, 76, 85, 149–150, 257, 279.

ary legal elite that he knew intimately and whose values he shared. Furthermore, the scope and nature of Adams' legal learning are just plain interesting. Adams was the man sent in 1784 to negotiate the crucial five million guilder loan from the Dutch bankers in the dark hours for America.[3] What did he know about the civil law of Europe?

II. YOUNG JOHN ADAMS AND HIS "PICK AX": EARLY
LEGAL TRAINING (1756–1761)

The young Adams frequently felt sorry for himself. This was particularly so when his first writ was abated, a crisis for any adolescent attorney. He lamented: "[I]t is my Destiny to dig Treasures with my own fingers. No Body will lend me or sell me a Pick axe."[4] And, to an astonishing degree, Adams really was self-taught.

Adams' *Diary* indicates almost exactly what he read in the period from 1756 to 1758 in Worcester and in the period from 1758 to 1760 in Braintree.[5] During the earlier period Adams was technically a student and apprentice, but Putnam was an indifferent teacher.[6] During the later period Adams was technically a full-fledged practitioner, but, in fact, business was slow starting. Under the informal tutelage of Jeremiah Gridley, a great teacher, Adams filled the empty hours between clients with an extensive course of study.

There was quite a difference between the books read in Worcester, which were largely common law classics and abridgements, and Adams' Braintree reading under Gridley's influence. In Adams' words: "I have read no small Number of Volumes, upon the Law, the last 2 Years [1758–1760]. Justinians Institutes I have read, thro, in Latin with Vinnius's perpetual Notes, Van Muydens Tractatio Institutionum Justiniani, I read thro, and translated, mostly into English, from the same Language. Woods Institute of the Civil Law, I read thro. These on the civil Law; on the Law of England I read Cowells Institute of the Laws of England, in Imitation of Justinian, Dr. and student, Finch's Discourse of Law, Hales History, and some Reporters, Cases in Chancery, Andrews Etc. besides oc-

[3] See *Diary*, III, 154.

[4] *Diary*, I, 62–63, 64–65.

[5] Ibid., I, 173–174.

[6] Ibid., I, 63.

casional searches for Business. Also a general Treatise of naval Trade and Commerce, as founded on the Laws and Statutes."[7]

This is quite a list, with a strong civilian flavor. In particular, not only was there a heavy emphasis on Roman Law, but Dr. Cowell's *Institutes of the Laws of England* exposed Adams to England's leading civilian propagandist.[8] Cowell's *Institutes* laid out the entire English common law on the framework of Justinian's *Institutes*.[9] Furthermore, St. Germain's *Doctor and Student*, Mathew Hale's *History of the Common Law of England*, and the "general Treatise of the naval Trade," almost certainly Charles Molloy's *De Jure Maritime et Navali*, incorporated many references to civil and canon law.[1]

But did Adams really absorb this learning? By his own account, "All this series of Reading, has left but faint Impressions, and [a] very Imperfect system of Law in my Head."[2] First, Adams doubted his own grasp of common law principles. "I must form a serious Resolution of beginning and pursuing quite thro, the Plans of my Lords Hale, and Reeve. Woods Inst[itutes] of common Law I never read but once, and my Ld. Coke's Com[mentary] on Lit[tleton] I never read but once. These two Authors I must get, and read, over and over again. And I will get em too, and break thro, as Mr. Gridley expressed it, all obstructions."[3] Gridley clearly would have made a great football coach!

Adams was equally concerned about his civilian learning. "Besides, I am but a Novice in natural Law and civil Law. There are multitudes of excellent Authors, on natural Law, that I have never read,

---

[7] Ibid., I, 173–174. As to Gridley's career and famous pupils, such as William Cushing, James Otis, Benjamin Pratt, and Oxenbridge Thacher, see *Legal Papers*, I, ci.

[8] See D. R. Coquillette, "Legal Ideology and Incorporation I: The English Civilian Writers, 1523–1607," *Boston University Law Review*, LXI (1981), I, 71–81. (Hereafter cited as "Legal Ideology I.")

[9] Ibid., 71–73.

[1] See D. R. Coquillette, "Legal Ideology and Incorporation II: Sir Thomas Ridley, Charles Molloy, and the Literary Battle for the Law Merchant, 1607–1676," *Boston University Law Review*, LXI (1981), 315, 363 ff. (Hereafter cited as "Legal Ideology II.") Molloy's treatise was present in Adams' library. See Johnson, *Law Treatises*, 40.

[2] *Diary*, I, 174.

[3] Ibid.

indeed I never read any Part of the best authors, Pufendorf and Grotius."[4] This is consistent with Adams' awkward admission to Gridley, during Adams' interview for the bar, that he hadn't really read Grotius or Pufendorf.[5] "In the Civil Law, there are Hoppius, and Vinnius, Commentators on Justinian, Domat, Etc. besides Institutes of Cannon and feudal Law, that I have to read." Adams concluded by vowing, "Thus let me, every night before I go to bed, write down . . . [in my diary] what Book of Law, I have read."[6] Alas, the next entry reads, "I have not read one Word of Law, this Day."[7] Was it the distraction of Hannah Quincy again?

In addition to the listed volumes, Adams' *Diary* indicates that, during the 1759 to 1760 period, he did further reading in the Enlightenment authors, particularly Montesquieu's *Spirit of the Laws*,[8] and in 1761 Adams did indeed carry out his resolve to read canon law. "I borrowed of Mr. Gridley, the second Volume of the Corpus Iuris Canonici Notis illustratum. Gregorii 13 Iussi editum. . . . Mr. Gridley about 15 months since, advised me to read an Institute of the Cannon Law—and that Advice lay broiling in my Head, till Last Week, when I borrowed the Book."[9]

But that canon law book was borrowed by a very prejudiced man. Adams remarked: "I am very glad, that he gave, and I took, the Advice, for it will explain many Things in Ecclesiastical History, and open that system of fraud, Bigotry, Nonsense, Impudence, and Superstition, on which the Papal Usurpations are founded, besides increasing my skill in the latin Tongue, and my Acquaintance with civil Law, for in many Respects the Cannon Law is grafted on the civil."[1] One might have hoped that, on actually reading the book, Adams would change his good Congregationalist mind-set. Alas, no.

---

[4] Ibid.

[5] Cf. ibid., III, 271–272.

[6] Ibid., I, 174.

[7] Ibid., 175.

[8] See ibid., 115–117, 142, 123, note 19. Adams referred to Montesquieu as "Secondat," that being the baron's family name. Adams owned Nugent's translation, "Second Edition corrected and considerably improved" (London, 1752), a copy of which is still in the family. Ibid., 123, note 19.

[9] Ibid., 199.

[1] Ibid.

Two weeks later Adams remarked, "This Institute is a curious Monument of Priestly Ambition, Avarice and sublety. Tis a system of sacerdotal Guile."[2] As will be seen, Adams' "A Dissertation on the Canon and Feudal Law," written in 1765, reflected the same kneejerk prejudice.

Was all of Adams' civilian reading a facade to conceal such preconceived views of the world? Fortunately, we have more concrete evidence of how much he learned. The most important evidence will be analyzed in Parts III, IV, and VI of this paper. That was Adams' actual application of canon and civil law authority in his legal practice and political writing.

And there is other evidence. In Adams' *Earliest Diary* there are his laborious notes on Justinian's *Institutes* 2.1.12 and 3.14.3 through 3.18.pr.[3] The notes are clearly based on the Van Muyden *Tractatio . . .* 3d ed. Utrecht, 1707. This book, again, was an abridgement of Justinian's *Institutes,* and almost certainly the copy lent to Adams by Gridley.[4] While these notes are hardly polished, they demonstrate serious effort. The editors of the *Earliest Diary,* doubtless in despair over Adams' "cramped" writing, allege that Adams, in abstracting and translating, "seems to have been satisfied at times with gibberish."[5] How true, but the notes bear a striking resemblance to my own painful efforts as a student of Roman law at Oxford, and, I am sure, the same could be said of countless other law students. Furthermore, as will be seen, Adams actually applied *Institutes* 2.1.12 in a famous case, *Doane* v. *Gage* (Court of Vice Admiralty 1768–1769)[6] and his understanding of the Roman *jus naturale* and *jus gentium* concepts in *Institutes* 2.1.12 and 3.14.3 *ff.* appears to have had a direct influence on his famous *Novanglus* letters.[7]

We also have Adams' student "Commonplace Book" and a fragment of his "Student Notes."[8] The "Notes" reveal that Adams was

[2] Ibid., 200.

[3] *Earliest Diary,* 53–59.

[4] Ibid., 58, note 2. See the Illustration above, 365.

[5] Ibid., 58–59, note 2.

[6] See *Legal Papers,* II, 73 *ff.*

[7] See below, 408–416.

[8] *Legal Papers,* I, 2 *ff.*

well aware of the passages in *Coke on Littleton,* folio 11b (E. Coke, *The First Part of the Institutes of the Lawes of England,* London, 1628), which set out the use of civil law in the ecclesiastical, Constable and Marshal, and Admiralty jurisdictions. There is also mention of the Laws of Oleron, the early sea laws, which would continue to fascinate Adams.[9] Questions over the proper choice of civil law in key jurisdictions, particularly in Admiralty, probate, and divorce cases, would later be a feature of Adams' law practice.[1] Adams' "Commonplace Book" also demonstrated a good knowledge of Roman contract and bailment principles, and had at least one reference to Christopher St. German, the pioneer of English comparative law studies.[2]

Adams' *Diary* itself contained crabbed passages that were evidence of painful agony over Wood's *New Institutes of the Imperial or Civil Law* and Van Muyden's *Tractatio.*[3] Again, the editors of the *Adams Papers* were not impressed with Adams' accuracy, suggesting that "the diarist's mind was not on his books when he made these memoranda, but was 'roving from Girls to friends' and other matters not closely related to law."[4] But there can be no doubt that Adams was actually *reading* the books. And, again speaking as one who has also studied the *Institutes* as examination set texts, it *is* agony. As Adams later recalled: "At this time October 1758 the Study of the Law was a dreary Ramble, in comparison of what it is at this day [1802]. The Name of Blackstone had not been heard, whose Commentaries together with Sullivans Lectures and Reeves's History of the Law, have smoothed the path of the Student, while the long Career of Lord Mansfield, his many investigations and Decisions ... have greatly facilitated the Acquisition of it."[5]

Blackstone and Mansfield might "smooth the path" for law stu-

[9] Adams enjoyed a chance to see the Island of Oleron, although from a distance, during his first trip to Europe. See *Diary,* II, 291.

[1] See *Legal Papers,* II, 173 *ff.*, 275 *ff.*, 335 *ff.*; *Legal Papers,* I, 228–230, 245–247, 280–285.

[2] See ibid., 6, 7, 10, 11, 18, 24. As to St. German, see Coquillette, "Legal Ideology I," 39–49.

[3] See *Diary,* I, 104–106.

[4] Ibid., 122, note 4.

[5] *Diary,* III, 273–274.

dents, but in his later career, both legal and political, Adams found reason to distrust both. On several occasions he used the knowledge he had gained by a hard slog through original sources to contradict what Jefferson called "the honeyed Mansfieldism of Blackstone."[6] Indeed, in both "The Clarendon Letters" and "The Novanglus Letters," Adams attacked the principles of parliamentarianism that Blackstone held most dear.[7] Proximate to the "gibberish" so taxing to Adams' editors are also some gems of insights, most particularly that the ultimate justification of all law is human reason and that principles of government must be adapted to new conditions.[8]

Adams had some rivals in this early period, and he was terribly sensitive about competition. One was Robert Treat Paine. "Bob Paine is conceited and pretends to more Knowledge and Genius than he has."[9] Adams once told Paine that he, Adams, was reading Vinnius, a "Dutch Commentator" on the *Institutes*. Paine was not suitably impressed and retorted, "Vinnius . . . you cant understand one Page of Vinnius."[1] Adams did not take this lightly. "He must know that human Nature is disgusted with such incomplaisant Behaviour. Besides he has no Right to say I dont understand every Word in Vin-

---

[6] See Richard B. Morris, "Legalism versus Revolutionary Doctrine in New England," in *Essays in the History of Early American Law*, D. Flaherty, ed. (Chapel Hill, N.C., 1969), 431. See also below, 415–416, note 5. Adams wrote that he "had a low Opinion of the Compilers, Abridgers, and Abstract makers. We had better draw science from its fountain in original Authors." *Diary*, I, 177. Nevertheless, Adams did find Wood's *New Institute of the Imperial or Civil Law* and Van Muyden's *Tractatio* to be useful. "Have this moment finished Woods new Institute of the Imperial or civil Law. It is a great Help in the study of Van Muyden and Justinian. I understand Wood much better for having read Van Muyden, and shall now understand Van Muyden much better for having read Wood." Ibid., 103.

[7] See below, 408–416.

[8] Thus Adams wrote in his diary: "Law is human Reason. It governs all the Inhabitants of the Earth; the political and civil Laws of each Nation should be only the particular Cases, in which human Reason is applied." Adams continued: "Let me attend to the Principle of Government. The Laws of Britain, should be adapted to the Principle of the british Government, to the Climate of Britain, to the Soil, to its situation, as an Island, and its Extent, to the manner of living of the Natives as Merchants, Manufacturers and Husbandmen, to the Religion of the Inhabitants." *Diary*, I, 117.

[9] Ibid., 59. See Stephen T. Riley's fine essay "Robert Treat Paine and John Adams: A Colonial Rivalry" in *Sibley's Heir*, vol. 59, *Publications*, Colonial Society of Massachusetts (1982), 415–429.

[1] *Diary*, I, 59.

31. Robert Treat Paine (1731–1814) by Edward Savage and John Coles (*circa* 1796–1801). Justice, Supreme Court; Attorney General. Courtesy, Massachusetts Historical Society.

nius ... for he knows nothing of me."[2] Both Adams' law practice and his political writing will demonstrate that he did understand a little Vinnius and perhaps even more Van Muyden.[3]

Adams had another rival, Peter Chardon. "He has a sense of the Dignity and Importance of his Profession, that of the Law. ... He talks of exulting in an unlimited field of natural, civil, and common Law. ... This fellows Thoughts are not employed on Songs and Girls. ... He will make something."[4] Adams wanted to be like him, "exulting in an unlimited field of natural, civil, and common Law" and filled with the dignity and importance of being a lawyer.

III. The *Sodalitas* Club: The Intellectual Elite at the Pre-Revolutionary Boston Bar (1761–1765)

"Last Monday [prior to 8 January 1761], had a passionate Wrangle, with Eb Thayer, before Major Crosby. He called me a *petty* Lawyer. This I [Adams] resented."[5] And so he should. Adams was making steady progress at the bar by 1761. In November 1761 he was "admitted an attorney in the Superior Court," the highest step then available.[6] In 1762 as a result of Chief Justice Thomas Hutchinson's desire "to add dignity to the proceedings of that [the Superior] Court, all members of its bar were formally called as barristers at the August term."[7] "Adams was among those who thereafter appeared in 'Gowns and Bands and Tye Wiggs.'"[8]

Great was the difference that Adams perceived between his be-wigged self and "petty Lawyers." Indeed, the period of Adams' first success corresponded with a new offensive, at least in his diary, attacking his more "base" rivals. "Looking about me in the Country, I found the practice of Law was grasped into the hands of Deputy

[2] Ibid. Robert Treat Paine became a signer of the Declaration of Independence, Attorney General of Massachusetts, and a Justice of the Supreme Judicial Court. See *Legal Papers*, I, cvi.

[3] "[S]et down to Van Muyden in Earnest. His latin is easy, his deffinitions are pretty clear, and his Division of the subject, are judicious." *Diary*, I, 57.

[4] Ibid., 47. Peter Chardon died young in Barbadoes in 1766. See ibid., 48, note 2.

[5] *Diary*, I, 189 (emphasis added).

[6] *Legal Papers*, I, lviii; *Diary*, I, 224.

[7] *Legal Papers*, I, lviii.

[8] Ibid.; *Diary*, III, 276.

Sheriffs, Petty-foggers and even Constables, who filled all the Writts upon Bonds, promissory notes and Accounts, received the Fees established for Lawyers and stirred up many unnecessary Suits. I mentioned these Things to some of the Gentlemen in Boston, who disapproved and even resented them very highly. I asked them whether some measures might not be agreed upon at the Bar and sanctioned by the Court, which might remedy the Evil?"[9]

The answer, even in 1761, was the "Association" and "the Club." Civilized professional men could join together and set down the standards of decent behavior and practice. "A Meeting was called and a great Number of regulations proposed not only for confining the practice of Law to those who were educated to it and sworn to fidelity in it, but to introduce more regularity, Urbanity, Candour and Politeness as well as honor, Equity and Humanity, among the regular Professors. Many of these Meetings were the most delightfull Entertainments, I ever enjoyed. The Spirit that reigned was that of Solid Sense, Generosity, Honor and Integrity: and the Consequences were most happy, for the Courts and the Bar instead of Scenes of Wrangling, Chicanery, Quibbling and ill manners, were soon converted to order, Decency, Truth and Candor."[1] When Adams' colleague and Gridley's friend, Benjamin Prat, rode away to New York in November of 1761, "to take his Seat as Chief Justice of that State," his final words to his comrades were "Brethren above all things forsake not the Assembling of yourselves together."[2]

But there were Clubs and, then, there were *Clubs*. On 24 January 1765 Adams was approached in court by Samuel Fitch. The news was electrifying: "[T]hat Mr. Gridley and he had something to communicate to me, that I should like, in Sacred Confidence however."[3] Adams went to Gridley's office "after many Conjectures what the secret might be" and heard the news:

That He and Mr. Fitch had proposed a Law Clubb—a private Association, for the study of Law and oratory.—As to the Bar, he thought of them, as he did think of them—Otis, Thatcher, Auchmuty. He was con-

[9] *Diary*, III, 274.

[1] Ibid.

[2] Ibid. As to Benjamin Pratt (1711–1763) see *Legal Papers*, I, cvi.

[3] *Diary*, I, 251.

32. Benjamin Prat (1711–1763) attributed to John Smibert. Chief Justice, Province of New York; Moderator, Boston Town Meeting. Courtesy, Harvard Law School Art Collection.

sidering, who was for the future to support the Honour and Dignity of the Bar. And he was determined to bring me into Practice, the first Practice, and Fitch too. He could easily do it, by recommending. And he was very desirous of forming a Junto, a small sodality, of himself and Fitch and me, and Dudley if he pleased might come, in order to read in Concert the Feudal Law and Tullies orations. And for this Purpose he lent me, the Corpus Juris Civilis in 4 Partes distinctum, eruditissimis Dionysii Gothofredi J.C. clarissimi notis illustratum, at the End of which are the Feudorum Consuetudines Partim ex Editione vulgata partim ex Cujaciana vulgata, appositae, as also the Epitome Feudorum Dionysio Gothofredo Authore.[4]

The Club was called the "Sodalitas, A Clubb of Friends." Adams was thrilled. Regular meetings were arranged; reading projects were designed, with a heavy emphasis on legal classics:

We accordingly agreed to meet the next Evening [10 January 1765?] in one of Ballards back Chambers and determine upon Times, Places, and studies. We accordingly met the next Evening, Mr. Gridley, Fitch and I, and spent the whole Evening. Proposals were to read a Reign and the statutes of that Reign, to read Hurds Dialogues and any new Pieces. But at last we determined to read The Feudal Law and Cicero only, least we should loose sight of our main Object, by attending to too many. Thursday Nights were agreed on, and to meet first at Mr. Gridleys office. There we accordingly met on the Thurdsday Night [17 January 1765] following, and suffered our Conversation to ramble upon Hurds Dialogues, the Pandects, their Discovery in Italy by Lotharius in 1127, in the Reign of Stephen, upon Lambard de priscis Anglorum Legibus, in Saxon and Latin, upon Ld. Kaims [Kames], Mr. Blackstone &c. But we agreed to meet the next Thursday night at Mr. Fitch's, and to read the Three first Titles of the feudal Law, and Tullies oration for Milo.[5]

The next meeting was at Samuel Fitch's on 24 January 1765. "We read the 3 first Titles of the feudal Law, and We read Gothofreds Notes and We looked into Strykius for the Explanation of many

---

[4] Ibid.

[5] Ibid., 251–252. Adams' copy of Richard Hurd's *Moral and Political Dialogues* (3d. ed., London, 1765) is in the Boston Public Library. At one point Hurd describes the kind of person who is "[i]n a word, both in mind and person the furthest in the world from any thing that is handsome, gentlemenlike, or of use and acceptance in good company!" Besides this description, Adams later wrote: "An exact description of a Dartmouth educated Schollar." Ibid., 252, note 5.

hard Words in those 3 Titles—The Valvasors, Capitanii, Guardia and Guastaldi. This Strykius wrote an Examen Juris feudalis, by Way of Question and Answer. His account of the original of the Consuetudines Feudorum is, that they were collected and written by Gerardus Niger, and Obertus, the Consulls of Milan.—We read also Part of Tully's Milo—and are to read the 4th. and 5th Title of The Feudal Law, and the rest of that oration next Thursday night [31 January 1765]."[6]

Adams was in seventh heaven. "I expect the greatest Pleasure from this sodality, that I ever had in my Life—and a Pleasure too, that will not be painfull to my Reflections."[7] How unlike his memories of other "Pleasures," particularly with Hannah Quincy![8] Adams missed the next Sodalitas meeting at Joseph Dudley's on 31 January 1765,[9] but the following meeting, on 21 February 1765, was his turn to be host. He entertained the Club "at Blodgets":

We were never in better Spirits, or more Social. We began the 13th. Title of the feudal Law De Alienatione Feudi and read three Titles. Gridley proposed that we should mark all those Passages, which are adopted by the English Law, that when we come to read Ld. Coke we may recur back upon Occasion, to the originals of our Law.[1]

This was an important meeting in the development of Adams' political thought and jurisprudence. The topic of conversation was the feudal system, and Adams had brought up Rosseau's hostility to feudal institutions. This sparked a lively analysis of the merits and defects of feudalism.[2] Later, in writing "A Dissertation on the Canon and Feudal Law," Adams would reflect on this conversation and re-call the writing of Strykius on the *ius gentium* and the function of the feudal law as a component of the *ius gentium*.[3] In Adams' opinion

[6] Ibid., 252–253.

[7] Ibid., 253.

[8] Adams had bittersweet memories of Hannah. See ibid., I, 72–74. Hannah married Bela Lincoln, not a happy match. Ibid., 176–177.

[9] Joseph Dudley (1732–1767) married Gridley's daughter. See *Legal Papers*, I, c.

[1] *Diary*, I, 253.

[2] Ibid., 254.

[3] See the full analysis of this debate in connection with Adams' "A Dissertation on the Canon and Feudal Law," below, 401–403.

there was no "absurdity" in the institutions of the feudal law taken by themselves. At certain times such institutions had served a necessary purpose. It was the survival of these laws and institutions into different times and conditions which made them unjustifiable. Laws and institutions, Adams reflected, must continue to justify themselves, by reason or consensus, or they become oppressive.[4]

Gridley returned the conversation to self-improvement by producing "a Book intituled in Herennium Commentarius, as an Introduction to Tully De Oratore":

Gridley. Our Plan must be, when we have finished the feudal Law, to read Coke Littleton, and after him a Reign and the Statutes of that Reign. It should also be a Part of our Plan, to improve ourselves in Writing, by reading carefully the best English Writers, and by Using ourselves to writing—for it should be a part of our Plan to publish Pieces, now and then. Let us form our Style upon the Ancients, and the best English Authors.[5]

Adams concluded: "I hope and expect to see, at the Bar, in Consequence of this Sodality, a Purity, an Elegance, and a Spirit, surpassing any Thing that ever appeared in America. Fich [Fitch] said that he would not say he had Abilities, but he would say he had Ambition enough to hope for the same Thing."[6]

---

[4] *Diary*, I, 254–258.

[5] Ibid., 255. Gridley's suggestion that it "should be a part of our plan to publish Pieces, now and then . . ." may well have inspired Adams' "A Dissertation on the Canon and Feudal Law."

[6] Ibid. The Sodalitas Club was not unique. In Boston many lawyers certainly dined together during this period as informal groups. These included James Otis (1725–1783), Robert Auchmuty (1723–1788), and Oxenbridge Thacher (1719–1765), who often ate with Adams, Gridley, and the others. Indeed Richard B. Morris lists them as members of the Sodalitas Club. See R. B. Morris, "Legalism versus Revolutionary Doctrine in New England," in *Essays in the History of Early American Law*, D. H. Flaherty, ed. (Chapel Hill, N.C., 1969), 425. Cf. Page Smith, *John Adams* (Garden City, N.Y., 1962), I, 77–78. Thacher died in 1765. Otis was a great patriot, but plagued by madness. He was killed by lightning in 1783. Auchmuty, like Fitch, became Advocate General in Admiralty and Judge of the Vice Admiralty Court, a post held by his father. He was a leading loyalist and fled to Halifax and England in 1776. See *Legal Papers*, I, xcvi.

In New York the prestigious "Moot" Club, copied from the famous after-dinner moot association at Gray's Inn, met regularly in the eighteenth century. So did New Jersey's Institutio Legalis. See A-H Chroust, *Rise of the Legal Profession*, II, 130, note 1. The descendants of these associations, the famous "library companies,"

Ironically, this is the last account of the Sodalitas in Adams' *Diary*. Gridley died shortly thereafter, in 1767, as did Joseph Dudley, the same year at the age of only thirty-five.[7] Samuel Fitch and Adams alone survived. Fitch chose royal preferment as Advocate General in Admiralty from 1770 to 1776, and as Solicitor to the notorious American Board of Customs Commissioners.[8] In 1776 Fitch sailed to Halifax and then to England.[9] Adams took the other fork in the way and became President of the United States.

IV. Dead Whales, Smuggled Madeira, and Applied Civilian Learning in Adams' Legal Practice (1766–1774)

After the question of whether a lawyer like Adams ever read his civil law books, the next logical question is whether they ever did him any good.

Of course, there are many conceivable ways such legal learning might do a lawyer like Adams some "good." It might be of direct help in his practice, with immediate application to certain kinds of legal problems. Or it could assist in his definition of himself as a professional, or in his conception of what should characterize the best features of any lawyer or association of lawyers. Or it could influence his fundamental *ideas* about the operation of the legal system, such as his ideas about the ways in which law and lawyers ought to relate to political society as a whole. The latter I will call "legal ideology."

Regrettably, even with the splendid edition of the *Legal Papers of John Adams*, we still do not know as much about Adams' legal ideas as we would like.[1] But we do know something. The obvious place to start would be to see if there was any evidence that Adams'

such as the Library Company of Philadelphia (1802), and Boston's Social Law Library (1804), did much lasting practical good. Ibid., 130, note 1.

[7] *Legal Papers*, I, c. According to Adams' Autobiography the "little Clubb" met "once a Week," but for how long is unclear. *Diary*, III, 285. On Gridley's death, Adams characteristically wrote, "He was a great Admirer of Barbeyrac: thought him a much more sensible and learned Man than Puffendorf. I admired the facility with which he translated and criticised the Greek Passages in the Notes." *Diary*, III, 286.

[8] Ibid., I, c.

[9] Ibid.

[1] See *Legal Papers*, I, xciii–xciv.

study of Roman or Enlightenment civilian sources had a direct application in his law practice.

In England, as Adams carefully noted in his "Student Notes," civil law was applied "in certain Cases, not only in Courts Ecclesiastical, but in the Court of the Constable and Marshal, and of the Admiralty."[2] There is clear evidence that he read, in his travails with *Coke upon Littleton,* the famous section defining—perhaps a bit narrowly—the scope of civil law authority in English Courts.[3] He must have been at least aware of the existence of Doctors' Commons in London—the last stronghold of English civilian practice.[4] Was civil law applied in Massachusetts in analogous cases? Did Adams at least attempt it? The first sensible places to look would be the Admiralty cases, as well as any cases touching on the traditional ecclesiastical jurisdictions of domestic law and non-realty probate.[5]

A. *The Case of the Whale: Doane v. Gage (1766–1769)*[6]

The colonial vice-admiralty courts were "primarily to provide a forum for enforcement of the Acts of Trade and Navigation, with which England sought to control colonial commerce for the benefit of the Mother Country."[7] Most admiralty cases in Adams' Massachusetts were smuggling and revenue cases. But Adams did have one classic civil jurisdiction (i.e. non-revenue or non-criminal) admiralty case, *Doane* v. *Gage,* the "Case of the Whale."

This was a truly fabulous squabble over which whale ship was entitled to a dead whale. The whale had been hit by a harpoon from a boat launched by a ship captained by Adams' client, a Captain Doane.

---

[2] Ibid., 3.

[3] See E. Coke, *The First Part of the Institutes of the Lawes of England* (London, 1628), *11b. Indeed, Adams' notes are a paraphrase, as the editors point out.

[4] For a list of the standard scholarly sources on English civilian specialists, monopolies, and a brief description, see Coquillette, "Legal Ideology and Incorporation I," 19–22.

[5] See ibid., and Coquillette, "Ideology and Incorporation II," 346–363.

[6] *Legal Papers,* II, 68–97 (Case No. 43).

[7] Ibid., 68. See the excellent account by L. Kinvin Wroth, "The Massachusetts Vice Admiralty Court," in *Law and Authority in Colonial America: Selected Essays,* G. Billias, ed. (Barre, Mass., 1965), 32 *ff.* See also L. Kinvin Wroth, "The Massachusetts Vice Admiralty Court and the Federal Admiralty Jurisdiction," *American Journal of Legal History,* VI (1962), 250–268, 347–367.

The whale, quite sensibly, took off for the bottom. At some later point he returned to the surface and was hit by another harpoon. This harpoon came from a boat launched by a rival ship, commanded by a Captain Gage. At some other point—either before or after Gage's "iron" hit—Doane's boat's line came free. Under the custom of the whalers, a whale "belonged" to the boat that first struck it, even if another struck it later, *if* the first harpoon's line was attached to its boat at the time of the second hit. But "if the whale became 'loose' without having been struck a second time," the new harpoon gained full possession.[8]

So the key issue was simply whether Doane's boat was attached to the whale when Gage struck it, or whether the whale was a "loose" whale. No less than seventy-four witnesses, thirty-four for Doane and forty for Gage, would testify. John Adams represented Captain Doane and Robert Treat Paine and James Otis represented Captain Gage.[9] Never was a dead whale given such posthumous dignity. He was fought over by seventy-four eyewitnesses, two signers of the Declaration of Independence—one a future President of the United States—and the great James Otis!

For this case Adams prepared a truly remarkable "Notes of Authorities," with lengthy quotations on ownership of wild animals from Grotius' *De Jure Belli ac Pacis* and Justinian's *Institutes.* Adams' key point—rather contrary to the whalers' custom—was that once a wild animal was acquired by possession (presumably by being hit with his client's harpoon) that "Property acquired by Possession does not cease with the Loss of Possession." This proposition came directly from Grotius.[1] But Adams' notes contained a contrary rule from the Roman law sources themselves. "Ferae igitur Bestiae et Volucres, et Pisces, et omnia animalia, quae mari, Coelo, et Terra nascuntur: simulatque ab aliquo capta fuerint, jure gentium, statim illius esse incipiunt. Quod enim ante nullius est, id, naturali Ratione, occupanti conceditur." "Wild animals, birds, and fish, that is to say all the creatures which the land, the sea, and the sky produce, as soon as they are caught by any one become at once the property of their

---

[8] *Legal Papers,* II, 71–72.

[9] Ibid., 71.

[1] Ibid., 73.

captor by the law of nations; for natural reason admits the title of the first occupant to that which previously had no owner."[2] (Justinian's *Institutes*, 2:1:12). But the *Institutes* add: "[c]um vero tuam evaserit Custodiam, et in Libertatem naturalem sese receperit, tuum esse definit, et rursus occupantis fit," "An animal thus caught by you is deemed your property so long as it is completely under your control; but so soon as it has escaped from your control, and recovered its natural liberty, it ceases to be yours, and belongs to the first person who subsequently catches it."[3] This, of course, was a rule more in keeping with the whalers' custom.

Adams did not leave it there. He checked the *Institutes'* passage against the *Digest*, thus demonstrating both a degree of sophistication about the Roman law and access to a copy of the entire *Corpus Juris Civilis*. There he located the section (*Digest* 41:1:5) describing a controversy between Trebatius and Justinian's compilers. Trebatius was of the opinion that one who wounded a wild beast immediately became owner, and that "he must be held to retain the ownership so long as he kept on following the animal up, but that, if he relinquished the pursuit, his ownership ceased ... so that if, at any moment while the pursuit lasted, some other person should capture it ... he must be held to have committed a theft on the person first mentioned."[4] This was certainly a view which would appeal to Captain Doane. Justinian's compilers, however, indicated that "[a] good many authorities hold that the party does not become owner unless he captures it, because there is a considerable chance of the capture not being made; and this is a better view to take."[5] Here was a view that would surely appeal to Captain Gage!

Regrettably, no one seems to have recorded who won. There is only Paine's cryptic note on 27 October 1769, "Whale case finished."[6] Lengthy depositions survive, however, and they tend to indicate more concern with whalers' customs, such as "mateship," than with

[2] Ibid., 74, note 23.

[3] Ibid., 73, 74, note 24.

[4] Translation of *Digest* 41:1:5 from *De Adquirendo: Translation of Justinian's Digest, Book 14, Title* I, 3 (Cambridge, trans. C. H. Monro, 1900), set out in *Legal Papers*, II, 75, note 26.

[5] Ibid.

[6] Ibid., 73. The parties agreed to arbitration in April, 1769.

Roman law. There is no indication that Adams' classical learning was ever brought to bear. This result would have amused Herman Melville—who described the unwritten law of whaling as "a system which for terse comprehensiveness surpasses Justinian's Pandects and the By-laws of the Chinese Society for the Suppression of Meddling with other People's Business . . .

> I. A Fast-Fish belongs to the party fast to it.
> II. A Loose-Fish is fair game for anybody who can soonest catch it."[7]

But Adams certainly did get his Roman law books out for the case, and doubtless would have tried to see if the Court of Vice Admiralty would have listened to those arguments, even in Boston in 1768. This would have been particularly true if the Roman law had clearly cut his way. Equally significant, the lengthy testimony and depositions that definitely did take place were all in the form of written interrogatories, a civilian practice adopted "in deference to the civil law procedure followed in the High Court of Admiralty in England, or for convenience in a hearing four years after the event. . . ."[8]

B. *The Case of John Hancock's Remarkable, Vanishing Madeira: Sewall v. Hancock (1768–1769)*[9]

John Hancock, according to the sworn testimony of His Majesty's Commissioners of Customs, claimed that he could land wine from his vessel, the good sloop *Liberty*, without, alas! actually paying His Majesty's customs. The wine seemed to disappear between the point of arrival and the subsequent inspection by royal officers. This maneuver legally was known as "landing goods before entry."[1]

On 9 May 1768 the *Liberty* arrived at Boston from Madeira and made entry of "twenty-five pipes of madeira wine, upon which the duties were paid."[2] Cynics that they were, almost nobody in authority around the Boston waterfront took this declaration seriously. The case of the vanishing Madeira was on.

[7] H. Melville, *Moby Dick* (1950 ed.), 393–394, quoted by the editors of the *Legal Papers*, II, 72, note 27.

[8] *Legal Papers*, II, 72.

[9] Case No. 46, *Legal Papers*, II, 173–210.

[1] See ibid., 174–177.

[2] Ibid., 174.

The revenue officers' problem was getting witnesses. It was not easy. To make a long story short, one Thomas Kir, a tidesman who at the time of the *Liberty*'s arrival had reported nothing, became willing to testify that he had been locked in the *Liberty*'s steerage while Hancock's men illegally unloaded wine. There was no corroborating testimony, as his fellow tidesmen were "variously reported as asleep or drunk."[3] But the Commissioners of Customs, with the help of the powerful H.M.S. *Romney,* seized the *Liberty* in Boston harbor.

Adams represented Hancock. A lengthy and complex case followed in the Court of Admiralty, "and a painfull Drudgery I had of his [Hancock's] cause":

There were few days through the whole Winter, when I was not summoned to attend the Court of Admiralty. It seemed as if the Officers of the Crown were determined to examine the whole Town as Witnesses. Almost every day a fresh Witness was to be examined upon Interrogatories. They interrogated many of his [Hancock's] near Relations and most intimate Friends and threatened to summons his amiable and venerable Aunt, the Relict of his Uncle Thomas Hancock, who had left the greatest Part of his Fortune to him. I was thoroughly weary and disgusted with the Court, the Officers of the Crown, the Cause, and even with the tyrannical Bell that dongled me out of my House every Morning.[4]

The litigation featured the in-chamber examination and interrogatory procedure of the civil law, rather than common law procedures. Further, Adams at least twice employed extensive civilian authorities to advance his client's cause, and used them to illuminate two separate questions of legal principle. First, Adams stated that "[w]e are here to be tryed by a Court of civil not of common Law."[5] This meant that "we are therefore to be tryed by the Rules of Evidence

---

[3] Ibid., 175. A riot had driven the commissioners to Castle William.

[4] *Diary,* III, 306.

[5] *Legal Papers,* II, 203. In another context Adams was not so sure. "But disregarding order, for the present let me record the Controversy We had last Week, Concerning the Rules of Law which were to govern this Case. The Court of Admiralty is originally a Civil Law Court. Jurisdiction of a Crime, is given to it in this Case by Act of Parliament. The Question is whether it is to proceed by the civil Law?" *Legal Papers,* II, 206. As to the early choice-of-law doctrine in the colonies, see William E. Nelson, "The American Revolution and the Emergence of Modern Doctrines of Federalism and Conflict of Laws," below, 419–467.

that we find in the civil Law, not by those that We find in the Common Law."[6] In the absence of a jury trial right at civil law, the civil law insisted on certain strenuous rules of proof. One such rule was:

"The Number of Witnesses ought to be two at the least to make a full Proof, and these must be free from all Exceptions, Either as to their Persons or their Depositions. For the Testimony of a single Witness is of no Validity, tho the Person is of a great Character," &c. "For one Witness may mistake or lie, and be corrupted, and yet be consistent with himself, and so remain undiscovered; whereas two or three Witnesses may more easily be found in a Conspiracy by a prudent Judge if they are separately examined."

Adams quoted this key rule, which would destroy the Crown's single witness case, from Thomas Wood, *A New Institute of the Imperial, or Civil Law*, a book he had studied as a student.[7] Adams backed up this argument with an abundance of civilian authority, quoting the classic *Codex* maxim, "Simili modo sanximus, ut unius testimonium nemo Indicum, in quacunque causa facile patiatur admitti. Et nunc manifeste sanximus, ut unius omnino testis responsio non audiatur. . . . " (*Codex* 4:20:9:1). He also included some slightly inconsistent passages from the *Digest*, further sections from Wood's *New Institute of the Imperial, or Civil Law*, sections from Johannes Calvinus' *Lexicon Juridicum Juris Caesarei Simul et Canonici*, and references to the account of civil law procedures in Fortescue's *De Laudibus Legum Angliae*.[8]

Adams' second key argument was that in cases where the laws inflict specially severe penalties—as in the case of the smuggling laws

---

[6] Ibid., 203.

[7] Ibid., 206. As the editors of the *Legal Papers* alertly noticed, Adams omitted language from Wood making key exceptions from this rule: "unless he swears of his own Fact, and where there are other Circumstances to concur or corroborate, or unless he is a publick Officer; as a Notary, &c. deposing by Vertue of his Office. This is founded upon very good reason." Wood, *New Institute of the Civil Law*, 361 (2d ed. 1712). *Legal Papers*, II, 203, note 107.

[8] See *Codex* 4:20:9:1; *Digest* 22:5:12; Thomas Wood, *New Institute of the Imperial, or Civil Law*; J. Calvinus, *Lexicon Juridicum Juris Caesarei Simul et Canonici* (Cologne ed., 1622), 905; J. Fortescue, *De Laudibus Legum Angliae* (London, 1741, ed.), 38. See also *Legal Papers*, II, 203–204, notes 109, 116, 117. As the editors of the *Legal Papers* observe, Fortescue was, ironically, "pointing to" the rule "as a defect in civil-law procedure." *Legal Papers*, II, 205, note 117.

invoked against Hancock—these laws should be strictly construed. For this argument he cited Jean Domat's *The Civil Law In Its Natural Order* (Strahan trans., 1722):

Domat. V. 1. Page 13. Preliminary Book. Tit. I. Sect. 2 N. 15. "The Laws which restrain our natural Liberty, such as those that forbid any Thing that is not in itself unlawfull or which derogate in any other manner from the general Law, the Laws which inflict Punishments for Crimes and offences, or Penalties in civil matters; those which prescribe certain Formalities; *the Laws which appear to have any Hardship in them*" &c. "are to be interpreted in such a manner, as not to be applied beyond what is clearly expressed in the Law," &c. "We ought to give to such Laws all the Temperament of Equity and Humanity, that they are capable of." Notae: "Interpretatione Legum Poenae molliendae sunt, potius quam asperendae. In Poenalibus Causis benignius interpretandum est. In levioribus Causis proniores at Lenitatem Judices esse debent, in gravioribus Poenis, Severitatem Legum, cum aliquo temperamemto benignitatio subsequi."[9]

The last three sentences, as the editors of the *Legal Papers* observed, are quoted from a note in Domat from *Digest* 48:19:42; 50:17:155; 48:19:11. Adams also cited again, for the same proposition, Wood's *A New Institute of the Imperial, or Civil Law.*[1]

Adams concluded his analysis with an eloquent plea. He held that the Admiralty judge, his erstwhile dining partner Robert Auchmuty, could not have "his cake and eating it too" by choosing the worst from the common and civil law systems, at his discretion:

Shall We say that We are to be governed by some Rules of the common Law and some Rules of the civil Law, that the Judge at his Discretion shall choose out of each system such Rules as please him, and discard the rest. If so Misera Servitus est. Examinations of witnesses upon Interrogatories, are only by the Civil Law. Interrogatories are unknown at common Law, and Englishmen and common Lawyers have an aversion to them if not an Abhorrence of them. Shall We suffer under the odious Rules of the civil Law, and receive no advantage from the beneficial Rules of it? This,

---

[9] Jean Domat, *The Civil Law in its Natural Order* (Strahan Trans., 1722), 1:13–14, as set out in *Legal Papers*, II, 205.

[1] T. Wood, *A New Institute of the Imperial, or Civil Law* (3d ed., 1721), 310. See *Legal Papers*, II, 205.

instead of favouring the Accused, would be favouring the Accuser, which is against the Maxims of both Laws.[2]

Adams' arguments were not, in the end, successful,[3] but his knowledge of civilian authorities was certainly used directly to the aid of his client, John Hancock, and to the preservation of Hancock's excellent, but remarkably elusive, Madeira wine.

C. Divorces, Wills, and Harpooned Officers of the Royal Navy: Applications of Civil Law in Broadstreet v. Broadstreet (1771–1774); Clap's Will (1767–1768); and Rex v. Corbet (1769)

Adams' application of civil law was not limited to spectacular or unusual cases. His background proved useful in ordinary will and divorce problems. A good example is *Broadstreet* v. *Broadstreet* (1771–1774).[4] Poor Abigail Fuller married Dr. Joseph Broadstreet in February 1770. Within a few months, Broadstreet was making not-so-loving statements, such as "'he was a damned fool for having of her and that he should rather have married a Negro if She had money!'"[5] Domestic bliss diminished.

Abigail eventually sought a divorce before the Governor and Council, who had jurisdiction under the *Province Act of 3 Nov. 1692*, c. 25.[6] Represented by Jonathan Sewall, and probably by Adams as well, Abigail sought a divorce *a mensa* ("from Bed and Board"—the equivalent of a separation and maintenance decree) and "'thereby be intitled to the separate and sole use and improvement of her own Estate for the maintenance of herself and Child.'" Joseph, represented by Josiah Quincy, Jr., denied Abigail's "libel"— the civil law writ—and alleged that "'dark and mercenary Enemies to his household'" had by "'insinuating arts [withdrawn] the affections of his Wife.'" Two justices of the peace were assigned

---

[2] Ibid., 207.

[3] Robert Auchmuty's Interlocutory Decree (probably 1 March 1769), which rejected Adams' arguments, also referred extensively to the *Digest*. See *Legal Papers*, II, 207–209.

[4] Case No. 22, *Legal Papers*, I, 280–285.

[5] Ibid., 280.

[6] Ibid., 281, note 6. For an excellent discussion of the colonial Massachusetts law of divorce, see the editorial note at ibid., 280–284.

to take testimony . . . , depositions were read and the parties heard.[7]

The critical issues were whether a separation should be ordered and whether alimony was due. Adams' notes, as carefully analyzed by the editors of the *Legal Papers*, make it clear that "the canon law, as applied in the ecclesiastical courts in England, was an important source of the Massachusetts law of divorce."[8] The key sources examined were a treatise by a distinguished English civilian, John Godolphin's *Repertorium Canonicum* (London, 3d ed., 1687), Richard Burn's famous *Ecclesiastical Law* (London, 2nd ed., 1767), and, again, Thomas Wood's *A New Institute of the Imperial, or Civil Law* (4th ed., 1730).[9] Abigail, incidentally, won. She got a separation, plus costs and 25 pounds sterling alimony a year.

The Governor and Council also sat as the Supreme Court of Probate.[1] *Clap's Will* (1767–1768) was a case about one Samuel Clap, who allegedly "had not been himself for the last year of his life."[2] The issue was whether Clap, during his last year, was capable of making a will which disinherited his eldest living son, William. Evidence was taken according to the procedure and form of civil law interrogatories. Adams, who appeared in defense of the will and Clap's sanity, referred in his case notes to William Nelson's *Lex Testamentaria* (London, 2d ed., 1724) and John Godolphin's *The Orphan's Legacy* (London, 4th ed., 1701), both basic civil law texts of Doctors' Commons.[3] Adams apparently relied on Godolphin's statement of presumptions in favour of sanity when "the testator is known to have intervals of lucidity, or if the will is 'wisely and orderly made.'"[4] He also referred to both Godolphin and another leading English civilian, Henry Swinburne, in making notes of the

---

[7] Ibid., 283.

[8] Ibid.

[9] Ibid., 284–285. See W. Holdsworth, *History of English Law*, v (London, 3d ed., 1945), 12–15; ibid., xii (1st ed., 1938), 425–427.

[1] See *Legal Papers*, I, 245–247 for another excellent editorial note.

[2] Case No. 15, ibid., 245–254.

[3] Ibid., 254. At least according to the editors of the *Legal Papers*, the notation by Adams "in a heavier hand" suggests that "these are authorities for his position." Ibid., 254, note 17.

[4] Ibid., 254, note 20.

case of *Gardiner* v. *Purrington* (1763) in his *Diary*.[5] Swinburne's leading treatise, *A Treatise of Testaments and Last Wills, compiled out of the laws ecclesiastical, civil and canon* . . . (5th ed., 1728) was a great civilian text and was in Adams' law library.[6]

Even more striking examples of applied civilian learning were provided by Adams' cases on the criminal side of the Admiralty. The statute of 28 Hen. 8. c. 15 (1536) established a "criminal jurisdiction" for the Admiralty, encompassing various criminal offenses committed at sea. Provision was included for jury trial. During the days of Adams' practice in Massachusetts, such trials were held before a Special Court of the Admiralty under a commission issued on 14 January 1762.[7]

On 22 April 1769 the British warship, H.M. Frigate *Rose*, intercepted the brig *Pitt Packet* off Marblehead. The brig was boarded, apparently to press sailors. The crew hid in the forepeak, and, when confronted by the British lieutenant, Henry Panton, one sailor, Michael Corbet, drew back a harpoon and impaled the British officer, killing him instantly.[8] Lieutenant Panton is now in a King's Chapel, Boston, grave.

Adams, with James Otis, was hired to represent the seaman.[9] The key issue was whether the killing was justifiable homicide and, if so, was there any appropriate punishment at civil law. In his preparation for the case Adams scoured the civil law authorities on self-defense and provocation. Among the sources listed in his "notes of Authorities" and/or quoted in his "Argument and Report" are John Calvin's *Magnum Lexicon Juridicum*, title "culpa" (Geneva, 1734); Jean Domat's *The Civil Law in its Natural Order: Together with the Public Law* (1st ed. Strahan trans., 1722); Thomas Wood's *A New Institute of the Imperial, or Civil Law* (3d ed., 1721); Robertus Maranta's *Praxis, sive de ordine judiciorum . . . vulgo speculum aureum et lumen advocatorum* (Cologne, 1614); and Andreas Gail's

[5] See *Diary*, I, 243–244. As to Henry Swinburne's distinguished career as an English civilian, see J. Duncan M. Derrett, *Henry Swinburne* (?1551–1624), *Civil Lawyer of York* (York, England, 1973), a useful piece for biography and bibliography.

[6] See Johnson, *Law Treatises*, 52.

[7] See "Editorial Note," *Legal Papers*, II, 275–276.

[8] Ibid., 276–279.

[9] Ibid., 278.

*Practicarum observationum tam ad processum judiciarum praeser-
tim imperialis camerae quam causarum decisiones pertinentium*
(Cologne, 1721).[1]

At trial, on 14 June 1769, Adams came prepared to argue that the
homicide was a justified response to the threat presented by press
gang officers to an innocent seaman, who only wished to stay with his
ship:

> In these Circumstances what could he do? but defend himself, as he did?
> In these Circumstances what was his Duty? He had an undoubted Right,
> not merely to make a push at Lt. Panton, but to have darted an Harpoon,
> a dagger thro the Heart of every Man in the whole Gang.[2]

Adams invoked the *Codex*, 9:16:2, for the right to kill in self-defense. "'De eo, qui salutem suam defendit. Is qui *aggressorem* vel
quemcunque alium, in dubio vitae discrimine constitutus occiderit,
nullum ob id factum, calumniam metuere debet.'"[3] He also invoked
the Scottish civil law authority, Barrington's *Observation upon the
Statutes* (London, 2nd ed., 1766). "'By the Law of Scotland there
is no such Thing as Man Slaughter, nor by the civil Law; and therefore a criminal indicted for Murder, under the Statute of Henry the
Eighth, where the Judges proceed by the Rules of the civil Law,
must either be found guilty of the Murder or acquitted.'"[4]

Furthermore, reasoned Adams, if the governing law was civil law,
then the killing was punishable by death only if it were murder,
there being no civil law death penalty for unjustifiable homicide
without malice. The equivalent common law crime of manslaughter
was more risky, as it might be argued that the seamen were not entitled to benefit of clergy before a Special Admiralty Court.[5] Adams

---

[1] Ibid., 283 (Calvin); ibid., 283, 326 (Domat); ibid., 283, 326 (Wood); ibid.,
283, 329–330 (Maranta); ibid., 330, note 118; ibid., 283, 327–329 (Gail); ibid.,
328, note 116.

[2] Ibid., 330–331. See also ibid., 280.

[3] Ibid., 326 (emphasis Adams'). "Of those who defend their own safety. He who,
when in danger of his life, kills his aggressor or anyone else, should have no fear of
prosecution on this account." Ibid., 326–327, note 115.

[4] Ibid., 334. Adams had a copy of Barrington's book in his library. See Johnson,
Law Treatises, 5.

[5] *Legal Papers*, II, 278–279, 331.

also discovered a statute forbidding impressment of American seamen and moved for jury trial.[6]

The result was dramatic. Adams had only just begun his closing argument to the Special Court of Admiralty when, suddenly, Lieutenant Governor Hutchinson called for an adjournment. Four hours later the Special Court returned. A verdict of justifiable homicide was announced. The seamen were set free.[7]

D. *Conclusion*

There are many other examples of Adams' use of civil law authorities in his practice. In the bizarre criminal admiralty case, *Rex* v. *Nickerson* (1772–1773), Adams invoked the *Codex*, Maranta, Domat, Gail, Wood, and Francis Bacon in a brilliant and successful defense against a charge of piracy. There he obtained an acquittal on the grounds that the evidence against his client was either wholly circumstantial, or inadmissible under the applicable civil law.[8] And there were cases on slavery, where Gridley cited the *Institutes*[9] and Adams cited Voltaire and Montesquieu.[1] There were also routine Admiralty revenue cases where Adams cited civilian sources.[2] A close examination of the record would find many more.[3]

True, some of Adams' accounts were nearly comic searches for authority. "I went upon the first Appeal that has been yet made and prosecuted before Judge Auchmuty, and as it is a new Thing the Judge has directed an Argument, and a Search of Books concerning the Nature of Appeals by the civil Law. I found Time to look into Calvins Lexicon Title Appellatio and Provocatio, and into Maranta,

[6] Ibid., 278, 323–324.

[7] Ibid., 280. Later, Hutchinson would write that the Special Court believed the homicide to be justified. Ibid., 280.

[8] Case No. 57 (1772–1773), ibid., 335–351. For the importance of Francis Bacon as a conduit for civilian learning into the common law, see D. R. Coquillette, "Legal Ideology I," 9–10.

[9] *Slew* v. *Whipple*, Case No. 38 (1766), ibid., 52–55 (Whether "Jenny Slew" was wrongfully kept in "Servitude as a Slave" by "John Whipple Jnr. of . . . Ipswich.").

[1] *Newport* v. *Billing*, Case No. 39 (1768), ibid., 55–57 (Plaintiff claims he was capable of bringing "Trespass and false Imprisonment" action, as he was "no slave but a freeman.").

[2] Ibid., 104.

[3] See, for example, ibid., III, 257–258, in the context of the famous case of *Rex* v. *Wemms* (Case No. 64), the "Boston Massacre" case (1770).

who has treated largely of Appeals. Borrowed Ayliff, but there is no Table and could find nothing about the Subject. Domat I could not find."[4]

At other times, Adams clearly evaded the issue of choice of law between common law and civil law jurisdictions. "I shall not enter into any enquiry, how far the Admiralty sessions in England, or a Special Court of Admiralty in America ought to proceed by the rules of civil law, though it is a question of immense importance to Americans."[5] But Adams certainly did employ his civil law books and his civilian learning in the "trenches" of active practice, and he employed them effectively. Of that there can be no doubt.

V. ADAMS AND PROFESSIONAL ELITISM: THE FOUNDING OF THE SUFFOLK COUNTY BAR ASSOCIATION AND OTHER RESTRICTIVE PRACTICES (1762–1774)

In his *Earliest Diary* the young Adams reflected anxiously and characteristically on "Proof of Genius," i.e. how he could prove his own. It occurred to him that "Order, Method, System, Connection, Plan, or whatever you call it, is the greatest Proof of Genius, next to Invention of new Wheels, Characters, Experiments, Rules, Laws, which is perhaps the first and greatest."[6] Although Adams' energy turned up but a few original ideas, he was a great systematizer of what he knew. Nowhere was this more evident than in his attempts to impose a "system" on the entire local legal profession.

From 1762 through 1774 Adams supported attempts to impose a formal structure on the Boston bar.[7] His youthful aversion to the "pettyfoggers" who competed with him in Braintree led him to welcome more restrictive criteria for practice and more stringent standards for legal education.[8] It is not clear that he went so far as to support the attempt in 1762 by the tory Chief Justice, Thomas Hutchinson, to establish the rank of barrister and to require gowns and wigs. But Adams did show up in court, bewigged and all, and

[4] *Diary*, II, 56, quoted in *Legal Papers*, II, 104.

[5] Ibid., III, 258, note 218.

[6] *Earliest Diary*, 72–73.

[7] See *Legal Papers*, I, lxxvii–lxxxiii.

[8] See *Diary*, I, 136–137; ibid., III, 274.

1

Boston. January 3rd 1770. Wednesday Evening. The Gentlemen of the Bar, met at Mr Ingersols, viz

Benjamin Kent, James Otis, Samuel Fitch, William Reed Samuel Swift, Samuel Quincy, John Adams, Andrew Cazneau and Daniel Leonard Esquires, Barristers, and Francis Dana, Josiah Quincy and Simpson Blowers Attorneys, and voted.

1. That the Barristers and Attorneys at the Superiour Court, belonging to this and the Neighbouring Towns will form themselves into a Society or Law Clubb, to meet at Mr Ingersols, on the Evening of the first Wednesday of every Month, for the Year ensuing.

2. That the eldest Barrister present, preside for the Evening and if no Barrister be present, the eldest Attorney, & that Mr Kent accordingly take his Place for this Evening as the eldest Barrister

3. That a Secretary be chosen to record all Votes and Transactions of this Society, who accordingly proceeded to make Choice of a Person for that Purpose by written Votes, and John Adams Esqr was declared by the President to be chosen.

33. First page of the Bar Book, Suffolk County (1770), in the hand of John Adams, its first Secretary. Courtesy, Massachusetts Historical Society.

from 1762 onward he was present at the core of every effort to establish a formal bar association.[9] In January 1770 the Suffolk County barristers and attorneys formed a new Suffolk County Bar Association. Not surprisingly, Adams was elected its first secretary. The Association met regularly until the courts were closed in 1774.[1]

In 1763 new rules were devised by senior members of the bar that would have limited practice in the Inferior Court to "sworn attornies." The necessary consensus, however, was blocked by the unexpected opposition of the brilliant and eccentric James Otis. Adams was disgusted. "Thus with a whiff of Otis's pestilential Breath, was this whole system blown away. But the Barr was in a great Rage!"[2] Adams continued to lobby tirelessly for "a regular Progress, to the Gown" with a long "State of Probation."[3]

In July 1766 the Boston bar finally introduced a "regular Progress." It was a seven-year stretch, including three years of apprenticeship, two years as an Inferior Court of Common Pleas attorney, and two years as a Superior Court attorney. Of course Adams was enthusiastic.

At Boston. A Meeting of the Bar at the Coffee House, for the Admission of Three young Gentlemen, Mr. Oliver, Mr. Quincy and Mr. Blowers, and another Meeting appointed next Fryday sennight, to consider of some Measures for Limitation, making a Pause, &c. They [young lawyers] swarm and multiply. Sed, The Country grows amazingly, and the Time will not be long e're, many who are now upon the Stage will be in their Graves. . . . Within 4 Years possibly some of all these Ranks may depart. But the Bar has at last introduced a regular Progress, to the Gown, and seven Years must be the State of Probation."[4]

[9] See *Legal Papers*, I, lxxviii–lxxix; *Diary*, I, 235–236. See also G. W. Gawalt, *The Promise of Power*, 33, note 29.

[1] *Legal Papers*, I, lxxix.

[2] See *Diary*, I, 235–236. "Mr. Otis arose and said he had the Credit of the Motion, but he never had moved for any such Rules as these, for they were vs. the Province Law, vs. the Rights of Mankind, and he was amazed that so many wise Heads as that Bar was blessed with could think them practicable, and concluded that he was for one, entirely against them. And said that all schemes to suppress Petty fogger's [sic] must rest on the Honor of the Bar. Foster Hutchinson asked why then was the Court troubled with the Motion? Judge Watts said if the Bar was not agreed the Court could do nothing. And at last they determined to consider till April." Ibid., I, 236.

[3] Ibid., I, 316. See *Legal Papers*, I, lxxix.

[4] *Diary*, I, 316.

It was a far more rigorous path than Adams' own training and apprenticeship. Adams doubtless thought that such was progress. Even so, the new restrictions were not completely effective, and attempts by the Boston lawyers to gain bar concurrence throughout the province failed. There is no need to duplicate here the able work of John Murin, Gerard Gawalt, and Charles McKirdy on the development of the Massachusetts legal profession as a whole during this period.[5] But three points should be made about Adams in particular. First, Adams was a genuine elitist concerning the legal profession. He aspired to make it an aristocracy of talent and learning, excluding both those who sought advancement through family and wealth and those who were uneducated and uncultured. Second, Adams believed that humanist learning in general, and neoclassical legal studies in particular, were useful in achieving this goal. He pursued these studies himself and imposed them on his students and apprentices. "[T]he great works of the civil law should be studied—not only Justinian and his commentators, but Wood, Domat, Ayliffe, and Taylor," because, as Adams advised his student Jonathan Mason in 1776, "this was a study 'so interspersed with History, Oratory, Law, politics, and Warr, and Commerce, that you will find Advantages in it, every day.'"[6]

Finally, if Adams encouraged high standards and restrictions on bar membership, he surely did not advocate a narrow view of legal education. In his advice to others, or in his own development, Adams

[5] See John M. Murin, "The Legal Transformation of the Bench and Bar in Eighteenth Century Massachusetts," in *Colonial America: Essays in Politics and Social Development*, S. Katz, ed. (Boston, 1971), 415–449; Gerard W. Gawalt, *The Promise of Power: The Emergence of the Legal Profession in Massachusetts 1760–1840* (Westport, Conn., 1979); G. W. Gawalt, "Massachusetts Legal Education in Transition, 1766–1840," *American Journal of Legal History*, XXVII (1973), 27; G. W. Gawalt, "Sources of Anti-Lawyer Sentiment in Massachusetts, 1740–1840," *American Journal of Legal History*, XIV (1970), 283; G. W. Gawalt, *Massachusetts Lawyers: A Historical Analysis of the Process of Professionalization, 1760–1840*, 1969 Ph.D. thesis, Northwestern University; Charles R. McKirdy, "Before the Storm: The Working Lawyer in Pre-Revolutionary Massachusetts," *Suffolk Law Review*, XI (1976), 46; C. R. McKirdy, "A Bar Divided: The Lawyers of Massachusetts and the American Revolution," *American Journal of Legal History*, XVI (1972), 206; C. R. McKirdy, *Lawyers in Crisis: The Massachusetts Legal Profession 1760–1790*, 1970 Ph.D. thesis, Northwestern University. See also C. R. McKirdy, "Massachusetts Lawyers on the Eve of the American Revolution: The State of the Profession," above, 313–358.

[6] *Legal Papers*, I, lxxxiii.

envied cosmopolitan legal learning.[7] His avid development of his personal law library and his encouragement of other such libraries emphasized what today would be called comparative law, public international law, and political philosophy.[8] "I am mostly intent at present, upon collecting a Library, and I find, that a great deal of Thought, and Care, as well as Money, are necessary to assemble an ample and well chosen Assortment of Books.—But when this is done, it is only a means, an Instrument. When ever I shall have compleated my Library, my End will not be answered. Fame, Fortune, Power say some, are the Ends intended by a Library. The Service of God, Country, Clients, Fellow Men, say others. Which of these lie nearest my Heart?"[9] In all events, Adams built a great law library. He could fairly, if not modestly, say that "at any Sacrifice . . . and Accordingly by degrees I procured the best Library of Law in the State."[1] His was a "profoundly intellectual approach to the law."[2]

Of course it could also be argued that Adams' professional elitism and his emphasis on intellectualism were not-so-subtle devices to promote a narrow professional monopoly. They probably were. But, as McKirdy has observed, learning was the one and only way that the then humble, but able, Adamses, Gridleys, and Danas could compete with the great families of patronage and wealth, such as the

---

[7] Ibid., lxxxii–lxxxiii. One attraction of civilian learning to Adams and other Americans may have been the systematic, digestible civilian treatises. This must have been particularly attractive, given the absence of American law schools, the limited usefulness of apprenticeships, and the relative scarcity of readable common law treatises and law reports. I owe this suggestion to John Leubsdorf. See H. A. Johnson, *Imported Eighteenth-Century Law Treatises in American Libraries 1700–1799* (Knoxville, 1978) for the impressive extent of civilian titles present in America.

[8] Adams was a fanatic book collector. Wherever he went, he bought books and inspected the libraries of others. See his comments on Miers Fisher's law library in Philadelphia, *Diary*, II, 126; the Dickinson library in Fairhill, ibid., 133; George III's library (which Adams inspected), ibid., III, 150, note 3; Putnam's library, ibid., 264; and, of course, Gridley's great library, much of which Adams purchased, ibid., 271. He bought books in France, ibid., II, viii, 195 facing illustration; Spain, ibid., 426; New York, ibid., 109; and London, ibid., III, 149, note 3, 189. According to Adams, this was all at great expense and was a struggle. See ibid., I, 337.

[9] Ibid.

[1] Ibid., III, 274.

[2] *Legal Papers*, I, xciv.

Lyndes, Stoddards, and Sewalls.[3] If this was a restrictive practice, its restriction emphasized talent and training, not wealth and privilege.

Gerard Gawalt has stated that "the individualism that marks the American legal profession today can be traced to the triumph of competition over the corporate spirit that had motivated eighteenth-century organizers of the professional bar in Massachusetts."[4] Without arguing whether the great corporate firm of today's elite practice emphasizes any kind of "individualism," it certainly was true that Adams would have mourned the loss of the highly interrelated elite bar of his day. He believed such a bar could effectively encourage quality, learning, and the exchange of ideas.[5]

It is probably much too great a leap to try to link Adams' professional self-image with his civilian training, although the emphasis of the civilian tradition on learned elitists, on jurists, and on breadth of legal study certainly invites comparison.[6] Adams did say that "[t]he Roman Lawyers were good Writers. Justinians Institutes were pure as Classicks."[7] The ability to read and write well and to think analytically about the law were directly tied in Adams' mind to classical training. "By studying the classic treatises he hoped to grasp the theory of the law...."[8]

Adams, throughout his life, promoted a corporate, restrictive bar that would require, or reward, such intellectual training. It was not all a question of economic self-interest. In Adams' view such an elite bar could and should encourage its individual members to master the universals of legal culture. It could be a force for public good. It could be a force for change, even revolutionary change.

---

[3] Charles R. McKirdy, *Lawyers in Crisis: The Massachusetts Legal Profession, 1780–1790*, 1970 Ph.D. thesis, Northwestern University, 40.

[4] Gerard W. Gawalt, *The Promise of Power*, 6.

[5] See above, pages 376–381.

[6] See D. R. Coquillette, "Legal Ideology I," 22–35.

[7] *Diary*, II, 375.

[8] *The Earliest Diary*, 41. For descriptions of Adams' classical skills and readings, see A. Iacuzzi, *John Adams, Scholar* (New York, 1952); D. M. Robathan, "John Adams and the Classics," *New England Quarterly*, XIX (1946), 91–98, and C. B. Schulz, "John Adams on 'The Best of All Possible Worlds,'" *Journal of the History of Ideas* (1983), 561–577.

VI. ADAMS AND LEGAL IDEOLOGY: "A DISSERTATION ON THE
CANON AND FEUDAL LAW" (1765) AND "THE LETTERS
OF NOVANGLUS" (1775)

"In spite of his dogmatisms and inconsistencies he [John Adams] remains the most notable political thinker—with the possible exception of John C. Calhoun—among American statesmen." Thus Vernon Parrington has lauded John Adams' political thought, and Parrington has hardly been alone.[9] We have examined Adams' youthful training in civil law sources, his application of those sources in practice, and the influence of his neoclassical education on his self-image as a lawyer and his view of lawyers as an intellectual elite. But what of his politics? There remains the difficult question of what influence, if any, his early civilian training and knowledge had on Adams' fundamental ideas about the legal system and the politics of his day.

It certainly should be no surprise that the Sodalitas Club played a large role in this regard. Indeed Adams' first serious writing about law and politics was originally intended to be a paper for a Sodalitas dinner. This was the so-called "A Dissertation on the Canon and Feudal Law," a most remarkable mix of sober analysis and raging invective.

A. "A Dissertation on the Canon and Feudal Law" (1765)

The first surviving version of the "Dissertation" is a fragment in Adams' Diary "D/JA/10"—the same manuscript "Paper book No.

---

[9] Vernon L. Parrington, *The Colonial Mind 1620–1800* (New York, 1927), 320. Adams has been described as one of the "great triumverate" of American revolutionary thinkers, with Thomas Jefferson and James Wilson. See Charles F. Mullett, *Fundamental Law and the American Revolution 1760–1776* (New York, 1933), 179–188. Parrington praised Adams as a political "realist," the "political counterpart of Dr. Johnson." Parrington, *Colonial Mind*, 307. See also Robert J. Taylor's fine essays on Adams' political thought: "John Adams: Legalist as Revolutionist," *Proceedings of the Massachusetts Historical Society*, LXXXIX (1978), 55–71; and "Construction of the Massachusetts Constitution," *Proceedings of the American Antiquarian Society*, XC (1980), 326–346. For a scholarly analysis of the contributions of Adams to the 1773 constitutional arguments between Governor Thomas Hutchinson, the Massachusetts Council, and the House of Representatives, see *The Briefs of the American Revolution*, J. P. Reid, ed. (New York, 1981), 45–73, 119–143.

10" that contained the first records of the Sodalitas.[1] Judging only from its context, the fragment was written following the 21 February 1765 Sodalitas meeting which Adams himself hosted "at Blodgets. We were never in better Spirits, or more Social."[2]

Between drinks at Blodgets that February night Gridley proposed another rather strenuous discussion topic: feudalism. "We began the 13th. Title of the feudal Law De Alienatione Feudi and read three Titles."[3] Adams quoted to his brethren "the Preface to the Historical Law Tracts, 'The feudal Customs ought to be the Study of every Man, who proposes to reap Instruction from the History of the modern European Nations,'" but then quoted Rousseau *Du Contrat Social* (1762), which defined the feudal system as "'that most iniquitous and absurd Form of Government by which human Nature was so shamefully degraded.'"[4] This caused quite a stir and a debate. Fitch said that the feudal system was a military necessity, "a wise and good system, for a martial People in such Circumstances." Adams replied, "I think that the Absurdity and Iniquity lies in this, that Nations at Peace and in Plenty who live by Commerce and Industry, have adopted such a system." Gridley agreed, adding cryptically "that Rousseau is shallow."[5] Thus Adams began to think about the imposition of old systems of law and custom on societies which no longer required such laws as a matter of practical necessity, assuming that they ever did. Revolutionary musings!

Right after these Sodalitas notes, Adams wrote in his Diary that "[t]his Sodality has given rise to the following Speculation of my own, which I commit to writing, as Hints for future Enquiries rather than as a satisfactory Theory."[6] Thus begins the "Dissertation," and it is an extraordinary piece. Adams lambasted the "Cannon and Feudal Law" as the shrine of the "Desire of ... Dominion, that encroaching, grasping, restless, and ungovernable Principle in hu-

---

[1] See *Diary*, I, 255–258; ibid., 252, note 1.

[2] See ibid., 253–255.

[3] Ibid., 253. This was another reference to the "Feudorum Consuetudines Partim ex Editione vulgata partim ex Cujaciana vulgata appositate, as also the Epitome Feudorum Dionysio Gothofredo Authore" mentioned by Adams at ibid., 251.

[4] Ibid., 254.

[5] Ibid.

[6] Ibid., 255.

man Nature, that Principle which has made so much Havock and Desolation, among the Works of God. . . ."[7] Despite the caution of Fitch and Gridley, Rousseau was on the throne in the torrential attack that followed. No hint of any recognition of the reasons or justifications or even the civilization represented by the feudal and canon law systems emerged, and certainly no indication that here was a man who could and did read canon law in Latin.[8] "[O]f all the . . . Nonsense, Delusion, and Frenzy that had ever passed thro the Mind of Man, none had ever been more glaring and extravagant than the Notions of the Cannon Law, of the indellible Character, the perpetual succession, the virtuous and sanctified Effluvia from Episcopal Fingers, and all the rest of that dark Ribaldry which had thrown such a Glare of Mistery, Sanctity, Reverence and Right Reverence, Eminence and Holiness around the Idea of a Priest."[9]

The basic contrast was, of course, with America. "I always consider the settlement of America with Reverence and Wonder."[1] There the stalwart Puritan heroes "[a]fter their Arrival here . . . pursued their Plan both of Ecclesiastical and Civil Government in direct Opposition to the Cannon And the feudal systems."[2] This was great rhetoric, but was it educated? And was it loyal? If it had been given as a Sodalitas paper, what would Gridley have said?

The fine work of the editors of the recently published *Papers of John Adams* allows us to follow easily the subsequent history and drafts of the "Dissertation."[3] It was never presented to the Sodalitas. Instead, the approval of the Stamp Act by Parliament in March 1765 (in Adams' words that "enormous Engine . . . for battering down all the Rights and Liberties of America")[4] incited Adams to a new idea. He would publish the "Dissertation" in the Boston *Gazette*.[5]

[7] Ibid., 255–256.

[8] See above, 371–372.

[9] *Diary*, I, 258.

[1] Ibid., 256–257.

[2] Ibid., 256.

[3] See *Papers of John Adams*, I, 103–128.

[4] Ibid., 104. See *Diary*, I, 263.

[5] Adams, in his *Autobiography*, described the production of the "Dissertation" in the *Gazette* version:

It was a slightly cooler version that was finally published in the *Gazette* as a series in August, September, and October of 1765. The *Gazette* version actually acknowledged that there just might have been a reason for the feudal system.[6] And it did omit the "Reverence and Wonder" passage about America.[7] But it still was a polemic, a hard-hitting piece. Not only were the corrupt customary laws of Europe contrasted with the ideals of righteous American settlers, but also with *universal principles of law and reason,* namely, "the principles, of the best, and greatest, and wisest legislators of antiquity."[8]

Now what did Adams mean by this? What standard of law did he intend to hold up against Europe's "dark ribaldry of hereditary indefeasible right?"[9] The truth was that young Adams was not too certain. But he had an idea. "[N]o such unworthy dependences took place in the ancient seats of liberty, the republic of Greece and Rome." Bad history, but Adams meant something more. What really contrasted with the medieval European oppression of church and state was the reason of the Enlightenment. And this, in Adams' mind, was built on the classical, civilian notions of universal legal principles, the rights and duties of the *ius gentium.* "[E]very writer, who would allow the people to have any right to life or property, or freedom, more than the beasts of the field, and who was not hired or inlisted under *arbitrary lawless power,* has been always willing to admit the

"On the 14 day of July of this Year 1765, Mrs. Adams presented me with a Daughter in her confinement in her Chamber, I was much alone in (*the Parlour below*) my Office of Evenings and Mornings. The Uneasy State of the public Mind, and my own gloomy Apprehensions, turned my Thoughts to writing. Without any particular Subject to write on, my Mind turned I know not how into a Speculation or rather a Rhapsody which I sent to the Boston Gazette, and was there published without Title or Signature, but which was afterwards reprinted in London under the Title of a dissertation on the Cannon and Feudal Law. It might as well have been called an Essay upon Forefathers Rock. Writings which appear mean enough at the present day, were then highly applauded, in proportion to their Zeal rather than their Merit, and this little production had its full Share of praise." (*Diary,* III, 284.)

[6] "[P]erhaps, for the necessary defense of a *barbarous* people...." *Papers,* I, 112.

[7] To Charles Francis Adams' dismay. See C. F. Adams, *The Works of John Adams,* 10 vols. (Boston, 1850–1856), III, 452. (Hereafter cited as *Works.*)

[8] *Papers,* I, 115.

[9] Ibid., 117.

feudal system to be *inconsistent with liberty and the rights of mankind*."[1]

In the third and fourth installments of "A Dissertation," in the Monday, 30 September 1765 *Gazette,* and the Monday, 21 October 1765 *Gazette,* Adams unveiled an important political and legal theory about the colonists' proper relationship with the British Crown. The colonists, in Adams' theory, "were contented therefore to hold their lands of their King, as their sovereign Lord . . . but to no mesne or subordinate Lords, nor were they willing to submit to any of the baser services."[2] This rather confused version of feudal theory laid the groundwork for Adams' later assertion that loyalty to the Crown did not automatically require consent to the taxation of Lords and Commons. Adams continued further that "Rulers are no more than attorneys, agents and trustees for the people; and if the cause, the interest and trust is insidiously betray'd, or wantonly trifled away, the people have a right to revoke the authority, that they themselves have deputed, and to constitute abler and better agents, attorneys and trustees."[3]

Were these doctrines rebellious? Not in Adams' view. They were but a proper assertion of a legal order against an "arbitrary lawless power." But what was the source of this legal order? It clearly could not be the Parliament. "Let it be known, that British liberties are not the grants of princes or parliaments, but original rights, conditions of original contracts, coequal with prerogative and coeval with government. . . ." And where could this constitution be found? "[M]any of our rights are inherent and essential. . . . Let them search for the foundations of British laws and government in the frame of human nature, *in the constitution of the intellectual and moral world*."[4]

For Adams, therefore, the *ius gentium* of the classical legal tradition and, more significantly, the continental Enlightenment were obvious sources of intellectual authority to resist the arbitrary power of the Parliament. "Let them all become attentive to the grounds and principles of government, ecclesiastical and civil. Let us study the law

---

[1] Ibid. (Emphasis added.)

[2] Ibid., 118.

[3] Ibid., 121.

[4] Ibid., 127. (Emphasis added.)

of nature; search into the spirit of the British constitution; read the histories of ancient ages; contemplate the great examples of Greece and Rome. . . ." Most particularly, "Let the Bar proclaim, 'the laws, the rights, the generous plan of power,' delivered down from remote antiquity. . . ."[5]

Adams surely had reasons to take pride in "A Dissertation." It may have been terrible legal history, but it had a useful and coherent political thesis. The four installments in the *Boston Gazette* were published anonymously.[6] But, to Adams' delight, they were re-printed at once in England, through the efforts of Thomas Hollis, who placed them in the *London Chronicle*.[7] Further, to Adams' even greater pleasure, the pieces were regarded as so learned they were attributed generally to Jeremiah Gridley. When the installments of the "Dissertation" were collected and published together in 1768 in *The True Sentiment of America*—again through Hollis' influence—they were attributed to "Jeremy Gridley, Esq; Attorney General of the Province of *Massachuset's Bay*."[8]

It was a proud thing to be mistaken for Gridley, but Adams, natu-rally, had to put the record straight. What could be a better oppor-tunity than a letter to the talented historian and pamphleteer, Mrs. Catharine Macaulay? Adams simply oozed false modesty:

Indeed it was rather a Mortification to me to find that a few fugitive

[5] Ibid., 126.

[6] 12, 19 August 1765; 30 September 1765; and 21 October 1765. See ibid., 103.

[7] Ibid., 105. Thomas Hollis (1720–1774) was an extraordinary man. Heir to a fortune from manufacturing, Hollis was a dissenter and a whig who supported republican causes, including undertaking to rebuild the library of Harvard College after the fire of 1764. Thanks to the assistance of William H. Bond, the leading expert on Hollis, it can be said with certainty that Hollis caused the publication in the *London Chronicle* of what Hollis called a *"master"* dissertation, although he did not know who wrote it. Unpublished Diary of Thomas Hollis, Nov. 21 [1765] (Hollis emphasis). Hollis also caused Adams' "Dissertation" to be published again by way of addition to the *Appendix to the Journal of the House of Representatives of Massachusetts Bay* "now reprinting here by Almon, by my [Hollis'] means. . . ." Ibid., June 21 [1768]. Hollis still did not know the author. Ibid., June 26 [1768]; July 19 [1768]; Hollis quoted from Adams' "Dissertation" in a letter published in the *London Chronicle* on July 28, 1768 to "Katharina Alexieuna, Empress of all the Russias, ever magnanimous." Ibid., July 24 [1768] and July 28 [1768]. All of the above information is thanks to William H. Bond.

[8] There is a Boston Athenæum copy, EB5 F68–9H7. See ibid.; *Diary*, I, 360–361. See also ibid., 258, note 1.

Speculations in a News Paper, had excited your Curiosity to enquire after me. The Production, which some Person in England, I know not who, has been pleased to intitle a Dissertation on the cannon and the Feudal Law, was written, at Braintree about Eleven Miles from Boston in the Year 1765, written at Random weekly without any preconceived Plan, printed in the Newspapers, without Correction, and so little noticed or regarded here that the Author never thought it worth his while to give it Either a Title or a signature. And indeed the Editor in London [Thomas Hollis], might with more Propriety have called it The What d ye call it, or as the Critical Reviewers did a flimsy lively Rhapsody than by the Title he has given it.

But it seems it happened to hit the Taste of some one who has given [it] a longer Duration, than a few Weeks, by printing it in Conjunction with the Letters of the House of Representatives of this Province and by ascribing it to a very venerable, learned Name. I am sorry that Mr. Gridleys Name was affixed to it for many Reasons. The Mistakes, Inaccuracies and Want of Arrangement in it, are utterly unworthy of Mr. Gridleys great and deserved Character for Learning and the general Spirit and Sentiments of it, are by no Means reconcilable to his known Opinions and Principles in Politicks.

It was indeed written by your present Correspondent, who then has formed Designs, which he never has and never will attempt to execute. Oppressed and borne down as he is by the Infirmities of ill Health, and the Calls of a numerous growing Family, whose only Hopes are in his continual Application to the Drudgeries of his Profession, it is almost impossible for him to pursue any Enquiries or to enjoy any Pleasures of the literary Kind.[9]

Hollis himself was eventually corrected by Andrew Eliot as to the true identity of the author, and Hollis added to his own copy that "This Dissertation ... was written by John Adams, Esq., a young gentleman of the law. . . . He has a large practice, and will probably be soon at the head of his profession."[1]

[9] *Diary*, I, 360–361.

[1] *Works*, III, 447. The "Dissertation" continued to serve Adams well. It formed part of Adams' contribution to the Massachusetts House of Representatives' "Rejoinder" of 2 March 1773 to Governor Thomas Hutchinson's constitutional arguments. See *The Briefs of the American Revolution*, J. P. Reid, ed. (New York, 1981), 119–143. On the occasion of Adams' appointment as Minister Plenipotentiary to the States General of the United Netherlands, he encouraged a new edition, which was published in 1782 in London, *A Collection of State-Papers, Relative to the First Acknowledgment of the Sovereignty of the United States of America, and the Reception*

B. *"The Letters of Novanglus"* (*1775*)

David R. Chesnutt, an able historian with an obvious musical streak, recently has stated that the "simple theme" of Adams' "A Dissertation" contrasts to Adams' later "Novanglus" letters as "the Pachelbel *Kanon*" contrasts to "the Bach *Brandenburgs.*"[2] "A Dissertation" was certainly simplistic, but it was a young work. As the times became increasingly intense, Adams became a more sophisticated ideologue, and his appeal to neoclassical jurisprudence for universal principles of law became more explicit and more precise.

The "Novanglus" letters were the culmination of Adams' revolutionary thought. They were written right up to the outbreak of the fighting.[3] While earlier letters published by Adams evoked civilian authority and delved tentatively into jurisprudence, none could match "Novanglus" for learning and style.[4]

There were twelve "Novanglus" letters, published anonymously in the *Boston Gazette* between 23 January and 17 April 1775. A thirteenth letter was never published, because of the suspension of

of *Their Minister* [*Plenipotentiary,*] by [*their Mightiness*] *the States General of the United Netherlands, By An American. Like an Essay on Cannon and Feudal Law, by John Adams, Esq.* See *Papers,* I, 105. It attracted favorable comment, *Works,* III, 447; *Papers,* I, 104, and was republished by Robert Bell in Philadelphia in 1784. *Works,* III, 447. It was republished again in 1851 in the classic *The Works of John Adams,* edited by Charles Francis Adams. *Works,* III, 447–464. It has now been republished yet again, in a definitive edition, in the *Papers of John Adams* (Cambridge, Mass., 1977). *Papers,* I, 103–128.

[2] See D. R. Chesnutt's review of the *John Adams Papers,* vols. 1 and 2, in *American Journal of Legal History,* XXV (1981), 82, 83. "His [Adams'] 'Dissertation' of 1765 is like the Pachelbel *Kanon* which is built around a simple theme. The Novanglus letters of 1775 are more like the Bach *Brandenburgs* which bring forth a variety of themes hammered home through complex orchestration. (The editors wryly describe the plethora of legal citations in Novanglus as a veritable 'thicket.')" Ibid., 83.

[3] The last letter was published 17 April 1775, two days before the hostilities at Concord and Lexington. See *Papers,* II, 373. Adams, with Joseph Hawley and Samuel Adams, probably also wrote the answer of the Massachusetts House of Representatives in 1773 to Governor Thomas Hutchinson's famous "Address" of 1773. See the excellent edition by John Phillip Reid, *The Briefs of the American Revolution* (New York, 1981), 25–73.

[4] See, for example, the drafts of the "Clarendon/Pym Letters" (1765–1766), *Diary,* I, 272, 274–275, 281–282, 287–292, 296–299. These include a marvellous reference to Grotius' *De Jure Belli ac Pacis,* never published in the newspapers, on the issue of modifying covenants and rules to allow for cases of necessity and impossibility — here put in a context of "a Failure of Justice" that equals an "Abdication of the Crown and Throne." Ibid., 289.

printing following the battles at Lexington and Concord on 19 April 1775.[5] The "Novanglus" letters were provoked by, and responded to, another series of letters. These were written by Daniel Leonard, under the pen name "Massachusettensis," and were published anonymously in consecutive issues of the *Massachusetts Gazette* and the *Boston Post-Boy* and *Advertiser* from 12 December 1774 to 3 April 1775.

Leonard, a successful lawyer from Taunton, had been a close friend of Adams.[6] He also had been a supporter of Samuel Adams and James Otis, but was turned from the popular party by the Boston Tea Party and subsequent events, which were too hot for his taste. He became a loyalist. By August of 1774 he had been driven from his Taunton home by enraged patriots and had settled with his family in the safety of Boston.[7] His letters, commencing three months later, emphasized the practical benefits of subordination to Britain and the "inconsistency of whig reasoning on the relationship between Parliament and the colonies."[8] It was never clear whether Adams recognized, at the time, that his anonymous adversary was his old friend.[9]

Adams' editors have given Leonard an edge in the contest. "In this encounter at least, Leonard understood better the art of public persuasion. Adams sought to bowl over his opponent with an astonishing display of legal scholarship that might have impressed lawyers but would certainly have left ordinary readers bewildered, exhausted, and finally bored."[1] Nevertheless, at least from this impressed

---

[5] *Papers*, II, 222.

[6] See the excellent "Editorial Note," *Papers*, II, 216–226.

[7] In August 1774 Leonard accepted appointment from General Gage as one of the mandamus councilors. *Papers*, II, 217. He later became solicitor to the Customs Commissioners in 1775, sailed to Halifax in 1776, and continued his service to the Commissioners there and in England. From 1782 to 1806 he was Chief Justice of Bermuda, and he was a leading barrister in London from 1806 until his death in 1829. See *Legal Papers*, I, ciii.

[8] Ibid., II, 219.

[9] Leonard was correctly identified in 1775 by Adams' former law clerk, John Trumbell, but Adams later expressed surprise that "Massachusettensis" was other than another old loyalist friend, Jonathan Sewall, who sailed for London in August 1775. Ibid., 221–222. See ibid., I, cx. Sewall's son became Chief Justice of Lower Canada. Ibid.

[1] Ibid., II, 219.

lawyer's perspective, Adams was juristically and intellectually superior, and, in fact, in a class by himself.

Adams' purpose in writing the "Novanglus" letters was to establish a legal justification for a Commonwealth status for American colonies under a constitutional monarch. His first target, therefore, was the theory that the Crown's theoretical dominion in the colonies brought with it the unlimited power of Parliament.

[A]fter the maxim was established, *quod principi placuit legis habet vigorem,* and so far from including the two houses of parliament in the idea of this imperial crown, it was intended to insinuate that the crown was absolute, and had no need of lords or commons to make or dispense with laws. Yet even these court sycophants when driven to an explanation, never dared to put any other sense upon the words imperial crown, than this, that the crown of England was independent of France, Spain, and all other kings and states in the world.[2]

In the process of making this argument, Adams demonstrated a mastery of both colonial and English seventeenth-century constitutional history, together with an understanding of England's historical relations with Scotland, Wales, and Ireland, and of the history of British provincial law,[3] including the *post nati* controversy and *Calvin's Case.*[4] But the essence of Adams' argument was not the doubtful precedents of English colonial history. The core of the argument was the application of three legal principles of the *ius gentium*, namely: (1) that under the law of nature and nations resistance to arbitrary power is allegiance to the principles of law, i.e. "[r]esistence to lawful authority make rebellion";[5] and (2) that under the law of nations and the law of the English constitution itself

---

[2] Ibid., 251.

[3] See, for example, ibid., 250–252, 258–265, 337–385.

[4] Ibid., 309. *Calvin's Case*, VII, Coke's Reports (1608), I, concerned James I's desire to have the *post-nati*, i.e. those born after his accession to the English throne, naturalized in both England and Scotland. The English Parliament was unwilling, and a collusive action was brought by Calvin, a Scottish *post-natus*. A majority of the Exchequer Chamber held that Calvin was a natural-born subject of the King of England, and not an alien, and that allegiance to a sovereign and protection by a sovereign were reciprocal rights. For a concise account, see D. Walker, *The Oxford Companion to Law* (1980), 170; W. Holdsworth, *A History of English Law*, IX (3rd ed., 1944), 79–80.

[5] *Papers*, II, 269.

there was no lawful parlimentary authority over the colonies, whether under the pretext of an "imperial crown" or otherwise,[6] i.e. "if the colonies are feudatory to the kings of England, and subject to the government of the king's laws, it is only to such laws as are made in their general assemblies, their provincial legislatures"; and (3) therefore, resistance to attempts to subordinate colonial government to parliamentary edicts was, as a matter of universal legal principle, an affirmation of legal order.[7]

Throughout Adams resorted extensively to civilian, comparative law and Enlightenment sources. He began with his "principle one," that resistance to arbitrary power was lawful by the law of nature and nations. He turned first to Grotius' *De Jure Belli ac Pacis:*

> Be it remembered then, that there are tumults, seditions, popular commotions, insurrections and civil wars, upon just occasions, as well as unjust. Grotius B. I. c. 3 § I. observes "that some sort of private war, may be lawfully waged. It is not repugnant to the law of nature, for any one to repel injuries by force."[8]

Adams then turned to Baron Pufendorf's *Law of Nature and Nations,* and the attached notes of Jean Barbeyrac, the French jurist:

> Pufendorf's law of nature and nations L. [Bk.] 7. c. 8 § 5 and 6. Barbeyrac's note on §6. "[I] When we speak of a tyrant that may lawfully be dethroned, we do not mean by the people, the vile populace or rabble of the country, or the cabal of a small number of factious persons; but the greater and more judicious part of the subjects of all ranks. Besides the tyranny must be so notorious and evidently clear, as to leave no body

---

[6] Ibid., 251. See also ibid., 337–354.

[7] Ibid., 372.

[8] Ibid., 288–289. This quotation is from the 1738 translation, found in Adams' library. Ibid., 306, note 1. The quotation from Grotius continued: § 2. "The liberty allowed before is much restrained, since the erection of tribunals: Yet there are some cases wherein that right still subsists; that is, when the way to legal justice is not open; for the law which forbids a man to pursue his right any other way, ought to be understood with this equitable restriction, that one finds judges to whom he need apply," &c.

Adams referred as well to Sidney's *Discourses,* which also cited Grotius: "The same course is justly used against a legal magistrate, who takes upon him to exercise a power which the law does not give: for in that respect he is a private man, (Quia,) as Grotius says, (eatenus non habet imperium,) and may be restrained as well as any other, because he is not set up to do what he lists, but what the law allows, so the same law limits and directs the exercise of that which he has." Ibid., 291.

any room to doubt of it, &c. Now a prince may easily avoid making himself so universally suspected and odious to his subjects: for as Mr. Locke says, in his treatise of civil government c. 18.§.209. 'It is as impossible for a governor, if he really means the good of the people, and the preservation of them and the laws together, not to make them see and feel it; as it is for the father of a family, not to let his children see he loves and takes care of them.' And therefore *the general insurrection of a whole nation does not deserve the name of rebellion.*"[9]

Adams concluded by invoking the full greatness of the Enlightenment against poor old "Massachusettensis": "Surely Grotius, Puffendorf, Barbeyrac, Lock, Sidney, and LeClerk, are writers, of sufficient weight, to put in the scale against the mercenary scriblers in New-York and Boston, who have the unexampled impudence and folly, to call these which are revolution principles in question, and to ground their arguments upon passive obedience as a corner stone."[1]

Adams then turned to his "second" principle — the absence of any lawful parliamentary authority over the North American colonies. Again, he appealed to the universal law of nations, as the law of "right reason,"[2] and to classical antecedents:

Is America incorporated into the realm? Is it a part of the realm? Is it a part of the kingdom? Has it any share in the legislative of the realm? The constitution requires that every foot of land should be represented, in the third estate, the democratical branch of the constitution. How many millions of acres in America, how many thousands of wealthy landholders, have no representative there?

But let these "best writers" say what they will, there is nothing to the law of nations, *which is only the law of right reason, applied to the conduct of nations,* that requires that emigrants from a state should continue, or be made a part of the state.

The practice of free nations only can be adduced, as precedents of what the law of nature has been thought to dictate upon this subject of colonies.

---

[9] Ibid., 291. (Emphasis added.)

[1] Ibid., 293.

[2] Ibid., 311. Adams confused the three separate classical concepts of *ius gentium, naturalis ratio,* and *ius naturale.* See below, 413, note 3. But so did the Roman jurists. See C. F. Mullett, *Fundamental Law and the American Revolution,* 1760–1776 (New York, 1933), 16–17. See also D. R. Coquillette, "Legal Ideology I," 22–24.

Their practice is different. The senate and people of Rome did not inter-
fere commonly in making laws for their colonies, but left them to be
ruled by their governors and senates. Can Massachusettenis produce from
the whole history of Rome, *or from the Digest,* one example of a *Senatus
consultum,* or a *Plebiscitum* laying taxes on a colony.[3]

Thus in Adams' view there was an explicit source of "the law of
nations" directly relevant to the lawfulness of his positions: namely,
"the practice of free nations" as "precedents of what the law of nature
has been thought to dictate . . . ," and "the opinions of the best writers
upon the law of nations," including Justinian's *Digest*.[4] This authority was not only relevant, but, in Adams' view, it supported
a single particular rule as to foreign territories. "I deny therefore
that the practice of free nations, or the opinions of the best writers
upon the law of nations, will warrant the position of Massachusettenis, that when a nation takes possession of a distant territory, that
becomes a part of the state equally with its ancient possessions. The
practice of free nations, and the opinions of the best writers, are in
general on the contrary."[5] Furthermore, this universal authority, in
Adams' view, indicated a practical and just solution to the American
"problem." The provincial governments were commonwealths, with
legislative independence, but they owed allegiance to the Crown as a

---

[3] *Papers,* II, 311–312. (Emphasis added in first two instances.) Adams continued to
emphasize that Parliament's claims were not supported by "the practice of nations":
  "The practice of nations has been different. The Greeks planted colonies, and
neither demanded nor pretended any authority over them, but they became distinct
independent commonwealths.
  The Romans continued their colonies under the jurisdiction of the mother commonwealth—but, nevertheless, she allowed them the priviledges of cities. Indeed
that sagacious city seems to have been aware of the difficulties similar to those under
which Great Britain is now labouring; she seems to have been sensible of the impossibility of keeping colonies planted at great distances, under the absolute control of her
senatus consulta. Harrington tells us, Oceana p. 43, that 'the commonwealth of
Rome, by planting colonies of its citizens within the bounds of Italy, took the best
way of propagating itself, and naturalizing the country; whereas if it had planted
such colonies without the bounds of Italy, it would have alienated the citizens, and
given a root to liberty abroad, that might have sprung up foreign, or savage and
hostile to her; *wherefore it never made any such dispersion of itself, and its strength,*
till it was under the yoke of the emperors, who disburdening themselves of the people,
as having less apprehension of what they could do abroad than at home, took a
contrary course.'" Ibid., 311.

[4] Ibid., 312, 313.

[5] Ibid., 313.

constitutional sovereign. Rule by an absolutist parliament, in which the colonists had no voice, violated this natural law and the "law of nations, which is only the law of right reason, applied to the conduct of nations."[6] Only if the natural lawful order were recognized would a peaceful society, based on true principles of law be possible. Quoting James Harrington's *The Oceana* (3d ed., 1747), Adams concluded:

> "A faithful peace was to be expected from men whose affections were conciliated—nor was any kind of fidelity to be expected from slaves." The consul exclaimed, *Eos demum, qui nihil praeterquam de libertate, cogitent, dignos esse qui Romani fiant.* That they who regarded nothing so much as their Liberty, deserved to be Romans. *Itaque et in senatu causam obtinuere, et ex auctoritate patrum, latum ad populum est, ut privernatibus civitas daretur.*[7]

Adams was not writing the "Novanglus" letters to urge "precipitating us into a civil war."[8] On the contrary he had a compromise in mind. It was a compromise most ironically suggested by his study of the traditional dividing line between the civil law admiralty jurisdiction and common law jurisdictions, i.e. the "low water mark" of the ocean:

> And therefore I contend, that our provincial legislatures are the only supream authorities in our colonies. Parliament, notwithstanding this, may be allowed an authority supreme and sovereign over the ocean, which may be limited by the banks of the ocean, or the bounds of our charters; our charters give us no authority over the high seas. Parliament has our consent to assume a jurisdiction over them. *And here is a line fairly drawn between the rights of Britain and the rights of the colonies, viz. the banks of the ocean, or low water mark. The line of division between common law and civil, or maritime law.* If this is not sufficient—if parliament are at a loss for any principle of natural, civil, maritime, moral or common law, on which to ground any authority over the high seas, the Atlantic especially,

---

[6] Ibid., 311.

[7] Ibid., 312.

[8] Ibid., 314. Adams argued that: "In one word, *if public principles* and motives and arguments, were alone to determine this dispute between the two countries, *it might be settled forever, in a few hours;* but the everlasting clamours of prejudice, passion and private interest, drown every consideration of that sort, and are precipitating us into a civil war." Ibid., 314.

let the colonies be treated like reasonable creatures, and they will discover great ingenuity and modesty. . . .[9]

"Massachusettensis" had argued that there was "no possible medium between absolute independence and subjection to the authority of parliament."[1] Adams replied:

If this is true, it may be depended upon that all North America are as fully convinced of their independence, their absolute independence, as they are of their own existence, and as fully determined to defend it at all hazards, as Great Britain is to defend her independence, against foreign nations. But it is not true. An absolute independence on parliament, in all internal concerns and cases of taxation, is very compatible with an absolute dependence on it in all cases of external commerce.[2]

Until fighting actually began, Adams was looking for universal legal principles to resolve the dispute, perhaps resolve it "in a few hours," even as those principles also justified the continuing American resistance, leading to war.

A staggering compilation of common law authority on the rights of parliament and the nature of the Crown graced the concluding "Novanglus letters." Adams' argument incorporated *Calvin's Case*, the *post nati* dispute,[3] and extended into the most learned dissertations on the legal status of Wales and Ireland, Guernsey and Jersey, and the Counties Palatine.[4] His citations ranged from Coke's *Reports* and *Institutes* to the latest *Burrow's Reports* and the decisions of Lord Mansfield.[5] It was all a convincing demonstration of

[9] Ibid., 313–314. (Emphasis added.)

[1] Ibid., 335.

[2] Ibid.

[3] Ibid., 309, 347–348. As to *Calvin's Case*, see above, 410, note 4.

[4] Ibid., 373–376.

[5] See, for example, ibid., 363–369. Adams' "love-hate" relationship with Mansfield, who argued against repeal of the Stamp Act, could be the subject of another article. On one occasion, rich with irony, Adams was technically Mansfield's guest at the House of Lords! See *Diary*, III, 149–151, setting out Adams' letter to the *Boston Patriot* of 17 February 1812:

"Mr. Copley, another of my countrymen, with whom I had obtained without so much royal protection, a reputation not less glorious; and that by studies and labours not less masterly in his art, procured me, and that from the great Lord Mansfield, a place in the house of lords, to hear the king's speech at the opening of parliament [11 November], and to witness the introduction of the Prince of Wales, then arrived

Adams' ability to do serious research. Not only was this research remarkably accurate for its day, but it led Adams to propose a "royal Commonwealth" model which, in different times, would prove to be both practical and successful.[6] The "Novanglus" letters were an attempt to apply universal principles of law both to justify an ordered freedom and to prevent war. They demonstrated a genuine and cosmopolitan legal learning, and they represented, then and now, the legal mentality at its best. But even as Adams began writing the thirteenth "Novanglus" letter in April 1775, men were training on the Green at Lexington.

C. Conclusion: An Ideology of Universal Legal Principles

Adams tried to sound like Cicero.[7] His legal ideas were neoclassical too. He believed that there were universal principles of law

at the age of twenty one. One circumstance, a striking example of the vicissitudes of life, and the whimsical antithesis of politics, is too precious for its moral, to be forgotten. Standing in the lobby of the house of lords, surrounded by a hundred of the first people of the kingdom, Sir Francis Molineux, the gentleman usher of the black rod, appeared suddenly in the room with his long staff, and roared out with a very loud voice—'Where is Mr. Adams, Lord Mansfield's friend!' I frankly avowed myself Lord Mansfield's friend and was politely conducted by Sir Francis to my place. A gentleman said to me the next day, 'how short a time has passed, since I heard that same Lord Mansfield say in the same house of lords, "My Lords, if you do not kill him, he will kill you."' Mr. West said to me, that this was one of the finest finishings in the picture of American Independence.

Pope had given me, when a boy, an affection for Murray. When in the study and practice of the law, my admiration of the learning, talents and eloquence of Mansfield had been constantly increasing, though some of his opinions I could not approve. His politics in American affairs, I had always detested. But now I found more politeness and good humor in him than in Richmond, Cambden, Burke or Fox." Ibid., III, 150–151.

Adams' friendship with Copley had another ironic twist. Copley's son, John Singleton Copley, Baron Lyndhurst (1772–1863), became Lord Chancellor of England. See *The Compact Edition of the Dictionary of National Bibliography* (1975 ed.), I, 1107–1114.

[6] See, for example, Geoffrey Marshall, *Parliamentary Sovereignty and the Commonwealth* (London, 1957), 47–138; K. C. Wheare, *The Constitutional Structure of the Commonwealth* (Oxford, 1960), 1–113; R. L. Watts, *New Federations Experiments in the Commonwealth* (London, 1966), 17–37.

Other contemporaries of Adams had reached almost identical conclusions. See, for example, Thomas Jefferson's *A Summary View of the Rights of British America* (Philadelphia, 1774).

[7] See Stephen Botein, "Cicero as Role Model for Early American Lawyers: A Case Study in Classical 'Influence,'" *Classical Journal*, LXXIII (1977–1978), 313, 316–319.

applicable to all intelligent, civilized peoples and that these legal principles curbed arbitrary power.[8] This was nothing new in Massachusetts. Even John Winthrop "asserted the dependence of all civil laws upon natural law, and implied that a test of the law of nature was its agreement with the needs of the society to which it is applied."[9] Still the young Adams sounded the call of fundamental law with a new assurance, and the notes were resonant with civilian learning and the spirit of the continental Enlightenment.

What was the ultimate significance of civilian learning in Adams' own view? It was not just as a symbol of professional elitism, although Adams truly believed in the virtue of elitism.[1] Nor was it merely a useful tool in practice and advocacy, although it had stood him in good stead in cases from dead whales to affairs of state. Nor did Adams freely apply civilian precedents outside those cases concededly governed by civil law to fill in the gaps of the common law, much less to attack or subvert common law rules.[2] Rather, such learning was, to Adams, the mark of the whole intellectual lawyer. It linked the struggling, ambitious young apprentice in the Worcester office with the juristic world.

It was a world of legal principles, not just legal rules and procedures. It encompassed the jurisprudence of Grotius, Montesquieu, Ayliffe, Pufendorf, Vattel, Babeyrac, Domat, and Burlamaqui.[3] It

---

[8] See above, 404–415. See also Charles F. Mullett, *Fundamental Law and the American Revolution 1760–1776* (New York, 1933), 181–188. Mullett correctly observed that the *ius gentium* of Gaius, "universal, rational and equitable," was hardly adopted by later civilians, and that these terms had much ambiguity in colonial America. Ibid., 17. Nevertheless, Mullett acknowledged that "Grotius, Pufendorf, and Vattel" did much toward identifying *ius gentium* and natural law among American colonials. Ibid., 17. See also Peter Stein "The Attraction of the Civil Law in Post Revolutionary America," *Virginia Law Review*, LII (1966), 403, 404–407.

[9] George Lee Haskins, *Law and Authority in Early Massachusetts* (New York, 1960), 160.

[1] See above, 376–381. See generally, John M. Murin, "The Legal Transformation: the Bench and Bar in Eighteenth Century Massachusetts," in *Colonial America: Essays in Politics and Social Development*, S. Katz, ed. (Boston, 1971), 415–449.

[2] It was in Adams' political writing that he frequently turned to civilian authority as a source of broadly applicable, natural law principles. I am indebted to John Leubsdorf for the suggestion in the text.

[3] See above, 382–395. For an excellent general account of the contents and nature of these eighteenth-century civil law treatises, see A. W. B. Simpson, "The Rise and Fall of the Legal Treatise: Legal Principles and the Forms of Legal Literature," *University of Chicago Law Review*, XLVIII (1981), 632, 656–657. For an excellent

extended to the renaissance of Bacon and Selden, and even to those ultimate classical symbols of humanist aspiration in the law, the classical Roman jurists, Justinian's compilers, and Cicero.[4] It encouraged a provincial lawyer to dare to think "big," to aspire to have universally valid ideas.

When Adams, as a battle-scarred seventy-year-old Federalist, took up his pen to continue writing his "Autobiography," he recalled an incident nearly forty-seven years in the past.[5] It was that day in October 1758 when the young Adams went to seek support and advice from the patriarch of the Boston bar, Jeremiah Gridley.

[Gridley] "Have you read Grotius and Puffendorf?"

[Adams] "I cannot say I have Sir. . . ."

[Gridley] "You will do well to do so: they are great Writers. Indeed a Lawyer through his whole Life ought to have some Book on Ethicks or the Law of Nations always on his Table. *They are all Treatises of individual or national Morality and ought to be the Study of our whole Lives.*"[6]

general account of their influence on American revolutionary thought, see Thomas C. Grey, "Origins of the Unwritten Constitution: Fundamental Law in American Revolutionary Thought," *Stanford Law Review*, XXX (1978), 843, 850, 860–863, emphasizing the influence of Pufendorf, Burlamaqui, Vattel, and Rutherforth. See also Erwin C. Surrency, "The Lawyer and the Revolution," *American Journal of Legal History*, VIII (1964), 125, 132, emphasizing Pufendorf, Grotius, and Wood's *Institutes of Civil Law*.

[4] Of these, only Bacon's influence on Adams has not been illustrated by this essay. As to this, see *Diary*, I, 177, 186, 266, 286; *Diary*, II, 375, 386; *Diary*, III, 264; *Diary*, IV, 212.

[5] The exact dates when the "Autobiography" was written remain unclear. See *Diary*, I, xliv. The section with the Gridley quote follows a mark in the text stating "Continued November 30, 1804." See *Diary*, III, 261.

[6] *Diary*, III, 271–272. (Emphasis added.) For a slightly different account in Adams' contemporary diary, see ibid., I, 54–55. See also above, 363, note 8.

WILLIAM E. NELSON

The American Revolution and the Emergence of Modern Doctrines of Federalism and Conflict of Laws

THE received learning about the history of conflict of laws in America tells us that conflicts rarely, if ever, occurred during the colonial period and that it was only the creation during the War of Independence of a "confederation of states, each of which was legally independent, [that] turned the attention of lawyers to the practical solution of the necessarily resulting conflicts."[1] Having no other model to which to turn for that "practical solution," Americans, it is suggested, borrowed doctrinal concepts from Continental law and transplanted them in the New World.[2]

A study of conflicts cases arising in the colonial, state, and federal courts of Massachusetts between 1760 and 1830 indicates that the story was much more complex. Conflicts problems did occur in colonial Massachusetts, but they were of a different sort from the problems with which we are familiar today. There was, moreover, a body of English law dealing with the problems, which offered an alternate model upon which modern American conflicts law could have been erected. A central historical question is why that English model was rejected.

After a preliminary inquiry as to why conflicts of the sort with which we are now familiar rarely arose in colonial Massachusetts,

Note: Citations to published source materials of a legal nature conform to *A Uniform System of Citation* (Cambridge, Mass., 13th ed., 1981), which is available at most law libraries. The author is indebted to Morton J. Horwitz for his helpful comments and criticisms and to the Law Center Foundation of New York University for research support.

[1] Joseph H. Beale, *A Treatise on the Conflict of Laws*, vol. 3 (New York, 1935), 1911. But see Kurt H. Nadelmann, "Joseph Story's Contribution to American Conflicts Law: A Comment," *American Journal of Legal History*, 5 (1961), 230, 234–235.

[2] Willis L. M. Reese and Maurice Rosenberg, eds., *Cases and Materials on Conflict of Laws* (Mineola, 7th ed., 1978), 4–5.

34. Old State House, Boston, by James B. Marston (1801). For many years it served as the seat of the Superior Court of Judicature, and was the heart of the "legal district." John Adams and other lawyers lived near by. Courtesy, Massachusetts Historical Society.

this essay will turn to the conflicts which did arise and the legal model under which they were analyzed. Next it will describe the stresses to which that model was subjected during the Revolutionary War years—stresses under which the model broke down. Finally, it will consider the attempt made at the Constitutional Convention to readjust the model to post-Revolutionary American conditions and the ultimate failure of that attempt in the early nineteenth century. A consequence of that failure was that federal-state conflicts and interstate conflicts, which the readjusted model treated as parallel and indistinguishable questions, came to be analyzed as separate problems—the former to be resolved largely as a matter of federal constitutional law and the latter, largely as a matter of state law.

I. English Law in the New World

A. The Legal Unity of the Anglo-American World

Before the War of Independence had fragmented the political unity of the Anglo-American world, conflicts problems, as we know them, arose only infrequently. The nature of Anglo-American law in the eighteenth century accounted to some degree for the lack of modern choice-of-law doctrine. Especially in eighteenth-century New England, the power to determine the rules of law by which cases were decided was lodged in juries rather than judges.[3] Although juries in some cases may have been faced with questions about the applicability of a rule other than that of the forum, the fact that the reasons underlying jury verdicts were never recorded meant that no body of doctrine about how juries should choose law could emerge. Issues about choice of substantive law were determined and doctrine was created only in occasional cases in which a question of substance lurked in the interstices of the procedural and pleading rules which were the chief concern of the eighteenth-century judiciary.

The political unity of the English-speaking world also contributed to the legal unity of that world. Considering themselves Englishmen, the American colonists demanded all the rights of Englishmen,

---

[3] See William E. Nelson, *Americanization of the Common Law: The Impact of Legal Change on Massachusetts Society, 1760–1830* (Cambridge, Mass., 1975), 21–35; William E. Nelson, "The Eighteenth-Century Background of John Marshall's Constitutional Jurisprudence," *Michigan Law Review,* 76 (1978), 893, 902–924.

one of the most important of which was the right to have disputes resolved by the common law. Whatever the doubts of Blackstone and the imperial hierarchy,[4] the common law had been received by the mid-eighteenth century in each of the thirteen colonies. "The common law of England," one English lawyer wrote, "is the common law of the plantations . . . [as far] as the nature of things will bear,"[5] for, as another explained, "if there be a new and uninhabited country not found out by *English* subjects, as the law is the birthright of every subject, so, wherever they go, they carry their laws with them, and therefore such new country is to be governed by the laws of *England*."[6] Judges in Massachusetts were in full agreement: Peter Oliver, later a chief justice, thought that "we brought over both the Common Law and Statute with us,"[7] while Edmund Trowbridge, another judge, argued that officials must follow "the Rule at Common Law; unless that Rule be altered by some Statute or Law of the Province."[8] The inclination of Massachusetts judges to look to Westminster for precedent was further confirmed by the absence of published Massachusetts law reports, which left them with no other choice. As a result, an essentially uniform common law existed throughout the colonies; in fact, during the fifteen years before the Revolution, no record exists of a single Massachusetts case in which a common-law choice of law question was raised.

[4] Blackstone argued that the American plantations had been acquired by conquest, not settlement, and therefore were not subject to the common law. See William Blackstone, *Commentaries on the Laws of England*, vol. 1 (Oxford, 1765), 105. See generally Elizabeth G. Brown, *British Statutes in American Law, 1776–1836* (Ann Arbor, 1964), 12–14.

[5] Opinion of Richard West, Counsel for Board of Trade (1720), in George Chalmers, *Opinions of Eminent Lawyers on Various Points of English Jurisprudence*, vol. 1 (London, 1814), 194–195.

[6] Anonymous, 2 P. Wms. 75, 24 Eng. Rep. 646 (Ch. 1722). Accord, Blankard v. Galdy, 2 Salk. 411, 91 Eng. Rep. 356 (K.B. 1693). See generally Brown, *British Statutes in American Law*, 10–11; Joseph H. Smith, *Appeals to the Privy Council from the American Plantations* (New York, 1950), 482–484. Brown finds any conclusions as to reception tenuous. See Brown, *British Statutes in American Law*, 19–21.

[7] Baker v. Mattocks, Quincy 69, 72 (Mass. 1763).

[8] Richmond v. Davis, Quincy 279, 293 (Mass. 1768). Accord, Baker v. Mattocks, Quincy 69, 70 (Mass. 1763) (opinion of Russell, J.); Hendricks v. Ashley, Hampshire Super. Ct., September 1772 (allegation of false imprisonment "against the Custom of England and this province").

To what extent did choice of law problems arise during this same period as a result of conflicting statutes? The increasingly sophisticated debate in which Americans were engaged about the applicability of acts of Parliament in the colonies[9] suggests that the colonists were aware of the existence of numerous legislative bodies in the Anglo-American world and of the possibility that their statutes could come into conflict. But, in fact, only one choice-of-law case emerged in Massachusetts out of conflicting statutes.[1] For Americans, in the day to-day ordering of private legal affairs, usually forgot sophisticated constitutional doctrines and adopted a simpler argument, analogous to that made to secure reception of the common law, that, as Englishmen, they were entitled, "as part of their birthright," to all the rights of Englishmen, including the benefits of English legisla-

---

[9] See generally Bernard Bailyn, *Pamphlets of the American Revolution, 1750–1776*, vol. 1 (Cambridge, Mass., 1965), 115–138; Lawrence H. Gipson, *The Coming of the Revolution, 1763–1775* (New York, 1954), 69–89, 110–115, 172–195; G. H. Guttridge, *English Whiggism and the American Revolution* (Berkeley, 2d ed., 1963), 58–90.

[1] See Jones v. Belcher, Quincy 9 (Mass. 1762), which involved a conflict between a Massachusetts statute and an act of Parliament. But the analysis would have been similar if two colonial statutes had been involved. The issue was whether, upon a bond executed by a Massachusetts debtor to pay a debt due in England, interest should be allowed at the rate provided by the Massachusetts or by the English statute. The court could not make the typical arguments and merely apply the English rule, since a local rule was in direct conflict. See below, 423, notes 2–7 and accompanying text. But its approach was equally simplistic. Declining the opportunity to rule generally upon the applicability of acts of Parliament in the colonies, it held merely that "as the Bond was given to a Person here, (not the Creditor in England), and the Debt was become his, New England Interest ought to be granted." Ibid., 9. Residence of the parties thus appears to have been the deciding factor in determining what law to apply, but the brevity of analysis and the lack of other cases make it impossible to determine if the holding was representative of any general rule. But see Jonathan Elliot, ed., *The Debates in the Several State Conventions, on the Adoption of the Federal Constitution* (Philadelphia, 2d ed., 1836), 2:556–557, where John Marshall noted some twenty years later that in such a case the *lex loci contractu* would apply. There was some support for Marshall's approach in mid-eighteenth-century English cases. See Robinson v. Bland, 2 Burr. 1077, 1079, 97 Eng. Rep. 717, 718 (K.B. 1760) (dictum); Note, Interest Money, 1 Eq. Cas. Abr. 286, 288–289, 21 Eng. Rep. 1049, 1051 (cc. 1700). Jones v. Belcher itself could be so analyzed. But, as Lord Mansfield observed, "the law of the place where the thing happens does not always prevail." Robinson v. Bland, 2 Burr. 1077, 1084, 97 Eng. Rep. 717, 721 (K.B. 1760). See also Roach v. Garvan, 1 Ves. Sen. 157, 27 Eng. Rep. 954 (Ch. 1748). Both Robinson and Roach involved transactions entered into in France by English subjects to which English courts hesitated to apply French law. See generally Part I, B, below, for a possible explanation as to why.

tion.[2] The Maryland Assembly, for one, "deemed the General Statutes of England to have the force of Laws of Maryland ... [for] it would be a great Absurdity to advance that we are intituled to all the Rights and Liberties of British Subjects and that we Can't have the Benefits of the Laws by which those Rights and Liberties are Reserved."[3] And the highest colonial courts, ignoring the refined theories of English judges, text writers, and privy councillors, almost invariably agreed. One colonial judge in Massachusetts, as already noted, believed "we brought over both the Common Law and Statute with us,"[4] while a colonial court held "all general statutes of [England] ... not by express words restrained [thereto] ... to be of force and to have always been received as such,[5] unless, as in the case of the common law, they were inapplicable to local conditions."[6] Statutory conflicts were further minimized by the tendency of colonial legislatures not to enact statutes of more than local effect unless, as in the case of the Statute of Frauds, they copied them from Parliamentary acts.[7] The relatively small amount of intercolonial intercourse during the 1760's, compared with that occurring even fifteen years later,[8] also helped to keep conflicts at a minimum.

[2] Allison v. Long, Jamaica Ct. Errors, January 1710, quoted in part in Smith, *Appeals to the Privy Council*, 477.

[3] Proceedings and Acts of the General Assembly of Maryland, October 1720–October 1723, quoted in Brown, *British Statutes in American Law*, 18–19.

[4] Baker v. Mattocks, Quincy 69, 72 (Mass. 1763). Judge Trowbridge's statement in Richmond v. Davis, Quincy 279, 293 (Mass. 1768), see text at 422 above, is not inconsistent with the statement quoted here in the text, for by statute Trowbridge meant an act of Parliament as distinguished from a provincial law. See ibid., 293.

[5] Allison v. Long, Jamaica Ct. Errors, January 1710, quoted in part in Smith, *Appeals to the Privy Council*, 477.

[6] The qualification concerning inapplicability to local conditions is based on a somewhat broad reading in Smith, *Appeals to the Privy Council*, 485–486, of two Rhode Island cases. The important point to note is that these cases do not put in question the general rule that acts of Parliament were in force in the colonies. Read broadly, as Smith reads them, they merely place a qualification upon that rule, that only legislation applicable to local conditions would be in force in the colony. Read more narrowly, they suggest only that an act of Parliament which does not expressly name the colonies could be overridden by local legislation. Moreover, as Smith himself notes, "many years were to pass before ... [any broad] challenge of Parliament's right to legislate was to become current." Ibid., 486.

[7] See E. Allen Farnsworth, *Contracts* (Boston, 1982), 371.

[8] See Curtis P. Nettels, *The Emergence of a National Economy, 1775–1815* (New York, 1962), 39–40, 43–44, 251.

The unity of the Anglo-American world was also reflected in the respect which courts of one province accorded to judgments of courts of another. Except in certain types of cases, particularly cases involving title to land in which suit had to be brought before the courts and in accordance with the law of the jurisdiction within which the land was located,[9] a plaintiff could bring suit on a claim anywhere in the British world where he could find the defendant, and the courts throughout that world would enforce the judgment so obtained. Massachusetts courts, for example, rejected an argument that New York and Massachusetts were "Distinct provinces" having "no Metropolitan, who presides over and has a Right to Exercise Jurisdiction about the Probate of Wills &c. in both," and treated New York probate decrees as they would their own, ruling that an administrator of a New York decedent who procured New York letters could sue in Massachusetts without first obtaining ancillary letters.[1] Courts of one portion of the British empire likewise gave effect to assignments in bankruptcy judicially sanctioned in another portion.[2] Finally, in Massachusetts, the courts permitted plaintiffs to bring writs of debt upon judgments recovered in other provinces of British North America.[3] While it was not clear at common law whether such judg-

[9] See Rickards v. Hudson, Privy Council, 1762, quoted in Smith, *Appeals to the Privy Council*, 491 n.99; Wright v. Searl, Berkshire C.P., September 1767, where the court held that an action for breach of a warranty relating to land in Connecticut could be heard only in Connecticut, since "divers facts and matters in issue which are local . . . must have existed and Taken Place in . . . Connecticut." It should be noted that even in some types of suits not involving land, litigants were required to show that the cause of action accrued within the jurisdiction of the court before which they were bringing suit. See, e.g., Freeman v. Eddy, Bristol Super. Ct., October 1768 (suit for maintenance of bastard child dismissed since child neither begotten nor born within the county).

[1] Fonda v. Burghardt, Berkshire C.P., April 1764. The matter quoted in the text was contained in Ross v. Willson, Berkshire C.P., September 1766, which was dismissed on other grounds. For analogous cases from colonial Pennsylvania, see Hyam v. Edwards, 1 Dallas 1 (Pa. Sup. Ct. 1759); Weston v. Stammers, 1 Dallas 2 (Pa. Sup. Ct. 1759).

[2] See Rickards v. Hudson, Privy Council, 1762, discussed in Smith, *Appeals to the Privy Council*, 490–491; Cuyler v. Vanschaack, Hampshire Super Ct., September 1773, Suffolk Files No. 158004. For an opinion in Maryland according a limited effect to a judgment of bankruptcy obtained in Great Britain, see Burk v. M'Clain, 1 H. & M. 236 (Md. Prov. Ct. 1766).

[3] Douglass v. Douglass, Berkshire C.P., September 1768; Henshaw v. Phelps, Hampshire C.P., August 1761. See generally, *Legal Papers of John Adams*, L. Kinvin Wroth and Hiller B. Zobel eds. (Cambridge, Mass., 1965), I, 79–80.

ments could be collaterally attacked in the Massachusetts proceedings,[4] whatever doubts may have existed were definitively settled when the General Court in 1774 enacted that debt could be brought in a Massachusetts court upon "a judgment . . . [recovered] in any court in . . . his majesty's neighboring colonies in America" and that such judgments were to be given the same effect as if they "had been rendered . . . in the court where such action of debt shall be brought and depending."[5] Just as the Revolution was breaking out, the policy of legal unity was coming to its fullest fruition.

That political boundaries within the Anglo-American world were of much less legal significance than subsequent state lines does not, however, mean that jurisdictional conflicts never occurred during the colonial period. Most colonial conflicts, however, were of a different sort from those with which we are now familiar. To understand the difference, it will be necessary to inquire into the judicial structure of contemporary England and the kinds of conflicts problems which that structure generated.

B. English Jurisdictional Conflicts

As in the Middle Ages, litigants in eighteenth-century England still could choose from "a prodigious variety of courts, some with a more limited, others with a more extensive jurisdiction."[6] A litigant's choice was an extremely significant one, however, for choice of court generally determined choice of law as well. The central courts of common law, chancery, and admiralty, as is well known, each applied their own peculiar brand of law; so did the courts of lesser jurisdiction. The Court of Chivalry, for example, applied its own "'usages and customs'";[7] church courts, the canon and civil law;[8] borough courts, a varying mixture of common law and borough

[4] See Kurt H. Nadelmann, "Full Faith and Credit to Judgments and Public Acts: A Historical-Analytical Reappraisal," *Michigan Law Review*, 56 (1957), 33, 37, 40.

[5] Province Laws of 1773–1774, ch. 16 (1774), in *Acts and Resolves . . . of the Province of Massachusetts Bay*, vol. 5 (Boston, 1886), 323.

[6] William Blackstone, *Commentaries on the Laws of England*, vol. 3 (Oxford, 1768), 24.

[7] Ibid., 103.

[8] See ibid., 100.

custom;[9] and university courts, either the common law or their own custom, at their discretion.[1] Choice of court and choice of law, then, were intertwined — so intertwined, indeed, that eighteenth-century Englishmen saw no distinction between them. Subject matter jurisdiction was conceived of as the power to enforce one particular body of law and no other.[2] Thus, the King's Bench in one case held that it "ha[d] no Jurisdiction" to remove a case pending before a local court possessing equitable powers, since its "power and commission ... [were] legal only" and "the proceedings ... [were] in an equitable, Chancery way,"[3] while in another case, the Lord Chief Justice thought it "very material" whether plaintiff's claim was "founded on the canon law," since if it were, "this Court has nothing to do in it, but the party must take his remedy by appeal to some superior Ecclesiastical Court."[4] It was likewise clear that courts which were not common law courts could not hear common law matters; thus, a suit in an admiralty court for damage to goods on a transatlantic crossing — a transaction over which admiralty normally had jurisdiction — was prohibited, since the libel sounded in assumpsit for breach of the promise to transport the goods safely — a form of action which only the common law could enforce.[5]

The identification of choice of law with choice of court meant that an English court normally was not confronted with an issue about what law to apply. That issue was subsumed under the determination of which of two or more competing courts had jurisdiction to try a

[9] See ibid., 80–81; Adolphus Ballard and James Tait, eds., *British Borough Charters, 1216–1307* (Cambridge, 1923), 145–155.

[1] See William Blackstone, *Commentaries on the Laws of England*, vol. 3 (Oxford, 1768), 83.

[2] See Edith G. Henderson, *Foundations of English Administrative Law* (Cambridge, Mass., 1963), 118–119; David J. Sharpe, "The Origins of American Admiralty and Maritime Law," S.J.D. dissertation, Harvard Univ., 1969, 140; Alexander W. Sack, "Conflicts of Laws in the History of English Law," in *Law: A Century of Progress, 1835–1935* (New York, 1937), 3:342, 356–357. For some exceptions to this rule in the field of maritime law, see Sharpe, "Origins of American Admiralty," 146–149. Common law courts would, of course, enforce some other law as custom.

[3] Commins v. Massam, King's Bench, 1642, discussed in Henderson, *Foundations of English Administrative Law*, 119–120.

[4] King v. Bishop of Litchfield, 7 Mod. 217, 219, 87 Eng. Rep. 1200, 1201 (K.B. 1734).

[5] Caule v. Cook, 2 Keble 498, 84 Eng. Rep. 313 (K.B. 1669).

case—a determination ordinarily made by the Court of King's Bench. King's Bench understood that it had authority to "examine the proceedings of all jurisdictions erected by an Act of Parliament ... to the end that this Court may see, that they keep themselves within their jurisdiction: and if they exceed it, to restrain them."[6] King's Bench also exercised a like power over other courts, such as the Censors of the College of Physicians, which derived their jurisdiction from a source other than Parliamentary statute.[7] As Blackstone explained, it was the duty of King's Bench to "keep ... all inferior jurisdictions within the bounds of their authority."[8] "In short, the common law ... [was] the one uniform rule to determine the jurisdiction of courts,"[9] both in cases of horizontal competition between two courts, neither of which was a common law court, and in cases of vertical competition between such a court and a common law one, even the King's Bench itself.

The choice-of-law-choice-of-court identification also meant that questions of jurisdiction possessed substantive as well as procedural significance. Changes in the jurisdiction of the courts altered substantive legal rights; as a result, Englishmen viewed inter-court rivalries as attempts to destroy vested legal rights. Sir Edward Coke's jurisprudence epitomized the thought process by which petty jurisdictional disputes were magnified into constitutional crises; in discussing admiralty's claim to jurisdiction over transactions occurring upon a river, haven, or creek, for example, he argued that it would be "dangerous and penall ... for them to deal in these cases," for that would be to "hold plea of things done within the body of the County, which are triable by verdict of twelve men, ... determinable by the Common Law, and not ... according to the Civil Law." Admiralty's assumption of jurisdiction, he contended, would "change and alter the laws of the realm," for it would affect not only the forum but the substantive law, the mode of finding and weighing

---

[6] Rex v. Inhabitants in Glamorganshire, 1 Ld. Raym. 580, 91 Eng. Rep. 1287, 1288 (K.B. 1701).

[7] See Groenvelt v. Burwell, 1 Ld. Raym. 454, 91 Eng. Rep. 1202 (K.B. 1700).

[8] William Blackstone, *Commentaries on the Laws of England*, vol. 3 (Oxford, 1768), 42.

[9] Ibid., 87.

facts, and other procedures as well.[1] It was the magnitude of the change which required "that ... particular jurisdictions, derogating from the general jurisdiction of the courts of common law, ... [be] ever taken strictly" and "prohibited from exceed[ing] the limits so prescribed them."[2]

C. *American Jurisdictional Conflicts*

Americans viewed their own conflicts problems, most of which were with prerogative courts similar to those against which the common law had struggled in England, against this English background. They believed that the reasons for restraining prerogative courts were the same and "as strong in *New England* as in *Great Britain*," for those courts infringed upon the "Privilege of an *Englishman* ... to be try'd by his Country and the Laws of the Land."[3] Beneath this argument still lay the old assumption that choice of forum determined choice of law—an assumption articulated by John Adams as late as five years before the Revolution, when he argued that, in a proceeding in a court of vice admiralty, a civil law court, no reference could be made to the common law and all issues had to be determined in accordance with civil law rules.[4] Provincials continued to

[1] Edward Coke, *The Fourth Part of the Institutes of the Lawes of England*, IV (London, 6th ed., 1681), 135–136. Cf. Thomlinson's Case, 12 Co. Rep. 104, 77 Eng. Rep. 1379 (C.P. 1605).

[2] William Blackstone, *Commentaries on the Laws of England*, vol. 3 (Oxford, 1768), 85, 87.

[3] Jeremiah Dummer, *A Defense of the New-England Charters* (Boston, 1745), 27. For further examples of colonial attacks on prerogative courts like admiralty and chancery as contrary to the rights of Englishmen, and, in the case of chancery, as dilatory and expensive, see James Alexander, *A Brief Narrative of the Case and Trial of John Peter Zenger* (Cambridge, Mass., Stanley N. Katz, ed., 1968), 3–4, 111, 205–206 n.8; Stanley N. Katz, *Newcastle's New York: Anglo-American Politics, 1732–1753* (Cambridge, Mass., 1968), 65 n.10, 67, 81; Carl Ubbelohde, *The Vice-Admiralty Courts and the American Revolution* (Chapel Hill, 1960), 143–146; Sewall v. Hancock, 1768–1769, in Wroth and Zobel, *Legal Papers of John Adams*, II, 174, 199–200; Charles M. Andrews, "Introduction: Vice-Admiralty Courts in the Colonies," in Dorothy Towle, ed., *Records of the Vice-Admiralty Court of Rhode Island, 1716–1752* (Washington, D. C., 1936), 1–79; Solon D. Wilson, "Courts of Chancery in the American Colonies," in Association of American Law Schools, ed., *Select Essays in Anglo-American Legal History* (Boston, 1908), II, 779, 793–795. For similar attacks in seventeenth-century England, see William S. Holdsworth, *A History of English Law* (London, 1923), I, 432–433, 558–559.

[4] See Sewall v. Hancock, 1768–1769, in Wroth and Zobel, *Legal Papers of John Adams*, II, 173, 203. See also "A Journal of the Times," 24 February 1769, in ibid., II, 208 n.131.

think in seventeenth-century English categories even in their analysis of the Appeals Committee of the Privy Council, which they viewed merely as another prerogative court. Thus, as late as 1769, they were arguing that "appeals . . . to the King in Council, whereby the lands, tenements, and hereditaments of British subjects may be questioned by the Lords of the . . . Council, [were] contrary to the Petition of Rights,"[5] since appeals "from the Verdict of their Equals and Neighbors" deprived them "of the important Privilege of a Trial by their Peers."[6]

The Massachusetts materials show that in their contests with the prerogative, colonial common law courts acted much as their English counterparts had acted, even using the same weapons. In dealing with admiralty, for example, writs of prohibition were the most obvious weapon,[7] but the common law courts also possessed further powers in that they could take cognizance of borderline matters over which admiralty also claimed jurisdiction[8] and could entertain suits against admiralty and customs[9] as well as other royal officials[1] for allegedly

[5] Thomas Pownall to Rev. Dr. Cooper, 25 February 1769 and 9 October 1769, in Smith, *Appeals to the Privy Council*, 208.

[6] Anonymous, *Remarks on the Review of the Controversy between Great Britain and Her Colonies* (London, 1769), 122–123. See also Smith, *Appeals to the Privy Council*, 143, 163, 208.

[7] See Scollay v. Dunn, Quincy 74 (Mass. 1763); L. Kinvin Wroth, "The Massachusetts Vice-Admiralty Court," in George A. Billias, ed., *Law and Authority in Colonial America* (Barre, Mass., 1965), 32, 45–48, 54–56; L. Kinvin Wroth, "The Massachusetts Vice-Admiralty Court and the Federal Admiralty Jurisdiction," *American Journal of Legal History*, VI (1962), 250, 347, 355, 358–360; Ubbelohde, *Vice-Admiralty Courts*, 18–19.

[8] See Lyman v. Alvord, Hampshire C.P., August 1763, holding that admiralty does not have exclusive jurisdiction of actions regarding the cutting of naval mast trees. On the admiralty claim to jurisdiction, see "Editorial Note," in Wroth and Zobel, *Legal Papers of John Adams*, 2:247.

[9] See Erving v. Cradock, Quincy 553 (Mass. 1761); Francis Bernard to Earl of Halifax, 2 December 1763, in Quincy 392, 394 (Mass. 1763). As to similar suits in other colonies, see Ubbelohde, *Vice-Admiralty Courts*, 50–51, 165–168. Such suits were in accord with the apparent English rule "that in these cases the officer seizes at his peril, and that a probable cause is no defense." Leglise v. Champante, 2 Str. 820, 93 Eng. Rep. 871 (K.B. 1728). See also the discussion in Wroth and Zobel, *Legal Papers of John Adams*, II, 125, n.62. The legal and political significance of the rule is attested by the Revenue Act of 1764, 4 Geo. 3, ch. 15, sec. 46, reversing the rule in America.

[1] As to suits against other royal officials, see Goodspeed v. Gay, Quincy 558 (Mass. 1763); Brown v. Switser, Suffolk Super. Ct., August 1760 (suit against "an Officer

acting contrary to the common law. Likewise, the claim of the Massachusetts Superior Court that it alone, "by the Clauses in our Charter relative to this Matter, is to judge of the Limitations of Appeals"[2] and the frequent denials of appeal made in reliance on that claim[3] gave the provincial court considerable leverage over the scope of the Privy Council's appellate jurisdiction. Although a party who had been denied an appeal could obtain leave for one directly from the Council,[4] that remedy was of little avail, for the Massachusetts court did not recognize the legitimacy of appeals so taken and would, in such cases, either refuse to assist the appellant in putting evidence in writing for transmission to the Council or decline to order execution of the Council's final judgment.[5] Thus, the Massachusetts court, like the common law courts in England, effectively insured its own determination of the jurisdictional limits of the other courts.

Americans also sought to analyze intercolonial judicial relation-

---

of the Forces now serving in America" for recruiting a man claimed as an indentured servant); Harrington v. Fletcher, Worcester Super. Ct., September 1770 (suit against enlistment recruiter on his promise to pay the plaintiff for granting permission to his son to join the army); Cowdin v. Brewer, Worcester C.P., May 1760 (suit against army captain on his promise to pay the plaintiff the wages earned by his apprentice in the army, if the apprentice enlisted). On the common law liability of officials in eighteenth-century England, see William S. Holdsworth, *A History of English Law* (London, 1923), X, 157. On the common law liability of provincial and other local officials in Massachusetts, see Nelson, *Americanization of the Common Law*, 13, 17–18.

[2] Scollay v. Dunn, Quincy 74, 81 (Mass. 1763). The provision of the Charter was as follows:

And whereas we judge it necessary that all our subjects should have liberty to appeal to us, our heirs and successors, in cases that may deserve the same, we do by these presents ordain, that in case either party shall not rest satisfied with the judgment or sentence of any judicatories or courts within our said province or territory, in any personal action, wherein the matter in difference doth exceed the value of three hundred pounds sterling, that then he or they may appeal to us, our heirs and successors, in our or their privy council.

Quoted in Scollay v. Dunn, supra, at 81 n.4.

[3] See, e.g., Scollay v. Dunn, Quincy 74 (Mass. 1763); Dudley v. Dudley, Quincy 12, 25 n.2 (Mass. 1762); Hancock v. Bowes, Suffolk Super. Ct., August 1766. Appeals were allowed only in personal actions in which the plaintiff sought over £300 damages. See Erving v. Cradock, Quincy 553, 557 (Mass. 1761), for a case in which an appeal was granted.

[4] See Smith, *Appeals to the Privy Council*, 160–163.

[5] See ibid., 163–165, 328–344. See also Anonymous, *Review of the Controversy*, 63, for an argument that, at least in chartered colonies, the crown had "no Way to put" a Privy Council judgment "in Execution."

ships against the background of the English judicial system. This is suggested by the case of *Whipple v. Mattoon*,[6] where the issue was the enforceability in Massachusetts of a common law judgment obtained in New Hampshire. A brief for one of the parties,[7] although incoherent in its resolution of this issue, contains numerous citations to English cases concerning the effect to be given in one English court to a judgment rendered in another. One case, for example, discussed the effect to be given in Common Pleas to a judgment rendered in the "Court of Kingston-upon-Hull";[8] another, the effect to be given in the "Court of Bristol" to a judgment rendered in King's Bench;[9] a third, the effect to be given in one London court to a judgment rendered in another.[1] These citations suggest that the lawyer who drew up the brief did not see any difference between cases which involved two or more political entities, such as Massachusetts and New Hampshire, and cases which did not;[2] counsel — indeed, the

[6] Adams Trust Ms., March 1771, Microfilm Reel No. 185, Massachusetts Historical Society, Boston, Mass.

[7] The brief does not indicate whether it was written for plaintiff or defendant.

[8] Jevens v. Harridge, 1 Wms. Saund. 8, 85 Eng. Rep. 8 (K.B. 1666) (dictum). Accord, Adney v. Vernon, 3 Lev. 243, 83 Eng. Rep. 671 (C.P. 1685). Cf. Chetley v. Wood, 2 Salk. 659, 91 Eng. Rep. 560 (K.B. 1703) (effect in King's Bench of judgment rendered in Common Pleas).

[9] Pitt v. Knight, 1 Lev. 222, 1 Wms. Saund. 97, 83 Eng. Rep. 379, 85 Eng. Rep. 105 (K.B. 1667). Accord, Shuttle v. Wood, 2 Salk. 600, 91 Eng. Rep. 510 (K.B. 1703). Cf. Anon., 1 Salk. 209, 91 Eng. Rep. 187 (K.B. 1712) (effect in Marshalsea of judgment rendered in King's Bench or Common Pleas).

[1] Mico v. Morris, 2 Lev. 234, 83 Eng. Rep. 666 (K.B. 1685). Other arguably relevant cases cited by counsel were Lucking v. Denning, 1 Salk. 201, 91 Eng. Rep. 180 (K.B. undated) (limits of jurisdiction of "Court of the Sheriffs of London"); Stannian v. Davis, 1 Salk. 404, 91 Eng. Rep. 350 (K.B. 1704) (limits of jurisdiction of "Palace-Court"); Anon., 2 Salk. 439, 91 Eng. Rep. 381 (K.B. 1698) (limits of jurisdiction of Marshalsea); Wharton v. Musgrave, Cro. Jac. 331, 79 Eng. Rep. 283 (Ex. Ch. 1613) (whether *scire facias* should be brought in county where original judgment rendered); Hewson v. Brown, 2 Burr. 1034, 97 Eng. Rep. 692 (K.B. 1760) (mode of bringing Common Pleas judgment into King's Bench).

[2] Counsel did cite Vaughan's "Concerning Process out of the Courts at Westminster into Wales of Late Times, and How Anciently," Vaughan 395, 124 Eng. Rep. 1130 (undated), to the effect that "a judgment given in Wales shall not be executed in England." Vaughan at 398, 124 Eng. Rep. at 1131. See also Vaughan at 412–413, 417, 124 Eng. Rep. at 1138–1139, 1141. But these citations do not indicate that counsel saw an analogy between the English-Welsh boundary and provincial boundaries in America. See Walker v. Witter, 1 Dougl. 1, 6, 99 Eng. Rep. 1, 4 (K.B. 1778), where Lord Mansfield thought the "Courts in Wales" analogous to

common law as a whole — viewed the effect to be given to judgments primarily as a problem between courts within a single political entity rather than a problem between courts of separate political entities. The potential legal significance of provincial boundaries was simply passed over.

D. *Readjusting English Law to American Conditions*

We should not look too harshly, however, upon the confusion of counsel in *Whipple v. Mattoon*, because his confusion stemmed in large part from the fact that the English model which he was seeking to apply in America did not match with certain American legal realities. Those realities, in fact, were beginning to force lawyers to readjust the model in two significant respects.

One of the readjustments was caused by the presence in the British imperial system of potentially divisive structural elements which the common law had never before encountered. Unlike England, which possessed one supreme legislature — Parliament — and one supreme common law court — the King's Bench, the American colonies had thirteen legislatures and thirteen supreme courts administering common law. British North America possessed no unifying institutions resting atop a hierarchy of local institutions: the common law, which was at the top of the hierarchy and therefore curbed local independence in England, was at the bottom of the hierarchy and thereby had potentially the opposite effect in America. Meanwhile the agencies of the royal prerogative, which sought to serve as unifying forces, were, as we have seen, surely not much stronger and, perhaps, even weaker than local, common law institutions.[3]

---

local "Courts in England not of record," and William Blackstone, *Commentaries on the Laws of England*, vol. 3 (Oxford, 1768), 77, where Welsh courts were viewed merely as "a fifth species of private courts of a limited . . . jurisdiction," analogous to the courts of the duchy of Lancaster and the counties palatine. See ibid., 77–78. Counsel also cited cases discussing whether English courts could take jurisdiction of suits involving foreign corporations, Henriques v. General Privileged Dutch Co., 2 Ld. Raym. 1532, 1535, 92 Eng. Rep. 494, 496 (K.B. 1729), or contracts made in Wales, Ireland, Scotland or Europe, Dutch West-India Co. v. Henriques, 1 Stra. 612, 93 Eng. Rep. 733 (C.P. 1725); Errington v. Thompson, 1 Ld. Raym. 183, 91 Eng. Rep. 1018 (K.B. 1697). Of course, English courts declined jurisdiction in such cases when they could not administer foreign law. See above, 426–427. It is difficult to see what counsel's citation of these cases indicates other than confusion.

[3] See above, 422–424, notes 7–9, 1–5 and accompanying text.

35. Fourth Court House, Harvard Square, Cambridge, 1758. Served as Courthouse until 1816. Moved 1841. Demolished 1930. Courtesy, Cambridge Historical Commission.

Gradually and almost imperceptibly during the course of the eighteenth century Americans became aware of these divisive elements and perceived that they were witnessing, not merely a conflict between common law and prerogative courts, but a struggle to define relationships between different levels of government within an imperial system in some ways structurally akin to the future federal system.[4] The first vague perception of the struggle occurred surprisingly early in the century. In 1700, for example, one American argued that a Parliamentary bill to deprive Connecticut of its "judicial autonomy" by authorizing appeals to the Privy Council was, in fact, "a designe to take away all the proprietie of Governments at one blow...."[5] Some years later another American argued that Parliament lacked power to enact such a bill, for "the *American* Charters are of a higher Nature, and stand on a better Foot, than the Corporations in *England*."[6] Americans likewise argued that the Crown lacked power to establish prerogative courts in the colonies and that their provincial legislatures alone possessed such power.[7] Nevertheless, despite these preliminary insights into the fact that two levels of government were competing for control of their judiciary, colonial Americans failed to articulate a coherent philosophy of federalism until they were compelled by the constitutional debates of the 1760's, 1770's, and 1780's to do so.[8] It is important to note that, until 1787, they proposed to weaken, rather than strengthen, central institutions capable of counteracting the divisive elements in their political and legal structure.

A new understanding of the relationship between choice of court and choice of law also began to develop during the pre-Revolutionary constitutional debate. Although the absence of chancery courts had made New Englanders aware from an early date that common law

---

[4] See generally Bailyn, *Pamphlets*, 115–138.

[5] Statement of Sir Henry Ashurst, Colony Agent, quoted in Smith, *Appeals to the Privy Council*, 143, n.57, 147, n.85.

[6] See Dummer, *Defense of the New-England Charters*, 4.

[7] See Alexander, *Trial of John Peter Zenger*, 205–206 n.8; Katz, *Newcastle's New York*, 66–67; Wilson, "Courts of Chancery," 794–795, 801. Cf. Frederick B. Wiener, "Notes on the Rhode Island Admiralty, 1727–1790," *Harvard Law Review*, 46 (1932), 44, 59.

[8] See Bailyn, *Pamphlets*, 120, 136–138.

courts could administer equity,[9] reasoned analysis of the choice-of-court-choice-of-law relationship first occurred in 1769 in the politically sensitive case of *Sewall v. Hancock*.[1] This was a suit for a penalty for smuggling brought by the Crown against John Hancock, under the provision of the Townsend Acts giving Vice Admiralty courts jurisdiction over certain common law causes of action. One issue in the suit was whether the Crown had to sustain the higher civil law burden of proof, or the less stringent common law burden, in order to recover the penalty. John Adams, representing Hancock, made the usual argument that, since trial was in a civil court, the civil law was determinative of all legal issues.[2] The Court ruled, however, that since "the process now in question . . . [was] founded on an Act of parliament, originally intended to be guided by the Rules of the common Law," it would determine the case "according to those rules."[3]

As the Revolution approached, it was not, then, clear whether Americans would adhere to the English doctrine tying choice-of-law to choice-of-court. The decision in *Sewall v. Hancock*, the administration of equitable remedies in several colonial common law courts, and the fact that even in England the common law was sometimes applied in local courts[4] indicate that Americans might not have followed the doctrine in interstate conflicts cases. On the other hand, it is clear that American lawyers were aware of the English doctrine and thought it applicable, at least in some instances.

What ultimately led to Americans' rejection of the English rule was its potential for complete fragmentation of the American legal system. For in America, unlike England, there existed no body of accumulated rules directing plaintiffs to sue in one court rather than another; a plaintiff was free to sue in whatever province he could find a defendant's person or property. England's rules could not be imported because of the immense differences between the English

[9] See Dummer, *Defense of the New-England Charters*, 21.

[1] See D. R. Coquillette, "Justinian in Braintree: John Adams, Civilian Learning, and Legal Elitism, 1758–1775," above, 386–390. *Legal Papers of John Adams*, II, 173.

[2] Ibid., 203.

[3] Ibid., 208.

[4] See above, 432.

and American judicial structures. Nor did Americans possess the equivalent of a Court of King's Bench atop their judicial structure which was capable of formulating new rules. Adherence to the choice-of-court-choice-of-law tie could only lead to forum shopping of the worst sort as soon as America's thirteen legal systems began to apply their own differing rules of law to whatever cases plaintiffs chose to bring before them. Only the unity of substantive law throughout the thirteen colonies made it possible to avoid such fragmentation during the pre-Revolutionary period. But the potential for fragmentation—a potential soon to be realized—remained.

II. Revolution and Fragmentation

A. *Rejection of the Choice-of-Court-Choice-of-Law Tie*

The collapse of royal power and institutions at the outset of the War of Independence might have produced immediate fragmentation, but the state courts permitted the Continental Congress to step into the void and assume many of the old imperial government's powers. From the outset of the struggle with England, Congress was treated by state judges as a government:[5] at "the moment of their association, the United States necessarily became a body corporate" having "no superior from whom that character ... [was] derived"[6]—a body against which treason and other crimes could be committed[7] and whose agents, like the agents of the crown, were immune from suit upon contracts made in its behalf.[8] It was also recognized that the new government, of necessity, possessed legisla-

[5] See Gordon S. Wood, *The Creation of the American Republic, 1776–1787* (Chapel Hill, 1969), 355; Curtis P. Nettels, "The Origins of the Union and of the States," *Massachusetts Historical Society Proceedings*, 72 (1957–1960), 68, 69–70.

[6] Respublica v. Sweers, 1 Dallas 41, 44 (Pa. Sup. Ct. 1779). Congress accordingly had the right to bring suit in state courts. See, e.g., United States v. Foster, Suffolk Sup. Jud. Ct., August 1788; Hillegas v. Silber, Suffolk C.P., April 1782.

[7] See Government v. Lyon, Hampshire Super. Ct., April 1777 (treason); Government v. Baker, Barnstable Sup. Jud. Ct., May 1780 (sedition); Commonwealth v. Smith, Bristol Sup. Jud. Ct., November 1782 (sedition).

[8] See Hammett v. Warren (1783), in William Cushing, "Notes of Cases decided in the Superior and Supreme Judicial Courts of Massachusetts from 1772 to 1789," ms. in Harvard Law School Library, Cambridge, Mass., 61–62, citing Melchart v. Halsey, 3 Wils. K.B. 149, 95 Eng. Rep. 982 (K.B. 1771). Accord, Bingham v. Cabot, Essex Sup. Jud. Ct., November 1801, in Francis Dana, "Minute Book," ms. in Massachusetts Historical Society, Boston, Mass.

36. Council Chamber, Old State House, Boston. The Superior Court of Judicature met in this room on frequent occasions in the eighteenth century. Courtesy, Bostonian Society.

tive powers. In 1776, for example, the commissions of certain justices of the peace still containing the royal style were adjudged invalid, since they had not yet been "alter'd agreeable to the Act of Independency establish'd by the Congress,"[9] while a decade later a Massachusetts judge told a grand jury that the authors of the Confederation had "intended that ye recommendations of Congress should have ye force of Laws."[1] Many Congressional acts were, in fact, accorded the force of law in state courts, among them treaties entered into with foreign powers[2] and various exercises of the war power, including seizures of property in war zones[3] and regulations for the distribution of prizes[4] and the governance of the army.[5] Another Congressional power given effect in the state courts was that of emitting

[9] Final Record, Plymouth Gen. Sess., October 1776. See also James Sullivan, *Observations upon the Government of the United States of America* (Boston, 1791), 24, which refers to the Declaration of Independence as the "act of Congress" which established independence. But see Wood, *Creation of American Republic*, 356, who notes that seven states thought it necessary to enact the Declaration of Independence to give it the force of law. See also Province Laws, 1775–1776, ch. 22 (1776), *Acts and Resolves*, 5:484, which made provision for court styles.

[1] Charge to the Grand Jury, cc. 1790, in the N. P. Sargeant Papers, ms. in Essex Institute, Salem, Mass. See also "Notes of subjects in debate in Convention," January 1788, Cushing Papers, ms. in Massachusetts Historical Society, Boston, Mass., which notes that the Confederation had "many, if not most of the great powers, now inserted in the proposed Constitution, such as making war & peace, borrowing money without bounds upon ye Credit of the united States—building & equipping a navy—demanding men & money without limitation—& of appropriating *money*." See generally "Note: The United States and the Articles of Confederation: Drifting Toward Anarchy or Inching Toward Commonwealth?," *Yale Law Journal*, 88 (1978), 142.

[2] See Commonwealth v. Bartlett, Cumberland Sup. Jud. Ct., June 1784 (prosecution for sale of goods to British army during war dismissed under amnesty provision of peace treaty).

[3] Respublica v. Sparhawk, 1 Dallas 357, 362–363 (Pa. Sup. Ct. 1788); Wilcox v. Henry, 1 Dallas 69, 71 (Pa. Sup. Ct. 1782) (dictum).

[4] See Warren v. Sloop Speedwell, Cumberland Sup. Jud. Ct., July 1780, in N. P. Sargeant, "Court Minutes," ms. in Essex Institute, Salem, Mass. (two Congressional resolves pleaded); Buffington v. Brig Susanna, Middlesex Sup. Jud. Ct., November 1780, in Sargeant, "Court Minutes" (Congressional resolve instructing ship captain pleaded). See generally Henry J. Bourguignon, *The First Federal Court: The Federal Appellate Prize Court of the American Revolution, 1775–1787* (Philadelphia, 1977), 45–47, 52–75. In some instances, Congressional recommendations were effective only because state legislation specifically made them so. See ibid., 58–75.

[5] See Hall v. Langdon, Cumberland Sup. Jud. Ct., July 1783 (rules for government of American army pleaded). See generally Wood, *Creation of the American Republic*, 355; Nettels, "The Origins of the Union," 69–70.

money.[6] Finally, there was the power of entering into and enforcing contracts.[7]

These powers and the institutions created pursuant to them gave the new federal government considerable influence during the War of Independence over the daily lives of its citizens — more influence, perhaps, than the old imperial government had ever possessed. The most obvious example of this influence is the army: courts martial had jurisdiction not only over service-connected offenses of soldiers,[8] but also over crimes committed by soldiers against civilians,[9] spying committed by civilians,[1] and other offenses committed by civilians within war zones.[2] Moreover, Congress used its powers broadly; it learned very quickly, for example, to insert in its distributions of contractual largess stipulations compelling contractors to carry out government policy — stipulations to which state courts accorded the force of law.[3]

In addition to enforcing federal law, the Massachusetts courts dur-

[6] The cases suggest that Congressional bills of credit had many of the attributes of money. See, e.g., Government v. Fisk, Hampshire Super. Ct., September 1778 (indictment for counterfeiting Congressional bills); Morey v. Moris, Suffolk Common Pleas, April 1783, appeal dism. for want of prosecution, Suffolk Sup. Jud. Ct., August 1783 (not necessary in civil action to plead specie value of federal bills); Government v. Clark, Hampshire Gen. Sess., August 1777 (indictment for refusing to accept Congressional bills in discharge of debt—*nolle pros*—entered at November 1777 term). See generally Nettels, "The Origins of the Union," 70.

[7] See Hillegas v. Silber, Suffolk C.P., April 1782. See generally Bourguignon, *The First Federal Court*, 93–94.

[8] See, e.g., United States v. Fulton, October 1776, in Heath Papers, Microfilm Reel No. 28, Massachusetts Historical Society, Boston, Mass. (desertion); United States v. Snow, October 1776, in ibid. (leaving guard); United States v. Looly, December 1776, in ibid. (minor accused of sleeping at post discharged by reason of nonage and other inabilities); United States v. Horton, December 1776, in ibid. ("behaving in an infamous & Scandalous Manner unbecoming an Officer or a Gentlm."); United States v. Harman, January 1777, in ibid. (enlisting twice); United States v. Spring, March 1778, in ibid. (abusing officer); United States v. Lyon, March 1782, in Heath Papers, Microfilm Reel No. 29 (desertion and forging pass).

[9] See United States v. Nowel, December 1776, in Heath Papers, Microfilm Reel No. 28 (larceny from traveller on road); United States v. Galloway, December 1777, in ibid. (parading in streets with swords drawn and threatening civilians).

[1] See United States v. Strong, January 1777, in ibid.; "Guard Report," 17 October 1778, in Miscellaneous Bound Manuscripts (ms. in Massachusetts Historical Society, Boston, Mass.) (Peter Murry, a transient, suspected of being a spy).

[2] See Hall v. Langdon, Cumberland Sup. Jud. Ct., July 1783 (providing intelligence to British).

[3] See the cases cited above, 437, note 8.

ing the late 1770's and 1780's gave effect in several cases to rights created by the law of other states. They continued, for example, to permit litigants to bring suit on out-of-state judgments.[4] They also dismissed suits which were already pending before or properly cognizable in the courts of other states at the time proceedings were commenced in Massachusetts.[5] Finally, there were two Massachusetts cases in which out-of-state statutes were given effect. In one, a Connecticut act which had been applied by a Connecticut court so as to confiscate a Tory's intangible as well as tangible property was applied in Massachusetts in order to bar the Tory from recovering upon a promissory note,[6] while in the other, a New York statute granting immunity to Justices of the Peace for certain acts committed in pursuance of their duty was applied so as to bar a suit in trespass for seizure of the plaintiff's goods.[7]

The immediate significance of state judicial recognition of federal law and of the law of other states was that it permitted the American war effort to be sustained. But it also had a long-term consequence for American conflict of laws, for it dissolved the link between choice of court and choice of law. By the late 1780's it was clear that a plaintiff's choice of court did not automatically determine the law that would be applied to his case; there had been too many cases in which courts had made that determination independently and chosen law other than their own. A potentially fragmentary element thus had been removed from the American legal system.

B. *Fragmentation*

But another potentially fragmentary element remained—the thirteen legislatures and thirteen supreme courts of each of the states—whose existence threatened to destroy the unity of substantive law that had existed throughout the colonial period and to subject Americans with interstate connections to uncertainty about the

[4] See Peine v. Thayer, Worcester Common Pleas, June 1784.

[5] See Commonwealth v. Brown, Barnstable Sup. Jud. Ct., May 1789; Roberdeau v. Fitzgerald, Suffolk Common Pleas, January 1787, appeal dism. on nonappearance of both parties, Suff. Sup. Jud. Ct., February 1787.

[6] Apthorp v. Henshaw, Suffolk Sup. Jud. Ct., February 1786.

[7] Spencer v. Worthington, Berkshire Sup. Jud. Ct., October 1789. See also Worthington v. Spencer, Hampshire Sup. Jud. Ct., September 1789, in Dana, "Minute Books."

rules of law which would govern their conduct. During the Revolution, this potential for fragmentation became real, as state courts, despite the many occasions on which they treated the acts of Congress and of the other states as law, nonetheless exercised a residual power to reject such law when it came into conflict with their own local law or local policy.

As in the colonial period, admiralty was a major source of conflict. As soon as war with Britain had begun, Congress established first a Committe on Appeal and then a Court of Appeals in Cases of Capture to review state prize cases.[8] The need for such an appellate jurisdiction was obvious from the effect which state-controlled privateering could have upon the subjects of friendly and neutral nations during a war in which America needed every friend it could get.[9] The new appellate bodies, however, were soon subjected to the old jurisdictional attacks. Like the old admiralty courts, the new federal bodies were accused of depriving litigants of the right to trial by jury — a right which, since the Revolution, had generally been granted in state admiralty courts.[1] To protect this common law right and thereby save their citizens from nonjury trials in a far-off court,[2] the legislatures of most states placed a variety of limitations upon appeals to the federal court.[3] Like the Privy Council before them, the Committee and later the Court of Appeals contended that the scope of their jurisdiction was a matter of federal law: "the judgment and decree of this court," the Court of Appeals observed, "must be directed by the resolves and ordinances of congress. . . ."[4] State courts, however, simply acted as colonial courts had acted before them: they denied

[8] See Bourguignon, *The First Federal Court*, 79–134.

[9] See ibid., 97–100, 133–134.

[1] See ibid., 105, 109–110; Sharpe, "The Origins of American Admiralty," 204. On Congress' recommendation to the states that jury trial be granted in admiralty cases and on the states' responses thereto, see Bourguignon, *The First Federal Court*, 46, 58–75.

[2] See ibid., 65–66, 105, 108–110, discussing Pennsylvania's provision that facts found by juries could not be reexamined on appeal.

[3] See ibid., 74–75.

[4] Miller v. Ship Resolution, 2 Dallas 1 (Fed. Ct. App. 1781). Accord, Luke v. Hulbert, 2 Dallas 41 (Fed. Ct. App. 1787); Bourguignon, *The First Federal Court*, 107, 314.

appeals to litigants requesting them[5] and refused to levy execution on federal judgments with which they disagreed.[6] Although the federal court could grant an injunction if its decree was disobeyed, such an injunction was meaningless since the federal government lacked institutions capable of enforcing it.[7]

Results in cases involving the army and other federal officials, although not as clear cut, were similar. In dealing with the army, state courts possessed two powers—the power of habeas corpus and the power to take cognizance of suits against the military for alleged violation of common law rights. These powers, like the power to limit the jurisdiction of the federal Court of Appeals, were thought essential for the preservation of liberty within the several states. Americans universally agreed that there was no "worse state of thraldom than a military power in any government, unchecked and uncontrolled by the civil power";[8] the absolute danger to liberty lay in making "the civil subordinate to the military," as Jefferson put it in 1774, "instead of subjecting the military to the civil power."[9] Thus, the state courts did not hesitate to use their powers; on two occasions, writs of *de homine replegiando* and habeas corpus were sought to procure the discharge of prisoners in military custody,[1] one of them allegedly a soldier,[2] while there were several instances of common law suits against military agents and officers—for assault,[3] for false imprisonment,[4] for back pay,[5] for death benefits granted by

[5] Williams v. Schooner Polly, Suffolk Sup. Jud. Ct., February 1778, in Sargeant, "Court Minutes." See Bourguignon, *The First Federal Court*, 303.

[6] See ibid., 105–106, 307–318.

[7] See ibid., 317–318.

[8] Samuel Seabury, *An Alarm to the Legislature of the Province of New-York* (New York, 1775), quoted in Bailyn, *Pamphlets*, 42.

[9] Thomas Jefferson, *A Summary View of the Rights of British America* (Philadelphia, 1774), quoted in Bailyn, *Pamphlets*, 41.

[1] Whitney v. Russell, Middlesex Sup. Jud. Ct., April 1782, in Sargeant, "Court Minutes"; Motion of Scot, Worcester Super. Ct., September 1777.

[2] Whitney v. Russell, Middlesex Sup. Jud. Ct., April 1782, in Sargeant, "Court Minutes."

[3] King v. Shattuck, Hampshire Common Pleas, April 1782. This suit was dismissed, however, upon a plea that the remedy for the assault lay solely within the jurisdiction of a court martial.

[4] Hall v. Langdon, Cumberland Sup. Jud. Ct., July 1783.

[5] Locke v. Thomas, Essex Common Pleas, December 1784.

a Congressional resolution,[6] and for failing to forward a plaintiff's commission whereby the plaintiff lost his promotion.[7] The Massachusetts courts also reserved power in criminal cases to determine the validity of defendants' claims that they were under military jurisdiction and therefore entitled to a court martial.[8] In view of these state-court powers, federal officials who acted contrary to local sentiment always ran a risk of civil and even criminal liability at the hands of local juries. That risk insured that liberty—that is, the common law and, through the jury system, local, communal control of government policy—would be preserved, but at the cost of making enforcement of unpopular though necessary federal policies difficult, if not impossible. Old libertarian arguments were not only having libertarian effects, but were beginning to fragment the legal system as well.

The jurisdictional conflicts so far discussed were, however, only a minor problem for the federal government. A much greater difficulty lay in the fact that state common law courts were the ultimate interpreters of federal law, in large part because of the fact that they were almost invariably the last court to hear any suit. A 1780 suit for money had and received, in which a defendant claimed the money under Congressional regulations as the commander-in-chief's portion of a prize taken by a Continental ship, is an explicit example of the state courts' interpretative power: the court's judgment rested on a finding that the defendant "Cannot be Considered as the Commander in Chief in the sense of those regulations."[9] Possession of this ultimate interpretative power meant that federal policy could be overridden whenever the exigencies of local policy so required—a danger which several Massachusetts cases arising under the peace treaty with Great Britain demonstrate.

Three provisions of the treaty affected the states. The first provision—that which "recommend[ed that] ... the Legislatures of the respective States ... provide for the restitution" of confiscated

---

[6] Mitchel v. Prichard, Suffolk Sup. Jud. Ct., August 1783.

[7] Cushing v. Vose, Suffolk Common Pleas, October 1785.

[8] Commonwealth v. McGregory, 14 Mass. 499 (1780).

[9] Johonnot v. Tucker, Suffolk C.P., April 1780.

property of certain categories of British subjects and Loyalists[1] — did not require, but merely urged, the states to restore confiscated lands. In Massachusetts, at least, no land was returned.[2] But a second provision — that British creditors would "meet with no lawful impediment to the recovery of the full value in sterling money, of all bona fide debts"[3] — caused more difficulty. Massachusetts recognized its obligation to permit such creditors' suits,[4] but, pursuant to statute, barred the creditors from recovering the interest which had accrued during the course of the War of Independence.[5] The payment of such interest, according to the General Court, would have been "repugnant to the spirit and intendment of the fourth article in the treaty of peace, which provides only for the payment of *bona fide* debts."[6] Local policy considerations were also vindicated in the only cases in which recovery of the debt itself was denied.[7] They involved statutes which had confiscated plaintiffs' intangible as well as real property; although these cases at first glance fit under the treaty's provision covering debts, they were from the state's point of view more like the land confiscation cases. For to restore confiscated property — real or intangible — would either put its local purchasers to a loss, or require the state's taxpayers to reimburse them. The outcome, upon such analysis, was clear.

The greatest difficulties came in the interpretation of the third

[1] Definitive Treaty of Peace with Great Britain, 3 September 1783, art. V, 8 Stat. 80, 82 (1783).

[2] See, e.g., Gibbs v. Apthorp, Hampshire Sup. Jud. Ct., May 1785, where a purchaser from the state pleaded the confiscation in defense to a suit brought by the Tory to recover his land. The plea was rejected, however, probably because the defendant did not allege title in himself by virtue of the confiscation.

[3] Treaty of 1783, art. IV.

[4] See Knights v. Park, Middlesex Sup. Jud. Ct., October 1787; Brattle v. Taylor, Middlesex Sup. Jud. Ct., October 1787; Brattle v. Hinckley, Worcester Sup. Jud. Ct., September 1786; Caner v. Houghton, Worcester Sup. Jud. Ct., September 1786; Bancroft v. Kent, Suffolk Sup. Jud. Ct., February 1786.

[5] Mass. Laws of 1784, ch. 77. See Caner v. Houghton, Worcester Sup. Jud. Ct., September 1786; Bancroft v. Kent, Suffolk Sup. Jud. Ct., February 1786; Bliss v. Bascom, Hampshire C.P., May 1786. But see Lane v. Jones, Suffolk Sup. Jud. Ct., February 1787, where British creditors did recover interest accruing between 1775 and 1783.

[6] Mass. Laws of 1784, ch. 77.

[7] Pepperell v. Cutler, Suffolk Sup. Jud. Ct., August 1786; Apthorp v. Henshaw, Suffolk Sup. Jud. Ct., February 1786.

provision — "that there shall be no future confiscations made, nor any prosecutions commenced against any person or persons for, or by reason of the part which he or they may have taken in the present war, ... and the prosecutions so commenced [shall] be discontinued."[8] The Massachusetts courts accepted this provision in cases in which it was clearly applicable. Thus, a prosecution, which had been pending on the effective date of the treaty, for sale of provisions to the British army was dismissed,[9] for it was clear that the defendant was being prosecuted solely on account of the aid he had rendered to the British. In sedition cases, however, the basis for halting prosecution was not so clear. Surely the treaty did not bar prosecution of a defendant who had threatened a tax collector "that if he came into that Street ... to collect any Rates that he Would be rode on a Rail,"[1] even if, in addition to his lack of money, his reasons for not paying his taxes included a belief that America's new governors were guilty of treason.[2] Likewise, the treaty arguably did not bar prosecution of a defendant who had observed that, if independence were won, he "would not give a farthing for all the Estate ... [he] had." This defendant also had observed that a dictator was to be appointed for all the United States and asked if it would "be better to be under a Dictator, than to be under the King of Great Britain," whose right to make laws and levy taxes he was willing to recognize, particularly since "it was in vain for the people to pursue their measures any longer against Great Britain ... and [was] impossible to carry on the War any longer," when "we cannot raise an army" and "can never pay our taxes."[3] Another defendant was similarly war-weary; he refused to "pay anything for such a Government as this," and was certain that "King George will ... overcome," since the people were revolting and going over to him. He urged there was "no other way but to refuse paying Taxes, for as long as we pay taxes the War will Continue."[4] A final defendant similarly combined tory and radical

[8] Treaty of 1783, art. VI.

[9] See Commonwealth v. Bartlett, Cumberland Sup. Jud. Ct., June 1784. Cf. Respublica v. Gordon, 1 Dallas 233 (Pa. Sup. Ct. 1788).

[1] Commonwealth v. Phelps, Hampshire Sup. Jud. Ct., April 1783.

[2] Commonwealth v. Whitney, Worcester Sup. Jud. Ct., April 1783.

[3] Commonwealth v. Williams, Hampshire Sup. Jud. Ct., April 1784.

[4] Commonwealth v. Appleton, Essex Sup. Jud. Ct., June 1783.

whig ideas. He urged that "there must be a revolution," since "America's little finger is heavier than the British Loins" and its "Government . . . broke by the General Court." With his "motto" that "Great Britain and America [should] ever be united," he predicted that "there will soon be the greatest revolution there has been Yet," in which royal troops would triumph, amnesty would be proclaimed, and the people would "see better times than they ever had."[5] Despite the fact that its pro-British sentiments appeared to place it within the scope of the peace treaty's amnesty provisions, such language put in doubt the very survival of government and, in view of government's fragility,[6] was too dangerous to ignore. The Massachusetts courts under such pressure permitted sedition prosecutions to continue. The amnesty clause was accordingly applied only to cases in which a defendant was being prosecuted solely "for . . . reason of the part" which he had taken in the war; if any other local policy or governmental interest was served by a prosecution, the amnesty clause was forgotten.

The Massachusetts courts also applied the provision concerning future land confiscations narrowly.[7] Although no new cases were commenced, confiscation proceedings which had been instituted prior to the effective date of the treaty were permitted to progress to judgment thereafter;[8] the treaty was, after all, somewhat vaguely written on this issue. The treaty's vagueness also permitted the courts to adhere to the common law rule which barred aliens from holding realty for their own use,[9] on the theory that otherwise "the nation might in time be subject to foreign influence."[1] No one, of course, was prepared to argue that the common law was confiscatory, but the

---

[5] Commonwealth v. Wright, Hampshire Sup. Jud. Ct., April 1784.

[6] See generally Oscar Handlin and Mary F. Handlin, *Commonwealth: A Study of the Role of Government in the American Economy: Massachusetts, 1774–1781* (Cambridge, Mass., 1947), 33–48.

[7] See above, 446, note 8 and accompanying text.

[8] See, e.g., Taylor v. Commonwealth, Suffolk Sup. Jud. Ct., February 1783.

[9] See Moore v. Patch, Worcester Sup. Jud. Ct., April 1792, in Dana, "Minute Books"; Herrick v. Hart, Essex Sup. Jud. Ct., December 1788. But see Gibbs v. Apthorp, Hampshire Sup. Jud. Ct., April 1785, where a plea in abatement alleging that one of two administrators of the plaintiff estate was an alien was overruled.

[1] William Blackstone, *Commentaries on the Laws of England*, vol. 1 (Oxford, 1765), 360.

effect of following it clearly was to confiscate any remaining British land holdings and to prevent future land acquisitions by British subjects.[2]

Other states also construed the 1783 treaty in ways that impeded former supporters of the British cause from protecting their American interests. In South Carolina, for example, the state Supreme Court held that the treaty's provision against future prosecutions and confiscations only barred "criminal prosecutions at the suit of the state," but that it did "not exonerate ... persons from damages in civil suits."[3] Pennsylvania held that the same provision barred a loyalist whose property had been confiscated from recovering on a pre-Revolutionary debt on the theory that the state had confiscated the debt prior to the date of the treaty even though the state had never brought suit to recover or otherwise exercised control over the debt.[4] Other cases were also resolved against those who had sided with the British during the war,[5] although there were also a few cases decided in favor of British sympathizers.[6]

The same localism that manifested itself in federal-state conflicts also appeared during the Confederation period in interstate conflicts cases. The largest group of such cases in Massachusetts arose out of the collision between the creditor-oriented economic policies of the Commonwealth and the debtor-oriented policies of Rhode Island. The most notorious phase of this collision occurred when Rhode Island made its own depreciated paper currency legal tender for the payment of out-of-state creditors.[7] That legislation soon led to fur-

[2] Article 9 of Jay's Treaty, 8 Stat. 116, 122 (1794), reversed the common law rule as to then existing British land holdings in the United States. See Commonwealth v. Sheafe, 6 Mass. 441 (1810).

[3] Whitaker v. English, 1 Bay 15, 16 (S.C. 1784).

[4] Camp v. Lockwood, 1 Dallas 393 (Pa. Ct. Com. Pl. 1788).

[5] See Respublica v. Gordon, 1 Dallas 233 (Pa. 1788); Marks v. Johnson, Kirby 228 (Conn. 1787); Beckman v. Tomlinson, Kirby 291 (Conn. 1787).

[6] See Rutgers v. Waddington, New York Mayor's Court 1784, in Richard B. Morris, ed., *Select Cases of the Mayor's Court of New York City, 1674–1784* (Washington, D. C., 1935), 302; State v. Johnston, 2 H. & M. 160 (Md. 1786).

[7] Frank G. Bates, *Rhode Island and the Formation of the Union* (New York, 1898), 121–140; Merrill Jensen, *The New Nation* (New York, 1950), 323–325. An analogous issue that did not arise in Massachusetts during the Confederation period concerned the effect to be given to out-of-state discharges in bankruptcy. For cases from other states, see Taylor v. Geary, 1 Kirby 313 (Conn. 1787); Miller v. Hall,

ther legal fragmentation, when the Massachusetts General Court, in response, permitted Massachusetts residents to pay their Rhode Island creditors in the same Rhode Island paper,[8] and the Massachusetts courts upheld the local policy.[9] Another example of retaliatory legislation in the Massachusetts-Rhode Island dispute was the Rhode Island statute of 1780 prohibiting appeals to Congress in prize cases in which one of the parties was from a state, such as Massachusetts, which itself restricted appeals.[1] Localism was also evident in a Massachusetts case brought to recover Massachusetts land in which the defendant pleaded a title obtained from the original Rhode Island owner pursuant to an English and a Rhode Island bankruptcy act. The court rejected the plea on the ground "that the said Act of Assembly of the late Colony of Rhode Island and the said Statute of the twenty first of James are not nor never were of force within the late Province now State of Massachusetts Bay"[2] — a rather cavalier treatment of out-of-state legislation which would have been unlikely to have occurred during the pre-Revolutionary period before the trend toward localism had set in. Nor were the cases involving Rhode Island the only ones in which the Massachusetts courts in the advancement of local policy denied relief to out-of-state claimants. The most politically sensitive of all, perhaps, occurred in 1783, when Massachusetts granted habeas corpus to a runaway slave from South Carolina, over an objection that his release had some "Connection with, or relation to *puritanism*" and constituted "an attack upon the *Spirit, freedom, dignity, independance, Sovereignty* of S.C."[3] The Massachusetts judges, of course, denied the charge, but their argument that their decision had been based upon the un-

---

[1] Dall. 229 (Pa. Sup. Ct. 1788); Jones v. Allen, 1 Dallas 188 (Philadelphia C.P. 1786).

[8] See Mass. Laws of 1786, ch. 29.

[9] See Bruce v. Chapin, Suffolk C.P., January 1788, modified on other grounds, Suffolk Sup. Jud. Ct., February 1789. According to the Connecticut case of Mumford v. Wright, 1 Kirby 297 (Conn. 1787), Rhode Island applied its legislation only to payments made by Rhode Island debtors to Rhode Island creditors.

[1] See Bourguignon, *The First Federal Court*, 63.

[2] Whipple v. Winsor, Bristol Common Pleas, September 1779.

[3] "Justices to Gov. Hancock," 20 December 1783, in Cushing Papers (ms. in Massachusetts Historical Society, Boston, Mass.).

availability of procedures for committing runaways was patently un-
true.[4] As the South Carolinians sensed, Massachusetts was merely
advancing its own policy of abolitionism.

These federal-state and interstate conflicts cases, most of which
were, as we have seen, products of conflicting state statutes oriented
toward local, particularistic social and economic policies, made explicit the legal fragmentation implicit in the colonial system's thirteen supreme courts and thirteen legislatures—"a hydra in government, from which nothing but contradiction and confusion . . .
[could] proceed."[5] By introducing the element of statutes into the
law, the Revolution had destroyed the unity of American substantive
law—a unity which during the colonial period had obscured the
structural fragmentation which had occurred merely in transplanting
English judicial institutions to America. By the late 1780's, Americans, surveying the "rival, conflicting and angry regulations" of the
states[6] and the federal laws which "ye States ha[d] disregarded . . .
with constancy & without Blushing,"[7] were well aware that fragmentation had occurred.

As against this fragmentation, the rejection of the English doctrine
tying choice of law to choice of court paled into insignificance. For
that rejection had merely brought about a shift from a potentially
rigorous conflicts rule of applying the *lex fori* in every case to a more
flexible, but still divisive approach of analyzing whether local governmental policy required such application. This new approach, however, by no means eliminated the danger that "from the gradual
conflicts of State regulations, . . . the citizens of each, would at length
come to be considered and treated by others in no better light

---

[4] See Exeter v. Hanchet, Hampshire Sup. Jud. Ct., September 1784, in Sargeant,
"Court Minutes," in which a year after the South Carolina case procedures for committing runaways were mentioned as existing. No statute creating such procedures
intervened between the two cases.

[5] *The Federalist* No. 80 (Middletown, Conn., Jacob E. Cooke, ed., 1961), 535
(Hamilton).

[6] James Madison, "Preface to Debates in the Convention of 1787," in Max Farrand,
ed., *The Records of the Federal Convention of 1787* (New Haven, 1911), III, 539,
547.

[7] "Charge to Grand Jury," ca. 1790, Sargeant Papers.

than that of foreigners and aliens"[8]—a "danger ... much to [be] dread."[9]

III. Conflict of Laws in a Federal System

A. *The Program of the Framers*

The importance which federal-state and interstate conflicts problems had assumed made it "necessary," many Americans believed, "to establish one court paramount to the rest—possessing a general superintendence, and authorised to settle and declare in the last resort, an uniform rule of civil justice."[1] The justices of the Supreme Court, for example, "deemed [it] essential to the due administration of Justice, that some national Court or Council, should be instituted or authorized to examine the Acts of the ordinary Tribunals, ... it being important that these Tribunals should be confined to the limits of their respective Jurisdictions, and that they should uniformly interpret and apply the Law in the same Sense and manner."[2] Such federal superintendence and control were needed to "preserve the harmony of the states, and that of the citizens thereof";[3] all practices having "a tendency to disturb the harmony" were, *The Federalist* argued, "proper objects" of such national control.[4]

The framers always kept in mind the "constant tendency in the States to encroach on the federal authority ... [and] to infringe the rights & interests of each other...."[5] Their initial response to this tendency was to confer upon Congress a power to negative all state laws, but this solution was rejected on the ground it would per-

[8] *The Federalist* No. 22, 137 (Hamilton).

[9] Charles C. Pinckney, "Observations on the Plan of Government Submitted to the Federal Convention in Philadelphia," in Farrand, *Records of the Federal Convention*, 106, 115.

[1] *The Federalist* No. 22, 143–144 (Hamilton). See also Elliot, *Debates in the State Conventions*, 4:147 (remarks of Mr. Iredell).

[2] "Justices of the Supreme Court to President Washington," September 1790, in Cushing Papers, ms. in Massachusetts Historical Society, Boston, Mass.

[3] Farrand, *Records of the Federal Convention*, 1:238 (remarks of Mr. Randolph).

[4] *The Federalist* No. 80, 537 (Hamilton). See also Farrand, *Records of the Federal Convention*, 1:22 (resolution proposed by Mr. Randolph), 224 (resolution of Convention), 237 (report of Committee of the Whole); 2:46 (resolution of Convention); Elliot, *Debates in the State Conventions*, 4:159 (remarks of Mr. Davie).

[5] Farrand, *Records of the Federal Convention*, 1:164 (remarks of Mr. Madison). See also Elliot, *Debates in the State Conventions*, 3:66 (remarks of Mr. Randolph).

mit national interference in purely local affairs; as George Mason argued, "[N]o road nor bridge ... [could] be established without the Sanction of the General Legislature," which would be required "to sit constantly in order to receive & revise State Laws."[6] The Convention then responded with two narrower provisions, which sought to reach only those state laws which came into conflict either with federal law or with the law of another state.[7] The provision dealing with federal-state conflicts was the supremacy clause, which made "the laws of the general government ... binding on the state[s]...."[8] To deal with the problem of interstate conflicts, the Convention incorporated the full faith and credit clause of the Articles of Confederation into the new Constitution, but with two amendments which sought to insure its application to "acts of the Legislatures" as well as to "Judgments"[9]—the only two interstate conflicts problems which legal thinkers had yet perceived.[1] Finally,

[6] Farrand, *Records of the Federal Convention*, 2:390. See generally ibid., 2:27–29 (debate on proposed negative).

[7] See Elliot, *Debates in the State Conventions*, 2:481 (remarks of Mr. Wilson).

[8] "The Letters of Luther Martin," in Paul L. Ford, ed., *Essays on the Constitution of the United States Published during its Discussion by the People, 1787–1788* (Brooklyn, 1892), 361.

[9] Compare U. S. Constitution, art IV, sec. 1, which applies to "the public Acts, Records, and judicial Proceedings of every other State," with Articles of Confederation, art. IV, which applied to the "records, acts and judicial proceedings of the courts and magistrates of every other State." But see Nadelmann, "Full Faith and Credit," 54–56, where the argument is made, on the basis of language stricken out of Madison's Notes referring to state acts of insolvency, that the full faith and credit clause was intended to apply only to private laws, not to the public laws of the states. Nadelmann bases his argument on the assumption that all state insolvency legislation during the Confederation period consisted of private acts. But this assumption is unsound, for several states, such as New York, passed general insolvency acts. See An Act for giving Relief in Cases of Insolvency, N.Y. Laws of 1788, ch. 92 (1788). In any event, it is difficult to understand how the framers, who for a decade had been witnessing statutory reconstruction of their entire legal system, could have conceived of legislation as anything but public acts. See Nelson, *Americanization of the Common Law*, 90–92.

The second amendment to the full faith and credit clause gave Congress power to legislate concerning the effect to be given to statutes as well as to judgments. See generally Farrand, *Records of the Federal Convention*, 2:486–489.

For the quotation in the text, see ibid., 2:447 (remarks of Mr. Wilson and Dr. Johnson).

[1] On the fact that lawyers in the 1780's were not generally aware of developing differences between the common law of the various states, see Morton J. Horwitz, *The Transformation of American Law, 1780–1860* (Cambridge, Mass., 1977), 11–14.

the Convention made provision for the creation of a federal judiciary since "the Courts of the States . . . [could] not be trusted with the administration of the National laws."[2]

When one looks at the framers' statements against the background of the problem they were seeking to solve, one senses that they had a vaguely defined, general goal of creating a new body of federal law and a new federal institution capable of imposing jurisdictional limits on state courts and legislatures,[3] much as the common law and the Court of King's Bench had imposed limits on the jurisdiction of local courts and local law in England. There seemed to be no other solution. No one had, as yet, conceived of the possibility of dealing with federal-state and interstate conflicts as different issues; indeed, on most occasions when the framers spoke about the problems, they spoke about them together. Moreover, the states had failed equally in dealing with both. No alternative existed to creating a new institution — a Supreme Court which would administer federal law[4] setting limits upon the jurisdiction of the states, both as against itself and as against each other.

The framers did not think about conflicts problems in more precise terms than this. Aware of "the difficulty in establishing the powers of the judiciary,"[5] they left to the future the demarcation of precise boundaries between various courts and various laws in America. "Time, reflection, and experience," they realized, would "be necessary to suggest and mature the proper regulations on this subject."[6] Accordingly they wrote the relevant constitutional provisions in

[2] Farrand, *Records of the Federal Convention*, 2:46 (remarks of Mr. Randolph). See also Elliot, *Debates in the State Conventions*, 2:491–492 (remarks of Mr. Wilson); 4:156 (remarks of Mr. Davie), 164 (remarks of Mr. Maclaine).

[3] See ibid., 2:258 (remarks of Mr. Hamilton). Cf. ibid., 3:542 (remarks of Mr. Henry).

[4] Scholars who have studied the history of full faith and credit have debated whether the courts or only the Congress would have power to create such a body of law—that is, whether the full faith and credit clause is self-executing. The debate has been particularly pointed in regard to legislation, as distinguished from judgments. The arguments are summarized in Nadelmann, "Full Faith and Credit," 62–73. The issue, however, is historically a spurious one, since the record left by the framers is too thin for close analysis.

[5] Farrand, *Records of the Federal Convention*, I, 238 (remarks of Mr. Randolph). Cf. Elliot, *Debates in the State Conventions*, II, 488 (remarks of Mr. Wilson); IV, 150 (remarks of Mr. Johnston), 165 (remarks of Mr. Iredell).

[6] Ibid., II, 488 (remarks of Mr. Wilson).

rather broad and general language. One critic, in speaking of the jurisdiction of the federal courts and of federal law, observed that it was "impossible for human nature to trace its extent,"[7] while Madison's statement about the first sentence of the full faith and credit clause — that it was "extremely indeterminate; and can be of little importance under any interpretation it will bear"[8] — describes perfectly the state in which posterity would find the record left by the framers. In resolving conflicts problems, posterity accordingly would turn to other sources in addition to that record.

B. *The Common Law as a Guide to Constitutional Interpretation*

The source to which legal thinkers initially turned was the common law. The Massachusetts legislature, for one, assumed that the limits of federal jurisdiction were to be "found in the application of the principles and usages of the common law,"[9] for, as a Massachusetts representative in Congress explained, "when the people of the United States convened for the purpose of framing a federal compact, they were all habituated to this common law, to its usages, its maxims, and its definitions."[1] It was therefore "natural to conclude that, in forming the Constitution, they kept in view the model of the common law, and that a safe recourse may be had to it in all cases that would otherwise be doubtful."[2] "Without this law," another Congressman argued, "the Constitution [would] become ... a dead letter."[3]

It was, indeed, natural to turn to the common law. Lawyers of moderate intelligence and conservative temper who dared not think bold new thoughts had little else to which to turn. The common law, however, produced strange and unacceptable results in three of the instances upon which courts did have recourse to it.

1. Federal Diversity Jurisdiction. — One instance of recourse to

---

[7] Ibid., III, 565 (remarks of Mr. Grayson).

[8] *The Federalist* No. 42, 287 (Madison).

[9] Elliot, *Debates in the State Conventions*, 4:536 (answer of Massachusetts legislature to Virginia Resolutions of 1798).

[1] *Annals of Congress*, VIII, 2146 (1798) (remarks of Representative Otis).

[2] Ibid., VIII, 2146 (1798) (remarks of Representative Otis). See also ibid., VIII, 2252 (1799) (remarks of Representative Bayard).

[3] Ibid., XI, 614 (1802) (remarks of Representative Bayard).

the common law was the adoption by federal courts, hearing diversity cases, of common law rules concerning waiver of jurisdictional defenses. The common law distinguished between subject matter jurisdiction, which a defendant could not waive, and other jurisdictional matters, which he could waive, thereby consenting to jurisdiction. By subject matter jurisdiction, English lawyers meant jurisdiction to administer the sort of law under which the plaintiff was seeking a remedy; the concept had reference to the choice of court-choice of law relationship—to the fact that a common law court, for example, could not administer ecclesiastical remedies.[4] Pleas, on the other hand, alleging improper venue or that a defendant was privileged not to be sued in a particular court, were of the sort which could be waived.[5] Since lack of diversity was factually more analogous to the latter than to the former English concept, there were many early cases in the federal courts of Massachusetts in which diversity was waived and jurisdiction consented to—suits, for example, between two foreigners;[6] between two citizens of Massachusetts,[7] one of whom, in one case, pleaded that he was a citizen of Massachusetts who resided overseas;[8] and between a Massachusetts citizen and a citizen of another state residing in Massachusetts.[9] Moreover, during the first seven years of the diversity jurisdiction

[4] See Anon., Y.B. 11 Hen. 4, f. 47, pl. 21 (1409) (opinion of Thirning, J.). See also Marshall's Case, Cro. Car. 9, Latch 83, 79 Eng. Rep. 613 (K.B. 1625); Alexander W. Renton, ed., *Encyclopaedia of the Laws of England* (London, 1897), III, 357–358.

[5] See Camfield v. Warren, 1 Lutwyche 639, 125 Eng. Rep. 335 (C.P. 1700); Unston v. Milner, 1 Show. K.B. 49, 89 Eng. Rep. 440 (K.B. 1689); Barnes v. Ward, 1 Sid. 29, 82 Eng. Rep. 950 (K.B. 1661); John Comyns, *A Digest of the Laws of England*, vol. 1 (London, 1762), 5.

[6] Nebon v. DeBellerive, Cir. Ct. D. Mass., May 1790. Cf. Prince v. Parker, Cir. Ct. D. Mass., June 1798 (New York plaintiff v. Virginia defendant).

[7] Browne v. Read, Cir. Ct. D. Mass., October 1795; Wells v. Freeman, Cir. Ct. D. Mass., October 1794.

[8] Clarke v. Wilder, Cir. Ct. D. Mass., June 1794 (jury verdict that overseas resident not a citizen of Massachusetts).

[9] Douglass v. Enos, Cir. Ct. D. Mass., October 1792; Parkman v. Langdon, Cir. Ct. D. Mass., October 1796. Cf. Lyman v. Amory, Cir. Ct. D. Mass., June 1796 (Massachusetts plaintiff v. Massachusetts defendant and foreign defendant resident at Boston). See also Gray v. Spellman, Cir. Ct. D. Mass., October 1798 (Massachusetts plaintiff v. defendant "of New Haven . . . , now residing in Boston & citizen of the State of New York"); Apthorp v. Rogers, Cir. Ct. D. Mass., October 1792 (New York administrator of Massachusetts decedent v. Massachusetts defendants).

in Massachusetts, only one dismissal occurred for want of diversity alone, and then, only after the want of diversity had been pleaded.[1] Instead, in one case which was dismissed for lack of jurisdiction,[2] the defendant had made the identical plea he would have made at common law to challenge the jurisdiction of a state court[3]—that neither of the parties lived nor did the cause of action arise within the territorial limits of the court.[4] The hiatus between that plea, which is almost analogous to a modern plea of improper venue, and the modern concept of diversity is further demonstrated by a suit between an English plaintiff and a Massachusetts defendant, which was nonetheless dismissed upon a plea of lack of jurisdiction solely because the cause of action had arisen in England.[5]

2. *Federal Jurisdiction of Common Law Crimes.*—Another instance of recourse to the common law was the federal courts' assumption of jurisdiction over common law crimes during the 1790's and early 1800's. The theory upon which jurisdiction was assumed was that the government had "an implied power to preserve its own existence and promote the end and object of its creation";[6] as one district judge observed, the federal government "could no longer be called an independent government, if, for the punishment of offenses of this nature, tending to obstruct and pervert the administration of its affairs, an appeal must be made to the state tribunals."[7] Like the independent state governments, the federal government accordingly

---

[1] Folger v. Barker, Cir. Ct. D. Mass., October 1792.

[2] Walton v. McNeil, 29 Fed. Cas. 141 (C.C.D. Mass. 1794).

[3] See Froud v. Robbins, Suffolk C.P., January 1805; Irving v. Derby, Essex C.P., October 1794.

[4] Upon such a plea fact questions were determined by a jury. See Duffield v. Greenleaf, Cir. Ct. D. Mass., October 1797.

[5] Fields v. Taylor, 9 Fed. Cas. 41 (C.C.D. Mass. 1799). Cf. Irving v. Derby, Essex Common Pleas, October 1794, in which an analogous plea was upheld in a state court suit between a Massachusetts plaintiff and an English defendant.

[6] United States v. Hudson, 11 U.S. (7 Cranch) 32, 34 (1812) (dictum).

[7] United States v. Worrall, 2 Dallas 384, 395 (C.C.D. Pa. 1798) (opinion of Peters, D.J.). See also Henfield's Case, 11 Fed. Cas. 1099, 1103–1105 (grand jury charge of Jay, C.J.), 1120 (petit jury charge of Wilson, J.) (C.C.D. Pa. 1793). See generally Horwitz, *Transformation of American Law*, 9–15; Leonard W. Levy, *Legacy of Suppression: Freedom of Speech and Press in Early American History* (Cambridge, Mass., 1960), 234–248; James M. Smith, *Freedom's Fetters: The Alien and Sedition Laws and American Civil Liberties* (Ithaca, 1956), 188–220.

turned to the common law, bringing a series of criminal prosecutions that have been chronicled in detail by historians.

3. State-Court Suits Against Federal Officials.—Lawyers also continued to look to state common law to provide relief against abuses of power by government officials. State writs of habeas corpus[8] and *de homine replegiando*[9] accordingly were used on numerous occasions to test the validity of military enlistments, and in the majority of the cases the enlistees were released. Such state writs, of course, carried with them the power to interpret the federal statutes by which the validity of enlistments was determined[1]—a power which Justice Story thought was used by Massachusetts to defeat federal legislative policy during the War of 1812.[2] Few legal thinkers, however, saw the issue as one of federal-state power. Most, instead, saw state control over the military as a *"practice"* based upon the principle that "in a free country, the civil power must predominate"—a practice which would "secure and preserve our liberties from the inroads of a standing army."[3] Analogous policy considerations were involved in the power of state courts to entertain common law damage suits against federal officials. Such suits were brought upon contract claims,[4] for allegedly illegal seizures of plaintiffs' goods,[5] and for allegedly unlawful sales of real estate for nonpayment of taxes.[6] State-court suits were also commenced against federal officials in their

[8] Commonwealth v. Cushing, 11 Mass. 67 (1814); Commonwealth v. Harrison, 11 Mass. 63 (1814); Commonwealth v. Sumner, Suffolk Common Pleas, April 1827. Habeas corpus to obtain the release of a man in military service could, of course, also be brought in the federal court. See, e.g., United States v. Bainbridge, 24 Fed. Cas. 946 (C.C.D. Mass. 1816).

[9] Bassett v. Ross, Berkshire Common Pleas, April 1813.

[1] See Commonwealth v. Cushing, 11 Mass. 67, 71 (1814), where the court determined the "true construction" of the statute.

[2] See United States v. Bainbridge, 24 Fed. Cas. 946 (C.C.D. Mass. 1816), where Justice Story noted that he had "never been able to bring . . . [his] mind to assent to the construction put upon . . . [federal enlistment legislation] in some of the cases in the Massachusetts Reports. Com. v. Cushing, 11 Mass. 67." 24 Fed. Cas. at 952.

[3] Isaac Maltby, *A Treatise on Courts Martial and Military Law* (Boston, 1813), 160–161.

[4] Freeman v. Otis, 9 Mass. 272 (1812); Brown v. Austin, 1 Mass. 208 (1804).

[5] Hoit v. Hook, 14 Mass. 210 (1817); Coolidge v. Harris, Suffolk Common Pleas, October 1822.

[6] Holden v. Eaton, 8 Pick. (25 Mass.) 436 (1829).

capacity as private citizens.[7] These suits gave state courts significant leverage over federal policy, particularly in view of the trial court's power to find facts and initially to accept or reject defenses.[8]

The results which the common law produced in the areas of diversity, criminal law, and suits against government officials made sound analytical sense to common lawyers and were consistent with precedent. Moreover, the results were unbiased: sometimes, as in diversity and criminal law, the common law made federal jurisdiction broader than we now know it; at other times, as with suits against government officials, that jurisdiction was narrowed. Nonetheless, the common law failed as a guide to interpreting the Constitution's jurisdictional provisions. The difficulty was that its results were unacceptable to politically significant groups. Thus, reference to the common law rendered people with strong fears of centralized power subject to prosecution at the hands of that power for essentially political crimes, such as sedition[9] or taking sides in a European war which many Americans saw as a struggle between liberty and tyranny.[1] The common law as used in interpreting the diversity jurisdiction, meanwhile threatened the state courts, again enhancing central at the expense of local institutions. On the other hand, as events during the War of 1812 proved, the common law rendered the federal government potentially incapable of enforcing national

[7] Sprague v. Carter, Middlesex Common Pleas, May 1801 (suit against marine for personal debt); Discharge of Richardson, Worcester Sup. Jud. Ct., September 1800 (writ of habeas corpus granted on behalf of soldier imprisoned pursuant to writ of execution). The two members of the military, who were exempt from imprisonment for debt by virtue of federal statute, see An Act for the Better Organization of the Troops of the United States §4, 1 Stat. 749, 751 (1799), were discharged from custody.

[8] See Freeman v. Otis, 9 Mass. 272 (1812), where the state court rejected the defense of official immunity on a government contract upon a finding that the defendant had prevented the plaintiff from obtaining redress from the government, and Holmes v. Hastings, Plymouth Common Pleas, April 1802, rev'd on discontinuance by plaintiff, Plymouth Sup. Jud. Ct., June 1802, where the court rejected a plea by a Boston postmaster that he was too busy to come to Plymouth to defend a suit brought against him there.

[9] See Levy, *Legacy of Suppression*, 234–248; Smith, *Freedom's Fetters*, 188–220.

[1] See, e.g., Williams' Case, 29 Fed. Cas. 1330 (C.C.D. Conn. 1799) (joining crew of French privateer); Henfield's Case, 11 Fed. Cas. 1099 (C.C.D. Pa. 1793) (joining crew of French privateer).

policies in time of crisis.[2] The common law, in short, hindered the establishment of the constitutional system—promoting both national tranquility and local liberty—which the framers had sought to create. Legal thinkers accordingly turned elsewhere in their search for principles with which to clothe the Constitution.

C. *Politics as a Guide to Constitutional Interpretation*

Americans finally derived the principles with which they clothed the Constitution from the political theory and political reality of the early nineteenth century. Many of the great constitutional issues of the period—the extent of national legislative power and the jurisdiction of the Supreme Court over state appeals, for example—were, at their root, questions of political theory—questions over which people disagreed. There existed, however, a common core of political assumptions to which nearly all Americans assented. These assumptions, in turn, influenced the direction which the courts took during the nineteenth century in several conflicts matters and which courts today still continue to take.

One political assumption upon which nearly all Americans agreed was that the federal government was a government of limited powers. This was true of all its agencies; the courts, for example, possessed "only . . . such portions of power as were conceived necessary for the public welfare,"[3] and, in fact, had been denied added powers because such powers would have been dangerous to that welfare. From this it followed that a litigant could, "by no means, give a jurisdiction to . . . [a] court of the United States, which that court . . . [did] not possess by the constitution of . . . [its] power from the people of all the states."[4]

1. Federal Diversity Jurisdiction.—Recognizing that jurisdictional limitations existed for constitutional reasons of greater importance than the convenience of individual litigants, federal diversity courts refused after 1797 to permit litigants to consent to

---

[2] See above 457, notes 1 and 2, and 458, note 8 and accompanying text.

[3] John B. McMaster and Frederick D. Stone, eds., *Pennsylvania and the Federal Constitution, 1787–1788* (Philadelphia, 1888), 302.

[4] James Sullivan, *Observations upon the Government*, 31. Cf. Marbury v. Madison, 5 U.S. (1 Cranch) 137, 174–176 (1803).

jurisdiction and began to dismiss *sua sponte* suits in which diversity did not appear upon the record.[5] By the 1820's the courts were applying an essentially modern rule that "where the want of jurisdiction is apparent . . . , it is fatal at all times, and may be insisted upon by way of motion or otherwise, in any stage of the cause, and even upon appeal."[6] They also had forged modern rules prohibiting suits between parties, neither of whom was a resident of the district,[7] and requiring total diversity between all parties on each side of any matter.[8]

2. *Federal Jurisdiction of Common Law Crimes.*—Recognition of the limitations of federal power also assisted in the destruction of the federal courts' jurisdiction over common law crimes. The first step occurred in 1798 in *United States v. Worrall*,[9] where Justice Chase argued that federal courts could not have such common law jurisdiction because neither the Constitution nor the Congress had made the common law a part of federal criminal jurisprudence.[1] Two years later James Madison improved upon this argument. He contended that the adoption of the common law by the federal courts would have one of two unconstitutional results. If the common law were held, "like other laws, liable to revision and alteration by the authority of Congress," then "the authority of Congress . . . [would be] coextensive with the objects of common law; that is to say, with every object of legislation . . . [and] no longer under the limitations

---

[5] See Bingham v. Cabot, 3 U.S. (3 Dallas) 382 (1798); Emory v. Greenough, 3 U.S. (3 Dallas) 369 (1797). Cf. Borden v. Borden, Cir. Ct. D. Mass., June 1806 (remanded to state court from which previously removed since want of diversity apparent upon record even though diversity properly pleaded).

[6] Dodge v. Perkins, 7 Fed. Cas. 798, 799 (C.C.D. Mass. 1827), where in dictum Justice Story added that, if the want of diversity were not apparent, it must be pleaded by the defendant before the court reached the merits of the controversy.

[7] Picquet v. Swan, 19 Fed. Cas. 609 (C.C.D. Mass. 1828).

[8] Strawbridge v. Curtiss, 7 U.S. (3 Cranch) 267 (1806).

[9] 2 Dallas 384 (C.C.D. Pa. 1798).

[1] 2 Dallas at 394–395. Chase also observed that federal courts could not adopt state common law, since the common law of the various states was different. Ibid., 394–395. Other lawyers were first coming to this realization at about the same time. See Brown v. Van Braam, 3 U.S. (3 Dallas) 344, 352–354 (1797) (argument for defendant in error), discussed in Charles Warren, "New Light on the History of the Federal Judiciary Act of 1789," *Harvard Law Review*, XXXVII (1923), 49, 89 n.85. See generally Horwitz, *Transformation of American Law*, 11–15.

marked out in the Constitution."[2] On the other hand, if the common law were held "paramount and irremediable by the legislature," that "would confer on the judicial department a discretion little short of a legislative power."[3] In either case, adoption of a federal common law "would overwhelm the residual sovereignty of the states, and, by one constructive operation, new-model the whole political fabric of the country."[4]

With Madison's party in power during the next decade, so few federal common law prosecutions occurred that, when the Supreme Court was called upon in 1812 to determine the legitimacy of such prosecutions, it considered the question "as having been long settled in public opinion" and in "the general acquiescence of legal men," and accordingly held in *United States v. Hudson*[5] that such prosecutions were impermissible. There was, however, an answer to Madison's argument — an answer vaguely perceived by James Sullivan in 1801 and clearly articulated by Justice Story in *United States v. Coolidge* in 1813[6] — namely, that federal common law jurisdiction could be limited to those substantive crimes over which Congress had legislative power. Such a limitation, of course, would not have upset the balance of federalism. On the basis of Story's analysis, the Supreme Court was willing to reconsider its decision in *Hudson*, but the Madison administration declined in *Coolidge* to argue on behalf of the government, and the Court refused to overrule *Hudson* without hearing argument.[7] Administrative decision-making thus joined with constitutional analysis to end the federal courts' jurisdiction over common law crimes.

3. State-Court Suits Against Federal Officials. — A third area in which courts had had recourse to the common law was that of state-

---

[2] "Madison's Report on the Virginia Resolutions" (1800), in Elliot, *Debates in the State Conventions*, IV, 546, 565–566.

[3] Ibid., 566.

[4] Ibid., 566.

[5] 11 U.S. (7 Cranch) 32 (1812).

[6] See United States v. Coolidge, 25 Fed. Cas. 619 (C.C.D. Mass. 1813); James Sullivan, *A Dissertation upon the Constitutional Freedom of the Press* (Boston, 1801), 40–41, 48–54. Cf. United States v. Smith, 27 Fed. Cas. 1147 (C.C.D. Mass. 1792) (common law prosecution incident to federal statute).

[7] United States v. Coolidge, 14 U.S. (1 Wheat.) 415 (1816).

court suits against federal officials. But, during the War of 1812, the propriety of this jurisdiction became a matter of political rather than legal concern, largely as a result of state-court obstruction of federal war policies.[8] The result was a series of temporary statutes in 1815, which permitted most sorts of federal officials to remove to a federal court proceedings brought against them in their official capacities in a state court. Some of these temporary acts remained in force for several years, and in 1833 a permanent removal statute for federal officials was finally enacted in response to South Carolina's attempt to nullify the Tariff of 1832.[9] It was not until the Civil War era, however, that state courts were forbidden to grant habeas corpus to prisoners in federal custody.[1]

4. Interstate Conflict of Laws.—A fourth subject upon which political considerations had an effect was that of interstate conflict of laws. At the Constitutional Convention, the expectation had been that interstate, as well as federal-state conflicts, would be resolved as matters of federal law.[2] But, in fact, few interstate conflicts were so resolved. Interstate choice of law questions, both statutory[3] and non-statutory,[4] for example, all became questions of state law; no one

[8] See above, 457, notes 1 and 2, and 458, note 8 and accompanying text.

[9] See generally *Hart and Wechsler's The Federal Courts and the Federal System*, Paul M. Bator, Paul J. Mishkin, David L. Shapiro and Herbert Wechsler, eds. (Mineola, N.Y., 1973), 1336.

[1] See Tarble's Case, 80 U.S. (13 Wall.) 397 (1872); Ableman v. Booth, 62 U.S. (21 How.) 506 (1859).

[2] See above, 451–453, notes 1–9, 1–2 and accompanying text.

[3] See Byrne v. Crowninshield, 17 Mass. 55 (1820) (foreign statute of limitations rejected); Blanchard v. Russell, 13 Mass. 1 (1816) (bankruptcy law of state of which creditor a citizen rejected); Bradford v. Farrand, 13 Mass. 18 (1816) (foreign bankruptcy statute rejected since contract made in Massachusetts); Walsh v. Farrand, 13 Mass. 19 (1816) (foreign insolvency statute applied when all parties citizens of foreign state); Phelps v. Decker, 10 Mass. 267 (1813) (Pennsylvania statute invalidating warranty on Pennsylvania land rejected in suit for breach thereof); Wilson v. Bourne, 10 Mass. 337 (1813) (foreign insolvency statute rejected when plaintiff a Massachusetts citizen); Baker v. Wheaton, 5 Mass. 509 (1809) (foreign insolvency statute applied in suit by Massachusetts endorsee); Pearsall v. Dwight, 2 Mass. 84 (1806) (foreign statute of limitations rejected); Proctor v. Moore, 1 Mass. 198 (1804) (foreign bankruptcy statute rejected since contract not made in foreign state and plaintiff not a citizen thereof).

[4] See Winthrop v. Carleton, 12 Mass. 4 (1815) (foreign interest rate applied upon money advanced in foreign state); Wellman v. Nutting, 3 Mass. 433 (1807) (factor in foreign country liable according to its law); Powers v. Lynch, 3 Mass.

in Massachusetts and, perhaps, no one in the rest of the nation as well, ever argued during the last decade of the eighteenth century or the first three decades of the nineteenth that such problems were of federal dimension.[5] Out-of-state law was applied in choice of law cases only as a matter of "comity"[6] — a concept borrowed from continental law.[7] Likewise, most questions concerning the effect to be given in one state to a judgment rendered in another were resolved as matters of state law. For instance, the Massachusetts courts, reversing the colonial rule,[8] rejected the argument that letters of administration were within the scope of full faith and credit[9] and held that an administrator who had received letters under the authority of another state could not sue in Massachusetts without first obtaining ancillary letters.[1] They similarly held that a criminal conviction in another state was not entitled to full faith and credit and accordingly did not render the convict incompetent as a witness in Massachusetts,[2] observing that "a judgment on a criminal prosecution cannot be carried into effect, beyond the jurisdiction of the state, within which the offense was committed," and that it was "hardly possible to conceive" that a contrary rule would "ever be adopted, so long as any portion of sovereignty remains with the states."[3] Massachusetts

77 (1807) (endorsee of bill of exchange drawn in foreign country liable according to laws of that country).

[5] None of the Massachusetts cases makes any argument that full faith and credit was applicable in choice of law cases. Neither did Justice Story, either in his treatise on conflicts or in his treatise on the Constitution; in both he talks about the full faith and credit clause only in connection with judgments. See Joseph Story, *Commentaries on the Constitution of the United States*, vol. 3 (Boston, 1833), secs. 1297–1307; Joseph Story, *Commentaries on the Conflict of Laws* (Boston, 3d ed., 1846), 1004–1005. As to the remainder of the United States, see Nadelmann, "Full Faith and Credit," 73.

[6] The doctrine of comity is discussed in Tappan v. Root, 15 Mass. 419 (1819); Hanover v. Turner, 14 Mass. 227 (1817); Greenwood v. Curtis, 6 Mass. 358, 377 (1810). See also Story, *Conflict of Laws*, 11–12.

[7] See Nadelmann, *Joseph Story's Contribution to Conflicts*, 230–232.

[8] See above, 423, note 1 and accompanying text.

[9] Sherburn v. Emery, York Sup. Jud. Ct., June 1792, in Dana, "Minute Books."

[1] Goodwin v. Jones, 3 Mass. 514 (1807). See also Stevens v. Gaylord, 11 Mass. 256, 263–264 (1814) (dictum). Cf. Cutter v. Davenport, 18 Mass. (1 Pick.) 81 (1822).

[2] Commonwealth v. Green, 17 Mass. 515 (1822).

[3] 17 Mass. at 546–547.

courts also analyzed out-of-state divorce decrees not as a matter of full faith and credit, but as a matter of whether to "permit another state to govern our citizens, in direct contravention of our own statutes" — a result which could be "required by no rule of comity."[4]

There was, in fact, only one problem to which the full faith and credit clause was held applicable — that of the effect to be given in one state to a judgment in a civil suit rendered in another.[5] Even upon this question, the courts at first had doubts, and many early cases held that the clause and the Congressional legislation pursuant to it provided only for a method of authenticating out-of-state judgments and said nothing about the effect to be given them.[6] Only after 1810 did it become clear that federal law required the state in which an out-of-state judgment was pleaded to give it conclusive effect, provided that the court rendering the judgment had had jurisdiction of the suit.[7]

Why, except for the problem of civil judgments, did interstate conflicts problems become questions of state rather than federal law? Part of the answer lies in the realm of political theory. A common assumption shared by all political theorists in the first half of the nineteenth century was that sovereignty in America had been divided between the states and the federal government. Although overlap occurred in those areas where the two governments possessed concurrent powers, the Constitution, as a general rule, was thought to have dispensed "certain powers on the state governments, and certain other powers on the national government."[8] The states were "no more subject within their respective spheres to the general authority, than the general government . . . [was] subject to them in its own

---

[4] Hanover v. Turner, 14 Mass. 227 (1817). But compare Barber v. Root, 10 Mass. 260 (1813).

[5] See Hall v. Williams, 23 Mass. (6 Pick.) 232 (1828); Hull v. Blake, 13 Mass. 153 (1816); Jacobs v. Hull, 12 Mass. 25 (1815).

[6] See Bartlett v. Knight, 1 Mass. 401 (1805). For similar cases in other states, see Nadelmann, "Full Faith and Credit," 63–66.

[7] See Mills v. Duryee, 11 U.S. (7 Cranch) 481 (1813); Bissell v. Briggs, 9 Mass. 462 (1813).

[8] M'Culloch v. Maryland, 17 U.S. (4 Wheat.) 316, 326 (1819) (argument of Mr. Webster, counsel for M'Culloch). See also McMaster and Stone, *Pennsylvania and the Federal Constitution*, 302 (remarks of Mr. Wilson).

sphere."[9] The now familiar expedient of giving the federal government power, usually under the Fourteenth Amendment, to set minimum standards within which state law must then operate in regulating particular subject matters was foreign to the early nineteenth-century legal mind, which tended instead to consider power over any particular subject matter either as exclusively federal or as exclusively state. Given contemporary predilections for decentralized government, such an analysis led irresistibly toward giving the states jurisdiction over interstate conflicts problems. Everyone agreed that the states had jurisdiction over their "internal police and economy"[1]—that is, over "ye laws about last wills & Testaments, descent of real estates, laws respecting contracts, respecting debts, conveyances, &c." and "ye mode of conducting & bringing actions, & seeking redress of private injuries & wrongs."[2] It followed that, if each state was to "give . . . the supreme law within its own dominions on all [such] subjects,"[3] the states must have exclusive cognizance of all conflicts questions.

The courts could, of course, have departed from this mechanistic analysis; indeed, they did depart from it in dealing with the problem of out-of-state judgments. Analysis of how that problem differed from other conflicts problems indicates why no other departures were made.

One difference was that, in 1790, for reasons which the scantity of the legislative record make it impossible to determine, Congress had enacted legislation about judgments, but not about other interstate conflicts problems. This difference became crucial when the Supreme Court in 1813 rested its holding in *Mills v. Duryee*,[4] that out-of-state judgments were to be given conclusive effect, upon the legislation rather than the underlying constitutional provision. The

[9] Timothy Ford, *An Enquiry into the Constitutional Authority of the Supreme Federal Court* (Charleston, S.C., 1792), 13. See also Sullivan, *Government of the United States*, 39. See also M'Culloch v. Maryland, 17 U.S. (4 Wheat.) 316, 405–406 (1819).

[1] Cohens v. Virginia, 19 U.S. (4 Wheat.) 264, 293–294 (1821) (argument of counsel for Virginia).

[2] "Grand Jury Charge," ca. 1790, in Sargeant Papers.

[3] Story, *Conflict of Laws*, 12.

[4] 11 U.S. (7 Cranch) 481 (1813).

absence of other legislation under full faith and credit was, however, also symptomatic of a more basic historical fact—that such legislation was not needed. For the other great conflicts problems which had arisen during the Confederation period were dealt with under other provisions of the Constitution—the currency cases, under the commerce power and the prohibition upon the states against issuing any paper money;[5] the fugitive slave cases, under the provision for the return of those slaves;[6] and the insolvency cases, under the contract clause.[7] In cases like *Swift v. Tyson*,[8] where the defendant argued in a federal court in New York that New York law should be applied to a negotiable instrument uttered in Maine; *Prigg v. Pennsylvania*,[9] where Pennsylvania sought to prosecute a Maryland resident who had entered Pennsylvania to recapture an alleged fugitive slave; and *McMillan v. McNeill*,[1] where it was decided that a Louisiana statute could not affect the obligation of a contract made in South Carolina, nineteenth century courts continued to face conflicts problems similar to those of an earlier era. The courts analyzed such cases, however, not as general conflict of laws cases, but as interstate commerce cases, fugitive slave cases, and contract clause cases. As a result, the cases did not give birth to a body of national conflict of laws doctrine. Nor did the residuum of conflicts problems, which essentially were problems of private law, where the public policies of various states rarely clashed and where the extension of comity by one state to the law of another could and, in fact, did lead to fair and just results.[2] The fact that Congress legislated only upon the problem of judgments was, finally, symptomatic of one other fact—the difficulty of framing other conflicts rules. As the Founding Fathers had realized, "time, reflection, and experience" would "be necessary to suggest and mature proper regulations"[3] on the subject of interstate

[5] U.S. Constitution, art. I, sec. 10.

[6] U.S. Constitution, art. IV, sec. 2.

[7] U.S. Constitution, art. I, sec. 10.

[8] 41 U.S. (16 Pet.) 1 (1842).

[9] 41 U.S. (16 Pet.) 539 (1842).

[1] 17 U.S. (4 Wheat.) 209 (1819).

[2] See above, 463–464.

[3] See above, 453, note 6 and accompanying text.

conflict of laws. This "time, reflection, and experience" were gained by leaving most of the subject to the states.

IV. Conclusion

When one disengages from the preconceptions of one's own time and looks backward over the long, complex process by which the subject of interstate conflict of laws became a matter primarily of state law, rather than federal constitutional law, it becomes clear that the process was not logically ordained. On the contrary, the logical solution both for federal-state and for interstate conflicts was that conceived by the framers — to place a supreme court administering a supreme law atop the national judicial structure with a mandate to resolve all intercourt conflicts.

Logic, however, is rarely the sole determinative force in any legal development. Much more important are people's needs and wants. It is therefore not surprising that the mode of resolving interstate conflicts, like the scope of federal jurisdiction, was determined largely by one of the dominating impulses of early nineteenth century America — localism, or the urge on the part of nearly all Americans to govern their own affairs without interference from outsiders unacquainted with the details of those affairs. This localism, which initially influenced the law of conflict of laws during the era of the American Revolution, continues by inertia to influence it today.

Sources

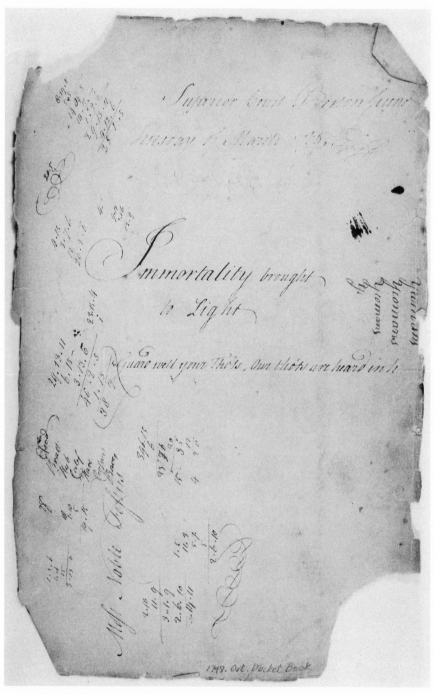

37. Inscription on 1749 October Docket Book. Although the page is entitled "Superior Court," it was used for the Inferior Court of Common Pleas, Suffolk. Courtesy, Social Law Library, Boston.

ROBERT J. BRINK

"Immortality brought to Light": An Overview of Massachusetts Colonial Court Records

I T has been fashionable to describe the colonial period as "the dark ages of American law."[1] Competent legal historians for this period have been hampered by a dearth of available primary source materials. Now that Massachusetts court records have been largely inventoried, after centuries of being "buried"[2] in courthouse basements, "some way will have to be found for getting scholars and colonial court archives together."[3]

It is hoped that these articles on sources will encourage researchers to use the colonial court records of Massachusetts. They will provide scholars with a county-by-county survey of early court materials in Massachusetts, jurisdictional outlines of the courts, a glossary of commonly used legal terms, a guide to common law rules of pleading and procedure, and discussions of data contained in the court records

[1] Lawrence M. Friedman, *A History of American Law* (New York: Simon and Schuster, 1973), 29.

[2] William E. Nelson, *Americanization of the Common Law: The Impact of Legal Change on Massachusetts Society, 1760–1830* (Cambridge: Harvard University Press, 1975), vii. Of course the term "buried" does not include the so-called "live" records of the probate courts and registries of deeds, which can readily be found in the respective clerks' offices.

This article attempts to provide a review of recent remedies to records management abuses and to suggest some research uses. It should be noted that actual examples and references to colonial court cases are generally limited to the Inferior Court of Common Pleas for Suffolk County. For a detailed guide to this collection, see Catherine Menand, *The Records of the Suffolk Inferior Court of Common Pleas*, available at the Supreme Judicial Court Records Preservation Project, fifteenth floor, Suffolk County Court House, Boston, MA 02108.

[3] William Jeffrey, quoted by George L. Haskins, "Law and Colonial Society," *Essays in the History of Early American Law*, ed. David H. Flaherty (Chapel Hill: The University of North Carolina Press, 1969), 41. Michael S. Hindus notes in *The Files of the Massachusetts Superior Court* (Boston: G. K. Hall and Company, 1980), 4, that "colonial court records [are] vital because they [are] frequently the only relatively complete historical source for the entire colonial period. In the late nineteenth and twentieth centuries, court records were only one of many historical sources, and thus their value as collateral sources of information is not nearly as great as for the colonial and early national periods."

for non-legal historians. There are also listings of relevant primary and secondary materials at four major research institutions in Massachusetts for colonial legal studies.

The publication of these articles on sources is not the Colonial Society's first attempt to lead researchers to court records. In addition to publishing the excellent early volumes of Massachusetts court records, one of the Society's prominent early members must be credited with the conservation of a collection which has been variously described as "a legal and historical treasure"[4] and "the best single collection"[5] of colonial court records in the country. John Noble, Clerk of the Supreme Judicial Court of Massachusetts and Editor of Publications for the Colonial Society at the turn of this century, directed the conservation and indexing of these files between 1883 and 1907. Generally known as the *Suffolk Files*, the collection comprises minute books, extended record books, and 1,289 volumes of file papers, mostly from the Superior Court of Judicature. It also includes other miscellaneous papers from County Courts, the Court of Assistants, General Sessions, Common Pleas, and Admiralty. Located in the Office of the Clerk of the Supreme Judicial Court for Suffolk County, fourteenth floor, Suffolk County Court House, Boston, the *Suffolk Files* have adequately been described by Noble and other scholars.[6]

Discussing the custodial provenance of these papers and records in an 1897 article, Noble observed that "one of the [clerks] cared little for such accumulations of the past, the other cared much."[7] Thus, Noble unwittingly explained why most of the Commonwealth's colonial court records have received little custodial attention over the

---

[4] *The Legal Papers of John Adams*, ed. L. Kinvin Wroth and Hiller Zobel, 3 vols. (Cambridge: Harvard University Press, 1965), I, xxxiii.

[5] David H. Flaherty, "The Use of Early American Court Records in Historical Research," *Law Library Journal*, LXIX (1976), 345. See *Records of the Suffolk County Court*, Colonial Society of Massachusetts, *Publications*, XXIX, XXX (1933); W. C. Ford, A. Mathews, "Bibliography of the Laws of Massachusetts Bay, 1641–1776," Colonial Society of Massachusetts, *Publications*, IV (1910), 297–480.

[6] John Noble, "The Early Court Files of Suffolk County," Colonial Society of Massachusetts, *Publications*, III (1895–1897), 317; Flaherty, "Court Records in Historical Research"; Robert J. Brink, "The Use of Court Records in Biographical Research," *Biography*, I (1978), 79.

[7] Noble, "Early Court Files," 318.

centuries, while several select collections have received considerably more. This fact was amplified by an incident more than half a century later. In 1954, Elijah Adlow, then Chief Justice to the Boston Municipal Court, was informed by the clerk's office that there was desperate need for space and that the "rubbish" in "an old vault in the basement" should be burned. Adlow was then led "down into the dark, cavernous basements of the old building" where he discovered, much to his "amazement," nearly thirteen thousand papers from the eighteenth and nineteenth centuries. Among these "crumbled and dust ridden sheets," Adlow found a complete set of quarterly returns of the Suffolk County Jailer for the period 1770 to 1820, listing prisoners confined there during the entire Revolutionary period. There was a voucher written by Sheriff Frobisher certifying his outlays for lodging and "victuallying" the jury that tried Captain Preston and other participants in the Boston Massacre. There were also records of Justice of the Peace Stephen Gorham, minutes of the Court of General Sessions for Suffolk County, and complete files of the Town Court of Boston, a tribunal unknown to any of Adlow's contemporaries.[8] The Adlow Collection is now at the Boston Public Library.

It should be noted that "the old courthouse" to which Judge Adlow had referred was also the seat of the Supreme Judicial Court in Boston, the very same building in which John Noble had served as clerk over a half century earlier, and is still in use. Recently, and again in the same building, the Librarian of the Social Law Library, Edgar J. Bellefontaine, saved from destruction the file papers of the Suffolk Inferior Court of Common Pleas for the period 1730–1817. Beginning in 1976, the Social Law Library sponsored a four-year project to organize and conserve the over 360,000 file papers, minute books, and extended record books. In so doing the Social Law Library publicized the need for preservation of such papers, which for centuries had been stored in precarious conditions in courthouse cellars throughout the Commonwealth.

Also in 1976 the Honorable Edward F. Hennessey, Chief Justice of the Supreme Judicial Court, appointed a Judicial Records Committee composed of clerks, scholars, librarians, and archivists. The

[8] Elijah Adlow, *Threshold of Justice: A Judge's Life Story* (Boston: Court Square Press, 1973), 272–275.

Committee was mandated to appraise the condition of the Commonwealth's judicial archives and formulate enlightened records management and archival policies. A number of projects have been undertaken, including an inventory of records of the Superior Court and
its colonial predecessors. That inventory, the relevant parts of which
are published in this volume (see below, 531–540), identified court
records throughout the state which "have been in storage, unused,
for up to 350 years. . . . Many records are in such fragile shape that
to use them without proper precautions would be tantamount to destroying them."[9] There are now plans to collect and centralize all
the pre-1859 materials in a special judicial archives section of the
Massachusetts Archives building now under construction. Moreover,
under the leadership of Chief Justice Hennessey, the Social Law
Library's professional conservation laboratory and its staff of con-
servators and archivists have been adopted by the Supreme Judicial
Court as the nation's only official court records preservation and management facility. Chief Justice Hennessey has thus committed the
Supreme Judicial Court to continue this "Noble" enterprise.

Scholarly Neglect in the Past

With relevant records kept for centuries in the kind of "dark"
basements to which Judge Adlow alluded earlier, it is understandable why the judicial history of the colonial period has been dimly
understood for so long. Unfortunately, the lack of research into legal

[9] Michael S. Hindus, *The Records of the Massachusetts Superior Court and its Predecessors: An Inventory and Guide* (Boston: Archives Division, Office of the Secretary
of the Commonwealth, 1977), 3. See the following for information on the development of a records program for the Massachusetts courts. Robert J. Brink, "The
Suffolk Inferior Court Files: An Historical Treasure Turning to Dust," *Boston Bar
Journal*, XX (1976), 6; Robert J. Brink, "Boston's Great Anthropological Documents," *Boston Bar Journal*, XXII (1978), 6; Robert S. Bloom, "Judicial Records:
The Formulation of a Statewide Records Preservation Program," *Boston Bar Jour-
nal*, XXII (1978), 23; Michael S. Hindus, "Designing Projects for Maximum Im-
pact: Saving the Early Court Records of Massachusetts," *The American Archivist*,
XLII (1979), 307; Robert J. Brink, "Deferred Maintenance of Court Records," *Law
Library Journal*, LXXIII (1980), 997; Catherine Menand, "Archival Processing of
Court Records," *Law Library Journal*, LXXIII (1980), 1003; Michael S. Hindus,
"The Massachusetts Superior Court Records Project," *Law Library Journal*, LXXIII
(1980), 1007; Michael S. Hindus et al., *The Files of the Massachusetts Superior
Court, 1859–1959: An Analysis and a Plan for Action* (Boston: G. K. Hall and
Company, 1980); and Robert J. Brink, "Saving the Court Records of Massachu-
setts," *Boston Bar Journal*, XXVI (1982), 16.

records themselves has led to erroneous explanations about law in the colonial period—erroneous explanations which exert enormous influence and which persist to this day.[1] Roscoe Pound popularized the misconception that under colonial conditions there was only "a rude administration of justice."[2] The title of his famous book *The Formative Period of American Law* (Boston, 1938) (referring to 1775 to 1860) has become accepted in the lexicon of our legal history to mean that "[f]or most practical purposes American judicial history begins *after* the Revolution."[3] Adjudication, asserted Pound, was left to "untrained magistrates who administered justice according to their common sense and the light of nature with some guidance from legislation."[4]

Thus several generations of scholars were dissuaded from delving into serious studies of law during the colonial period.[5] Pound's view became the established view, which to some extent still endures. Grant Gilmore, for instance, in his relatively recent book *The Ages of American Law* (New Haven, 1977), reflects a similar misconception concerning colonial legal studies:

[T]here can hardly be a legal system until the decisions of the courts are regularly published and are available to the bench and bar. Even in the seaboard colonies, where the practice of law had, during the eighteenth

[1] See Michael G. Kammen, "Colonial Court Records and the Study of Early American History: A Bibliographical Review," *American Historical Review*, LXX (1964–1965), 738. See also Zechariah Chafee, Jr., "Colonial Courts and the Common Law," *Essays in the History of Early American Law*, ed. David H. Flaherty (Chapel Hill: The University of North Carolina Press, 1969), 66.

[2] Pound, quoted by Chafee, "Colonial Courts," 66.

[3] Pound, quoted by Chafee, "Colonial Courts," 67. (Emphasis added.) See R. Pound, *The Formative Era of American Law* (Boston, 1938), 3–8; *The Spirit of the Common Law* (Boston, 1963), 113.

[4] Pound, quoted by Chafee, "Colonial Courts," 67. See R. Pound, *The Spirit of the Common Law*, 113.

[5] G. Edward White's book *Tort Law in America: An Intellectual History* (New York: Oxford University Press, 1980), xiii, explains that "scholarship is implicitly directed toward areas about whose relevance and soundness a tacit consensus exists and away from areas tacitly judged to be unpromising. The direction of research is a function of largely unarticulated value choices made by influential scholars." In this context, Michael Kammen commented that "Dean Pound's enormous influence on the study of American law also tended to persuade potential scholars that the period before independence was not worth close examination." See Kammen, "Colonial Court Records," 738.

century, became professionalized, there were no published reports; consequently there was nothing which could rationally be called a legal system.[6]

One of the first uses of court records is to test such theories against the true record of our colonial tradition. The work of George Haskins and others has taught us that to learn the facts of our colonial legal heritage we must *un*learn such fictions as that there was "nothing which could rationally be called a legal system."[7] Gilmore's logic overlooks the work historians have done in tracing the development of colonial doctrines from "unpublished judicial opinions, lawyers' notes, and, most commonly, records of pleadings, judgements, and other papers incorporated into official court files."[8] Although decisions of the colonial period were not regularly published, they were regularly recorded. In all Massachusetts counties, clerks from the Superior Court of Judicature, Courts of Common Pleas, and Courts of General Sessions kept extended record books, sometimes called judgment books, in which clerks summarized transcriptions of parties' pleadings and motions, the juries' verdicts, and the courts' judgments. In this context it should be noted that although there were no published court reports until after the Revolution, lawyers did, on occasion, prepare and circulate among themselves collections of local cases.[9] For more detailed information scholars are turning their attention to file papers to trace changing practice styles, which in turn substantiate changes in substantive law. The articles published in this volume often demonstrate the use of such records and the relative sophistication of the legal system they represent.

Scholars like William E. Nelson are finding that important "formative" doctrinal developments of the nineteenth century actually had important antecedents *before* the Revolution. For example, the

[6] Grant Gilmore, *The Ages of American Law* (New Haven: Yale University Press, 1977), 9.

[7] Ibid.

[8] Nelson, *Americanization of the Common Law*, vii. Professor Nelson states that his "research disclosed that the law of Massachusetts did change substantially in the seventy years between 1760 and 1830 in a variety of ways." Ibid.

[9] Friedman, *A History of American Law*, 282. See Josiah Quincy, *Reports of Cases Argued and Adjuded in the Superior Court of Judicature of the Province of Massachusetts Bay, between 1761 and 1772* (Boston, 1865).

development of a generalized negligence theory in torts superseded the particularized and technical pleadings of the common law writ system. The "conventional explanation" for the demise of the writ system is that the nineteenth-century codification movement suddenly abolished the writ system's forms of actions.[1] Specifically, scholars have identified the 1848 enactment of David Dudley Field's New York Code of Civil Procedure as the "catalytic agent" which, almost "at one blow," pronounced "the death sentence" on common law pleadings.[2] "Unfortunately, *insufficient scrutiny* of the writ system has taken place to justify this conventional explanation."[3] In fact, Nelson's study of common law pleadings in Massachusetts suggests that the reform was gradually modified over a long period and that, when the state legislatively abolished writ pleading in 1851, the reform was already realized in practice.[4]

Colonial records may also help to explain the development of the consideration doctrine in contract law. Some scholars, such as William E. Nelson and Morton J. Horwitz, have suggested that eighteenth-century common law courts discouraged competitive commercial transactions through an analysis of what in essence was consideration, whereby agreements were scrutinized for substantive equality of the exchange.[5] Such a mechanism for policing the fairness of exchanges may have protected the unsuspecting against bad bargains, but could have been a burden to the burgeoning business interests of the late eighteenth century. Horwitz has suggested that businessmen apparently "endeavored to find legal forms of agreement with which to conduct business transactions free from the equalizing tendencies of courts and juries. Of these forms, the most im-

---

[1] White, *Tort Law in America*, 8. See Nelson, *Americanization of the Common Law*, 69–88.

[2] Friedman, *A History of American Law*, 341.

[3] White, *Tort Law in America*, 9. (Emphasis added.)

[4] Ibid. See also William E. Nelson, "The Reform of Common Law Pleading in Massachusetts, 1760–1830: Adjudication as a Prelude to Legislation," *University of Pennsylvania Law Review*, CXXI (1973), 97.

[5] See generally Nelson, *Americanization of the Common Law*, 54–63; Morton J. Horwitz, *The Transformation of American Law, 1780–1860* (Cambridge: Harvard University Press, 1977), 167–168.

portant was the penal bond."[6] Such bonds "precluded inquiry into the adequacy of consideration for exchange"[7] and "allowed parties to determine their own damages free from judicial intervention."[8] Except for this general overview of the use of penal bonds, we must await more detailed, empirical studies of court records to explain more fully the influence of penal bonds on the judiciary's changing concern away from the adequacy of consideration to a non-protective inquiry confined to the presence of mere formal consideration. As David H. Flaherty has pointed out, for "the colonial era ... civil litigation remain[s] almost unstudied."[9]

Early court records can also help scholars to evaluate the impact or implementation of legislation. Two examples come to mind. Some scholars have speculated that the passage of the Stamp Act may have hindered the developing practices of young lawyers, and thus in some measure may have encouraged these young men to revolt — a difficult action in an otherwise conservative profession which teaches reverence for law, not revolution.[1] Young John Adams was anxious and annoyed by the whole affair:

So sudden an Interruption in my Career, is very unfortunate for me. I was but just getting into my Geers, just getting under Sail, and an Embargo is laid upon the Ship. Thirty Years of my Life are passed in Preparation for Business. I have had Poverty to struggle with—Envy and Jealousy and Malice of Enemies to encounter—no Friends, or but few to assist me, so that I have groped in dark Obscurity, till of late, and had but just become known, and gained a small degree of Reputation, when this execrable Project was set on foot for my Ruin as well as that of America in General, and of Great Britain.[2]

[6] Horwitz, *Transformation of American Law*, 167. See also Nelson, *Americanization of American Law*, 61.

[7] Horwitz, *Transformation of American Law*, 167.

[8] Ibid., 168.

[9] Flaherty, "Court Records in Historical Research," 344. Although Flaherty made this statement in 1976, it is still largely true today. In Massachusetts, the poor storage conditions of courthouses combined with the poor physical condition of early court records have discouraged in-depth analysis of developing pleading practices and doctrine by all but the most enterprising researchers.

[1] See Erwin C. Surrency, "The Lawyer and the Revolution," *American Journal of Legal History*, VIII (1964), 125.

[2] *Diary and Autobiography of John Adams*, ed. L. H. Butterfield, 4 vols. (Cambridge, Mass.: Belknap Press, 1961), I, 264–265, quoted in Hiller B. Zobel, "The Joys and

What exact impact did the Stamp Act have on the careers of Adams and others, as well as on the courts generally?[3] Did fewer lawyers begin practice during the year the Stamp Act was in effect? How many fewer cases did Adams handle in court, or, for that matter, how many fewer cases were generally heard?[4] Given that geographically there were whig and tory strongholds within the colony,[5] did the Stamp Act affect lawyers and courts in different counties differently? Court records provide empirical data from which to make term-by-term, year-by-year, and county-by-county comparisons.

Such examination of early court records is essential with respect to understanding the implementation, as well as all the implications, of various other legislative initiatives. The plight of Tory property demands such a look at litigation. The loyalists who fled Boston at the beginning of the American Revolution left their lands—and indeed their beloved homes—at the mercy of the very patriot leaders and neighbors who forced their departure. In 1779 the General Court passed two confiscation bills. The first was "An Act to Confiscate The Estates of Certain Notorious Conspirators." (*Acts & Resolves*, v, chap. 48, 966–967.) Punitive in nature, it confiscated without any legal process the estates of twenty-nine notable loyalists.

The second, less vituperative bill was aimed at a wider class of "certain persons commonly called absentees." (*Acts & Resolves*, v, chap. 49, 969–971.) Ostensibly it aided the state's coffers and creditors by establishing a judicial procedure for the condemnation and sale of Tory estates, under which the attorney general issued a complaint in the inferior courts of common pleas. In addition to interesting tidbits (John Adams' country seat in Quincy, "Peacefield," was a confiscated

Uses of Legal History," Massachusetts Historical Society, *Proceedings*, LXXXIV (1972), 59.

[3] David H. Flaherty has noted in "An Introduction to Early American Legal History," *Essays in the History of Early American Law*, ed. David H. Flaherty (Chapel Hill: The University of North Carolina Press, 1969), 17, that "there remains both opportunity and need for the study of the role that lawyers played in the American Revolution. The definitive works have not yet appeared." This is still true.

[4] "The largest source of information about John Adams' legal career," the editors of his personal legal papers point out, exists, strangely enough, not in the legal papers themselves but in court records. *Legal Papers of John Adams*, xxxiii. This observation must also be true for other lawyers.

[5] See Charles Robert McKirdy, "A Bar Divided: The Lawyers of Massachusetts and the American Revolution," *American Journal of Legal History*, XVI (1972), 205.

Tory estate), research in the court records has revealed, to one scholar at least, "an inside story of corruption, self interest and plunder in Massachusetts' confiscation policy."[6] Despite concepts of due process envisioned in the legislation, its implementation tells a rather sordid story. The lesson for historians is that public policy may be enunciated by the legislature but, as revealed by court records, can still be undermined by the judicial process.

The Records Series

Court records consist of three distinct record series: minute books, extended record books, and file papers. All students of colonial law

38. Colonial Court records of the Inferior Court of Common Pleas, Suffolk. Illustrated are a minute book, a record book, and file papers. In other counties, colonial file papers are still in their original case rolls.
Courtesy, Social Law Library, Boston.

should be aware of these record types, their relation to one another, and the kind of information which can be gleaned from them. The following generalized description is drawn from the Suffolk Common Pleas court records, since no chronological or colony-wide com-

[6] David E. Maas, "Honest Graft in Revolutionary Massachusetts," *Boston Bar Journal*, XXIII (1979), 7.

parisons of clerks' practices have been undertaken. In fact, as noted by the editors of the *Legal Papers of John Adams*, there is still "embarrassingly little knowledge of the way in which the Massachusetts courts regulated their business and conducted their trials."[7]

Clerks regulated their court business primarily through the use of minute books, and they constitute the only index to the file papers. Somewhat like the docket books of today, minute books recorded basic information about the court's work load. Although a single minute book may sometimes cover a period of more than a year, they are organized by four terms most frequently held in January, April, July, and October. The first page for each term would indicate the day and month beginning the term, identify the sitting judges, and usually enumerate the first and second petit juries then serving.

Civil cases are listed by ascending number in a typical plaintiff *versus* defendant fashion. Some clerks in some years meshed the continued actions of previous terms in the same numerical sequence, while other clerks in other years maintained separate continued action lists. It should be noted that the minute book number corresponds to the case number for that term and would be written on the back side of the writ. In the event of a continuance, the case papers were held and grouped with the cases for the next term; the old number was scratched out and a new minute book number assigned. Thus some cases with multiple continuances will have numerous scratched-out minute book numbers, by which one may trace the case back to earlier terms.

In the right margin of the common pleas minute books, the plaintiffs' attorneys are listed. The early books generally do not mention any pleas, while some of the nineteenth-century books do. Minute books do mention, however, the determination of cases in a shorthand, skeletal fashion. Also it was not uncommon for referees to be appointed, and clerks would indicate this in similar cryptic fashion. The left margin seems to have been kept clear for post-trial filings, most often executions and appeal bonds.

On the last page of the term the clerk customarily indicated the date court adjourned, as well as special court business. It was not

---

[7] *Legal Papers of John Adams*, ed. Wroth and Zobel, I, x, viii. The editors also note that a "thorough treatment of the court system must ... await ... documentary exhumation. ..." Ibid., xxxviii.

unusual for the clerk to note the swearing in of attorneys, or to take minutes of special motions, or to post new rules promulgated by the court. The last pages of the 1738 July term of the Suffolk Inferior Court of Common Pleas indicate that the justices entertained a number of oral motions for fees and costs. For example, "The Memorial of Robert Auchmuty and others, . . . relating to the allowance of their fees having been considered by the Court was not granted they being divided in their opinion concerning the same." Perhaps impatient with such motions, the court ordered "that henceforth all motions for costs shall be made in writing & the like fee be paid to the court as for other complaints." As their last act in 1738, the justices levied new fees, which were to be split between the court and the clerk, on "proving a deed in Court."

In addition, minute books provide much statistical and procedural information about the business of the court. They record the length of terms, the number of cases handled, the frequency of referring cases to referees, the number of continuances, court rules ordered by the justices, the frequency of appeals, and the levels of practice of particular lawyers.

Although skeletal in nature, these minute books tell *who* was in court and how often. In fact, biographers are beginning to believe that court records are of "extraordinary value."[8] A brief look at the lawyers and litigants on the final page of the 1758 minute book for the Suffolk Inferior Court of Common Pleas offers a remarkable example. In a few brief entries we find Jeremiah Gridley, tutor to such as John Adams, James Otis, and William Cushing, was involved as a plaintiff representing himself. Two signers of the Declaration of Independence, Robert Treat Paine and John Adams, are present in court as well. Paine was participating as a plaintiff in a minor civil case; Adams and Samuel Quincy were beginning distinguished careers at the bar as they were "admitted as Attorneys in Law in this Court to Act as Such and accordingly tooke the Oaths of an Attor-

[8] Kenneth Silverman, "Cotton Mather and the Howell Estate," *Boston Bar Journal*, XXVI (1982), 5. See also Robert J. Brink, "The Use of Court Records in Biographical Research: A Descriptive and Prescriptive Look at the Suffolk Files," *Biography*, I (1978), 79. For an example of the use of court records in tracing the legal career of lawyers see Hugh F. Bell, "James Otis's First Big Case: *Fletcher* v. *Vassall*," *Boston Bar Journal*, XXV (1981), 7.

Gridley 216 Jere. Gridley vs Oliver Pratt Default
Ex. Nov.13.1758. Jud. £.6. 0. 0. Costs Grid. 7 ₰.

217. James Reid Ex. vs Will. Calder. Cont. from last court —— Grid
Cont. no depat

Dana. 218. James Pitts vs Abraham Norwell Default
Ex. Nov.13.1758.— Jud. £. 107. 5. 1 ¾ 0 Cost Dana
At march 9: 1759.
at. April 24. 1759.
Swift 219 John Champney vs Eleazer Williams Jug. vac.
a Scire facias ordered

Swift 220 Sam. Swift vs John Deckor Jug. vac.
a Scire facias ordered

Price 221 Rob. Treat Paine vs Rebecca Pope Jug. vac.
Scire facias ordered

Mess. Samuel Quincey & John Adams are admitted
as Attorney in Law in this court to act as such and accordingly
took the Oaths of an Attorney

Borough taken Nov. 11: 1758.
before Fost. Hutchinson Esq.

Nov. 10: 1758. The Court Enter'd up Judgments on the
Defaults & Verdicts, tax'd Bills of Cost, and then

Adjourn'd without Day

Att. Ezek. Goldthwait Cler.

39. Docket Book, Inferior Court of Common Pleas, Suffolk, 1758
October, showing the admission of John Adams and Samuel Quincy
as attorneys on 6 November 1758. Note the signature of Ezekiel
Goldthwait, Clerk, and the names of Jeremiah Gridley, Foster
Hutchinson, and Robert Treat Paine. Courtesy,
Social Law Library, Boston.

ney." The session is presided over by Foster Hutchinson, brother of the royal governor driven into exile by the Revolution that Paine and Adams helped to start.

Clerks also maintained extended record books. These are large folio volumes, sometimes called judgment books, and constitute the formal, official record of the courts' actions on adjudicated cases. They are arranged in yearly volumes with plaintiff name indices and page reference numbers at the beginning of each book. They are not cross-referenced to the minute books or the file papers, since the order of entries is according to the courts' final actions. They also do not reflect the flow of court business, as they record only adjudicated cases. They do, however, provide an important summary of each case and mention the parties' names, places of residence, and occupations or professions. This is important demographic data, which is clearly set forth and easily coded for computer analysis. These records also summarize the legal written pleas and oral pleadings of the facts of the cases. They provide the courts' final determination of cases and also indicate when executions were issued and whether appeal bonds were filed. This information overlaps that of the minute books to some extent, especially with respect to the end-of-term orders of the court.

The Suffolk County Court of General Sessions displayed a respect for its records in its decision to replace the courthouse of 1764–1766 with a new building designed by Charles Bulfinch in 1810. In reaching its determination to build a new courthouse, the general sessions justices heard the following report, noted in the 1807 extended record book. "The Committee beg leave further to report that from the increase of population in the Capital and the accumulation of business in the Courts, it is no longer possible for the various courts to do their business in one small Court House (besides further provision ought to be made for public offices and for securing public papers.)"[9] As a historian of this Bulfinch building cleverly noted, "the corset could no longer hold the body."[1]

---

[9] Quoted in Charles A. Hammond, "Bulfinch and the Suffolk County Court House of 1810," *Boston Bar Journal*, XXII (1978), 12, note 7.

[1] Ibid., 11. Dr. Hammond's article and its appendices suggest the considerable significance of court records to architectural historians. Not only do the records show reports of the various committees, which provide insights into the workings of town

The extended record books are the easiest records series to use since they are sturdy and well bound and generally complete. Many minute books are extant, but these quarto waste books are much more fragile. File papers, to be discussed below, are the most difficult to use but also the most promising. Except for the Suffolk and Essex Files, most extant file papers have been left exactly as they were soon after adjudication. It was the practice of clerks to fold file papers in tripartite, bundle and label them by term and year, and tie them with linen string into case rolls. Subsequent clerks stuffed these upright into the same cramped topless file tins in which they survive today. "As we take the court documents from their original packages," Hiller B. Zobel has observed, "we literally unfold our history."[2]

The Documents

The documents have great intrinsic historical value. Catherine Menand, Chief Archivist of the Massachusetts Supreme Judicial Court, notes that "the sheer aesthetics of these early documents are important independent of their content and they provide a source of cultural and technological history."[3] For example, documents were demanded at every stage in the legal process, but paper was often in short supply. By examining watermarks—the papermakers' unique signatures or trademarks—one can trace the importation of paper as

and county governments, but the records detail exactly what materials were used, their suppliers as well as their costs.

Courts today have not lost their appetite for litigation or legal papers; and our courthouses, too, have been stretched, like corsets, to their limit. As a result, "[c]ourt records have been in a condition of crisis for a long time. The records of the Massachusetts Superior Court, the major trial court of the state, are housed in fourteen county courthouses, most of them built in the nineteenth century. . . . These records date from the earliest settlement of the Massachusetts Bay Colony in the 1620's. . . . There [is] no disagreement about the conditions of storage; in nearly every county they [are] inadequate, and in some counties deplorable." Michael S. Hindus et al., *The Files of The Massachusetts Superior Court, 1859–1959*, 3. As described at the beginning of this article, much is now being done to remedy the records problems. This digression into the deplorable condition of court records is to put scholars on notice that there are problems in using them.

[2] Hiller B. Zobel, "The Pompeii of Paper," *Boston Bar Journal*, XXII (1978), 21.

[3] Catherine Menand, "Archival Processing of Court Records," *Law Library Journal*, LXXIII (1980), 1006. Ms. Menand notes that one "can learn almost as much from the character of the documents as from the contents: evidence of literacy, of physical vigor, and something from the quality of the paper and the arrangement of the text. Only the originals can do this."

40. Watermark, Inferior Court of Common Pleas, Suffolk, 1790 OCT c. 288.
Courtesy, Social Law Library, Boston.

41. Watermark, Inferior Court of Common Pleas, Suffolk, 1797 OCT 88.
Courtesy, Social Law Library, Boston.

well as the establishment of local mills. Paper from England dominates the Suffolk County Inferior Court collection, but there is also paper from France and Denmark. A look at English and American watermarks shows the differences and disparities between old England and New England. Generally speaking, English watermarks are majestic crests, sometimes shield-shaped, with ornamental ridging and armorial bearing. Early American papermakers relied on simpler symbols, almost primitive when compared to their English counterparts. They pictured plows and Indians, doves, with and without olive branches, and eagles.[4] One telling watermark simply states "Save Rags"—a plea about the near-constant shortage of the raw material necessary for the manufacturing of rag paper.[5]

Watermarks are clearly visible only when paper is held to light. Thus they can sometimes hide, or heighten, historical ironies. For example, on 1 May 1776, two full months before the signing of the Declaration of Independence in Philadelphia, the Massachusetts General Court ordered that all legal papers, processes, and proceedings no longer mention the monarch's lengthy title: "George the Third, by the Grace of God of *Great Britain, France* and *Ireland,* KING, Defender of the Faith, etc." (See illustration below, 544.) Soon thereafter, in Suffolk County, either the clerks of court or lawyers unceremoniously scratched out, by hand, the foregoing title from writs and other formal papers and wrote in its place: "The Government and People of the Massachusetts Bay in New England."[6] Massachusetts may have declared its independence from the mother country, but as the manuscripts are held to light, and English watermarks are overwhelmingly revealed, it shows that the colony's legal process still very much depended on English paper.

The records have other interesting physical features. Embossed filing stamps were not uncommon on bonds, indentures, and other documents. Designs on provincial filing stamps, for example, were derived from important economic resources and appear to have re-

[4] Records of the Suffolk Inferior Court of Common Pleas (in the custody of the Social Law Library, Boston), Case of 1791 April c (Continued Action). 111; ibid., Case of 1792 January, 187; Case of 1790 October c. 288.

[5] Ibid., Case of 1797 October 88.

[6] See Robert J. Brink, "Massachusetts Declares Independence," *Boston Bar Journal,* XXII (1978), 32.

42. Embossed four-penny filing stamp, Inferior Court of Common Pleas, Suffolk, 1771 OCT c. 49. Courtesy, Social Law Library, Boston.

43. Embossed tuppence filing stamp, Inferior Court of Common Pleas, Suffolk, 1761 JAN 128. Courtesy, Social Law Library, Boston.

44. Heraldic embossed seal of Richard Jenneys "Notary & Tabellion Publick by Royal Authority...in Boston," Inferior Court of Common Pleas, Suffolk, 1760 OCT 134. Courtesy, Social Law Library, Boston.

45. Embossed three-penny filing stamp, Inferior Court of Common Pleas, Suffolk, 1755 OCT 173. Courtesy, Social Law Library, Boston.

mained constant for long periods: a cheerful codfish with the motto "STAMP OF THE MASSACHUSETTS" on the tuppence stamp; a flourishing pine tree on the three-penny stamp with the motto "PROVINCE OF MASSACHUSETTS"; and a trim two-masted schooner with the motto "STEADY—STEADY" on the four-penny stamp.[7]

An amazing variety of intricate, rich, red-wax seals has survived on the surfaces of these documents. They provide visible and tangible evidence of a person's stature and authority. Public officials frequently assumed a heraldic coat of arms as their seal, as did merchants and other wealthy and worldly persons. The papers bearing these seals provide excellent evidence documenting British mercantile connections within the empire. Decorative monograms, rebuses, unmarked tabs of paper, ink marks—even finger prints—were used by less eminent persons not entitled to coats of arms.

The variety of such seals makes a most interesting study, and as with watermarks, understanding sometimes unveils otherwise hidden ironies. The embossed, heraldic seal of Richard Jenneys "Notary & Tabellion Publick by Royal Authority duly Admitted & sworn dwelling and Practicing in Boston" shows as his crest a hand clasping olive branches surmounted by an eagle erect.[8] Hugh Clark's *Short and Easy Introduction to Heraldry* (London, 1788) defines these "technical terms" thus: "Hands signify power, equity, fidelity and justice"; the "olive tree is the emblem of peace and concord"; and the "Eagle is accounted the King of birds, and signifies magnaminity and fortitude of mind, who seeks to combat with none but his equals." Another seal, the crest of a swan, according to Clark's *Introduction to Heraldry* representing "Appollo's bird, the emblem of sincerity," ironically appears on Malachy Satter's unpaid promissory note of 1778.[9]

Artistic engravings also adorn many of the merchant accounts entered as evidence in actions to recover unpaid bills. Patriot and silver-

[7] Records of the Suffolk Inferior Court, Case of 1761 January 128; Case of 1755 October 173; Case of 1771 October c. 49.

[8] Ibid., Case of 1760 October, 134.

[9] Ibid., Case of 1778 July c. 39; Hugh Clark's *Short and Easy Introduction to Heraldry* (London, 1788) has an alphabetical listing of "technical terms" beginning on page 89.

smith Paul Revere was an engraver too. "He was especially fond of elaborate Chippendale borders and mantling and evidently copied the designs of English cards. [How unpatriotic!] ... But few of Revere's cards have survived to the present day. Of a dozen or more which he is known to have engraved, only five are to be found, four of them unique examples."[1] Another of these rare Revere engravings, a billhead, has turned up in the Suffolk common pleas papers. It is a profile engraving of "O. Cromwell's Head," the symbol of Joshua Brackett's well-known inn located on School Street.[2]

Other engravers, perhaps less renowned than Revere—even obscure to the point of anonymity—often applied their artistic skills to merchant billheads preserved in early court papers. Some engravings visually explain work processes and expound patriotic sentiments in the years immediately following the Revolution. The billhead of Eben Clough's "Boston Paper Staining Manufactory" illustrates the basic steps in wallpaper making during the eighteenth century while, at the same time, proclaiming "Americans, Encourage the Manufactories of your Country, if you wish for its prosperity."[3] The picture depicts the actual production processes of early wallpaper making. Catherine Lynn Frangiamore's *Wallpaper in Historic Preservation* explains:

[T]he gentleman wielding a large brush in either hand is laying on the ground color. Immediately to the left of the tablet describing the business, a printer with his left hand under the handle on a carved woodblocks raises a mallet with his right hand to strike a firm impression. The boy standing to his left prepares the color between each impression, spreading it on a pad. The man of the far left, with the assistance of yet another boy, is probably rolling and trimming paper in standardized lengths for sale.[4]

Of course the colonial and early republican court papers are primarily valuable for their contents, not their aesthetic character. An exhaustive survey of each and every document type, litigant, and legal plea is beyond the scope of this paper. But a sample from a

[1] Clarence S. Brigham, *Paul Revere's Engravings* (Worcester: American Antiquarian Society, 1954), 116.

[2] Records of the Suffolk Inferior Court, Case of 1772 misc., *Brackett v. Joy.*

[3] Ibid., Case of 1801 April c. 380.

[4] Catherine Lynn Frangiamore, *Wallpapers in Historic Preservation* (Washington, D.C.: Office of Archeology and Historic Preservation, National Park Service, 1977), 8.

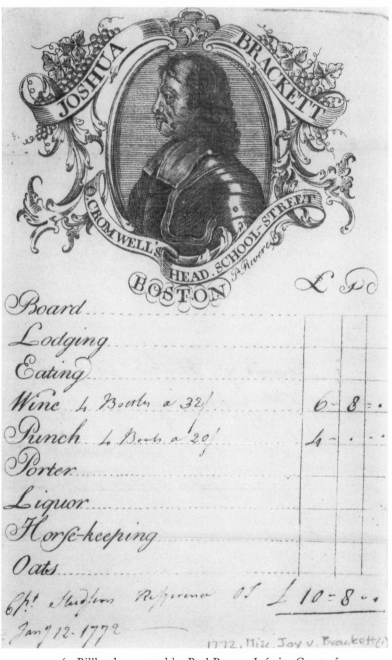

	£	s	d
Board			
Lodging			
Eating			
Wine 4 Bottles a 32/	6	8	
Punch 4 Bots a 20/	4		
Porter			
Liquor			
Horse-keeping			
Oats			
Cpt Hudsons Reffrence os £	10	8	

Jan.y 12- 1772

1772. Misc. Joy v. Brackett(1)

46. Billhead, engraved by Paul Revere, Inferior Court of
Common Pleas, Suffolk, 1772 JUL Misc. *Joy v. Brackett*.
Courtesy, Social Law Library, Boston.

Americans, Encourage the Manufactories of your Country, if you wish for its prosperity.

47. Engraved billhead illustrating the basic steps in making wallpaper. It encourages customers to buy American goods. See above, 490. Inferior Court of Common Pleas, Suffolk, 1801 APR c. 380. Courtesy, Social Law Library, Boston.

single term should be enough to encourage further examination, especially with the other articles on sources as research aids. Take, for example, the 1765 July term of the Suffolk County Court of Common Pleas. Most of the actions are of first instance in the inferior court, although there is at least one judgment on appeal from a justice of the peace and several litigants suing on executions from earlier, yet unsatisfied, judgments.

Every court term saw luminaries involved in litigation. For instance, Samuel Adams was involved in several suits during the July term of 1765. In at least three separate actions he was acting in his official capacity as "a Collector of Taxes" for the years 1759 through 1763. Defendants in these actions were "Jack a free Negro," and housewrights William Moor and Samuel Avery.[5] Each was in arrears for several years on their ratable "proportion of Province County and Town taxes," which Adams' declarations detailed in exact amounts. Adams' attorney in each action was James Otis, Jr., that famous "flame of fire" who argued in the great Writs of Assistance Case of 1760. There is no evidence from the file papers that defendants Moor or Avery were represented by counsel, but "Jack"

[5] Records of the Suffolk Inferior Court, Case of 1765 July 375; Case of 1765 July c. 123; Case of 1765 July 374.

was represented by Samuel Fitch. Otis found authority for the actions "by force of an Act of this our Province made in the forth Year of our Reign entitled an Act to enable . . . Collectors of Taxes in the Town of Boston to sue for and recover the Rates & taxes given them to collect in certain Cases. . . ."

File papers generally do not, in themselves, record the results of these suits, although in some cases there are jury slips indicating judgments. Scholars must turn to the extant extended record books and minute books. The papers do, however, provide important information from a number of perspectives. There is both personal and professional biographical significance. Thus, these records reveal a long-term professional relationship, as between the two famous patriots, tax collector Adams and lawyer Otis. Further, Otis' reliance on legislation as authority on which to maintain the litigation may help to show the state of trial practice, as well as illustrate the general background, influence, and impact of this tax-related act. Adams' actions and Otis' arguments to enforce these taxes passed by the provincial legislature are in contrast to the revolutionary cry "no taxation without representation."

Government agents like Adams were not only plaintiffs, but sometimes defendants too. The "Proprietors of the East & West Wings so called the North half of the Township of Rutland in our County of Worcester" were sued in 1765 by Stephan Minot, administrator to the Estate of Jonas Clark, Esquire. It seems that Clark "by a Vote of the Proprietors was appointed and at their Special request became their Clerk . . . during [which] . . . time [he] faithfully served them in that Office and trust, duly attended their several meetings, kept their books & accounts & regularly entered all their Notes and orders and their Planns and Surveys and transacted their business abroad. . . ." Clark's administrator claimed that he was never paid for the foregoing services, some of which were detailed in an attached account. Such details provide valuable insights into the administration of colonial government.[6]

Litigants throughout these records came from all counties, colonies, and points of the compass. Especially interesting are the cases relating to the sea. Boston's waterfront swarmed with wharfingers,

[6] Ibid., Case of 1765 July 296.

coasters, and shoremen, as well as boatbuilders, shipwrights, ship carpenters, caulkers, mastmakers, blockmakers, ropemakers, riggers, sailmakers, oarmakers, and carvers. All appeared in the court records, as do the mariners, sailors, officers, and pilots manning these ships. Their cases touched upon complex issues, issues as diverse as impressment, articling of underage seamen, wages, and cargoes lost to privateers and storms. Such cases connected Boston to points of call in Africa, South America, the Pacific Northwest, the East Indies, and China.

The 1765 July term had several controversies related to seagoing and international commerce. Robert Robins, "Master of the Good Schooner called the Polley," sued "Daniel Arthur of the City of Lisbon in the Kingdom of Portugal Merchant" for breach of a written covenant.[7] The agreement was recounted in the declaration of Captain Robins' writ of attachment and was drawn by another famous lawyer, Josiah Quincy. It described a trade route, import and export goods, and the voyage's expected time and pay schedules. Robins claimed that the outward cargo of wine and fruit was delivered pursuant to the agreement to Boston via Halifax ("the wind not proving favorable"), but Daniel Arthur's agents broke the agreement by not having a required cargo of fish ready to return to Lisbon. For this Robins asked judgment of four hundred pounds.

"Landlubbers" in commerce appeared in court records too. "Historians would learn far more about economic life in Boston from an analysis of the civil court records of the Superior Court or the Suffolk County Court, than from almost any extant efforts at writing the economic history of this community."[8] Currency shortages were not

[7] Ibid., Case of 1765 July 197. The agreement provided that at the "River Tagus" in Lisbon "the said Brig (meaning said Schooner) being tight, stained and strong manned tackel'd and provided fit for Merchants service . . . should load, receive, and take on board . . . WINE & FRUIT or any other Goods, as they should tender to be laden not exceeding what the said Schooner could reasonably stow and carry over & above her Tackle, Apparel and furniture therewith as the Wind & Weather would permit should sail and proceed to Boston in New England, but if the Wind proved favorable to touch first at Halifax Nova Scotia . . . there deliver . . . said cargo . . . proceeding with the Residue to Boston . . . where said Master was to receive and take on board said Schooner a Cargo of fish to proceed from thence to Lisbon allowing Forty working days for landing her outward Cargo at the aforesaid Ports taking her return Cargo of fish at Boston & unloading it there viz at Lisbon. . . ."

[8] Flaherty, "Court Records in Historical Research," 344. John Noble described the numerous variety of legal and non-legal papers typically found in colonial court

uncommon. Although some colonists tried counterfeiting, most relied on each other for liberal credit or were content with poor commerce. Despite signed bonds and promissory notes with compound interest, debtors were often dilatory, and creditors demanded payment in their formal "pleas of debt" filed in the Inferior Court of Common Pleas. If no bonds or promissory notes had been extracted from debtors, creditors often had detailed accounts of sales or services which corroborated their "plea of the case" claims. Such accounts accompanied the more formal legal papers and revealed much detail about colonial life.

In addition to the accounts and inventories which preserved the external details of colonial life, other documents immortalized the personal sentiments, the spirit, and even the speech of litigants centuries dead. Depositions, now called affadavits, told harrowing tales of human travails. For example, the rambling deposition of John Martin Randell recounted his voyage, as boatswain, "on board the ship Ulysses... David Lamb Commander... some time in the Month of August 1798 Bound from Boston to the North West Coast of America, from these to Canton and back to Boston...." It seemed that at the voyage's very beginning the commander tried to dispel his cantankerous reputation "the first Night after we made Sail, When We Was about oposite the Ligh[t] House in Boston Harborer the Capt. Called All Hands, Officers and Men aft... and informed them that he had been formerly called a Tyrant, but now he was going to alter his conduct and behave better... and everything seemed to past. Harmonious until we arrived at St. Iago." There the captain "left one half of the people go on shore at a time that they might buy some... stores...." But the captain began to show how little he cared for his crew when one sailor, Charles Reed, did not return. "We went on board the Ship, all Hands were ordered to Supper, directly after Supper [the first mate] asked if all Hands were on board.... he was told that Charles Reed was left on Shore, [the first

files: "They are made up not only of the original pleadings in the cases, but also of exhibits, evidence, copies of records and documents used in the trial of those cases, and of all sorts of collateral matter introduced therein. Besides these files of court there are great numbers of miscellaneous papers, records, wills, deeds, correspondence, and papers of every sort of legal and historical character...." Noble, *Early Court Files*, 317.

mate] then asked Capt. if he Should Send a boat on Shore for Charles Reed? No Sd the Capt. if My own Father was on Shore I would not send for him, ... then the Capt. ordered ... Charles Reed's Chest and Baggage aft into the cabin to him which was done, and his Chest was Opened directly and things were all overhauled, and some Money was found in the Chest which the Captain took. ..."

During the passage from St. Iago to the Falkland Islands, "Our allowance of Provisions was ... diminished daily, Until it became so Small, and our Duty so hard" that the crew began to complain. There were several savage episodes, including the beating of the carpenter "to Such a degree that he was all over Bloody, and brused very much, and almost out of his Sences ..." merely because "the Bread-room door was loose. ..." On another occasion, "While we were heaving at the Windlis the Hands were so exhausted for want of Sleep and refreshing, and some with sore throats that they could not Sing out While heaving and the Capt. said Why don't you Sing ... and then he called for his pistols ... and walked forward within about Seven or Eight passes of where we were ... and Stopt and cocked his pistols and he Leveled them at our Heads, and said if you don't heave up ... I will blow your brains out. ..." Relations between Captain and crew deteriorated as the *Ulysses* "passed from the Falkland Islands round Cape Horn." Randell's deposition describes episodes on the voyage for eight pages. Finally, at one point, "the Capt. kept up his tirannical behavior to such a degree and being intoxicated by Liquor at the same time, that the whole crew were afraid for their lives, and two days before we came to anchor they were obliged to confine him, to save their own lives. ..."[9] Thus, the captain was imprisoned by his crew!

There are many depositions among court documents which, like that of boatswain Randell, narrate misbegotten thoughts, words, and deeds. In litigation, as in life, we all must wonder what unknown witnesses are listening or looking on. One unknown court clerk must have been harboring such paranoid thoughts when he wrote, in large and florid pen strokes, the following inscription on the title page of the minute book for October 1748: "*Immortality brought to Light.*" Court records do bring the "dark ages" of colonial law to light, and

[9] Records of the Suffolk Inferior Court, Case of 1801 January 98.

will immortalize men and women long since dead. But our clerk was concerned with judgment day in another court, the court of very last resort: *"Guard well your Tho'ts,"* he added, *"Our tho'ts are heard in h———."*

Conclusion

James Willard Hurst has declared that "[t]he greatest difficulties for legal history lie in relating the formal operations of law—passing statutes, deciding cases, making administrative orders or rules—to the life that flowed outside the legal forms." He called for a "hyphenate legal history: legal-economic history, legal-religious history, legal-class-and-caste history."[1] In other words, legal history should no longer divorce doctrine from day-to-day living. In this context court records help reconcile law with the rest of life. They reflect not only the final solutions of judges and juries, but also the initial human problems of people suing over matters of personal concern. Much can be learned from cases involving common yeomen, carvers, coopers, confectioners, cordwainers, butchers, bakers, housewrights, husbandmen, tailors, weavers, hatters, periwigmakers, doctors, distillers, dancing masters, mathematical instrument makers, and myriad others who make up the mosaic of colonial life. Almost as if anticipating Hurst's "hyphenate legal history," John Noble noted 1897 that court records "are something of a study in government, economics, sociology, education, religion, politics, public and private life."[2]

[1] James Willard Hurst, "Legal Elements in United States History," *Law in American History*, ed. Donald Fleming and Bernard Bailyn (Boston: Little Brown and Company, 1971), 14–15.

[2] Noble, "Early Court Files," 325.

WILLIAM E. NELSON

Court Records as Sources for Historical Writing

COURT records are obviously the most useful kind of source material available to historians of the law. They are also, perhaps, the most promising untapped body of sources for historians of American social, economic, and institutional history. As Zechariah Chafee wrote, court records:

have great value for historians, especially those who are seeking to learn how the colonists lived, acquired and managed property, and engaged in quarrels. An old author or newspaper often tells us disappointingly little about some of the most important features of human conduct at the time. The writer knew that such matters would be taken for granted by those for whom he was writing. In an old lawsuit, however, much less was taken for granted. The facts of everyday life had to be presented in the complaint or the testimony of witnesses, so as to let the judges know the nature of the dispute.[1]

Moreover, a surprising quantity of material is often readily available to historians without travel or other great expense. Much valuable data, for example, is often available at a law library associated with a historian's university or at other nearby law libraries. Much manuscript material has been microfilmed by the Genealogical Society of Utah and can be obtained at the Society's more than 150 branch libraries.[2]

This brief essay is designed to provide historians with a basic guide to the use of court records. First, it will take note of the kinds of data contained in court records that non-legal historians might find interesting. Second, the essay will provide an introductory sketch of the rules of pleading that a historian must understand in order to make

[1] Zechariah Chafee, Jr., "Preface," in William Jeffrey, Jr., *Early New England Court Records: A Bibliography of Published Materials* (Cambridge, Mass., 1954), 3–4. See also Zechariah Chafee, Jr., "Introduction," Colonial Society of Massachusetts, *Publications*, XXIX (1933), xvii–xciv.

[2] See Larry R. Gerlach and Michael L. Nicholls, "The Mormon Genealogical Society and Research Opportunities in Early American History," *William and Mary Quarterly* (3d ser.), XXXII (1975), 625.

use of court records. Finally, the essay will take note of certain major bibliographies that exist for New England court records.

Data Contained in Court Records

The Civil War in seventeenth-century England established a principle to which Anglo-American jurisdictions still adhere, that government may not coerce individuals either through bodily imprisonment or property seizures unless the government action is subject to review in an ordinary court of common law. The only exception to this principle occurs when martial law is imposed through suspension of the writ of habeas corpus.

From the seventeenth until the nineteenth century, when England and America lacked the large-scale bureaucracies they possess today, this principle meant that government generally acted against a person by commencing either a civil or a criminal proceeding in a court of law.[3] Court records are accordingly the best source for studying the activities of government over that two-century period. Even today, when government bureaucrats often act on their own initiative without seeking the aid of a court, the fact that their actions are subject to judicial review makes court records a good source for learning the rules to which the executive branch of government is supposed to adhere.

Obviously the historian of some institution of government, such as seventeenth-century municipality or an office such as that of sheriff, will find court records an invaluable collection of sources. There are also other ways in which institutional historians can find court records helpful. On occasion, for instance, court records will illustrate the impact of political acts, such as the Declaration of Independence, made by the highest levels of government. Thus court records tell us that "at the moment of their association, the United States necessarily became a body corporate" having "no superior from whom that character . . . [was] derived"[4] and that the commissions of certain

---

[3] See William E. Nelson, *Americanization of the Common Law: The Impact of Legal Change on Massachusetts Society, 1760–1830* (Cambridge, Mass., 1975), 14–18; William E. Nelson, "The Eighteenth-Century Background of John Marshall's Constitutional Jurisprudence," *Michigan Law Review*, LXXVI (1978), 893, 902–904.

[4] *Respublica* v. *Sweers*, 1 Dallas 41, 44 (Pennsylvania Supreme Court, 1779).

local judges which, in October 1776, had not yet been "alter'd agreeable to the Act of Independency establish'd by the Congress," were void.[5]

A deeper understanding of the functioning of the courts, derived from study of court records, can give historians new perspectives on significant historical events. New England court records make it plain, for example, that juries in the eighteenth century had power to determine law as well as fact in the cases that came before them.[6] Knowledge of this power of juries, together with knowledge of eighteenth-century rules of jurisdiction, pleading, and procedure, gives a new perspective on the pre-Revolutionary struggle between American Whigs and the British imperial government in New England. It enables historians to see that the imperial government had legal limits on its power and that its enforcement failures may have stemmed more from those limits than from any incompetence on the part of imperial officials.[7]

Court records can be equally valuable for economic historians. Records contain considerable data about the kinds of money in circulation, the value of that money, and the value that litigants and, at times, a court or a jury place upon various commodities. Court records also reveal how law has been used to promote economic growth. Massachusetts records, for example, provide detailed information about the construction of the roads, canals, railroads, and mills that constituted the foundation on which the Commonwealth's nineteenth-century economy was erected. Some court records may even provide information about the quality and quantity of economic growth occurring during some period in the past, as the work of J. Willard Hurst on the Wisconsin lumber industry suggests.[8]

Finally, the value of court records to social historians must not be

[5] Final Record of Court of General Sessions, Plymouth County, Mass., October 1776 (ms. in Pilgrim Hall, Plymouth, Mass.).

[6] See Nelson, *Americanization of the Common Law*, 21–30; Nelson, "Eighteenth-Century Background," 904–917.

[7] For an example of how legal knowledge can generate new historical insight, see John P. Reid, *In a Defiant Stance: The Conditions of Law in Massachusetts Bay, the Irish Comparison, and the Coming of the American Revolution* (University Park, Pa., 1977).

[8] J. Willard Hurst, *Law and Economic Growth: The Legal History of the Lumber Industry in Wisconsin, 1836–1915* (Cambridge, Mass., 1964).

overlooked. At least in New England, manuscript records normally contain information about the social rank or occupation of the litigants—information which makes it possible, for instance, to examine changing patterns of deference in seventeenth- and eighteenth-century society.[9] If a researcher has information from outside court records about the religious affiliation of individuals, the records also can be used to examine the relationship between Congregationalists and dissenters—to learn, for example, whether dissenters served as court officials or jurors and whether dissenters found themselves involved in litigation with Congregationalists.[1]

Common Law Rules of Pleading and Procedure

Institutional, economic, and social historians can put old court records to significant use. But in order to do so they must know enough law to interpret the records properly. In particular, they must know common law rules of jurisdiction, pleading, and procedure which, until the second half of the nineteenth century, constituted the skeleton around which court records were constructed.

The basic pattern in the American colonies was for three types of court to exist in any one geographical entity. One was the equivalent of the Court of General Sessions of the Peace in England, which had jurisdiction within a single county to engage in a wide variety of administrative activities and to hear all but the most serious criminal matters. A second court in a given locality typically would possess the jurisdiction of the Court of King's Bench in England to hear disputes between individuals and the most serious criminal cases. Sometimes, as in Massachusetts, the jurisdiction of King's Bench would be divided among two courts, with jurisdiction over serious crimes and appellate jurisdiction over civil disputes being reserved for the higher court and original typical jurisdiction over civil disputes reserved for the lower court. The third court in most localities was the one-man court of the justice of the peace, which heard petty civil and criminal cases. In addition, chancery courts existed in some colonies, together

[9] For an illustration of one effort to do so, see William E. Nelson, *Dispute and Conflict Resolution in Plymouth County, Massachusetts, 1725–1825* (Chapel Hill, 1981), 80–86.

[1] See generally Nelson, *Dispute and Conflict Resolution.*

48. Wax Seal from His Majesty's Superior Court of Judicature for the Province of New Brunswick, found on documents delivered to the Massachusetts Courts in October 1758. Suffolk Files, Cabinet Collection No. 143101. Restored, Kathryn M. Carey. Courtesy, Supreme Judicial Court.

with admiralty courts prior to the Revolution, and various federal courts thereafter.[2]

This essay will focus on pleading and procedure in the Court of General Sessions and in courts having original jurisdiction over civil disputes. Most of what is said will be applicable, however, to proceedings before justices of the peace, who tended to mimic procedures of the higher courts, and to proceedings in nineteenth-century federal courts, which were required to follow the essentials of state procedure. Only admiralty and chancery courts followed procedures substantially different from those about to be described.

Most of the administrative business of General Sessions is recorded in a straightforward manner that a historian with no legal training can readily understand. Whatever difficulties occur in understanding court records that deal with matters such as poor relief, road construction, local finance, licensing, and location of mills is just as likely to stem from not comprehending the technology or social reality of the past, as from not understanding its law. The technology involved in the construction and operation of mills can, in particular, be quite difficult to penetrate. Perhaps the only necessary warning to the historian who is about to use administrative records of a Sessions Court is to beware of assuming that all the orders issued by the Court were, in fact, carried out. Many court orders were simply never obeyed.

Criminal business also tends to have been recorded in a readily comprehensible manner. Many of the common crimes of the seventeenth, eighteenth, and nineteenth centuries remain common and familiar today: homicide, rape, assault, theft, drunkenness, contempt of authority, and violation of license laws. Nor should a historian have any difficulty comprehending the meaning of adultery, sodomy, fornication, drunkenness, profanity, and breach of the sabbath, even though such activities rarely result in criminal prosecution today. Only a few technical concepts need to be mastered before using criminal records. One is the distinction between murder and manslaughter: the former is an intentional homicide committed with premeditation and deliberation, whereas the latter is an intentional homicide

---

[2] For a survey of early American court jurisdictions, see Lawrence M. Friedman, *A History of American Law* (New York, 1973), 32–49, 122–126.

committed on the spur of the moment.[3] A second important concept is that of robbery, which is a taking of an item of value through the use of force. A third concept is burglary, which is the breaking and entering of a dwelling house in the nighttime with intent to commit any crime, whether it be theft or rape, therein. Burglary is to be distinguished from the lesser crime of breaking and entering, which may be deemed to occur if a structure is entered in the daytime, is not a dwelling house, or is entered without any specific criminal intent.

The prospective user of criminal records requires warning that some of the language contained in pleadings will be fictitious in nature and ought not be taken literally. Consider, for example, a prosecution brought in colonial Massachusetts against one Anna Donham, accused of "being a person of ill fame, Character and conversation and having a wicked and diabolical intent to corrupt and debauch the morals of divers of his majesties subjects and to excite them to commit lewdness, Fornication and adultery with her." She was accused more specifically of permitting an unknown man "to lay her down on her back on the floor of" a barn they had entered together and then "to lay himself upon her Body and to continue in that posture for the space of a quarter of an hour." She was charged with similar behavior on other occasions, but she was not accused of having sexual intercourse with any man. The allegations against Anna Donham should not, however, be taken too literally. At the time of the events in question, her husband was "drawing near death."[4] If she had had sexual intercourse with the unknown man, she would have been guilty of adultery — then and there a capital offense. Juries, however, generally refused to allow people to be executed for adultery; instead of returning a verdict of guilty of adultery, they would usually find a couple guilty only of lying together without having intercourse. In the Donham case the prosecutor simply obtained an indictment for an offense for which he might get a conviction. There is every reason, however, to believe that, despite the language of the indictment, she was guilty of adultery if she was guilty of anything.

There is also little reason to believe the other allegations about

---

[3] See George P. Fletcher, *Rethinking Criminal Law* (Boston, 1978), 253–256.

[4] *King* v. *Donham*, Plymouth General Sessions, October 1763, in David T. Konig, ed., *Plymouth Court Records, 1686–1859* (Wilmington, Del., 1978), III, 59.

Anna Donham's intent and about her engaging in similar activities on other occasions. Such allegations were mere surplusage that the prosecution need not prove in order to obtain a conviction: the crime of lewdness is established merely by showing that a married person lay in an embrace in a secret place with a person of the opposite sex not his or her spouse. Indeed, it is quite common for criminal indictments to contain surplus, often ritualistic language, especially in assault cases, where exaggerated allegations of physical violence are not uncommon.

The departures from social reality that have been noted are, however, insignificant ones that should not make it difficult for historians without legal training to use criminal and administrative court records. In civil litigation, on the other hand, the allegations appearing in the court records depart further from actual facts. The reason is that, until the procedural reforms of the mid-nineteenth century, civil litigants had to fit their cases within one of the common law forms of action. Each form of action was a precise pigeonhole broad enough to encompass only one type of case that a plaintiff might decide to bring. Under the common law writ system, a plaintiff had little flexibility in choosing the form of action he would bring. He had to bring the form appropriate to his claim, and he had to squeeze the facts of his case into the appropriate pigeonhole by casting those facts in the terminology proper for his chosen writ.

By the end of the seventeenth century *ejectment* had become the most common writ used to litigate title to land. In ejectment a plaintiff was required to allege that he had the legal right to possession of the land and that John Doe, a person who had leased the land from him, had been ousted from possession by Richard Roe, who had acted on behalf of the defendant who, in turn, was now in possession of the land. The allegations of a lease to John Doe and ouster by Richard Roe are benchmarks of the writ of ejectment. Nonetheless, the historian should not take Doe and Roe seriously, for both were fictitious persons; the real essence of the writ of ejectment was merely that the plaintiff was the rightful possessor of the land in question but that the defendant was occupying it adversely to him.[5]

---

[5] See Benjamin J. Shipman, *Handbook of Common-Law Pleading* (St. Paul, Minn., 3d ed. by Henry W. Ballantine, 1923), 183–185.

Another writ commonly used to litigate title to realty was the *writ of entry*. The basic allegation of the writ of entry was the existence of some recent, specified flaw in the defendant's title: for example, that the defendant had purchased from some individual who had forcibly ousted the plaintiff from the land. Entry came in many varieties. In Maitland's words:

there is one applicable to almost every conceivable case in which a tenant has come to the land by some title in which a recent flaw can be pointed out—we hear *e.g.* of a form of action as a writ of entry *"sur disseisin* in the *per,"* a writ of entry *"sur disseisin* in the *per* and *cui."* In 1267 the Statute of Marlborough . . . in effect abolished the restrictions on the formation of writs of entry—but it only did this by adding to their number. If since the unlawful entry the land had passed through several hands a writ of entry "in the post" might be used—the demandant might allege that the tenant only had entry *post* (after) a disseisin committed by someone without showing how the land had passed from the disseisor to the tenant.[6]

Other actions for recovery of land that might occasionally be found in court records were writs of novel disseisin, mort d'ancestor, and dower and even writs of right. Another fairly frequent proceeding was the common recovery, a procedure used to bar what was known as an *entail*. An entail was a device by which a landowner granted land to a particular family line and attempted to prevent that family line from conveying the land outside the line. The common recovery was the device used by the person in the family line holding the land to convey the land to another. The procedure was for the purchaser of the land to bring a collusive suit, usually in ejectment, against the seller who, in fact, did not have a good title to sell. The seller would allege, however, that he did have a good title and he would call upon a fictitious person, typically John Doe or Richard Roe, to warrant his title. After the fictitious person had made the warranty, the seller would then default and the court would find that the purchaser had a full and complete title to the land. The person who held the right to the land following failure of the entail was effectively deprived of his rights by the common recovery, since

---

[6] F. W. Maitland, *The Forms of Action at Common Law* (Cambridge, 1936), 42. See also *ibid.*, 44, 85–86.

he was permitted to sue only the fictitious person who had falsely warranted the defendant's title for damages resulting from the false warranty.[7] Until entails were abolished legislatively after the American Revolution, common recoveries were not unusual in most American jurisdictions.

One final writ that was also commonly used to litigate title to real estate was the *writ of trespass.* But before this use of trespass can be understood, it is first necessary to understand the three main functions of this writ.

The first purpose for which a plaintiff would normally use the writ was to recover damages for a bodily injury. Such writs were adorned with formulary allegations, such as that a defendant "with Force and armes an assault on the Body of the Plantf Did Make and . . . with a Certain Club Did Strike the Plant on the Head and Beate him Down to the Ground and Drew Much Blood so that Life was Despared of."[8] If a plaintiff won a suit founded on such a writ, a historian could be confident that the defendant had struck the plaintiff on the head with a club, but beyond that much is merely formulary allegation. The allegation of force and arms, for example, had to be made in order for a court to have jurisdiction over a writ of trespass, and hence the allegation will be found even in writs in which no armed force could conceivably have been used, such as in carriage collision cases or in cases involving the equivalent of modern medical malpractice. Another fictitious allegation made in every writ of trespass, including a portion of the above writ not quoted, was that the defendant acted "against the peace."[9] This also was required for the old royal court jurisdiction in trespass. Some of the other allegations, such as the one that the defendant drew much blood or that the plaintiff's life was despaired of, did not have to be pleaded in order for the court to have jurisdiction to hear the plaintiff's suit, and thus their presence in the writ cannot be accounted for on the theory that they

[7] For an illustration of the pleadings in a common recovery, see *Angier* v. *Harris,* Plymouth Common Pleas, January 1786, in Konig, *Plymouth Court Records,* xvii, 23. See generally A. W. B. Simpson, *An Introduction to the History of the Land Law* (Oxford, 1961), 121–129.

[8] *Wanno* v. *David,* Plymouth Common Pleas, December 1732, in Konig, *Plymouth Court Records,* iv, 537.

[9] See Maitland, *The Forms of Action,* 49–50.

had to be there. But neither can the historian be confident that the allegations were true, since a plaintiff did not have to prove them in order to recover a verdict in his favor. The allegations are probably best understood as having been placed in the writ by the plaintiff's lawyer when he was not yet fully cognizant of the facts of the case. Since the lawyer could offer in evidence only facts which had been previously pleaded, a lawyer who was drafting a pleading had to include whatever facts he might be able to prove at trial even if it subsequently happened that little of what he alleged had actually occurred.

A second form of trespass was the *quare clausum fregit* form — trespass for breaking and entering the plaintiff's close or parcel of land. In such a writ, a plaintiff in addition to formulary allegations claimed that he was in possession of land and that the defendant entered and interfered with his possession, as, for example, by cutting and taking away crops growing on the land. This second form of trespass could be used in effect to litigate title if the defendant instead of denying that he took the goods pleaded that he did take them because they were growing on his land. Then a jury would determine whether the land on which the crops were growing belonged to the plaintiff or the defendant — a determination that for most purposes would resolve the question of title.[1]

The third variety of trespass was the writ *de bonis asportatis* — for taking and carrying away the plaintiff's goods. Again this variant of the writ will contain ritualistic allegations that the defendant acted with force and arms and against the peace of the king or later of the state, even though the only force required was that involved in physically taking possession of the plaintiff's goods.[2] Again, the historian should be aware that a judgment in favor of the plaintiff does not necessarily establish the truth of every fact alleged in the recorded pleading. A plaintiff might, for example, have alleged the theft of 100 bushels of corn valued at $1.00 each and the jury might have returned a verdict for only $50.00, suggesting that only 50 bushels were taken or that each of the 100 bushels taken was worth only $ .50. Normally there is no way of knowing from pleadings alone

[1] See Nelson, *Americanization of the Common Law*, 74.

[2] See Shipman, *Common-Law Pleading*, 213.

what the precise facts of a case actually were, although a guess can be hazarded if a historian knows from other sources that a bushel of corn was worth, for instance, $ .50 at the time of the verdict.

Trespass was not the only writ available by which a plaintiff could recover damages from a defendant who was in wrongful possession of the plaintiff's goods. Another form of action available for that purpose was *trover*, which lay when a defendant had come into possession of goods lawfully but then retained them unlawfully. Trespass *de bonis asportatis*, it will be recalled, lay when a defendant came into possession of goods unlawfully. Hence trover did not contain a fictitious allegation that the defendant had acted with force and arms and against the peace. Instead, the plaintiff in trover always alleged fictitiously that he had "casually lost" his goods, that the defendant had subsequently "found" them, but that the defendant had refused to return them.[3]

If a plaintiff wanted to recover, not damages for the taking of his goods, but the goods themselves, he would bring either a *writ of replevin* or a *writ of detinue*. In both writs, a plaintiff had to allege and prove that he was entitled to possession of goods that were in the possession of the defendant at the time of the commencement of suit. In addition, in replevin he had to allege that the defendant had wrongfully taken the goods in question. In detinue, a plaintiff could recover the goods even if they had come into possession of the defendant lawfully and he had merely retained them unlawfully. Detinue, however, unlike replevin, would not lie to recover fungible goods like cattle or grain. It was available only to recover goods capable of being specifically identified.[4] If fungible goods were merely unlawfully retained by a defendant, a plaintiff's only remedy was a suit for damages by way of a writ of trover.

Various forms of the *writ of trespass on the case*, or simply *case*, lay to recover damages for torts or wrongful conduct by defendants. The special quality of the action on the writ of case was that it lay when no other writ was available to a plaintiff, but he nonetheless could allege facts for which he ought to have a remedy.[5] As a result,

case of trespass on the case

---

[3] See Maitland, *The Forms of Action*, 71, 92.

[4] See Shipman, *Common-Law Pleading*, 114–131.

[5] See Maitland, *The Forms of Action*, 66–68.

most varieties of the writ of case that were used to recover damages for torts contain little in the way of fictional pleading. In case, plaintiffs usually alleged only facts that the law required them to prove or that they hoped to prove. Hence a jury verdict in a plaintiff's favor in a writ of case usually indicates that the facts pleaded in the writ were true.

It is impossible to do more than mention the most common varieties of the writ of case for tort. One was case for defamation, where a plaintiff alleged injury to his reputation. Another was case for malicious prosecution. A third was case for negligence. A fourth was case for an indirect injury to a property right, such as the right to operate a mill. All of these forms of case, together with many others, usually contain straightforward allegations of fact which a historian with slight legal training should have little difficulty comprehending.

So far, attention has focused on actions for recovery of land and goods and actions for what modern lawyers label tort. In addition, a whole series of forms of action existed to recover for what modern lawyers would label breach of contract. These contract actions, which contain a great deal of technical and often fictitious pleading, accounted for the overwhelming bulk of litigation in most American jurisdictions. To use court records effectively, historians must come to grips with them.

Among the most ancient and least frequently used actions was the *writ of covenant*. Covenant lay when a defendant, in a written instrument to which he had attached his seal, promised to perform some act, other than giving some item of fixed value such as money, for the plaintiff and subsequently failed to perform. A plaintiff in covenant thus had to allege and prove the execution of a sealed instrument, the promise to perform some act of no fixed value such as building a house, and the breach of the promise.[6] Covenant was thus a straightforward form of action with little fictitious pleading. It applied, however, only to contracts of uncertain value executed with the formality of a seal and few such contracts were so executed at any time in American history. Writs of covenant, therefore, appear only occasionally in American court records.

Another ancient action was the *writ of debt on a bond*. A bond,

[6] See Shipman, *Common-Law Pleading*, 141–143.

like a covenant, was an instrument to which a defendant had attached his seal, but unlike an instrument sued upon in covenant, a bond contained a promise to pay to the plaintiff something of fixed value, usually money. Bonds, unlike covenants, were often used by businessmen to formalize contracts, and court records therefore reveal a good deal of litigation over bonds.

When a contract simply called upon a defendant to pay a sum of money, an action of debt on a bond was simple. A plaintiff merely pleaded execution of the bond under seal, the promise to pay the money due, and the nonpayment. Unless the defendant could prove that he did not execute the bond (in Latin, *non est factum*, or, as commonly translated into English, that it was "not his act and deed"), the court gave judgment for the plaintiff for the sum stated in the bond. If the defendant claimed that he rightfully owed less than the sum stated in the bond, the common law court which had heard the action of debt could not reduce the damages to the rightful sum. In England, a defendant had to bring a separate action in the High Court of Chancery to obtain a reduction of damages. In America, this particular equitable power was sometimes given by statute to common law courts. Nevertheless, once a defendant had lost an action of debt on a bond, he could obtain a reduction in damages only by petitioning a court with the appropriate equitable power to "chancer the bond."

Businessmen often used bonds, not to secure payment of a sum of money, but to secure performance of a promise of uncertain value. They sought, that is, to have a bond and the action of debt on the bond perform the work of a covenant and of the action of covenant. The method they used was to make the bond conditional. They did this by executing a bond under seal for a specified sum of money and then placing a provision on the back of the bond declaring it void if a specified act was performed. For example, a building contractor might promise to pay $10,000 unless he completed a specified construction job by a specified date. Indeed, a borrower might enter into a bond to pay $10,000 unless he returned the $5,000 he had borrowed plus interest to the lender by a specified date.

Suits on conditional bonds produced court records of considerable complexity. Such records begin like all records of debt on a bond, with the plaintiff alleging the execution of the bond under seal, the promise to pay the sum due, and the nonpayment. But the defendant, instead of pleading *non est factum* or admitting his liability, would "pray oyer" of the condition of the bond—that is, he would ask to have the condition heard in open court. The condition on the back of the bond, which often details a business transaction of interest to economic historians, would then be read into the record, after which the defendant would plead performance of it. If he proved his plea, the case would end, but if he failed to prove it judgment would be given for the plaintiff subject to the defendant's right to pray chancery of the bond. Normally defendants did petition the court to chancer the bond. When they did, further proceedings were held to determine the actual value of the act the defendant had failed to perform. Court records generally indicate at least the outcome of those proceedings.[7]

The action of debt was available not only against a defendant who had executed a bond under seal, but against any defendant who was indebted to a plaintiff for a fixed sum. The writ was commonly used against defendants who had become indebted to plaintiffs by virtue of statutes, such as the customs laws, imposing penalties for their breach. Such statutes typically divided the penalty among several persons, such as an informer, a public official, the crown, or later the state. Any person eligible to receive a portion of a penalty could bring the action of debt. In such actions, court records will usually describe the statute that was breached as well as the nature of the breach. Writs of debt were also commonly used to revive judgments which were not otherwise enforceable in the jurisdiction in which the writ was brought. Debt was also available for other purposes, but for reasons not germane to most users of American court records, its use for those purposes had become obsolete prior to the founding of the American colonies.[8]

The writ that made debt obsolete and became the principal vehicle for the litigation of matters of contract in America was *assumpsit*, a variety of the action of case. Some court records will refer to the action as assumpsit; other records will refer to it simply as case.

[7] See A. W. B. Simpson, "The Penal Bond with Conditional Defeasance," *Law Quarterly Review*, LXXXII (1966), 392.

[8] See Nelson, *Americanization of the Common Law*, 80.

Assumpsit, in turn, came in many varieties, and often a plaintiff joined several varieties together in one pleading, thereby saving to himself the possibility of proving that his transaction lay within whichever variety the evidence at trial fit best.

The variety of assumpsit that had superseded debt by the early seventeenth century was *indebitatus assumpsit*. Translated this meant that the defendant, having become indebted to the plaintiff, assumed the obligation to pay what was owed. The allegation of a subsequent promise to pay was a fictitious one that the plaintiff did not have to prove at trial. Thus, indebitatus assumpsit lay whenever a defendant had become indebted—that is, whenever the writ of debt lay. Because plaintiffs found indebitatus assumpsit more advantageous procedurally, they brought it instead of debt.[9]

Indebitatus assumpsit itself had several varieties known as the common counts, which encapsulated the common sorts of ways in which one individual became indebted to another for a fixed sum. The common counts were (1) for money had and received to the defendant for his use, (2) for goods sold and delivered to the defendant, (3) for work done for the defendant, (4) for money lent to the defendant, and (5) for money paid by the plaintiff to a third party to the use of the defendant. At least by the nineteenth century, most American jurisdictions permitted plaintiffs to join these common counts, which overlapped, together alternatively in a single action. Thus a historian who finds in court records an action of assumpsit for $5 for money had and received, $5 for money lent, and $5 for money paid to the use of the defendant should recognize that only one $5 transaction between the parties had occurred and that the plaintiff's lawyer, unsure of the category into which the facts would fit, was pleading the three common counts in the alternative so that he could prove whichever count turned out to be easiest to prove at trial.[1]

Another variety of assumpsit was *special assumpsit*, which lay

---

[9] See Maitland, *The Forms of Action*, 68–70. In particular, debt permitted the ancient and obsolete proof by wager of law, i.e. by the defendant swearing an oath of innocence with supporting oaths by a fixed number of others. Plaintiffs usually wished to avoid wager of law, which was not abolished in England until 1833. Ibid., 69–70.

[1] See Morton J. Horwitz, *The Transformation of American Law, 1780–1860* (Cambridge, Mass., 1977), 171–173; David T. Konig, "Editor's Introduction," in Konig, *Plymouth Court Records*, I, 139, 154–156.

whenever a defendant had made an express promise to make a payment or perform an act. The most common form of special assumpsit was assumpsit to recover on a promissory note, where the plaintiff had to plead and prove that the defendant had executed the note, that the note had been given in return for some valuable "consideration," that the plaintiff had demanded payment, and that the defendant had refused to pay.[2] Special assumpsit also lay to enforce labor contracts. Two other frequent forms of special assumpsit were assumpsit on an account annexed to the writ, which lay when litigants had been keeping an account on sheets of paper which a plaintiff could attach to his writ, and assumpsit on a book account, which lay when the account was being kept in a book which could not be attached to the writ, but could be introduced in evidence at trial. These last two forms of special assumpsit were distinct from indebitatus assumpsit for goods sold and delivered and from older, medieval actions of account that occasionally appear in American court records.[3]

Two other forms of assumpsit known by the names *quantum meruit* and *quantum valebant* appear frequently in American records. They were brought when a defendant was indebted for an amount of money that was not fixed or precisely ascertainable. Quantum meruit lay when a plaintiff had performed services for a defendant and was seeking to recover as damages as much as he merited or deserved to have. Quantum valebant lay when a plaintiff had delivered goods and sought to recover as much as they were worth.[4]

The forms of action outlined above were by far the most common ones used in American courts prior to the procedural reforms of the mid-nineteenth century, after which plaintiffs were generally required merely to plead the facts they expected to prove at trial. A few words must still be said, however, about pleas available to defendants. Defensive pleas were essentially of three sorts. First were *dilatory pleas* which led merely to a dismissal of a plaintiff's action, but normally did not bar him from reinstituting the action. Examples of dilatory pleas are *pleas to the jurisdiction*—that the plaintiff has brought his suit in the wrong court—and *pleas in abatement*, which

---

[2] See Nelson, *Americanization of the Common Law*, 54–55.
[3] See Konig, "Editor's Introduction," 154–155.
[4] See *ibid.*, 155.

allege some technical defect in the writ, such as that the plaintiff has misspelled the defendant's name. A second possibility open to a defendant was a *demurrer*. In order to interpose a demurrer, a defendant had to admit the truth of all the allegations contained in the plaintiff's writ. By his demurrer he contended, however, that even if all the plaintiff's allegations were true, the law did not give him the remedy he sought. A defendant's third option was a *plea in bar*. A plea in bar could take the form of a general denial, such as a plea to a writ of assumpsit that the defendant never promised, which had the effect of denying all the facts alleged by the plaintiff and submitting the case to the jury. Or a defendant could plead specially — that is, assert some new fact which he contended should bar the plaintiff's recovery. If a defendant pleaded specially, the plaintiff could reply to his plea, the defendant could rebut the replication, and so forth.[5]

A historian who is familiar with the common writs used by plaintiffs and with the basic options open to defendants should have little difficulty reading court records in a knowledgeable fashion. If more detailed information is needed, the following sources are suggested:

FIFOOT, C. H. S. *History and Sources of the Common Law: Tort and Contract* (London, 1949).

Still the best available collection of source materials on the history of tort and contract and on the development of the writs of trespass, case, and assumpsit. Some thoughtful commentary is appended to the sources.

HORWITZ, MORTON J. *The Transformation of American Law, 1780–1860* (Cambridge, Mass., 1977).

Essentially a study of change in substantive American law, this book relates substantive change to change in the forms of action, especially in the fields of tort and contract.

KONIG, DAVID T. "Editor's Introduction," in *Plymouth Court Records, 1686–1859* (Wilmington, Del., 1978), I, 141–183.

A useful summary written by a historian for other historians. It concerns the various common law forms found in the Plymouth, Mass., court records.

---

[5] See Shipman, *Common-Law Pleading*, 277–449.

MAITLAND, FREDERIC W. *The Forms of Action at Common Law* (Cambridge, 1936).

This is the classic work on the forms of action, describing in less than a hundred pages how they developed and were used over time. A glossary of common writs is appended to Maitland's text.

MILSOM, S. F. C. *Historical Foundations of the Common Law* (2d edition, London, 1981).

Revises much of Maitland's earlier work on the forms of action, especially in regard to the fields of tort and contract. Milsom's is a large and deep book.

NELSON, WILLIAM E. *Americanization of the Common Law, 1760–1830* (Cambridge, Mass., 1975).

Like Horwitz's, a study of substantive legal change over the period in question. Chapter 5 is the most detailed study yet published of how common law pleading worked in an American jurisdiction, and how it came to be abolished.

SHIPMAN, BENJAMIN I. *Handbook of Common-Law Pleading* (St. Paul, Minn., 3d ed. by Henry W. Ballantine, 1923).

A detailed one-volume treatise on the rules of common law procedure as they stood at the end of the nineteenth century. The book was aimed primarily at an audience of law students seeking to learn the rules, and often fails to address historical questions.

SIMPSON, A. W. B. *An Introduction to the History of the Land Law* (Oxford, 1961).

The best up-to-date summary of the English law of real property and of the property writs. Third impression was in 1973.

Bibliographies of New England Court Records

WILLIAM JEFFREY, JR., *Early New England Court Records: A Bibliography of Published Materials* (Cambridge, Mass., 1954).

A reasonably up-to-date list of published New England materials, with a brief statement of the contents of each. Two items not in print when the bibliography was prepared are David T. Konig, ed., *Plymouth Court Records, 1686–1859*, 16 vols. (Wilmington, Del., 1978–1982), and Joseph H. Smith, *Colonial Justice in Western Massachusetts, 1639–1702: The Pynchon Court Record* (Cambridge, Mass., 1961). Cf. William Jeffrey, Jr., "Early American Court Records—A Bibliography of

Printed Materials: The Middle Colonies," *University of Cincinnati Law Review*, XXXIX (1970), 685–710.

DAVID H. FLAHERTY, "A Select Guide to the Manuscript Court Records of Colonial New England," *American Journal of Legal History*, XI (1967), 107.

An annotated list. Flaherty has also done a comparable list for Virginia. See David H. Flaherty, "A Select Guide to the Manuscript Court Records of Colonial Virginia," *American Journal of Legal History*, XIX (1975), 112.

CATHERINE S. MENAND, *The Records of the Suffolk County Inferior Court* (Boston, 1981).

A guide to the Papers of the Suffolk County Inferior Court of Common Pleas in the custody of the Social Law Library, Boston, Massachusetts. Available at the Social Law Library, Boston, Massachusetts.

MICHAEL S. HINDUS, *Inventory and Guide to the Records of the Massachusetts Superior Court and Its Predecessors* (Boston, 1977).

An inventory of the location and contents of all major Massachusetts trial court records. Available at the Social Law Library, Boston, Massachusetts.

KATHRYN M. CAREY, CATHERINE S. MENAND, *Supreme Judicial Court Records Preservation Laboratory* (Boston, 1981).

An archival and conservation analysis of the pre-1800 records of the Massachusetts courts. Available at the Social Law Library, Boston, Massachusetts.

MICHAEL S. HINDUS

A Guide to the Court Records of
Early Massachusetts

I N 1977 the Commonwealth of Massachusetts, funded by a grant
from the National Historical Publications and Records Commission, inventoried the records of the major trial court of the state,
the Superior Court and its predecessors.[1] The records included in
this inventory spanned over three and a half centuries, excluding
only the lesser trial courts, specialized courts, and the "Suffolk Files"
records of the highest courts—the Superior Court of Judicature and
the Supreme Judicial Court.[2]

This article is designed to supplement and complement the 1977
inventory for researchers wishing to use early (pre-1859) records.
Because it was not possible to revisit every courthouse, this inventory,
based on the 1977 field survey, is restricted to the records of the
major trial courts.[3] Nevertheless, this guide to using court records
and the history of the courts will aid researchers using Massachusetts
court records which are not included in the inventory.

The following summary of history of the courts and their jurisdictions in Massachusetts up to 1859 is not intended as definitive.
Rather, it is intended to aid the researcher to determine which court's
records are appropriate for a particular research task.

[1] Michael S. Hindus, *The Records of the Massachusetts Superior Court and Its
Predecessors: An Inventory and Guide* (Boston, 1977). The inventory project was
commissioned by the Judicial Records Committee of the Massachusetts Supreme
Judicial Court. Many of the pre-1860 records inventoried here will be included in
the judicial archives scheduled to be deposited in the new State Archives building at
Columbia Point, Boston, in late 1985.

[2] For a full description of the Suffolk Files, see John Noble, "The Early Court Files
of Suffolk County," Colonial Society of Massachusetts, *Publications*, III (1900),
317, and "The Records and Files of the Superior Court of Judicature, and of the
Supreme Judicial Court, Their History and Places of Deposit," Colonial Society of
Massachusetts, *Publications*, V (1902), 5.

[3] Similarly, although an earlier ending point might have been more appropriate for
this volume, it was impossible to use a different cut-off date without replicating at
great expense the field work for the 1977 inventory.

The Organization and Jurisdiction of Early Massachusetts Courts

Although the names and powers of the courts in Massachusetts changed significantly from the founding of the colony to the Civil War, the history of the jurisdiction of the various courts is not complicated. One basic principle was in place throughout most of that period—a three-tiered system of courts, with jurisdiction based primarily, but not exclusively, on the seriousness of the dispute or criminal charge. Appeals from a lower-tier court could generally be heard at the next higher tier. At almost every point in Massachusetts history there was: (1) a person or court to handle minor civil and criminal matters (commissioner, justice of the peace, or municipal court; (2) a trial court for most of the remaining jurisdiction (County Court, Court of Common Pleas, Superior Court); and (3) a high court which was primarily appellate, but which also had some original jurisdiction (Court of Assistants, Superior Court of Judicature, Supreme Judicial Court).

The three-tiered structure was by no means static. Jurisdiction frequently shifted, particularly in the direction of narrowing the original jurisdiction of the highest court. In addition, the courts themselves were frequently reorganized and renamed. Finally, specialized courts, such as the Strangers Court created in 1639, were established to deal with an increasingly complex economy and society and the greater role of the law in those spheres.

The first trial courts in Massachusetts were the county courts, established in 1636. Located in Cambridge, Boston, Ipswich, Salem, Springfield, and York (now Maine), these Inferior Quarter Courts, as they were also known, were circuit quarterly courts of general civil and criminal jurisdiction staffed by local magistrates appointed by the General Court. County courts heard civil cases involving disputes greater than 40 shillings and not exceeding £10, as well as all criminal cases other than those punishable by banishment or loss of life or limb.[4]

Cases under 40 shillings could be heard initially by magistrates

---

[4] David T. Konig, *Law and Society in Puritan Massachusetts: Essex County, 1629–1692* (Chapel Hill, 1979), 26, 35–36; Zechariah Chafee, Jr., "Introduction" to *Records of the Suffolk County Court, 1671–1680*, Colonial Society of Massachusetts, *Publications*, XXIX (1933), xvii–xx; George Lee Haskins, *Law and Authority in Early Massachusetts* (New York, 1960), 32–34.

and, after 1647, by one-person commissioner's courts in towns without magistrates. The criminal jurisdiction of the commissioner's courts included drunkenness, lying, swearing, and theft. Commissioners were also empowered to lay out highways, appoint masters of the correction houses, license innkeepers, and maintain highways. Appeals from these courts could be heard by the county courts.[5]

The next level was the Court of Assistants, also known as the Greater Quarter Court, composed of the governor, deputy governor, and twelve Assistants. This same group also functioned as the Governor's Council. The Court of Assistants met twice a year for judicial business, hearing criminal cases punishable by loss of life or limb, divorces, and civil cases above the jurisdictional level of the county courts.[6] The Court of Assistants also heard appeals from the county courts.

The county courts, commissioner's courts, and the Court of Assistants comprised the three-tier model described earlier. But in the half-century under the original charter, the aptly named General Court, while primarily a legislative body, had an adjudicative function as well, acting as a supreme court for appeals from the Court of Assistants.[7] The General Court was composed of the Court of Assistants plus the deputies from the towns.

The revocation of the charter in 1684 led to a reorganization of *[handwritten: after first charter —]* the courts, with the three-tiered structure retained, but names, structures, and jurisdictions altered. In 1692 the Inferior Court of Common Pleas replaced the old county courts. The Court of Common Pleas was a quarterly circuit court composed of four justices in each county, three of whom were a quorum. Its jurisdiction extended to all civil cases above forty shillings. Cases below that amount which did not involve land titles were heard by constables and justices of the peace, but were appealable to Common Pleas.[8] The Court of Com-

---

[5] The lower jurisdiction was 20 shillings from 1638 to 1647 when cases were heard by magistrates. Haskins, 32; Konig, 36; Chafee, xix.

[6] Chafee, xx–xxi; Charles J. Hilkey, *Legal Development in Colonial Massachusetts, 1630–1686* (New York, 1910), 29–36.

[7] See Barbara Black, "The Judicial Power and the General Court in Early Massachusetts, 1634–1686," unpublished Ph.D. dissertation, Yale University, 1975; Konig, 36–37n; Chafee, xxi.

[8] Much of the legislation relating to the courts was disallowed by the English Privy Council between 1692 and 1699. The basic scheme appears in 1692–3 Massachu-

mon Pleas was the main trial court in Massachusetts until 1859, although it underwent slight changes in name and more significant changes in structure over the 167 years.

Contemporaneous with the establishment of Common Pleas, a new court was created — the Court of General Sessions of the Peace. Composed of the justices of the peace in each county sitting collectively, this court had both administrative and adjudicatory functions. In its adjudicatory capacity, it heard criminal cases not punishable by death, as well as criminal appeals from justices of the peace. In its administrative capacity, it handled inns and liquor licensing; issues of settlement, poor relief, and bastardy; and control of highways and roads.[9] This court succeeded to the functions previously performed by commissioners.

At the top, the Superior Court of Judicature replaced the Court of Assistants. It was a circuit court composed of a chief justice and four associate justices, any three of whom were a quorum, with original jurisdiction in matters involving the Crown and in many probate and land matters. It also heard appeals from both the Inferior Court of Common Pleas and the Court of General Sessions of the Peace. The Superior Court of Judicature retained jurisdiction over serious crimes, but "matters relating to the peace" became the province of General Sessions. Unlike the Court of Assistants, which prior to legislation of 1660 and 1672 had original jurisdiction in cases above the jurisdictional limit of the County Courts, Common Pleas apparently had no such limitation until the nineteenth century. Accordingly, the Superior Court of Judicature had no original jurisdiction based solely on the amount in dispute.[1]

Although it may appear that by the end of the seventeenth century, Massachusetts had constructed a rational system of courts of progressively greater jurisdiction, in fact this system was the height of in-

---

setts *Acts and Resolves,* Chapter 9 and Chapter 33 and was finally passed as 1699 Massachusetts *Acts and Resolves,* Chapters 1–3.

[9] 1699 Massachusetts *Acts and Resolves,* Chapter 1; see also the excellent analysis of Hendrik Hartog, "The Public Law of a County Court: Judicial Government in Eighteenth Century Massachusetts," *American Journal of Legal History,* xx (1976), 282.

[1] 1699 Massachusetts *Acts and Resolves,* Chapter 3; Hilkey, 34; *The Legal Papers of John Adams,* Wroth and Zobel, eds., 1 (Cambridge, Mass., 1965), xli.

efficiency. The problem was a system of trials *de novo*, which presented litigants up to three chances to have a fact finder try a case. A party could bring an action in Common Pleas and, if he lost, receive a new trial before the Superior Court of Judicature. The party losing before this court could seek another trial before that same court, providing he had not also lost below. Thus it was possible for a case to be tried three times.[2]

Despite the widely perceived and lamented inefficiencies of this system, it survived the eighteenth century and the Revolution with only slight changes. In 1780 the Superior Court of Judicature was reconstituted as the Supreme Judicial Court. This became the state's major appellate court, retaining original jurisdiction only over capital offenses, divorces, and some land cases. The full court of five justices traveled yearly to every county, twice a year to the populous ones. The Supreme Judicial Court continued the inefficient system of trials *de novo*, hearing appeals in cases where the appellant had not already suffered two adverse decisions.

Attempts to reduce the inefficiencies and delay endemic to this system resulted only in fine tuning. In 1799 the Supreme Judicial Court was increased to seven members, any three of whom could constitute a quorum. The following year the quorum requirement was reduced to two, and in 1804 the court was empowered to hold *nisi prius* terms, where cases could be heard by a single judge. All these measures increased the number of cases the court could hear, but did not solve the problem of delay.[3]

Other changes in the post-Revolutionary years merely shifted jurisdiction among the various courts. For example, in 1783 justices of the peace were authorized to hear all cases under £4 (changed to $20 in 1807) in which land title was not an issue. Common

---

[2] William Nelson suggests that this characterization was exaggerated. In his view, parties were interested primarily in getting a decision from the highest court and would raise sham pleading points in order to avoid trial in a lower court. William E. Nelson, *Americanization of the Common Law: The Impact of Legal Change on Massachusetts Society, 1760–1830* (Cambridge, Mass., 1975), 16.

[3] 1780 Massachusetts *Acts*, Chapter 17, 1782 Massachusetts *Acts*, Chapter 9; Richard E. Ellis, *The Jeffersonian Crisis: Courts and Politics in the Young Republic* (New York, 1971), 184–87; Michael Stephen Hindus, *Prison and Plantation: Crime, Justice, and Society in Massachusetts and South Carolina, 1767–1878* (Chapel Hill, 1980), 12–14.

Pleas was expressly forbidden to hear such cases except as appeals from justices of the peace.[4] Justices of the peace were also given jurisdiction over assaults and batteries, affrays, riots, and disturbing the peace.[5]

A later change of greater significance was the demise of that unwieldy hybrid, the Court of General Sessions. In 1809 its adjudicatory functions were transferred to Common Pleas; four years later they were transferred back again. In 1813 most Courts of General Sessions were abolished, but this, too, was only a temporary move. In 1818 Sessions was reestablished, but the trend was clear. In 1827 Sessions was abolished for good, and its administrative functions were transferred to the County Commissioners.[6]

By the early nineteenth century, then, the three-tiered system was still intact. Justices of the peace heard minor civil and criminal matters; Common Pleas heard the rest; and the Supreme Judicial Court was primarily, but not exclusively, an appellate court. Boston had a Municipal Court to hear criminal cases heard in other counties by Common Pleas. This modification demonstrates the creation of specialized courts where the press of business demanded it.

The political and legal environments which caused the reorganization of Massachusetts courts are beyond the scope of this brief introduction. Scholars have studied many aspects of this story, particularly from an institutional perspective. But a functional history of Massachusetts courts, based on an analysis of their actual business, remains to be written. The records described in this inventory will be an important part of that research.

How to Use the Records

The key to utilizing court records is to understand what information can be obtained from each type of record and how different records series are interrelated. The type of information found in a particular record series is a product of the purpose for which the record was created.

---

[4] 1783 Massachusetts *Acts*, Chapter 42; 1807 Massachusetts *Acts*, Chapter 123.

[5] 1783 Massachusetts *Acts*, Chapter 51.

[6] Hartog, 329, n. 145.

A basic source is the minute or docket book.[7] These contain the name of the case, what type of action it was (i.e., assumpsit, trespass, and the like), the procedural history of the case, and its resolution. A case reappeared on a docket at every court session until it was disposed of, either by trial, dismissal, motion, or other means. These books generally detail all motions and all appearances of attorneys. However, the information is in a skeletal format; the facts supporting an action, motion, or decision are not included. Dockets and minute books are rough guides to the volume and nature of civil litigation and criminal prosecutions. While providing much information on the procedural history of actions, the administrative history of the courts, and even the growth of the legal profession, minute books and dockets shed little light on the nature and flavor of legal disputes. They serve as a guide to court procedure and legal practice, as well as a type of index to other court papers, especially files, by giving a barebones account of every case. Thus, a researcher studying a particular type of legal dispute—for example, assumpsit—could use minute or docket books to identify cases in that category, but could not determine the nature of the case or the business relationship between the litigants.

A narrative description of a lawsuit or criminal prosecution frequently appears in extended record books, described in the inventory as "Records." These oversize volumes contain a capsule summary of the dispute or crime as well as the ultimate disposition of the case. While informative and accessible to the layman, these narratives are still only summaries of what brought the parties into court and how it was that they left. Detailed facts such as summaries of testimony are not to be found in record books. Records, too, can serve as an index to other records series.

The third major record series are the case files. Unlike dockets, minutes, and records, the files follow no prescribed form. They are the papers filed with the court for each case. They include writs, bonds, pleadings, bills of costs, and executions of judgment. But they can include other documents related to a case which have little legal significance, but may be of great historical value. The eclecticism of case files is what makes them so appealing to historians who use them

---

[7] Minute books and docket books are described in the inventory as dockets.

not only as a guide to legal history, but to reconstruct societies in the past.[8] Files may contain almost any sort of document — from surety bonds to guarantee appearances to summaries of witness testimony. In debt cases the files may include the actual note or other evidence of a debt, or the account indicating payment due. In disputes over real estate the files frequently include maps or surveys of the area in question. Miscellaneous documents, also described in the inventory, offer a flavor of the range of business which courts handled, from licenses to vital records.

Prior to the establishment of police forces, beginning in Boston in 1837, courts were probably the form of secular authority with which the citizenry had the greatest contact. Early court records, accordingly, mirror almost every aspect of civil authority.

How to Use the Inventory

The inventory is arranged by county and court. The first listing will be a County or Quarter Court, if its records survived and if the county had one. The next listing will be the Court of General Sessions of the Peace, followed by the Court of Common Pleas. No distinction is made in this inventory between the colonial Inferior Court of Common Pleas and the post-Revolutionary Circuit Court of Common Pleas because, from a records perspective, this was primarily only a change in nomenclature.

The inventory within each court for each county is divided into two main parts. The first comprises the primary or major record series: dockets, files, and records. The second part, labelled "Miscellaneous" in the inventory, comprises the secondary record series. Each entry gives a short title of the series, the inclusive dates, and the number of cases, volumes, or boxes which comprise the series. Indexes which are interfiled with a series are included in the entry. Indexes which are kept as a separate record series have their own listing.

As the volume of court business expanded, counties gradually introduced specialized record-keeping. In particular, criminal cases began to be recorded separately from civil. The point at which such

[8] Robert J. Brink, "Boston's Great Anthropological Documents," *Boston Bar Journal*, XXII (September, 1978), 6.

specialization occurred varied with the size of the county. In Suffolk, for example, criminal cases were separated—and indeed heard in a separate court—as early as 1800; in Norfolk it did not occur until 1847. When criminal cases were separated from civil in 1847 in Norfolk, that did not create two new record series. Instead, a criminal series was established and the old series was continued, containing now only civil cases. To show this specialization and to stress that the series which formerly had contained all cases continued with only civil and with no indication of any change, the inventory uses the following notation—the example is from Norfolk County:

Dockets, 1794–1859   Civil and Criminal, 1794–1847; Civil, 1847–
               1859, 54v
             Criminal, 1847–1859, 5v

The term "box" as used in the inventory refers to all manner of boxes, ranging from the common one cubic foot archive box found in 1977 in the State Records Center and Middlesex County to large

49. Case files of the Inferior Court of Common Pleas, Suffolk, showing the tins in which many colonial court records are still stored. Courtesy, Social Law Library, Boston.

open wooden and cardboard boxes in Berkshire. "Small metal case" refers to a metal case *or* drawer, the most common way of storing case files. Whether a closed case, open case, or drawer, the dimensions are usually 5" wide, 12" high, and from 17" to 24" deep.

In 1977 court records were found not only in courthouses, but also in private and public libraries, historical societies and institutions, and in the State Records Center. By the mid-1980's, however, all historic judicial records will be transferred to the judicial section of the new state archives building, now under construction. Accordingly, the location indicators of 1977 will soon be obsolete and have been excluded from this inventory. Researchers wishing to use court records prior to their move to the archives buildings should consult the clerk of the court in the county in which the research will take place. For a copy of the 1977 inventory, which includes specific locations of records, usually by room, and both in and out of courthouses, researchers should write to Social Law Library, 1200 Courthouse, Boston, Massachusetts 02108. Records in fragile or deteriorating condition undergoing or awaiting conservation may be temporarily unavailable.

ABBREVIATIONS

BMC	Boston Municipal Court
c.	circa
C.	century
CCP	Court of Common Pleas
	Circuit Court of Common Pleas
	Inferior Court of Common Pleas
fd	File Drawer (5"–8" wide)
lfd	Large File Drawer (13"–17" wide)
ms	Manuscript
SC	Superior Court
Sessions	Court of General Sessions of Peace
SJC	Supreme Judicial Court
v	Volume
WPA	Works Progress Administration

GLOSSARY

Accounts	Various expenses owed by the court.
Affidavit	Written sworn statement of facts introduced as evidence in trial.
Appeal	Resort to a higher court to redress supposed error or injustice of lower court.
Attachment	Process of seizing chattels or taking title to real property by virtue of a writ; frequently used to satisfy judgment or to guarantee appearance at trial.
Bail	The process of obtaining the release of a person under arrest by assuming responsibility for his appearance at time and place specified; also refers to money pledged to guarantee this appearance.
Bastardy bonds	Money pledged to court to guarantee that bastards do not become public charges; usually paid by putative father.
Bill of costs	A certified, itemized statement of the amount of costs in an action or suit.
Bond	A promise to pay; used here, it refers to money paid to court for a specific purpose, usually to prosecute and appeal (appeal bond) or for bail (bail bond).
Declaration	The first pleading on the part of the plaintiff in a lawsuit; usually states the specific complaints alleged against the defendant.
Demurrer	Statement by defendant that truth of plaintiff's allegations are not sufficient to make demurring party answer them or not sufficient to require answers or to allow cause to proceed.
Deposition	Sworn written testimony of witness taken by interrogation, but not in court.
Docket	Outline of case prepared by clerk of court; gives dates of major pre-trial, trial, and post-trial actions.
Estreat	A copy of an extract from the rolls of any court in which the fines, recognizances, and the like, imposed or taken by that court upon or from the accused are set down,

and which are to be levied by the bailiff or other officer of the court.

Exception   Objection to a decision made by the court.

Execution   A writ putting into effect a final judgment of the court.

Files   Papers accompanying a case or action, usually including writs, complaints, answers, and bonds.

Fine   Sum of money paid at end of a case, usually as a penalty.

Index   Alphabetical or chronological listing of cases or parties referred to in a given record series; as used here, usually compiled at the time the records were created and intended to be used with them.

Indictment   Accusation in criminal case found and presented by grand jury.

Innholders and Retailers   Provisioners to whom Court of General Sessions granted licenses, particularly to serve liquor.

Inquest   Coroner's investigation into a death.

Jury Bills   Costs for maintaining jury (in this usage, distinct from grand jury bill, or finding of sufficient evidence to prosecute).

License   Permission to sell liquor, granted by General Sessions.

List of entries   List of cases formally entered on to court docket or records.

Mittimus   Order of court or magistrate to sheriff commanding him to take the person therein named to jail and to the jailer commanding him to keep the prisoner until further notice.

Motions   Applications made for consideration and hearing of a certain point.

Non-Entries   Writs issued in cases which were satisfied or dropped before coming to court.

Partition   Division of land between co-owners or co-proprietors.

Pleading   Process performed by parties in a suit, alternately presenting written statements of their contention, responding to preceding contentions.

Presentment   Writing containing the accusation presented by grand jury.

Recognizance | Obligation entered into before some court with condition to perform some particular act as to appear in court, keep the peace, pay a debt, and the like.

Record | As used here, the extended account of a case, including a prose summary of the proceeding, but generally lacking substantive summaries of testimony and evidence.

Remand | The sending of a case back to a lower court by a higher court.

Return Day | Day named in writ by which an officer is required to return it.

Revolutionary Pensions | Applications by Revolutionary War veterans for pensions, c. 1820; include important information about applicants' finances.

Scire Facias | Process based on court records, to execute on a judgment, or to revive either a judgment or the original action.

Sentence | Judgment formally pronounced in criminal cases.

Session Book | List of cases heard in a given period or court session; more skeletal than docket; similar to trial calendar.

Summons | Writ notifying person to appear in court on a given day.

Venire | Order by court to sheriff to summon a jury.

Warrant | Writ requiring sheriff to arrest a person and to bring him to court on a given day for an offense with which person is charged.

EARLY MASSACHUSETTS TRIAL COURT RECORDS

BARNSTABLE COUNTY—FOUNDED: 1685

Court of General Sessions of the Peace

Records, 1783–1791 | Records, 1783–1791, 2v (includes CCP dockets)

Court of Common Pleas

Dockets, 1783–1859 | Dockets, 1783–1791, 2v (includes Sessions records)

Miscellaneous | Rule Book, 1782, 1v

BERKSHIRE COUNTY—FOUNDED: 1761

Court of General Sessions of the Peace

Dockets, 1761–1827	Dockets, 1761–1796, 1808–1815, 1822–1827, 4v (WPA typescripts, 1761–1795, 2v)
Files, c. 1762–1827	Files, 1762–1827, 34 bundles and 1 box
	Licenses, 1763–1827, 17 bundles
	Writs, c. 1780–1827, 29 bundles
Records, 1761–1827	Records, 1761–1822, 2v (WPA typescripts, 1761–1827, 3v)
	Records, 1769–1770 (1875 ms copy), 1v
Miscellaneous	Minutes, 1799, 1v

Court of Common Pleas

Dockets, 1799–1859	Civil, 1799, 1803; Civil and Criminal, 1810, 1815 (includes Sessions), 1841; Civil, 1848–1859, 18v
Files, 1761–1859	Criminal, 1797–1859, 6 boxes
	Executions, 1762–1768, 6 boxes
	Executions, 1781–1782, 1789–c. 1827, 3 bundles and 4 boxes
	Writs, 1761–1859, 7 bundles and 21 boxes
Records, 1761–1859	Civil, 1761–1774, 1782–1804; Civil and Criminal, 1804–1849; Civil, 1850–1859, 84v
	Executions, 1767–1785, 2v

BRISTOL COUNTY—FOUNDED: 1685

Court of General Sessions of the Peace

Files, 1704–1827	Files, 1704–1762, 1764–1765, 1769–1780, 15 metal cases; Files, 1748, 1773–1827, 3 boxes
Records, 1697–1827	Records, 1697–1827, 16v (includes CCP and Marriages)

Court of Common Pleas

Files, 1652–1859	Civil, 1765–1804; Civil and Criminal, 1804–1834; Civil, 1834–1859, 234 metal cases
	Executions, 1765–1859, 63 bundles; Miscellaneous Writs, Bills, and Bonds, 1652–1820, 22 metal cases
Records, 1702–1859	Executions, 1721–1722, 1v (includes Sessions);

| | Records, 1702–1776, 1783–1859, 61v (includes Sessions) |
| Miscellaneous | Index, 1730–1767, 6v |

Vital Records

Marriages, 1699–1805, 1 metal case (includes Sessions)
Marriages, 1700–1798, 3v

DUKES COUNTY—FOUNDED: 1695

Quarter Court

| Records, 1665–1692 | Records, 1665–1692, 1v (includes Sessions and CCP) |

Court of General Sessions of the Peace

| Files, c. 1765–1827 | Files, c. 1765–1827, 3 metal cases (includes CCP) |
| Records, 1692–1827 | Records, 1692–1715, 1722–1827, 5v (includes Quarter Court and CCP) |

Court of Common Pleas

Dockets, 1772–1859	Dockets, 1722–1859, 22v (includes Sessions)
Files, c. 1777–1855	Files, c. 1777–1855, 7 metal cases including:
	Decisions and Orders, 1841–1855,
	Executions, 1770–1855,
	Indian wills, 1669–1812,
	Indictments, 1781–c. 1827,
	Petitions, 1777–1853,
	Warrants and Complaints, 1778–1837,
	Writs, 1790–1795, 1813–1842 (includes Sessions)
Records, 1692–1859	Records, 1692–1715, 1722–1859, 6v (includes Sessions), Index; 1851–1859, 1v
	Proprietors Record, Farm Neck, 1707–1827, 1v

ESSEX COUNTY—FOUNDED: 1643

County Court

| Files, 1636–1694 | Files, 1636–1694, 58v |
| Records, 1637–1748 | Records, 1637–1748, 5v |

	Records (Ipswich), 1645–1692, 5v
	Records (Norfolk), 1648–1680, 2v
	(Pulsifer copies [David Pulsifer was a Clerk of Court], 1648–1654, 1672–1679, 2v)
	Records (Salem), 1636–1642, 1647–1656, 1673–1685, 4v
Miscellaneous	Index, 3v
	WPA Index, 1636–1694, 4v

Court of General Sessions of the Peace

Files, 1693–1827	Accounts, 1737–1755, 1780, 1792–1800, 1802–1813, 1816, 1818–1827, c. 25 boxes and 1 bundle
	Bastardy, 1707, 1801, 1 box
	County Orders, 1798, 1 box
	Files, 1693–1827, 49 metal cases and 1 envelope (includes CCP)
	Files, 1793, 1797–1799, 1805, 1819, 3 boxes
	Indictments, 1797–1801, 1 box
	Innholders and Retailers, 1799–1813 (Sessions), 1809–1811 (CCP), 1812–1813 (Sessions), 1814–1818 (CCP), 1819–1827 (Sessions), 2v
	Licenses, 1750, 1813, 1 box
	Presentments of the Grand Jury, 1726, 1732 1734–1750, 2 boxes
Records, 1692–1827	Records, 1692–1795, 10v
	Records, 1796–1827, 5v
Miscellaneous	Index, 1695–1696, 1726–1744, 2v

Court of Common Pleas

Dockets, 1692–1859	Civil, 1692–1726, 6v
	Civil, 1721–1804; Civil and Criminal, 1804–1812; Civil, 1812–1831, 1833–1859, 92v
Files, 1693–1859	Accounts 1703, 1720, 1780, 1793, 1795–1802, 1804–1815, 1817–1819, 1824–1831, 1833–1839, 1841, c. 50 boxes
	Attachments, c. 1790, 1 box
	Bonds and Notes, c. 1770–c. 1780, 1 box
	Executions, 1719–1737, c. 1830, 3 boxes

Executions, 1793–1859, 67 metal cases

Files, 1693–1859, 448 metal cases and 1 envelope

Grand Jurors Records, 1797–1803, 1834, 1 box

Larceny Cases, 1708, 1 box

Mittimuses, 1722, 1736, 1739, 1798, c. 1820–c. 1830, 3 boxes

Non-Entered Writs, 1726–1729, 1732–1742, 1744–1748, 1750, 1756–1767, 1770, 1773–1774, 1778, 1787–1791, 1793–1794, 1798, 1801–1815, 1817–1818, 1823–1839, 1851, 1859, c. 150 boxes

Recognizances, 1733–1734, 1789, 1798, 1800, 1801, 1825–1826, 3 boxes

Scire Facias, 1736, 1763, 1 box

Summons, 1694–1695, 1703–1704, 1734–1735, 1767, 1772–1774, 1789–1790, 1799, 2 boxes

Venires, 1736, 1777–1780, 1783, 1794–1801, 1804–1805, 1824–1825, 1827, 1830–1831, 1833, 2 boxes

Records, 1680–1858   Civil, 1696–1698, 1v

Civil, 1749–1804; Civil and Criminal, 1804–1835, 74v

Executions, 1680–1783, 2v

Miscellaneous   Consolidated Index, 1749–1904, 8v (includes SC)

Vital Records

Births, Marriages and Deaths, 1636–1795, 5v

Witchcraft

Miscellaneous Papers, 1692–1693, 1 box

Miscellaneous Papers, 1692, 2v

Hampshire County (Springfield Sitting)

Sessions and Quarter Sessions Records, 1681–1739, 1v

Sessions, Quarter Sessions and Court of Com-

mon Pleas Records, 1692–1706, 1710–1729,
2v

Sessions and Court of Common Pleas Records,
1707–1714 (typed), 1724–1726, 2v

Sessions and Court of Common Pleas Files and
Miscellaneous Documents, 1720–1812, 3v

County Court, Sessions and Court of Common
Pleas Records, 1720–1727, 1664–1812
(typed), 2v

HAMPSHIRE COUNTY—FOUNDED: 1662

Court of General Sessions of the Peace

Files, 1721–1827	Files, 1721–1827, 41 metal cases
Records, 1677–1827	Records, 1677–1827, 16v (includes CCP)

Court of Common Pleas

Files, 1712–1859	Civil, 1712–1804; Civil and Criminal 1804–1850
	Civil, 1850–1859, 387 metal cases
Records, 1677–1859	Civil, 1677–1798, 21v (includes Sessions)
	Civil, 1797–1804; Civil and Criminal, 1804–1853
	Executions, 1715–1764, 1v
Miscellaneous	Index, c. 1700–1859, 17 fd

MIDDLESEX COUNTY—FOUNDED: 1643

County Court

Files, c. 1648– c. 1777	Executions, 1658–1699, 1 metal case
	Files, c. 1648–c. 1777, 650 envelopes (includes CCP) (photocopies of envelope contents, 67v)
Records, 1649–1699	Records, 1649–1663, 1671–1686, 1658–1699, 4v (includes CCP) (Pulsifer copies, 1649–1663, 1681–1686, 2v)
Miscellaneous	Abstract, 24 fds

Court of General Sessions of the Peace

Files, c. 1650–1827	Files, c. 1650–1827, 154 metal cases
Records, 1686–1827	Records, 1686–1688, 1692–1761, 1790–1802,

	1809–1827, 9v (photostatic copies, 1686–1688, 1692–1723, 1735, 4v)
	Records, 1722–1729 (includes CCP), 1761–1790, 1796–1799, 1801–1808, 5v
Miscellaneous	Licenses, 1791–1810, 1v

Court of Common Pleas

Dockets, 1728–1859	Civil, 1728–1731, 1v (includes Sessions)
	Civil, 1738–1804; Civil and Criminal, 1804–1844; Civil, 1844–1859, 151v
Files, 1648–1859	Civil, 1723–1804; Civil and Criminal, 1804–1859, 1207 metal cases
	Executions, 1700–1858, 361 fd
	Files, c. 1648–c. 1777, 650 envelopes (includes County Court)
	Files, c. 1650–1802, 15 metal cases (includes Sessions)
Records, 1699–1852	Civil, 1699–1770, 1780–1792, 1799; Civil and Criminal, 1805–1844; Civil, 1844–1859, 116v
	Civil, 1728–1731 (includes Sessions), 1770–1780, 1792–1795, 1799–1804; Civil and Criminal, 1804, 1805, 1809, 1829, 1839, 16v
	Executions, 1751–1767, 1v
	Executions, 1767–1784, 1v
	Partitions, 1785–1815, 1837–1856, 2v
Miscellaneous	Venire Abstract, c. 1650–c. 1700, 1 fd

Vital Records

	Births, Deaths and Marriages, 1778–1793, 1v (Pulsifer Copies, 1632–1677, 1673–1745, 2v)
	Births, Marriages and Deaths Abstract, 1652–1699, 2 fd
	Marriages, 1733–1767, 1v
Files, 1794–1827	Files, 1794–1827, 10 metal cases

Court of Common Pleas

Dockets, 1794–1859	Civil and Criminal, 1794–1847; Civil, 1847–1859, 54v (Index, 1806–1810, 1827–1859, 85v, interfiled)

Files, 1793–1859   Civil and Criminal, 1794–1847; Civil, 1847–
1859, 206 metal cases
Executions, 1794–1859, 29 metal cases
Non-Entries, 1794–1832, 6 metal cases
Records, 1794–1859   Records, 1794–1859, 56v (Index, 57v)

Vital Statistics
Marriages, 1793–1795, 1v

PLYMOUTH COUNTY—FOUNDED: 1685
Plymouth Colony Records
Court Orders, 1620–1697, 6v

Court of General Sessions of the Peace
Records, 1686–1827   Records, 1686–1692; 1698–1818, 12v
(includes Marriages)

Court of Common Pleas
Dockets, 1745–1859   Dockets, 1745–1749, 1796–1802, 3v
Files, 1687–1859   Civil, 1798–1804; Civil and Criminal, 1804–
1849, 113 metal cases (Sessions interfiled)
Executions, 1735–1855, 1 box
Files, c. 1700–1843, 29 metal cases
Recognizances, 1687–1859, 1 metal case
Venires, 1702, 1797, 1800–1859, 7 metal cases
(includes SC)
Warrants, 1701–1857, 1 metal case
Writs, 1701–1859, 8 metal cases
Writs, 1714–1835, 1v
Records, 1702–1859   Records, 1702–1859, 38v

Vital Records
Births, Marriages, Deaths, 1620–1697
(Plymouth Colony Records), 1v
Marriages, 1726–1737, 1v (includes Sessions)

SUFFOLK COUNTY—FOUNDED: 1643
County Court
Records, 1680–1692   Records, 1680–1692, 2v (photostatic copies)

Court of General Sessions of the Peace

Dockets, 1727–1822   Dockets, 1743–1758, 1764–1773, 5v (fragments, 1727–1728, 1733–1741, 1759, 1762–1763, 1776–1780)

Files, 1793–1816   Files, 1793–1796, 1 box

Records, 1702–1822   Records, 1702–1732, 4v

Records, 1718–1720, 1v

Records, 1796–1822, 5v

Court of Common Pleas

Dockets, 1720–1824   Dockets, 1720–1722, 1726–1731, 1733–1735, 1740–1746, 1749, 1751–1759, 1763–1764, 21v

Dockets, 1738, 1767–1771, 1776, 1779, 1783, 1785–1788, 1790–1799, 1805, 1808, 1816, 1822–1824, 78v

Dockets, c. 1790–1805, c. 30v

Files, 1709–1855   Civil, 1730–1774, 1776–1817, 436 metal cases

Civil, 1806–1819, 1832, 5 boxes

Depositions, 1692–1766

Executions, 1709–1855, 83 boxes

Non-Entries, 1730–1855, 13 boxes

Writs, 1770–1822, 116 boxes

Records, 1692–1855   Partitions, 1782–1832, 1837–1855, 5v

Records, 1692–1701, 1706–1715, 6v

Records, 1701–1706, 1715–1718, 1720–1722, 1724–1751, 1776, 1780, 1782–1791, 1793–1855, 250v (Index, 1852–1855, 1v)

Worcester County—Founded: 1731

Court of General Sessions of the Peace

Minutes, 1777–1803   Minutes, 1777–1780, 1782–1785, 1792–1799, 1801–1803, 38v (includes CCP)

Files, 1776–1827   Files, 1776–1827, 51 metal cases

Records, 1731–1827   Records, 1731–1827, 9v

Court of Common Pleas

Dockets, 1777–1859   Civil, 1777–1780, 1782–1785, 1792–1799, 1801–1803, 1851–1852, 53v (includes Sessions)

	Civil, 1781–1783, 1855–1859, 27v
	Civil, 1785–1792, 1794–1796, 1798–1801, 1803–1804; Civil and Criminal, 1804–1826, 1828–1831, 1833–1834; Civil, 1837–1844, 1846–1850, 1853–1854, 251v
Files, 1731–1859	Civil, 1731–1859, 827 metal cases
	Civil, 1735–1804; Criminal, 1804–1859, 70 metal cases and 14 bundles
Records, 1731–1859	Appeals, 1785–1806, 1v
	Civil 1731–1804; Civil and Criminal, 1804–1835; Civil, 1835–1859, 131v
	Civil, 1779–1782, 1v
	Executions, 1744–1792, 2v

Vital Records

Marriages, 1746–1796, 2v

CATHERINE S. MENAND

A "magistracy fit and necessary":
A Guide to the Massachusetts Court System

T HE course of colonial history in Massachusetts was marked by a consistent concern for establishing legal authority and the rule of law. George Haskins has pointed out that one of the first acts of the Massachusetts Bay Company's officers in the new settlement was to grant to some of their members the powers of justices of the peace. Within a few years, the three-tier hierarchy of courts, which still exists, was established.[1] The full panoply of judicial administration was slower to emerge, as conflicts over equity and probate jurisdiction were resolved, but nonetheless the judicial history of Massachusetts has been an unbroken evolution.

Each step in creating the court structure in Massachusetts has been based on specific legal authority and enactment; the history of the judiciary can, and should, be traced from the establishing act through subsequent enabling statutes. The initial authority for erecting courts in the colony was cited by the General Court at its meeting in London on 30 April 1629. It was that passage in the charter which empowered the company to settle the "forms and ceremonies of government and magistracy fit and necessary" and allowed for the "imposition of lawful fines, mulcts, imprisonment, or other lawful correction" to the end that the colony might be "religiously, peaceably, and civilly governed."[2] The first meeting of the Court of Assistants in the colony, on 23 August 1630, ordered that "in all civil actions, the first process or summons by the beadle or his deputy shall be directed by . . . a justice of the peace; the next process to be a capias [indictment] or distringas [distrain], at the discretion of the Court."[3] Thus, not only was the colony never without legal of-

[1] See in this volume George Haskins, "Lay Judges, Magistrates, and Justices in Early Massachusetts," above 44–45, and Michael Hindus, "A Guide to the Court Records of Early Massachusetts," above, 520.

[2] Charter, Massachusetts Records, I, 16 and 17, spelling modernized.

[3] Massachusetts Records, I, 73.

ficers, it was never without institutions to impose the rule of law and procedures to administer justice.[4] Courts of record sat to hear civil and criminal causes from the first, and at no time did the religious authority of the Puritan theocracy replace the secular rule of English law.[5]

County courts were established in 1636, with a bench composed of magistrates of the county sitting together. They heard civil causes under ten pounds and criminal causes not subject to the original jurisdiction of the General Court, which were all cases not involving life, member, or banishment. Appeal from the county courts lay to the Court of Assistants.[6] These same magistrates, sitting singly in their towns, heard civil causes under twenty shillings and minor criminal causes. After 1638 they were augmented by commissioners, invested with "like power," who sat in panels of three, with two a quorum.[7] Divorce cases were heard in the county courts, with appeal to the Court of Assistants. Probate, too, was in the county courts, and inquests on deaths were held before a magistrate with a jury.

A Strangers' Court, for the "speedy dispatch of all causes" involving transients who could not stay for the ordinary courts, was established in 1639. After 1650 strangers were allowed to sue in any court, and the special court fell into disuse.[8] Equity was judged upon application to the General Court until 1685 when, "for ease," it was transferred to the county courts, which were "empowered as a court

[4] The titles of recent studies emphasize law and authority, tending to obscure the importance of the court structure itself. For example, while Thomas Konig offers a fine discussion of the county courts, his title is *Law and Society in Puritan Massachusetts* (Chapel Hill, 1979). His bibliography lists Thomas Barnes, "Law and Liberty (and Order) in Early Massachusetts," (1975), George Haskins, *Law and Authority in Early Massachusetts* (1960), and Edwin Powers, *Crime and Punishment in Early Massachusetts* (1966). The seventeenth-century judicial system has been more heavily studied than the eighteenth; Joseph Smith's introduction to *Justice in Western Massachusetts* (Cambridge, Mass., 1961), which provides an excellent outline of the courts, ends at 1692.

[5] Descriptions, such as in P. S. Reinsch, *English Common Law in the Early American Colonies* (1899), of a legal system resembling a Biblical patriarchy have been revised by historians examining statutes and court records.

[6] Massachusetts Records, I, 169. Before counties were established in 1643, these courts were also called Inferior Quarter Courts.

[7] Ibid., I, 239.

[8] Ibid., I, 264. John Noble, "Notes on Strangers' Courts," Colonial Society of Massachusetts, *Publications*, VI, 283, says special courts were eliminated in 1672.

of chancery."[9] This was the court structure under the first charter.

The brief Dominion period which followed disrupted many things in the public life of Massachusetts, but had little impact on court organization in the lower tiers. The elected magistrates became appointed justices of the peace and the county courts continued much as before. The General Court was, of course, abolished, and its legislative functions exercised by the Governor and Council.[1] The Superior Court of Judicature, established in 1687, became the highest court.[2]

The second charter, in 1692, transformed the colony into a royal province and gave the legislature authority to establish courts. This authority had limits, however, for the first three comprehensive judiciary acts were disallowed by the Privy Council.[3] Statutes passed in 1699–1700 replaced the county courts with courts of general sessions of the peace for criminal causes and courts of common pleas for civil; the Superior Court of Judicature was continued as an appellate court. Justices of the peace continued to administer justice at the local level, with appeal lying to the inferior courts of sessions and common pleas.[4]

The Governor and Council were given power over probate by the 1692 charter, but they appointed a judge of probate to sit in each county and heard only appeals.[5] Equity was heard in common pleas. Coroners courts were established and reported to general sessions.[6]

The Constitution changed the name of the Superior Court of Judicature to the Supreme Judicial Court, but structurally nothing

[9] Massachusetts Records, V, 477.

[1] Dudley Commission 8 October 1685 (in Colonial Society of Massachusetts *Collections*, II, 39).

[2] Council Minutes 1 March 1687. After the Revolution the Superior Court of Judicature became the Supreme Judicial Court (Statute 1780, chapter c. 17). The 1780 Constitution expressly stated the separation of legislative, executive, and judicial branches.

[3] Province Laws 1692, chapter 33; 1692–1693, chapter 9; and 1697, chapter 9 were all disallowed. Stanley Katz, "The Politics of Law in Colonial America," *Perspectives*, V (1971), ascribes the reason to the Privy Council's view that equity courts were the prerogative of the crown and not to be established by legislatures.

[4] Province Laws 1699–1700, chapter 1 (general sessions); chapter 2 (common pleas); chapter 3 (Superior Court).

[5] Charter in Colonial Society of Massachusetts *Collections*, II, 23.

[6] Province Laws 1700–1701, chapter 3.

else. The same court system continued into the nineteenth century.

Research in court records should be guided by the original statutes defining the jurisdictions and procedures of each court and by the succeeding legislative acts which redefined that court's authority.[7] Times and places of sittings, as well as court fees, were set by the legislature. Even the authorized text for court forms can be found in the printed Acts and Resolves. No matter how reliable secondary sources may be, they are no substitute for information on actual court jurisdictions and powers set out in the statutes themselves.

The following list of the Massachusetts courts, grouped by jurisdiction and citing each establishing statute, illustrates an evolutionary history that flows without interruption from the first days of settlement. Massachusetts court records over the years show old writ headings crossed out and new ones penned in and docket books economically filled up, with only the names changing as the business of administering justice in Massachusetts proceeds through its fourth century.

50. Section of Writ of Attachment, 25 June 1776, Inferior Court of Common Pleas, Suffolk. It shows George III's title crossed out and replaced with "The Government and People of the Massachusetts Bay in New England." This, and similar writs, were issued before the signing of the Declaration of Independence on 4 July 1776. See above, 487. Courtesy, Social Law Library, Boston.

---

[7] A word of caution: references to the administrative authority of general sessions, for example, before these duties were assumed by county commissioners in 1827, are scattered throughout legislation on such subjects as elections, taxation, poor relief, and the incorporation of new towns. Researchers would need to conduct a wider search than the single index heading of the court's name in the laws.

THE MASSACHUSETTS COURTS
Underlined courts are still in operation as courts

APPELLATE COURTS

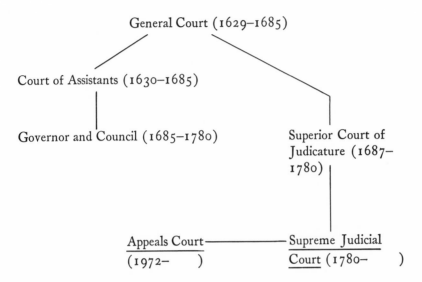

General Court (1629–1685)

Court of Assistants (1630–1685)

Governor and Council (1685–1780)

Superior Court of Judicature (1687–1780)

Appeals Court (1972–   )

Supreme Judicial Court (1780–   )

General Court: Charter of 1692
Court of Assistants: Records 23 August 1630
Governor and Council: Dudley's Commission 8 October 1685
Superior Court: Council Minutes 1 March 1687
Supreme Court: Constitution, Chapter III; St. 1780, c. 17
Appeals Court: St. 1972, c. 740

TRIAL COURTS

SUPERIOR COURT DEPARTMENT

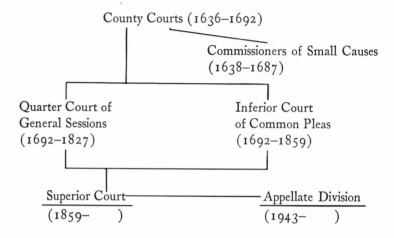

County Courts (1636–1692)

Commissioners of Small Causes
(1638–1687)

Quarter Court of
General Sessions
(1692–1827)

Inferior Court
of Common Pleas
(1692–1859)

Superior Court
(1859–   )

Appellate Division
(1943–   )

County Court: Colony Laws 3 March 1636
Commissioners: Colony Laws 6 September 1638
Sessions: Province Laws 1699–1700, c. 1
Common Pleas: Province Laws 1699–1700, c. 2
Superior: St. 1859, c. 196
Appellate: St. 1943, c. 588, § 1

DISTRICT COURT DEPARTMENT

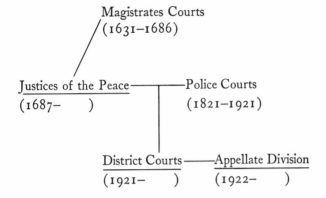

Magistrates: Colony Laws 14 June 1631
Justices: Council Minutes 3 March 1687
Police: St. 1821, c. 109
District: St. 1921, c. 430
Appellate: St. 1922, c. 532, § 8

BOSTON MUNICIPAL COURT DEPARTMENT

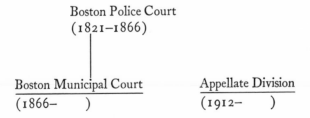

Boston Police: St. 1821, c. 109
Boston Municipal: St. 1866, c. 279
Appellate: St. 1912, c. 649, § 8

SPECIAL COURTS

Strangers Court (1639–1672)
Coroners Court (1700–1877)
Admiralty Court (1685–1775)

Strangers: Colony Laws 6 June 1639
Coroners: Province Laws 1700–1701, c. 3
Admiralty: Dudley's Commission 13 November 1685

PROBATE AND FAMILY COURT DEPARTMENT

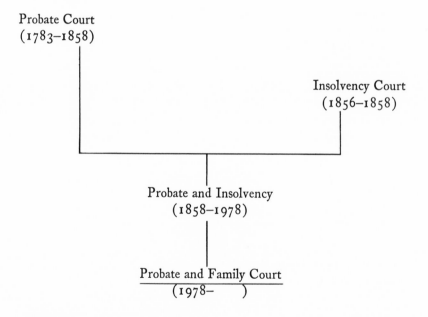

Probate Court
(1783–1858)

Insolvency Court
(1856–1858)

Probate and Insolvency
(1858–1978)

Probate and Family Court
(1978–   )

Probate: St. 1783, c. 46, § 1–2
Insolvency: St. 1856, c. 284, § 1
Probate and Insolvency: St. 1858, c. 93
Probate and Family: St. 1978, c. 478, § 128

JUVENILE COURT DEPARTMENT

Boston (1906–   )
Springfield (1969–   )   elsewhere handled
Worcester (1969–   )   by District Courts
New Bedford (1972–   )

Boston: St. 1906, c. 489
Springfield: St. 1969, c. 859
Worcester: St. 1969, c. 859
New Bedford: St. 1972, c. 731

LAND COURT DEPARTMENT

Land Court (1898–   )

Land Court: St. 1898, c. 562

HOUSING COURT DEPARTMENT

Boston (1971–   )
Hampden (1973–   )

Boston: St. 1971, c. 843
Hampden: St. 1973, c. 591

Sources for Study

SOURCES FOR THE STUDY OF LAW IN COLONIAL MASSACHUSETTS AT THE AMERICAN ANTIQUARIAN SOCIETY, WORCESTER, MASSACHUSETTS

By Kathleen A. Major

The American Antiquarian Society is a learned society founded by Isaiah Thomas in 1812 in Worcester, Massachusetts. The third oldest historical society in the country, it is the first to be national rather than regional in its purposes and in the scope of its collections. The library contains twenty miles of bookshelves on which are preserved more than 600,000 volumes, an equal number of manuscripts, maps, engravings, broadsides and prints, and two million seventeenth-, eighteenth-, and nineteenth-century American newspapers. The American Antiquarian Society holds two-thirds of the total pieces known to have been printed in this country between 1640 and 1821 and possesses useful source materials and reference works printed since that period.

The card catalogue of the Society's collection of manuscripts has been published in a four-volume set: *Catalogue of the Manuscript Collections of the American Antiquarian Society* (Boston: G. K. Hall & Company, 1979). The printed catalogue in turn acts as a comprehensive index to the more detailed, unpublished collection descriptions filed in the manuscripts department and in the main reading room.

For an inquiry into the development of law in colonial Massachusetts, the manuscript holdings of the American Antiquarian Society can be best divided into four categories: (1) Lawyers' Papers, (2) Justice of the Peace Records, (3) Court Records, and (4) Town Records. The Society's holdings of early Lawyers' Papers are limited, but noteworthy. The first lawyer in the colony was Thomas Lechford, whose notebook, 1638–1641, is located in the Society's manuscripts department. (See Thomas G. Barnes, "Thomas Lechford and the Earliest Lawyering in Massachusetts, 1638–1641," above, 3–38.) Lechford became a controversial figure. After he was censured in 1639 for attempting to influence a jury outside the court, he returned to England, where he published *Plain Dealing: or Newes from New-England*. Lechford's notebook is a detailed record of every legal document and/or transaction drawn by him in Boston. He also included accounts of compensation he received for his work. The records reveal much concerning seventeenth-century New England political and legal history. The notebook has been published in the *Transactions and Collections of the American Antiquarian Society*, vol. 8 (1885).

Two other manuscript collections may be placed in the category of Lawyers' Papers. Although John Winthrop (1587/88–1649) and Samuel Tompson (1630–1695) were not strictly speaking members of that profession, their manuscripts are representative of the type of work that is often performed by counsel today. Governor Winthrop certainly influenced the development of law in seventeenth-century Massachusetts Bay. The Winthrop manuscript, dated 1642, is apparently a contemporary copy of Governor Winthrop's brief in the famous Sow Case of 1642, which led to the establishment of a bicameral colonial legislature in 1644. The manuscript details Winthrop's support of the magistrates in the case and includes a history or "breaveate" of the case and the general opinion of the court. It has been published in the *Proceedings of the American Antiquarian Society*, vol. 30 (1920).

The notebook, 1678–1695, of Samuel Tompson of Braintree, Massachusetts, is entitled "Magnum Parvo; or, the Pen's Perfection," and contains instructions for the preparation of legal forms, such as bonds, subpoenas, bills, and wills, and several copies of legal documents, such as bills of sale and articles of agreement.

The manuscript records of justices of the peace reflect the responsibilities and powers of colonial judges in Massachusetts. The Society's holdings include "Justice of the Peace Records" for Suffolk County, 1731–1763. These contain notes on forms and precedents relating to the office and duty of the magistrates, and papers of a wealthy Charlestown merchant, Joseph Lemmon (1692–1750), who served as Justice of the Peace in Middlesex County, land deeds, summonses, and other legal documents issued by Lemmon, 1708–1767. The "Justice of the Peace Records" also include the account book, 1758–1802, of Leominster merchant Thomas Legate (1735–1807) containing entries concerning his duties as Justice of the Peace, such as debtor records, fees paid for his magisterial services, and marriages performed; and several papers, 1750–1777, of Jedediah Foster (1726–1779) in the Foster Family Papers. The Foster Papers document his position as Justice of the Peace in Brookfield and include business letters, warrants, and writs issued by him.

Colonial Court Records include (a) those legal documents that are found in many collections of family papers, such as wills, land deeds, court summonses, petitions, powers of attorney, and the like; and (b) actual court logs. The American Antiquarian Society possesses, as an example of the latter, the Hampshire County Court Records, 1677–1696. These two volumes document the probating of wills and court trials for a wide variety of offenses, both civil and criminal. The Worcester County Papers also contain judicial records for 1731 to 1775, including warrants, declarations of indebtedness and examinations of the poor, criminal indictments, summonses, petitions, probate records, writs of attachment, court orders, jury lists, transcripts of court testimony, and colonial jail records for the period 1748 to 1775.

Family collections also provide information relating to courtroom law in colonial Massachusetts. Examples are the Lincoln Family Papers, 1731–1937, and the Thayer Family Papers, 1735–1836. William Lincoln (1801–1843), noted Worcester lawyer, historian, and librarian, collected four volumes of material, 1731–1840, relating to the judicial process, including a volume of memoranda, 1731–1743, from the records of the Worcester County Court of General Sessions, and three volumes of miscellaneous legal papers, 1750–1840, such as briefs and case studies. The Thayer family of Mendon included members who appear to have participated often in the judicial process through lawsuits, receipts of debt settlements, wills, and land deeds. There are other collections of family papers in the manuscripts department that contain similar material. These have not been necessarily catalogued under the usual legal history subject headings in the published catalogue because of the broad scope and content of those collections.

The fourth category is "Town Records." Their value lies in the information they provide concerning the quasi-judicial function that town officials often exercised. In the Worcester, Massachusetts Collection, 1686–1775, are records that deal with the poor laws, license records, vital records, and other forms of colonial regulation. The Shrewsbury, Massachusetts Papers, 1723–1877, include court summonses and arrest warrants, while many other manuscript collections of local records contain similar legal material, as well as occasional records of proprietors' meetings. Among these are the papers of Sudbury, 1642–1834; Sutton, c. 1683–c. 1868; Shutesbury, 1742–1781; and Brookfield, 1673–1860. For more information concerning the Society's holdings in all of these areas, the researcher should consult the published manuscripts catalogue under the subject headings: "Court Records," "Local Records," "Law," and "Lawyers."

SOURCES FOR THE STUDY OF LAW IN COLONIAL MASSACHUSETTS AT THE ESSEX INSTITUTE, SALEM, MASSACHUSETTS

By Caroline Preston

The Essex Institute, originally founded as the Essex Historical Society in 1821, is one of the oldest and largest independent historical societies in the United States. The primary focus of the Essex Institute is the history and culture of Essex County, Massachusetts. The Institute's library contains approximately 300,000 books, pamphlets, broadsides, and maps, as well as 4,000 linear feet of manuscripts.

The Essex Institute has a substantial quantity of manuscript material pertaining to the development of law in colonial Massachusetts. These can be divided into four categories: 1. Court Records; 2. Justice of the Peace Records; 3. Notary Public Records; and 4. Lawyers' and Judges' Records.

I. Court Records*

In 1980 the Essex County Superior Court temporarily deposited all pre-1800 court records at the Essex Institute. These include the Norfolk County Court Records, 1648–1680; the Essex County Court Records, 1636–1694; the documents of the 1692 Court of Oyer and Terminer; the records of the Essex Court of General Sessions of the Peace, 1692–1827; and the Essex Court of Common Pleas Records, 1692–1800.

1. County Court (Norfolk County)

Old Norfolk County was defined in 1643 as the area north of the Merrimac River. It included Haverhill and Salisbury in Massachusetts and Hampton, Exeter, Portsmouth, and Dover in New Hampshire. The county was divided into two Court jurisdictions; Dover and Portsmouth formed one and the other towns formed the other, with Salisbury as the shire town. In 1680 the four northern towns joined the royal province of New Hampshire, and the towns of Haverhill and Salisbury were added to

---

* [These court records were deposited at the Essex Institute under an agreement with the Supreme Judicial Court and remain under the control of the Court and of the Clerk of Courts for Essex County. Except for the witchcraft trial records, which are on permanent deposit at the Institute, by late 1985 it is anticipated that these records will be moved to the State Archives building now under construction at Columbia Point, Boston, as part of a new judicial archives which will contain all pre-1860 court records. FSA, Jr., DRC.]

Essex County. The records on deposit at the Institute are those from the southern jurisdiction. The old Norfolk records contain two records volumes, 1648–1680, and one box of court file papers, 1654–1679. Transcriptions of the Norfolk records volumes were included in *Records and Files of the Quarterly Court of Essex County, Massachusetts, 1636–1686*, ed. George Francis Dow.

2. *County Court (Essex County)*

The 15 County Court records volumes cover the period from the Court's inception in 1636 to its dissolution in 1692. There also are 57 boxes of file papers which include presentments, depositions, correspondence, deeds, wills, inventories of estates, contracts, apprentice indentures, inquests, writs, and executions. Transcriptions of the records books were compiled in *Records and Files of the Quarterly Court of Essex County, Massachusetts, 1636–1686*, which was edited by George Francis Dow, and published by the Essex Institute in 9 volumes. The file papers were transcribed and indexed by the W.P.A. in the 1930's. This 54-volume set of unpublished typescripts is also on deposit at the Institute.

3. *Court of Oyer and Terminer*

By far the most significant early court records at the Institute are the legal documents of the Court of Oyer and Terminer, the special court formed in 1692 to hear the Salem witchcraft trials. The Essex County Superior Court placed 527 witchcraft documents on permanent deposit at the Institute in 1980. The documents include declarations, arrest warrants, indictments, examinations of the afflicted and the accused, summonses, mittimuses (writs instructing jailers to hold prisoners), and a single death warrant. Transcriptions of all extant Salem witchcraft documents in the possession of the Essex Institute and other repositories were published in *The Salem Witchcraft Papers: Verbatim Transcripts of the Legal Documents of the Salem Witchcraft Outbreak of 1692*, Vols. 1–3, edited by Paul Boyer and Stephen Nissenbaum (New York, 1977).

4. *Court of General Sessions of the Peace*

In 1692 the Court of General Sessions of the Peace was formed to handle criminal and administrative business. The General Session Courts were superseded by 1827 and replaced by the County Commissioners. The Essex County records consist of 13 record volumes, 1692–1795, 22 boxes of file papers, 1701–1795, and 14 boxes of administrative papers, 1792–1862.

5. *Court of Common Pleas*

The Inferior Court of Common Pleas was formed in 1692 to hear civil cases. The Essex County Common Pleas records contain 21 docket books, 1721–1800; 19 extended records volumes, 1686–1800; 200 boxes of file papers, 1693–1799; and approximately 220 boxes of non-entered writs and miscellaneous material.

II. JUSTICE OF THE PEACE RECORDS

The Essex Institute has the records of numerous Essex County justices of the peace dating from the colonial and early federal period. These are: Thomas Bancroft, J. P. Records, 1776–1803; Joseph Bowditch, J. P. Salem, Records, 1753–1762; Edward Bowen, J. P. Marblehead, Records, 1790–1795; Nathan Bowen, J. P. Marblehead, Records, 1782–1817; John Choate, J. P. Ipswich, Records, 1788; A. C. Cleaveland, J. P. Topsfield, Records, 1788–1790; Samuel Curwen, J. P. Salem, Records, 1756–1773; Nathaniel Lovejoy, J. P. Andover, Records, 1787–1795, 1797–1800; Isaac Mansfield, J. P. Marblehead, Records, 1787–1799; Nathaniel Marsh, J. P. Salem, Records, 1796–1800; Daniel Noyes, J. P. Ipswich, Records, 1787–1793; Isaac Osgood, J. P., Records, 1788–1795; John Perkins, J. P. Lynnfield, Records, 1787–1788; Edward Pullin, J. P. Salem, Records, 1786–1790; William Pynchon, J. P. Salem, Records, 1746–1789; Ichabod Tucker, J. P. Salem, Records, 1787–1812; and unidentified J. P., Records, 1776–1784, 1787–1789.

III. NOTARY PUBLIC RECORDS

Two early volumes of Salem Notary Records primarily concern marine protests and contain descriptions of shipwrecks and other disasters at sea. Volume 1, covering the period 1696 to 1722, was kept by Salem notary Stephen Sewall. Volume 2, covering the period 1723 to 1769, was kept by notaries Samuel Sewall, 1723–1725; Mitchell Sewall, 1727–1748; James Jeffrey, 1749–1754; and Jonathan Notting, 1757–1769. Transcriptions of the early Salem Notary volumes were published in the *Essex Institute Historical Collections*, Volumes 42–48.

IV. LAWYERS' AND JUDGES' RECORDS

The Curwen Family Papers contain one folder of records of Judge Jonathan Curwen (1640–1718). Curwen was a Justice of the Court of Common Pleas, 1690–1708; Judge of Probate, 1698–1702; and

Judge in the 1692 Court of Oyer and Terminer. The legal papers reflect his tenure as a Judge in Salem and include depositions from Salem residents and a 17 January 1692 letter from Reverend Samuel Parris concerning a parishioner's loss of estate. The Bowen Family Papers include one volume of Court of Common Pleas minutes, 1762–1767, kept by Nathaniel Bowen, Sr., of Marblehead. The Nathaniel Peaslee Sargeant (1731–1791) Papers record the legal activities of the second Chief Justice of the Supreme Court of Massachusetts. The one-box collection contains court minutes, 1770–1794, for the Superior Courts at Springfield, Boston, Barnstable, Ipswich, and Worcester, and legal notebooks and notes.

The Institute has one box of the papers of Beverly lawyer Nathan Dane (1752–1835). The collection contains a book of executions, 1782–1817; a ledger, 1825–1834; and two office day books, 1800–1823.

John Prince (1782–1848) was a clerk for the Essex County Courts, a notary public, a justice of the peace, and an attorney active in Salem. The John Prince Collection contains 7 boxes of professional case files, 1770–1825, which concern administration of estates, cases of debt, bankruptcy, and spoliation cases. Prince's professional papers contain legal correspondence, case notes, and background material relating to legal cases.

SOURCES FOR THE STUDY OF LAW IN COLONIAL MASSACHUSETTS AT THE HARVARD LAW SCHOOL CAMBRIDGE, MASSACHUSETTS

By Edith G. Henderson

The Harvard Law Library, located in Langdell Hall, Cambridge, has an unusually full collection of seventeenth- and eighteenth-century legal materials, both English and American. In general, English imprints up to 1700 and American imprints to 1820 are housed in the Treasure Room, while most eighteenth-century English imprints are kept in other closed stack areas.

Statutes

A useful starting point for research is the collection *Charters and General Laws of the Colony and Province of Massachusetts Bay*. It was edited by Nathan Dane, Joseph Story, and William Prescott, and published in Boston in 1814. This was an official compilation based on public records and early printed books, with a brief but useful statement of method in the preface. Dates were given for each act or provision where possible. After 1692 the collection appears to be a complete reprint of the session laws, year by year through 1779. There is an index and an appendix, the appendix containing more statutory matter whose relation to the main body of the book is not entirely clear.

Other statutory compilations:

The only known copy of *The Capitall Lawes of New-England,* a broadside reprinted in London, 1643, from an original printing "first in New England." It seems highly unlikely that some of these "laws" were ever enforced, and the whole work seems more like some good Puritan's notion of what the laws ought to be than actual legislation.

A photographic facsimile of the Huntingdon Library's unique *Book of The General Lawes and Libertyes Concerning The Inhabitants of the Massachusets* (Cambridge, Mass., 1648.)

The Book Of The General Lawes and Libertyes (Cambridge, Mass., 1660, also the revision of 1672 as printed in Cambridge, Mass., 1672, and London, 1675.)

Laws of the Dominion of New England, 1686, a pamphlet, reprinted in Concord, N. H., 1928, from the only known copy of the original edition. It deals largely with the judiciary.

Book of the General Laws for New Plymouth, 1672 (facsimile) and 1685.

Acts and Laws, 1699, 1710, 1721, 1726, 1759, 1781. *Perpetual Laws to 1788* (Worcester, Isaiah Thomas). These give the impression that they were compiled on the "statutes now in force" principle, and so are useful only for years close to their publication dates.

We have also the *Whitmore* compilations of colonial laws from 1660 to 1686 (Boston, 1889.)

Charters are generally printed at the beginning of compilations of statutes. We have also the 1780 constitution: The *Debates* on its adoption are in the "open" stacks in an 1832 reprint.

Session laws (published year by year as the General Court met): Our collection is fairly full from 1661 to 1680 and 1699 to 1774 as well as for later years, but there are some gaps. We have also a series of Massachusetts *Resolves,* from 1776 to 1806, a series of *Temporary Acts,* 1743 to 1774, and a few volumes of collected *Tax Acts.*

Miscellaneous legislative and governmental material:

Collection of the Proceedings of the Great and General Court, 1729.

Massachusetts Bay, Council. *Proclamation for Proroguing the General Court* (25 Sept., 1757) (broadside.)

Conference between the Commissaries of Massachusetts-Bay and the Commissaries of New-York at New-Haven, 1767.

Proceedings of the Council and the House of Representatives, 1770 (relative to having the House meet outside Boston, for example, in Cambridge.)

Continuation of the Proceedings of the House of Representatives, 1770 (likewise.)

Case Law

As is well known, it is more difficult to find American case law before 1800 than English cases of the thirteenth century. We have (in the Treasure Room, unless otherwise stated):

Josiah Quincy, Jr.'s *Reports of Cases Argued and Adjudged in the Superior Court,* covering cases 1761–1772, printed Boston, 1865, including some grand jury charges and a learned appendix attributed to Horace Gray, J., on the Writs of Assistance.

The Legal Papers of John Adams, 3 vols., edited by Kinvin Wroth and Hiller Zobel, Boston, 1965, on the "open" shelves.

The Pynchon Manuscript, a notebook kept by William Pynchon and others as Justices of the Peace in Springfield, about 1639–1690. This was edited by Joseph H. Smith and printed under the title *Colonial Justice in Western Massachusetts (1639–1702): The Pynchon Court Record* (Cambridge, 1961.)

Notebook of Nathaniel Blagrove, probate judge in Bristol County, with notes of cases from 1733 to 1737. The individual notes are very brief, little more than listings.

The (William) Cushing Manuscript of cases heard in the Supreme Judicial Court from 1772 to 1789.

Photographic copies of the original papers for cases heard in the Middlesex County Court, 4 vols., approximately 1649–1664. These copies were made when the papers had been neatly pasted into books as a WPA project; they are numbered and the arrangement is roughly chronological, but there is no index or table of contents.

A small group of bills of lading for shipments from London to Boston, 1766 to 1771. (These are printed forms, bound into a little book.)

Extracts of leases from the Selectmen of Boston, 1678 (manuscript.)

Bridgman, Sarah, Testimonys Taken on Behalf of Sarah, the Wife of James Bridgman of Northampton (11 August 1656) (manuscript). (This includes the testimony of several people, including "Goodwyfe Bridgman," as to the acts of one Mary Parsons, accused of witchcraft and tried in Springfield.)

Parsons, Theophilus, Office Book; Docket. (1774–1800) (manuscript.) (This is a list of court cases for each court term during the period in question.)

———, *Precedents*. (Top right of first page dated Sept. 1775) (manuscript.) (These are samples of the forms necessary for bringing various causes of action.)

Trials

The Harvard Law School Library has quite a large collection of individually printed trials. Those printed in this country before 1820 are in the

Treasure Room, together with the English imprints before 1700. Not many of them relate to Massachusetts, but if the defendant's name is known, and it is a trial that might have been printed, it could be worth investigating. The following is an attempt at a complete list for Massachusetts before 1800. We have rather more for 1800–1820.

The trial of William Wemms, James Hartegan, William McCauley, Hugh White, Mathew Killroy, William Warren, John Carrol, Hugh Montgomery, Soldiers in His Majesty's 29th Regiment of Foot for the Murder of Crispus Attucks, Samuel Gray, Samuel Maverick, James Caldwell, and Patrick Carr. (Boston, 1770.) (These are the "Boston Massacre Trials." John Adams and Josiah Quincy, Jr., represented the defendants. Quincy's brother, Samuel Quincy, appeared with Robert Treat Paine for the Crown.)

The state of the action brought by William Fletcher against William Vassall, for defaming him. Tried in the Superior Court at Boston August term, A.D. 1752 and now pending by Appeal to his Majesty in Council. (Boston, 1753.) (A collection of documents concerning an action of trespass on the case for defamation, with a preface by the plaintiff. James Otis appeared for the defense, while his father "Colonel" Otis represented the plaintiff.)

Flagg, James, *A short vindication of the conduct of the referees in the case of Gardiner versus Flagg, against the unjust aspersions contained in two anonymous pamphlets lately published and handed about.* (Boston, 1767.) (This is an interesting account of litigation growing out of the rental and maintenance of a mill dam owned by Dr. Sylvester Gardiner. It is significant both for the use of other businessmen as referees to settle the dispute, and the use of pamphlets to gain public support for each side.)

Chisholm v. *Georgia.* (Boston, 1793.) (This account of the famous case on whether a state could be sued by a private citizen of another state was printed for the Massachusetts legislature at its direction.)

The interesting trials of the pirates, for the murder of William Little, Captain of the ship American Eagle. (Newburyport, 1796.) (This was an Admiralty trial held at the Old Bailey. The ship was an American vessel.)

The proceedings of a general court martial, held at Cambridge, on Tuesday the Twentieth of January, and continued by several adjournments to Wednesday the 25th of February, 1778. Upon the trial of

Colonel David Henley. (Boston, 1778.) (These were court martial proceedings against an American officer for mistreatment of British prisoners.)

Trial of Jeremiah Hill, Esq. for heresy, before the Church of Christ in Biddeford May 2, 1793. (There is no place or date of printing. This was not a judicial proceeding, but a meeting of the "Association" of the Church of Christ.)

A narrative of the Life and conversion of Alexander White, Aet. 23. who was executed at Cambridge, November 18, 1784 for the murder of a Captain White, at sea. (Boston, 1785.) (This is not an account of a trial, but rather of the religious conversion and repentance of the defendant while awaiting trial. One paragraph describes the defendant's confession at trial.)

Treatises

The Treasure Room is famous for its collection of sixteenth-century English legal treatises. It also has a very full collection of English and American legal treatises of the seventeenth and eighteenth centuries. Coke, Dalton, Matthew Hale, and Blackstone are merely examples of the well-known authors represented. If it concerns colonial law, the chances are very good that it is in the Treasure Room.

Editions printed in the United States before 1821, and in England before 1701, are kept in the Treasure Room, while eighteenth-century English editions, with a few exceptions, are in another closed area of the stacks.

Some Massachusetts Imprints (Other than Massachusetts Statutes and Trials) From 1620 to 1800. The list is intended to be complete up to 1774, but for later years it is not. The treatises are grouped by place of printing.

Boston, Massachusetts:

Boone, Nicholas, *Military discipline: the compleat solder*. (Boston, 2d ed., 1706.) (This is a guide to soldiering, with a section on the military law of Massachusetts Bay.)

————, *The constable's pocketbook, being a guide to their keeping the peace*. (Boston, 1710, 2d ed., 1727.) (This is a guide to constables in the form of a dialogue between an old and a new constable. It contains samples of warrant forms.)

Breton, William, *Militia Discipline*. (Boston, 1733.)

Dummer, Jeremiah, *Defense of the New England Charters.* (Boston, 1745, 1765.) (First printed in 1721, the defense is in response to attempts in Parliament to curtail the colonial charters.)

Whitefield, George, *A brief account of the occasion, process, and issue of a late trial at Gloucester, March 3, 1743, 4 between some of the people called Methodists Plaintiffs and certain persons of the Town of Minchin-Hampton, in said county, defendants.* (Boston, 1744.) (Reprinted from a London print, 1744.) (The Methodist plaintiffs were victims of riots and successfully sought redress in court. Whitefield, one of the most important Methodist preachers of his day and a leader in the Great Awakening, took part in the trial.)

Sever, Nicholas, *A speech on the occasion of Col. Lothrop's death, delivered at the opening of the Court of Common-Pleas at Plymouth, on the 15th of May 1750.* (Boston, 1750.) (Sever was Chief Justice of the Court of Common Pleas. Isaac Lothrop was justice of the same court. The book also contains a speech by Peter Oliver, another justice of the court and later chief justice.)

Mathew, Jonathan, *A discourse occasioned by the death of the honourable Stephen Sewall, Esq.* (Boston, 1760.) (Sewall was Chief Justice of the Superior Court of Judicature, Court of Assize, and General-Gaol-Delivery, and a member of His Majesty's Council for the Province of the Massachusetts-Bay in New England. The discourse is a eulogy with enlightening comparisons between Samuel Sewall and his Old Testament namesake.)

Observations on Several Acts of Parliament passed in the 4th, 6th, and 7th years [1763, 1766, 1767] *of his present Majesty's reign: and also on the conduct of the Officers of the customs, since those Acts were passed, and the Board of Commissioners appointed to reside in America. Published by the merchants of Boston.* (Boston, 1769.) (The Acts in question imposed duties and bonding requirements on the importation of goods.)

The County and Town Officer; or an Abridgment of the Laws of the Province of the Massachusetts. (Boston, 1768.)

Hawles, Sir John, *The Englishman's right, or a dialogue between a barrister at law and a jury man.* (Boston, 1772.) (The "right" mentioned is the right to trial by jury, and the tract is an attempt to educate the populace on how to be good jurors. There is also a 1798 Philadelphia printing which also contains Francis Bacon's "An Introductory essay on the moral duty of a judge." This tract was originally printed in London.)

Hutchinson, Thomas, *A collection of original papers relative to the history of the colony of Massachusetts-Bay*. (Boston, 1769.) (Contains various documents pertaining to the history of the colony, including "An abstract of the laws of New England," originally published in England in 1655. In the preface Hutchinson wrote: "He who rescues from oblivion interesting historical facts is beneficial to posterity as well as to his contemporaries and the prospect thereof to a benevolent mind causes that employment to be agreeable and pleasant which otherwise would be irksome and painful.")

————. *Speeches of his excellency Governor Hutchinson*. (Boston, 1773.)

Parsons, Theodore and Pearson, Eliphalet, *A forensic dispute on the legality of enslaving the Africans, held at the public Commencement in Cambridge, New-England, July 21st 1773 by two candidates for the Bachelor's degree*. (Boston, 1773.)

Eliot, Andrew, *Christ's promise to the penitent thief. A sermon preached the Lord's Day before the execution of Levi Ames, who suffered death for burglary, Oct. 21, 1773 Aet. 23*. (Boston, 1773.) (This sermon was delivered at the desire of the prisoner, who was present at the occasion.)

[Francis] Hargrave, *An argument in the case of James Sommerset, a Negro, largely determined by the Court of King's Bench: Where in it is attempted to demonstrate the present unlawfulness of domestic slavery in England*. (Boston, 1774.) (Originally printed in England. Sommerset was a slave from Virginia who had left his master's service in England and later was seized by men in the employ of his master, with the intention of taking him to Jamaica and selling him. Lord Mansfield granted a writ of habeas corpus and heard the case. Hargrave was one of Sommerset's counsel. Sommerset was discharged from the custody of his former master.)

French, Jonathan, *A practical discourse against extortion, from Ezekiel XII, 12*. Delivered at a lecture in the South Parish in Andover, 1 January 1777. (Boston, 1777.)

Backus, Isaac, *Government and Liberty described; and ecclesiastical tyranny exposed*. (Boston, 1778.)

The lawyer's promotion. To an excellent new tune. (n.p.n.d., ca. 1780.) (This is the story of a rich woman who persuades a lawyer to marry her. "Now he's cloathed in rich attire/Not inferior to a Squire./ Thus you see he raised his Fame,/But I can't relate his name.")

Warren, Mercy Otis, *Observations on the new constitution, and on the federal and state conventions.* (Boston, 1788.) (This was formerly ascribed to Elbridge Gerry.)

Freeman, Samuel, *The Massachusetts justice: being a collection of the laws of the Commonwealth of Massachusetts, relative to the power and duty of justices of the peace.* (Boston: Isaiah Thomas and Ebenezer Andrews, 1795.) (This also includes legal forms and rules for converting pounds, shillings, pence, and farthings into dollars and cents. There was a second edition in 1802, and a third edition in 1810.)

————, *The probate auxiliary: or director and assistant to probate courts, executors, administrators and guardians.* (Portland, Me., 1793.) (This contains sample forms. There was a second edition in 1806, and a third edition in 1812.)

————, *The town officer: or power and duty of selectmen, town clerks, town treasurers, etc., as contained in the laws of Massachusetts, with forms.* (Portland, Me., 1791.) (Subsequent editions were printed in Boston: 1793, 1794, 1799.)

————, *A valuable assistant to every man: or American clerk's magazine, containing the most useful forms.* (Boston, 1794.) (There was a second edition in 1795; third edition in 1797; and a fourth edition in 1800.)

Minot, George R., *Continuation of the history of the province of Massachusetts Bay (1748–65.)* (Boston, 1798–1803, 2 vols.)

Worcester, Massachusetts:

Jackson, Jonathan, *Thoughts upon the political situation of the United States—by a native of Boston.* (Worcester: Isaiah Thomas, 1788.)

Blackstone, Sir William, *Commentaries on the laws of England.* (Isaiah Thomas: Worcester, 1790.) (This work was the first edition of Blackstone's *Commentaries* published in Massachusetts. Equally interesting was its publisher, Isaiah Thomas. With only six weeks of formal education, Thomas eventually became one of the most important printers of his day. Thomas was a staunch opponent of the royal government. The British occupation of Boston in 1775 drove him from the city. In April of that year, he moved to Worcester. During the same month he joined Paul Revere and others in alarming the countryside, and fought as a minuteman at Lexington and Concord. Thomas' business prospered in Worcester. There were 150 employees, seven printing presses, a paper mill, and a bindery. Thomas founded the American Antiquarian Society in 1812.)

Montesquieu, Charles Louis de Secondat, baron, *The Spirit of Laws*. (Worcester: Isaiah Thomas, Jr., 1802.) (This is the first American edition, taken from the fifth London edition.)

Thomas, Isaiah, *History of Printing in America with a biography of printers*. (Worcester: Isaac Sturtevant, 1810.)

Portland, Maine:

Freeman, Samuel, *The town officer*. (Portland: Benjamin Titcomb, 1791.)

———, *The probate auxiliary*. (Benjamin Titcomb, Jr., 1793.)

———, *General directions to executors and administrators in the county of Cumberland*. (n.p., 1805.)

Raithby, John, *The study and practice of the law—By a member of Lincoln's Inn*. (Portland: T. B. Wait, 1806.)

Blackstone, Sir William, *Commentaries*. (Portland: T. B. Wait, 1807.)

Bath, Maine:

Luders, Alexander, *Tracts on various subjects in the law and history of England*. (Bath: Richard Cruttwell, 1810.)

Kennebunk, Maine:

Peirce, Charles, *The American citizen's sure guide*. (Kennebunk, Me., 1804.) (This was a compilation of documents, including the Declaration of Independence, the Articles of Confederation, and the United States Constitution.)

Historical records:

We have quite a respectable collection of the publications of various historical societies, including the Massachusetts Historical Society, the Colonial Society of Massachusetts, and the Essex Institute of Salem. Those volumes published by the Massachusetts Historical Society before 1820 are in the Treasure Room; the others are on "open" shelves.

SOURCES FOR THE STUDY OF LAW IN COLONIAL MASSACHUSETTS AT THE MASSACHUSETTS HISTORICAL SOCIETY

By John D. Cushing

Introduction

In its almost two hundred years of existence the Massachusetts Historical Society has amassed an impressive collection of source materials for the study of American history that has made it one of the leading repositories in the country. It has been estimated that there are ten million items in its manuscript collections, while its library, though not so astronomical in size, has an extraordinary collection of printed material with many items that are unique. The Society's holdings relevant to a study of law in colonial Massachusetts are extremely rich, in part because many members of the Society in its early years were judges, attorneys, and governmental officials, in part because members of the Society played a prominent part in collecting and publishing many of the great nineteenth-century documentary works dealing with the early history of Massachusetts.

While the Society's holdings of materials for the study of law in colonial Massachusetts represent only a small fraction of the total, they are nonetheless substantial—far too extensive to be listed by individual items here. During the period 1969–1980 the Society published nine large volumes (Boston: G. K. Hall) listing some four hundred thousand items in its manuscript collections, arranged alphabetically. Though this listing covers only the cream of the crop, so to speak, a student of law in colonial Massachusetts will find a careful examination of these volumes very rewarding. The Society has not published a similar listing of its printed material, but the card catalogue of its library is readily available to scholars.

A high point of the Colonial Society's Conference on Law in Colonial Massachusetts was a reception and exhibition held at the Massachusetts Historical Society in the late afternoon of the first day of the conference. The exhibition had been prepared by our fellow-member, John D. Cushing, Librarian at the Society. Included here are samples of some of the extraordinarily interesting titles that made up part of the exhibition, arranged under three headings—Legislature, Executive, and The Courts and The Bar. This will record one of the important parts of the Colonial Society's conference, and demonstrate the richness of the collections of the Massachusetts Historical Society. What follows, then, is a listing of the descriptions of some of the items exhibited for the conference, prepared by John Cushing and his staff.[1]

FREDERICK S. ALLIS, JR.

Legislature

An Abstract Or the Lavves of Nevv England, As they are novv established.

London, Printed for F. Coules, and W. Ley at Paules Chain, 1641.

This little book, attributed to John Cotton, was long thought to be the first compilation of Massachusetts laws. Modern scholarship has demonstrated that it never served that purpose, but may have been prepared by Cotton, ca. 1636–1639, when he and Nathaniel Ward were appointed by the General Court to draw up a body of fundamentals upon which a code of laws could be based. It has been assumed that one of Cotton's London correspondents received a copy of the manuscript, supposed it to be the law of the Bay colony, and had it printed. It was Ward's contribution, known as "The Body of Liberties," that served as the basis for the first compilation of Massachusetts laws in 1648.

An Abstract Of Laws and Government. Wherein as in a Mirrour may be seen the wisdome & perfection of the Government of Christs Kingdome . . . Collected and digested into the ensuing Method, by that Godly, Grave and Judicious Divine, Mr. John Cotton, of Boston in New-England, in his Life-time, and presented to the Generall Court of the Massachusets. And now published after his death, by William Aspinwall.

London, Printed by M.S. for Livewel Chapman, and are to be sold at the Crown in Popes-head Alley, 1655.

Aspinwall's edition of Cotton's *Abstract* confirmed the latter's authorship, and lamented that the work had not been adopted as the law of the Massachusetts colony. Aspinwall inserted numerous scriptural citations in support of various temporal laws, and thus enlarged the edition by 23 pages.

The Book of the General Lavves and Libertyes Concerning the Inhabitants of the Massachusets, Collected Out Of The Records Of The General Court, For the Several Years Wherein They Were Made And Established.

Cambridge, Printed according to Order of the General Court. 1660.

Until the discovery in 1909 of the still unique copy of the 1648 edition of

---

[1] Mr. Cushing wishes to acknowledge the assistance of Anne E. Bently, Catherine S. Craven, and Robert V. Sparks, all of the staff of the Massachusetts Historical Society, in the mounting of this exhibition.

the laws, this was considered to be the first plenary compilation of Massachusetts statute law. The title page contains a quotation from Romans XIII: "VVhosoever therefore resisteth the Power, resisteth the Ordinance of God, and they that resist, receive to themselves damnation." The passage was intended to support the discretionary, even arbitrary, power of the colony magistrates in administering justice.

The General Laws And Liberties of the Massachusetts Colony: Revised & Re-printed. . . .

Cambridge Printed by Samuel Green, for John Usher of Boston. 1672.

When the laws of 1660 and their supplements (of which no copies survive) became too cumbersome to use, the General Court appointed John Usher, of Boston, to see a revised edition through the press. Usher's compensation was a monopoly on the distribution and sale of the edition; thus it was the first book to be copyrighted in North America.

The Book of the General Laws of the Inhabitants of the Jurisdiction of New-Plimoth; Collected out of the Records of the General Court And lately revised, and with some Emendations and Additions, Established and Disposed into such Order as they may readily conduce to general use and benefit, And published by the Authority of the General Court for that Jurisdiction, held at Plimouth, the sixth of June, Anno Dom. 1671.

Cambridge: Printed By Samuel Green. 1672.

The first printed laws issued by the Plymouth settlement did not appear until the year that Massachusetts issued its third edition. Because the settlement was never granted a charter, the government was not always certain of the extent of its authority, as is attested by the use of the term "Jurisdiction of New-Plimouth," rather than the "colony" of New-Plimouth.

[Colony Seal.] *At A Council Held at Boston the 22d. of August 1678.* [A special tax act to provide for ransoming prisoners taken by the Indians.] Broadside.

[Cambridge: Samuel Green, 1678.]

The unique copy of this special tax act was once used as a wrapper for pamphlets, hence its battered appearance, with portions missing at the former fold.

The order made provision for defraying the expenses of a party appointed to ransom the captives taken by the Indians at Hatfield in September 1676. Because the order does not appear in the records of the General Court, this is the sole source of detailed information on the episode.

[Dominion Seal.] *A Proclamation By The President and Council For the Orderly Solemnization of Marriage.* Broadside.

Boston Printed by Richard Pierce, Printer to the Hounourable His Majecty's President & Council of His Majesties Teritory & Dominion of N-England. [1686.]

This broadside act was issued by the Dominion of New England after the revocation of the Massachusetts Colony charter, and was intended to make the "Solemnization of Marriage" more conformable to the practice of the Church of England, thus eroding the Puritan view of marriage as a civil contract. Very little of the legislation of the Dominion of New England was ever printed, and very little of that survives.

Acts And Laws, of Her Majesties Province of the Massachusetts-Bay in New-England.

Boston in New-England: Printed by B. Green, Printer to His Excellency the Governour & Council, for Benjamin Eliot and Sold at his Shop on the North side of King's Street. 1714.

This volume is representative of the various compilations of province laws that were issued at irregular intervals between 1692 and 1759.

Journal of the Honourable House of Representatives of His Majesty's Province of the Massachusetts-Bay in New-England, Begun and Held at Boston, on Wednesday the Twenty-Seventh Day of May, Anno Domini, 1724.

Boston: Printed by Bartholomew Green and Samuel Kneeland, Printers to the Hounourable House of Representatives. 1724.

The *Journal* records the day-to-day business conducted in the House, including votes, memorials, orders, and ordinary "housekeeping" activities. It was regularly published from 1715 to 1776, and was later resumed by the Commonwealth government.

The Committee of the General Court appointed the 21st of February last, to Receive and Consider any Scheme or Projection, for Retrieving the Value of Bills of Credit. . . . Broadside.

Boston, March 15. 1727,8.

This broadside appears to be the only surviving evidence of a scheme to provide the province with a circulating medium of exchange at a time when hard money was in short supply.

Acts & Laws, of His Majesty's Province of the Massachusetts-Bay in New-England.

Boston, in New-England: Printed by S. Kneeland, by Order of His Excellency the Governor, Council and House of Representatives. M,D,CC,LIX.

The 1759 edition of the province laws was the last plenary retrospective compilation to be issued before the outbreak of the American Revolution.

The County and Town Officer: Or An Abridgment of the Laws Of The Province of the Massachusets-Bay. . . . By a Gentleman.

Boston: Printed by T. and J. Fleet, and Sold at the Book-Store in Union-Street, 1768.

This 149-page manual was intended as a working guide for Justices of the Peace, Sheriffs, Selectmen, and a spate of other town and county officers. It abstracts from the statutes the duties of those officers, listed in alphabetical order, from Assay Masters to Wood Corders.

State Of Massachusetts-Bay. In the House of Representatives, February 6, 1777. Whereas there may be . . . an Omission to renew the Appointment of Committees of Correspondence, Inspection and Safety. . . . Broadside.

[Boston: 1777.]

This is one example among many in the Society's collections of legislation issued in broadside format during the Revolutionary years.

In Pursuance of an Act of the General Assembly of this State, entitled "An Act to prevent Monopoly and Oppression". . . . Broadside.

Boston, Feb. 19th, 1777.

The Revolutionary state government endowed the towns with the authority to fix prices. The Society's collections are very rich in such materials.

An Act, Laying Duties of Impost and Excise, on Certain Goods, Wares and Merchandize, Therein Described; And for repealing the several Laws heretofore made for that Purpose.

Boston: Printed by Adams and Nourse, in Marlborough Street, 1783.

A separate printing of an act that established a customs service and tariff scheduled for the newly formed commonwealth. The text of the act eventually appeared as chapter 12 of the legislation enacted at the May session of the legislature; this advance printing made its substance immediately available to all who were concerned with its provisions.

The Perpetual Laws Of The Commonwealth of Massachusetts, From the Commencement Of The Constitution . . . To The Last Wednesday in May, 1789.

Boston: Printed By Adams and Nourse, Printers to the Honourable General Court. M,DCC,LXXXIX.

This folio publication was one of several retrospective editions designed to publish all viable public acts and thus supplant the session laws. It contrasts markedly with commercial editions, such as a pocket-size volume issued by Isaiah Thomas.

Private and Special Statutes of the Commonwealth of Massachusetts, From The Year 1780, to the Close of the Session of the General Court, Begun And Held on The Last Wednesday In May, A. D. 1805. . . . 3 vols.

Boston: Printed For The State, By Manning & Loring. 1805.

This special compilation, issued according to a resolve of 1803, selected from the morass of Session Laws and Resolves all then viable private and special legislation. The work, executed chiefly by John Davis, was carefully done, well indexed, and contains a useful list of then obsolete acts.

Executive

The governor dep: govr. & assistants doe hereby declare . . . [1644].

From the Winthrop Papers.

This declaration proclaimed that the Magistrates were to administer the law of the colony, and that the Governor and Assistants were to be the duly elected legislators. It was the first approach, however feeble, to defining the separation of powers.

[Colony Seal.] *At A Council Held at Charlestown, June the 20th, 1676.* Broadside.

[Cambridge: Samuel Green, 1676.]

Although the proclamation of 1644 separated the judicial and administrative functions of government, the executive powers were exercised by the Council and the Governor, as this thanksgiving broadside attests.

Accompt of John Usher Esqr Treasurer and Receiver Generall of all of His Majesty's Revenues, Arising within His Majesty's Territory and Dominion of New England . . . From the first day of July 1688. To the First Day of January 1688/9.

This treasurer's report, a parchment more than eighteen feet in length, was the last to be issued under the government of the Dominion of New England. It appears to have been Usher's retained copy and was purchased by the Society in 1853 for twenty dollars.

Anno Regni Regis & Reginae Gulielmi & Mariae Secundo. By The Governour & Council. Broadside.

[Boston: 1690.]

Following the overthrow of the Dominion of New England, and before the establishment of the province government, the officers of the former colony formed a temporary administration. Here the Governor and Council prepare for a military expedition to Canada under the command of Sir William Phips, who became governor the following year.

[William Stoughton, *et al.*] *A Narrative Of The Proceedings Of Sir Edmond Androsse and his Complices. . . .*

[Boston:] Printed in the Year 1691.

This twelve-page pamphlet contains a critical analysis of the arbitrary government of Sir Edmund Andros and the Council of the Dominion of New England. It purports to treat "but a small part of the Grievances justly complained of by the people . . . ," and was written "to vindicate Their Majesties Loyal Subjects."

[Royal Arms.] *By the Honourable the Council of His Majesties Province of the Massachusetts-Bay in New-England. A Declaration.* Broadside.

Boston: Printed by B. Green, Printer to the Honourable Council. 1714.

Upon the death of Queen Anne, all commissions issued by her authority became vacant at the end of six months. In February 1715, Governor Paul Dudley was ousted by the Council because his new commission from George I had not arrived. On 14 March Dudley, who had served since 1702, published a critique of the Council, which was answered on the 18th. The new commission arrived on the 21st.

The Accompt of Jeremiah Allen Gent: Treasurer and Receiver General of his Majties Revenue within the Province of the Massachusetts Bay in New England. [1714–1716.]

This is a meticulous account of revenues received from all sources, and expenditures made by order of the Governor and Council.

Jonathan Belcher. Letterbook. Volume II. September 1731–November 1732.

The twelve volumes of Belcher letterbooks document many phases of provincial political activity, and contain source materials not easily found elsewhere.

Province of the Massachusetts-Bay, ss. [Royal Arms.] *Harrison Gray, Esq; Treasurer & Receiver General for His Majesty's said Province. . . .* [Tax warrant for £412:3:3, levied on the town of Dorchester.] Broadside.

[Boston: 1757.]

This is the only known copy of a tax warrant dated 2 November 1757, and is representative of a very large number in the Society's collections. Equally rich is the collection of tax acts, companion pieces to the warrants.

Copy of the Complaint Of the House of Representatives of Massachuset's-Bay, against Sir Francis Bernard: With Sir Francis Bernard's Answer.

[Boston: 1770.]

Harbottle Dorr, sometime Boston Selectman and a keen observer of the political scene, kept a collection of newspapers and pamphlets published during the years of the American Revolution, which he carefully annotated. His marginal notes are valuable in leading the researcher to other sources.

Copy Of Letters Sent to Great-Britain, by his Excellency Thomas Hutchinson, the Honourable Andrew Oliver, and several other Persons, Born And Educated Among Us.

Boston: Printed. Salem: Re-printed and sold by S. & E. Hall. 1773.

Many Massachusetts governors have been unpopular with their constituents, and Thomas Hutchinson was no exception. These letters, intercepted in England by Benjamin Franklin and published in Boston, hopelessly tarnished his career.

In Provincial Congress, Watertown, April 30, 1775. Whereas an Agreement has been made between General Gage and the Inhabitants of the Town of Boston, for the Removal of the Persons and Effects of such ... as may be so disposed.... Broadside.

[Watertown: Benjamin Edes, 1775.]

With the standard machinery of government dismantled, both legislative and executive functions came to be exercised by the Provincial Congress.

Thomas Gage. [Royal Arms.] *By The Governor. A Proclamation.* [requiring Boston inhabitants to surrender their firearms to the government.] Broadside.

[Boston: 19 June 1775.]

Thomas Gage, although commandant of Boston and holding all reins of government in his hands, issued proclamations under his authority as civil governor.

Commonwealth [State Seal] *of Massachusetts. By His Excellency James Bowdoin, Esquire, Governour of the Commonwealth of Massachusetts. A Proclamation.* Broadside.

[Boston: 1786.]

Executive proclamation seeking support for the government at the outbreak of Shays' Rebellion.

The Courts and The Bar

James Russell's Commonplace Book, ca. 1680–1710. Manuscript.

This book, compiled by James Russell, of Charlestown, sometime colony Treasurer, Justice of the Peace, and Councilman, is characteristic of similar compilations made by many justices of the peace for their own guidance. It contains forms of writs and warrants, copies of important legislation, assignments of wills and administrations, and other useful information.

We whose nams Are heareunto subscribed being desired by goodman Nurse to Declare what we know concerning his wives conversation for time past.... [1692.] Manuscript.

The deposition of Israel Porter and 38 other brave Salem residents attesting the good character of Rebecca Nurse, an accused witch. Despite this impressive support, Mrs. Nurse was convicted and executed.

The Examination of Alice Parker 12 May. 1692. Manuscript.

This is a summary of the testimony given by several neighbors who advanced spectral evidence attesting the guilt of Alice Parker, indicted for witchcraft.

The Jurors for our Soveraigne Lord and Lady the King and Queen.... [1692.] Manuscript.

The indictment of George Burroughs by the special inquest upon the accusation of Elizabeth Hubbard, who was "tortured, afflicted . . . Consumed, wated and tormented" by Burroughs' practice of "detestable Arts called Witchcraft or Socery."

Cotton Mather. The Examination of Geo: Burroughs. 9. May. 1692. Manuscript.

Cotton Mather here summarized the spectral evidence presented against George Burroughs during his trial for witchcraft. Burroughs was convicted and executed.

Cotton Mather. *The Wonders of the Invisible World. Observations As well Historical as Theological, upon the Nature, the Number, and the Operations of the Devils.*
Boston Printed by Benj. Harris for Sam. Phillips. 1693. [i.e., 1692.]

When the Salem witchcraft trials cast a pall over New England in the summer of 1692, Mather was commissioned by the province government to write an account of the affair that would demonstrate the fairness of the trials. This account considers the broader aspects of witchcraft, and also reports the trials of five of the accused. The reports, the first court reports printed in North America, contain detailed information that would not necessarily appear in the file papers, most of which have long since been "expurgated" by descendants of the accused.

Thomas Maule. *Nevv-England Pesecutors Mauld VVith their own VVeapons.*
[New York: William Bradford, 1697.]

Thomas Maule, a much persecuted Salem Quaker, was arrested in 1695 on charges of publishing a book containing "notorious and wicked Lyes and scandals" against the Province government. Called to Boston to answer before the Governor and Council, he denied their authority to examine him and demanded a trial in his own county. When tried before the Essex County session of the Superior Court, he managed his case with sufficient adroitness to convince the jury to acquit him. Tried forty years before the celebrated Zenger case, this may have been the first American case involving freedom of the press that resulted in the acquittal of the defendant.

Samuel Sewall. "Arithmetick and Common Place Book." Manuscript.

Commonplace books abound at the Society, and frequently contain a variety of data concerning legislation and litigation that cannot be found elsewhere, as attests a humble example in this manuscript, in Judge Sewall's hand: "a Copy of the Bounds Levied by execution upon 500 acres of Land at Dudley by Danl Gookin Sheriff."

Deposition of Zachariah Collman, of Scituate, 25 December 1701. Manuscript.

The aged Collman was cheated out of a parcel of land and here begins an action with a complaint to the local justices of the peace. No evidence survives that this matter ever was tried in any court, but the Plymouth County court papers have been ravaged by fire.

The Trials Of Eight Persons Indited for Piracy &c.
Boston: Printed by B. Green, for John Edwards, and Sold at his Shop in King's Street. 1718.

Eight would-be pirates captured a coastal trader, imprisoned the crew, impounded the cargo, and drank so freely of wine that they were ingloriously shipwrecked and apprehended by the authorities. This account is a detailed report of the trials.

"Rich[ar]d Dana's Writ-Book for Suffolk County. July 1752–July 1756." Manuscript.

Writ books or dockets, such as this one, although not indexed, can be of assistance to the patient researcher tracing litigation that originated in the Court of General Sessions of the Peace and that may, or may not, have subsequently been heard by the Superior Court of Judicature.

Josiah Quincy, Junior. Law Reports, 1762–1763. Manuscript.

Although Massachusetts has the oldest judicial system in continuous existence in North America, it was not until 1804 that there was a reporting system. Attorneys kept their own notes of trials. Shown here are the notes kept by the youthful Josiah Quincy, Jr. (1744–1775). Quincy's notes, which included the years 1761–1772, were recorded in such a formal manner that one suspects the reporter intended to publish them. If that was his intent, it was frustrated by an early death. They were not fully published until 1865.

Samuel M. Quincy, ed. *Reports of Cases Argued and Adjudged In The Superior Court of Judicature of the Province of the Massachusetts Bay. . . . By Josiah Quincy, Junior.*
Boston: Little Brown, And Company. 1865.

Josiah Quincy's reports for 1761–1772 finally saw print nearly a century after they were compiled, when his grandson issued this edition.

51. Samuel Quincy (1734–1789) by John Singleton Copley (*circa* 1767).
Solicitor General, Justice of the Peace. Proscribed in 1778.
Courtesy, Museum of Fine Arts, Boston.

Robert Treat Paine. Papers on the Cause of *Tyng vz. Gardiner* (1763). Manuscript.

Tyng vz. Gardner was one suit in a tangled web of litigation that became the most complex civil action in the annals of early Massachusetts law. At stake was a huge tract of land in Maine, originally owned by the Plymouth Company and later sold to the Kennebec Proprietors.

[Richard Dana] "Records of judgmts & Proceedings before me in the county of Suffolk begining ye 20th day of April 1767. . . ." Manuscript.

This is one of a series of record books kept by Richard Dana as a justice of the peace. Because J.P. courts were courts of no record, the proceedings were the property of the individual J.P. There was no system for preserving them, and thus very few have survived.

Most cases involved assault and battery, jumping ship, petty larceny, and violation of the license laws. Note case number 101, a complaint against one Elizabeth Clark for selling a mug of cider without a license, and continued to the following day at six o'clock—A.M. or P.M.?

John Adams. Notes for use in the Boston Massacre Trials. Manuscript.

Adams undertook the unpopular assignment of defending the British Captain Thomas Preston, wherein the central question was whether Preston had ordered the troops to fire on the civilian mob at the "Boston Massacre."

Dom. Rex v Capt. Thos. Preston. for Murder of Saml. Maverick & Lemuel Gray. . . . 1770–1771. Manuscript.

Notes taken by Robert Treat Paine (1770) who represented the Crown at the Boston Massacre trials. The testimony recorded in these notes alone is sufficient to reconstruct in detail the events that transpired on the night of the massacre.

Robert Treat Paine's address to the jury at the conclusion of the trial of Captain Preston. Manuscript.

Paine's summary of the evidence, documented in his notes of the trial, reduced the question to whether or not Preston had ordered the troops to fire on the civilians and, if so, whether extenuating circumstances could reduce "the crime to a lower species of homicide than Murder."

Robert Treat Paine. Minutes of Law Cases, 1760–1774. Manuscript.

Robert Treat Paine (1730–1814) and his contemporaries kept notes of important law cases in addition to those in which they participated. The pocket-size notebooks were crudely bound together to form a series by a nineteenth-century descendant.

Edmund Trowbridge. Notes on legal actions and extracts from cases. (Undated.) Manuscript.

Edmund Trowbridge (1709–1793) was considered to be the most able Massachusetts attorney of his times. His notes on legal actions, of which the item shown is but one example, are copious, extensive, and detailed.

Francis Dana. Law Minutes. (Undated.) Manuscript.

Both as an attorney and a jurist, Francis Dana (1743–1811) made notes on many points of law and sought accurate definitions and detailed precedents, all of which he arranged in one alphabetical sequence for future reference.

Robert Treat Paine. Law Notes. (Undated.) Manuscript.

Paine, like most attorneys of his time, also kept small notebooks which were, in effect, miniature law dictionaries, containing definitions, rules, and useful precedents.

William Cushing. Judicial Notebook, 1783. Manuscript.

In 1783 a series of lawsuits involving a Negro slave, Quock Walker, culminated with the case of *Commonwealth* v. *Jennison*, tried by the Supreme Judicial Court sitting at Worcester. In summing up the evidence for the jury, Chief Justice Cushing noted that slavery had never been officially instituted in Massachusetts, and that the Constitution of 1780 "sets out with declaring that all men are born free and equal. . . . The Idea of Slavery is inconsistent with our . . . constitution & there can be no such thing as perpetual servitude of a rational creature." The Jury returned a verdict accordingly.

Chief Justice William Cushing to an unknown correspondent. [December, 1785?] Manuscript.

With a piracy case pending before the Supreme Judicial Court at Salem, the Chief Justice combed Coke, Blackstone, Wood, Selden, State Trials, and other sources in an effort to distinguish between, and define, mutiny and piracy. This is representative of efforts made by many jurists to evaluate the customary English law against the needs of a new republic. Cushing later became one of the first appointments to the new Supreme Court of the United States.

Francis Dana. Advisory opinion of the Supreme Judicial Court to the Massachusetts Senate. [1787.] Manuscript.

The Massachusetts Constitution empowers the legislative and executive branches of the government to request advisory opinions from the Supreme Judicial Court on important questions of law. Exhibited here is an opinion, re-

52. William Cushing (1732–1810) by Max Rosenthal (1889) from a portrait by James Sharples. Associate Justice, Supreme Court of the United States; Chief Justice, Supreme Judicial Court. Cushing was appointed Chief Justice, Supreme Court of the United States, but could not serve for health reasons. Courtesy, Harvard Law School Art Collection.

quested by the Senate, on the locus of the pardoning power. In later years the court would deliver opinions on such matters as veterans' benefits, the eight-hour day, and the exclusion of women from Chinese restaurants.

Robert Treat Paine. Attorney General Papers. 1787. From the Paine Family Papers.

Attorney General Paine kept full records of all cases prosecuted for the Commonwealth. In the nineteenth century his descendants gathered those records together to form rather crude notebooks, such as this one concerning Shays' Rebellion.

Robert Treat Paine. Charges to Grand Juries, 1790–1804. Manuscript.

All sessions of the Supreme Judicial Court opened with charges to the Grand Juries from the bench. The charges usually began with a short discourse on the nature of government, surveyed the nature of criminal and capital offenses, and sometimes took cognizance of current civil or political disturbances.

This is one of Justice Paine's charges, wherein he extols the virtues of the social compact and the obligations of citizens in a republican government.

Reports of Cases Argued And Determined In The Supreme Judicial Court of the State of Massachusetts, From September 1804 To June 1805. By Ephraim Williams, Esq. [Williams' Reports.]
Northampton, Published By S. & E. Butler. 1805.

In response to an increasing demand for a reporting system the legislature, in March of 1804, authorized the appointment of a reporter of decisions for the Supreme Judicial Court. Williams produced the first volume in a series that continues to the present day.

757   Mr Samuel Phillips to William Story —   Dr

April 1	To filling writ &sum. ag.t m.r Million blanks &c. &c.	0 . 7 . 4
1758 Janry	To disbursem.ts in your action ag.t English	1 . 8 . —
	To advice &attend.ce in English's 2 Actions ag.t you	18 . —
	To disbursem.t &c in your action ag.t Quill & Bixon	1 . 16 . 4
	To ditto in your action ag.t Goddard	1 . 15 . 10
July	To filing writ &sum. ag.t Tuckerman &blanks	5 . —
20	To draw.g 2 deeds from m.r Goddard to you	5 . 4
26	To my attend.ce on you in Torrey's action	8 . —
	To disbursem.ts &c in your action ag.t Guniter & Bixon	2 . 19 . —
Oct.r 2	To ditto in your action ag.t m.r Mellon	1 . 15 . 8
1759	To advice &attend.ce in m.r Mellons 2 actions ag.t you	8 . —
Janry	To advice &attend.ce on you in Torreys action preparing papers for your defence at sundry times	16 . —
Feb.y 7.16.	To my attend.ce at the Court &before referees in Torreys action at several times &arguing your defence before them	16 . —
	To my disbursem.t &c in m.r Mellons 2 actions at the last Court	12 . —
	To ditto in appeal &c	4 . —
Aug.t 16	To disbursements &c in Haws action ag.t Carneau	3 . 2 . 6
	To disbursem.t &c to m.r Auchmuty in Carneaus actions ag.t you	18 . —
	To my attend.ce on you &at the Court in 3 actions of Carneaus	12 . —
	To disbursem.t for entry copys &c in m.r Mellons actions	1 . 7 . —
Sep.r 29	To draw.g bonds of submis.n w.th m.r Penning my attend.ce upon that affair draw.g discharges &c	1 . —
1760		
Janry 22	To my attend.ce on Carneaus 4 actions &upon you rel.t &c	12 . —
		£ 22 . 4 . 6

53. Attorney's Bill, 1760. When this volume was in page proof, the editors discovered that there was no illustration and almost nothing in the text to indicate that colonial lawyers ever got paid. To remedy this oversight we close the volume with an attorney's bill. The litigious Samuel Phillips, who owed this substantial sum for legal expenses, was "Esquire" Phillips, the father of the founder of Phillips Academy, Andover, and one of the wealthiest men in the Province. Inferior Court of Common Pleas, Suffolk, 1760 APR 166. Courtesy, Social Law Library.

INDEX

Index

Unless otherwise indicated, all place names are in Massachusetts
(including Maine)

A

Adam, 219, 227 *n*.5

Adams, Abigail, 318 *n*.9

Adams, Ferdinando, 13–15

Adams, John, xl, xlv, xlvi *n*.5, xlvii,
l–li, lxii, 104, 105, 204, 219, 230,
273, 276, 317 *n*.7, 318 *n*.1, 323–
324, 325 *n*.6, 327, 339, 344, 355,
356, *illus.* 361, *illus.* 396, 420,
479, 481–484 *passim.*, 493, 562;
admiralty cases, 382–395; and Boston Massacre trial, 270, 581; and
Boston Tea Party, xliii *n*.2; on civil
law, lii *n*.6; and jurisdictional conflict, 429; on lawyers, 289, 360,
376; legal career, 359–418; library, 244; *Novanglus*, li, 372,
374, 401, 408–416; papers at Massachusetts Historical Society, 581;
and *Sewall* v. *Hancock*, 436; and
Stamp Act, 478

Adams, John, 302

Adams v. *Dade*, 17

Adams, Samuel, 408 *n*.3, 409, 492

Addington, Isaac, 114, 329

Adjournments and continuances, 139

Adlow, Elijah, 473, 474

Administrative actions, 149

Admiralty Court, 548

Adultery, 505

Afro-Americans, *see* Blacks

Alexander, James, 270

Allen, James, 114 *n*.9

Allen, Jeremiah, 575-576

Allen, John, 253, 267, 339

Allen, Jonathan, 339

Allen, Josiah, 182

Allen, Neal W., xxxviii, xliii–xlv, lxv

Allen, Samuel, 284

Allestree, Paul, 21

Allis, Frederick S. Jr., lxi–lxii

Allum, John, 130

Almshouses, *see* Poverty, law of

American Antiquarian Society, resources for legal history, 551–553

American Eagle (ship), 562

American Revolution, and legal history, xl, xlv *ff.*, lii *ff.*, 419–467;
and fragmentation of court system,
437–451; pamphlet literature, 272.
See also Conflict of laws; Federalism

Andros, Edmund, xxi, xxxiii, xxxiv,
66, 265, 575

Angier, Oakes, 339

Antinomian movement, xxvi, lx, 265,
268

Appeals, 126–127, 140, 212–214

Appeals Court, 545

Appellate Courts, 545

Appellate Division, 546, 547

Apprenticeship, legal, 326 *ff.*

Arnold, Benedict, 342

Arnold, Oliver, 342

Arrowsic, 296, 306

Arthur, Daniel, 494

Articles of Confederation, 452

Arundel, 307

Ashley, John, 339

Ashurst, William, 63 *n*.3

Aspinwall, William, 3, 33

Assistants, Court of, 5, 21, 43–46, 48,
51–53, 521, 522, 541, 542, 545

Assizes, Court of, 192 *ff.*, 204–207,
218–219, 227

Assumpsit, 18, 513–516

Atkins, Thomas, 130

Attorneys, *see* Lawyers

Attucks, Crispus, 270, 562

Auchmuty, Robert, xxxiii, xliii, 103,
194–195, 198–203, 210–215,
218, 227, 233, 235 *n*.4, 339–340,
351, 389, 390 *n*.3, 394; acting Attorney General, 220; and bail hear-

590   INDEX

ings, 218; and benefit of clergy, 237; and English law, 231–232; memorial, 482.

Auditors, 139

Austin, Benjamin, 340

Austin, Jonathan Williams, 340

Avery, Samuel, 492

B

Bacheller v. *Brocke*, 29, 30

Bail hearings, 217–218

Baker, Mary, 141

Baker, Nathaniel, 141

Bancroft, Thomas, 557

Bane, Jonathan, 298, 307

Bankes (Attorney General), 13–14

Bankruptcy, 425

Barnes, Thomas G., xxvii, xxix, xxxvi, lxv

Barnet, John, 114 *n*.9

Barnstable, 237, 558

Barratry, 7

Barret, John, 159, 160

Barret, Margaret, 159

Barrett, Samuel, 340

Barristers, 16, 25. *See also* Lawyers; Solicitors

Barry, Mary, 225

Bastwick, John, 12

Bath, 567

Belcher, Jonathan, 58, 102, 201–202, 288, 576

Belcher, Jones v., 423 *n*.1

Bell, Robert, 256, 408 *n*.1

Bell, Sarah, 175 *n*.1

Bellefontaine, Edgar J., 473

Bellingham, Richard, xxviii, 7, 9, 10, 42, 51

Bellomont (Governor), 67–68

Benefit of clergy, 236–239

Bentley, William, 168–169, 170

Berkshire County, list of records, 532

Bermuda, BWI, 23

Bernard (Governor), 352

Bernard, Francis, 576

Berwick, 210, 275–307 *passim*

Beverly, 558

Biddeford, 301, 307, 563

Billings, Joseph, 142–143

Billing, Newport v., 394 *n*.1

Bisbee, Elisha, 194 *n*.1, 317 *n*.7

Black, Barbara A., xxx–xxxiii, xxxviii, xli, lxv

Blackburn, Joseph, Otis portrait, *illus.* 320

Blacks, xli *n*.9, 128–129, 141

Blackstone, *Commentaries*, 205–206, 243, 256, 428

Blagrove, Nathaniel, 63 *n*.3, 77 *n*.5, 80–88, 90–98, 100–102

Blin, James, 212 *n*.7

Bliss, Daniel, 340

Bliss, Jedediah, 340

Bliss, Jonathan, 340

Bliss, Moses, 340–341

Blood, Phineas, 235

Blood, Samuel, 235

Bloomfield, Maxwell, xxv

Blowers, Sampson Salters, 341

Blyth, Benjamin, Adams portrait, *illus.* 361

Body of Lawes and Libertyes, 31, 41, 47

Bollan, William, 194 *n*.1, 200–201, 235

Bond, William H., lxi

Bond, writ of debt, 511–513

Boone, Nicholas, *Constables Pocket-Book*, 255

Borland, John, 221

Boston, 11, 14, 19, 20, 21, 30, 34, 36, 58, 59, 68, 82, 108–151 *passim*, 164–188 *passim*, 194–236 *passim*, 246–271 *passim*, 273, 277, 288, 293, 322, 360, 363, 386, 396, 397, 403, 406, 409, 418, 473, 479, 490, 493, 494, 495, 520, 547, 549, 558, 562, 563, 564, 566, 570, 571, 572, 577, 581

Boston Massacre, xlvi, 473; trial, 269–270, 562

Boston Municipal Courts, 547

Boston, Old State House, *illus.* 420, *illus.* 438

Boston Police Court, 547
Boston Tea Party, xlviii *n*.2, 409, 581
Botein, Stephen, xxv
Bourn, Silvanus, 194 *n*.1
Bourne, Shearjashub, 341
Bowditch, Joseph, 557
Bowdoin, James, 577
Bowen, Edward, 557
Bowen, Nathan, 557
Bowen, Nathaniel Sr., 558
Brackett, Joshia, 490
Brackett, Joy v., 491
Bradbury, Theophilus, 289 *n*.4, 341, 349
Bradford, Andrew, 254
Bradford, William, xxvii *n*.5, 254, 271
Bradstreet, Simon, xxviii, 20, 48 *n*.9, *illus.* 50
Braintree, 164, 165, 172, 360, 362, 369, 552
Brattle, Elizabeth (Hayman), 86, 95, 97
Brattle, William, 86–87, 341–342
Breach of peace, 117, 118, 124
Breaking and entering, 505, 509
Briar, Richard, 286, 289
Bridger, John, 276–277, 281, 284
Bridges, John, 159
Brink, Robert J., xviii, xxiv, xxxvii, lxi, lxiii, lxv
Bristol, 58–102 *passim*, 227, 235, 237
Bristol County, list of records, 532–533
Broadstreet, Abigail (Fuller), 390–391
Broadstreet, Joseph, 390
Broadstreet v. *Broadstreet*, 390–391
Brocke, Bacheller v., 29, 30
Brockus, John, 134
Bromfield, Edward, 114
Brookfield, 552, 553
Brookfield papers, 553
Brooklyn (Brookline), 134
Brown, Daniel 342
Brown, John, 342
Browne, William, 332

Buckminster, Joseph, 209
Bulfinch, Charles, 484
Bull, Job, 130, 138, 141
Buller, *Nisi Prius*, 244
Burglary, 505
Burnet (Governor), 102
Burnham, Job, 297 *n*.8, 301
Burrel, George, 130
Burrel, Samuel, 135
Burrill, John, 304
Burroughs, George, 578
Burton, Henry, 12
Burton, Stephen, 70, 72
Butterfield, Robert, 218
Butters v. *Stoughton*, 29
Buttley, John, 133
Byfield, Deborah (Clark), 58
Byfield, Nathaniel, xxx, xxxii–xxxiii, xxxviii, xli, 56–105, *illus.* 56; coat of arms, *illus.* 105
Byfield, Richard, 58
Byfield, Sarah (Leverett), 58, 103
Byng, Admiral, 267
Byrd, William II, 244

C

Caldwell, James, 270, 562
Calhoun, Daniel, xxv
Calhoun, John C., 401
Callender, Joseph, 121
Calvinism, xxxvi
Cambridge, 161, 168, 180, 201, 392, 558
Cambridge, Fourth Court House, *illus.* 434
Cambridge Platform, xxvi, xxx
Came, Samuel, 292, 294, 297, 302, 306
Campbell, Barnet, 169–171
Campbell, Sarah, 169–171
Canals, 501
Canon law, 403
Care, Henry, 258, 260; *English Liberties*, 257–258, *illus.* 259
Carol, John, 562. *See also* Carrol, John
Carr, Patrick, 270, 562

Carrol, John, 270. *See also* Carol, John

Carver, Anna, *see* Richards, Anna (Carver)

Case files, 525, 526. *See also* File papers

Cavet, William, 119

Cazneau, Andrew, 342

Chadwick, John, 137

Chafee, Zechariah, Jr., xvii–xviii, xxii, xxx, xxxii, xxxiii, xxxv, xxxvi, xxxvii

Chancery Court, 16

Chandler, John, 342

Chandler, Nathaniel, 342

Chandler, Rufus, 342

Chapman, Jonathan, 235

Chardon, Peter, 376

Charlestown, 150, 199, 201, 221, 235, 574

Charters, Massachusetts, 253–254, 265

Chase [Samuel], 460

Chauncey, Charles, 58, 61–62

Checkley, Anthony, xxxiv, xl

Checkley, John, 232

Checkley, Samuel, 134

Chesebrough, William, 20

Child, John, *New Englands Jonas*, 249, 250–251

Child, Robert, xxvi, 265, 268

Chisholm v. *Georgia*, 562

Choate, John, 557

Choice of law/choice of court, lv, 427–428, 429, 436, 437

Chroust, Anton-Hermann, xxv, xxxiv–xxxv

Cicero, 359, 416

Citizenship, 249

Civil law, 135–148, 367 *ff.*, 382 *ff.*, 506 *ff.*

Clap(p), Samuel, 159, 391

Clap, William, 391

Clap's Will, 391

Clark, Daniel, 217, 222

Clark, Deborah, *see* Byfield, Deborah (Clark)

Clark, Hugh, 489

Clark, John, xxxviii, 107–151; Judi-cial Book, 111 *ff.*, *illus.* 112, *illus.* 131

Clark, Jonas, 493

Clark, Timothy, 114 *n.*9

Cleaveland, A. C., 557

Clement, Augustin, 22 *n.*5

Clough, Eden, 490

Cockerell v. *Cockerham*, 26 *n.*4

Cockerham, Cockerell v., 26 *n.*4

Cockshutt, John, 13

Coffin, William, 143

Cogan, John, 23

Cogan, Foxwill v., 28

Cohen, Morris L., xxviii–xxxi, xxxviii, xlv, lv–lxvi

Coke, Edward, 9, 47, 48, 228; *Booke of Entries*, 25; *Institutes*, 230, 231; on jurisdictional conflict, 428

Colcord, Edward, 3

Cole, Elizabeth, Francis Doughty v., 33 *n.*6

Cole, William, 30

Cole, William, Francis Doughty v., 33 *n.*6

Coleman, Dr., 62–63 *n.*9

Coles, John, Paine portrait, *illus.* 375

Collman, Zachariah, 579

Commissioner's courts, 521

Commissioners of Small Causes, 546

Common law, 47, 136 *ff.*, 422, 454–458

Common Pleas, 6, 16

Common Pleas, Inferior Court of, 521–522, 523, 524, 546; records, *illus.* 470, 480, 483, 486, 488, 492, 527, 544, 585

Commonwealth status, 410

Commonwealth v. *Jennison*, 582

Conflict of laws, liv–lv, 419–467

Congregationalism, 41, 502

Connecticut Colony, legal publications, 253

Constables, 124–125, 174, 176, 179, 183

Constitution, American, 452, 454–467

Continental Congress, 437–441, 442

Contracts, 440, 511 *ff.*

Conveyancing, xxxv–xxxvi
Cook, Alice, 121
Cooke, Elisha, 66–69, 108, 109, 110, 114, 329
Coolidge, Lawrence, lxi
Coolidge, United States v., 461
Coomer, John, 135
Cooper, John, 161
Copley, John Singleton, 416 n.5; Goldthwait portrait, illus. 203; Quincy portrait, illus. 580
Copley, Matthew, Jr., 213–214
Coquillette, Daniel R., xix, xxi–lxiii, lxvi
Corbet, Michael, 392
Corbet, Rex v., 392–394
Coroners Court, 548
Costs, court, 140
Cotton, John, 7, 12, 13, 15, 20, 38, 42, 251; Moses his Judicials, 250
Council for the Safety of the People and the Conservation of the Peace, xxxiii
Counterfeiting, 495
County courts, 542, 546
Court House, Fourth, Cambridge, illus. 434
Courts: organization and jurisdiction, 520–524; records at American Antiquarian Society, 552–553. See also names of courts (e.g., Assistants, Court of)
Courts-martial, 440
Covenant, writ of, 511, 512
Cox, Anna, 181–182
Cox, Elisha, 181–182
Crackbone, Benjamin, 161 n.7
Criminal law, xxxviii, xlii–xliii, 146, 191–242, 504 ff.
Croke, George, 14
Crosby, Major, 376
Cross, Joseph, 303
Currency cases, 466
Curtis, Joseph, 298, 305
Curwen, Jonathan, 557–558. See also Curwin, Jonathan
Curwen, Samuel, 557

Curwin, Jonathan, 329. See also Curwen, Jonathan
Cushing, John, lxi, lxvi, 330, 342, 569
Cushing, John, Jr., 330
Cushing, Roland, 342
Cushing, William, xl, 314 n.5, 325 n.6, 332, 342–343, 370 n.7, 482, 582, illus. 583
Customs, 386 ff.
Cutt, Eleanor, see Phipps, Eleanor Cutt

D

Dade, Henry, 13, 14, 17
Dade, Adams v., 17
Daftorn, Isaac, 142
Daftorn, Mary, 142
Dalton, Michael, Countrey Justice, 111, 117, 121, 144, 229, 288
Dana, Francis, 343, 582, 583
Dana, Richard, 328 n.7, 343, 579, 581
Dane, Nathan, 558, 559
Danforth, Thomas, 329
Davenport, Addington, xxxiv, xliv, 330
Davenport, Addington, Jr., 194 n.1, 286
Davis, James, 254
Davis, John, 297 n.8
Davis, Woodcock v., 26 n.3
Dawson, John P., xxv, xxviii
Day, Ezekiel, 158–159
Day, Matthew, Book of the General Lawes and Libertyes, xxix–xxx, 6, 10, 251, 252, illus. 252
Day, Steven, 247, 248, 250, 253
De bonis asportatis, 509–510
Debt, writ of, 511–513, 515
Declaration of Independence, 487, 500
Dedham, 223
Defamation, 511
Defense counsel, 204–216, 217 ff.
Defensive pleas, 515–516
Demurrer, 516

Dennett, John, 302
Detinue, writ of, 510
Dewey, Israel, 171
Dewin, Henry, 121
Dick, 129
Dickenson, Eben, 224
Dickenson, Sarah, 224
Dilatory pleas, 515
Dissenters, 268, 275, 502
District Court Department, 547
Divorce cases, 390–391
Doan, John, 228 n.8
Doane, Captain, 383, 385
Doane v. *Gage*, 372, 383–386
Docket books, *see* Minute books
Doctors, xl n.8
Dodge, Richard, Jr., 159
Dominion of New England, 265
Donham, Anna, 505–506
Dorchester, 149, 150
Dorman, Jesse, 222
Dorr, Harbottle, 576
Double jeopardy, 125 n.5
Doubleday, Elijah, 137
Doughty, David, 218, 238
Doughty, Francis, William and Elizabeth Cole, v., 33 n.6
Dover, NH, 555
Dower right, 507
Downing, Emmanuel, xxviii n.6, 9
Draper, Rich, 114 n.9
Dudley, Joseph, 59, 66, 68, 85, 88, 101–102, 120, 217, 229, 265, 289, 379, 380, 382, 575
Dudley, Paul, xl, xliv, xxxiii n.3, xxxiv, 9, 87–88, *illus.* 196, 197, 217, 283, 286, 330
Dudley, Thomas, xxviii, 48, 51
Dukes County, list of records, 533
Dummer, Jeremiah, 59, 62 n.9, 63 n.3, 114, 231
Dummer, Samuel, 118
Dummer, William, 63 n.3, 296
Duncan, Jeremiah, 118
Dunster, Henry, 34, 248, 253
Duryee, Mills v., 465
Dyer, Gyles, 114 n.9
Dyer, Mary, lx

E

Economic growth, and legal history, 501
Edgartown, 214
Edwards, Constable, 308
Edwards, Jonathan, 344, 354
Edwards, Malachi, 291, 296–297, 308–311
Egremont, 176
Ejectment, 506
Ela, Daniell, xxxv
Election sermons, 264
Ellis, Mrs., 233–234
Ely, John, 343
Ely, Justin, 343
Endicott, John, 48, *illus.* 49, 129
England, civil war, xxvi; courts, 5, 6, 16; legal profession, 9; rural legal system, 4. *See also* English law
English, Philip, Sr., 222
English law, xxix *ff.*, xxxvi, xxxix *ff.*, xlv, lii, 143 *ff.*, 147–148, 227 *ff.*, 257, 421–429, 433–437. *See also* England
Engravings, on file papers, 489–490
Enlightenment, 359, 371, 383 *ff.*, 404 *ff.*, 417
Entail, 507–508
Entertainment laws, *see* Settlement, law of
Essex, Joseph, 139
Essex County, xxx, xxxiii, xxxiv, xlvii; list of records, 533–536; records in Essex Institute, 556
Essex Institute, resources for legal history, 555–558
European law, 419
Eusden, John D., xxix
Execution sermons, 265
Exeter, NH, 276, 282, 555

F

Fairwether, John, 114 n.9
Falmouth (Portland), 275, 296, 299, 306, 307, 567
Family Court, 548

Family responsibility for poor, 158 ff., 174
Family violence, 129–130
Farmer, Thomas, 161 n.7
Farnham, Daniel, 343, 350
Faulkner, Eliza, 123–124
Federal-state jurisdictional conflict, 451–454. See also Conflict of laws
Federalism, 419–467
Fees, for attorneys, 240; bill, illus., 585
Feke, Benjamin, Sewall portrait, illus., 331
Fennison, Margaret, 236
Fernald, Nathaniel, 301, 308
Fessenden, Stephen, 314 n.5
Feudalism, 380, 402 ff.
Field, David Dudley, 477
File papers, 480–481, 485–497, illus., 527
Fines, 125–126
Fitch, Joseph, 343
Fitch, Samuel, xl, xlvii, 343–344, 377, 379, 382, 403, 493
Fitzpatrick, Edward, 236
Flag, Ester, 120 n.4
Flagg, James, 269, 562
Flaherty, David H., xxxviii, xlii–xliii, lxvi, 478
Flanders, Mary, 161 n.5
Fleet, Thomas, 270
Fletcher, William, 269, 562
Fletcher v. Vassall, 318 n.9
Fortes, John, 110
Fortune telling, 128
Foster, Jedediah, 552
Foster, John, 114 n.9
Fowles, John, 236
Foxcroft, Thomas, 59, 61
Foxwill v. Cogan, 28
Frame, Benjamin, 116
Franklin, Benjamin, 324, 576
Franklin, James, 258
Frauds, statute of, 424
Freeman, Enoch, 344
Freeman, Samuel, 344
French and Indian Wars, xxxviii, xxxix n.2, 154

Frobisher, Sheriff, 473
Froe, Priscilla, 160–161
Frogley, Mr., 139
Frost, Catherine, see Hammond, Catherine (Frost)
Frost, Catherine, see Leighton, Catherine (Frost)
Frost, Charles, 286, 288, 289, 297, 299, 310
Frost, Margaret, 303
Frost, Nicholas, 281, 282
Frost, Simon, 282
Fuller, Abigail, see Broadstreet, Abigail (Fuller)

G

Gage, Captain, 384–385
Gage, [Thomas] (General), 576–577
Gage, Doane v., 372, 383–386
Gaine, Hugh, 254
Gambling, Benjamin, 283, 285, 309
Gardiner, Sylvester, 269, 562
Gardner, Constable, 125
Gardner, Tyng v., 581
Gawalt, Gerard, xxv, l
Gee, Mr., 142
Gee, Lately, 213
General Court (Massachusetts), 5, 10, 29–30, 44–45, 52, 521, 541–543
General Gaol Delivery, 192
General Session of the Peace, Court of: Maine, xliv; Massachusetts, 192, 502 ff., 522, 524
George, Amos, 161
Georgetown, 285
Georgia, Chisholm v., 562
Gibbs, Robert, 114 n.9
Giddings, Daniel, 155 n.7
Gilbert, Evidence, 244
Gilbert, Felix, lvii
Gilmore, Grant, lix, 475, 476
Glossary, 529–531
Gloucester, 138, 180, 564
Glover, Jesse, 248
Glover, Jesse (Mrs.), 248, 250
Godsoe, William, 286–287, 289

Goebel, Julius, xxii
Goffe, Edmund, 355
Gold, David, 212
Goldthwait, Ezekiel, *illus.* 203, 483
Gooch, Joseph, 194 *n*.1
Goodere, John Dinely, 267
Goodere, Samuel, 267
Gookin, Nathaniel, 142
Gordon, Robert, lviii
Gorges, Sir Ferdinando, 275, 278, 279
Gorges, Thomas, 278–280
Gorham, David, 344
Gorham, Shubael, 344
Gorton, Samuel, 265, 268
Gould, Stephen, 246–247
Goulding, Peter, xxxv
Government institutions, in court records, 500–501
Governor and Council, 521, 543, 545
Gowen, James, 286
Gowen, Nicholas, 286, 289
Grand Remonstrance, 37
Grant, Daniel, 305
Grant, James, 129
Graves, Thomas, 330
Gray, Harrison, 576
Gray, Lemuel, 581
Gray, Samuel, 270, 562
Great Awakening, lvi, *n*.1
Great Barrington, 161, 169, 170, 171
Greater Quarter Court, 521
Green, Bartholomew, 253
Green, John, 122–123
Green, Samuel, 253, 264
Green, Thomas, 260
Greenleaf, Joseph, 96, 254, 255–256, 257
Gridley, Benjamin, 344
Gridley, Jeremiah (Jeremy), xl, lxii, 319 *n*.3, 343, 348, 355, 360, 363, 366, 369–370, 377, 379, 381, 382, 394, 399, 402, 403, 406, 418, 482, 483
Groton, 159
Guildhall (London), 6

H

Hadley, 224
Hale, Matthew, *Pleas of the Crown*, 228–229
Hamilton, Alexander, 270
Hammond, Catherine (Frost), 282
Hammond, Joseph, Sr., 282, 289, 290, 296, 302, 304, 305, 307, 310
Hammond, Joseph, Jr., 287, 289, 290, 294, 296, 299, 300, 302, 304, 307, 310
Hammond, William, 282–283, 296
Hampden, 549
Hampshire County, court records, 536, 553
Hampton, NH, 555
Hancock, John, 386–390
Hancock, Thomas, 387
Hancock, Sewall v., lii *n*.6, 436
Hargrave, Francis, 269
Harris, Benjamin, 257, 258, 260
Harris, John, 141
Hartegan (Hartigan), James, 270, 562
Harvard College, xxvi; professions of graduates, xxxiv, xlix, 333–336
Harvard Law School, resources for legal history, 559–568
Harvey, Thomas, 303
Haskins, George, xxii, xxiii, xxv, xxvii, xxviii, xxix, lxvi–lxvii, 476
Hatch, Rucke v., 27, 28
Hatfield, 571
Hatt, Giles, 18 *n*.5
Hatt, John, 18, 19, 26
Haverhill, 161, 555
Hawkins, William, *Pleas of the Crown*, 229 *n*.7, 233
Hawles, Sir John, *Englishman's Right*, 257
Hawley, Joseph, 315, 325 *n*.5, 344–345, 354, 408 *n*.3
Hawthorne, John, 329
Hayman, Elizabeth, *see* Brattle, Elizabeth (Hayman)
Hayman, Mary, 86–88, 95, 97

Hayman, Nathan, 70, 81–83, 86, 95, 97, 101
Heard, John, 304
Heath, Joseph, 296
Henderson, Edith G., lxvii
Henley, David, 563
Hennessey, Edward F., xxiv, lxi, 473–474
Henry, Hugh, 301
Hett v. *Shave*, 26
Hett v. *Tose*, 26
Hewes, Dr., 124
Heylyn, Peter, 13 *n*.3
Highways, 134, 501
Hill, Jeremiah, 563
Hill, John, 296
Hill, Joseph, 308–309
Hill, Roger, 296
Hill, Valentine, 21
Hiller, Joseph, 194 *n*.1, 223
Hindus, Michael S., xxiv, lxvii
Hitchburn, Thomas, 142
Hittee, 231, 234–235
Hoar, William, 75 *n*.7
Hoddy, Mary (Plaisted), *see* Phipps, Mary (Plaisted) Hoddy
Hodgkins, Francis, 176
Hollis, Thomas, 406–407
Holmes, Oliver Wendell, lviii–lix
Holmes, Silas, 237
Homicide, *see* Murder
Hooper, John, 303
Hopkins, Mark, 345, 352
Hopkins, Timothy, 345
Horton, Sarah, 137
Horwitz, Morton J., lii, liv, lv *n*.8, 477–478
Housing Court Department, 549
Hovey, James, 317 *n*.7, 319, 321, 323, 345
How, Daniel, 230
Hubbard, Elizabeth, 578
Hubbard, Nathaniel, 330
Hudson, Seth, broadside, *illus.* 185
Hudson, United States v., 461
Hue, Simon, 237
Humfry, John, xxvii, *n*.6, xxviii, 42, 51

Hunt, Thomas, 121
Hurst, James Willard, xxiii, xxv, 501
Hutchinson, Anne, lx, 268
Hutchinson, Elisha, 114
Hutchinson, Foster, 332, 483, 484
Hutchinson, Susannah, 280
Hutchinson, Thomas, lvi–lvii, 204, 227 *n*.6, 232–233, 271, 321 *n*.7, 332, 340 *ff. passim.*, 376, 394, 395, 407 *n*.1, 408 *n*.3, 576

I

Idleness, 128
Immigrants, 174–175, 186
Indebitatus assumpsit, 514
Indians, xxxii, xxxviii, xliii, xli *n*.9, 126, 129, 141, 172, 271–272, 275
Inflation, 154
Ingersoll, David, 345
Inns of Chancery, 15–16
Inns of Court, 15–16
Insolvency, 466
Insolvency Court, 548
Institutio legalis, 381 *n*.6
Interstate jurisdictional conflicts, 448–451. *See also* Conflict of laws
Ipswich, 6, 164, 172, 183, 520, 558
Ius gentium, 404, 405, 410 *ff.*

J

Jack, 492–493
Jamestown, VA, 246
Jefferson, Thomas, 244, 324, 401 *n*.9
Jeffrey, James, 557
Jenneys, Richard, 488, 489
Jennison, Commonwealth v., 582
Jephson, William, 139
Jewett, Amos, Jr., 162–163
Jewett, Ann (Noyes), 162
Johnson, Isaac, xxviii, 42, 48, 51
Johnson, Jonathan, 302
Johnson, Margaret, 126
Jolliffe, John, 20
Jones (Justice), 13
Jones, Douglas L., xxxviii, xlii, lxvii
Jones v. *Belcher*, 423 *n*.1

Jones v. *Leeke*, 26 *n*.4
Jordan, Captain, 305
Jordan, John, 307
Joy v. *Brackett*, 491
Judges, role of, liii–liv. *See also* Lay judges and magistrates; magistrates
Judgment books, *see* Record books
Judiciary, federal, 453
Jurisprudence, European, 359, 368
Jury, role of, liii, 501
Justice (symbol), *illus.* frontispiece and title page
Justices of the peace, 46–47, 54, 113 *ff.*, 143 *ff.*, 504 *ff.*, 524, 543, 547; records at American Antiquarian Society, 551, 552; records at Essex Institute, 557. *See also* Judges; Lay judges and magistrates; magistrates
Juvenile Court Department, 549

K

Kelley, Michael, 303
Kennebunk, 567
Kent, Benjamin, 225, 328, 333, 345, 360
Kent, Joseph, 345
Keyser, George, 3
Kilroy, Matthew, 270, 562
King, Esther, 161
King, Peter, 231
King, William, 161
King Philip's War, xxxii
King William's War, xxxviii
King's Bench, lv, 6, 16
Kir, Thomas, 387
Kittery, 275–302 *passim*
Kneeland, Samuel, 260
Konig, David, xxiv, xxvi, xxx, xxxii, xxxiii, xxxvii

L

Labor contracts, 515
Lamb, David, 495
Lambard, *Eirenarcha*, 111
Lancaster, Duchy of, 16

Land Court Department, 549
Land title, 506, 507
Lane, Andrew, 194 *n*.1
Lane, John, 228
Langdell, Christopher Columbus, lviii
Langdon, Timothy, 345
Larkin, George, 257
Laud, William (Archbishop), 6, 11, 13–14
Laver, William, 20
Law, colonial, xvii *ff.*, xxi *ff.*, xxvi *ff.*; social value, 147. *See also* Lawyers; headings beginning Legal . . . ; specific subjects (*e.g.*, names of courts, types of law, legal issues)
Law libraries and reports, xl
Lawson, Deodat, 267
Lawson, George, 229
Lawton, Christopher Jacob, 213
Lawyers, xxxii, 3, 4–7, 9, 16, 29–30, 143, 210; in Assizes, 193 *ff.*; in civil cases, 211 *ff.*; in criminal cases, 191–242; fees, xxxi–xxxv; geographic distribution, xlix–l, 337–338; Maine, xliii–xliv, 276 *ff.*; professionalization, xxiv *ff.*, xxxiii *ff.*, xxxix ff., xliii–xliv, xl, xlvii, 1, 19, 39, 164–171, 191, 207, 212, 244–245, 313–358, 368, 476; papers at American Antiquarian Society, 551; public opinion, 41, 200–201, 207, 254, 395–400. *See also* Barristers; Solicitors
Lay judges and magistrates, xxv *ff.*, xxxviii–xxxix, xli–xliii, 39–55. *See also* Judges; Justices of the peace; magistrates
Leach, Mrs., 129
Lechford, Richard, 11
Lechford, Thomas, xxvi–xxvii, xxxvi, 3–38, 40, 551–552; *Notebook*, 271; *Plain Dealing*, 35, 36, 37; scriveners book, *illus.* 24
Lee, Philemon, 184
Leeke, Jones v., 26 *n*.4
Legal education, *see* Legal training
Legal history, xxiii *ff.*, lvii–lx, 270–271; sources, 471–584

Legal literature, xxviii *ff.*, xxx, xxxviii, 243–272
Legal profession, *see* Lawyers
Legal publication, *see* Legal literature
Legal training, xxviii, xxxii, xxxv *n*.5, xl, xlvii, lviii–lix, 200, 369 *ff.*
Legal unity, 426
Legate, Thomas, 552
Leighton, Catherine (Frost), 304 *n*.2
Leighton, John, 305–306
Lemmon, Joseph, 552
Leominster, 552
Leonard, Daniel, xlvii, li, 342, 345–346, 409. *See also* Massachusettensis
Leonard, Elkanah, 194 *n*.1
Leonard, Ephraim, 346
Leonard, George, 346
Leonard, Zephaniah, 346
Leverett, Hudson, xxxv *n*.5
Leverett, John, 91, 100, 329
Leverett, Sarah, *see* Byfield, Sarah (Leverett)
Libby, Samuel, 301
Libel, 117, 120
Liberty (ship), lii *n*.6, 386 *ff.*
Lidgett, Madam, 74
Lilly, John, 229 *n*.7
Lincoln, William, 553
Liquor sales, 126, 132–133
Litchfield Law School, 1
Little, Isaac, 234–235
Little, William, 562
Little, Woodbridge, 346, 347
Littleton, 159
Livermore, Matthew, 239
Long, H., 161 *n*.5
Lonyon, Thomas, 126
Lord, Benjamin, 303
Lord, Robert, 3
Loring, Israel, 346
Loring, Jonathan, 346–347
Lovejoy, Nathaniel, 557
Lowell, John, 347
Loyalists, xlvii, 445–448, 479
Lucy, 128–129
Ludlow, Roger, xxviii, 42, 48, 51
Lumber industry, 501
Lyde, Byfield, 58

Lyde, Edward, 58
Lyman, Phineas, 344, 357
Lymon, Henry, 32
Lymon, Wolcot v., 32
Lynde, Benjamin, xxxiv, xl, 194 *n*.9, 233, 330
Lynde, Benjamin, Jr., 330
Lynde family, 400
Lyndery, Ralph, 142
Lyndsey, Eleazer, 238

M

Macaulay, Catharine, 406
McCauley, William, 270, 562
MacDonald, John, 237
McKirdy, Charles, xxv, xxxiv, xlix–l, lv, lxvii
McLane, Elizabeth, 159, 160
McMillan v. McNeill, 466
McNeill, McMillan v., 466
Madeira case, 386–390
Madison, James, 460–461
Magistrates, 39–55, 145, 543. *See also* Judges; Justices of the peace; Lay judges and magistrates
Magistrates Courts, 547
Maine, xxxviii, xliii–xliv, 273–312
Mainwaring and Frost v. Shores, 285
Major, Kathleen A., lxvii
Malicious prosecution, 511
Malynes, Gerald, xxxi *n*.7
Manchester, 165
Mangent, Jemima, 226
Mansfield, Isaac, 557
Mansfield, Lord, 269
Manslaughter, *see* Murder
Marblehead, 161, 168, 180, 201, 392, 558
Marion, Joseph, 194, *n*.1
Marsh, Nathaniel, 557
Marshfield, 234
Marston, James B., 420
Maryland Assembly, 424
Mason, Arthur, 114 *n*.9
Mason, George, 452
Mason, Jonathan, 398

Massachusettensis, 409, 412, 415. *See also* Leonard, Daniel

Massachusetts: court records, 471–497, 499–540; court system, 541–544; and New Hampshire, 201, 204, 279. *See also* Massachusetts Bay headings; names of courts; specific subject headings

Massachusetts Bay Colony, xxvi *ff.*, xxxii–xxxiii, xxxvii, xxxviii, xxxix *n.*2, lvi, 3–10, 21, 25, 29–30, 32, 37, 42, 144–146. *See also* Massachusetts

Massachusetts Bay Company, 43–44

Massachusetts Historical Society, resources for legal history, lxi, 569–584

Massachusetts Judicial Records Committee, lxi

Masters, Giles, xxxiv

Mather, Cotton, 63 *n.*3, 67, 108, 209, 261–264; *Bonifacius*, xxi, 207, 263; *Magnalia Christi Americana*, 271, *illus.* 274; sermons, 264–265; *Wonders of the Invisible World*, 268

Mather, Increase, xxxiii, 63 *n.*3, 108, 261, 264; *Crisis of Conscience*, 268

Mattoon, Whipple v., 432, 433

Mauduit, Israel, 271

Maule, Thomas, 578

Maverick, Samuel, 270, 581

Mayhew, Jonathan, *Discourse*, 265–266

Medad, 239

Medicine, xl *n.*8

Menand, Catherine, xviii, xxiv, lxi, lxiii, lxviii, 485

Menzies, James, 289

Menzies, John, xl

Middlesex County, list of records, 536–538

Militia, 133–134

Miller, Perry, xxiii, xxiv

Millet, Nathan, 138

Milliken, Harry, xviii

Mills, 501

Mills v. *Duryee*, 465

Minot, Stephan, 493

Minute books, 480–484, *illus.* 470, *illus.* 483, 493

Mitchell, David, 347

Mitchell, Jacob, 347

Money, 439–440, 501

Monsky, John, lxi

Montgomery, Hugh, 270, 562

Moody, Samuel, 291, 293, 296, 299, 306

Moor, Mrs., 128–129

Moor, Sarah, 162–164

Moor, William, 492

Moore, Francis, 22, 23

Moot Club, 381 *n.*6

Morals laws, 147

Morison, Samuel Eliot, xxii

Morris, Richard B., xxii

Morrison, Daniel, 291, 296–297, 308–311

Mort d'ancestor, 507

Morton, Perez, 347

Morton, Thomas, xxvii *n.*5

Moulton, Jeremiah, 294, 298, 306

Moulton, Sheriff, 312

Mount Hope, 70, 73, 74

Municipal Court, Boston, 524

Murder, 392–394, 504–505

Murphy v. *Pinchbeck, illus.* frontispiece

Murray, Daniel, 347

Murrin, John M., xxv, xxxix *ff.*, lii

Muyden, Johannis van, *see* Van Muyden, Johannis

N

Nantucket, 237

Native Americans, *see* Indians

Neal, John, 303

Neal, Robert, 238

Necho, George, 239

Negative vote conflict, 52

Negligence, 511

Negroes, *see* Blacks

Nelson, John, 195

Nelson, William, *Office and Authority of a Justice of Peace*, 117, 229 *n.*7

Nelson, William E., xviii, xxiv, xxxvii, liii–liv, lxviii, liv *ff.*, 477
Neoclassicism, 368
New Bedford, 549
New Castle, NH, 283
New England, Dominion of, 265
New Hampshire province, 253, 275–276, 279; and Massachusetts, 201, 204
New London, CT, 214
New Milford, CT, 197
New York, NY, 246, 247, 254, 261, 269, 270, 466, 477
Newbury, 162
Newburyport, 176
Newcastle, Duke of, 202
Newport v. *Billing*, 394 *n*.1
Newton, John, 219
Newton, Thomas, xxxix–xl, xliii–xliv, 194–195, 205, 211–212, 221, 227 *n*.5, 230, 283 *n*.4, 286, 288
Nickerson, Rex v., 394
Nimeno, John, 175 *n*.1
Noble, John, *illus.* v, 347–348, 472, 474, 497
Nolan, Dennis, xxv
Nonamesset, 214
Noodle Island, 151
Norfolk County, records in Essex Institute, 555–556
Norridgewock, 298
North Carolina, 254
Northampton, 159, 164, 165, 180, 184, 561
Notary public records, 557
Notting, Jonathan, 557
Novel desseisin, 507
Nowel, Peter, 303–304
Nowell, Increase, 20
Noyes, Ann, *see* Jewett, Ann (Noyes)
Noyes, Daniel, 557
Nurse, Rebecca, 577

O

Oakes, Josiah, 228, *n*.8
Oath of a Free-Man, 248–250; *illus.* 249

Old State House, Boston, *illus.* 420, *illus.* 438
Oliver, Andrew, 105
Oliver, Captain, 303
Oliver, Daniel, 348
Oliver, Nathaniel, 70, 72, 81
Oliver, Peter, 105, 332, 340, 348, 422
Osgood, Isaac, 557
Osgood, Russell K., xxxviii, xli, lxviii
Otis, James, xlv, 317 *n*.7, 318 *n*.9, 319 *n*.3, 203–204, 327, 328, 348, 351, 352, 360, 366, 370 *n*.7, 377, 381 *n*.6, 384, 392, 409, 482, 493, 562
Otis, James, Jr., xl, 233, 318 *n*.9, *illus.* 320, 348, 352, 357, 492
Otis, John, Jr., 214
Overing, John, xliii, 194–195, 199–201, 213–215, 222

P

Paddleford, Seth, 348
Paine, Robert Treat, xl, 314 *n*.5, 318 *n*.9, 321 *n*.8, 348–349, 374, *illus.* 375, 376, 384, 482, 484, 562; papers, 581–584
Paine, Thomas, 349
Paity, Peter, 116, 125
Panton, Henry, 392–393
Parker, Chief Justice, 231
Parker, Alice, 577
Parker, James, 299, 301
Parker, Joseph, 237–238
Parker, William, 352
Parks, William, 254
Parliamentarianism, 374
Parris, Samuel, 558
Parrot, Samuel, 138
Parsons, Moses, 349
Parsons, Theodore, 269 *n*.7
Parsons, Theophilus, 289 *n*.4, 349
Peak, John, 129
Pearson, Eliphalet, 269 *n*.7
Pedley, John, 139
Pelham, Herbert, xxviii
Pemberton, Mr., 123

Penhallow, John, 285, 306
Penhallow, Joseph, 296
Penhallow, Mary, *see* Phipps, Mary (Penhallow)
Penn, William, 244
Pennsylvania, Prigg v., 466
Pepperrell, William, 281, 289, 298
Pepperrell, William, Jr., 282, 287, 288, 297, 298, 299, 300, 303, 304, 306
Perkins, John, 557
Peters, Hugh, 14
Petition, right of, 79 *ff.*
Phenix, Jeremiah, 235
Philadelphia, PA, 243, 246, 256, 257, 564
Phillips, Samuel, bill to, *illus.* 585
Philpot, Rebeccah, 133
Phipps, Eleanor Cutt, 285
Phipps, Mary (Penhallow), 285
Phipps, Mary (Plaisted) Hoddy, 285
Phipps, Thomas, 285–286, 311, 312
Phips, Spencer, 230
Phips, William, xxxviii *n.*2, 63 *n.*3, 67, 575
Physicians, *see* Doctors
Pickering, John, 284
Pickering, Timothy, 349
Pillory, *see* Stocks
Pinchbeck, Murphy v., *illus.*, frontispiece
Piracy, 266–267, 394
Pitt Packet (brig), 392
Pitts, John, 138
Plaisted, Elisha, 282, 302, 303, 306
Plaisted, Hannah (Wentworth), 282
Plaisted, Hannah (Wheelwright), 282
Plaisted, Ichabod, 281, 282
Plaisted, John, 276, 281, 284
Plaisted, Mary, *see* Phipps, Mary (Plaisted) Hoddy
Plaisted, Samuel, 282
Plea bargaining, 219–222
Plea in bar, 516
Pleading: rules of, 502–516; bibliography, 516–517
Pleadings, written, 25

Pleas in abatement, 515–516
Pleas to the jurisdiction, 515
Plymouth, 71, 75, 145, 146, 233, 319, 564, 571
Plymouth Colony, legal publications, 253
Plymouth County, liv, 144–146; Court Records Project, liv *n.*3, xxiv; list of records, 538
Police Courts, 547
Police forces, 526
Political theory, on jurisdiction, 459–467
Polley (schooner), 494
Poor laws, *see* Poverty, law of
Popish plot, 257
Population, and economic conditions, 153; and legal history, xxxii, xxxvii
Porter, Eleazer, 184
Porter, Elisha, 349
Porter, Israel, 577
Porter, Samuel, 349–350
Portsmouth, NH, 276, 283, 285, 309, 555
Pound, Roscoe, 475
Poverty, law of, xxxviii, xlii, 134, 153–190
Powers, Edwin, xxxii
Prat(t), Benjamin, xl, 230, 349, 350–351, 356, 360, 363, 366, 370 *n.*7, *illus.* 378
Preble, Abraham, 281, 306
Preble, Mary, 306
Prerogative, 429 *ff.*, 435
Presbyterians, 265
Prescott, William, 559
Preston, Captain, 473
Preston, Caroline, lxviii
Preston, Thomas, 270, 581
Preston, Rex v., 318 *n.*9
Prigg v. *Pennsylvania*, 466
Primus, 129
Prince, John, 558
Printing, 246 *ff.*
Probate, 425
Probate and Family Court Department, 548
Procedural pleas, 222 *ff.*

Procedural reforms, 506
Profanity, 117, 118–119
Professionalization, see Lawyers: professionalization
Property law, 147, 189
Property right, 511
Prout, Joseph, 114 n.9
Providence, RI, 258
Prynne, William, 12, 13
Publishing, legal, see Legal literature; Printing
Pullen, Richard, 133
Pullin, Edward, 557
Puritans, xxvi ff., xxix, xlv, 4–7, 11, 31, 41, 262, 542
Putnam, James, 342, 350, 354, 362, 369
Pym, John, 37–38
Pynchon, William, 9, 111 n. 3, 113, 350, 356, 557
Pynchon Court Record, xxx

Q

Quakers, 265, 268
Quantum meruit, 515
Quantum valebant, 515
Quare clausum fregit, 509
Quarter Court of General Sessions, 546
Quarter Courts, Inferior, 520
Queen Anne's War, xxxviii
Quincy, 479
Quincy, Edmund, 330
Quincy, Hannah, 360, 371, 380
Quincy, Josiah, xl, xlvii, 226, 314 n.5, 347, 350, 494
Quincy, Josiah, Jr., 270, 318 n.9, 321 n.7, 350, 390, 562, 579, 580
Quincy, Samuel, xl, 219, 318 n.9, 350–351, 356, 482, 483, illus. 580

R

Railroads, 501
Ralph, Jeremiah, Jr., 237
Randell, John Martin, 495, 496
Randolph, Edward, xxi, xxxiv, 66, 67

Rastell, William, Collection of Entries, 25
Rawson, Edward, 253
Raynes, Nathaniel, 289–290
Read, John, xl, xlii, 194–195, 197, 198–204, 209, 212, 215, 227–228, 230, 232, 233, 288, 351; law library, 230, 244 n.7
Read, William, 351
Reasons of Appeal, xxxv, 221 ff.
Recognizance of the peace, 121–122, 126, 141, 143, 148
Record books, 480, 484–485, 493, 525
Reed, Charles, 495–496
Regulatory offences, 130 ff.
Reid, John, xxv, lv n.8
Religion, and legal issues, xxxix, lvi, 261–266. See also names of denominations
Religious offenses, 147
Remington, Jonathan, 194 n.1, 194 n.9, 330
Replevin, 139, 510
Residency, see Settlement, law of; Warning-out system
Respublica v. Sweers, 500 n.4
Revere, Paul, 488, 490
Revolution, American, see American Revolution
Rex v. Corbet, 392–394
Rex v. Nickerson, 394
Rex v. Preston, 318 n.9
Rex v. Wemm, 394 n.3
Reynolds, Nathaniel, 75 n.7, 80
Rhode Island boundary case, 202, 204
Rice, Gideon, 238
Richards, Anna (Carver), 116
Richards, John, 329
Richards, Joseph, 116
Richmond, 296, 306
Rishworth, Edward, 280, 287
Roads, see Highways
Robbery, 505
Robes, James, 120
Robie, Thomas, 201
Robie, William, 135

Robins, Robert, 494
Robinson, Jack, 348
Robinson, Robert, 195, 214–215, 223, 225, 233
Rogers, Jeremiah Dummer, 351
Rogers, John, 77 *n*.5
Roman law, 367, 370, 383 *ff*.
Ropes, Nathaniel, 332
Rose (frigate), 392
Rosenthal, Max, Cushing portrait, *illus*. 583
Rouse, William, 221. *See also* Rowse, William
Rousseau, [Jean Jacques], *Du Contrat Social*, 380, 402, 403
Rowell, Thomas, 161 *n*.5
Rowley, 162, 163, 164
Rowse, William, 302. *See also* Rouse, William
Roxbury, 150
Rucke v. *Hatch*, 27, 28
Ruddock (Justice), 327
Ruggles, Timothy, 319 *n*.1, 351
Rushbrook, Ovid, 209
Russell, Chambers, 330, 352
Russell, James, 577

S

Sabbath breaking, 117, 122, 124
Sack Cut, 238
Saco, 296
Saffin, John, 63 *n*.3, 71–77, 80, 81, 85–88, 219, 227 *n*.5, 329; "The Original of the Town of Bristol," 73
St. Georges, 290
Salem, 149, 150, 164–180 *passim*, 197, 237, 238, 520, 555, 557, 577, 582
Salem witchcraft trials, *see* Witchcraft trials: Salem
Salisbury, 555
Salkeld, *Kings Bench Reports*, 232
Salmon Falls, 276, 306
Saltonstall, Gurdon, 197
Saltonstall, Richard, 9, 48, 330
Saltonstall, Robert, 3

Sargeant, Christopher, 351
Sarjeant, Nathaniel Peas(e)lee, 351–352, 558
Satter, Malachy, 489
Savage, Edward, Paine portrait, *illus*. 375
Savage, Ephraim, 123
Scarborough, 301
Scituate, 579
Scriveners, Company of, 19
Scroggs, Chief Justice, 258, 260
Seahorse (ship), 132
Seals, on legal documents, 489, *illus*. 503
Sedgwick, Benjamin, 352
Sedgwick, Theodore, 352, *illus*. 353
Sedition, 446, 447, 458
Selectmen, 132 *ff*., 157 *ff*.
Senie, Elisabeth, 159
Sermons, printing of, 264–265
Sessions Courts, 162
Settlement, law of, xlii, 171–176
Sewell, David, 289 *n*.4, 352
Sewell, Hannah, 108
Sewall, Jonathan, xlvii, 201, 318 *n*.9, 352, 354, 390, 409 *n*.9
Sewall, Mitchel(l), 350, 557
Sewall, Samuel, xxxix *n*.2, 63 *n*.3, 88, 91–92, 107, 108, 114 *n*.9, 122, 123, 132, 194–195, 198–199, 207, *illus*. 208, 209, 212 *n*.8, 229–231, 273, 329, 557, 578–579
Sewall, Stephen, 330, *illus*. 331, 352, 557
Sewall family, 400
Sewall v. *Hancock*, lii *n*.6, 436
Sexual offenses, 117, 120–121, 124
Sharples, James, Cushing portrait, *illus*. 583
Shave, Hett v., 26
Shaw, J., *The Practical Justice of Peace*, 117
Shays' Rebellion, lvi
Shepard, John, 287
Sheppard, William, *England's Balme*, 289
Sherburn, 142
Shipton, Clifford, lx

Shirley, William, xxxiii *n*.3, 201, 235
  n.4, 236, 238
Shores, Mainwaring and Frost v., 285
Shove, Edward, 194 *n*.1
Shower, *Kings Bench Reports*, 232
Shrewsbury, 553
Shrewsbury papers, 553
Shurtleff (Dr.), 20
Shute, Samuel, 59, 63 *n*.3, 109, 110,
  198–199
Shutesbury, 555
Shutesbury papers, 553
Simpson, Daniel, 298, 306
Simsbury, 184
Skye, William, 126
Slavery, xli *n*.9, 269, 279, 394
Slaves, fugitive, 466
Slew v. *Whipple*, 394 *n*.9
Smibert, John, 60; Byfield portrait,
  illus. 56; Prat portrait, *illus.* 378;
  Sewall portrait, *illus.* 208
Smith, Benjamin, 183
Smith, John, 292, 302, 303, 304,
  312
Smith, Joseph, xxii, xxiii, xxx, xxxii,
  xxxvii
Smith, Mary, 133
Smith, Richard, 75–76
Smith, Samuel, 301
Smith, Thomas, 209
Social Law Library, lxi
Social status of litigants, 127–128,
  141, 145–146, 502
Sodalitas Club, lxii, 376–382, 401,
  402, 403
Soldiers, 187
Solicitors, 15, 17, 19. *See also* Bar-
  risters; Lawyers
Somers, John, *Security of English-
  men's Lives*, 260, 261
Somerset, James, 269
South Carolina, 254
Sow case, 552
Sparrow (ship), 23; license, *illus.* 24
Special assumpsit, 514–515
Special Courts, 548
Spencer, Isaac, 138
Spinney, Samuel, 287

Sprague, John, 354
Sprague, Timothy, 212
Springfield, 168, 180, 239, 520, 549,
  558, 561
Stackpole, John, 301
Stamp Act, xlvi, 478, 479
Stamps, on legal documents, 487, *illus.*
  488, 489
State courts, 442 *ff.*
Statutes, publication, 250–254
Stephens, Mary, 161
Stevens, Daniel, 237
Stevens, John, 114 *n*.9
Stevens, Robert, xxv
Steward, Edward, 303
Stocks, *illus.* 185
Stoddard, Anthony, 229
Stoddard, Solomon, 354
Stoddard family, 400
Stolen goods, 125
Stone, Benjamin, 291, 305
Stoneham, 212
Story, Charles, 283, 284–285, 288,
  289
Story [Joseph] (Justice), 327, 461,
  559
Stoughton, William, 329, 575
Stoughton, Butters v., 29
Strangers' Courts, 520, 542, 548
Stratton v. *Stratton*, 28
Strong, Caleb, 354
Strong, Nehemiah, 354
Strong, Simeon, 354
Sturgeon Creek, 281
Sturgeon, Robert, 214–215, 231
Sudbury, 553
Sudbury papers, 553
Suffield, 160, 213
Suffolk County: bar association, xlvii,
  322–323, 395, 400; bar book, li,
  illus. 396; records, xxx, xxxiii,
  xxxiv–xxxvi, 538–539
Suffolk Files, 472 *ff.*
Sullivan, James, 289 *n*.4, 317 *n*.7,
  354–355, 461
Sullivan, John, 289 *n*.4, 254–355
Superior Court Department, 546
Superior Court of Judicature, 192,

193, 204, 211–213, 522, 523, 543, 545; documents, *illus.* 503
Supreme Court, 453
Supreme Judicial Court, lxi, 523–524, 543–544, 545; inventory, 519, 526–528
Surrency, Erwin, xxv
Suspicious individuals, 117–118, 121
Sutton, 553
Sutton papers, 553
Sweers, Respublica v., 500 *n.*4
Swift, Samuel, 355
Swift v. *Tyson*, 466

T

Taggart, John, 218
Taggart, Patrick, 218
Tailer (Lt. Governor), 58
Tailer, William, 102
Taxation, 45, 175–176
Taylor, Ezra, 355
Tedman, John, 116, 125
Thacher, Oxenbridge, 347, 350, 360, 370 *n.*7, 377, 381 *n.*6
Thayer, Eb, 376
Thayer family, 553
Theft, 117, 124
Thomas, John, 352
Thomas, Nathaniel, xxxiv, 330
Thomas, William, 143, 233
Thompson, John, 302
Timon, 118
Tinker, John, 22 *n.*5
Title, to land, 506, 507
Tompson, Samuel, 552
Topsfield, 172, 222
Tories, *see* Loyalists
Tose, Hett v., 26
Town records, at American Antiquarian Society, 553
Townsend, Penn, 114
Townsend Acts, 436
Trade development, xxxii
Transients, *see* Poverty, law of; Settlement, law of
Travis, Betsy, 183
Trespass, 139, 508–511

Trial Courts, 546
Trials, published proceedings, 266–271
Triumphs Of Justice Over Unjust Judges, 258, 260
Trover, 510
Trowbridge, Edmund, xl, 332, 343, 349, 350, 355, 422, 582
Trowbridge, Thomas, 217
Trumbell, John, 409 *n.*9
Trumbull, J. Hammond, 17 *n.*2, 18 *n.*2
Tucker, Ichabod, 557
Tuckerman, John, 135, 136
Tudor, John, 355
Tudor, William, xlvi *n.*5, 355–356
Tufts, Mary, 169 *n.*6
Tunagain, John, 126
Tupper, Thomas, 214
Turland, Thomas, 126
Turner, James, 302, 303
Tuttle, Daniel, 209–210, 220, 233–234
Tyng v. *Gardner*, 581
Tyson, Swift v., 466

U

Ulysses (ship), 495
United States v. *Coolidge*, 461
United States v. *Hudson*, 461
United States v. *Worrall*, 460
Upham, Jabez, 356
Upham, Joshua, 356
Usher, John, 253

V

Valentine, John, xl, xliii, xliv, 194–195, 198, 205, 209, 221, 233, 283 *n.*4, 286, 288; law library, 244 *n.*7
Van Muyden, Johannis, *Compendiosa, illus.* 365
Van Schaak's Law School, 1
Vassall, William, 269, 562
Vassall, Fletcher v., 318 *n.*9
Virginia, 254

W

Wakefield, John, 136
Walker, Edward, 356
Walker, Isaac, 356
Walker, Quock, 582
Walker, Thomas, 77 *n*.5
Walley, John, 70, 72–76, 81, 91, 100, 329
Wallingford, CT, 221
Wallpaper making, 490, 492
Waltham, 181, 182
War of Jenkin's Ear, xxxviii
Ward, Artemas, 230
Ward, Nahum, 230
Ward, Nathaniel, xxviii, 5–7, 30, 42; *Body of Liberties*, 5–7, 9, 30, 31, 33, 42, 47, 250, 251
Wardell, Jonathan, 129
Warning-out system, xxxviii, 176–189; documents, *illus.* 177–178
Warren, Charles, xxv
Warren, John, 236
Warren, Mehetabel, 182–183
Warren, William, 270, 562
Watertown, 214, 231, 576
Watertown, tax protest, 45
Watson, John, xxxiv
Wealth, and residency, 181, 188–189
Webb, Christopher, xxxiv, 136
Webber, Thomas, 138
Welch, William, 305
Weld, Thomas, 268
Welfare, right to, 155, 188
Wells, Robert, 254
Wells, 239, 275, 281, 282, 291, 296, 298, 307, 309
Wemm, Rex v., 394 *n*.3
Wemms, William, 270, 562
Wenham, 158, 159, 165
Wentworth, Lord Deputy, 15
Wentworth, Hannah, *see* Plaisted, Hannah (Wentworth)
Wentworth, John, 282
West, *Symboleography*, 22, 23
Westfield, 180
Weston, 181, 182

Wetmore, William, 350, 356
Whales, 383–386
Wheeler, William, Jr., 236
Wheelwright, Hannah, *see* Plaisted, Hannah (Wheelwright)
Wheelwright, John, 268, 280–282, 289, 294, *illus.* 295, 296, 298, 299, 302, 308–309
Wheelwright, John, 282
Wheelwright, Samuel, 282
Whigs, 501
Whipple, Slew v., 394 *n*.9
Whipple v. *Mattoon*, 432, 433
White, Alexander, 563
White, Hugh, 270, 562
White, Samuel, 346
White Pine Acts, 69, 103, 105
Whiting, William, 169
Whittemore, Mr., 139
Whitton, Henry, 225
Widows, 306
Wilkes, John, 267, 345
Wilkins, John, 76–79, 81
Willard, Abel, 340, 354, 356
Willard, Samuel, xxxix *n*.2, 356
William and Elizabeth Cole v. *Francis Doughty*, 33 *n*.6
Williams, Ephraim, 584
Williams, John, 356–357
Williams, Jonathan, 356–357
Wilson, James, 401 *n*.9
Winchester, John, Jr., 217
Winchester, Josiah, 134
Winslow, John, 357
Winslow, Pelham, 357
Winter Harbor (Saco), 305
Winthrop, Adam, 125 *n*.2, 134
Winthrop, John, xxvii, xxx, lix, 6–9, *illus.* 8, 11, 21, 23, 35 *n*.3, 41–44, 47, 48, 104, 105, 142, 214, 249, 250, 268, 271, 417; papers at American Antiquarian Society, 552
Winthrop, John, Jr., xxviii *n*.6
Winthrop, Stephen, 23
Winthrop, Waite, 67, 329
Wise, Jeremiah, 288
Witchcraft trials, 268; Salem, xxxii, xxxviii *n*.2, 265, 267, 556, 578

Witham, Peter, 307–308
Wolcot v. *Lymon*, 32
Woodbridge, John, 291 *ff.*, 302, 304, 306, 312
Woodbridge, Nathaniel, 346
Woodbridge, Timothy, 170
Woodcock v. *Davis*, 26 *n.*3
Woodman, John, 301, 304
Woodman, Jonathan, 120
Woodsum, Joseph, 210
Worcester, 230, 362, 363, 369, 549, 551, 553, 558, 566, 567, 582
Worcester County, list of records, 539–540; papers, 553
Workhouses, *see* Poverty, law of
Worrall, United States v., 460
Worthington, John, 314 *n.*5, 340, 354, 357
Wright, Benjamin, 296
Wright, Henry, 134
Writ of entry, 507

Writ of attachment, *illus.* 544
Writ of right, 507
Writ of trespass, 508–511
Writ system, 477
Writs of Assistance case, xlv, 492
Wyer, David, 289 *n.*4, 357
Wyeth, John, 357–358
Wythe's Law School, 1

Y

York, 228, 237, 239, 275–311 *passim*, 520
York County (Maine), Court of General Sessions, 290–312; records, *illus.* 298, *illus.* 300

Z

Zenger, John Peter, 269–270
Zobel, Hiller B., 485

legislature; this advance printing made its substance immediately available to all who were concerned with its provisions.

The Perpetual Laws Of The Commonwealth of Massachusetts, From the Commencement Of The Constitution . . . To The Last Wednesday in May, 1789.

Boston: Printed By Adams and Nourse, Printers to the Honourable General Court. M,DCC,LXXXIX.

This folio publication was one of several retrospective editions designed to publish all viable public acts and thus supplant the session laws. It contrasts markedly with commercial editions, such as a pocket-size volume issued by Isaiah Thomas.

Private and Special Statutes of the Commonwealth of Massachusetts, From The Year 1780, to the Close of the Session of the General Court, Begun And Held on The Last Wednesday In May, A. D. 1805. . . . 3 vols.

Boston: Printed For The State, By Manning & Loring. 1805.

This special compilation, issued according to a resolve of 1803, selected from the morass of Session Laws and Resolves all then viable private and special legislation. The work, executed chiefly by John Davis, was carefully done, well indexed, and contains a useful list of then obsolete acts.

Executive

The governor dep: govr. & assistants doe hereby declare . . . [1644].

From the Winthrop Papers.

This declaration proclaimed that the Magistrates were to administer the law of the colony, and that the Governor and Assistants were to be the duly elected legislators. It was the first approach, however feeble, to defining the separation of powers.

[Colony Seal.] *At A Council Held at Charlestown, June the 20th, 1676.* Broadside.

[Cambridge: Samuel Green, 1676.]

Although the proclamation of 1644 separated the judicial and administrative functions of government, the executive powers were exercised by the Council and the Governor, as this thanksgiving broadside attests.

Acts & Laws, of His Majesty's Province of the Massachusetts-Bay in New-England.

Boston, in New-England: Printed by S. Kneeland, by Order of His Excellency the Governor, Council and House of Representatives. M,D,CC,LIX.

The 1759 edition of the province laws was the last plenary retrospective compilation to be issued before the outbreak of the American Revolution.

The County and Town Officer: Or An Abridgment of the Laws Of The Province of the Massachusets-Bay. . . . By a Gentleman.

Boston: Printed by T. and J. Fleet, and Sold at the Book-Store in Union-Street, 1768.

This 149-page manual was intended as a working guide for Justices of the Peace, Sheriffs, Selectmen, and a spate of other town and county officers. It abstracts from the statutes the duties of those officers, listed in alphabetical order, from Assay Masters to Wood Corders.

State Of Massachusetts-Bay. In the House of Representatives, February 6, 1777. Whereas there may be . . . an Omission to renew the Appointment of Committees of Correspondence, Inspection and Safety. . . . Broadside.

[Boston: 1777.]

This is one example among many in the Society's collections of legislation issued in broadside format during the Revolutionary years.

In Pursuance of an Act of the General Assembly of this State, entitled "An Act to prevent Monopoly and Oppression". . . . Broadside.

Boston, Feb. 19th, 1777.

The Revolutionary state government endowed the towns with the authority to fix prices. The Society's collections are very rich in such materials.

An Act, Laying Duties of Impost and Excise, on Certain Goods, Wares and Merchandize, Therein Described; And for repealing the several Laws heretofore made for that Purpose.

Boston: Printed by Adams and Nourse, in Marlborough Street, 1783.

A separate printing of an act that established a customs service and tariff scheduled for the newly formed commonwealth. The text of the act eventually appeared as chapter 12 of the legislation enacted at the May session of the